# Images of the Past

SIXTH EDITION

T. Douglas Price
*University of Wisconsin–Madison*

Gary M. Feinman
*The Field Museum*

The McGraw·Hill Companies

IMAGES OF THE PAST
Published by McGraw-Hill, an imprint of The McGraw-Hill Companies, Inc., 1221 Avenue of the Americas, New York, NY 10020. 

This book is printed on acid-free paper.

1 2 3 4 5 6 7 8 9 0 CCI/CCI 0 9

ISBN: 978-0-07-353105-2
MHID: 0-07-353105-7

Editor in Chief: *Michael Ryan*
Sponsoring Editor: *Gina Boedeker*
Marketing Manager: *Pam Cooper*
Managing Editor: *Nicole Bridge*
Developmental Editor: *Janice Wiggins-Clarke*
Production Editor: *David Blatty*
Manuscript Editor: *Thomas L. Briggs*
Design Manager: *Preston Thomas*
Cover Designer: *Mary-Presley Adams*
Photo Research: *Brian Pecko*
Production Supervisor: *Tandra Jorgensen*
Composition: *9.25/12 Palatino by Thompson Type*
Printing: *45# Pub Matte, Courier*

Cover Image: *Mexico, Tabasco, Parque-Museo La Venta, Olmec carved head. The Olmecs were of the first civilizations in Mexico and are renowned for their giant carvings of heads, some of which are up to 3 metres tall. © Robert Frerck/Stone/Getty Images.*

Credits: The credits section for this book begins on page C-1 and is considered an extension of the copyright page.

**Library of Congress Cataloging-in-Publication Data**

Price, T. Douglas (Theron Douglas)
Images of the Past / T. Douglas Price, Gary M. Feinman.—6th ed.
p. cm.
Includes bibliographical references and index.
ISBN-13: 978-0-07-353105-2
ISBN-10: 0-07-353105-7
1. Prehistoric peoples. 2. Antiquities, Prehistoric. 3. Archaeology.
4. Indians—Antiquities. I. Feinman, Gary M. II. Title.

GN740.P75 2010
930.1—dc22 2009040460

The Internet addresses listed in the text were accurate at the time of publication. The inclusion of a Web site does not indicate an endorsement by the authors or McGraw-Hill, and McGraw-Hill does not guarantee the accuracy of the information presented at these sites.

**www.mhhe.com**

*For Anne Birgitte Gebauer and Linda Nicholas*

# Brief Table of Contents

# Contents

## CHAPTER THREE
## *Out of Africa:* Homo erectus *73*

## CHAPTER FOUR
## *The Hunters 105*

## CHAPTER FIVE
## *Postglacial Foragers 165*

## CHAPTER SIX
## *The Origins of Agriculture 199*

## CHAPTER SEVEN
## *Native North Americans 267*

## CHAPTER EIGHT
## *Ancient Mesoamerica 321*

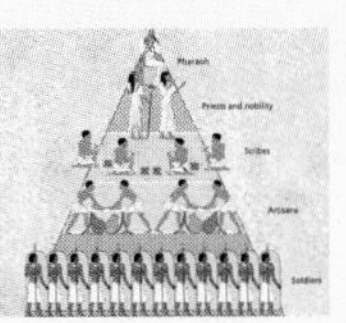

## CHAPTER ELEVEN
## *Prehistoric Europe 507*

## CHAPTER TWELVE
## *The Past as Present and Future 561*

# Preface

*Images of the Past* is an introduction to prehistoric archaeology that aims to capture the excitement and visual splendor of archaeology while at the same time providing insight into current research methods, interpretations, and theories in the field. To introduce our text, we offer some background on why we wrote the book, describe its organization and distinctive features, indicate what is new in this edition, provide some information on the various supplements, and, finally, acknowledge all those individuals and institutions that have contributed to *Images of the Past*.

## WHY WE WROTE THIS BOOK

Perhaps a short history of our own teaching experience and the motivation for this volume will help convey our intent. *Images* is the result of a combined total of more than 50 years of teaching archaeology. Some years ago, when our introductory archaeology curriculum was revamped with an advanced section for majors and a beginning course for other students, we decided to make interesting archaeological sites the focus of a survey of world prehistory. We would discuss a series of sites from the Pliocene (now Miocene!) to the present that reflected archaeological knowledge about the past and how that information was obtained. The emphasis on sites allowed us to cover time and space and certain methods and theories, as well as provide a general survey of world prehistory. Students generally enjoyed the course and completed the semester with a broad understanding of archaeology, the major questions in the discipline, and the ways that archaeologists think about the past.

But we were generally dissatisfied with the texts that were available for this introductory archaeology course. A number of introductory books on the subject already existed, of course. Such volumes generally took one of two directions: They provided either a comprehensive survey of world prehistory or a primer on method and theory. Back then, and still today, surveys of world archaeology summarized what archaeologists had learned, but they often tended to be rather dry encyclopedias of information on the many places and times that people lived in, in the past. That vast body of data is formidable to beginning students, and they have trouble discerning what is really important. Primers on method and theory, on the other hand, were compilations of the history, techniques, concepts, and principles of archaeology: how to search for archaeological remains, how excavations are done, how to determine the age of prehistoric materials, who Louis Leakey was, and the like.

Neither of these approaches met our needs, so we decided to write a text that followed the format that had been successful in our introductory class. We wrote a book that combined both survey and primer, but with an emphasis on archaeological sites. We believed then, and still do today, that a combination of what has been discovered and how archaeologists learn about the past is of value in introductory archaeology courses.

We also took a new tack in the book. Rather than try to cover all of archaeology, we chose to emphasize only certain discoveries that had produced major insights into prehistory. Our focus was, and still is, on some 80 archaeological sites from a variety of times and places around the world. These sites are signposts to the past and allow students to focus on what is important.

To play to our strengths, we divided up the writing according to our own areas of knowledge and activity. Doug Price is interested in prehistoric foragers and the transition to agriculture; Gary Feinman is interested in the rise of complex societies and the organization of states. Price works primarily in the Old World with stone tools, bones, and hunter-gatherers; Feinman does fieldwork largely in Mexico and China, where ceramics are a primary source of information. Our diverse interests allowed us to create a text with balanced coverage of the Eastern and Western Hemispheres.

We also took a new approach to the format and layout of the text. We divided the information into pieces, with more than 80 sites and numerous small sections on ideas, methods, people, and things. These short segments, while full of information, can be readily digested by the reader and allow the instructor to organize the readings in the book as best fits the course. The substantial number of illustrations helps convey both the diversity and splendor of archaeology.

Thus *Images* offers a visual, site-oriented look at human prehistory. What is important, we believe, is to convey the excitement, intrigue, and imagery of archaeology.

We think that *Images* does that and that it provides a rich introduction to archaeology. We hope that our interest in and enthusiasm for archaeology carry over to you in this book and that you will enjoy these *Images of the Past.*

## ORGANIZATION OF THE BOOK

Our journey begins with the evidence for the first humans, more than 5 million years ago, and concludes with the rise of great empires around the world. This survey of world prehistory is organized in 12 chapters, along chronological and/or geographical lines. Chapters 2–6 are in chronological order, from the earliest human remains several million years ago to the beginnings of farming around 10,000 years ago. These chapters follow the expansion of human beings from our original home in Africa to Asia, Europe, and eventually Australia and the Americas. Chapter 6 covers the beginnings of agriculture from a global perspective.

Chapters 7–11 are concerned with the rise of large, complex societies and early states and empires. This second half of the text has a geographical organization, with chapters on North America, Middle America, South America, Asia and Africa, and Europe. Within each of these chapters, we have generally followed the sequence of development through time, from earlier to later. Although the earliest state societies arose in the Old World, we have arranged the chapters from the New World to the Old in order to emphasize and compare the rise of states in both areas. This arrangement of the chapters is intended to enhance comprehension of major processes such as the spread of agriculture and the rise of more complex societies.

We have sandwiched these ten chapters of site-oriented survey between two distinctive bookends that introduce the field and convey some sense of the larger context of archaeology. Chapter 1 provides a brief overview of principles and methods. This information gives the reader a basic understanding of the kinds of things that archaeologists want to know and how they find them out. Chapter 12 has been substantially expanded as a conclusion for the book. This chapter considers why archaeology is important and the ethical responsibilities of being an archaeologist.

## HALLMARK FEATURES OF THE BOOK

Each of the chapters on world prehistory contains site and concept essays enclosed by an Introduction and by a concluding section called "Images and Ideas." The Introduction provides an overview of the major themes and discoveries in the chapter. The Introduction also contains essential maps and chronological charts for the chapter. The "Images and Ideas" sections provide a recapitulation of the chapter content and place that information in a larger context, often incorporating new concepts, theories, or comparisons. Examples of discussions in the "Images and Ideas" sections are the behavioral correlates of cold climate adaptations, the origins of language, and the nature of cultural complexity. The Introductions and "Images and Ideas" sections should be read with some care; they provide the glue that binds the site descriptions together.

Interspersed among the site descriptions are concept sections that cover some of the how and why of archaeology: essential methods, debates about archaeological interpretation, or certain spectacular finds. In these concept sections, we illustrate some of the more interesting questions archaeologists ask about the past and highlight various new methods that are employed to decipher the archaeological record.

Because prehistory is a very visual subject, we have incorporated more than 600 illustrations in this book—more than any other book on the market. It is essential to see and study the maps, plans, artifacts, and places that help make up the archaeological record. The basic framework of archaeology is the place of prehistoric materials in time and space. For this reason, we have included a series of coordinated maps and timelines to show readers where these sites and materials fit in terms of geography and chronology.

Throughout the text, we have included a number of learning aids to help students better understand the material. Chapter outlines lead off each chapter, giving students a preview of what is to come. Marginal quotes allow students to hear the voices of the field. A pronunciation guide lists difficult names and terms. Technical terms and important concepts in archaeology are indicated in **bold** type; these words can be found both in the adjacent margin of the text and in a glossary at the end of the book. The size and scale of archaeological sites and features is an important aspect. Where appropriate, we have tried to provide some sense of the size of areas and structures with reference to modern features such as city blocks, football fields, and buildings. An appendix offers some English–metric measure conversions and various equivalents to help make sizes more comprehensible.

Supplementary readings are essential for introductory courses, for several reasons: to provide interested students with directions for further study, to assist in the preparation of papers, and to elaborate on subjects that can be addressed only briefly in a textbook. In *Images of the Past,* a short list of Suggested Readings appears at the end of each chapter, appropriate to the subject matter. A more complete list of sources used in the preparation of the book can be found in the back pages. Specific citations were not used in the text itself for the sake of readability, but references for the information can be found under the name of the individual associated with the work in the bibliography at the back of the book. In addition, this bibliography appears in searchable format on the book Web site.

An important note on dates in this edition: Because of the long time span covered by archaeology, the age of archaeological materials is given in several ways. Dates older than 10,000 years ago are described in years before the present (B.P.) or in millions of years ago (m.y.a.). Dates less than 10,000 years ago are given in calendar years before Christ (B.C.) or anno Domini, "in the year of the Lord" (A.D.). Dates for the past 10,000 years have been corrected, or calibrated, for a known error in radiocarbon dating. Another term used for more recent periods of time is *millennium*, a period of 1000 years. We live today in the third millennium, the third 1000-year period after Christ. The millennia before Christ run in reverse—for example, the first millennium goes from 1000 B.C. to 1 B.C., and so on.

## WHAT'S NEW IN THIS EDITION

This sixth edition of *Images of the Past* is a welcome chance to make corrections, update material, and add new material. We have retained the basic structure of a site-by-site journey through the past, interspersed with blocks of text about places, methods, and things. We believe that this connected series of short modules serves the reading habits of our students well. At the same time, we have improved the quality of the book with this round of revisions.

In addition, we have substantially updated and revised all of the chapters, deleting dated material and adding new, hopefully even more interesting, information. We have made a strong effort to ensure that dates and periods are the same throughout the text. In part because of the many helpful comments and suggestions we have received, we have been able to revise this text in accordance with both new discoveries in archaeology and the interests of our readers. The past does not get old, and new discoveries and changing interpretations are a constant in archaeology. The pace of discovery and insight in modern archaeology is such that each year there are dramatic changes in our knowledge. We hope to keep *Images of the Past* as up-to-date as a book about the past can be.

In the first part of the book, new material has been added on extinct hominids, the first Americans, genetics, the origins of agriculture, and domestication. Several sites have been deleted (Trinil, Gatecliff, and Vindolanda), as they provided less information than others. Chapter 1, on the principles of archaeology, has been modified with some new illustrations and text. More discussion of the relationship between anthropology and archaeology has been added, and more on historical archaeology as well. Context, association, and provenience in archaeology get more attention in the chapter. Phytoliths and starch grains have been added to the microbotanical remains mentioned in the chapter. And field notes are illustrated.

Chapter 2, also on the first humans, has been revised slightly, with a new section on argon-argon dating, discussion of recent discoveries of early hominins, and the latest information on Atapuerca and the first Europeans. Chapter 3 contains further mention of the so-called hobbits from the island of Flores in Indonesia. We have added material on a number of new sites, including a discussion of the discovery of fire at Gesher Benot Ya'aqov in Israel, Kennewick, Hebior, and the Jomon.

In Chapter 4, several changes have been made. The sites of Pinnacle Point and Kibish in Africa have been added, in regard to the appearance of fully modern humans. Genetics continues to offer much new information—in this case, on body hair and skin color in early humans. In the Western Hemisphere, there is also news. The oldest site in North America, Paisley Cave in Oregon, contains elementary evidence of the first Americans. The Clovis phenomenon seems to have been a brief one. And a new argument that meteors caused extinctions of large game at the end of the Pleistocene is noted, but not accepted. A new box on the peopling of the Pacific has been added after the section on Australia to provide some information on this vast area of the world. Although the Pacific Islands were colonized late in human prehistory, the story of the expansion of humans across the Pacific is a remarkable one. There is a spectacular Jomon site, Sannai Maruyama, to replace the previous one. Nitrogen isotopes have been added to the discussion of paleodiet in Chapter 5.

Chapter 6 contains revised art and text, with new findings on the domestication of plants and animals in Peru, the Near East, China, Africa and Europe. The term *paleoethnobotany* has been changed to *archaeobotany* in keeping with consensus in the field. It also matches well with *archaeozoology* and conveys the very direct connection to archaeology.

The second half of the book includes new information and features. In Chapter 7, new findings concerning the introduction of corn into the American Southwest are presented. Chapter 8 presents new material on early Maya writing and new perspectives on the competition between different Maya states during the classic period. Chapter 10 incorporates new information on the mapping and size of Angkor. Chapter 11 has the latest on the Iceman, including the use of strontium isotopes to determine his place of origin. There are also exciting new data from the Stonehenge Riverside project, including interpretation of life and death contexts. Finally, we have expanded Chapter 12 again, with more material on CRM (some picked up from earlier chapters) and additional discussion of career options.

We have also added new art—photos and line drawings—to improve the visual impact of *Images of the Past.* There are more color illustrations in the book this time, and captions for all illustrations have been expanded. Maps and timelines have been updated along with the text. We hope that these visuals convey some of the excitement of these discoveries. In addition, the Suggested Readings for each chapter have been updated. The bibliography at the end of the book has been expanded and revised. Glossary terms for each chapter have been expanded. Figures have been numbered throughout the text so that specific reference can be made to them individually.

Throughout the volume, we have tried to improve the flow and accuracy of the text and to add to the connectivity of our story. We hope that the new content has resulted in a book that students will want to pick up and read. In addition to the changes in the text, the supplements for the book remain a strong component and are detailed in the next section.

## SUPPLEMENTS

### For the Student

*The Student's Online Learning Center* (by Adam Wetsman, Rio Hondo College). This free, Web-based student supplement features a large number of interactive exercises and activities, helpful study tools, links, and useful information (www.mhhe.com/priceip6e). The Web site is designed specifically to complement the individual chapters of the book. In-text icons guide students to information on a particular topic that is available on the Web site.

*Useful Study Tools*

- Chapter objectives and outlines—give students signposts for understanding and recognizing key chapter content.
- Multiple-choice and true/false questions—give students the opportunity to quiz themselves on chapter content and visuals.
- Essay questions—allow students to explore key chapter concepts through their own writing.
- Glossary—defines key terms.
- Audio glossary—helps students with words that are difficult to pronounce through audio pronunciation.

*Useful Information*

- FAQs about archaeology careers—give students answers to questions on available jobs, necessary education and training, and basic texts on the field, as well as picking a college or university, going on a dig, and getting more information.
- Career opportunities—offer students related links to useful information on careers in anthropology.

### For the Instructor

*The Instructor's Online Learning Center* (by T. Douglas Price, Gary M. Feinman, and Adam Wetsman). This indispensable, easy-to-use, password-protected instructor supplement provides a variety of features:

- Image Library—offers professors the opportunity to create custom-made, professional-looking presentations and handouts by providing electronic versions of many maps, tables, illustrations, and photos from the text. All images are ready to be used in any applicable teaching tools.
- PowerPoint lecture slides—give professors ready-made chapter-by-chapter presentation notes.
- Instructor's Manual—offers chapter outlines, chapter summaries, learning objectives, lecture launcher ideas, and suggested films and videos.

It also provides access to all of the student online materials. Visit our Online Learning Web site at www.mhhe.com/priceip6e to access these robust supplements.


## ACKNOWLEDGMENTS

Any large project like this is the culmination of the efforts and contributions of a multitude of individuals and institutions. We want to thank the many people who have helped with this book in a number of different ways—reviewing the text, providing new data, supplying photographs and art, locating materials and information, checking facts, and giving general support. With more than 600 illustrations, the task of finding artwork, obtaining copies and permissions, and organizing it all is enormous. We have done our very best to contact the copyright holders of the original work included herein and to secure their permission to reprint their material; if we have overlooked anyone, we offer our sincere apologies.

This project has been long and complex and would not have been possible or pleasurable without the help of these friends and colleagues: Kim Aaris-Sørensen, Melvin Aitkens, Niels Andersen, Larry Bartram, Gert Jan Bartstra, John Bennet, Pia Bennike, Peter Bogucki, Richard Bradley, Maggie Brandenburg, C. K. Brain, Robert Brightman, Göran Burenhult, Jim Burton, Brian Byrd, Christopher Chippendale, Tim Champion, Grahame Clark, Desmond Clark, Carmen Collazo, Meg Conkey, Lawrence Conyers, Nina Cummings, Erwin Cziesla, George Dales, Jack Davis, Hilary and Janette Deacon, John de Vos, Preben Dehlholm, Tom Dillehay, Christopher Donnan, Scott Fedick, Lisa Ferin, Kent Flannery, Melvin Fowler, George Frison, Anne Birgitte Gebauer, Henry George, Ted Gerney, Jon Gibson, Junko Habu, Peter Christian Vemming Hansen, Spencer Harrington, Sønke Hartz, Matt Hill, Ian Hodder, Brian Hoffman, Frank Hole, Vance Holliday, F. Clark Howell, Fang Hui, Tom Jacobsen, Dick Jeffries, Greg Johnson, Ken Karstens, Larry Keeley, Mark Kenoyer, Susan Kepecs, J. E. Kidder Jr., Richard Klein, François Lévêque, Katina Lillios, Henry de Lumley, Tom Lynch, Joyce Marcus, Alexander Marshack, Ray Matheny, Alan May, Roderick McIntosh, Susan McIntosh, Richard Meadow, James

Mellaart, A. T. M. Moore, Donna J. Nash, Chris O'Brien, Inger Österholm, David Overstreet, John Parkington, Peter Vang Petersen, Tom Pleger, Theron D. Price, Naomi Pritchard, Jeffrey Quilter, John Reader, Charles Redman, Merle Greene Robertson, Gary Rollefson, Ulrick Rossing, William Ruddiman, Denise Schmandt-Besserat, Sissel Schroeder, Kathie Schick, Jeff Shokler, Brian Siegel, Ralph Solecki, Charles Spencer, Dragoslav Srejovic, Sharon Steadman, Vin Steponaitis, Jim Stoltman, J. F. Thackeray, Helmut Thieme, David Hurst Thomas, Donald Thompson, Larry Todd, B. L. Turner II, Patty Jo Watson, John Weinstein, Huang Weiwen, J. Peter White, Joyce White, Edwin Wilmsen, Peter Woodman, and Tineke van Zandt.

Several individuals deserve special mention. Linda Nicholas helped greatly with many aspects of the project, especially finalizing large parts of the text and illustrations. Jennifer Blitz spent much of a year obtaining illustrations and permissions for the first edition with extraordinary energy and care. We are also very grateful to the teaching assistants we had over the years in our introductory course in archaeology at the University of Wisconsin for their input and comments.

Reviewers for the sixth edition provided lots of ideas and suggestions, and we gratefully acknowledge their contributions:

Charles Ewen, East Carolina University
Kristy Miller, Estrella Mountain Community College
Lisa Westwood, California State University–Chico
Nancy Marie White, University of South Florida
Slobodan Mitrovic, Brooklyn College
Timothy R. Pauketat, University of Illinois
Tina Thurston, SUNY Buffalo
Jennifer Taschek, San Diego State University
Mark A. Rees, University of Louisiana at Lafayette
Lisa Frink, University of Nevada–Las Vegas
Tineke Van Zandt, Pima Community College
Ellen E. Bell, California State University–Stanislaus
Alexia Smith, University of Connecticut
Alexandre Steenhuyse, Virginia Commonwealth University
Kerry Josef Pataki, Portland Community College–Sylvania

We thank our reviewers for the previous five editions, who provided help, ideas, and inspiration to revise and refine the text:

Douglas B. Bamforth, University of Colorado–Boulder
Timothy Baumann, University of Missouri–St. Louis
J. M. Beaton, University of California–Davis
Richard Blanton, Purdue University
Charles A. Bollong, University of Arizona
Scott Brosowske, University of Oklahoma
G. A. Clark, Arizona State University
Angela E. Close, University of Washington
Kathryn Cruz-Uribe, Northern Arizona University
Richard Effland, Mesa Community College
James Enloe, University of Iowa
Steven Falconer, Arizona State University
Kenneth L. Feder, Central Connecticut State University
Lynne Goldstein, Michigan State University
William A. Haviland, University of Vermont
John W. Hoopes, University of Kansas
John J. Killeen, Louis Berger and Associates, Cultural Resource Group
Steve Langdon, University of Alaska–Anchorage
Paul E. Langwalter II, Cypress College
Carole A. Mandryk, Harvard University
Marilyn Masson, State University of New York–Albany
Randall McGuire, State University of New York–Binghamton
Alan McPheran, University of Pittsburgh
Gary W. Pahl, San Francisco State University
Mary Pohl, Florida State University
David Pokotylo, University of British Columbia
Donald A. Proulx, University of Massachusetts–Amherst
John W. Rick, Stanford University
Lauren W. Ritterbush, University of Kansas
Ralph M. Rowlett, University of Missouri–Columbia
Katharina J. Schreiber, University of California–Santa Barbara
Michael P. Smyth, University of Kentucky
William Turnbaugh, University of Rhode Island
Peter S. Wells, University of Minnesota
Adam Wetsman, Rio Hondo College
Mary K. Whelan, University of Iowa
Randall White, New York University
Chip Wills, University of New Mexico
David J. Wilson, Southern Methodist University
Richard W. Yerkes, Ohio State University

This sixth edition has required a large group of talented individuals to put it together and we would like to heartily thank them. The McGraw-Hill staff included Gina Boedeker, Sponsoring Editor; Nicole Bridge, Managing Editor; David Blatty, Production Editor; Preston Thomas, Design Manager; Brian Pecko, Photo Permissions; Natalie Gibboney, Text and Art Permissions; Tandra Jorgensen, Production Supervisor; Thomas L. Briggs, Copyeditor; Kimberly McCutcheon, Proofreader; and Janice Wiggins-Clarke, Developmental Editor.

To all of these individuals go our deep and sincere thanks. We hope that you find the result worth your efforts and that you will continue to provide input, suggestions, and new discoveries that will improve the next edition.

T. Douglas Price
Gary M. Feinman

# About the Authors

Doug Price is Weinstein Professor of European Archaeology and Director of the Laboratory for Archaeological Chemistry at the University of Wisconsin–Madison, where he has been on the faculty for more than 30 years. He is also 6th Century Chair in Archaeological Science and a part-time member of the Department of Archaeology at the University of Aberdeen. His current research involves fieldwork on the beginnings of agriculture in Denmark and lab studies using strontium isotopes in human tooth enamel to address questions of prehistoric migration. He is the author of a number of books and articles on archaeology and has been involved in fieldwork in Ireland, Wisconsin, Michigan, the Netherlands, Peru, Israel, Guatemala, Mexico, and New Mexico. He likes archaeology, most children, cooking, college football, and the family dog, Bagel. He doesn't like long, self-promoting descriptions of the author of a book.

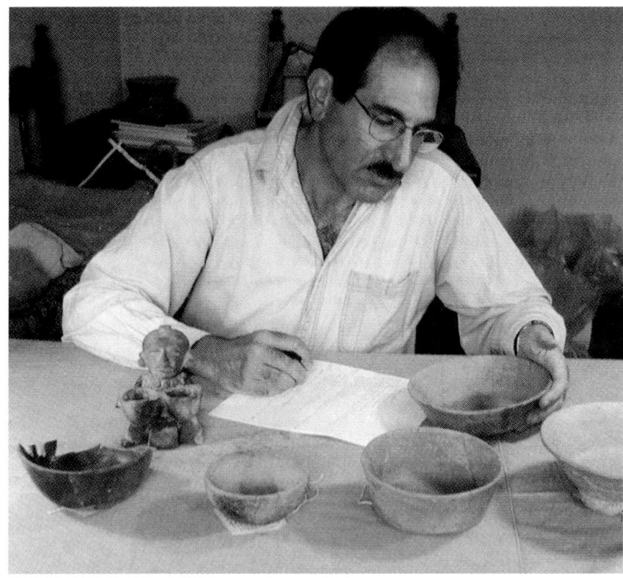

Gary Feinman is Curator of Mesoamerican Anthropology at The Field Museum in Chicago. He also is an Adjunct Professor of Anthropology at both the University of Illinois–Chicago and Northwestern University. Feinman's current research, which he directs with Linda Nicholas, is focused on understanding the economy and daily life at the time of the Monte Albán state in the Valley of Oaxaca, Mexico, primarily through excavations at the site of El Palmillo. He also is involved in a regional settlement pattern project in eastern Shandong Province, China, with colleagues from The Field Museum and Shandong University. Feinman is the author of various books and articles and also has conducted field research in the North American Southwest. He has taught postgraduate classes in Mexico and China. In addition to archaeology, Feinman enjoys sports, hiking, time with family and friends, travel, and communicating about science and archaeology to the public through diverse media and means.

## Also Available from McGraw-Hill

by T. Douglas Price

*Principles of Archaeology*, 2007

# CHAPTER ONE

**Figure 1.1** Excavations at Boxgrove, a Paleolithic site in England.

# Principles of Archaeology

## Introduction

Excavation is at the heart of the fascination of archaeology. Digging into the earth to reveal buried lives is an extraordinary undertaking. Excavations at the site of Boxgrove in southern England (Figure 1.1), for example, are uncovering human bones and stone tools from almost half a million years ago. Archaeology tells us about our human past.

This book, *Images of the Past,* is about archaeology and covers more than 7 million years and much of the planet. But it is simply not possible to write about all of human **prehistory** in a single volume such as this; that would be like trying to see all the attractions in Washington, DC, in 10 minutes. Because we can visit only a few of the more interesting places, we have chosen important archaeological sites that have substantially increased our understanding of the past.

We hope the pathway through the past that weaves through the following pages provides you with a sense of what archaeologists know about our global past and how they have come to know it. The trail that runs through this volume and ties the past to the present involves major trends in our development as a technological species—growth, diversification, and specialization. Growth is seen in the increasing number of people on the planet and in the greater complexity of human technology and organization. Diversity is observed in the variable roles and social relationships that exist in society and in the kinds of environments our species inhabits. Increasing specialization is witnessed in the tools and techniques used to obtain food and manufacture objects. The story of our human past, then, is the story of these changes over time as we evolved from small, local groups of people living close to nature to large nation-states involved in global trade, warfare, and politics.

**Archaeology** is the study of our human past, combining the themes of time and change. Those themes—change in our biology and change in our behavior over time—are also the focus of this book. Archaeology is the closest thing we have to a time machine, taking us backward through the mists of the ages. The fog becomes thicker the farther back we go, and the windows of our time machine become more obscured. In Chapter 2, we go as far back as humans can go, some 7 million years ago, when we took our first steps in Africa. Subsequent chapters trace the achievements of our ancestors as we migrated to new continents, developed innovative technologies for coping with cold climates, crafted more complex tools, imagined art, domesticated plants and animals, moved into cities, and created written languages. But first, in this chapter, we present an introduction for comprehending our human past—those themes of time and change—along with basic methods and principles of archaeology.

CHAPTER OUTLINE



**prehistory** In general, the human past; specifically, the time before the appearance of written records.

**archaeology** The study of the human past, combining the themes of time and change.

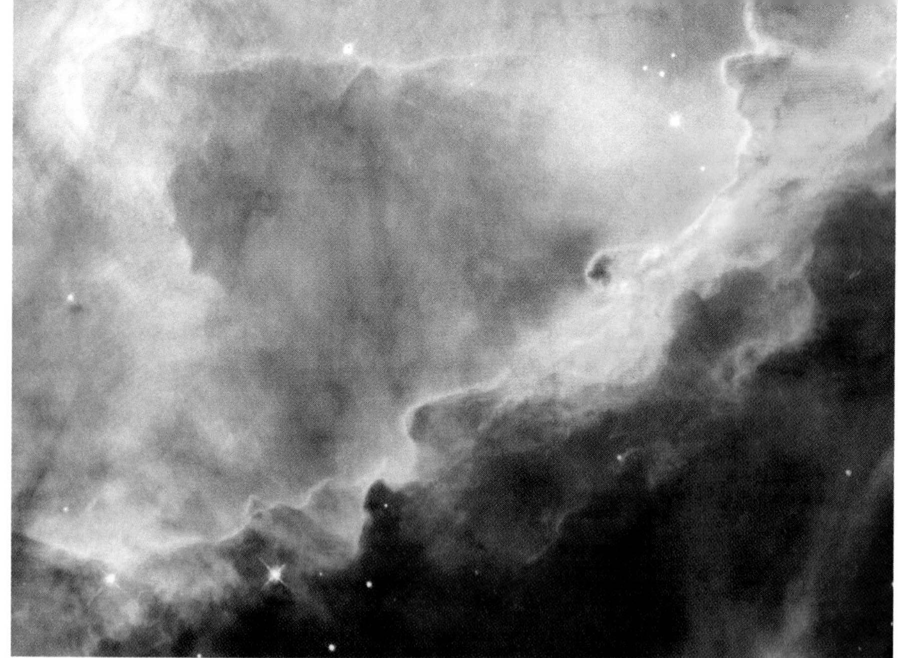

Figure 1.2 The Big Bang began the history of the universe, spewing space and time into the unknown.

## TIME

To understand time, it is necessary to imagine the unimaginable. Sometime between 10 and 15 billion years ago, an explosion of cosmic proportions ripped time and space apart and created our universe. Hydrogen and helium hurtled through the emptiness, cast out of that original Big Bang (Figure 1.2). Clouds of these gases began to coagulate, and as they were compacted by gravity, temperatures rose and the energy created in the nuclear furnaces of the first stars lit up the universe.

www.mhhe.com/priceip6e

For preview material for this chapter, see the comprehensive chapter outline and chapter objectives on your online learning center.

More complex reactions in these emerging stars gave rise to heavier atoms of carbon, oxygen, magnesium, silicon, sulfur, and the other elements. Huge eruptions and disintegrations tore these early elements out of the stars and spewed them across space, creating newer and heavier stars. Smaller conglomerations of elements, lacking the mass or the temperature to ignite, condensed and gathered around the edges of the brightly burning stars. Some of these cold outliers became hard, metallic globes; others, frigid balls of gas. The planets were born. Some gases remained on the harder planets and condensed into oceans or enveloped the surface as a primordial atmosphere. Violent electrical storms, driven by energy from the stars and cataclysmic volcanic activity, rifting the surface of the forming planets, tore apart and reconstituted these elements in the early seas and atmospheres.

On the planet we call Earth, formed about 4.6 billion years ago, this alchemy of primeval forces churned out new molecules in an atmosphere of methane, ammonia, hydrogen sulfide, water, and hydrogen. Among the multitude of chemistries created in the soup of the early earth's oceans was a remarkable combination of atoms. This was a strange molecule, able to reproduce itself—to make a copy of its original—to live. Life emerged shortly after 4 billion years ago. Like the broom of the sorcerer's apprentice in the film *Fantasia,* once begun, the copying process filled the seas with duplicates. These reproducing molecules grew, achieved more complex forms, and became the building blocks of more elaborate organisms that developed metabolic and sexual reproductive functions. Systems for eating and internal metabolism enabled organisms to obtain energy from other life-forms. Sexual reproduction allowed for a tremendous diversity in offspring and, thus, a greater capacity for adapting to changing environments and conditions.

*If you count one number per second, night and day, starting with 1, it would take 17 minutes to count to a thousand, 12 days to count to a million, and 32 years to count to a billion.*
—Carl Sagan (1987)

Plants appeared in the oceans and spread to the land. The atmosphere fed carbon dioxide to the plants, and they in turn replenished the air with oxygen through the process of photosynthesis. Swimming cooperatives of mole-

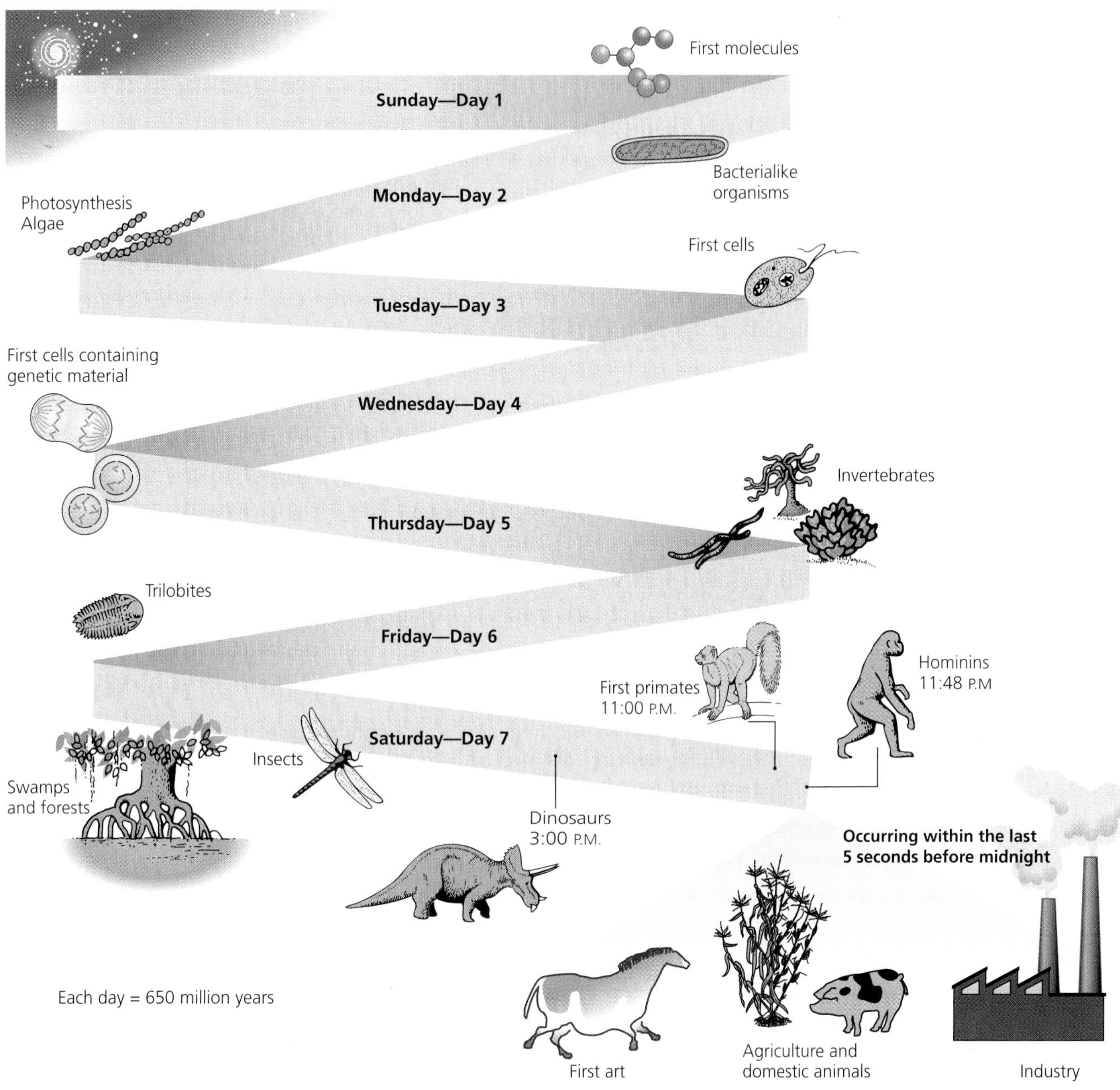


**Figure 1.3** The evolution of life on earth seen as a single week in time. Planet Earth forms at 12:01 on Sunday morning, life shows up for work on Monday morning, fish evolve on Saturday morning, and the first bipedal hominins show up at 11:48 Saturday night.

cules in the oceans moved onto the land and began to use the oxygen in the air for breathing and other metabolic functions. Fish, amphibians, reptiles, insects, mammals, and birds spread across the face of the earth. And then, only a moment ago in geological time, a human creature evolved as part of this great chain of living beings.

## Geological Time

Time is a very difficult concept. The universe is perhaps 10 billion years old. Earth is roughly 4.6 billion years old. The idea of 10 billion years, 4.6 billion years, or even 1 million years is impossible for us to comprehend. But to understand our past and our place in the cosmos, we need some way to appreciate such a vast span of time. If we could compact the eons that have passed into meaningful units of time, the events of our evolutionary history might make more sense.

Consider a single week, from Sunday morning to Saturday night, as a substitute for our countdown to today (Figure 1.3). One day in this 4.6-billion-year week would represent over 650 million years, a single hour would be 25 million years, a minute would be 400,000 years, and the passage of a single second would take more than 6000 years.

Roughly 4.6 billion years ago—the 7 days of our symbolic week—the earth formed in our solar system. The time was the first thing Sunday, 12:01 A.M. By Sunday evening, a primitive atmosphere and oceans had appeared, and the first molecules began to coalesce. By Monday morning, the first traces of life emerged in the shape of bacteria that evolved and multiplied. More complex bacteria and algae, using photosynthesis, began the task of converting the poisonous, primordial atmosphere to an oxygen base on Tuesday. Not until Thursday were the first cells carrying genetic material created. Late Friday morning, the first invertebrate animals—resembling jellyfish, sponges, and worms—evolved. Before dawn on Saturday morning, the seas were teeming with shell-bearing animals, such as the trilobites. Around breakfast time on Saturday, fish and small land plants appeared. By 11:00 A.M., amphibians began to move onto the land, and insects appeared in a warm landscape of swamps and forests. Late that same afternoon, the first dinosaurs crawled about. Smaller, warm-blooded dinosaurs began to produce live young and nurse them. The ancestors of modern mammals appeared shortly after 9:30 P.M. At 10:53 P.M., the common ancestor of apes and man made its home in the dense forests of Africa. The first recognizable human, walking on two legs, made an appearance at 11:48 P.M. The first art was created less than 5 seconds before midnight. Agriculture and animal domestication originated only 2 seconds before the end of the week, and the industrial revolution began just as the echoes of the last bell at midnight disappeared.

To help make this huge time span comprehensible, archaeologists and geologists have developed systems for breaking the vastness of time into smaller segments. Archaeologists deal with the period of humans on the planet, roughly the past 5 or 6 million years. Archaeologists use geological time, but they also have created a means of reckoning time that reflects changes in human behavior and artifacts. This archaeological system of chronology involves divisions such as Paleolithic, Neolithic, Bronze Age, and Iron Age and is discussed in more detail in a subsequent chapter. (See Chapter 3, p. 78.)

Geologists deal with the entire history of the earth and distinguish a series of **eras** representing major episodes, usually separated by significant changes in the plant and animal kingdoms (Figure 1.4). The Precambrian was the first major era of geological time, extending from the origin of the earth to about 600 million years ago (**m.y.a.**). The succeeding Paleozoic era witnessed the appearance of the first vertebrate species: fish and the first amphibians. Plants spread onto the land, and reptiles began to appear. Around 245 m.y.a., the Mesozoic era, the Age of Dinosaurs, began following a period of extinction. The Cenozoic, our current era, began about 65 m.y.a. with the expansion of modern mammals, birds, and flowering plants, following extinction of the dinosaurs. This episode of extinction is now thought to have resulted from the catastrophic impact of a meteor, causing major climatic and environmental disruption.

The Cenozoic is further divided by geologists into a series of seven **epochs,** only the last four of which are relevant to the evolution of the human species. The Miocene, which dates from 25 to 5.5 m.y.a., witnessed the emergence of our first humanlike ancestor near the end of the epoch. The Pliocene, beginning about 5.5 m.y.a., is the geological epoch in which a variety of hominins, or humanlike creatures, appeared. The Pleistocene, beginning about 2 m.y.a., was marked by a series of major climatic fluctuations. Completely modern forms of the human species appeared toward the end of this epoch. The Recent epoch—also called the Holocene (or the Postglacial or Present Interglacial)—began only

**era** A major division of geological time, tens or hundreds of millions of years long, usually distinguished by significant changes in the plant and animal kingdoms. Also used to denote later archaeological periods, such as the prehistoric era.

**m.y.a.** Abbreviation for *millions of years ago.*

**epoch** A subdivision of geological time, millions of years long, representing units of eras.

| Era | Period | Epoch | Millions of years ago (m.y.a) | Important Events |
|---|---|---|---|---|
| CENOZOIC | Quaternary | Recent (Holocene) | | Modern genera of animals. |
| | | | 0.01 | |
| | | Pleistocene | | Early humans and giant mammals now extinct; glaciation. |
| | | | 2.0 | |
| | Tertiary | Pliocene | | Anthropoid radiation and culmination of mammalian speciation. |
| | | | 5.5 | |
| | | Miocene | | Earliest apes. |
| | | | 25 | |
| | | Oligocene | | |
| | | | 38 | |
| | | Eocene | | Expansion and modernization of mammals. |
| | | | 54 | |
| | | Paleocene | | |
| | | | 65 | |
| MESOZOIC | Cretaceous | | | Dinosaurs dominant; marsupial and placental mammals appear; first flowering plants spread rapidly. |
| | | | 135 | |
| | Jurassic | | | Dominance of dinosaurs; first mammals and birds; insects abundant, including social forms. |
| | | | 180 | |
| | Triassic | | | First dinosaurs and mammal-like reptiles, with culmination of large amphibians. |
| | | | 245 | |
| PALEOZOIC | Permian | | | Primitive reptiles replace amphibians as dominant class; glaciation. |
| | | | 270 | |
| | Carboniferous | | | Amphibians dominant in luxuriant coal forests; first reptiles and trees. |
| | | | 350 | |
| | Devonian | | | Dominance of fishes; first amphibians. |
| | | | 400 | |
| | Silurian | | | Primitive fishes; invasion of land by plants and arthropods. |
| | | | 440 | |
| | Ordovician | | | First vertebrates, the jawless fish; invertebrates dominate the seas. |
| | | | 500 | |
| | Cambrian | | | All invertebrate phyla appear and algae diversify. |
| | | | 540 | |
| PRE-CAMBRIAN | | | | Oldest rocks; a few multicellular invertebrates; earliest fossils at 3.6 b.y.a. Single-cell organisms appear. |
| | | | 4600 | |

**Figure 1.4** The major periods of geological time and their principal characteristics.

11,000 years ago and witnessed the origins of agriculture, the first cities, and the industrial age, including our present time.

## CHANGE

Change, modification, variation—these themes describe the path of evolution from the first self-replicating molecules to fully modern humans of today. Most of the evolution of life on Earth is marked by biological evolution from one species to another in order to adapt to change. As humans, we have a second, unique system for adaptation that involves learned behaviors. **Culture** is a means of human adaptation based on experience, learning, and the use of tools. Cultural and biological responses to cold conditions provide an example. Humans built fires to stay warm, whereas body hair increased on other animals, such as the woolly mammoth. Within limits, culture enables us to modify and enhance our behavior without a corresponding change in our genetic makeup. As a consequence, biological evolution and natural selection alone cannot explain the culturally acquired traits of the human species.

The prehistoric record of our ancestors is characterized by both biological evolution and cultural developments (Figure 1.5). Biological, rather than cultural, changes dominated our first several million years of existence. The evolution of our earliest forebears was highlighted by key changes in movement, body

**culture** A uniquely human means of nonbiological adaptation; a repertoire of learned behaviors for coping with the physical and social environments.

Figure 1.5 Biological organisms and cultural artifacts change over time. The history of the automobile from A.D. 1910 to 2000. The evolution of the horse from *Hyracotherium,* 45 m.y.a., to *Equus,* 1 m.y.a.

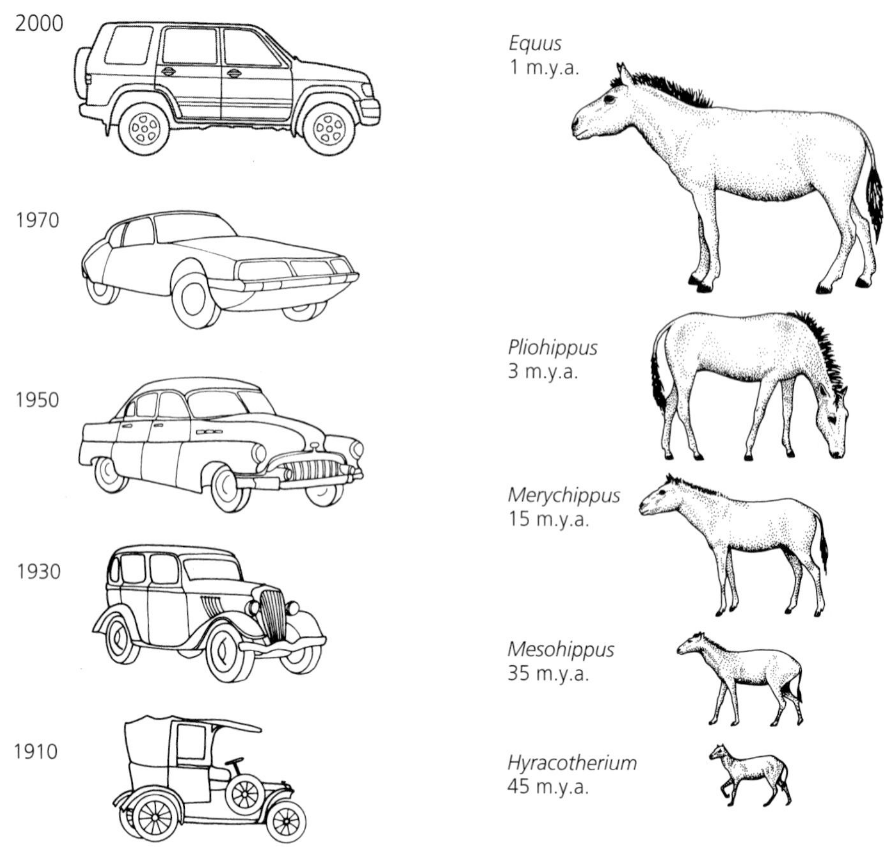


size, teeth, and the size and organization of the brain. The transmission of cultural traits through learning occurs much more rapidly than Darwinian evolution. The past hundred thousand years or so of our presence on the planet are marked primarily by cultural changes rather than biological ones. The story of archaeology—the search for evidence of our cultural development over time—is the subject of this book. The nature of biological evolution is briefly discussed in more detail before we return to the subject of archaeology.

## Biological Evolution

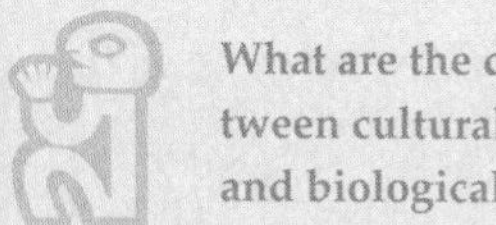

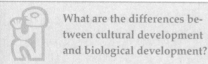

What are the differences between cultural development and biological development?

The theory of natural selection, formulated by Charles Darwin and Alfred Russel Wallace in the middle of the nineteenth century, describes this process of change. Wallace and Darwin were strongly influenced by the ideas of Thomas Malthus, an English clergyman and philosopher. In his *Essay on the Principle of Population* (1798), Malthus observed that the growth rate of the human population potentially exceeded the amount of food available. Malthus argued that famine, war, and disease limited the size of human populations, and for those reasons the number of people did not overwhelm the resources available to feed them. In essence, Malthus noted that not everyone who was born survived to reproduce.

Darwin coined the term *natural selection* to account for the increase in offspring of those individuals who did survive. He introduced the concept in his 1859 publication *On the Origin of Species by Means of Natural Selection.* During a global voyage of exploration aboard the HMS *Beagle,* Darwin had observed that most species of plants and animals showed a great deal of variation—that individuals were distinct and exhibited different characteristics. Following Malthus, Darwin pointed out that all organisms produce more offspring than can survive and that the individuals that survive do so because of certain advantageous characteristics they possess.

In other words, the surviving organisms are better adapted to the world that confronts them. For example, offspring with better hearing or eyesight can more effectively avoid predators. Nature's choice of better-adapted individuals—the "survival of the fittest," according to Darwin—leads to continual change in the species, as their more advantageous characteristics are passed genetically from one generation to the next. This basic process gave rise to the myriad creatures that occupy the world today. Evolutionary change is often described as differential reproductive success, and natural selection is the principal, though not the exclusive, mechanism responsible for it. Of course, as environmental conditions change, those physical characteristics that enhance survival and successful parenting also may vary.

Views on this process of **evolution** change over time, too. New mechanisms for evolution have been proposed, and there is ongoing discussion about the level in populations at which selection operates, whether on groups or on individuals. There is also debate about the pace of change—whether major evolutionary modifications occurred gradually, as Darwin emphasized, or rather abruptly and suddenly. Stephen Jay Gould and Niles Eldredge of Harvard University describe the uneven pace of evolution as "punctuated equilibrium." It now seems that some biological shifts occur gradually, as Darwin described, whereas others may occur in rapid spurts following long periods of stasis, or little change. A major theory such as evolution is modified over time, but the basic tenets of this view have withstood many tests and offer the best way to understand the emergence of life and early humans.

Does evolution happen slowly or quickly?

## FUNDAMENTALS OF ARCHAEOLOGY

As noted previously, archaeology is the study of our human past, combining the themes of time and change, using the material remains that have survived. Archaeology focuses on past human behavior and change in society over time. Archaeologists study past human culture across an enormous amount of time and space—essentially, the last several million years and all of the continents except Antarctica. In one sense, archaeology is the investigation of the choices that our ancestors made as they evolved from the first humans to the historical present.

Archaeology is also a detective story, a mystery far more complex and harder to solve than most crimes. The clues to past human behavior are enigmatic—broken, decomposed, and often missing. Piecing together these bits of information to make sense of the activities of our ancestors is a challenge. This challenge—and the ingenuity, technology, and hard work necessary to solve it—creates both the excitement and the frustration of archaeology.

Archaeology is a fascinating field, in part because the subject matter is highly diverse and highly human. There are so many times and places involved, and so many questions to be asked. Archaeology accommodates an extraordinarily wide range of interests: chemistry, zoology, human biology, ceramics, classics, computers, experiments, geology, history, stone tools, museums, human fossils, theory, genetics, scuba diving, and much, much more. Many of these subjects are discussed in the following chapters.

Another way to regard the nature of archaeology is to consider how it fits in among academic fields of study. There are different kinds of archaeology, and disciplinary homes vary. Archaeology is usually situated in the social sciences or humanities in a university setting. In the United States, archaeology is usually part of a Department of Anthropology, which combines archaeology with **biological anthropology** and **cultural anthropology,** all focused on humans and culture. Biological anthropology is the study of the biological nature of our nearest relatives and ourselves. Biological anthropologists study bones, blood, genetics,

**evolution** The process of change over time resulting from shifting conditions of the physical and cultural environments, involving mechanisms of mutation and natural selection.

**biological anthropology** The study of the biological nature of our nearest relatives and ourselves.

**cultural anthropology** The study of living peoples and the shared aspects of the human experience.

growth, demography, and other aspects of living and fossil humans and primates like the monkeys and apes. Cultural, or social, anthropologists study living peoples and focus on the shared aspects of the human experience, describing both the differences and the common characteristics that exist.

Archaeology in anthropology departments is sometimes designated as **anthropological archaeology,** or **prehistory.** Anthropological archaeology refers specifically to archaeological investigations that seek to answer the larger, fundamental questions about humans and human behavior that are part of anthropological enquiry. Prehistory refers to the time of humans before the written record placed us in history. Many archaeologists do study prehistory, but many also study literate societies such as the Maya and Aztec, and the urban civilizations of ancient Mesopotamia and China, where writing began. The term *prehistory* is often misused and applied to these early literate civilizations as well. **Historical archaeology**—archaeology in combination with the written record—borders on the field of history and usually refers specifically to the archaeology of civilizations of the Renaissance and industrial era.

## The Discovery of Archaeological Sites

Archaeologists study change in human culture, from the time of our early ancestors to the historical present. Much of the information about the past comes from artifacts and sites. **Artifacts** are the objects and materials that people in the past made and used. **Sites** are accumulations of such artifacts, representing the places where people lived or carried out certain activities. The process of discovery, analysis, and interpretation of artifacts and sites is the basic means through which archaeologists learn about the past.

Archaeological materials are most often discovered by accident. Digging and construction activities often uncover prehistoric objects; farmers and individuals in the outdoors come upon artifacts. Amateur archaeologists often know a great deal about the prehistory of their local areas and frequently find sites while walking fields. It is essential that these finds be reported to a local historical society, museum, or university. The past is too important not to share.

In addition to the chance discoveries, much of the information gathering for archaeological studies requires **fieldwork** that is intended to locate artifacts and sites. Artifacts and sites are found either on the surface or beneath the ground. **Surveys** (undertaken by archaeologists to discover artifacts on the ground) and **excavations** (used to expose buried materials) are the primary discovery techniques of professional field archaeology.

The discovery of archaeological sites depends in part on what is already known about the landscape, environment, and history of an area. Before beginning fieldwork, archaeologists check the relevant written material on the time period and place of interest. That research reveals the present state of knowledge, indicates what is not known, as well as what is, and helps establish directions for further research. Such library research is also essential to ensure that investigations similar to those planned have not already been completed.

The next step is to visit the local historical society or other archaeological institutions, such as museums or university departments, where records of the area are maintained. Such institutions generally keep archives of information on the location and contents of known archaeological and historical sites. Study of those archives indicates what types of sites are already known and perhaps their size and the general content of artifacts. Conversations with local amateur archaeologists and other interested individuals can provide additional useful information.

Maps are one of the most important tools for fieldwork. Topographic maps (showing the shape of the land surface with contour or elevation lines) are available for most areas and contain a great deal of information about longitude and latitude, elevation, slope, and the location of water, roads, towns, and other fea-

**anthropological archaeology (prehistory)** Archaeological investigations that seek to answer fundamental questions about humans and human behavior.

**historical archaeology** Archaeology in combination with the written record.

**artifact** Any object or item created or modified by human action.

**site** The accumulation of artifacts and/or ecofacts, representing a place where people lived or carried out certain activities.

**fieldwork** The search for archaeological sites in the landscape through surveys and excavations.

**survey** A systematic search of the landscape for artifacts and sites on the ground through aerial photography, field walking, soil analysis, and geophysical prospecting.

**excavation** The exposure and recording of buried materials from the past.

**Figure 1.6** An aerial photograph of an effigy mound in southern Wisconsin, approximately 800 years old. The mound has been outlined in white. See also the aerial photograph of Poverty Point, Louisiana, in Figure 7.4.

tures. In the United States, the U.S. Geological Survey compiles and distributes these maps.

Aerial photographs also can provide information on the location of archaeological sites (Figure 1.6). Old foundations or prehistoric agricultural fields, overgrown with vegetation and almost hidden on the surface, may appear in aerial photographs. When prehistoric structures were originally abandoned, the depressions often filled with rich topsoil, which provides better growth conditions for vegetation. In fields of wheat, for example, such different soil conditions might result in a distinctive pattern showing the outlines of houses or whole villages. In many parts of the world, such patterns are best observed from low-flying planes during a dry period in the early summer.

The next step in discovering the past involves fieldwork. An archaeological survey is a systematic search of the landscape for artifacts and sites (Figure 1.7). It is not always possible to make a complete survey of the entire area under investigation, because roads, forests, other vegetation, or construction often covers substantial parts of the landscape. It may be possible to thoroughly survey only a portion of the entire area, but that portion should be representative of the larger region under investigation. The larger the proportion of the research area that can be surveyed, the better.

**Figure 1.7** Field survey in Denmark. The small red flags mark the location of finds on the surface of the plowed field. This site was from the Neolithic period.

**Figure 1.8** Working a site. Intensive surface collections are made to pick up artifacts that may help date the site. One archaeologist holds a stadia rod used to measure the elevation.

The basic type of archaeological field survey involves systematic field walking. Field crews walk up and down cultivated fields and exposed surfaces. The intervals between the walks are determined by the size of the sites that may be in the area and the nature of the ground cover.

When an artifact is found, it is put in a bag, and the location of the find is recorded (Figure 1.8). The surrounding area should be searched carefully by walking back and forth at close intervals. It is important to determine whether the object is a single, isolated find or whether there are more artifacts. Surveyors also look for unusual discolorations on the surface that might indicate features such as fireplaces or pits. It is important to establish the area covered by artifacts to determine the size of the site and to obtain an estimate of the density of artifacts.

Information must be recorded about each find. These field notes should include such information as (1) location, site number, map number, which field, and position in the field; (2) the archaeological material found: types and number of artifacts, fire-cracked stones, charcoal, and so on; and (3) observations about the site—for example, discolorations in the soil that could indicate cultural layers or pits, the presence of mounds, stone foundations or walls, nearby streams or other sources of water, and other pertinent environmental information.

Archaeological remains are often buried beneath the sediments that have accumulated since their deposition. Objects found on the surface often have been brought up from deeper layers through agricultural or animal activities. Such materials usually provide only a partial indication of the information that can be obtained from a buried site.

Once buried sites have been located by survey and have been mapped, other kinds of fieldwork can be undertaken to learn more about them. Boring into the ground with an auger or corer brings up a column of soil showing the sequence of layers and samples of sediments at the site. Small test pits, perhaps 1 × 1 m in size, dug into the ground can provide similar information and may be necessary to determine if a buried site is present. A number of borings and/or test pits often are made, following a regular pattern over the surface of the site. Soil samples should be collected from all parts of the site and at varying depths.

Physical and chemical analysis of soil samples may provide information about the origins of the deposits, the water content and fertility of the soil, the amount of organic material, and the basic chemistry of the soil. These studies may provide further information on environmental and human activities involved in the formation and burial of the site and help to explain the conditions of preservation.

Phosphate analysis of the sediments from a site may reveal traces of human activities. Phosphate is found in bone, feces, urine, and other organic matters that accumulate in and around human habitation. Phosphate appears as a strong blue color in the soil sample when hydrochloric acid and ascorbic acid are added. Areas with higher concentrations of phosphate show up as stronger blue colors in such analyses. Phosphate testing may supplement surface surveys in areas where vegetation prevents observations of the surface or where cultural layers are buried deep under the topsoil. Within a known habitation area, these tests may be used to determine the extent of the site and to detect special areas such as house floors.

Other objects in the soil also are informative. Materials found in soil samples often include pieces of wood and plants, seeds, fragments of insects, mollusk shells, hair, or chips of bone or stone. Such items provide information on the formation of the layers, the local environment, and the nature of past human activities. For example, if small chips that result from the manufacture of arrowheads and other stone tools are present in borings and test pits, it is likely that tools were made or used in the vicinity and that other buried artifacts are present.

Geophysical prospecting can be used to detect disturbances in the subsoil and the presence of prehistoric features. These methods include measurements of magnetic variations in the ground and of the electrical conductivity (resistivity) of the soil, and the use of ground-penetrating radar. Metal detectors, for example,

(a)

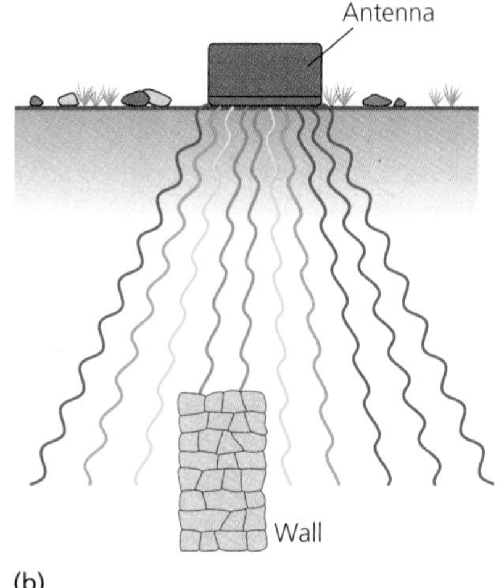

(b)

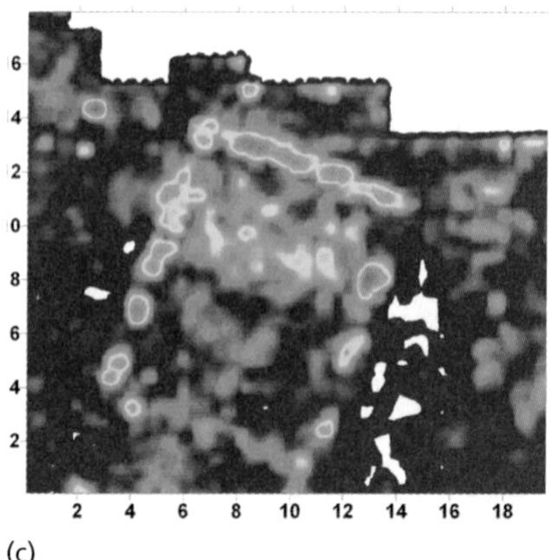

(c)

**Figure 1.9** Georadar in action. (a) Lawrence Conyers and assistant pulling the ground-penetrating radar (GPR) across an open area at Petra. (b) Schematic drawing of the instrument in use, emitting microwaves and measuring the response with an antenna. (c) A computer-generated display of the results of the magnetometer survey showing the outline of a rectangular structure buried in the middle of the open area. Test pits at this location revealed that stone walls were being recorded by the GPR.

register the presence of metal objects on the surface and buried in the soil. Metal detectors emit an electromagnetic field that is disrupted by the presence of metal objects in the ground. Magnetometers can provide a map of the magnetic anomalies in the ground and are very useful for finding buried structures.

The use of **ground-penetrating radar** (**GPR** or **georadar**) is standard practice on many archaeological excavations to look for features and structures before excavation. The use of ground-penetrating radar is a technique for studying buried archaeological sites (Figure 1.9). Electromagnetic waves in the form of georadar are sent into the ground, something like the sonar used in submarine hunts. Low-energy radar waves register anomalies in the subsoil, which are shown on a map or a graph. Excavation is often required to identify such irregularities.

In sum, prehistoric sites are often found through a combination of archival research and fieldwork. Archival research provides information on what is already known about an area. Fieldwork often results in the discovery of the unknown. When new sites are discovered, surface survey, testing, boring, and several geophysical methods are available to determine the size and possible contents of the prehistoric deposit. However, once a site is discovered and defined from the surface, excavations are often necessary to expose what lies beneath the surface of the ground.

## Archaeological Excavation

Excavation is the technique that archaeologists use to uncover buried remains from the past. Buried materials usually are more abundant and better preserved than those found on the surface. In excavations, accurate information can be observed on the arrangement and relationships of structures, artifacts, plant and animal remains, and other materials. The term *in situ* (Latin, "in place") is used to describe archaeological remains in their original position of deposition.

Excavation often is essential to obtain more information about the past. Excavations are conducted to answer specific questions that the archaeologist would like to answer: Who lived at the site? What did they eat? What did they do? Where did they get raw materials for making tools and equipment? What kinds of relations did they have with their neighbors? How was their society organized and structured? How did they understand the world around them? and so on.

*The Excavation Director* The direction of an excavation requires a variety of skills and knowledge for planning the field season, raising money to pay for the work, supervising and training a crew of volunteers or students, recording the

www.mhhe.com/priceip6e

For a Web-based activity on the opening of the tomb of Tutankhamen, see the Internet exercises on your online learning center.

**ground-penetrating radar (GPR or georadar)** An instrument for remote sensing or prospecting for buried structures using radar maps of subsoil features.

Figure 1.10 Excavations at a Mesolithic site in Denmark. Measuring, recording, studying.

information from the site with drawings and photographs, and measuring and mapping the location of all finds, samples, and features (Figure 1.10). The director must monitor progress in the field laboratory as well, where finds are washed, sorted, cataloged, and bagged for storage. Some knowledge of preservation techniques is necessary to conserve fragile objects.

Excavations require reams of drawings, recordings, and other paperwork. The director must keep an excavation log or diary, recording the course of the excavations, the work schedule, the number of people working, accounts of expenses, dimensions and positioning of excavation areas, layout of the measuring system, and all finds. There must be recording systems for all measurements, for observations and interpretations, and for all drawings, photos, and samples.

*The Field Crew* Archaeology is the science of the past, but it is also a social experience in the present. Excavation is a labor-intensive undertaking, and the field crew is the most important part of the project. This crew is a group of individuals involved in the actual digging process, unearthing the sites and artifacts. Crews are composed of a variety of individuals, young and old, ranging from professional archaeologists with advanced degrees to undergraduate and graduate students, and sometimes people just interested in the subject.

Fieldwork can require a few days, weeks, or months and can involve walking miles each day with one's head down in a survey of the ground or moving tons of earth to expose buried levels. Excavations are hard work, often in the hot sun. Frequently, they are carried out in remote places, requiring patience and endurance. Archaeology is also good dirty fun, and the experience of working, and relaxing, with others who enjoy the same things can be unforgettable. The discovery process is captivating, and sharing that excitement with colleagues and comrades enhances the entire experience.

Fieldwork is, finally, an extraordinary learning experience. One realizes the difficulties involved in recovering information from the past and comes to appreciate what has been previously learned. In addition, a constant stream of questions about the past and the significance of place, artifact, and context comes to mind during the process. All in all, archaeological fieldwork can be one of the most stimulating activities there is.

*Selecting Sites for Excavation* The choice of which site to excavate is determined by several factors, including potential danger to the archaeological remains. Archaeological sites are being destroyed at a rapid rate by the growth and development of modern civilization, and there is a serious and real concern about the loss of undisturbed sites for future research. Sites threatened by

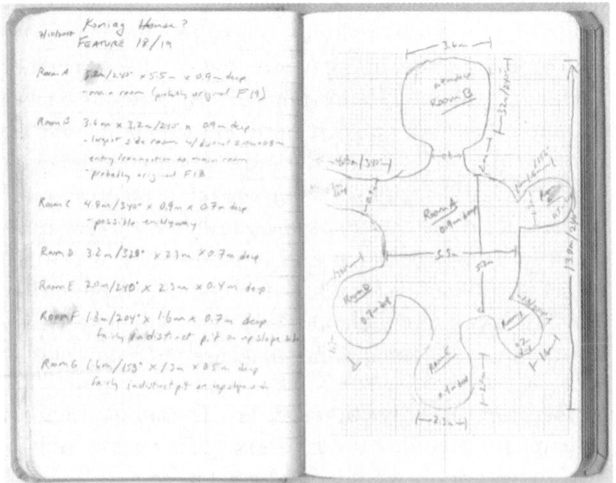

Figure 1.11 Archaeological field notes: two pages of information on an Alaskan koniag house and its features.

THEN

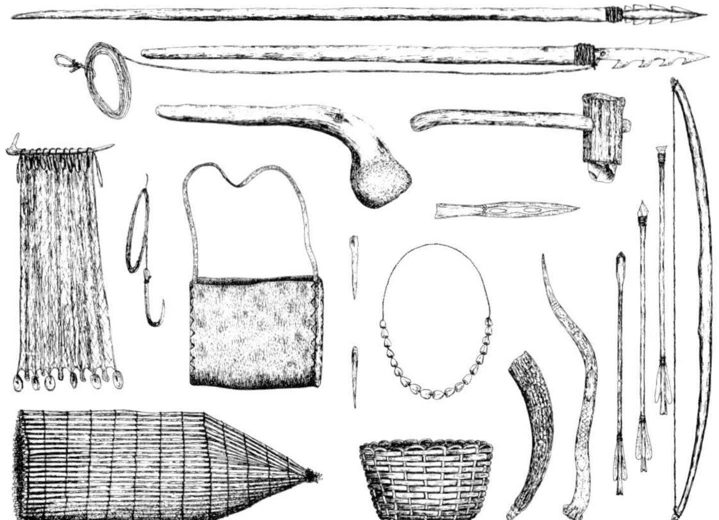

NOW

**Figure 1.12** The vagaries of preservation. Organic materials—wood, bones, features, antlers, hides, and the like—rarely survive in archaeological sites. The upper drawing shows some original material from the Stone Age in Scandinavia, including fishing and hunting spears, fishing nets, clubs and axes, a bow and arrows, baskets and bags, necklaces and pendants, and other tools. The lower drawing shows what would remain after the organic material decayed: the stone arrowheads, an axe, and the stone weights for the fishing net—only a tiny part of the total equipment that was in use in the past.

modern construction are often good candidates for excavation. The rescue excavation, intended to save information from such sites, is the most common type of project taking place today.

Sites are also chosen for excavation because they appear to be well preserved or to contain new information that will help us to better understand the prehistory of a particular region. The choice of a site for excavation is often based on the results of a survey. An initial survey of an area, including coring and testing, may indicate that one or several sites would be worth excavating. Careful surface collection and testing must be carried out at the site selected for excavation to make sure the site can provide the kinds of information that are needed and to assist in planning the excavation.

Historical archives may be studied over and over again, but archaeological sites are nonrenewable resources, something like endangered species. Excavations involve moving the earth and all its contents from a site. Every excavation means the destruction of all or part of an archaeological site. All that is left when an excavation is over are the finds themselves, the unexcavated parts of the site, and the samples, photographs, drawings, measurements, and other notes that the archaeologists made. Accurate notes and records of the layers, structures, and artifacts at a site are essential, not only for the investigator, but also to create a permanent archive of information about the site that is available to others (Figure 1.11).

Figure 1.13 A total station in use mapping an archaeological site in the highlands of Peru. Two members of the field crew work at the total station, and two others are locating and marking map points with the reflecting target for the total station. The total station uses a laser beam to measure the distance and angle between the instrument and the target and then calculates the exact position of the target.

www.mhhe.com/priceip6e

For a Web-based activity on the innovative area of GIS, see the Internet exercises on your online learning center.

**bioturbation** Activities of plants and animals in the earth, causing disturbance of archaeological materials.

**total station** A computerized surveying and mapping instrument that uses a laser beam or radio waves to measure the distance and angle between the instrument and the target and then calculates the exact position of the target.

**archaeological record** The body of material and information that survives for archaeologists to study.

**context** The association and relationships between archaeological objects that are in the same place.

The contents of a particular site are a matter of preservation (Figure 1.12). Important factors in preservation include the age of the site, the effects of erosion and deposition, **bioturbation,** and conditions of humidity and acidity. Archaeological sites vary from excellent conditions of almost complete preservation in extremely wet or arid conditions to poor acidic situations where almost nothing is left but inorganic objects of stone, pottery, and perhaps charcoal. Examples of extraordinary preservation can be seen in the Tollund Man from the waterlogged bogs of Denmark (see Figure 11.49) and the Iceman from the frozen glaciers of Alpine Italy (see Figure 11.10). Very old sites from the Paleolithic rarely have good conditions for preservation, and thus only stone tools and occasionally bones are preserved.

It is important to know as much as possible about a site before full-scale excavation in order to choose the best strategy for the project. At every excavation, the archaeologist is faced with a series of decisions about how to achieve the most and best-documented information. Under ideal circumstances, a site could be fully excavated and everything recorded in the finest detail. In the real world, however, constraints on time and funding and a need to leave a portion of the site for future archaeologists make it standard practice to excavate only a part of the total site.

*Maps and Grids* Accurate mapping of layers and artifacts is the key to the proper recording of information at an archaeological excavation. The exact topography, or shape, of the site must be recorded in the form of an accurate contour map made using a surveyor's level and the site grid. A grid is marked out across the surface of a site before excavation. This grid should be used for all horizontal measurements. A site grid represents a coordinate system, usually with lines running north-south and east-west at regular intervals. Intervals along the two axes of the grid are designated with a system of letters or numbers or both. The grid lines and measurements within each grid square are measured as distances in meters and centimeters north and east of the baselines at the edge of the excavations.

The site grid may also be oriented according to local topography or archaeological features such as mounds or middens. At coastal sites, trenches are sometimes excavated perpendicular to the coastline to study layers and site formation in relation to the coast. In a narrow cave, the grid is often aligned to the long axis of the cave.

Location of the site and the site grid in relation to global latitude and longitude must be determined. A control point, or site datum, must be located in the neighborhood of the excavation as a point of origin for vertical measurements. A preexisting datum point, such as a surveyor's benchmark, may be used if available. Otherwise, a permanent feature, such as a rock outcrop or a building foundation, may be marked and used as the datum point. The location and elevation of this point must be established in relation to known points, such as geographic features or distant benchmarks.

Vertical location in the excavation is best determined using a surveying instrument, set at a known elevation, and sighting on a vertical measuring rod. Measurements at the site should be converted to meters above sea level, or the elevation of the datum line may simply be recorded. In archaeology today, a **total station** is normally used to electronically map the site, record elevations, and determine the location of architecture, features, and artifacts (Figure 1.13).

## CONTEXT, ASSOCIATION, AND PROVENIENCE

The body of evidence that archaeologists work with is part of the **archaeological record**—the information about the past that has survived to the present. This record includes both past materials and the context in which they are found. **Context** is an essential aspect of archaeological information. Context involves the association and relationships between objects that are in the same place.

At a basic level, context concerns relationships among artifacts. Items that are found together in the same pit, the same layer, or the same sediment, for example, are assumed to be related in terms of time and activity. That is, objects in the same context are thought to have been in use together in time and geographic space, roughly contemporary, and involved in the same activities or resulting from similar behaviors.

In a broader sense, context is the physical setting, location, and association of artifacts and features. Context is of major importance in archaeology and provides much of the information necessary for the determination of authenticity and significance. Context is essential for learning about age, use, and meaning. The more that is known about the context of archaeological remains, the more that can be learned about the past, of both the artifacts themselves and the people who made them.

A distinction is made between primary and secondary context. An object in its original position of discard or deposition, in the place where it was left, is said to be in **primary context** or ***in situ*** (Latin, "in place"). Objects that have been moved from their original place of deposition are in secondary context and so are less useful for learning about the past. When artifacts are removed from their original location, without proper excavation and documentation, contextual information is lost forever. Looters are unconcerned with the context of archaeological materials. Peter Cannon-Brookes describes looted artifacts as "cultural orphans, which, torn from their contexts, remain forever dumb and virtually useless for scholarly purposes."

An important term in the realm of context is **provenience,** or place of origin. The provenience of an artifact—the place it was found—is very important. Provenience implies context, meaning that there is additional information available about the object of interest. Artifacts and other archaeological objects with an unknown provenience provide very little information for learning about the past.

**Figure 1.14** A section of an excavation trench exposing a stratigraphy of stream and lake deposits that succeeded one another as water levels changed in this area. The upper part of the deposit is recent blown sand.

*Test Pits* Preliminary examination of a site involves digging a series of one or more trenches or small, vertical test pits, perhaps 1 × 1 m in size, across the site. The test squares to be excavated may also be placed in rows or in a chessboard-like pattern across the site. Alternatively, their location may be chosen at random. The size and the number of test pits to be excavated depend on the kind of information being sought. In some cases, it is difficult to visualize the stratigraphy, or set of layers, observed in the small test pits. One or two long trenches across the site may provide a better view of the stratigraphy.

What are some of the important skills an archaeologist needs?

*Vertical Excavations* Excavations are generally either vertical or horizontal. Vertical excavation takes the form of test pits or trenches carefully placed across a site to expose the stratigraphy and artifact contents of a site (Figure 1.14). By studying the vertical walls (the sections) of such pits or trenches, archaeologists can identify stratified layers of soil sediments.

The stratigraphy, or layers, of natural sediments and human deposits reveals how the site was formed and how materials accumulated (Figure 1.15). The relationships between deposits in the stratigraphic sequence indicate the chronological arrangement of the layers. The bottom layer is deposited first as the oldest layer in the sequence. The subsequent layers are progressively younger—the law of superposition. The stratigraphic sequence provides a relative chronology whereby layers and the artifacts they contain can be determined to be "younger than" or "older than" other layers and artifacts in the same sequence.

The thickness of a layer is determined not so much by the length of time that it took to accumulate as by the natural and human activities involved in the deposition of the materials. Heaps of shells may accumulate very rapidly into high **shell middens** (large dumps of shells from mussels, oysters, or other species); the collapse of houses with earth or sod walls results in very thick layers; stone

**primary context (*in situ*)** An object found where it was originally located in antiquity, not redeposited.

**provenience** The place of origin for archaeological materials, including location, association, and context.

**shell midden** A mound of shells accumulated from human collection, consumption, and disposal; a dump of shells from oysters, clams, mussels, or other species found along coasts and rivers, usually dating to the Holocene.

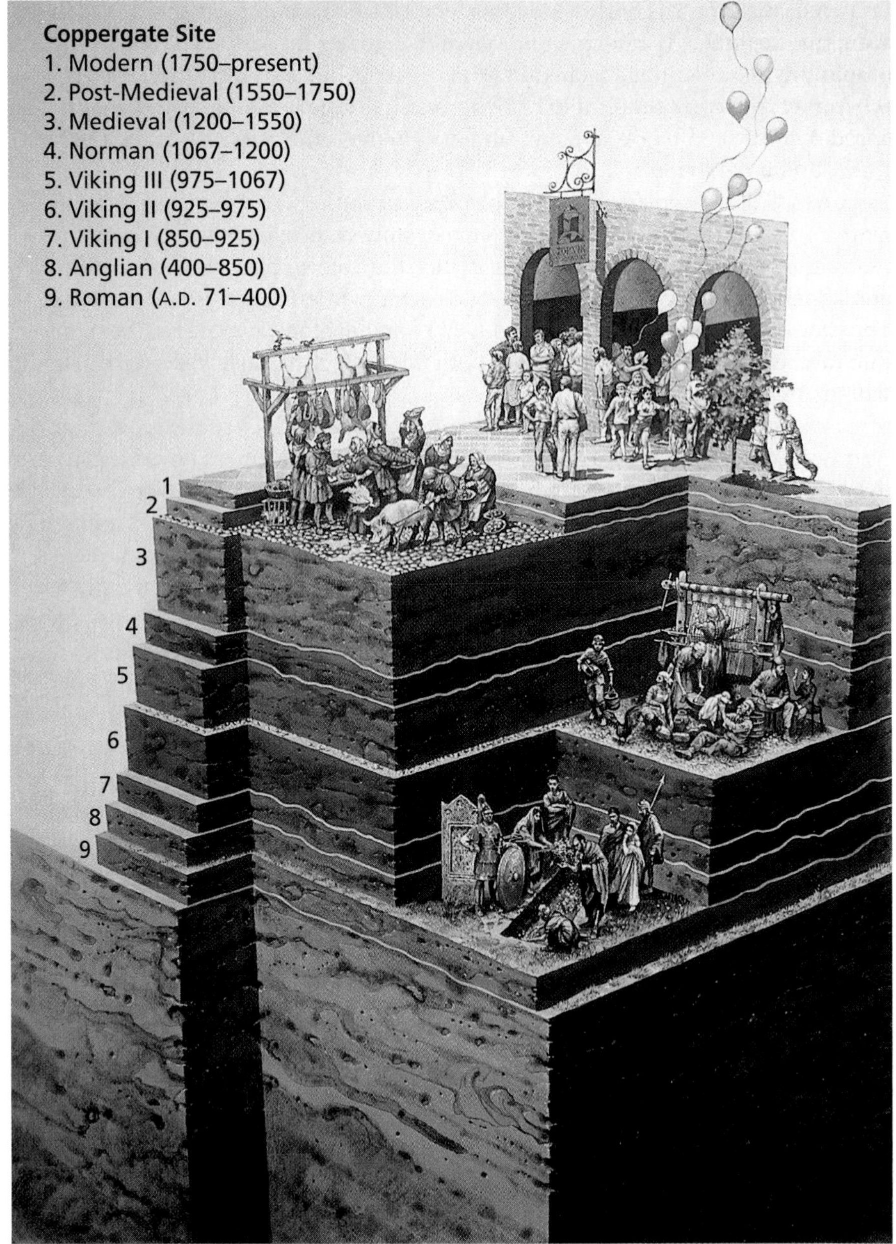


**Figure 1.15** Vertical excavation. Archaeological sites often were places of repeated human occupation. In this artist's reconstruction, several periods of settlement at the site of Coppergate in York, England, are shown in their stratigraphic context. The use of the site goes back almost 2000 years.

tool manufacture can produce extensive debris. On the other hand, the place where an animal was killed and butchered—a kill site—may leave almost no archaeological trace.

Evaluation of a stratigraphic sequence involves distinguishing between natural and human activities. Such environmental factors as soil erosion or flood deposits may add to the local accumulation but may also remove part of a layer. Younger features such as postholes or storage pits may have been dug into older deposits. Relationships between layers must be studied carefully to determine whether younger deposits are cut into older layers and whether animal activities, downed trees, floodwaters, or later construction has disturbed or destroyed the original stratigraphy.

Assessment of the context and relative position of layers allows an archaeologist to interpret the depositional history from the stratigraphic sequence. An actual calendar date of the layers may be derived from artifacts with a known date found in a particular layer. For example, a hubcap from a 1935 Ford would indicate that the layer could not have been formed before 1935. The ages of many types of pottery and stone tools are known and can be used to suggest an approximate date for archaeological levels. Layers and artifacts also may be dated by means of such absolute techniques as radiocarbon and other dating methods (see p. 145).

*It takes very special qualities to devote one's life to problems with no attainable solutions and to poking around in dead people's garbage: Words like "masochistic," "nosy," and "completely batty" spring to mind.*

—Paul Bahn (1989)

***Horizontal, or Area, Excavations*** Horizontal, or area, excavations are often the next step after initial vertical trenches reveal structures or features to be uncovered. Such excavations expose large areas of ground, one layer at a time. These horizontal layers are recorded and removed individually. Area excavations are intended to recover information on site arrangement and structures. Such excavations may expose actual prehistoric living floors and structures where a group of people carried out everyday activities (Figure 1.16).

When the site stratigraphy is relatively simple—with only one or two stages of occupation and thin cultural layers—it is possible to separate the remains from each stage of occupation. In such cases, it is advantageous to expose large surfaces of the same layer to get an overview of the distribution of features and artifacts at the settlement. Following removal of the topsoil, the surface is scraped with trowels or shovels, loose soil is removed, and features and artifacts are uncovered. The uncovered surface is then carefully recorded, usually in drawings and photographs. The sediments removed during the excavation are normally shaken or washed through fine screens to recover smaller items such as bone fragments and plant remains that otherwise may be missed (Figure 1.17).

Various kinds of samples are taken from different layers in the walls of the sections and from the occupation floor. The excavated soils are usually sifted through screens and/or washed with water to find even the smallest objects, fragments of bone, and plant remains. Soil samples are taken to help define and characterize the deposits at the site. Pollen samples are sometimes collected to assist in defining the vegetation in and around the site. At most sites, samples of charcoal and bone are taken for radiocarbon dating.

After removal of one layer of soil and artifacts, the procedure is repeated and a new surface is uncovered and recorded. One strategy for maintaining control of the stratigraphy is to leave a number of narrow sections untouched in the

**Figure 1.16** Horizontal excavation at a prehistoric village in Wisconsin. Only one-half of a feature is excavated at first. This feature, a house depression, is being excavated with trowels. The small wall in the middle is kept as a record of the feature's stratigraphy.

Figure 1.17 Soil from the excavation is sifted through a screen to recover small objects.

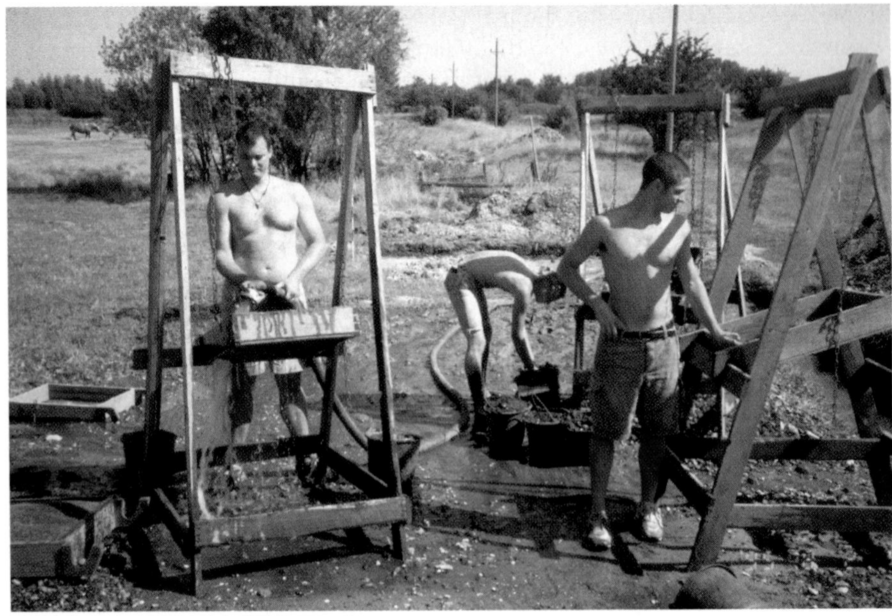

www.mhhe.com/priceip6e

For a Web-based activity on dating of archaeological material, see the Internet exercises on your online learning center.

excavation area. The walls of these sections are cleaned and studied as the excavation goes deeper. This kind of excavation aims at recording and then removing each horizontal layer individually.

Toward the end of the excavation, the sections are excavated. The surface of the sediments beneath the occupation layer is uncovered and cleaned. Unusual colors in the soil may reveal features such as pits and postholes, which are recorded by photos and drawings. Features are dissected by excavating one-quarter or one-half of the pit or posthole at a time to remove the contents and determine the function of the feature (Figure 1.18). This produces a vertical section through the middle of the feature.

Sections of all features are recorded by photos, drawings, and soil description. Postholes belonging to the same structure are grouped by examining the depth of the holes and the kind of soil present. Other features are studied to determine their function and mutual relationship. At the end of the dig, the excavated area has to be filled up and undisturbed portions of the site protected in the best possible manner.

## Analysis of Archaeological Materials

Analysis of recovered artifacts may begin concurrently with the fieldwork in a field laboratory, or records, artifacts, and samples may be shipped back to a home laboratory to be cleaned, cataloged, and prepared for analysis. More fragile objects will require careful conservation to protect them and ensure that they do not disintegrate.

After the fieldwork come more detailed analyses of the recovered materials, the writing of excavation reports, and the preparation of publications, all of which require much more work and time than the excavation itself. One estimate suggests 5 weeks of analysis and writing for each week spent in excavation. Final results of the investigations are made available to the public and to professional archaeologists through articles in scientific journals, in published reports, and in books.

Archaeological fieldwork produces several major categories of finds and information: (1) artifacts—portable objects altered by human activity; (2) **ecofacts**—the remains of plants, animals, sediments, and other unmodified materials that

Figure 1.18 Excavations expose postholes and the foundations of two houses, one built over the other. The dark rectangles mark the location of construction posts. Two fireplace pits can be seen at the center and right of the photo.

result from human activity; (3) **features**—the immovable structures, layers, pits, and posts in the ground; and (4) sites and settlements—the set of artifacts, ecofacts, and features that defines places in the landscape where activity and residence were focused.

A variety of specialists are needed in archaeology to examine and interpret the wide range of materials and information that is found at archaeological sites. There are specialists in archaeobotany, archaeometry, archaeozoology, bioarchaeology, classical archaeology, geoarchaeology, historical archaeology, paleoanthropology, theoretical archaeology, underwater archaeology, and many others. There are also specialists in certain classes of materials. For example, lithic specialists analyze the stone tools that are often a common object at archaeological sites. Ceramic specialists study the sherds of ancient pottery. Archaeobotanists (also known as paleoethnobotanists) study the plant remains, both visible and microscopic, that are found at a site. Archaeozoologists investigate the animal bones that represent the remains of meals and manufacturing activities. Bioarchaeologists are often trained in both archaeology and biological anthropology; they describe and interpret the human bones and teeth that may be found. Paleoanthropologists are archaeologists and physical anthropologists focused on the very earliest human fossils and artifacts. Geoarchaeologists and micromorphologists investigate the geological setting of sites and the details of the sediments encasing archaeological remains. Archaeometrists date those remains and undertake the chemical characterization of prehistoric materials to learn about their composition and source. Historical archaeologists and classical archaeologists work in specific time periods, with historical documents and with the classical civilizations of the Mediterranean (Rome, Greece, and others). Underwater archaeologists focus on shipwrecks and submerged archaeological sites (Figure 1.19).

Figure 1.19 Underwater archaeology—a growing part of fieldwork. Divers discover and excavate a variety of finds beneath the sea, including individual artifacts, shipwrecks, and entire settlements. In this case, divers in northern Germany are at work excavating a Mesolithic settlement from approximately 6000 years before the present.

*Artifacts* Each object from the excavations must be washed to remove dust and dirt (Figure 1.20). At some sites, each object is recorded by number in a catalog. At other sites, artifacts are recorded by material and context or by the excavation area where they were found. Numbering artifacts with permanent ink ensures that each item has a label with information on the site and location of the find (Figure 1.21).

The catalog description of each artifact includes a record of the kind of artifact, the type of raw material, the color, the overall shape and measurements, techniques of manufacturing, presumed function, decoration, and provenience

**ecofact** Any of the remains of plants, animals, sediments, or other unmodified materials that result from human activity.

**feature** An immovable structure or layer, pit, or post in the ground having archaeological significance.

Figure 1.20 Items from the excavation are washed, dried, and put in bags with labels showing their location in the site.

information. This description could be supplemented with an accurate drawing and a photograph of the artifact (Figure 1.22). An inventory of the materials from the excavation then can be made by counting and recording the number of artifacts in each category of material, such as chipped stone, ground stone, or pottery. Following this initial recording, artifacts are classified into other categories and types. Classification is a way of creating order in a mass of archaeological materials by dividing objects into groups on the basis of shared characteristics. One example of such classification is the initial division of the remains into artifacts, ecofacts, and features, described earlier. Another example is the division of chipped stone artifacts into axes, scrapers, knives, and arrowheads.

Three primary attributes are used to classify archaeological artifacts: (1) form—the size and basic shape of the object; (2) technology—the characteristics of raw material and manufacturing technique; and (3) style—the color, texture, and decoration of the object. Most of this information is recorded in the laboratory after the artifacts have been cleaned and cataloged.

*Ecofacts* Ecofacts are unmodified natural items, such as animal bones and plant remains, that are usually brought to the site by its occupants and useful for the study of past human activity. They are used to reconstruct the environment of the site and the range of resources that people used. Ecofacts are classified as organic (plants and animals) or inorganic (sediments and stone). These materials are usually studied by archaeologists or specialists with training in botany, zoology, or geology.

Plant remains from an archaeological site may include pollen, seeds, leaves, pieces of wood, and the like, depending on the quality of preservation. Visible (macroscopic) and invisible (microscopic) plant remains are distinguished. Invisible remains are often more likely to be preserved. Microscopic remains include pollen, phytoliths, starch grains, and other materials. Each type of plant produces distinctively different-looking pollen. Because of its long-distance distribution, pollen is likely to reflect the total environment around the site. Phytoliths are tiny pieces of the plant "skeleton" composed of silica. These plant parts can survive thousands of years and are often recognizable as to their

Figure 1.21 Sorting, numbering, and cataloging artifacts and other finds from an excavation are often a long and complicated process.

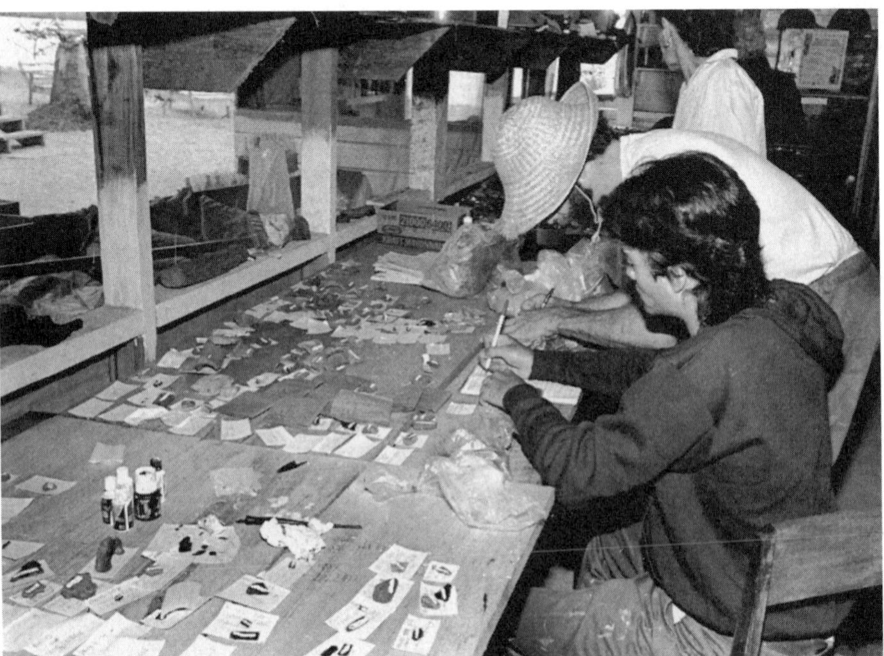

species. Many kinds of plants produce distinctive starch grains that can be preserved to the present.

Changes in the types of pollen at a site over time can be used to reconstruct the vegetation history of the area and to provide a record of climatic changes. Special growing requirements and other characteristics of certain plants may reflect certain climatic conditions or specific local situations such as an open rather than a forested environment around a site.

Macrofossils of botanical materials are visible remains, such as seeds and plant parts, that are more likely to be present at a site because of direct human utilization. Identification of these remains indicates what species of plants were present, whether they were wild or domestic, and in what context they were found. It is important to study the context of these remains to know how the plants were used. Plants may be collected for food, but they may also be used for production of textiles, mats, and baskets; for the manufacture of poison for arrowheads; or as drugs. Types of plants and their growing condition may also provide an indicator of the nature of the local environment and climate.

*Faunal analysis*, or archaeozoology, is the term used to describe studies of the animal remains from archaeological sites. Animal remains are tabulated by the kinds of bones, teeth, antler, and horn that are present (Figure 1.23). Species are identified and the numbers of individuals of each species are calculated. These studies show what animals were hunted and eaten and in what proportion. The amount of meat available from each animal also may be calculated to determine the animals' relative importance in the diet.

Faunal analysis also can provide an estimate of the ratio of adult to juvenile animals and of male to female animals. A predominance of certain age groups in a species such as deer may indicate that seasonal or selective hunting was practiced. For example, a site that contained a large proportion of 3- to 6-month-old deer would suggest the animals were killed primarily in the fall, since deer are born in the spring.

The presence or absence of certain parts of the animal skeleton may indicate the way animals were butchered and whether they were dismembered on the spot or killed elsewhere and selected steaks and chops brought back to the settlement. Not all animals are necessarily hunted for food. Nonfood items such as antler, fur, bone, and hides also are important materials from hunted animals.

**Figure 1.22** Recording the shape of flaked stone artifacts.

**Figure 1.23** Bones and teeth from an archaeological excavation, including domesticated sheep and pig.

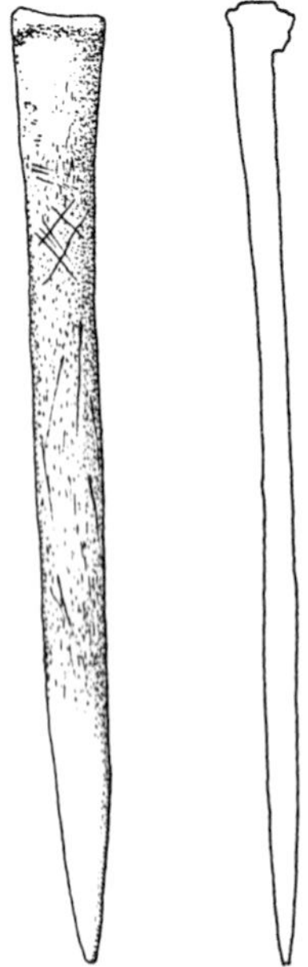

Figure 1.24 A bone point, Mesolithic Europe, 5000 B.C. This example is made from the leg bone of a small deer, split, ground, and polished to a point. It was then lashed to a wooden shaft for spearing fish.

Many different kinds of tools and equipment are made from animal products (Figure 1.24). Bone was a very important material for prehistoric peoples.

The most important inorganic ecofacts are the various sediments uncovered by excavation. Deposits of soils and sediments at human settlements result from both human and natural processes. These sediments and deposits are studied by geoarchaeologists. The types of sediments present may indicate the source of the material that was deposited. Examples include water-lain silts from a flood, volcanic ashes, and frost-cracked rocks from the ceiling of a cave. The study of soil chemistry is an important aspect of the analysis of soils and sediments.

***Features*** Features must be studied largely in the field, since they are fixed in the ground. Features may be structures such as houses or pits, or fences or field systems defining an area used for special purposes, or constructions for certain activities, such as drying racks, fireplaces, and traps. They are useful for understanding the distribution and organization of human activities at a site. For example, the size, elaboration, and location of dwellings or burials may suggest differences in wealth and status.

Some features result from the accumulation of garbage and debris, rather than from intentional construction. They include shell middens, heaps of waste material in workshops, and quarries. Studies of these features may indicate strategies for obtaining food or raw material, how the raw material was used and distributed, and whether it was scarce or abundant.

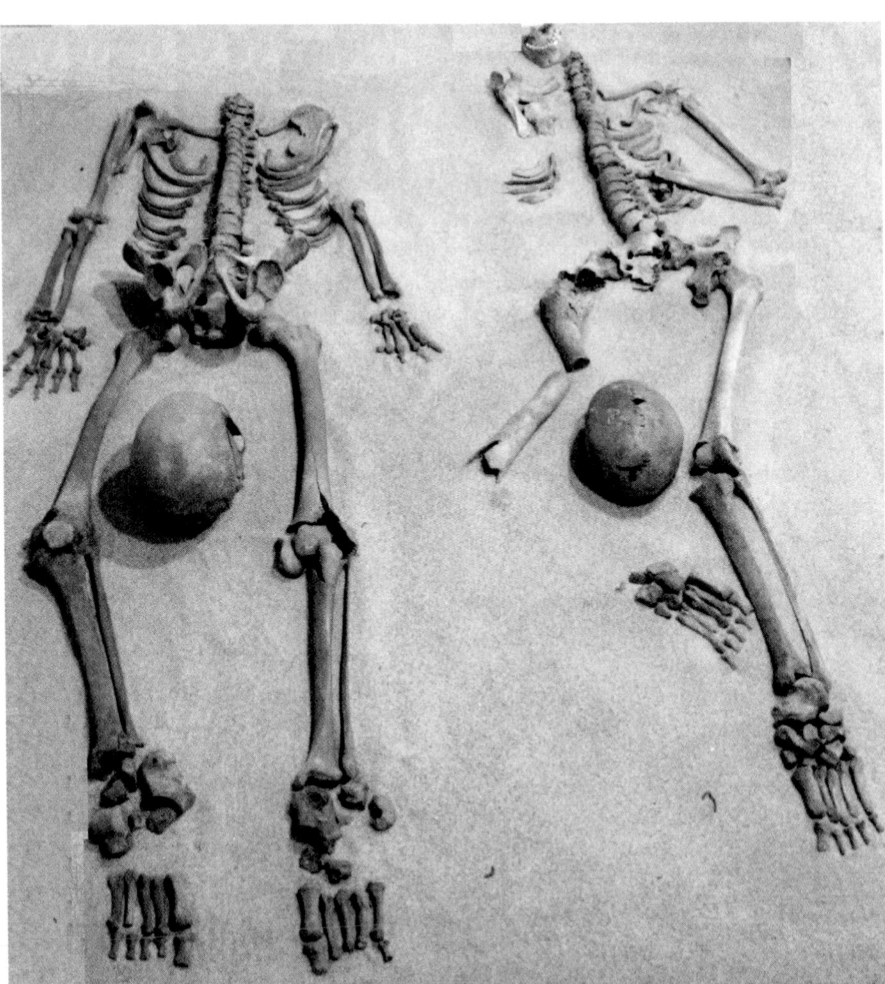

Figure 1.25 Two Viking-age burials from Denmark, A.D. 1000. These individuals were beheaded and buried with a bad view.

Burials and human bones are a special category of feature often found at archaeological sites. Several kinds of burials can be found (Figure 1.25). Simple inhumations represent the laid-out burial of the whole body. Such graves usually contain an articulated skeleton with all the bones in their correct anatomical positions. Secondary burials are the result of burial of some of the skeleton, after the flesh and soft tissue have disappeared. Usually, the skull and the larger bones are present, often in a small pile or bundle. Cremations are burials of the ash and small, carbonized bones from bodies that have been burned. Bioarchaeologists identify and analyze human remains. The sex of the skeleton can be determined by examining the size and shape of the pelvis and the skull and the thickness of the bones. The age at death can be estimated by the eruption sequence and wear of the teeth, the fusion (closing) of sutures between bones of the skull, and the fusion of the ends of the limb bones to the shaft.

The health status of past populations can be investigated by recording the incidence of trauma that affects the skeleton. Such diseases and injuries include bone fractures, arthritis, and periodontal diseases. Nutritional problems may be reflected in poorly developed bones and the low average height of the population. Cultural practices such as cranial deformation and dental mutilation (practiced in prehistoric America, for example) also show up in the skeletal remains.

***Sites and Settlements*** Settlement archaeology is the study of how and why prehistoric remains are distributed across the landscape. Investigations range from the analysis of the location of different activities within a single room to the distribution of sites in a region. There are at least three levels of locational information: (1) a room, a structure, or some other occupation surface, such as a cave floor; (2) a site or settlement; and (3) a series of sites within a larger region.

The spatial organization within a single structure defines areas for special activities such as grinding flour, cooking, weaving, or manufacturing tools, or for certain facilities such as those for sleeping or storage. Study of such organization may indicate a division of male and female space and activities, the number of people in a household, and the structure of the family—nuclear, extended, or polygynous, for example.

A settlement generally includes a habitation area with one or more houses and fireplaces; different activity areas for food preparation, curing of animal skins and hides, the manufacture of various artifacts, and perhaps storage equipment; and a midden or trash area. Spatial patterning within a site can provide information about the number of houses and people at the settlement and about their relationships with one another. In addition, most of the day-to-day activities of the occupants should be reflected in the various structures and activity areas found throughout the settlement (Figure 1.26). Structures at a site may be solid and substantial in the case of permanently settled communities in a village or townlike setting. Short-term or seasonal settlements, however, may leave little trace of construction. The size of a settlement in horizontal and vertical extent depends on the number of people who lived there, the length of time they lived there, and the kinds of activities that took place and structures that were erected, as well as environmental factors. Sites of similar size could have been created by a few permanently settled people or through the occasional use of the same spot by a larger group of people.

Differences in the size and architectural elaboration of houses may be evidence of status differentiation, a situation in which some people have more wealth and control over goods and labor than others. The arrangement of houses at a settlement also may reflect social organization in the separation of poor and wealthy households. Concerns for privacy and protection in the form of fences, palisades, or ditches may indicate private ownership or conditions of competition or warfare. In addition, settlement studies may reveal areas of economic specialization,

Figure 1.26 An early Neolithic site in northern Germany showing some of the activities and objects associated with the occupation. Clockwise from the top: bow hunting, wild elk and boar, pottery, a fishing spear, an antler axe, domestic sheep and cattle, domestic wheat, wild berries, tree felling, a dugout canoe and paddles, a ceramic lamp, flint blades, a groundstone axe, flint tools, and a fireplace.

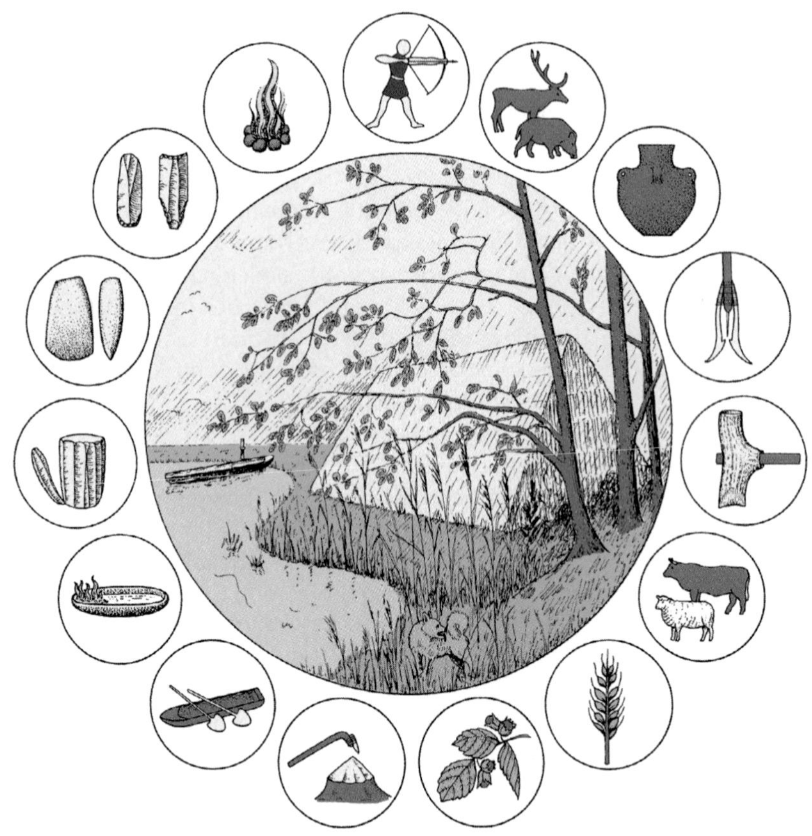

wherein certain materials were produced by skilled craftspeople, whereas other items were made in individual households.

Regional settlement patterns that are recorded in archaeological surveys can provide a variety of information on the prehistoric use of the landscape. Often, several kinds of sites are found in an area (Figure 1.27). Residential settlements of various sizes and durations are typical targets for investigation. Such sites can vary from camps to villages, towns, or prehistoric cities (Figure 1.28).

There are many other kinds of sites. Extraction sites are used for more specific, nonresidential purposes to obtain raw materials or resources, such as quarries for stone or copper and places where animals were killed and butchered. Distinct burial areas, outside settlements, are another kind of site. Cemeteries of inhumation graves, cremation urns, or individual burial mounds and tombs are some other types of sites. Ritual or ceremonial areas may be isolated localities on the prehistoric landscape—Stonehenge, for example.

## Interpretation of Archaeological Information

*The most difficult thing to predict is not the future, but the past.*

—Russian proverb

Archaeological information that is recovered from the ground and described and analyzed by specialists does not directly say very much about the past. The analyses may tell us what the items were, what they were made of, how they were used, and how old they are. But the questions that archaeologists seek to answer about the past concern larger concepts: the way of life of prehistoric peoples, the way human societies coped with their physical and social environments, and the way our predecessors viewed their world. Both the questions we ask and the ideas we use to find the answers are at the heart of interpretation in archaeology. The science and the creativity of archaeology lie in bridging that gap between the information we recover and the questions we seek to answer.

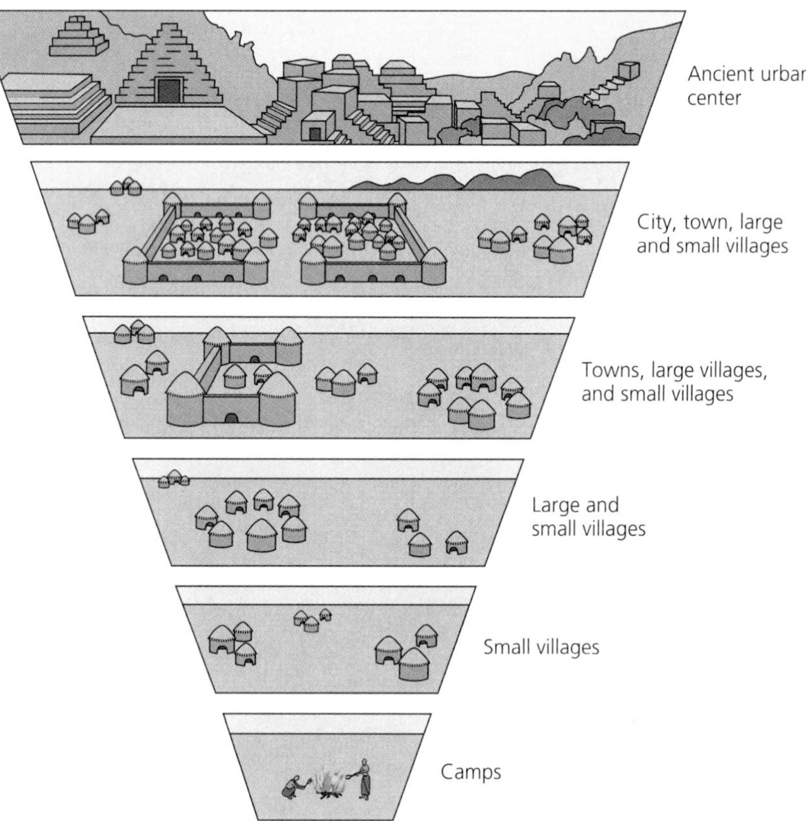


**Figure 1.27** A schematic representation of the changes in social systems from small bands to urban societies in prehistory. Note also that settlement patterns change over time and that bigger and more diverse communities emerge.

*The Science of Archaeology* The questions that archaeologists seek to answer are highly varied. Some questions are very specific: How was a flint scraper used? Others are very general: Why did humans domesticate plants and animals? Many questions arise from simple curiosity or common sense—the basic when, where, and what kinds of questions. Other questions—usually the how and the why kind—are much more difficult.

Some questions and some ideas come from our knowledge of living peoples. **Ethnographies**—anthropological descriptions of living or historically known groups of people in different parts of the world—are a prime source of information about human behavior and its variation. Archaeologists often look for comparisons in ethnographies to explain things. For example, knowing that the Northwest Coast Indians in North America lived in longhouses in the early twentieth century helps us make sense of buried structures built centuries earlier in that region. But ethnographic information has limitations, since past human behavior is much more diverse than what has been recorded in the anthropological literature about living peoples. As an extreme example of this situation, there are no ethnographies of Neanderthals.

*Archaeology is the search for fact. Not truth. If it's truth you're interested in, Doctor Tyree's philosophy class is right down the hall. So forget any ideas you've got about lost cities, exotic travel, and digging up the world. We do not follow maps to buried treasure and "X" never, ever, marks the spot. Seventy percent of all archaeology is done in the library. Research. Reading.*
—Indiana Jones (1989). *Indiana Jones and the Last Crusade.* Screenplay by Jeff Boam, story by George Lucas and Menno Meyjes.

Explaining human behavior in the past and its changes through time is a major goal of archaeology. Big questions about the past often come from our ideas about how things worked. Archaeological theories are bodies of ideas about human behavior in the past. There are also many theories about that past, but many of these tend to be related. There are, in fact, groups of theories that define schools of thought or perspectives in archaeology. The history and theoretical underpinnings of archaeology are beyond the scope of this book; several places to look for more information can be found in the Suggested Readings section at the end of this chapter. We can, however, look at some of the basic aspects of past societies and behavior that theories try to explain.

**ethnography** The study of human cultures through firsthand observation.

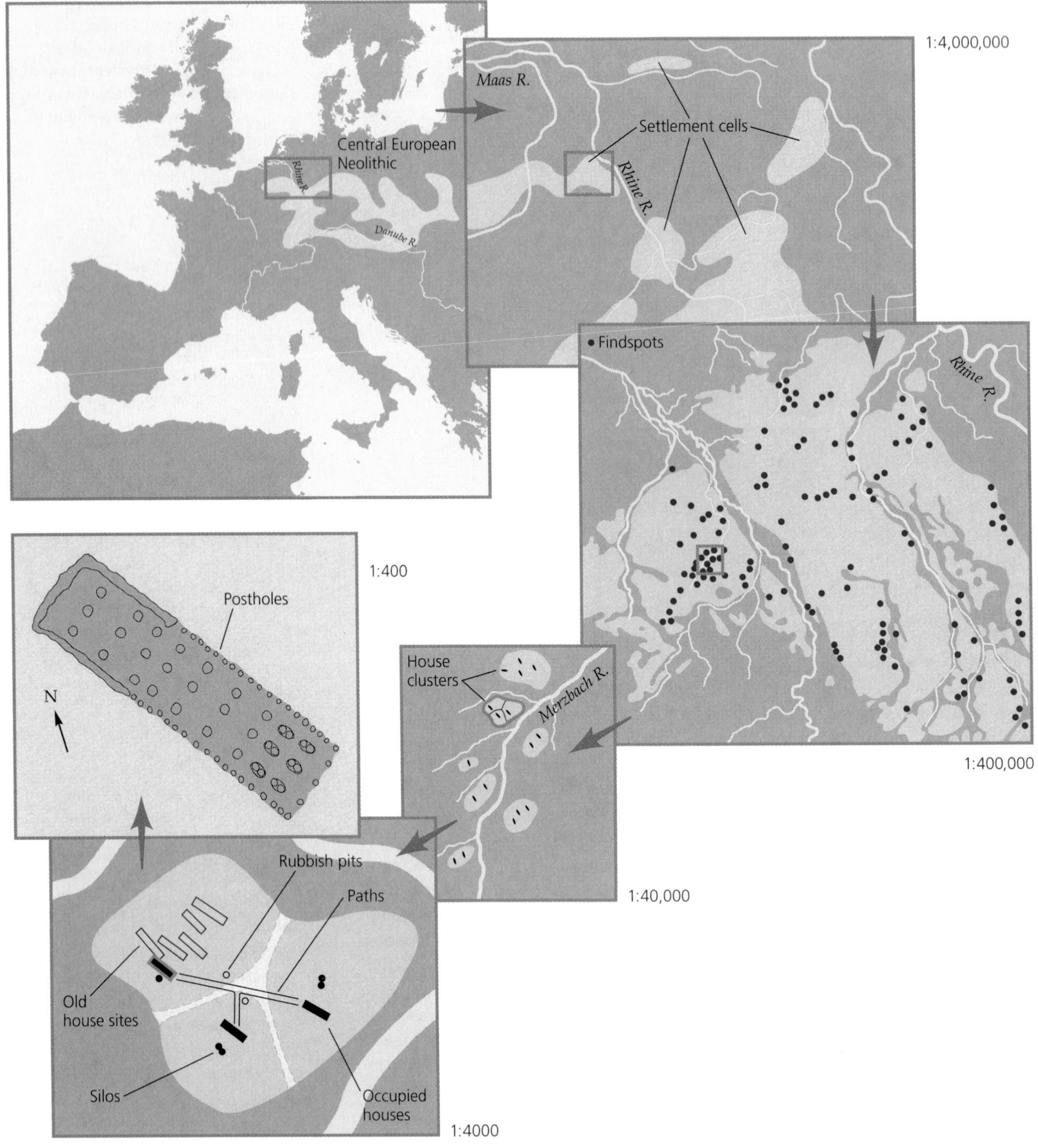


**Figure 1.28** A series of views of the distribution and pattern of settlement in the Early Neolithic of central Europe. These maps and plans show the nature of the Linearbandkeramik settlements approximately 7000 years ago.

Our theories and ideas are basically attempts to explain what took place in the past. The hard part of archaeology is connecting the facts (data) and the ideas (theories) to better understand what happened. The process of asking and trying to answer questions is essentially the process of learning. What makes archaeology science is rigorously testing or evaluating the answers to be confident that they are not wrong.

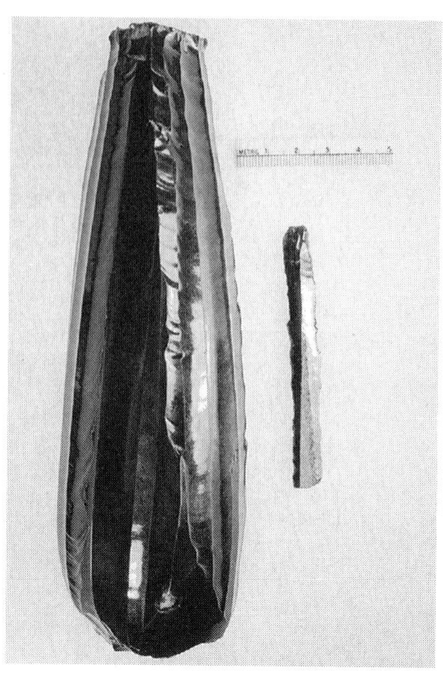

Figure 1.29 An obsidian core and blade.

*Aspects of Society and Behavior* The kinds of questions that archaeologists ask about past societies in general terms involve concepts such as technology, economy, organization, and ideology.

**Technology** is the set of tools, techniques, and knowledge that allows people to convert natural resources into tools, food, clothing, shelter, and other products and equipment they need or want. Technology is the means by which people interact directly with their natural environment. It is also the aspect of past culture that is most easily observed in archaeology. The fragments of the tools that people used in the past, made of durable materials such as stone, ceramic, and metal, are the most common archaeological remains (Figure 1.29). Changes in technology over time provide clear indicators of the development of our nonbiological means of adaptation.

**Economy** is a broad topic that involves how people obtain foods, materials, and goods to sustain their lives. One major aspect of prehistoric economies is subsistence—the activities and materials that people use to feed themselves. Archaeologists use the term *subsistence pattern* to describe the plants and animals that prehistoric people ate, the activities required to obtain those foods, and the procurement and preparation techniques and implements used to turn those plants and animals into food. The term *hunting and gathering* describes one general pattern in which wild animals are hunted and wild plants are collected or gathered for subsistence. *Agriculture* is a subsistence pattern that involves the herding of domesticated animals and the cultivation of domesticated plants.

Exchange is an important aspect of economy (Figure 1.30). When artifacts such as stone axes, obsidian knives, metal spearpoints, or certain kinds of food are passed from person to person or group to group, archaeologists talk about "exchange." One way to study such interaction within and between societies is to look at the distribution of items of exchange. Economic anthropologists distinguish three kinds of exchange: reciprocity, redistribution, and trade. Reciprocal exchange sometimes takes the form of gift-giving, whereby objects of relatively equal value are given to build alliances. Redistribution involves the movement of goods to a central place from which they are portioned out to members of a society. Such a system of redistribution may be used to support an army, or priests, or the pyramid builders of ancient Egypt.

Large-scale economic transactions known as trade often involve some sort of market economy and perhaps a monetary standard. Trade takes place in our own economic system today: Objects are imported and exported for the purpose of making a profit. This level of exchange usually involves a highly complex society with professional artisans, regular supplies of raw material, extensive transportation systems, protection of markets and traders against thieves, and enough customers to make the business worthwhile.

Archaeologists often examine exchange and interaction through the study of "exotic materials." The presence of objects and materials that are not available or locally produced in the study area provides immediate evidence of connections and interaction with others. Of greatest use in such investigations are artifacts or materials that come from a single location.

**Organization** refers to the roles and relationships in society and concerns relations between women and men and among different segments of society, such as families, age groups, labor units, or ethnic groups. Organization structures various aspects of society, such as social interaction, economic activity, and political relationships.

**technology** The combination of knowledge and manufacturing techniques that enables people to convert raw materials into finished products.

**economy** The management and organization of the affairs of a group, community, or establishment to ensure their survival and productivity.

**organization** The arrangements between individuals and groups in human society that structure relationships and activities.

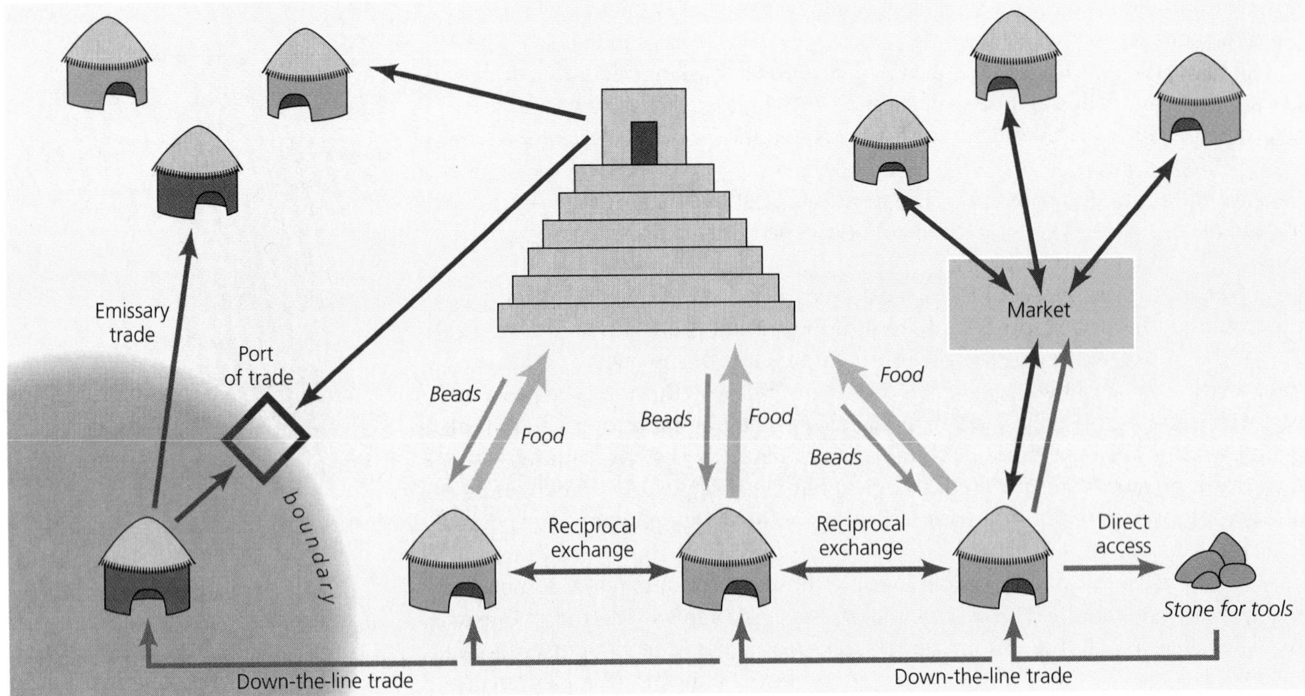


**Figure 1.30** The exchange of goods can take many paths in human societies. This diagram shows some of the methods for exchange in prehistoric economies. Such patterns reflect both economy and organization.

Kinship and marriage systems, lineage, rank, and class are important aspects of social organization and a means of structuring social relationships. Kinship defines the relationship between individual members in society on the basis of their family relationships. *Grandmother, brother, uncle,* and *cousin* are terms that relate us to other people through kinship. Marriage systems tie unrelated individuals together through sanctioned kinship; rules for these relationships are carefully defined in society. Lineages provide a means for calculating one's relationships through lines of ancestry. Such genealogies are a way to extend relationships and determine membership in a group. Members of the same lineage often work as a corporate group.

Rank and class distinguish individuals and groups of people within society. Many societies of hunter-gatherers are described as **egalitarian,** with essentially equal relations between all members of the group. Many agricultural societies are larger and exhibit distinctive groups within the society that are defined by inherited status differences. Higher status (resulting from prestige, wealth, and/or power) characterizes elite and privileged groups in a society. Rank and class are means of defining such status groups. **Rank** refers to inherited positions in societies in which everyone is ranked by status relative to all other people. The first-born of the highest-ranked group is the highest position in such a society. In ranked societies, each individual has a unique place in the order of relationships. **Class** societies are structured by distinctions between groups, or classes, of people that define levels, or strata, in society. Class is also usually inherited but defines large groups of individuals and may determine one's job, location of residence, marriage opportunities, and financial status. India under the caste system was an extreme example of a society structured by class.

**egalitarian** A term that refers to societies lacking clearly defined status differences between individuals, except for those due to sex, age, or skill.

**rank** A relationship of inequality between members of society in which status is determined by kinship relations of birth order and lineage.

**class** A relationship of inequality between members of society in which status is determined by membership in a level or class.

The economic activities of prehistoric peoples were organized in various ways. A fundamental mechanism for the organization of tasks is the division of labor. Separate groups or segments of society undertake different activities as part of the economic process. A basic example is seen in many groups of hunter-gatherers in which the division of labor is by sex; males are primarily hunters, and females are primarily gatherers. Both groups contribute foodstuffs to the subsistence economy of the group. Agricultural societies also see economic organization along gender lines, but the household becomes an important component of production for food and other necessary materials. Production becomes more specialized over time: Entire communities may be involved in the production of specific items, or specialist groups of producers—**craft specialists**—such as potters, metalsmiths, and beadmakers, may emerge. Production units can assume more formal structures, such as guilds or unions, in larger, more complex societies.

In a general sense, political organization is a reflection of the increasing complexity that is witnessed in human society over time. As societies became larger, organizational changes resulted in closer integration and more linear decision making.

One of the most significant changes in organization was the shift from egalitarian to hierarchical structures that often followed the origins of agriculture. **Hierarchical** organizations have one or more levels of control above the majority of the people in the society (Figure 1.31). These higher levels are seen in elite classes or ranks that control much of the wealth, power, and decision making in society. One way to imagine such a hierarchy is to recall the nature of military organization and the chain of command from generals to lieutenants to privates. Government also operates in a hierarchical manner, from local representatives to municipal government, state government, and federal government. The sphere of control and decision making varies with the level in the hierarchy. The municipal government repairs local roads; the federal government builds an interstate highway system.

There are several ways to describe or characterize such hierarchies in human society (Figure 1.32). The concepts of bands, tribes, chiefdoms, and states are often used to distinguish different kinds of political organizations. *Bands* and

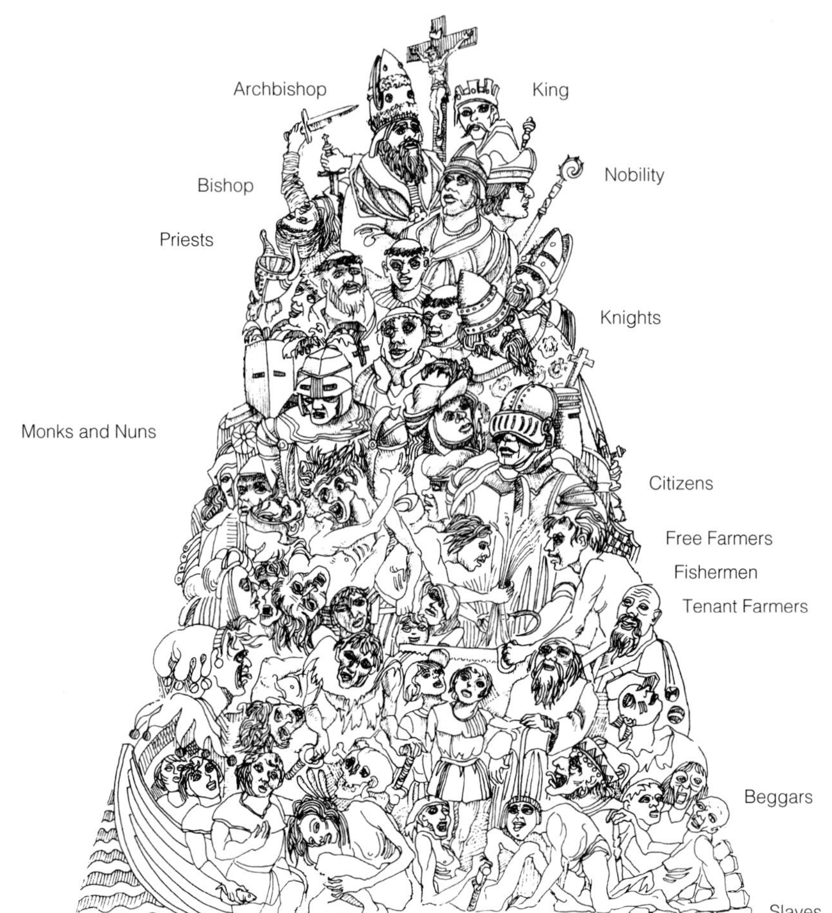


**Figure 1.31** Pyramid of the social layers in a medieval European population. Note also the symbols that mark positions in society—for example, the soldiers' helmets, the monks' haircuts, and the king's crown.

**craft specialists** (or **craft specialization**) Individuals involved in part- or full-time activities devoted to the production of a specific class of goods, often highly valued.

**hierarchical** A term referring to societies that have a graded order of inequality in ranks, statuses, or decision makers.

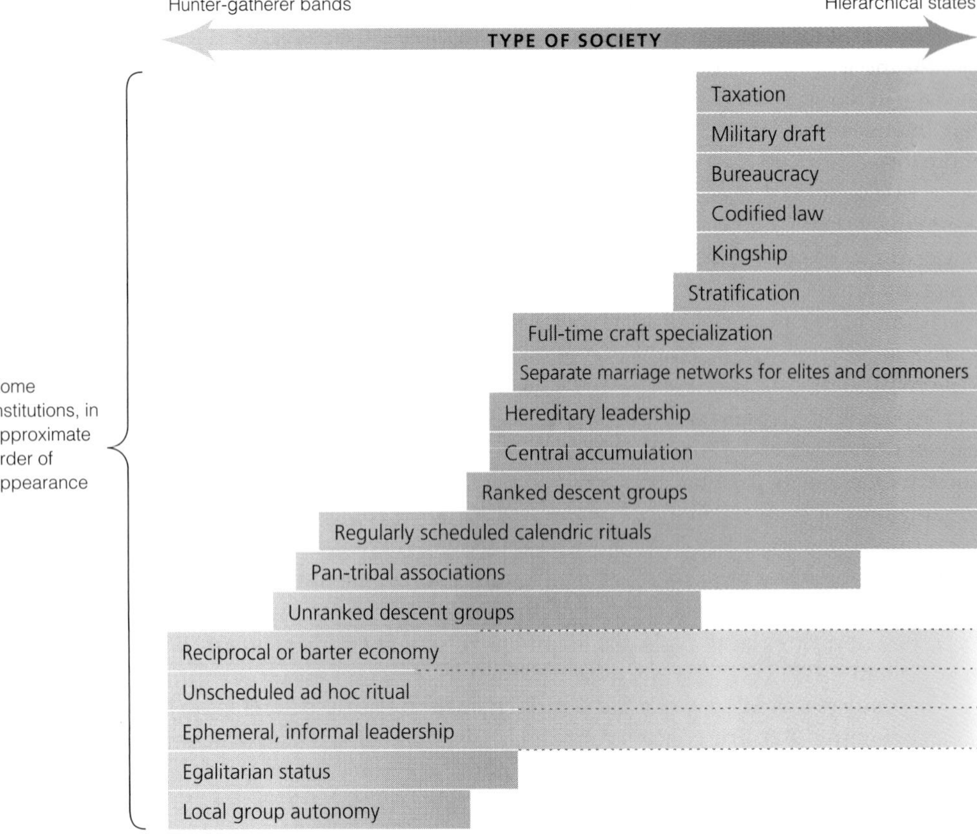


**Figure 1.32** Types of societies and the appearance of various institutions. This chart documents the emergence of many of the major institutions in human society on the path from small bands to more complex civilizations.

*tribes* describe relatively small societies of hunter-gatherers or farmers in which relationships are generally egalitarian and decision making is consensual. Power and property are distributed among all the members of the population. Status is earned through achievements and is ephemeral, held only by the individual who gained it. Chiefdoms and states are larger, often territorial, societies in which relationships are unequal and organization is hierarchical. Status is hereditary and assigned or ascribed by birth order or class affiliation.

One of the more apparent (though not always present) trends in the organization of human society is an increase in complexity over time. Complexity refers to more different units in society and more integration between those units. More units are a result of social, economic, and ideological specialization. Such differentiation is reflected in the distinctions between villages, towns, and cities that began to appear with chiefdoms and states. More integration is a result of hierarchical organization and the emergence of ranked or stratified groups within society whereby power and decision making are in the hands of a few. Some of the changes in social, economic, and political organization from bands to states are summarized in Figure 1.32.

**ideology** A conceptual framework by which people structure their ideas about the order of the universe, their place in that universe, and their relationships among themselves and with objects and other forms of life around them.

**cosmology** The worldview of a group or society, encompassing their understanding of the universe, their origins and existence, and nature.

**Ideology** refers to the means by which people structure their ideas about the universe, their own place in that universe, and their relationships with one another and with things and other beings around them. Ideologies are shared but also vary within and among groups of people. Ideology is the way that people view and understand their world. That view often affects many things they do. Ideology is reflected in the clothes we wear, the food we eat, and the places in which we live. Ideology encompasses the norms, values, and beliefs held by a society. Ideology is reflected in **cosmology**—explanations of the origins of the universe, of life, and of society. Roman cosmology invoked the twins Romulus and Remus, mythical beings raised by a she-wolf, as the founders of Rome.

Symbols and styles often are expressions of ideology and identity. School mascots, corporate logos, religious icons, national flags, and certain faces incorporate and display a wide range of concepts and ideas. Think of the importance attributed by thousands or millions of people today to the leprechaun of the University of Notre Dame, the circled star of a Mercedes, a statue of Buddha, the American flag, or a picture of Fidel Castro.

Symbols, styles, and ideologies often are expressed in art. Among hunter-gatherers, decoration often appears to have been individualistic, marking ownership or life events. Distinctive distribution of styles can be observed that probably mark the range of particular groups. For example, there were different zones of spearpoint styles in the late Paleolithic in northern Europe. From the beginning, there were distinctive styles of art. The first art appeared toward the end of the Paleolithic, about 30,000 years ago, in Europe, Africa, and Australia (Chapter 4, p. 105) and reflected the worldview of the people who produced it. Most of the cave paintings from the European Paleolithic are of large game animals, the major prey of these human groups—reindeer, bison, wild cows, and many other species. There are very few humans, plants, or scenes depicted. The cave and rock art of prehistory are of two major types. **Pictographs** were made by the application of pigment to rock surfaces (such as cave paintings); **petroglyphs** were made by removing the outer surface of a rock by carving or hammering (Figure 1.33).

**Figure 1.33** A rock carving of a Viking ship from Norway. Red has been used to highlight the carving.

Ideology is particularly clear in the art of larger civilizations, often in the form of propaganda. Distinctive motifs, like modern corporate icons, can be found everywhere the power of a particular political entity extends. This pattern can be seen in the double crown of the Egyptian pharaoh, the were-jaguar motif of the Olmec of Mexico (pp. 335–336), and many other contexts. Much of the art and decoration we know from past civilizations served both aesthetic and political purposes.

How does art function in the world today?

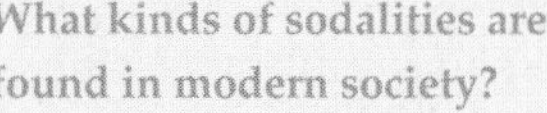

What kinds of sodalities are found in modern society?

Ideology is frequently expressed in ceremony and pageant surrounding important rites of passage through life: birth, adulthood, marriage, and death. Ideological norms and rules are usually stored and maintained in the older generation. Ideology is often embodied in specialists who maintain ritual knowledge and direct the ceremonies and activities that keep such ideology active and pertinent. In egalitarian societies, such individuals are known as witches and **shamans**—specialists in ritual and healing, seers of the future. In hierarchical societies, such specialists are found in powerful groups such as priesthoods, political organizations, and other **sodalities.**

These components of human society—technology, economy, organization, and ideology—are closely interrelated in prehistoric materials. A single artifact or object may contain aspects of each. A type of knife found exclusively in women's graves may hold information on the manufacture of tools, on the nature of women's work, on the distinction between sexes in the society, and on ideas about death. Technology, economy, organization, and ideology thus are different but related dimensions of past cultures and of human life and an important focus of archaeological investigations.

**pictograph** A written or painted symbol that more or less portrays the represented object.

**petroglyph** A drawing that has been carved into rock.

**shaman** An anthropological term for a spiritualist, curer, or seer.

**sodality** An alliance or association among some members of a society, often based on age and sex, with a specific function.

# *Images and Ideas*
## The Basics of Archaeology

This chapter has provided an introduction to the basic themes of archaeology—the study of past human behavior. Important concepts for thinking about the past are time and change.

Time is so vast that it is usually subdivided to make it more comprehensible, just as hours and minutes divide the day. Archaeologists utilize two systems for time, one geological and one archaeological. Geologists study the entire history of our planet: 4.6 billion years. They divide that time into major eras based primarily on changes in life-forms: Precambrian, Paleozoic, Mesozoic, and Cenozoic. The Cenozoic, the important one for humans, is divided into a series of epochs. The last four are the Miocene (when the first human ancestors separated from the apes), the Pliocene (when varieties of human fossil species emerge), the Pleistocene (the Ice Age, when humans leave Africa), and the Holocene (the past 11,000 years).

Archaeological time essentially covers the period of humans on earth, from the end of the Miocene. In fact, archaeological time really begins with the first artifacts, about 2.6 million years ago. The divisions in archaeological time are based on changes in the artifacts that people made in the past. In general, the important artifacts for chronology are made of stone, ceramic, or metal, hard materials that survive in the ground. Major divisions of archaeological time are based on the raw materials used for tools: stone, bronze, and iron. The Stone Age is divided into the Paleolithic, the Mesolithic, and the Neolithic, and these are further subdivided in many places.

In the context of time, archaeologists deal with change in human behavior. Such changes can be related to biology and/or culture. Biological changes are described as evolution. The earliest recognizable humans evolved from an ape-like ancestor and became more modern over time (Figure 1.34). The primary mechanism driving the biological changes in humans during the Miocene and the Pliocene was natural selection, the engine of evolution. The first artifacts—very simple, sharpened edges of stone—date to the end of the Pliocene. This is the initial evidence of culture. Culture is that uniquely human mode of adapting to the world around us. Culture is a buffer between us and the harshness of nature. Culture is learned behavior; culture is tools, information, organization, and action. Culture is stone-cutting implements; culture is building fires to stay

**Figure 1.34** A chimpanzee using a simple tool for immediate reward. An adult chimp uses a twig to extract insects from a hole in a tree. Humans make tools in order to make other tools for later use, a unique distinction.

warm; culture is an incest taboo. Cultural development became the main means of human adaptation during the Pleistocene period, replacing biology as our primary mechanism for coping with stress and change.

Archaeologists use theory and method to obtain information about human culture and behavior in the past and try to answer basic questions such as what, when, where, who, how, and why. Archaeological investigations generally follow a three-stage process involving discovery, analysis, and interpretation. Survey and excavation are the discovery components of fieldwork that are intended to find and recover artifacts, sites, and information. Analysis is the long and involved study of archaeological materials, describing, identifying, quantifying, compiling large quantities of data, and extracting answers to some of the easier of those basic questions. Interpretation is the difficult process of trying to make sense of the data and to understand what happened in the past. Interpretation usually involves the harder questions of how and why things happened and changed in the past.

*It's not what you find, it's what you find out.*

—David Hurst-Thomas (1989)

These big questions include the following: Why did we start to walk on two legs and become human more than 6 m.y.a.? What was responsible for the creative explosion in human behavior that was witnessed late in the Pleistocene? Why did we begin to domesticate plants and animals of the earth at the end of the Pleistocene? Why did inequality replace principles of egalitarianism? How did the first cities arise and operate? Why did empires die? The investigation of those questions and others is the subject of the remaining chapters in *Images of the Past.*

## DISCUSSION QUESTIONS

1. What are the two important chronological systems used in archaeology? Can you think of other methods for calculating time?
2. How does biological evolution work? How does one species evolve into another?
3. What are some of the main methods of archaeological fieldwork?
4. What are some of the kinds of sites that may be found during archaeological fieldwork?
5. What are some of the directions in which the analysis of archaeological materials can go?

**www.mhhe.com/priceip6e**

For more review material and study questions, see the self-quizzes on your online learning center.

## SUGGESTED READINGS

For Internet links related to this chapter, please visit our Web site at www.mhhe.com/priceip6e.


Bahn, P., and C. Renfrew. 1996. *The Cambridge illustrated history of archaeology.* Cambridge: Cambridge University Press. *An exceptionally well-documented depiction of the development of archaeology.*

Brothwell, D., and A. M. Pollard, eds. 2001. *Handbook of archaeological sciences.* London: Wiley Europe. *A comprehensive survey of the various aspects of archaeometry and archaeological science.*

Collis, J. 2001. *Digging up the past: An introduction to archaeological excavation.* Stroud, UK: Sutton.

Drewett, P. 1999. *Field archaeology. An introduction.* London: Routledge. *An up-to-date manual on field archaeology and its primary methods.*

Greene, K. 2002. *Archaeology: An introduction,* 4th ed. London: Routledge. *An excellent how-to introduction to archaeology.*

Hodder, I., ed. 2001. *Archaeological theory today.* Cambridge: Polity Press. *A series of papers on the present state of archaeological thinking assembled by a leading practitioner.*

Johnson, M. 1999. *Archaeological theory.* Oxford: Blackwell. *A discussion of current thinking in archaeology with comment and critique.*

Marcus, J., 2008. The archaeology of social evolution. *Annual Review of Anthropology* 37:251–266. *An up-to-date discussion of the evidence for social evolution in the past.*

Price, T. D. 2007. *Principles of archaeology.* New York: McGraw-Hill. *A new consideration of the major methods and theories of archaeology.*

Renfrew, C., and P. Bahn. 1998. *Archaeology: Theories, methods, and practice.* London: Thames & Hudson. *A popular textbook emphasizing how archaeologists learn what they know about the past.*

Sutton, M. Q., and B. S. Arkush. 1998. *Archaeological laboratory methods.* Dubuque, IA: Kendall/Hunt. *A guide to laboratory work in archaeology involving identification, conservation, and measurement.*

# CHAPTER TWO

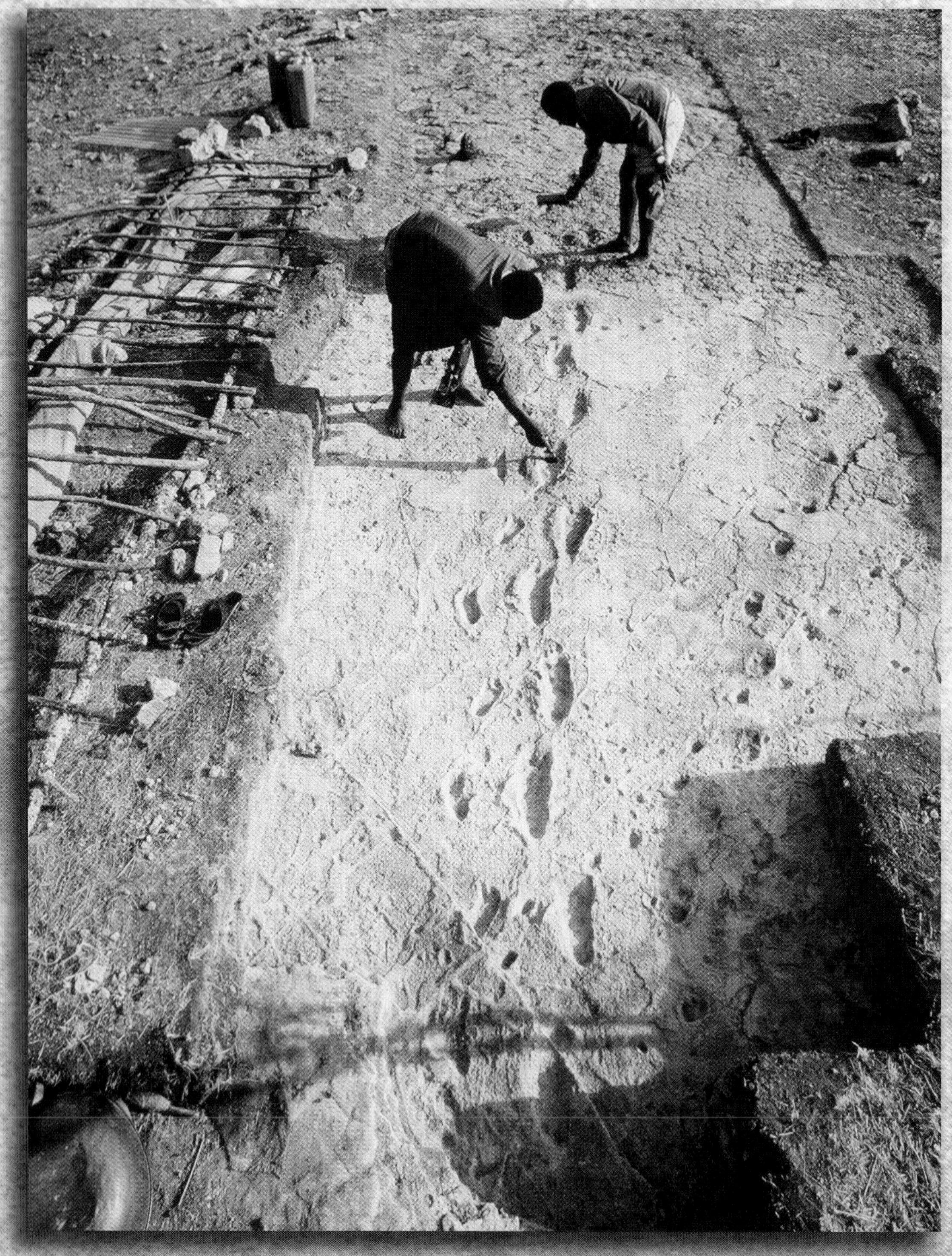

**Figure 2.1** The 3.75-million-year-old footprints discovered in East Africa at the site of Laetoli, Tanzania.

# The First Humans

## Introduction
## The Dawn of Humanity

The 3.75-million-year-old footprints found at the site of Laetoli in East Africa (Figure 2.1) are the most dramatic and important evidence we have of early humans as two-footed animals. Becoming bipedal appears to have been the first step we took in separating from our apelike ancestors. Our evolutionary path to being human is the subject of this chapter.

To comprehend the significance of this transformation, it is essential that we understand our place among the other animals. Zoologists classify the members of the animal kingdom according to their similarities and differences. We are animals because we move and eat with a mouth, we are vertebrates because of our backbone, and we are mammals because we have warm blood and breastfeed our offspring. We are **primates** because we have grasping hands, flexible limbs, and a highly developed sense of vision, which we share with the other members of the primate order: lemurs, tarsiers, monkeys, and apes. We are members of the family **Hominoidea,** the taxonomic group that includes apes and humans, because of the shape of our teeth, the absence of a tail, and our swinging arms. As humans, we share with chimpanzees and gorillas a common ancestor that lived sometime during the past 5–10 million years.

Present evidence suggests the following scenario for primate evolution during the Cenozoic. The first primates on Earth existed about 65 m.y.a. at the beginning of the Cenozoic, when the air temperature was warm and extensive tropical forests covered much of the land surface. These early primates began as tree-dwelling insect-eaters. They had adaptive characteristics such as stereoscopic color vision, which provided depth perception and enhanced their ability to move from branch to branch and to spot insects, and a grasping ability, so they could hold onto branches and grab bugs. This heritage has provided us with an extraordinary visual ability and large centers in the brain to process the enormous volume of information absorbed by the eyes. Along with the ability to hold and manipulate objects with dexterity came other changes. Arms and shoulders became more flexible for swinging in the trees, and internal organs and bones evolved toward a more vertical arrangement. This is evolution in action.

The earliest Hominoidea appeared approximately 25 m.y.a. Apes are generally distinguished from monkeys and other primates by larger size, distinctive teeth, greater sociability, the absence of a tail, and a reduced sense of smell. From one of these early apes, a new group of animals, known as the **dryopithecines,** emerged during the Miocene epoch some 17–12 m.y.a. These creatures had several features, known primarily from the fossil teeth that have survived, suggesting that they were the probable ancestors of both living apes and humans. Dryopithecines were apparently very successful in their arboreal adaptation, ranging over much of Africa, Asia, and Europe. During this time, the earth changed dramatically. Increased geological activity in the earth's crust created new mountain ranges.

CHAPTER OUTLINE



**primate** The order of animals that includes lemurs, tarsiers, monkeys, apes, and humans.

**Hominoidea** The taxonomic group (family) that includes the human and ape members of the primates, both fossil and modern forms.

**dryopithecine** The generic term for the Miocene fossil ancestor of both the living apes and modern humans, found in Africa, Asia, and Europe.

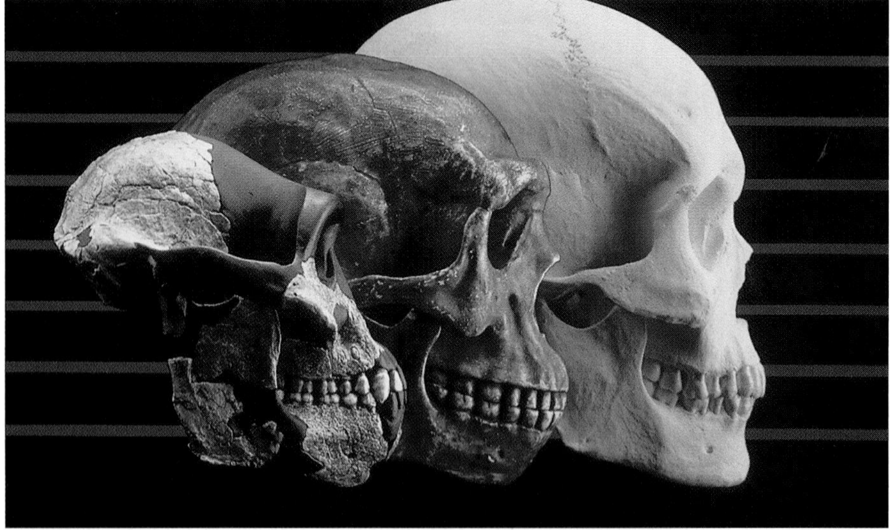

**Figure 2.2** The skulls of *Australopithecus afarensis* (left), *Homo erectus* (center), and *Homo sapiens sapiens* (right).

*Man is only one of the earth's "manifold creatures" and he cannot understand his own nature or seek wisely to guide his destiny without taking account of the whole pattern of life.*
—George Gaylord Simpson (1967)

**www.mhhe.com/priceip6e**

For preview material for this chapter, see the comprehensive chapter outline and chapter objectives on your online learning center.

Are humans really so different from other animals?

Between 9 and 4 m.y.a., the convergence of the Indian and Eurasian continental plates gave rise to the Himalayan Mountains and Tibetan Plateau. These massive new elevations rerouted the weather, and the climates from East Africa to East Asia became drier and more seasonal. Widespread tropical forests began to shrink, taken over by expanding grasslands and savannas. It is very possible that these events pushed some forest-dwelling apes in Africa toward the open savanna and along the human line (Figure 2.2).

At some point during the later Miocene epoch, after 10 m.y.a., one of these African primate species took the path toward humanness, as seen in the evidence for more upright posture and smaller canine teeth. The fossil record from this time period is very scanty. A fossil discovery in the Sumburu Hills of Kenya may be this creature (Figure 2.3). A fragment of an upper jaw, dating to 9–8 m.y.a., has characteristics of a generalized chimpanzee-gorilla-human ancestor. Genetic and molecular evidence indicates that early humans were most closely related to chimpanzees and that we began to diverge from the chimpanzee lineage between 6 and 5 m.y.a. Recent fossil evidence from Central and East Africa suggests that this date may be even earlier, before 6 m.y.a. Between 6 and 2 m.y.a., a variety of our early relatives made their appearance in Africa.

But what does it mean to be human? What makes us distinct from other species of animals?

**Figure 2.3** An artist's reconstruction of *Kenyapithecus*.

We are human because we have a skeleton designed for upright walking. We are human because we have grasping hands with opposable thumbs, capable of both strength and precision movement; we are also human because we have *lost* the grasping, opposable toes of the other apes. We are human because we have small, flat teeth and lack the large, slashing canines of other primates. We have a pronounced nose compared with that of apes and a face that sits beneath our brain case rather than in front of it. We are human because we lack fur and have more sweat glands than hair follicles. We have a conspicuous penis and breasts, and we have sex face-to-face and almost constantly compared with many other animals. We care for our young over a lengthy period of infancy and childhood. We are human because we make and use tools to alter our environment and make our lives more secure and comfortable. We are human because we

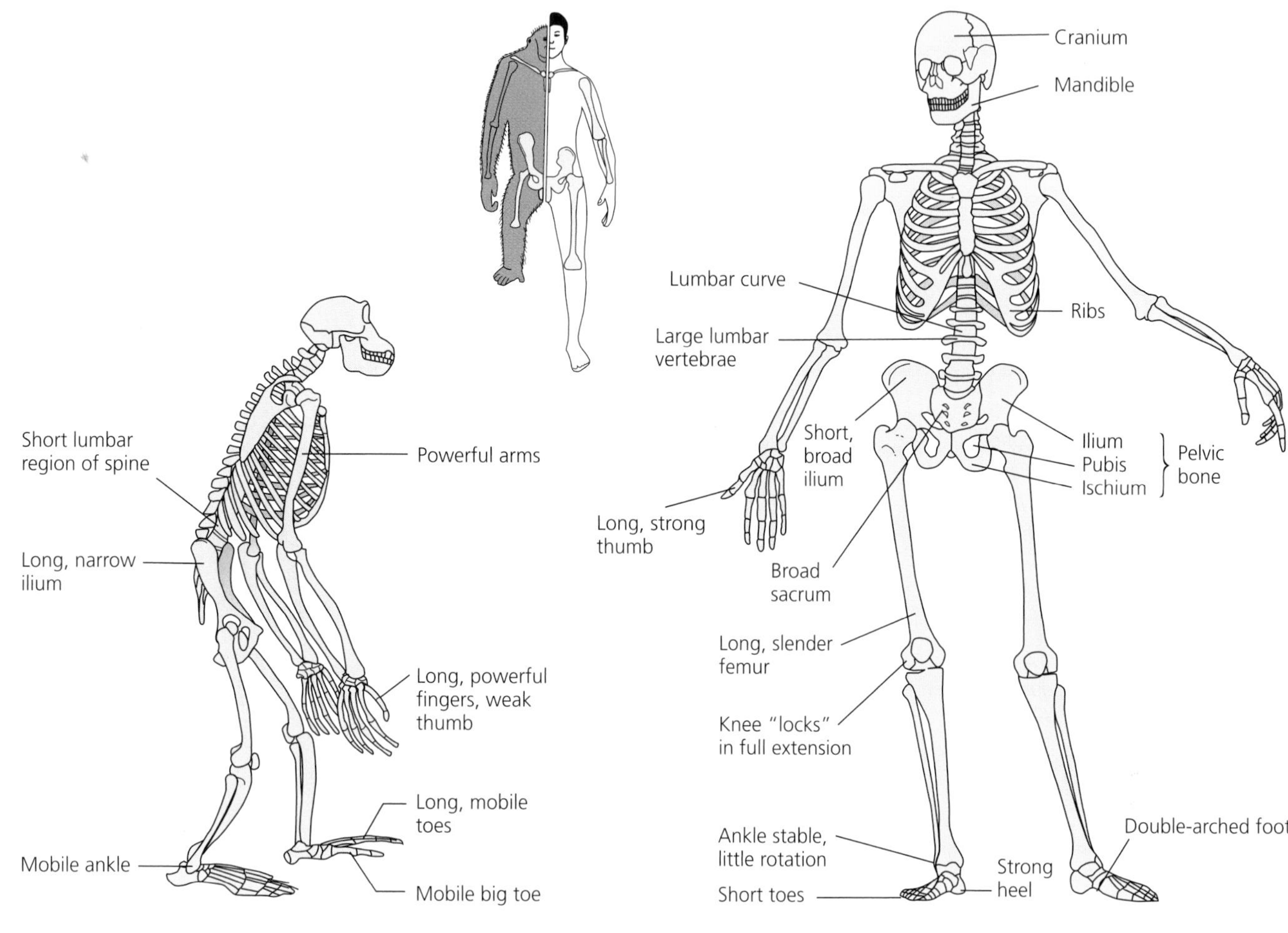


**Figure 2.4** Comparative skeletal anatomy of the chimpanzee and the modern human.

often act according to reason rather than on instinct. We have a large brain relative to our body size, and we have enhanced intelligence, as well as a complex repertoire of behaviors known as culture. We are human because we speak a language full of meaning and metaphor.

Many features, then, define us as human (Figure 2.4). But what characteristics can be identified in the fragmentary fossil bones and stone tools of our earliest ancestors? The markers of early humanness must be present in materials that can survive thousands and millions of years of exposure to the elements. Of all the characteristics of being human, the ones that can be found most readily in the fossil record are upright posture, larger brains, and tools. The major questions in human evolution, then, concern when, where, and why these distinctive characteristics appeared. What of us is preserved in the layers of geological time?

**Paleoanthropology,** the study of early human evolution, attempts to answer those and other questions, using evidence from **fossils** and artifacts. For this information, we must turn to Africa; our oldest ancestors are known only from that continent. Some of the best evidence comes from sites such as Hadar, Laetoli, Swartkrans, and Olduvai (Figure 2.5). We will visit these places in the following pages.

**www.mhhe.com/priceip6e**

For a Web-based activity on primate evolution, see the Internet exercises on your online learning center.

**paleoanthropology** The branch of anthropology that combines archaeology and physical anthropology to study the biological and behavioral remains of the early hominins.

**fossil** The mineralized bone of an extinct animal.

**Figure 2.5** Location of and timeline for early hominins in Africa.

*In each great region of the world the living mammals are closely related to the extinct species of the same region. It is, therefore, probable that Africa was formerly inhabited by extinct apes closely allied to the gorilla and chimpanzee; and as these two species are now man's nearest allies, it is somewhat more probable that our early progenitors lived on the African continent than elsewhere.*

—Charles Darwin (1871)

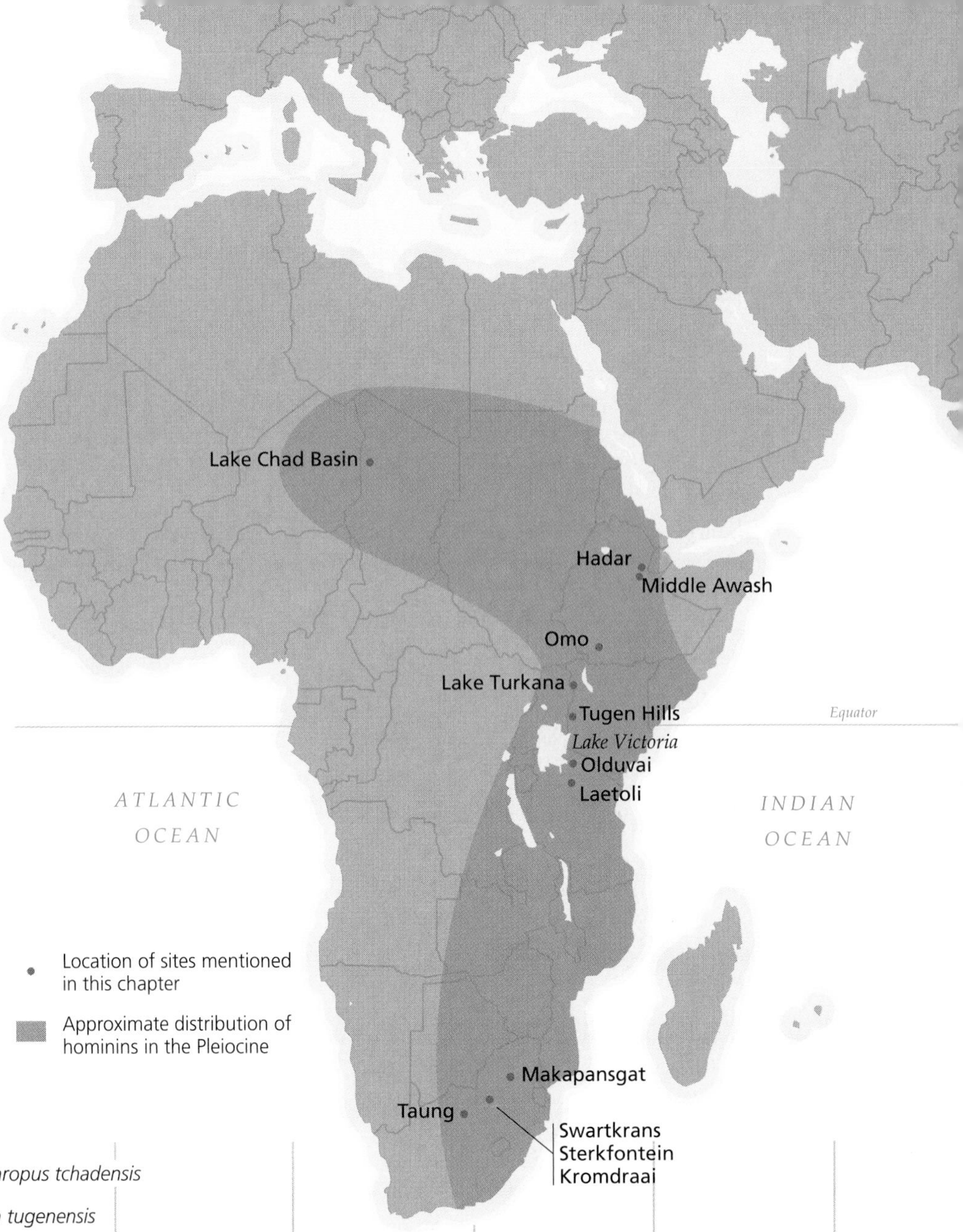

Lake Chad Basin
Hadar
Middle Awash
Omo
Lake Turkana
Tugen Hills
Equator
*Lake Victoria*
Olduvai
Laetoli
ATLANTIC OCEAN
INDIAN OCEAN
Location of sites mentioned in this chapter
Approximate distribution of hominins in the Pleiocine
Makapansgat
Taung
Swartkrans
Sterkfontein
Kromdraai

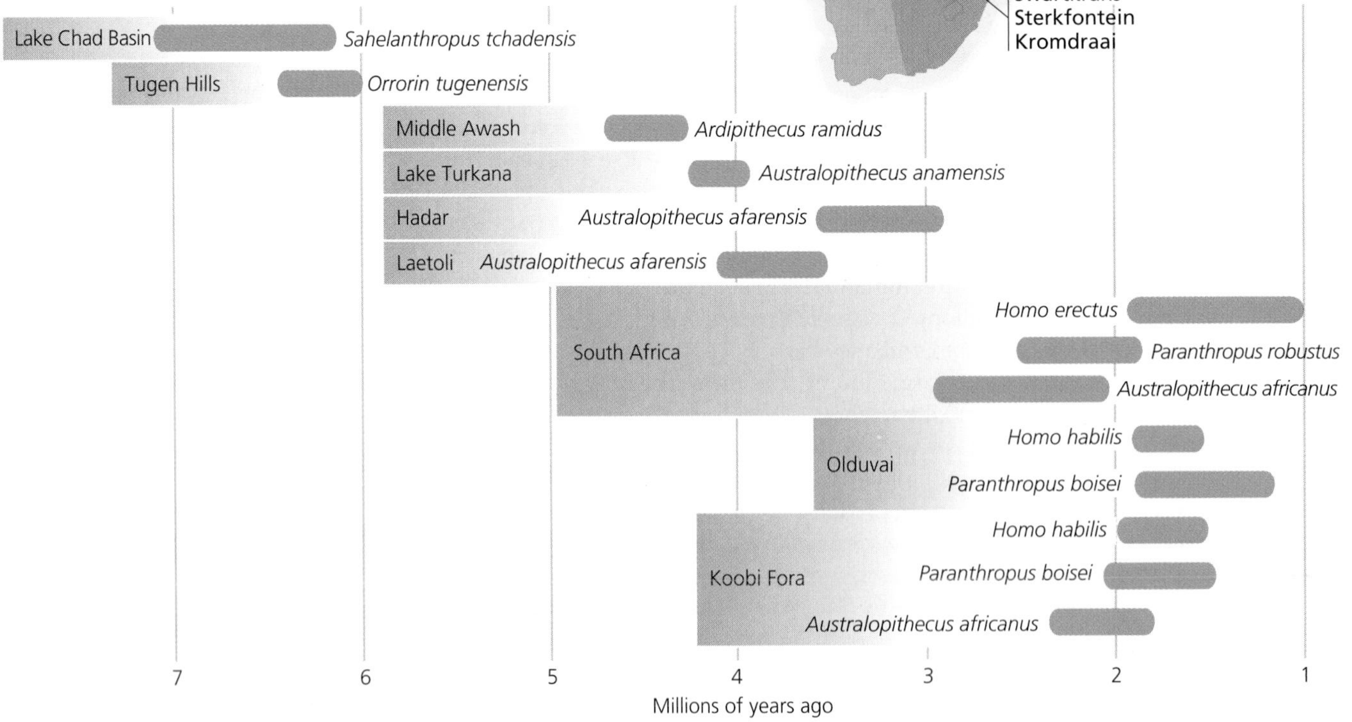

Lake Chad Basin — *Sahelanthropus tchadensis*
Tugen Hills — *Orrorin tugenensis*
Middle Awash — *Ardipithecus ramidus*
Lake Turkana — *Australopithecus anamensis*
Hadar — *Australopithecus afarensis*
Laetoli — *Australopithecus afarensis*
South Africa — *Homo erectus*, *Paranthropus robustus*, *Australopithecus africanus*
Olduvai — *Homo habilis*, *Paranthropus boisei*
Koobi Fora — *Homo habilis*, *Paranthropus boisei*, *Australopithecus africanus*

7 6 5 4 3 2 1
Millions of years ago

Concept

# The Family Tree

## *The evidence and interpretation of our earliest biology*

Human evolution—the changes in the skeleton and biology of our species over the past 7 million years—is a fascinating subject, but one for which there is only sparse evidence. In almost every instance, the fossil remains of our earliest hominin ancestors are very fragmentary, poorly preserved, and disturbed by natural forces—time and nature have taken their toll.

Since the initial work of the Swedish botanist Carolus Linnaeus during the mid-1700s, scientists have classified newly discovered members of the plant and animal kingdoms according to a system that organizes them into species, genus, family, order, class, phylum, and kingdom, from most specific to most general—a family tree of life. Modern humans are members of the family Homininae of the genus *Homo* and the species *sapiens.* Determining the genus and species of the fossil bones of early humans is very difficult. All the fragmentary early fossil finds represent only a few parts of a few hundred individuals. Determining the age of fossils is difficult, and questions remain about whether the species existed contemporaneously or sequentially. Not surprisingly, there are controversies over what to call these first hominin forms and how to identify them. As Richard Klein, of Stanford University, has noted, paleoanthropology is more like a court of law than a physics laboratory. It sometimes seems that whenever a new fragment is discovered, we have to reassess and even redraw our entire family tree. New fossils that modify current ideas are found almost every year. Disputes rage over the designation of species, the age of fossils, and the line of human ancestry.

Even the words to use to describe the category of early human ancestors are controversial. New fossil finds have forced a reconsideration of the terms because it becomes harder to distinguish the first humans from their closest relatives among the apes. The term **hominoid** refers to all present and past apes and humans. The word **hominid** has been used for many years as the

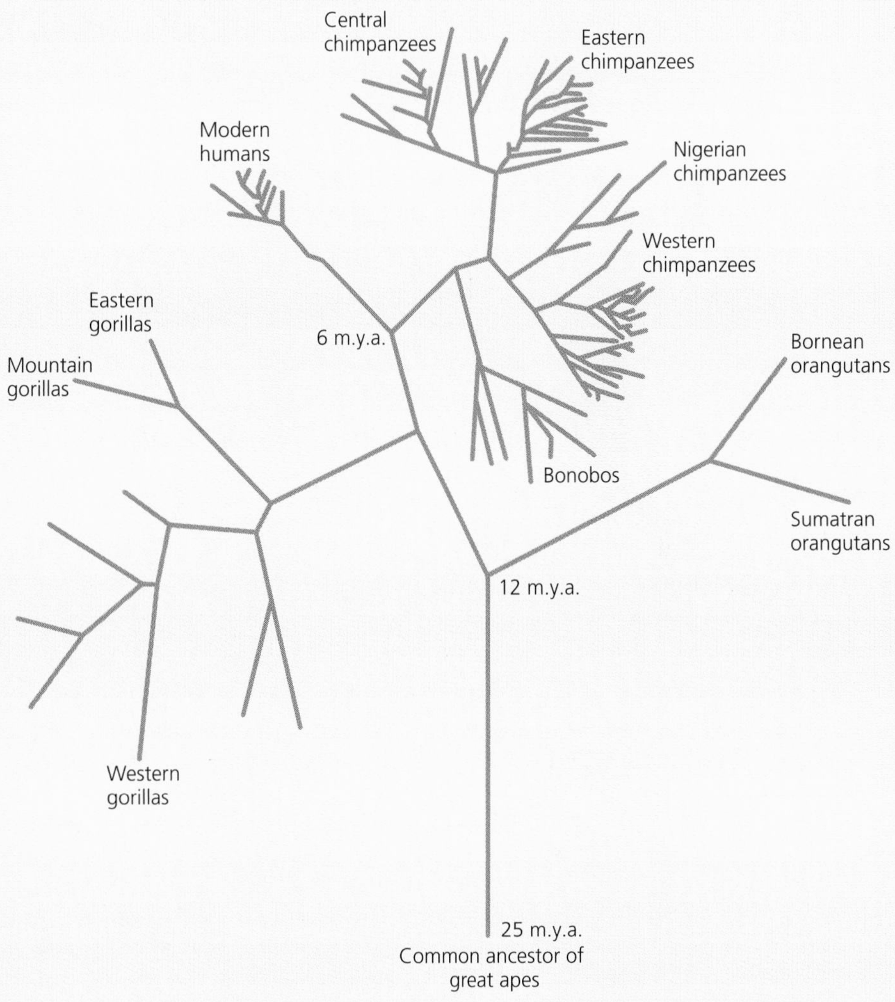


**Figure 2.6** An evolutionary tree for the great apes based on modern genetic studies. The length of lines shows genetic distance from one group to another. The diagram shows that our closest relatives are the chimpanzees and the **bonobos** and that we are not very far apart compared with some of the other species. Three estimates for the time elapsed since separation are shown on the diagram. Fossil evidence suggests that the separation of humans and an ape relative may be somewhat earlier than 6 m.y.a.

**bonobo** A small species of chimpanzee, closely related to humans.

**hominoid** A descriptive term for any human or ape, past or present, characterized by teeth shape, the absence of a tail, and swinging arms.

**hominid** An obsolete term that refers to the human members of the primates, both fossil and modern forms.

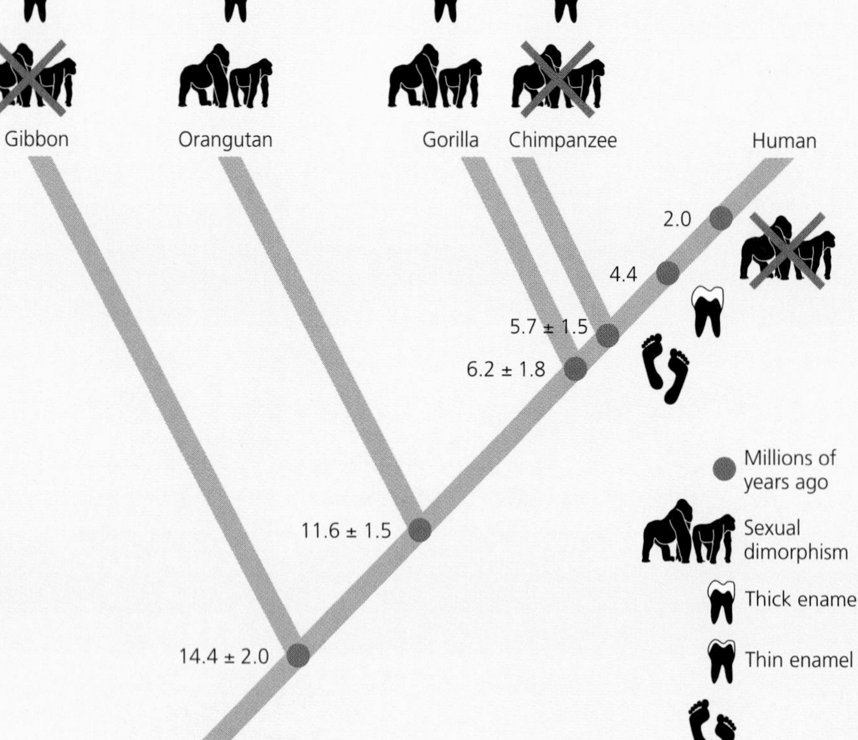


**Figure 2.7** A diagram showing the speciation of the great apes with chronology and some distinguishing characteristics. Humans, for example, exhibit bipedalism, thick enamel, and little sexual dimorphism. The red X indicates reduced sexual dimorphism.

*An ape-brained and small-canined creature, with dental enamel of unknown thickness. Large if male but smaller if female. May be spotted climbing adeptly in trees or walking bipedally on the ground. Last seen in Africa between 5 and 7 million years ago.*

—Pat Shipman (2002), describing the earliest humans

**hominin** A current term that refers to the human, chimp, and gorilla members of the primates, both fossil and modern forms.

**sexual dimorphism** A difference in size between the male and female members of a species.

generic term for present and past humans. However, a new term, **hominin,** is now being used in place of *hominid.* Genetic studies have shown that not all apes descended from a common ancestor (Figure 2.6)—that chimps and gorillas share a more recent ancestor with humans than they do with the orangutan, for example. That means that, on the strict taxonomic level, chimps and gorillas are hominins. The term *hominins,* then, is used to describe those species clearly in the line of human evolution, not other apes. All hominins are hominids, but not all hominids are hominins. Confusing, isn't it?

Recent years have seen major changes in the field of paleoanthropology—new discoveries, new dates, new species, and new disagreements. A flurry of fossil finds has spurred these changes and once again rewritten our understanding of the evolution of our earliest ancestors. These discoveries have come from an important new locale in Chad, in central Africa, and from the usual places in East and South Africa. Features of the fossil material such as thickness of tooth enamel, evidence for bipedalism and tree climbing, and size differences between the sexes—**sexual dimorphism**—play an important role in the discussion (Figure 2.7).

In Chad, a new, very old, and controversial fossil species has been found in the blowing sands of the Late Miocene deposits in the Lake Chad basin. This new form is designated as *Sahelanthropus tchadensis.* Although it combines ape and human characteristics, a flat face and "habitual bipedalism" distinguish the Chad specimen as a human ancestor. Habitual bipedalism means the species normally moves on two feet (e.g., humans). Facultative bipedalism means that the species is able to move on two feet (e.g., chimpanzees and gorillas). Dates on this bipedal individual lie between 7 and 6 m.y.a., making it our oldest known ancestor.

In East Africa, a spate of finds documents the diversity of our early ancestors. In the Middle Awash area of Ethiopia, seventeen fossils, including teeth, skull, and arm bones, were found by a research team directed by Tim White of the University of California, Berkeley. These fossils lie directly under a volcanic deposit dating to 4.4 m.y.a. Designated *Ardipithecus ramidus,* the species exhibits a combination of human and chimpanzeelike features. Since the initial discovery, leg bones have been found that suggest that this earliest ancestor likely walked on two legs. Meave Leakey and her colleagues have named a new genus and species, *Kenyapithecus platyops,* which has a flat, humanlike face but an ape-size brain. This fossil probably dates to 3.5 m.y.a.

An even earlier and more important find, from the Tugen Hills of Kenya, are fossils—named *Orrorin tugenensis*—that date to 6 m.y.a. A CAT scan of the fossil femur (thighbone) indicated habitual bipedalism. Like those of *Ardipithecus,* the arm bones suggest tree-climbing adaptations, but the two species differ in enamel thickness. *Orrorin* has thick enamel like a human's, whereas *Ardipithecus* has thin enamel more closely resembling that of other chimps and gorillas.

In South Africa, the big news is dating. New techniques have redated the deposits at several sites where varieties of **australopithecines** have been found and have pushed back the dates to almost 4 million years, twice as long ago as previously believed. These fossils are now easily as old as their counterparts in East Africa.

These recent fossil finds have pushed the antiquity of humans and their ancestors back to the end of the Pliocene into the Late Miocene, the oldest more than 7 m.y.a., aging our presence on the planet by several million years (Figure 2.8). The new finds have turned the tree of human evolution into more of a bush with a number of branches at the bottom as well. In addition, the finds have provided important new information on habitat, diet, and posture. The older fossil forms appear to have lived in forested environments, in contrast to the more open savanna that is thought to have been the habitat of the australopithecines. It now seems that bipedalism first appeared in the context of the forest rather than the plain.

Changes in diet are apparent in the fossil teeth. Relatively small molar size in chimps, *Ardipithecus,* and *Orrorin* indicates a diet primarily of fruit and vegetation. *Homo erectus* and *Homo sapiens* also have small molars relative to body size. Tooth enamel is thin in chimps, medium in *Ardipithecus,* and thick in *Orrorin, Australopithecus,* and *Homo.* Canine teeth in chimps and *Orrorin* are large, sharp, and V-shaped in cross section; canines are small, more rounded, and diamond shaped in *Ardipithecus* and later forms. The combination of thick enamel, large molars, and smaller canines first seen in the australopithecines is thought to show a change in diet from fruits and leaves to more roots, tubers, insects, and other small animals.

Microscopic analysis of wear patterns on fossil teeth by Alan Walker, of Pennsylvania State University, indicates that the tooth enamel among early hominins more closely resembles that of herbivores than that of carnivores (Figure 2.9). Examination of the anatomy of the wrist, shoulder, pelvis, and thigh of the early australopithecines indicates a pattern of movement, or **locomotion,** different from that of both the modern apes and humans. Henry McHenry, of the University of California–Davis, noting the curvature visible in hand and foot bones, concludes that these creatures must have spent some time in the trees. Sexual dimorphism was greatly reduced in *Homo erectus* and may reflect the emergence of monogamous mating systems, in which males and females each have a single mate for long periods of time.

*Australopithecus anamensis,* a transitional form between *A. ramidus* and *A. afarensis,* has recently been found at Lake Turkana, Kenya, dating to 4 m.y.a. Sometime around 3.9 m.y.a., *A. anamensis* evolved into *Australopithecus afarensis,* well known from Hadar, Laetoli, and elsewhere in East Africa (Table 2.1). *A. afarensis* exhibits more humanlike teeth and unquestionably walked upright, as seen in the footprints at Laetoli and in the fossil bones themselves.

The next series of fossil finds comes from a period generally referred to as the **Plio-Pleistocene.** This is a combined term for the late Pliocene

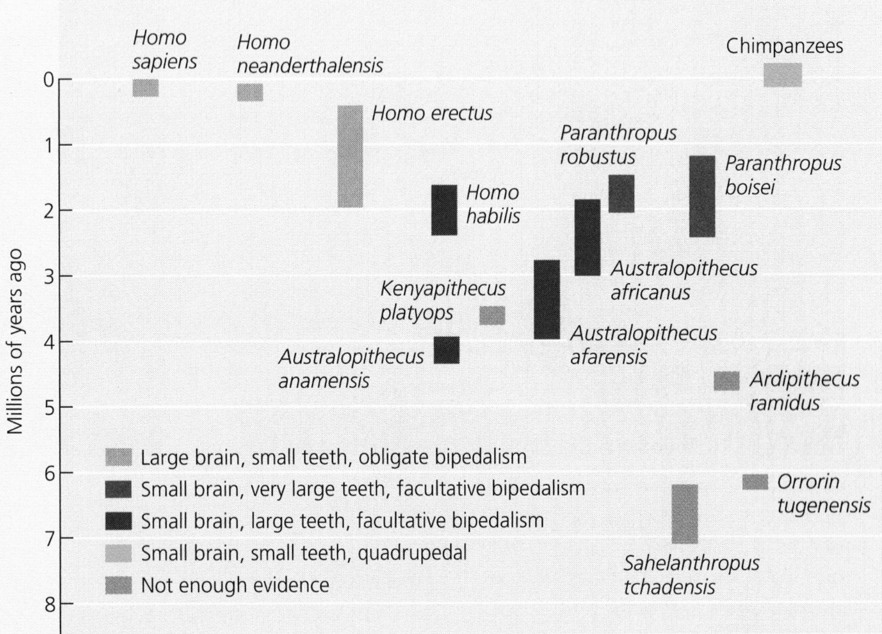


**Figure 2.8** Hominin evolution over the past 7 million years. The diagram shows only some of the major species and their major characteristics: brain size, tooth size, and bipedalism.

(Reprinted by permission from Macmillan Publishers Ltd: *Nature,* "Paleoanthropology: Hominid revelations from Chad" by Bernard Wood, Vol. 148, p. 134. Copyright 2002.)

**www.mhhe.com/priceip6e**

For a Web-based activity on the various hominin species, see the Internet exercises on your online learning center.

What advantages could bipedalism have provided for our ape ancestors?

**australopithecine** The generic term for the various species of the genus *Australopithecus,* including *A. ramidus, A. afarensis,* and *A. africanus.*

**locomotion** A method of animal movement, such as bipedalism.

**Plio-Pleistocene** A generic term for the period of the Pliocene and early Pleistocene, used to describe the age of fossil finds, approximately 3–1 m.y.a.

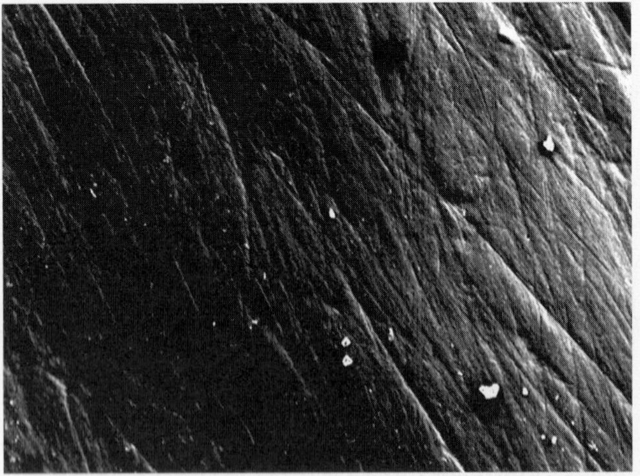

**Figure 2.9** Electron microscope photos of tooth wear on early hominins. The scratched surface from *Australopithecus africanus* (left) contrasts with the rough and irregular surface of the enamel of *Paranthropus* (right), thought to have eaten harder gritty foods such as roots and nuts.

*Stunning new fossils of hominins that lived three to four million years ago. . . . During this time, we're dealing with a warmer, wetter Africa that it seems was spawning hominins from the shores of Lake Chad to the caves of Sterkfontein.*

—Philip Tobias (2002)

***Paranthropus*** Genus of early hominins, contemporary with *Australopithecus,* that includes *boisei* and *robustus* as species.

and early Pleistocene, approximately 3–1 m.y.a. The generally accepted picture is that sometime between 3 and 2.5 m.y.a., *A. afarensis* split into two separate lineages. One of those lineages continued as the australopithecines (a generic term for various forms of *Australopithecus*). This line included both gracile and robust forms. The gracile form, with smaller teeth, skull, and body size, known as *Australopithecus africanus,* appeared shortly after 3 m.y.a. The robust forms, with big teeth and heavy jaws for chewing plant foods, are designated as genus ***Paranthropus.*** Several species have been identified, including *aethiopithecus, robustus,* and *boisei.* The robust forms have been found in both East and South Africa and eventually became extinct around 1 m.y.a.

The other lineage led to *Homo habilis,* the first members of our own genus. The earliest *H. habilis* is known from around 2.5 m.y.a. and is recognized by a clear increase in brain size. (The first *H. habilis* is very close in time to the earliest known stone tools; see "The First Tools," p. 63.) The 1986 discovery by Johanson and White of over 300 pieces of a skeleton in beds at Olduvai Gorge dating to 1.8 m.y.a. has filled in part of the picture of *Homo habilis.* For the first time, there were enough fragments of the arms and legs of an *H. habilis* creature to provide an indication of height and the proportions of the limbs. Surprisingly, this female *H. habilis* was less than 1 m (about 3 ft) tall and had very long arms, similar to Lucy and other australopithecines. Such evidence suggests that (1) *H. habilis* may still have been spending part of its life in the trees, (2) sexual dimorphism was still very pronounced, and (3) major changes in behavior and habitat of the early hominins may have taken place in the period between 2 and 1.5 m.y.a. Thus, it appears that *Homo habilis* "represents a mosaic of primitive and derived features, indicating an early hominin which walked bipedally . . . but also retained the generalized hominoid capacity to climb trees" (Susman and Stern, 1982, p. 931).

Richard Leakey, Alan Walker, and a few others suggest a different scenario. Louis Leakey always argued that the genus *Homo* had its roots deep in the Pliocene, and he eventually discovered several early *Homo* specimens at Olduvai and elsewhere. This view is maintained by his son Richard and others who would push the evolutionary split from a common ancestor of the *Australopithecus* and *Homo* lines much further back in time, perhaps near the beginning of the Pliocene, around 6 m.y.a. They imagine that two or more different australopithecine groups (*P. robustus* and *A. africanus*) and one line of *Homo* (*H. habilis*) evolved at this time.

The next stage in our family tree is relatively straightforward and uncon-

**TABLE 2.1 Major Characteristics of the Plio/Pleistocene Hominins**

| | *Australopithecus ramidus* | *Australopithecus anamensis* | *Australopithecus afarensis* | *Australopithecus africanus* | *Paranthropus robustus* | *Paranthropus boisei* | *Homo habilis* |
|---|---|---|---|---|---|---|---|
| Dates | 4.5–4.3 m.y.a. | 4.3–4.0 m.y.a. | 4.2–2.8 m.y.a. | 3–1.8 m.y.a. | 2.2–1.5 m.y.a. | 2.2–1 m.y.a. | 2.5–1.6 m.y.a. |
| Sites | Middle Awash | Lake Turkana | Hadar<br>Omo<br>Laetoli | Taung<br>Sterkfontein<br>Makapansgat<br>Lake Turkana (?)<br>Omo (?) | Kromdraai<br>Swartkrans | Olduvai<br>Lake Turkana<br>Omo | Olduvai<br>Lake Turkana<br>Omo<br>Sterkfontein<br>Swartkrans |
| Cranial Capacity | Unknown (400–450 cc?) | Unknown | 380–500 cc; average = 440 cc | 435–530 cc; average = 450 cc | 520 cc (based on one specimen) | 500–530 cc; average = 515 cc | 500–800 cc; average = 680 cc |
| Size | 100 lb? | 5' 110 lb (♂)<br>4'3" 70 lb (♀) | 3'6" 50 lb (♀)<br>(♂ to 100 lb?) | Similar to *A. afarensis* | 5'+ 150 lb | 5'+ 150 lb | Limited evidence; may have been size of *A. afarensis* |
| Skull | Large pointed canines, small molar crowns, thinner enamel; foramen magnum forward | Teeth and jaw hominin, but some similarities to chimpanzee | Very prognathous, receding chin, large teeth, pointed canines with gap, arcade between ape and human, hint of crest | Less prognathous than *A. afarensis;* jaw more rounded; large back teeth; canines smaller than *A. robustus,* larger than *A. afarensis;* no crest | Heavy jaws, small canines and front teeth, large back teeth, definite crest | Very large jaws, very large back teeth, large crest | Flatter face, less sloping forehead, teeth similar to *A. africanus,* no crest |
| Postcranial Skeleton | Arm bones with characteristics intermediate between great apes and hominins | Joints on leg bones indicate bipedal gait | Long arms, short thumb, curved fingers and toes, bipedal | — | Hands and feet more like modern humans', retention of long arms | — | Limited evidence, retention of long arms, maybe retention of primitive features of hand and foot |

*Source: Adapted from Feder and Park, 1997.*

tested. *Homo erectus* evolved from *Homo habilis* about 1.9 m.y.a., again in Africa. The earliest fossils of *H. erectus* are known from the eastern shore of Lake Turkana in northern Kenya. *H. erectus* is also the first early human form found outside Africa, in Asia and probably in Europe. In fact, a controversial date of 1.8 m.y.a. for an *H. erectus* fossil from China would suggest a very rapid spread of this species out of Africa. *Homo erectus* walked upright and had a brain size midway between that of *Australopithecus* and fully modern humans. The time period of *H. erectus* covers more than 1.5 million years, and there were a number of changes in the species during that period. In fact, there is some controversy today about the reliability of the *H. erectus* species designation.

Remarkably, and probably relatedly, a major innovation in the technology of stone tools, the appearance of the handaxe and other bifacial tools, occurred almost simultaneously with *Homo erectus* in Africa (see "The Acheulean Handaxe," Chapter 3, p. 99). The distribution of *Homo erectus* fossils and the archaeological evidence they produced are the subject of the next chapter.

*Homo erectus* gradually evolved in Africa and Asia, exhibiting slowly increasing brain size, for a million years, eventually expanding into Europe. *Erectus* forms evolved into *Homo heidelbergensis* after 600,000 years ago. At some point after, perhaps, 200,000 years before the present (B.P.), *Homo sapiens* began to appear. Suffice it to say here that *Homo erectus* is the ancestor of the first *Homo sapiens*—and ultimately of ourselves.

There is a great deal we don't know about our early ancestors. What would you like to know?

## Hadar

*A key place for finding the earliest humans*

All the evidence for the early hominins before 2 m.y.a. comes from Africa. Until 1970, there was relatively little evidence for the earliest human ancestors other than a few skulls and pieces of bone. The human characteristics of upright posture, large brain size, and tool use were thought to have evolved simultaneously as large primates moved out from the forest into the savanna. New fossil finds from Ethiopia, Kenya, and Tanzania have pushed back the age of the earliest known hominins and considerably modified our understanding of their behavior and appearance (Figure 2.10).

Shortly after 7 m.y.a., near the end of the Miocene, the first recognizable human began to appear in Africa. There are only a few examples of the earliest fossils. Most of the early hominin specimens date somewhat later, to the Pliocene and the beginning of the Pleistocene, a time often described as the Plio-Pleistocene.

One of the most productive areas of research is in a region known as the Hadar (huh-DAR), northeast of the

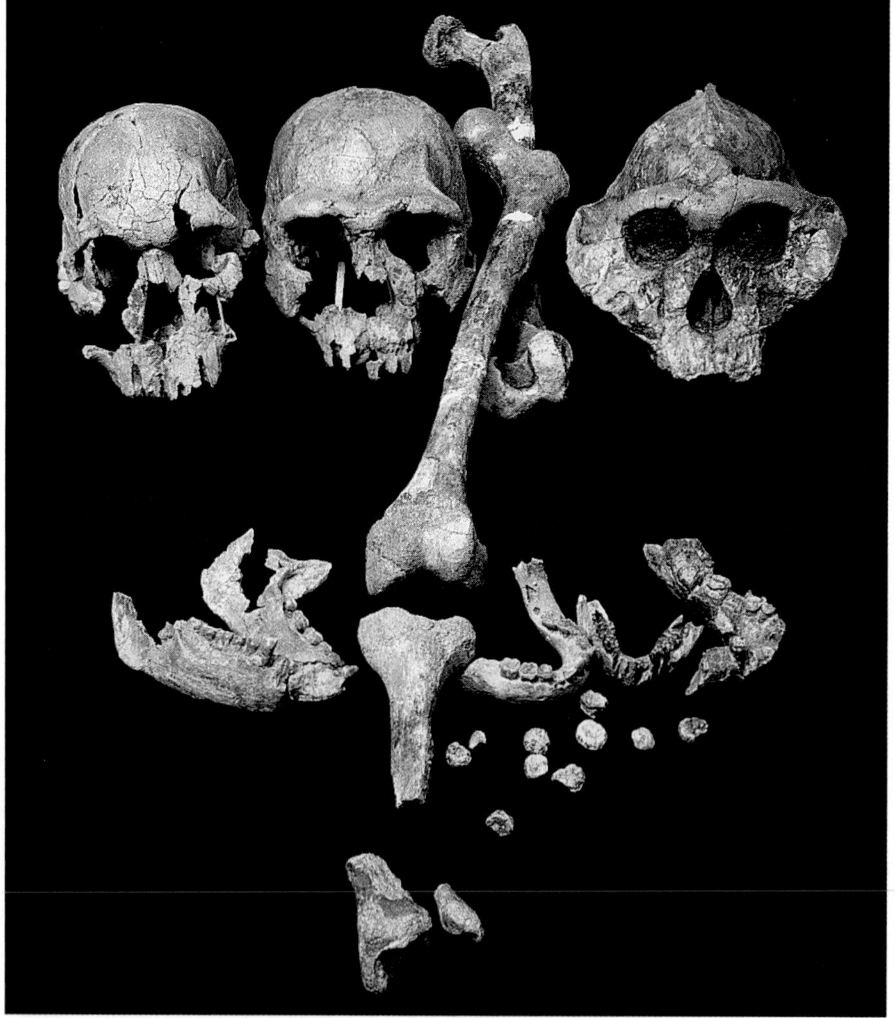

**Figure 2.10** Three early hominin skulls and other remains found by Richard Leakey and his co-workers in East Africa: *Homo habilis* (left), *Homo erectus* (center), and *Paranthropus robustus* (right). The discovery of these species in the same geological deposits suggests that they were roughly contemporary.

city of Addis Ababa in Ethiopia (Figure 2.11). In this geologically active zone, the combination of faulting, rapid deposition, and continued erosion has exposed numerous layers from the Pliocene that contain some of the earliest human fossils yet discovered (Figure 2.12). Donald Johanson, a paleoanthropologist now at the Institute for Human Origins in Tempe, Arizona (Figure 2.13), and French geologist Maurice Taieb began a search for early hominin fossils in this area in 1972. One of the most complete early human skeletons ever discovered was found by this team in 1974.

Johanson spotted a small arm bone on the ground while on a survey walk. He picked it up and immediately noticed bits of skull and bone. As he continued, he collected more pieces—fragments of vertebrae, limbs, and jaw. The next day he returned with a large crew and carefully sifted the earth at the site to recover all the fragments they could. The finds of Pliocene hominins usually consist of only a single tooth or at most a few bones. But after 2 weeks of searching and sifting,

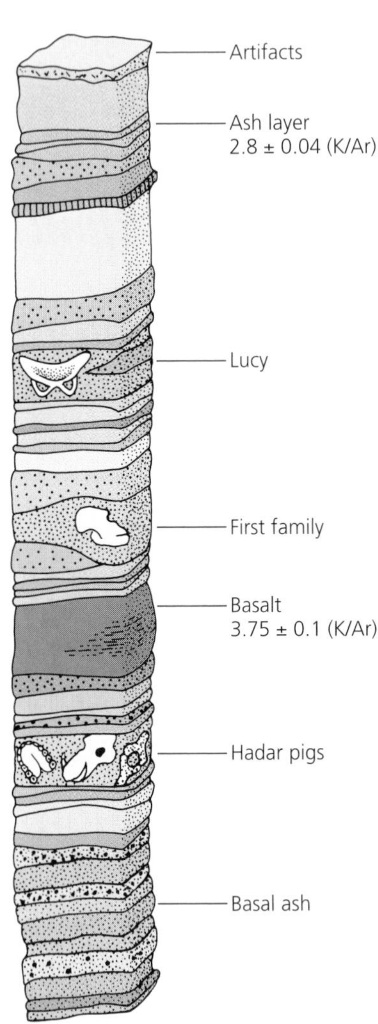


**Figure 2.11** The Pliocene stratigraphy at Hadar, showing the approximate age of the layers and where Lucy and the "first family" were found. These layers are exposed in the sides of gullies and on the surface by erosion. The fossils appear on the eroded surface. The number in the illustration followed by (K/Ar) provides the radiopotassium date for the layer in millions of years before the present (see "Dating Methods," p. 48).

**Figure 2.12** The severely eroded badlands of Pliocene and Pleistocene deposits in the Hadar region of Ethiopia. This is a part of the world where many fossil hominins have been found.

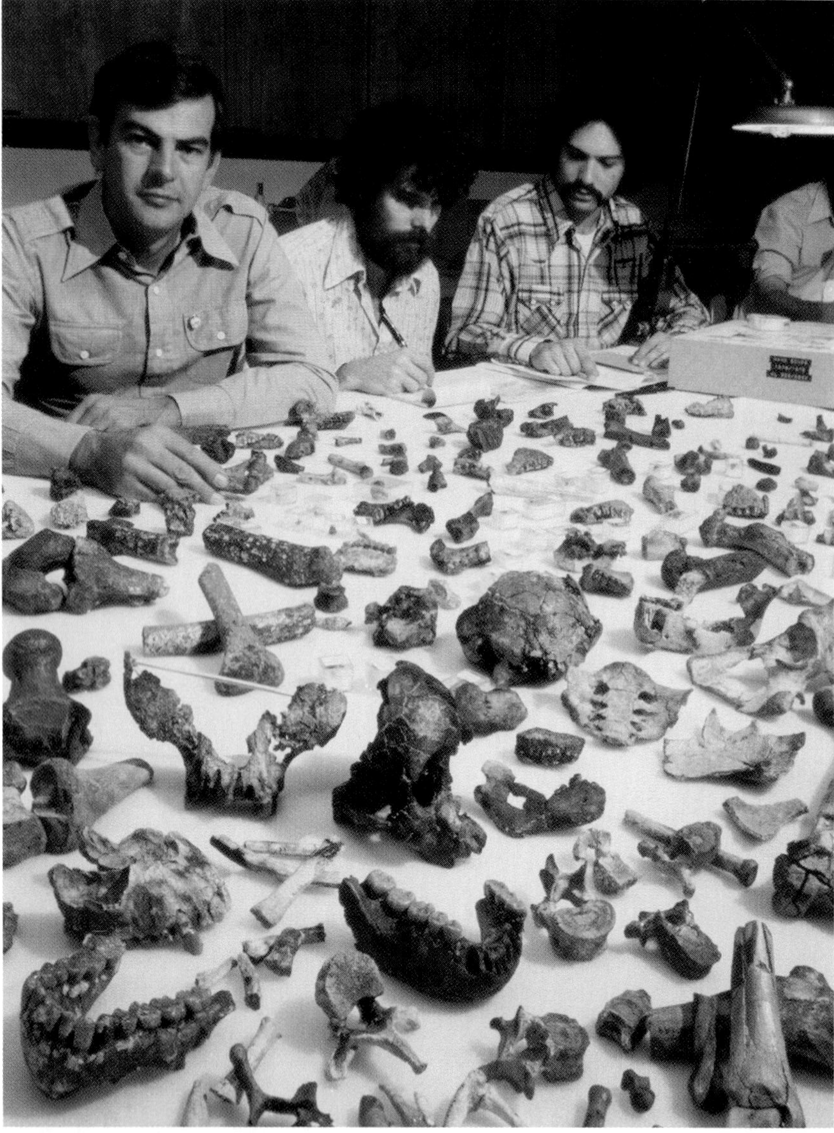

**Figure 2.13** Donald Johanson (left) and co-workers at the Institute for Human Origins with some of the fossil remains from Hadar.

Johanson's team found almost 100 fragments—about 40% of a complete hominin skeleton. Unfortunately, most of the skull was missing (Figure 2.14).

For the first time, a reasonably intact early hominin was available, enough to reconstruct virtually the entire skeleton. Lucy, as this individual was dubbed by her discoverers, provides much new detail on the anatomy of torso and limbs. Lucy was probably female, small in stature—1.2 m (just under 4 ft) tall—small-brained, and about 20 years old when she died. Absolute age for the skeleton is estimated as somewhat more than 2.9 million years. (Absolute dating is explained later in the chapter in "Dating Methods," p. 48.)

Earlier still from Hadar, possibly dating to 3.2 m.y.a., are the skeletal parts of what has been described as "the first family"—over 200 bones from at least seven individuals, five adults and two children, found together. This is an absolutely remarkable discovery. Johanson's own description of the discoveries conveys the excitement and the significance:

> *Anthropology student John Kolar spotted an arm-bone fragment. From some distance away, Mike Bush, a medical student, shouted that he had found something just breaking the ground surface. It was the very first day on survey for Mike.*
>
> *"Hominin teeth?" he asked, when we ran to him. There was no doubt. . . .*
>
> *Michèle Cavillon of our motion picture crew called to me to look at some bones higher up the hill.*
>
> *Two bone fragments lay side by side—one a partial femur and the other a fragmentary heel bone. Both were hominin.*
>
> *Carefully, we started scouring the hillside. Two more leg bones—fibulae—showed up, but each from the same side. The same side? That could only indicate two individuals. . . .*
>
> *Time was of the essence. Rainstorms during the months of our absence could wash away fragments that would be lost forever down the ravines. . . . Each day produced more remains. . . .*
>
> *So we had evidence of young adults, old adults, and children—an entire assemblage of early hominins. All of them at one place. Nothing like this had ever been found! (1976, pp. 805–811)*

These individuals apparently died as a group, possibly in a local flash flood, and their bodies were washed to a location where their bones were preserved until the present. The sediments in which the fossils were discovered are lakeshore and riverine deposits. There are very few remains from other species in these layers and no sign that the hominin bones had been gnawed or eaten by other animals.

The discovery of these bones from a *group* of individuals provides answers to

**www.mhhe.com/priceip6e**

For a Web-based activity on the Lucy specimen, see the Internet exercises on your online learning center.

**polygynous** Having more than one mate.

a number of questions. The presence of so many individuals together indicates that our earliest ancestors did indeed live in groups. The individuals were relatively small (1.2–1.5 m, or 4–5 ft, tall) but strong and sturdy. The small heads had human molars and small canine teeth. However, an apelike gap exists between the incisor teeth and the canines. The skeleton below the neck was almost completely human, but the arms were long and the bones of the hand were heavy, with large muscle attachments. The anatomy of the leg and pelvis indicates that they walked upright. Other information on early hominin patterns of growth, differences between children and adults and between males and females, the dexterity of the hands, and more, will emerge as the study of these extraordinary remains continues.

In 1994, fieldworkers in the Hadar region discovered the first intact skull of an *Australopithecus afarensis.* This skull confirmed the upright posture of a relative of Lucy's, dating to 3 m.y.a. More significant, the skull was a male's and documented significant sexual dimorphism, or size differences, among these early hominins. Pronounced differences in body size between the sexes in primates is generally correlated with **polygynous** mating systems, in which males compete for females. Males would have been approximately 1.5 m (5 ft) tall, weighing 50 kg (110 lb); females like Lucy were 1.0–1.2 m (3.5–4.0 ft) tall and weighed closer to 35 kg (75 lb). This difference between the sexes is also found in modern chimpanzees but is greatly reduced in more recent human species.

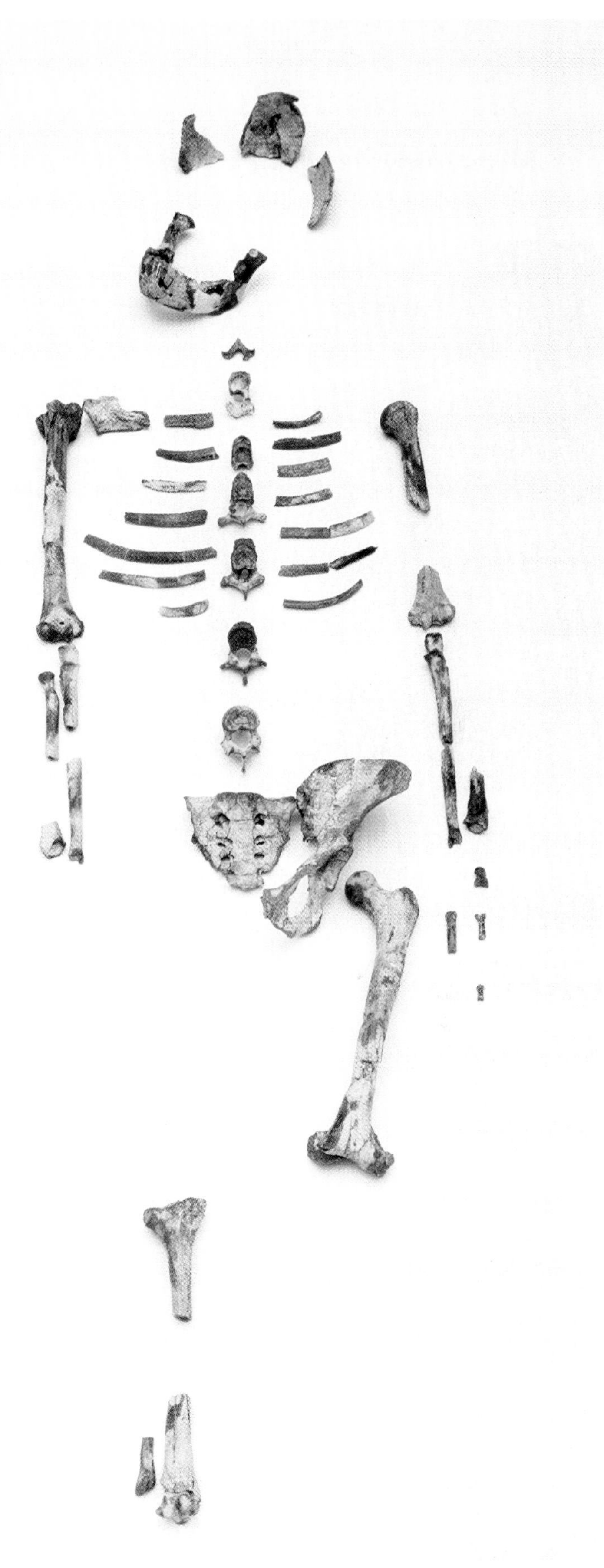

**Figure 2.14** The skeleton from Hadar known as Lucy, one of the most complete of an early hominin. Almost 40% of the bones are present. A member of *Australopithecus afarensis,* Lucy is approximately 1.2 m tall and 3 million years old.

*Concept*

# Dating Methods

## *Measuring the age of archaeological remains*

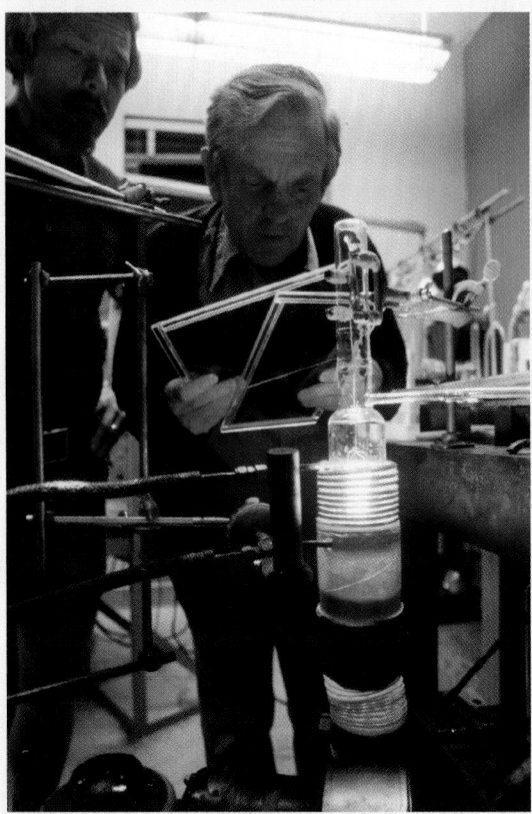

**Figure 2.15** Garniss Curtis, developer of the radiopotassium dating method, and his associate, Robert Drake (at left), examining the laboratory apparatus as a sample is heated to extract gases for the measurement of isotopes in a potassium-argon dating laboratory.

In the first half of the twentieth century, there was almost no way to determine the age of the remains of early humans and their artifacts. A few **relative dating** techniques were used to estimate the antiquity of bones and stones in a long sequence, but it was generally impossible to establish the absolute age of a layer or an artifact in calendar years. Relative dating methods often use stratigraphic relationships to sequence older and younger materials; lower layers of sediments in the ground, in caves, and elsewhere are, not surprisingly, older than the layers on top.

Relative dating methods also rely on the **association** of various items. For example, glass bottles have changed over the past 200 years. Bottles have become seamless, with shorter necks and narrower bodies. The known dates for certain types of bottles can be used to determine the age of other materials found with them. Similarly, the thickness of the stem and bore of clay smoking pipes from the eighteenth and nineteenth centuries steadily declined as the technology for manufacturing these items improved. Thus, the age of a historical trading post in Canada can be estimated by measuring the broken pieces of pipe stem found there. A photograph can be approximately dated by the known age of an automobile or other objects in the picture. The bones of extinct animals, such as elephants in France, found with stone tools were clear evidence that the artifacts were as old as the elephants, even if the exact age was uncertain.

Relative dating methods, however, are limited. It is often necessary to know the ages of archaeological materials more precisely in calendar years—**absolute dating**—to answer most questions about the past. Although many methods for determining absolute dates are now available, the most common techniques rely on the properties of radioactive decay in certain elements (Table 2.2). Many elements have both stable and radioactive atomic forms, known as **isotopes.** The techniques used for determining absolute dates with these elements are referred to as **isotopic techniques.** Perhaps best known among these is radiocarbon dating, but certain other elements—potassium, uranium, and calcium, for example—can also be used for dating purposes. Radiopotassium dating, or potassium-argon dating, used to determine the age of early human ancestors and their remains, is described in the following section. Radiocarbon dating, used to date archaeological materials and events that occurred within the past 40,000 years, is discussed in Chapter 4.

**relative dating** A technique used to *estimate* the antiquity of archaeological materials, generally based on association with materials of known age or simply to say that one item is younger or older than another.

**association** The relationship between items in an archaeological site. Items in association are found close together and/or in the same layer or deposit.

### RADIOPOTASSIUM DATING

**Radiopotassium dating,** also known as **potassium-argon dating,** is a technique of crucial importance for determining the age of the earliest human remains (Figure 2.15). This technique can date most of the earth's history and has been used to measure the age of the oldest rocks on our planet, as well as samples of moon rocks. The first potassium-argon dates from the lava at the base of Olduvai Gorge—1.75 m.y.a.—startled the scientific community in the 1960s. These fossil remains were almost 1 million years older than previously believed. Other early remains in East Africa from Laetoli, Koobi Fora, Hadar, and elsewhere have also been dated using the radiopotassium technique. Bones and artifacts are not themselves directly dated; rather, newly formed volcanic rocks or ash deposits that lie directly under or over the prehistoric

**TABLE 2.2 The Major Dating Methods Used in Archaeology**

| *Method* | *Materials* | *Range* | *Principle* | *Limitations* |
|---|---|---|---|---|
| Radiocarbon | Wood, charcoal, bone, carbonate | 100–40,000 years | Radioactive decay | Contamination, calibration |
| Radiopotassium | Volcanic rocks or minerals | Unlimited but approximate | Radioactive decay | Appropriate samples are rare |
| Uranium series | Coral, mollusks, travertine | 30,000–300,000 years | Radioactive decay | Few labs, technical problems, contamination |
| Geomagnetism | Undisturbed sediment or volcanic rocks | Unlimited but approximate | Alignment of particles with pole reversals | Few labs |
| Archaeomagnetism | Intact hearths, kilns, burned areas | 2000 years | Alignment with changes in location of the earth's magnetic pole | Few labs, calibration |
| Thermoluminescence (TL) | Pottery, heated stones, calcite | 1,000,000 years | Accumulation of TL in crystals | Environmental irradiation rate, few labs |
| Electron spin resonance | Heated crystalline stones, calcites, bones, shell | 1,000,000 years | Accumulation of unpaired electrons in crystals | Few labs, experimental technique |
| Obsidian hydration | Obsidian artifacts | 35,000 years | Accumulation of weathering rind on artifact | Requires local calibration |
| Dendrochronology | Tree rings in preserved logs and lumber | 8000 years | Counting of annual growth rings | Region-specific |
| Fission track | Volcanic rocks, crystalline materials | 100,000–1,000,000 years | Radioactive decay leaves microscopic track in crystals at known rate | Materials rare in archaeological context |

materials are analyzed. These dates thus bracket the archaeological materials in time.

The technique is based on the following principles. Potassium (chemical symbol K) is found in abundance in granites, clays, and basalts in the minerals of the earth's crust. Potassium occurs in several stable forms and has one radioactive isotope, $^{40}$K, with a half-life of approximately 1.3 billion years. **Half-life** is a measure of the rate of decay in radioactive materials; essentially, half of the radioactive material will disappear within the period of one half-life. Because this potassium isotope has such a very long half-life, it is usually not possible to date materials that are younger than about 500,000 years old, because too little decay would have taken place to measure.

The radioactive isotope $^{40}$K decays into argon ($^{40}$Ar), an inert gas, and calcium ($^{40}$Ca). The materials generally dated by the $^{40}$K/$^{40}$Ar technique are limited to rocks, volcanic ashes, and other substances that contain radioactive potassium and trap the argon gas that is produced. The molten state of the rock permits the release of trapped gas in the parent rock and resets the argon reservoirs in the new rock to zero. The $^{40}$Ar begins to accumulate as soon as a rock is formed. Using sophisticated counters that measure and record the amount of $^{40}$Ar compared with the amount of $^{40}$K remaining, researchers can determine how much $^{40}$K has decayed and thus the amount of elapsed time since the rock was created.

Advances in radiopotassium dating in recent years have greatly improved the method. Today a technique called **argon-argon dating** is used to measure the proportion of $^{40}$Ar to $^{39}$Ar. Using this method, the stable isotope of potassium $^{39}$K is converted to $^{39}$Ar by neutron bombardment in a nuclear reactor. Both argon isotopes can then be measured from the same sample. In addition, much smaller samples can be used. The improved precision of this technique allows samples younger than 100,000 years to be dated. In one recent study, an argon-argon date of A.D. 73 was obtained for the eruption of Mount Vesuvius, which buried the Roman town of Pompeii in A.D. 79.

**absolute dating** A method of assigning archaeological dates in calendar years so that an age in actual number of years is known or can be estimated.

**isotope** One of several atomic states of an element; for example, carbon occurs as $^{12}$C, $^{13}$C, and $^{14}$C, also known as carbon-14 or radiocarbon.

**isotopic technique** A method for absolute dating that relies on known rates of decay in radioactive isotopes, especially carbon, potassium, and uranium.

**radiopotassium dating** An absolute dating technique based on the principle of decay of the radioactive isotope of potassium, $^{40}$K. Also called *potassium-argon dating*.

**half-life** A measure of the rate of decay in radioactive materials; half the radioactive material will disappear within the period of one half-life.

**argon-argon dating** A more accurate method of potassium-argon dating that involves converting potassium to argon before the isotope ratios are measured.

# Laetoli

## *Conclusive evidence of our first steps*

*The study of fossil origin and evolution is a kind of mystery play, acted out in remote antiquity, in many scenes and in many places. The players have long ago departed the stage, and left their all too sparsely distributed and brittle bones buried deep in the rocks in a cave. The walking shadows, the poor players who have strutted and fretted their brief hours on the stage, have in most cases been heard from no more.*

—Ashley Montague (1964)

As we have noted, the three distinctive characteristics of being human are upright posture, a large brain, and tool use. The question of which came first has been dramatically answered by a discovery in East Africa. The evidence for this new posture comes not only from the fossil bones, however, but also from actual footprints preserved at the site of Laetoli (lay-TOE-lee) in Tanzania, discovered by Mary Leakey in 1976 (Figure 2.16). Laetoli is located about 70 km (40 mi) southeast of Olduvai Gorge. Sometime around 3.6 m.y.a., an active volcano near Laetoli covered the area with a layer of volcanic ash. Following a light rain shower, various animals moved across the damp layer of ash. A chemical reaction between rainwater and the ash quickly hardened their tracks; even the impressions of the raindrops are preserved in some areas at the site. Hares, birds, extinct elephants, pigs, buffalo, rhinos, a saber-toothed tiger, and many baboons left their footprints.

The numerous sets of tracks do not often overlap one another, suggesting that this layer of footprints was quickly buried by more ash, ensuring its preservation. Radiopotassium dating determined that the age of the ash layers, and therefore the footprints, was between 3.8 and 3.5 million years (see "Dating Methods," p. 48).

Early hominins walked across the fresh ash as well (Figure 2.17). The 70 or so human footprints continued over a distance of more than 6 m (20 ft) and were made by three individuals. The longest track contains about 30 prints of an individual walking on two feet with a stride and balance that is clearly human. A second, smaller individual followed in the footprints of the first, and a third set of prints lies alongside the first. The footprints look human, with a well-defined arch and an absence

**Figure 2.16** Mary Leakey recording the 3.6-million-year-old footprints of Laetoli.

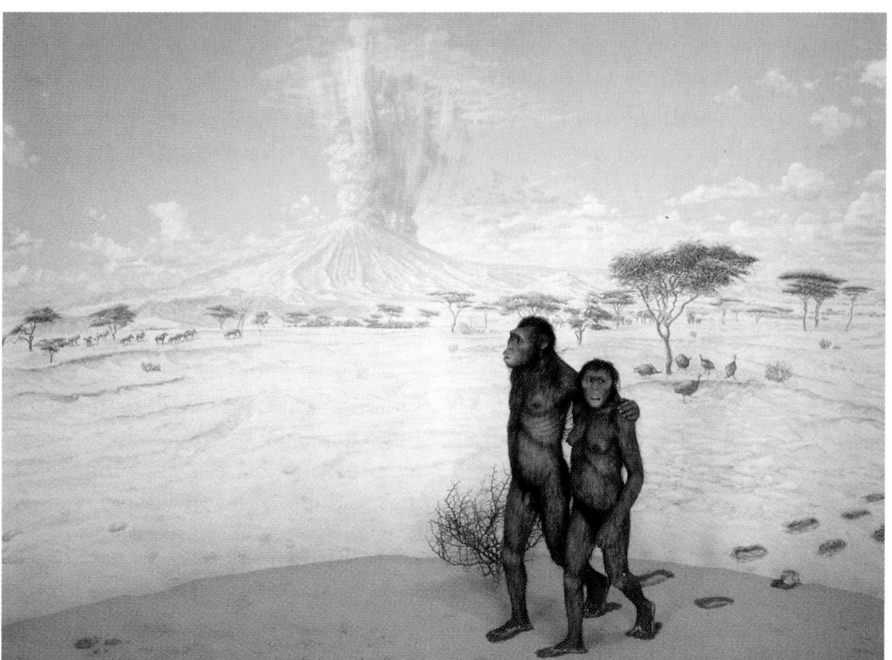

**Figure 2.17** An artist's reconstruction of the early hominins at Laetoli, walking across the volcanic ash 3.6 m.y.a.

of the diverging toe that is characteristic of great apes. Studies of the size and depth of the prints suggest that two of the individuals were approximately 1.4 m (4 ft, 8 in) tall, and the third 1.2 m (4 ft) tall. The footpath of the second individual indicates that this early hominin stopped briefly and turned slightly to the left before continuing. Mary Leakey, the excavator of these fossil footprints, speculated about the scene:

*This motion—the pause, the glance to the left—seems so intensely human, it transcends time. Three million six hundred thousand years ago, a remote ancestor—just as you or I—experienced a moment of doubt. (quoted in Lewin, 1988, p. 57)*

The brain of these earliest hominins from the Pliocene was no larger than that of modern apes, nor had their teeth changed a great deal from those of their ape ancestors. Fossil remains, particularly fragments of skulls from Laetoli and elsewhere in East Africa, demonstrate that the human brain had not yet begun its major expansion. No stone tools have been found in deposits of this age at Laetoli; such equipment was apparently not yet part of the human repertoire. What was different, however, was a shift to a new form of movement.

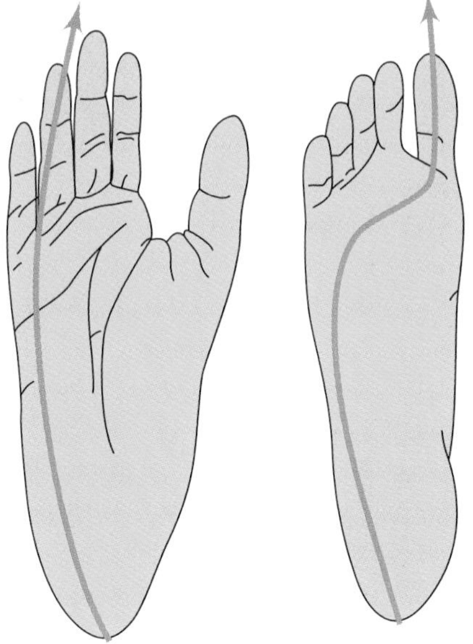

**Figure 2.18** The footprints at Laetoli are clearly from bipedal individuals. The weight distribution in ape feet is along the side of the foot (left). The big toe on apes is for grasping and does not carry weight. In humans, the weight is carried from the heel, along the side, and across the ball of the foot to the big toe (right).

The earliest human fossils give evidence of **bipedalism**—they walked on two feet, with a stride very similar to our modern one (Figure 2.18). In fact, these earliest humans might best be portrayed with the head and face of an apelike creature atop a small, upright human body, stepping into the future. As Mary Leakey went on to say, "The outstanding evolutionary question now is: What was the selection pressure that produced bipedalism?" (quoted in Lewin, 1988, p. 57).

*They are the most remarkable find I have made in my entire career. . . . When we first came across the hominid prints I must admit that I was skeptical, but then it became clear that it could be nothing else. They are the earliest prints of man's ancestors, and they show us that hominids . . . walked upright with a free-striding gait, just as we do today.*

—Mary Leakey
(quoted in R. Leakey, 1981)

**bipedalism** The human method of locomotion, walking on two legs.

## Swartkrans

*South African caves with many early human fossils*

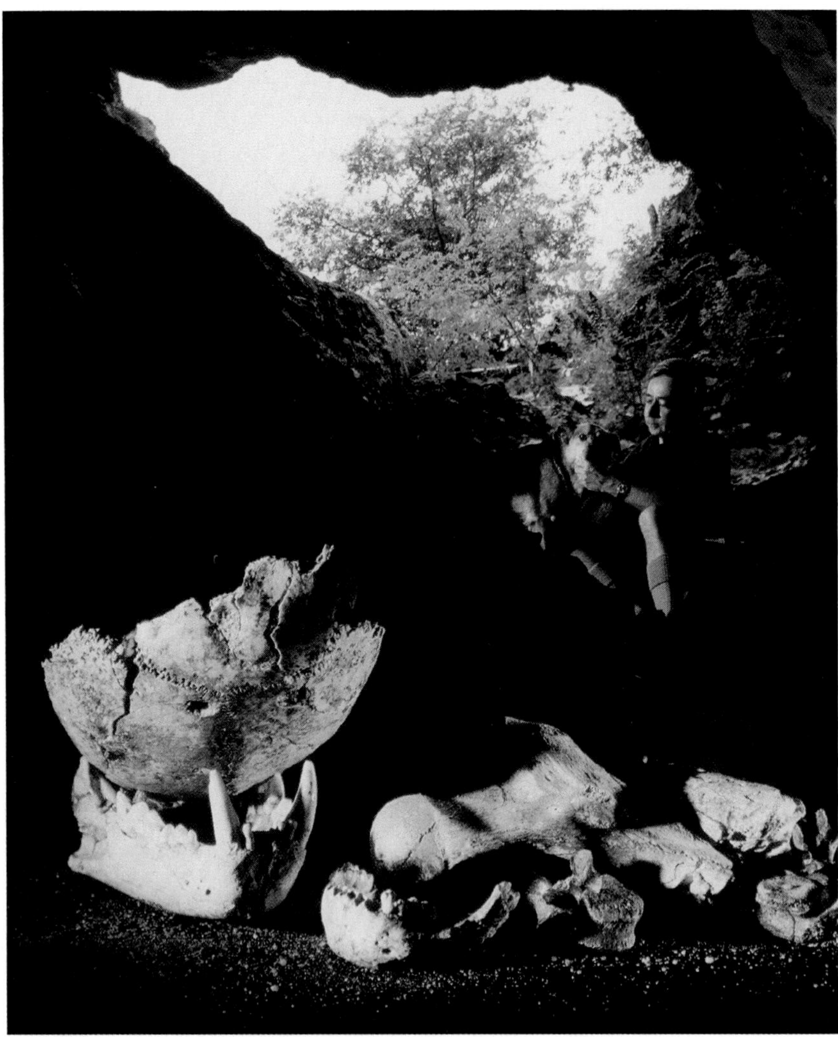

**Figure 2.19** C. K. Brain and some of the fossil remains at Swartkrans cave. The canine teeth of the leopard jaw precisely fit the two indentations in the skull, supporting Brain's theory that many of the early human bones are the remains of carnivore meals.

**breccia** The accumulated materials from cave deposits that harden into a conglomerate rock, including sediments, rocks, and animal bones.

Swartkrans (SWORT-kranz) is the name of one of several caves in the Transvaal region of South Africa that contain both human and animal fossils from the early Pleistocene. The Transvaal is a large area in the center of South Africa underlain with limestone bedrock. This soft, permeable stone is easily dissolved by running water, which creates underground rivers, caves, and sinkholes. Streams and heavy rains from the surface wash in a variety of surface sediments, debris, bones, and other objects, which gradually accumulate in these chambers. Other agents also add materials to these deposits. African porcupines, for example, collect bones at their nests and shelters, often within the confines of caves; hyenas carry bones and other objects to their dens. Some birds, such as owls and other birds of prey, regurgitate small pellets containing the bones of the small rodents they consume. The accumulated materials eventually harden into a fresh rock known as a conglomerate, or **breccia.**

Early fossils were first discovered when the breccias in these caves were commercially quarried for lime, used for making plaster and cement. Dense bone concentrations were discarded to obtain purer deposits. Eventually, the antiquity and the importance of these bones were recognized, and expeditions from museums and universities in South Africa and elsewhere conducted excavations to uncover more fossil materials. Collectively, these excavations have uncovered the remains of more than 150 individual hominins of several species.

There are four major problems associated with studying these materials: (1) extracting the fossils from the rock in which they are encased, (2) estimating the age of the fossils and the deposits, (3) determining the cause of death of the animals and how they got into the caves, and (4) designating the genus and species for the remains.

Removal of the fossils from these deposits is very difficult. The fossil bones are embedded in breccia and in fact have become rock themselves. Excavators have used jackhammers and even dynamite to break apart the breccia to get at the mineralized bones.

In recent years, large blocks of the breccia have been taken to a laboratory where acid treatments gradually dissolve the rock, thereby allowing the removal of the fossils.

Because these materials are buried in the earth, geological forces have modified and distorted the stone and the fossils. The weight of deposits sometimes flattens or warps bone or crushes materials together. The limestone deposits in these caves provide little that can be directly dated. There is no fresh volcanic ash or rock for potassium-argon dating. Most of the dates from the caves are based on the known ages of extinct animals that once existed throughout much of Africa. For example, changes over time in the size of the teeth of fossil pigs can be used to estimate the ages of the various deposits. Such dating is done by the association of remains with pig teeth of known age found in the same breccia. On this basis, the early Pleistocene breccia at Swartkrans was thought to date to between 1.7 and 1 m.y.a. However, new dating methods suggest that the earliest deposits may be as old as 3 million years, to between 2 and 4 million years, making them comparable in age to many of the finds from East Africa.

C. K. Brain, a paleontologist in South Africa, has been excavating at the site of Swartkrans for more than 20 years (Figure 2.19). Brain notes two major episodes of breccia accumulation, apparently of short duration, on the order of 10,000 years each. Dating of the deposits is complicated by the manner in which the breccias form. There is no simple stratigraphy in which materials are piled up in regular horizontal layers; continuing water flow erodes and partially dissolves older deposits, then new episodes of accumulation fill the cavities in the old deposits. Each cave thus contains a honeycomb of deposits from various periods.

These deposits are the source for fossils of both *Paranthropus robustus* (a late australopithecine) and *Homo erectus.* The partial remains of at least 80 *P. robustus* individuals have been recovered from the deposits at Swartkrans, along with fragments of bone and teeth from 6 individuals of *H. erectus.* These two hominin forms appear to be contemporaneous at Swartkrans, as at Olduvai. This astounding number of individuals from a single deposit raises the question of how so many came to be in one place—a question that has yet to be fully answered.

The shape and structure of the hand bones from several *P. robustus* individuals suggest that this hominin made and used some of the stone tools that are also commonly found in the cave deposits. In addition to the stone tools, there are bone artifacts with polishes that resulted from their being used as digging implements, probably to obtain the roots and bulbs of plants growing in the area. Recent data from Swartkrans, from approximately 1 m.y.a., suggest that the individuals in the cave used fire, perhaps to keep preying leopards at bay. If this evidence is reliable, it records the earliest instance of the intentional use of fire. There is also some evidence for the use of fire at Koobi Fora in East Africa perhaps 1.5 m.y.a., but this is less certain.

How the bones of so many early hominins ended up in the deposits also is not clear. This question has been the subject of lengthy debate. Raymond Dart, an anatomist in South Africa, studied the human and animal remains from the cave breccias for almost 50 years until his death in 1988. He proposed a number of theories about the life and times of *Australopithecus.* Professor Dart, the original discoverer of the australopithecines, believed that the early hominins were extraordinary predators, hunting many animals and bringing their carcasses back to the limestone caves. Dart argued that animal bones found in the caves were the remains of meals and evidence of the prowess of *Australopithecus* as a hunter of even the largest animals. Dart's graphic depiction conveys his image of our earliest ancestors: "Man's predecessors . . . seized living quarries by violence, battered them to death, tore apart their broken bones, dismembered them

**Figure 2.20** An artist's interpretation of the Swartkrans leopard hypothesis. A Pliocene leopard consumes a hapless australopithecine in a tree above the entrance to the Swartkrans depression.

(From C. K. Brain, *The Hunters or the Hunted?* Copyright © 1981 University of Chicago Press. Used with permission of the publisher, University of Chicago Press.)

Why was Africa such a propitious place for the emergence of humanity?

limb from limb, slaking their ravenous thirst with the hot blood of victims and greedily devouring living writhing flesh" (1953, p. 209). Dart further suggested that the high number of skulls in the caves, often with the bases broken away, was evidence that early humans also hunted their neighbors. The question is one of hunter or hunted, according to Brain. Brain's detailed studies provide numerous insights about the processes of deposition in the limestone caves, and they contradict some of the arguments of Dart. Many of the cracks and breaks in the fossil remains that Dart interpreted as evidence of violent death more likely resulted from geological distortion after burial, according to Brain. Brain argues that the vast majority of larger fossils came into the cave as the remains of carnivore meals, especially of leopards. Brain points out that leopards often drag their prey into trees, out of reach of other predators (Figure 2.20). The damp entrance shafts to caves such as Swartkrans would likely have been overgrown with trees, which may have been lairs for satiated leopards. Over 40% of the human fossils are immature individuals who may have been vulnerable to predator attacks. Brain also points to a skull with two crushing indentations in the forehead, punctures that fit precisely with the huge canine teeth of a leopard.

Investigations at this important South African cave document the contemporaneity of *Paranthropus robustus* and *Homo erectus*. Swartkrans finds demonstrate that *P. robustus* almost certainly made and used stone tools, that bone tools were an important part of the equipment for these early hominins, that plants were probably important in the diet, and that fire may have been used, at least for defensive purposes.

Concept

## Hunters or Scavengers?

### *Ways our early ancestors obtained their food*

What the early human diet consisted of is difficult to determine, because the remains of meals are generally not well preserved. The wild plants of East Africa probably provided a ready source of food for early humans, but plant materials are not preserved. The relative importance of fruits, nuts, and other plant foods in the diet is not yet known.

Another difficult matter, and a major controversy in paleoanthropology, is the issue of scavenging versus hunting: How did early hominins obtain meat? Some scholars believe that the first humans were primarily scavengers, visiting the kills of lions and other predators, and competing with hyenas and vultures for the morsels that remained. These scholars argue that the actual hunting of large animals is a relatively recent development in human prehistory. Others contend that early hominins were in fact hunters—stalking, killing, butchering, and eating the creatures of Plio-Pleistocene East Africa. The evidence is scanty and open to debate. Only a few facts are known: Chimpanzees and baboons occasionally hunt, kill, and consume small animals, and, by the end of the Pleistocene, humans were major predators and large-game hunters.

Evidence from numerous Plio-Pleistocene sites certainly suggests that humans brought various animal parts back to a common location and removed the meat and marrow with stone tools. In one instance, the large leg bone of an antelope-size creature was broken into ten pieces, in a fashion that modern hunters in the area today use to obtain the nutritious and tasty marrow. On this same bone, tiny scratches made by stone tools are also visible. Such **cutmarks** are sometimes found at places where large pieces of meat have been removed from the bone, suggesting that the animal was butchered for the meat (Figure 2.21). This evidence may indicate that early hominins were hunters with access to the best cuts of meat from their prey. But paleoanthropologists Richard Potts and Pat Shipman have observed that cutmarks are sometimes found over the marks left by the teeth of carnivores, suggesting the scavenging of animal carcasses. It seems clear that stone tools were used to butcher meat, but neither the presence of cutmarks indicating meat removal nor evidence of the extraction of marrow from bone demonstrates that the food was hunted, not scavenged. Recent studies of marks on bones from Olduvai Gorge suggest a sequence of large carnivore teeth, cut by stone tools, overlain by smaller carnivore tooth marks. Such a pattern suggests that the animal was killed by a large carnivore, scavenged by humans, and then eaten by smaller animals.

Comparisons of the kinds of animals represented at Olduvai Gorge and elsewhere with the prey of modern hunter-gatherers in the Kalahari Desert of South Africa support the argument that australopithecines were hunters. The range of prey types and their sizes are very similar in the two locations, suggesting that the Olduvai hominins may have been hunters, like people of the Kalahari, rather than scavengers.

Still, none of these pieces of evidence is definitive. Evidence for sites where large game animals were killed is not incontrovertible until much later in the Pleistocene, after 500,000 years ago.

(a)

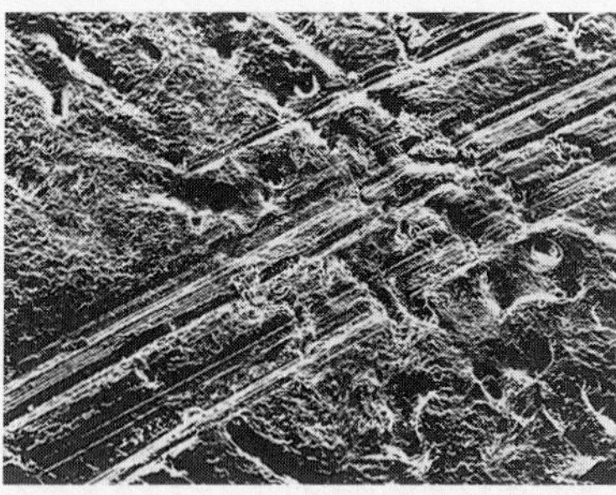
(b)

**Figure 2.21** Cutmarks on bones from Koobi Fora are a strong argument that our early ancestors were meat-eaters and hunters as well as scavengers. (a) A photomicrograph of round-bottomed grooves made by hyena teeth on modern bone. (b) A photomicrograph of a V-shaped cutmark made by a stone tool on modern bone.

**cutmark** A trace left on bone by a stone or metal tool used in butchering a carcass.

# Olduvai

## *A trail of biological and behavioral evolution from the early Pleistocene to the recent past*

Flying low across northern Tanzania, one crosses an enormous wilderness of grassland and solitary trees, a region filled with herds of wildebeest, giraffes, elephants, and many other animals. This is the fabled Serengeti (ser-in-GET-ee) Plain—the place of safari. The level surface of the plain results from the long, gradual accumulation of geological sediments, especially volcanic materials such as ash and lava. Two million years ago, this area was a large bowl-shaped basin, ringed by a series of volcanic mountains and uplands.

Active volcanoes filled the air with ash and covered the ground with molten lava, which hardened into new rock. The basin trapped rainfall, forming lakes and wetlands during the beginning of the Pleistocene. Silts and sands, carried by running water, were deposited in these lakes, which grew or disappeared over time as rainfall amounts varied with changes in cli-

**Figure 2.22** Olduvai Gorge, cutting 100 m into the Serengeti Plain and 2 million years into human evolution.

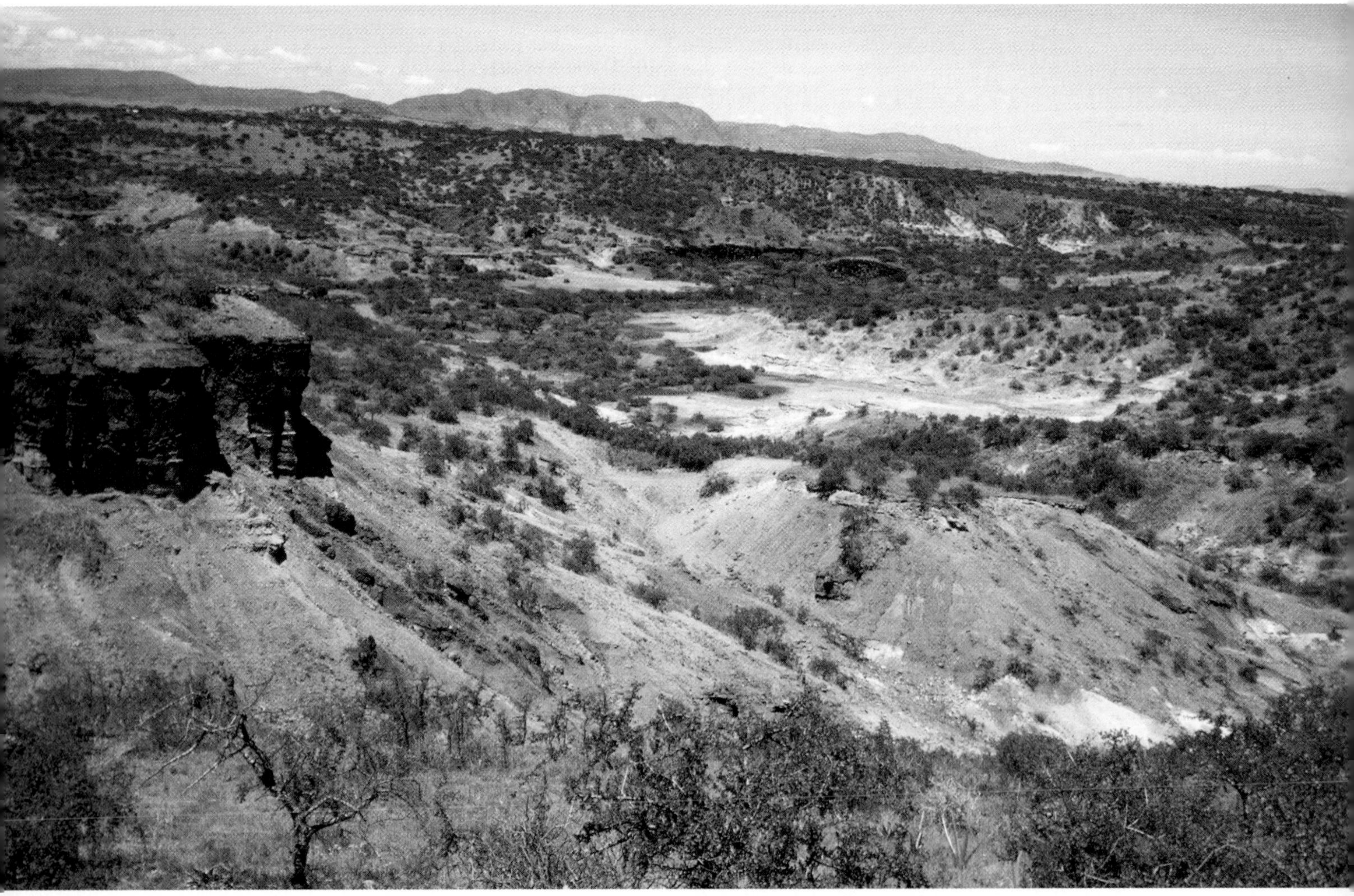

mate. Along the shores of these lakes, creatures of the early Pleistocene in East Africa found food, reproduced, and died; occasionally, their bones were buried and preserved in the accumulating layers of sediment.

The richness of the lakeshore environment is represented by the abundance of fossil animal bones that are found there. Antelope, giant buffalo, and wild sheep occur in large numbers, along with aquatic animals, such as the giant crocodile, the hippopotamus, and various species of fish and fowl. The layers of lava, ash, and lake deposits continued to build up until the basin became relatively level, resulting in the surface of the Serengeti Plain today.

About 200,000 years ago, a particularly violent series of earthquakes and volcanic activity opened a crack in the surface. Seasonal streams cut and eroded a large gully into the layers of sediment. Gradually, a canyon, some 40 km (25 mi) long and almost 100 m (325 ft) deep, wound its way from the top of the Serengeti Plain through the layer cake of deposits. This canyon is Olduvai (ol-dew-VIE) Gorge, one of the most famous prehistoric sites in the world (Figure 2.22). Each step down into the gorge takes us back 6000 years in time, toward the layer of basalt at the very bottom, dating to 1.9 m.y.a. (Figure 2.23).

Along the steep sides of this gorge, two archaeologists—Louis and Mary Leakey—began an extended vigil, in quest of the remains of the earliest humans. Starting in 1931, Louis and, later, Mary Leakey made the arduous journey from Nairobi each summer to spend several weeks at the rugged exposures of Olduvai. Accompanied by their dogs, and later their several children, they searched for fossil hominins. Louis Leakey had found numerous crude stone tools in the

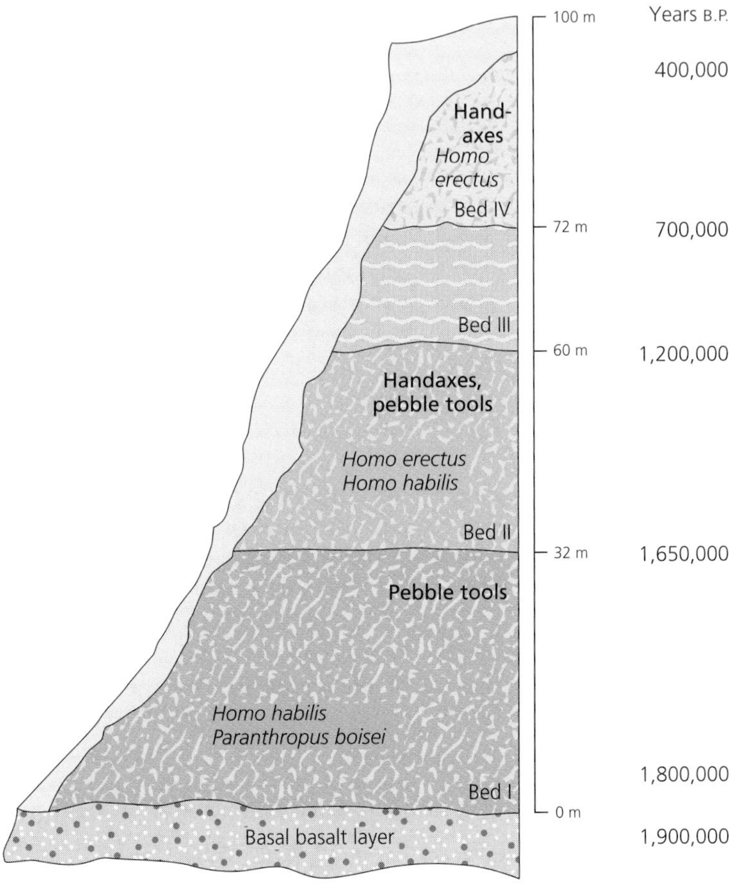


**Figure 2.23** A schematic cross section through the 100 m of deposits at Olduvai Gorge, naming the various fossil forms and types of stone tools, with approximate ages.

Figure 2.24 Some of the more common early Pleistocene animal species at Olduvai Gorge.

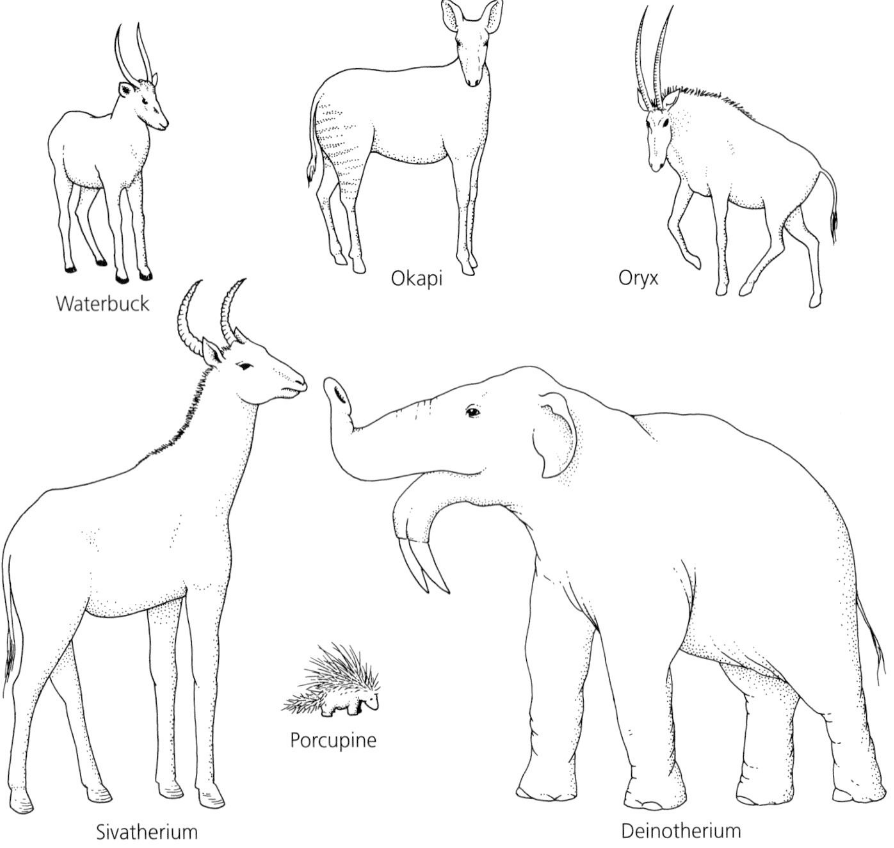


lower layers at the gorge and was convinced that the bones of the toolmakers would also appear in this remarkable series of deposits. Not until 1959, however, 28 years after Louis' first visit, was the persistence of the Leakeys rewarded by Mary's discovery of a very early fossil, initially named *Zinjanthropus.* At the time, the fossil was thought to be approximately 1 million years old—twice the age of the then-earliest-known remains from Java. Zinj, as this fossil is affectionately known (or *Paranthropus boisei,* as it is scientifically termed), actually dates closer to 2 million years old.

The Leakeys' discovery brought the search for the first humans to Africa and eventually back into the Pliocene epoch. Their discovery of Zinj also brought world recognition for their efforts in the form of acclaim and funding, which supported more extensive investigations at Olduvai. With that funding, the Leakeys were able to examine a larger area of the gorge in 2 years than had been possible in the previous 20 years. That intensive work paid off in the discovery of more fossils and a whole series of archaeological sites.

Very old standardized objects of human manufacture (stone artifacts) appeared in the lower layers at Olduvai. Olduvai provided the first clear documentation that crude stone tools and the bones of very early hominins occurred at the same point in geological time. Over 70 prehistoric localities with stones or bones, or both, have been recorded in the geological layers of the gorge to date; perhaps 10 of these represent actual living areas where tools were made and used. Some of the stones are unmodified and may have been used as anvils and for other purposes. Other stones were in-

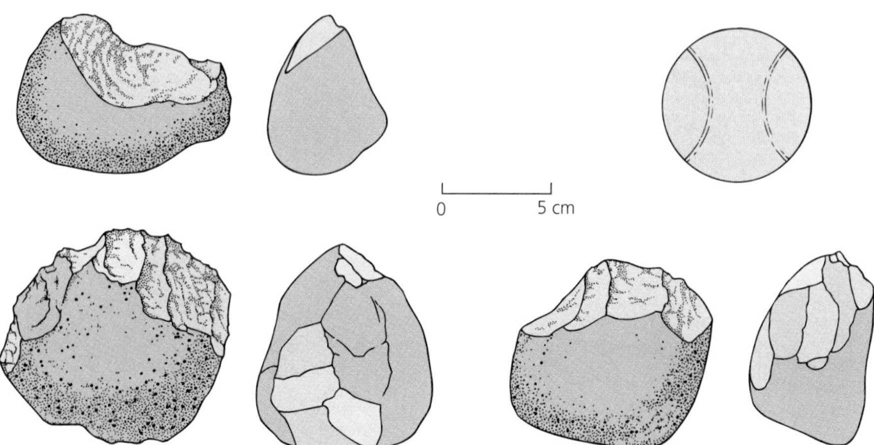


**Figure 2.25** Typical Oldowan pebble tools, shown with a tennis ball for scale.

tentionally bashed with another stone to shape and manufacture tools (Figure 2.25). These stone artifacts had strong, sharp edges, providing cutting equipment for a species lacking sharp teeth or claws.

The materials for these artifacts were often brought from the rocky hills some 10 km (6 mi) away. Raw materials were selected on the basis of specific properties. Fine-grained stone was used to make small cutting tools, and basalt and quartz were used for heavy chopping equipment. Tools described as choppers, spheroids, and discoids were created by knocking off flakes of stone from a rounded cobble or large pebble. These sharp-edged cobbles are about the size of a tennis ball and are known as **Oldowan** pebble tools, named after the gorge itself. The flakes that had been struck off these pebble tools also had sharp edges and were likely used as tools.

One of the Olduvai sites contains a large quantity of broken and fragmented bone, along with stone tools. Many of the bone fragments are clustered in an area of about 5 × 10 m (16 × 33 ft, the size of a large room), with an empty zone several feet wide surrounding this concentration. Perhaps a thorn hedge or barricade was placed in this area to protect the inhabitants in the center.

At another site in Olduvai Gorge is a group of several hundred rocks in a roughly circular arrangement, surrounded by the bones of giraffes, hippopotamuses, antelopes, and elephants (Figure 2.26). The reason for such concentrations is unknown; it is not even clear whether early hominins were responsible for killing the animals represented by the bones. However, the hominins almost certainly collected the bones. Two other sites at Olduvai are known to have been places of animal butchering. At one of the sites, known as FLK North, the bones of an elephant lie scattered on the ground along with stone artifacts. The elephant would have been much too heavy to move and was very likely butchered at the spot where it died. Most of the bones from the elephant are present, disarranged by the butchering and surrounded by stone tools and flakes. Striations and cutmarks on the bones document the use of stone flakes to remove meat from the skeleton. (The issue of whether the hominins at Olduvai actually hunted these animals was discussed earlier; see "Hunters or Scavengers?" on p. 55.)

Other evidence suggests that most of the living floors at Olduvai were occupied during the wet season. Tortoises hibernate during the dry season, making them difficult to capture, yet their remains are common at most of

**Oldowan** The name given to the assemblages of early pebble tools and flakes belonging to the Basal Paleolithic, derived from *Olduvai.*

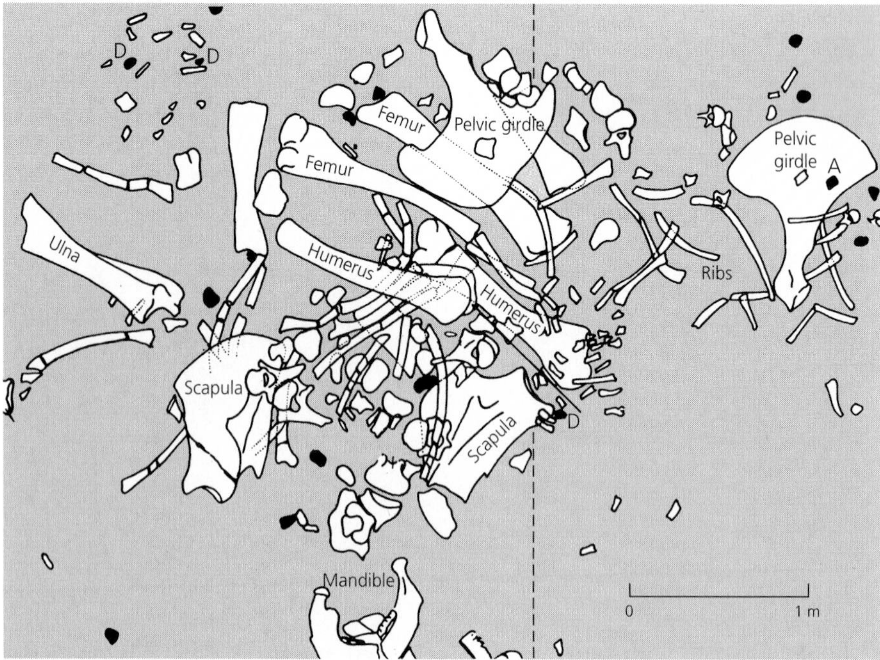


**Figure 2.26** The plan of part of an excavated deposit at Olduvai, containing a concentration of elephant and other bones, with stone tools shown in solid black. This site likely represents the place where parts of these animals were butchered.

**Figure 2.27** The Leakey family at work in Olduvai Gorge, ca. 1960.

the sites at Olduvai. Such information suggests that our early ancestors may have been absent from the Olduvai lakeshore during the dry season, pursuing other activities and perhaps game elsewhere in the region.

Olduvai will remain one of the most important archaeological sites in the world because it contains the information that helps answer many questions—the human fossils, the early Pleistocene deposits, the association of human bone and stone artifacts, and the fact that these materials are sometimes found where they were dropped by our early ancestors.

*Concept*

# The Leakey Family

## *A dynasty of paleoanthropologists*

Born to British missionary parents in Kenya in 1903, Louis Leakey became interested in prehistoric artifacts as a child. At age 16, he left for England to attend Cambridge University. A rugby injury forced a break in his studies, and he returned to East Africa on a year-long fossil-hunting expedition, engendering his interest in bones and paleontology. Leakey then returned to Cambridge, taking high honors in both archaeology and modern languages.

Leakey then received a 6-year research fellowship from Cambridge to conduct archaeological investigations in East Africa. One of his first expeditions centered on Gamble's Cave and provided the first sequences for the development of stone artifacts in East Africa. In 1931, Leakey led his third expedition to Olduvai Gorge. Here, early handaxes were found soon after his arrival, and a fragment of a human jaw was discovered nearby. Leakey argued for a great antiquity for this bone, but a British geologist, Percy Boswell, accused Leakey of incompetence in a letter to a scientific magazine. This incident left Leakey with a determination to be more exact in his statements.

Much of Leakey's research was guided by his belief that Africa was the cradle of the human race, in contrast to the generally accepted scientific view that East Asia held that distinction. One of the members of Leakey's fourth expedition was Mary Nicol, an archaeologist and illustrator, who would become his second wife in 1936. Together, Mary and Louis Leakey began their lifelong research on early humans in East Africa (Figure 2.28). The Leakeys continued their investigations at Olduvai Gorge because of its abundance of stone tools. Leakey was convinced that human fossils would also be found there, demonstrating the fact that early hominins had made the stone tools.

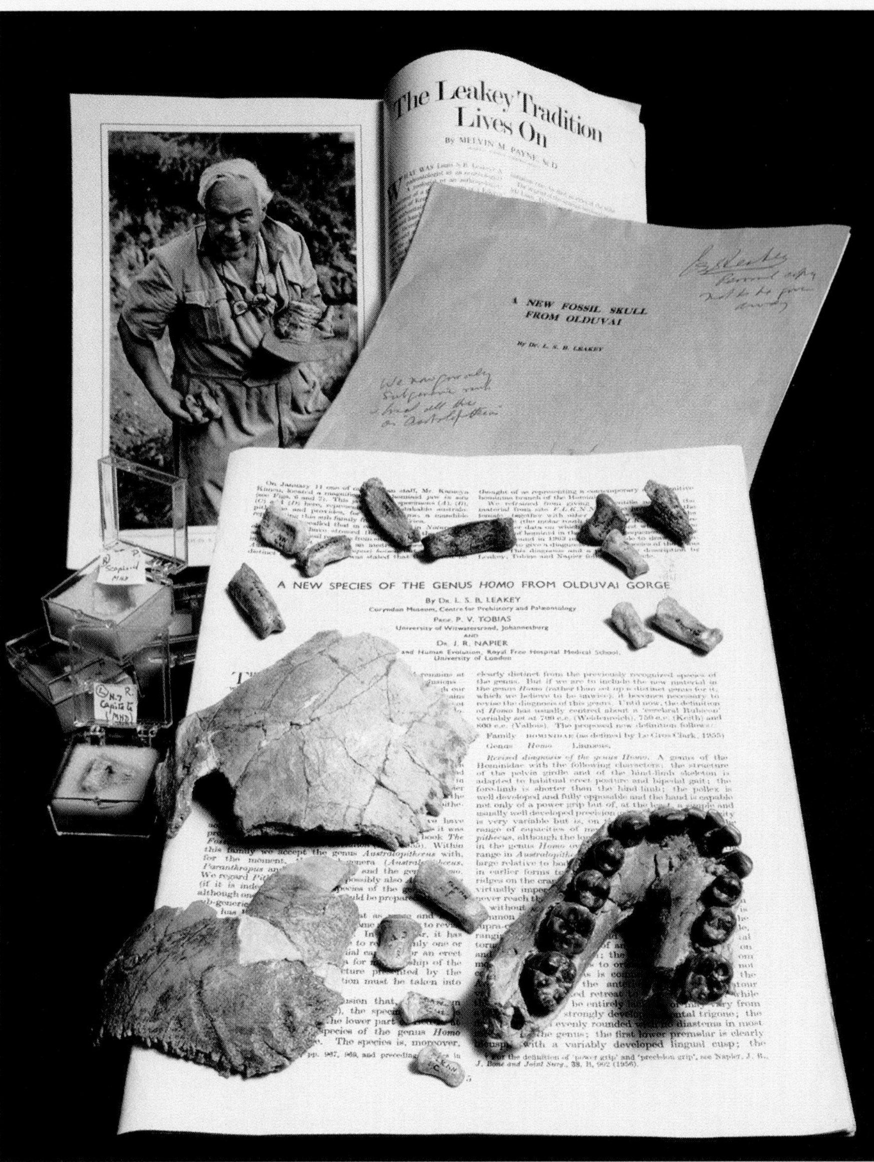


**Figure 2.28** Louis Leakey and the remains of *Homo habilis* from Olduvai Gorge. This discovery demonstrated that Africa was the cradle of early human evolution and brought fame to the Leakeys.

Leakey was appointed director of the National Museum of Kenya in Nairobi in 1945, and each summer the Leakeys would return to search for evidence of early humans in the layers of Olduvai Gorge. Finally, in 1959, after more than two decades of dogged and difficult prospecting, Mary Leakey spotted the fragments of the heavy jaw of Zinj, dating to the beginning of the Pleistocene.

The Leakeys proved that East Africa had indeed witnessed the emergence of the human species. In addition to the many important discoveries they have made, the Leakeys pioneered the study of early stone tools and animal remains in East Africa. Louis Leakey died in London on the first of October 1972.

After Louis' death, Mary Leakey and her children continued the search for human origins in Africa. Mary excavated at Olduvai, Laetoli, and elsewhere in East Africa, greatly enriching the record of early fossil animals and humans in this area. She compiled most of the important published descriptions of the prehistory of Olduvai. Mary Leakey died in 1996 at the age of 83. Her son Richard became the director of the National Museum of Kenya in Nairobi and a very famous paleoanthropologist in his own right. In spite of several calamities, including the loss of both legs in an airplane crash, Richard Leakey continues as a champion of the peoples and animals of his native Kenya. His debates with other scientists over the meaning of the fossil finds are the subject of several popular books. Richard's wife, Meave, is the head of the paleontological section of the National Museum of Kenya and has been involved in the search for fossil humans in the area around Lake Turkana for many years. Her daughter, Louise, a Ph.D. in archaeology from University College, London, is continuing the family tradition as director of the Koobi Fora project in northern Kenya.

# The First Tools

## *Simple, intentionally broken pebbles: the earliest preserved evidence for toolmaking*

Simple stone tools are the earliest human artifacts that archaeologists study. It is very possible that the first humans, like chimpanzees today, used tools of wood or bone. As our closest relatives, chimpanzees provide a good model for early humans. Chimpanzees in the wild, in fact, have frequently been observed killing and eating other animals and making and using tools. In West Africa, chimpanzees often use stone or wooden objects as hammers and anvils to open nutshells. They use twigs to remove marrow from bone cavities or to extract termites from their nests. Similarly, unmodified wood, bone, and stone objects may have been used long before the appearance of deliberately modified stone tools, but these either cannot be identified or have not survived.

Intentionally modified stone tools appeared first in Africa between 3 and 2 m.y.a., probably associated with the increasing importance of meat in the human diet. Such sharp flakes and cobbles provide access to the carcasses of animals, enabling early humans to cut through thick, tough skins to remove the meaty tissue—actions simply not possible without some kind of sharp implement. Stone tools provide useful cutting edges for a species that lacks both sharp teeth and claws for slicing meat, shredding plants, or digging. As Nicholas Toth says, "Sharp-edged stones became the equivalent of canines and carnassials [meat-cutting teeth] and heavier rocks served as bone-crunching jaws" (1987, p. 121).

The oldest dated stone tools were found in the 1990s along the Gona River in central Ethiopia, dating to 2.6 m.y.a. (see Figure 2.29). Cutmarks, made by stone tools, were found on animal bones at these sites, documenting their use for butchering carcasses. The earliest stone tools are remarkably simple, almost unrecognizable unless found together in groups or next to other objects. Small round cobbles, the size of a large egg or a tennis ball, 5–8 cm (2–3 in) in diameter, weighing about 1 kg (1–2 lb), were collected from streambeds, lakeshores, and beaches.

Figure 2.29 One of the earliest known stone tools from the Gona River region of Ethiopia, 2.6 m.y.a.

Early stone tools were created by striking one stone against another. This process, called **percussion flaking,** results in a **flake** being removed from the parent cobble, or **core,** by a blow from another stone, called a **hammerstone,** or some other hard object (Figure 2.30). Both the flake and the core then have fresh surfaces with edges sharp enough to be used for cutting. Initially, the fractured cobbles themselves were thought to be the intended artifact and were called pebble tools. The flakes were thought to be by-products of the manufacturing process, a kind of waste material, often referred to as ***débitage.***

**percussion flaking** A technique for producing stone artifacts by striking or knapping crystalline stone with a hard or soft hammer.

**flake** A type of stone artifact produced by removing a piece from a core through chipping.

**core** The stone from which other pieces or flakes are removed. Core tools are shaped by the removal of flakes.

**hammerstone** A stone used to knock flakes from cores.

***débitage*** A term referring to all the pieces of shatter and flakes produced and not used when stone tools are made.

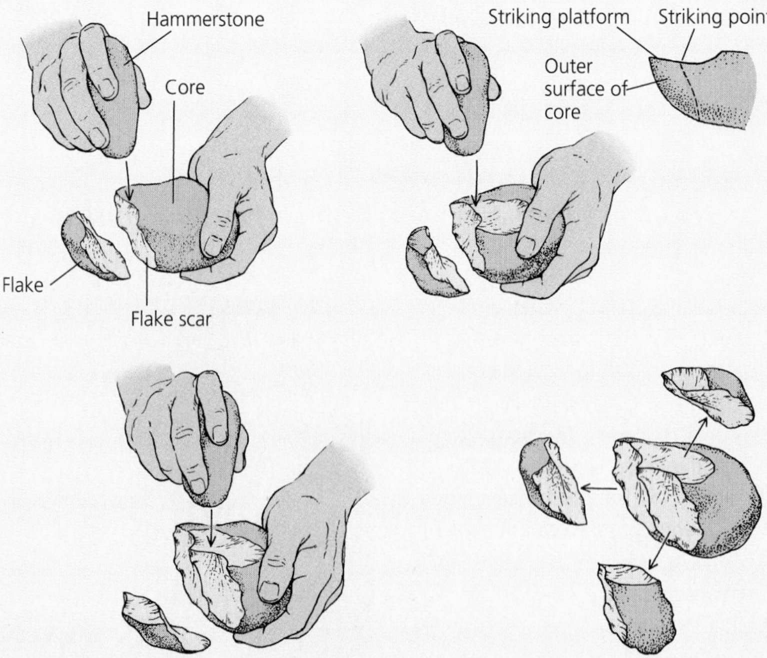


**Figure 2.30** Percussion flaking, used by early hominins to create cutting edges on stone tools. One stone (the hammerstone) was bashed against another (the core) to remove one or more flakes.

*Hello to all intelligent life forms everywhere . . . and to everyone else out there, the secret is to bang the rocks together, guys.*

—Douglas Adams (1980)

**flint** A fine-grained, crystalline stone that fractures in a regular pattern, producing sharp-edged flakes.

**flintknapping** The process of making chipped stone artifacts; the striking of stone with a hard or soft hammer.

**assemblage** The set of artifacts and other remains found at an archaeological site or within a specific level of a site.

**lithic** Pertaining to stone or rock.

**unifacial** A term describing a flaked stone tool in which only one face or side is retouched to make a sharp edge.

**bifacial** A flaked stone tool in which both faces or sides are retouched to make a thinner tool.

**retouching** The shaping or sharpening of stone artifacts through percussion or pressure flaking.

**handedness** Preferential use of the right or the left hand.

But it is now clear that flakes were equally important as cutting tools and tools for making other tools, such as shaping wood, bone, or antler into new forms for new purposes. The simple action of striking one stone against another to remove a flake and create a sharp edge was a very successful invention, one that was used and refined for more than 2 million years, until the introduction of metals just 6000 years ago.

The best raw materials for stone tools during the early Pleistocene were brittle enough to break but hard and smooth enough to provide a cutting edge. The stone also had to be fine-grained so that it would break in a predictable fashion, resulting in large flakes, rather than hundreds of shattered fragments. During this time, various rocks were used, including basalt (a hard volcanic lava), quartzite, and flint. **Flint** is one of the best and most common materials used for making stone tools. The term **flintknapping** is often used to describe the process of making stone tools.

The kinds of pebble tools found at Olduvai, at Koobi Fora, and elsewhere in Africa are described as Oldowan, a tradition of toolmaking. The term *Oldowan* is applied to the entire group, or **assemblage,** of different stone objects found together at sites from the end of the Pliocene and the first part of the Pleistocene. These stone, or **lithic,** artifacts include both **unifacial** pebble tools, flaked on one side only, and **bifacial** pebble tools, flaked on both sides. The flakes are also occasionally further modified by additional flaking, or **retouching,** along their edges, to shape them.

We have learned other kinds of information from stone artifacts, the most durable of the remains of our ancestors. Studies by Toth have suggested that many of these flakes were made by holding the core stone in the hand and striking it with a hammerstone. Indeed, Toth argues, on the basis of the shape of the flakes, most of the flakes from Koobi Fora were produced by right-handed individuals. This handedness is not seen in the very earliest stone tools from 2.6 m.y.a. but emerged in the period between 1.9 and 1.4 m.y.a., probably correlated with the changes in the organization of the brain. The brain of modern humans is divided into two hemispheres that control different areas of thought and behavior.

**Handedness** is a result of this lateralization of the brain. In right-handed people, the left hemisphere controls sequential abilities, such as speech, and more quantitative activities, and the right hemisphere regulates spatial conceptualization and more abstract behavior. These functions are reversed in left-handed people. Thus, the predominance of right-handedness in stone tool manufacture after 2 m.y.a. suggests that this organizational change had already taken place.

Studies by Nicholas Toth, of Indiana University, and Lawrence Keeley, of the University of Illinois–Chicago, have provided important clues about the use of these stone tools. Keeley used a high-powered microscope to examine the edges of stone artifacts from Koobi Fora. Experimental work demonstrated that different materials leave different kinds of traces in the form of polish on the edges of tools. At a magnification of 400×, Keeley observed microscopic polish and wear, indicating the cutting of meat, the slicing of soft plant material, and the scraping and sawing of wood, on about 10% of the flakes. Two of the flakes with evidence of meat butchering were found within 1 m (3 ft) of a large herbivore bone exhibiting cutmarks. Such evidence strongly supports the use of these stone artifacts as butchering tools. Evidence of woodworking suggests that wooden tools were also being made, perhaps crude digging sticks for finding roots and tubers. This indirect information is the only evidence for the use or consumption of plant materials.

**Tools** provide an interface between humans and the environment, enabling us to manipulate and change our surroundings. One of the most remarkable things about stone tools is the investment they represent—a vision of the future, an anticipation of action. An object was made at one time and place, often intended to be used later elsewhere.

**tool** Any equipment, weapon, or object made by humans to change their environment.

# *Images and Ideas*

## Bones, Stones, and Human Behavior

### *The evolution of our biology and our activities*

As we have noted, the late Miocene and Pliocene evidence for early hominins consists of pieces of bones and teeth, along with some small broken stones, from a few locations in Central Africa, East Africa, and South Africa. Although the evidence is fragmentary and rare, it is still possible to put together a picture of the evolutionary history of the hominins during the Miocene, the Pliocene, and the early Pleistocene. This period extends from approximately 7 to 2 m.y.a., from the earliest humans to the emergence of *Homo erectus.*

Many new varieties of African apes appeared in the late Miocene as the climate of this region became drier and the tropical rain forests shrank. Certain of these apes were becoming bipedal by the end of the Miocene. Only a very few examples of these Miocene hominins are known, including *Sahelanthropus tchadensis, Orrorin tugenensis,* and *Ardipithecus ramidus.* Their known characteristics reveal a mix of ape and more human features.

A variety of hominin forms appeared in the Pliocene, probably in response to the continued climatic trend to drier conditions. These new forms include the australopithecines and *Kenyapithecus.* Their bipedal locomotion is well documented, both in the fossil bones themselves and especially in the remarkable footprints from Laetoli, dating to 3.6 m.y.a. They were generally small-brained with large teeth.

Sometime between 3 and 2 m.y.a., our ancestors began to make stone tools, and near the end of the Pliocene, human evolution took two major paths. *Paranthropus* followed a dead-end street and disappeared before 1 m.y.a. *Homo habilis* started along the pathway to the present, a curious species with a mixture of traits, combining large teeth and small brains, with other, more evolved features. Determination of the correct species for *habilis*—whether *Australopithecus* or *Homo*—remains difficult and debated.

Whatever the case, *habilis* gave rise to *erectus,* a definite member of the genus *Homo,* exhibiting larger brains, thicker enamel, and a reduction in sexual

**Figure 2.31** Brain size and body weight in the higher primates and hominins. Body weight is estimated for the fossil forms. Notice the increase in both body weight and brain size in the line of human evolution.

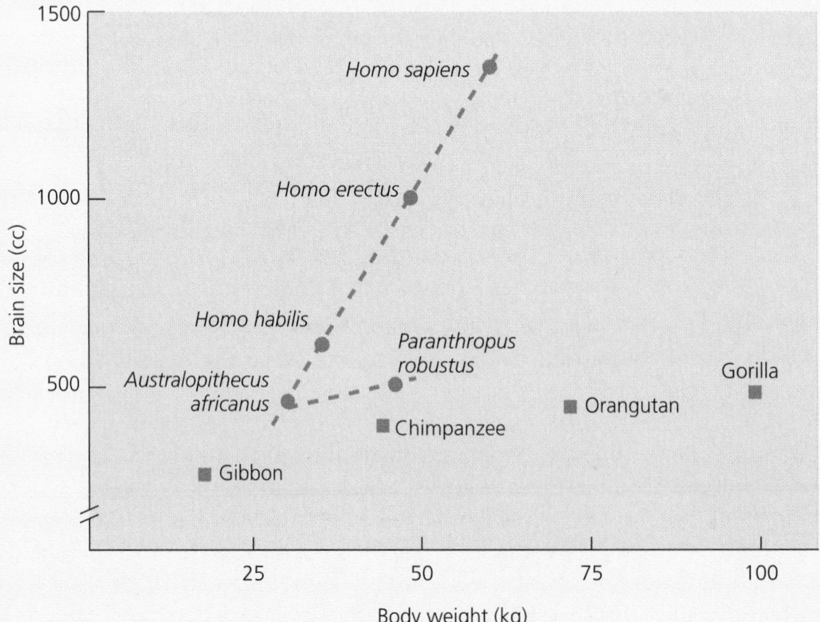

dimorphism. The rise of *erectus* also saw a doubling in brain size, a dramatic geographic expansion of the genus, and new species or subspecies (*neanderthalensis*) (Figure 2.31). *Homo erectus* was essentially human below the neck. The final stages in the evolution from *erectus* to *sapiens* took place in the cranium. These individuals almost certainly lived in small groups, evidenced by the clusters of animal bones and stone tools at Olduvai, Koobi Fora, and other sites. Early hominins ate both meat and plants. How they obtained the meat is unclear, but it appears that they may have hunted small animals and scavenged the marrow-rich bones and remaining meat from large-animal kills of other predators.

Beyond these few indications, however, there is very little direct evidence for reconstructing our early pedigree and behavior. The fact that there are any reasonable explanations of our earliest evolution is testimony to the diligence and ingenuity of the scientists who study those remains. In spite of the sparseness of evidence for the biology and behavior of early hominins, there are still a number of theories about how and why we became human. This understanding comes partly from comparisons with our nearest relatives, the chimpanzees, and partly from inferences made from the evidence of the stones and bones themselves.

**TABLE 2.3 Average Cranial Capacity of Some Primates and Fossil Hominins**

| *Species* | *Cubic Centimeters* |
|---|---|
| Modern humans | 1300–1400 |
| Neanderthals | 1300–1450 |
| *Homo erectus* | 800–1200 |
| *Homo habilis* | 500–800 |
| Australopithecines | 350–550 |
| Gorillas | 500–570 |
| Chimpanzees | 350–450 |
| Orangutans | 360–460 |
| Gibbons | 80–120 |

Much of the following discussion involves speculation about the evolution of human behavior, based on little evidence and vulnerable to considerable revision and modification. The brain size of modern humans is roughly 1000 cubic centimeters (60 cu in) larger than that of other primates (say, a large grapefruit compared with an orange) (Table 2.3). We have a much greater ratio of brain to body size than almost any other species, emphasizing the importance of our brain for survival. Brains are costly organs, requiring about 20% of the body's energy production to operate. Brain tissue needs more than 20 times the energy of muscle tissue to function. This means that humans may need food that is denser in calories and nutrients than most other species need.

Yet human infants are born with a remarkably small, underdeveloped brain, only some 25% of the adult size. Whereas a chimpanzee's brain at birth is about 65% of fully adult size, the human brain grows and develops largely after birth, because of the narrowness of the birth canal. Having an underdeveloped brain, a human infant requires a long period of maternal care and attention. In contrast, a newborn foal, for example, can run and feed itself within a few days. In humans, the long period of infant dependency fosters a strong bond between mother and child and also permits children to know their brothers and sisters. Kinship and learning may well be enhanced as a result of such extended and intimate relationships.

A lengthy period of maternal care, however, is expensive. Small children limit the mobility and activities of the mother, including the obtaining of food. Extended care and brain development also mean longer nursing and delayed weaning. In turn, such behaviors require more food for the mother; nursing alone may increase her metabolic demands by 50% or more. The average life expectancy among the australopithecines appears to have been low, around 20 years. Such an early age of death very likely meant that children were often orphaned and had to be nurtured by the group rather than by a single parent; communal childcare and feeding may well have been concomitant with the advance of our species.

Differences between humans and the apes are also represented in the secondary sex characteristics that differentiate males and females. Human female breasts are significantly larger than those of the male, a difference more pronounced than in most other species. Breast size is obviously not related to the effective feeding of offspring. The human male penis is far larger than that of other primates, including gorillas. Human females have softer skin and a higher voice and lack much of the body hair that often characterizes other primate females.

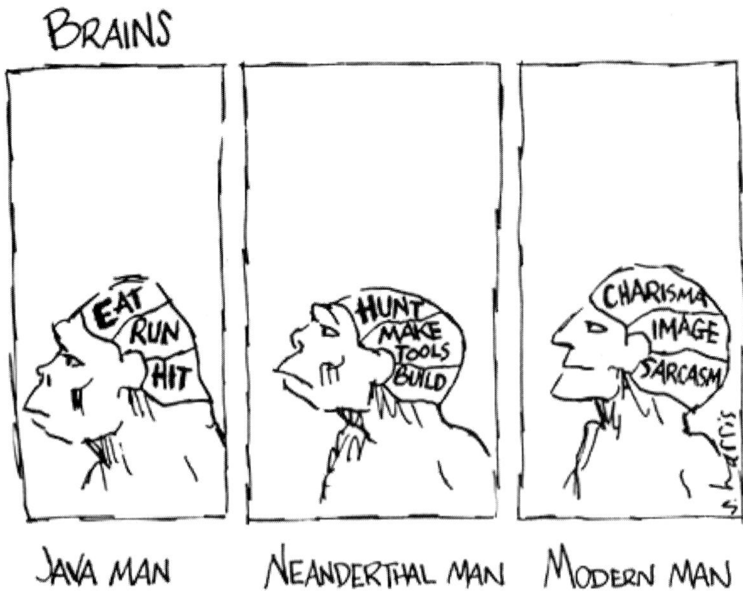


© 2004 by Sidney Harris. Reprinted with permission of ScienceCartoonsPlus.com.

**What were the conditions that gave rise to the steps toward human evolution?**

The vagina in the human female points sufficiently toward the front of the body to permit face-to-face sexual intercourse.

Another biological difference lies in the absence of an estrus cycle in human females. The female members of most animal species are sexually active only for limited intervals, a period known as **estrus,** a few days each month or each year. Female apes display sexual receptivity by means of flaring or brightly colored sex organs, but ovulation is concealed in human females. Clearly, there have been strong evolutionary selective forces favoring these characteristics.

Aside from biological similarities to and differences from other animals and our closest relatives among the apes, are we indeed closer to the angels? We possess other attributes that distinguish us from the animals. Our large brain and intelligence enable us to make decisions and act rationally, differently than the way our basic instincts might drive us to behave. Humans have moved from purely instinctual behavior to reason and thought. We may flee a fire, but we may also turn back into that fire to save others.

*With the stimulus of constantly available sex, protohominins had begun the most fundamental exchanges the human race would ever make. Males and females were learning to divide their labor, to exchange meat and vegetables, to share their daily catch. Constant sex had begun to tie them to one another and economic dependence was tightening the knot.*

—Helen Fisher (1982)

Humans have technology; we make and use a wide range of tools and other devices that increase our chances for survival. Tool use by humans is often considered to be the most distinctive characteristic of our species, even though other animals may use or even make simple tools. For example, the sea otter wields a rock to break open the shell of an abalone. Anthropologist Jane Goodall has observed chimpanzees using a variety of tools: thrashing about with branches for display, using clubs and missiles for defense, and selecting a twig and stripping its bark to probe the nests of termites and attract them to the stick in order to eat them. West African chimps use stone and wooden hammers to crack and open nutshells. Although tool use may not be unique to humans, using tools to make other tools does distinguish the human animal.

The evidence from Africa clearly indicates that our first step on the road to becoming human was the shift to bipedalism. It now seems clear from the African evidence that we had upright posture for several million years before either the use of stone tools or significant increases in the size of our brain. Apparently, standing upright was very important to our early survival.

**estrus** The cycle of female sexual receptivity in many species of animals.

Explanations for bipedalism focus on whether the feet or the hands were changing. Mary Leakey and her colleagues have suggested that we became upright to pursue migratory animal herds on the savanna. Bipedalism and powerful strides would be advantageous for moving long distances to follow herds for meat. And upright posture would free the hands for carrying young offspring. This hypothesis ignores the fact that australopithecine teeth seem adapted to an increasingly vegetarian diet, becoming bigger and flatter over time. Walking around on two feet could, however, be useful for collecting plant foods scattered across the landscape.

Other ideas regarding the evolution of bipedal locomotion relate to food getting, carrying, or sharing. Clifford Jolly, of New York University, has proposed that bipedalism was adaptive because it provided a means for gathering and eating young leaves, seeds, and pods of the African thornbush growing on the African savanna. Owen Lovejoy, of Case Western Reserve University, has proposed that our ancestors became two-footed because bipedalism enabled males to carry food back to a favored location to be shared with females, a concept known as male provisioning; this would have increased the birth rate and reproductive success of humans because females could support more than one dependent offspring at a time. Lovejoy wrote:

> *Both an advanced material culture and the Pleistocene acceleration in brain development are sequelae to an already established hominin character system, which included intensified parenting and social relationships, monogamous pair bonding, specialized sexual-reproductive behavior, and bipedality. . . . The nuclear family and human sexual behavior may have their ultimate origin long before the dawn of the Pleistocene. The proposed model accounts for the early origin of bipedality as a locomotor behavior directly enhancing reproductive fitness, not as a behavior resulting from occasional upright feeding posture. It accounts for the origin of the home base in the same fashion as it has been acquired by numerous other mammals. It accounts for the human nuclear family, for the distinctive human sexual epigamic features, and the species' unique sexual behavior. (1981, p. 350)*

We do not yet know why, in fact, certain apes became bipedal—and thus human. In the final analysis, however, it is culture that distinguishes the human creature. Culture is what anthropologist Leslie White called our "**extrasomatic** means of survival"—the nonbiological, nongenetic behavior and sociability that have carried us through the millennia and spread us into diverse environments across the planet. Clifford Geertz, of Princeton University, has described humans as "toolmaking, talking, symbolizing animals: Only they laugh; only they know when they will die; only they disdain to mate with family members; only they contrive those visions of other worlds called art. They have not just mentality but consciousness, not just needs but values, not just fears but conscience, not just a past but a history. Only they have culture" (1963, p. 2).

Culture is a constellation of ideas and actions that are learned and transmitted from generation to generation. Human culture embodies the totality of behaviors and experiences that are summarized in our language and taught us by our parents and peers—a kind of group personality that provides a repertoire of actions in situations of choice. It is as impossible to have human identity without social contact as it is to have biological existence without parents. Tarzan was an ape until he met Jane. Culture enables us to eulogize our place in the universe, to create gods, to anticipate death, to travel to the stars—and to study archaeology.

**extrasomatic** Literally, "outside the body"; nonbiological, nongenetic.

## DISCUSSION QUESTIONS

www.mhhe.com/priceip6e

For more review material and study questions, see the self-quizzes on your online learning center.

1. What are the more important clues for "humanness" in the fossil record?
2. What is the significance of stone tools? Were these the first tools?
3. What were the four most important changes that took place as apes evolved into humans?
4. What can we say about the diet of the earliest humans? How did they obtain food?
5. Which of the sites and fossils discussed in this chapter seems to be the most important and why?

## SUGGESTED READINGS

For Internet links related to this chapter, please visit our Web site at www.mhhe.com/priceip6e.


Aitken, M. J. 1990. *Science-based dating in archaeology.* New York: Longman. *One of the best and more comprehensive overviews of physical dating methods used in archaeology, including radiopotassium and radiocarbon.*

Campbell, B. G., and J. D. Loy. 2000. *Humankind emerging,* 8th ed. New York: Longman. *A well-illustrated textbook on human evolution and our early fossil ancestors.*

Cela-Conde, C. J., and F. J. Ayala. 2007. *Human evolution: Trails from the past.* New York: Oxford University Press. *An up-to-date review of the evidence for human evolution.*

Fisher, H. E. 1983. *The sex contract.* New York: Quill. *Another view of the origins of the species.*

Gamble, C. 2007. *Origins and revolutions: Human identity in earliest prehistory.* Cambridge University Press.

Gilbert, W. H., and B. Asfaw. 2009. *Homo erectus: Pleistocene evidence from the Middle Awash, Ethiopia.* Berkeley: University of California Press.

Lewin, R. 1998. *Principles of human evolution.* Oxford: Blackwell. *A popular and well-illustrated book on early humans.*

Stringer, C., and P. Andrews. 2005. *The complete world of human evolution.* London: Thames & Hudson. *The latest in color on fossil humans.*

Tattersall, I., and J. H. Schwartz. 2000. *Extinct humans.* Boulder, CO: Westview Press. *A book arguing that there have been many species of humans in the past and portraying their evolution.*

Taylor, R. E., and M. J. Aitken, eds. 1997. *Chronometric dating in archaeology.* New York: Plenum. *A scientific overview of a variety of absolute dating methods.*

Zimmer, C. 2001. *Evolution: The triumph of an idea.* New York: HarperCollins. *An exceptionally good book on the idea of evolution.*

# CHAPTER THREE

**Figure 3.1** Reconstruction of a woolly mammoth at the Royal British Columbia Museum in Victoria.

# Out of Africa

## Homo erectus

## Introduction

### From Hominin to Human

*Our ancestors begin to discover Asia and Europe 2 million years ago*

The magnificent creature shown in Figure 3.1 roamed the cold plains of Europe, Asia, and North America during the Pleistocene period. The woolly mammoth, a cold-adapted variety of elephant, typifies some of the adaptive challenges that emerged as the chill of the Pleistocene gripped the temperate zone, forcing plants, animals, and humans to change their location, appearance, and/or behaviors.

Our first several million years were spent in Africa. The earliest dates for the presence of humans outside Africa are less than 2 m.y.a., the beginning of the Pleistocene. Hominins began to move into the more northerly continents of Asia and Europe and to encounter new environmental conditions. The Pleistocene, also known as the Ice Age, was a time of climatic extremes in many parts of the world. Repeated, dramatic changes in temperature, sea level, and environment are hallmarks of this time (see "Climate and Environment in the Pleistocene," p. 81). The harsh environments of the Pleistocene Old World were the places we became more human, changing our habits, technology, and biology to adapt to these new conditions.

Our hands and simple tools had been sufficient to obtain the foods available in the benign warmth of Africa. But expansion out of the tropics at the beginning of the Pleistocene required new skills and inventions for surviving where cold weather and the lack of food or shelter could be fatal. It became necessary for our ancestors to begin to change nature to fit their needs and enhance their survival. The first reliable evidence for the controlled use of fire, for systematic hunting, and for the use of wooden spears appeared during this time.

Stone tools began to change as well. This is the period of the Lower Paleolithic, when core and flake tools replaced the pebble tools of the Basal Paleolithic. The handaxe was invented as an all-purpose tool (see "The Acheulean Handaxe," p. 99) and is a hallmark of the Lower Paleolithic.

The early migrants from Africa almost certainly belonged to *Homo erectus,* a new species of hominin, evolved from *Homo habilis* in Africa. Some researchers now separate the larger group of *erectus* into two distinct species, using the term *Homo ergaster* for early African varieties, and *Homo erectus* for later populations mainly in Asia and Europe. Fully modern humans first appeared in Africa some 200,000 years ago and likely evolved from *Homo ergaster* ancestors. For the sake of simplicity, we will use the general term *erectus* for this entire group of fossil humans.

**CHAPTER OUTLINE**



**www.mhhe.com/priceip6e**

For preview material for this chapter, see the comprehensive chapter outline and chapter objectives on your online learning center.

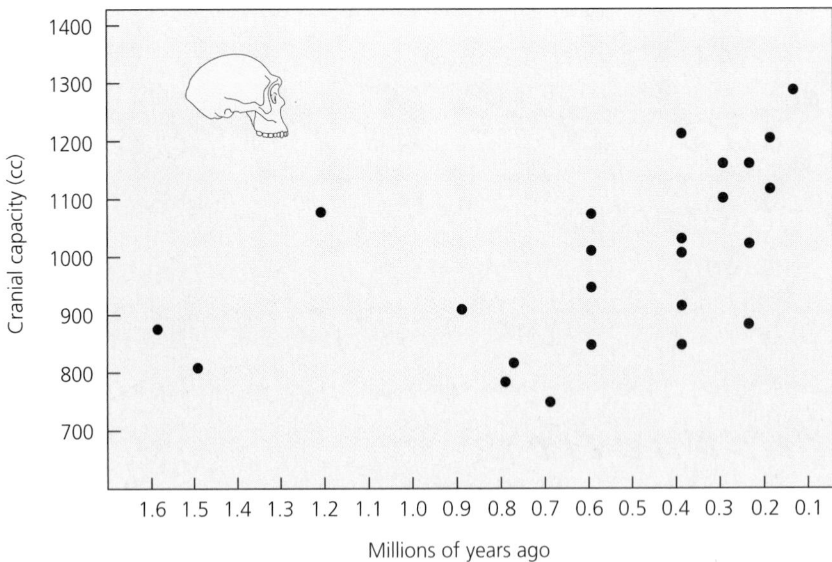


**Figure 3.2** Cranial capacity over time for *Homo erectus.* Two patterns emerge: (1) There is relatively little change between 1.5 and 0.5 m.y.a., and (2) there is a dramatic increase in cranial capacity after 0.5 m.y.a., perhaps associated with the rise of modern *Homo sapiens.*

**TABLE 3.1 Major Characteristics of *Homo erectus* vs. Modern Humans**

| *Trait* | Homo erectus | Homo sapiens sapiens |
|---|---|---|
| Forehead | Absent | Vertical and rounded |
| Face | In front of cranium | Under cranium |
| Cranial capacity | 900 cc | 1350 cc |
| Lower jaw | Larger and heavier; no chin | Smaller and lighter; distinct chin |
| Teeth | Larger | Smaller |
| Brow ridges | Heavy, across the eyes | Absent |
| Limb bones | Larger and heavier | Smaller and lighter |

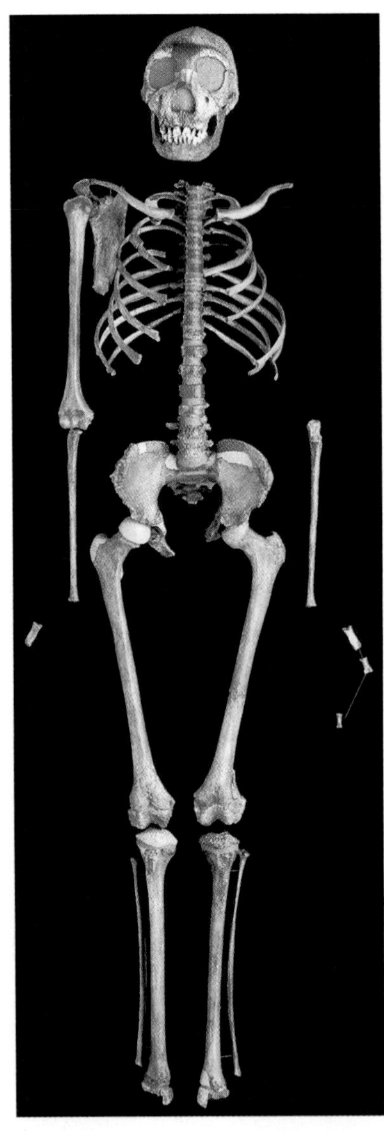

**Figure 3.3** The Nariokotome skeleton, a 1.6-million-year-old fossil of a 12-year-old *Homo erectus* (also known as *Homo ergaster*) boy from Kenya. One of the most complete fossil skeletons from the early Pleistocene.

The timing of the spread of populations out of Africa coincides closely with the appearance of *H. erectus.* The earliest *H. erectus* fossil comes from the western shore of Lake Turkana in northern Kenya, dating to approximately 1.8 m.y.a. *H. erectus* individuals were robust, with large bones and teeth; they also had larger bodies, more or less modern in size, and significantly larger brains—around 1000 cc—than their *H. habilis* ancestors (Table 3.1). These hominins were almost fully modern in movement and locomotion; they differed very little, if at all, from our own anatomy below the neck. Although their brain was twice as big as a chimpanzee's, it was only about the size of a 1-year-old modern human child's. *H. erectus* skulls are characterized by a low, sloping forehead; prominent brow ridges; and a protruding face. Cranial capacity changed very little in *H. erectus* during the period 1.8–0.5 m.y.a., after which a dramatic increase can be seen, perhaps in association with the rise of *Homo sapiens* (Figure 3.2). The trends in the development of *Homo erectus* show a number of similarities with modern *Homo sapiens,* including stature, increasing brain size, decreasing tooth and jaw size, and a vertical reduction in the size of the face.

One of the more important *erectus* fossils is the so-called Nariokotome boy, discovered by Richard Leakey and Alan Walker in Kenya in 1984 (Figure 3.3). Among the most complete early human skeletons, the 10- or 12-year-old boy lived approximately 1.6 m.y.a. The skeleton resembled a robust modern one below the neck. Most of the differences between *erectus* and modern are seen in the skull. The Nariokotome skull exhibited a cranial capacity of 880 cc and the earliest evidence for a projecting, external nose.

**Figure 3.4** A hypothetical reconstruction of the face of *Homo erectus*.

Several sites in Asia document the arrival of the first migrants to that continent. The site of Dmanisi (dim-an-EASE-see) in the country of Georgia, containing an *H. erectus* lower jaw and other skeletal remains, has been dated by radiopotassium methods to 1.7 m.y.a. 'Ubeidiya (UB-a-de-ya), located in Israel a few kilometers south of the Sea of Galilee, dates to approximately 1.5 m.y.a. 'Ubeidiya contains concentrations of handaxes and other stone tools, along with animal bones, on the shore of a former lake. In this area, geological activity has tilted the layers so that the archaeological deposits are almost vertical. Even earlier dates are known from Central and East Asia. Locations of *H. erectus* finds on Java, one of the islands of Indonesia, also have recently been dated using radiopotassium methods to roughly 1.2 m.y.a. A recent find from Longgupo in south-central China may go back even further. A fragment of a hominin jaw has been tentatively dated to 1.9 m.y.a.

www.mhhe.com/priceip6e

For a Web-based activity on the Nariokotome boy, see the Internet exercises on your online learning center.

If these early dates prove to be accurate, *Homo erectus* groups may have spread very quickly across Asia following their initial appearance in Africa. Even at a slow rate of expansion of, say, 16 km (10 mi) per generation of 20 years, it would take only about 20,000 years to cover the distance between East Africa and Southeast Asia—around 16,000 km (10,000 mi). That brief period is indistinguishable by current chronology techniques such as radiopotassium dating. The date of the movement of human populations into Europe is another question (see "The First Europeans," p. 89). The earliest dates for humans in Europe are just over 1 m.y.a., substantially later than the evidence from Asia.

Questions about the origins of and differences in human skin color are common. A recent study by Alan Rogers of the University of Utah provides some insight on this issue. Based on mutation rates in modern genes for skin color, Rogers and his colleagues calculated that humans have been relatively free of body hair for 1.2 million years. One of the characteristics of being human is a relative absence of body hair compared to the other apes. The assumption is that our hominin ancestors, like chimpanzees today, originally had fair skin and dark hair (Figure 3.4). Rogers and colleagues' thinking was that if humans have extensive body hair, there is no need for very dark skin color, which protects one from the harmful ultraviolet rays of the sun. Thus, the loss of body hair would have required that early humans in Africa develop dark skin color as protection against the sun.

Why did some of our early human ancestors leave the cradle of Africa?

*Homo erectus* was eventually replaced by *Homo sapiens* after 100,000 years ago. Most of our knowledge about the period between 700,000 and 120,000 years ago, known as the Middle Pleistocene, comes from Europe and the Near East. Caves and rock shelters in those areas have preserved remains, attracting archaeologists interested in this period. The precise chronology for this important period in human evolution is unclear. Because the Middle Pleistocene is too early for radiopotassium methods of determining ages and too late for radiocarbon methods, accurate dates are rare. Many archaeological sites from this period have barely survived the elements and the passage of time.

The sites described in this chapter document the discovery of these early humans and their activities (Figure 3.5). Zhoukoudian witnesses the presence of *Homo erectus* in East Asia. Atapuerca provides remarkable information on the first humans in Europe. Kalambo Falls and Olorgesailie demonstrate the continued development of the human species in Africa. These places take us through nearly 2 million years of human prehistory along our journey through time.

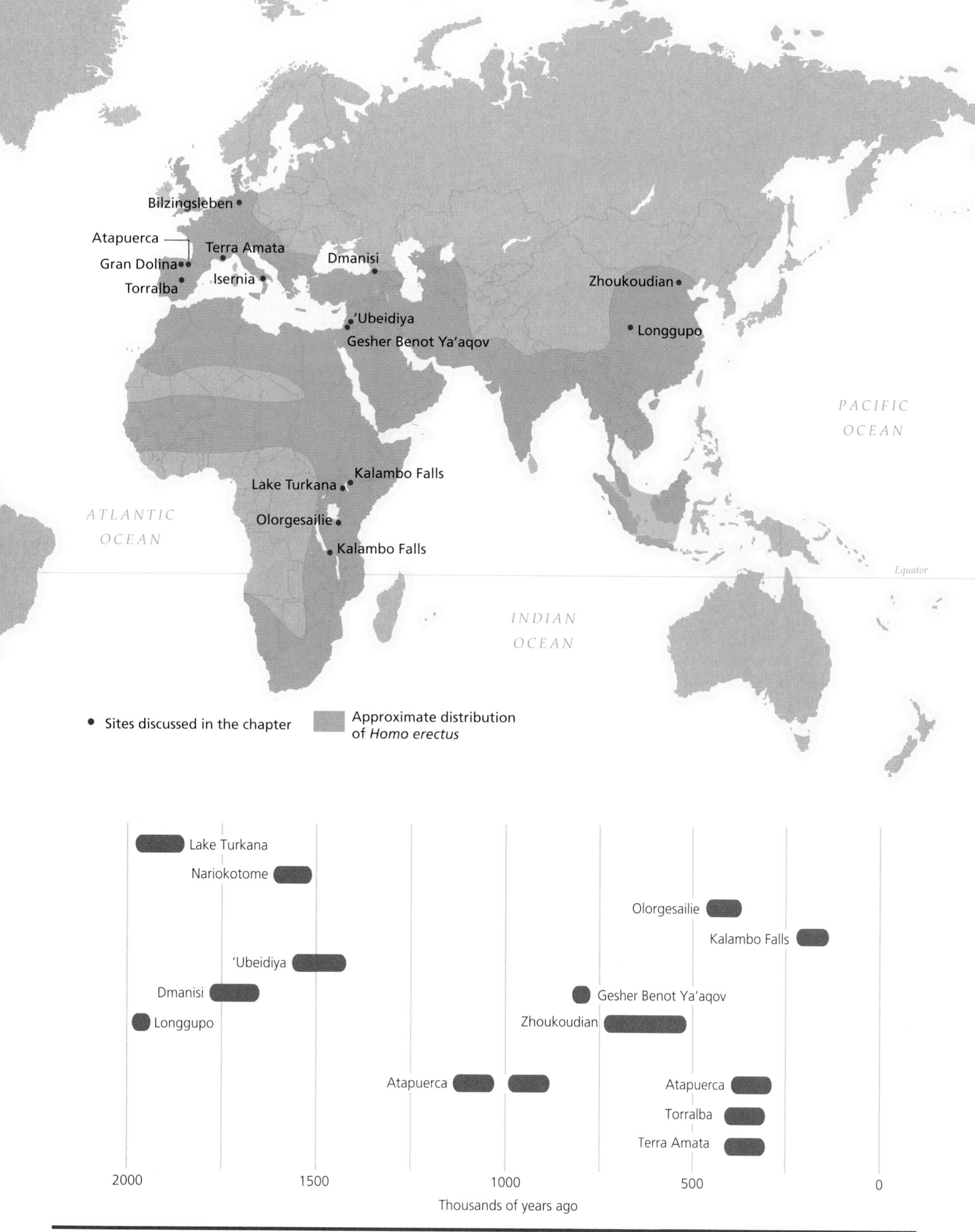


**Figure 3.5** Location of and timeline for *Homo erectus* in Africa, Europe, and Asia.

*Concept*

# The Paleolithic Period

## *Archaeological divisions of time*

Just as geologists divide the history of the earth into periods and epochs, archaeologists break up the prehistory of human society into smaller, more manageable and understandable units. The scheme used by archaeologists to compartmentalize prehistory focuses on changes in artifacts and material culture. Differences in the types of material used to make tools and changes in the shapes of tools are often the main criteria for distinguishing time periods (Figure 3.6).

The basic framework for dividing up the past was developed in 1836, when Christian Thomsen proposed an innovative three-age system for organizing the exhibits in the National Museum of Denmark, with separate display rooms for objects of stone, bronze, and iron. This system was quickly adopted elsewhere in Europe to designate the sequential ages of prehistory: Stone Age, Bronze Age, and Iron Age. These major divisions are still used in Europe and other areas of the world.

The Stone Age was further divided in 1865 by the English naturalist John Lubbock, who coined the terms *Paleolithic* and *Neolithic* to distinguish the Old Stone Age and the New Stone Age, respectively. The **Paleolithic** is characterized by tools of flaked flint (Figure 3.7), and the **Neolithic** is represented by polished stone tools and pottery. Further divisions of the Paleolithic were made as the antiquity and the complexity of the period were realized. In 1872, the French prehistorian Gabriel de Mortillet proposed three major subdivisions of the Paleolithic: Lower, Middle, and Upper.

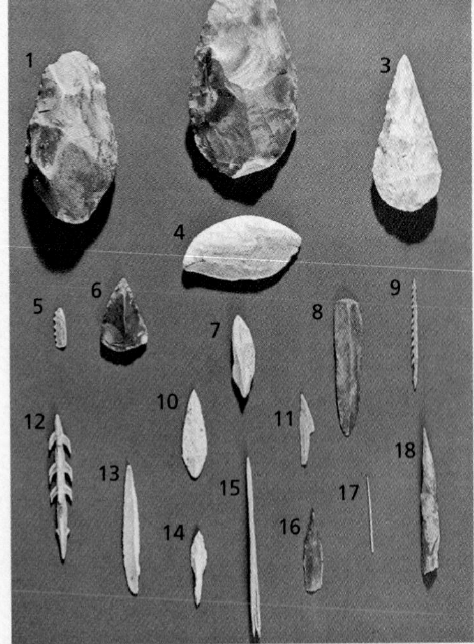


**Figure 3.6** Tools of the Paleolithic. 1–3: handaxes from the Lower Paleolithic. 4–6: side scraper, denticulated blade, and Levallois point from the Middle Paleolithic. 7–18: Upper Paleolithic tools. 7: flint point. 8: end scraper on blade. 9: barbed bone harpoon. 10–11: flint points. 12: barbed antler harpoon. 13: backed flint knife. 14: flint point. 15: bone point. 16: blade borer. 17: bone needle. 18: bone point. For scale, the handaxe at the top of the photo is approximately 20 cm (8 in) in length.

**Paleolithic** The first period of human prehistory, extending from the time of the first tools, more than 2.5 m.y.a., until the end of the Pleistocene, 10,000 years ago.

**Neolithic** The period of time of early farmers with domesticated plants and animals, polished stone tools, permanent villages, and often pottery.

0.5 kg of flint

From 0.5 kg of flint:
The pebble tool had 8 cm of cutting edge.

The handaxe had about 30 cm of cutting edge.

Mousterian flake tools provided about 90 cm of cutting edge.

Upper Paleolithic blade production resulted in up to 9 m of cutting edge.

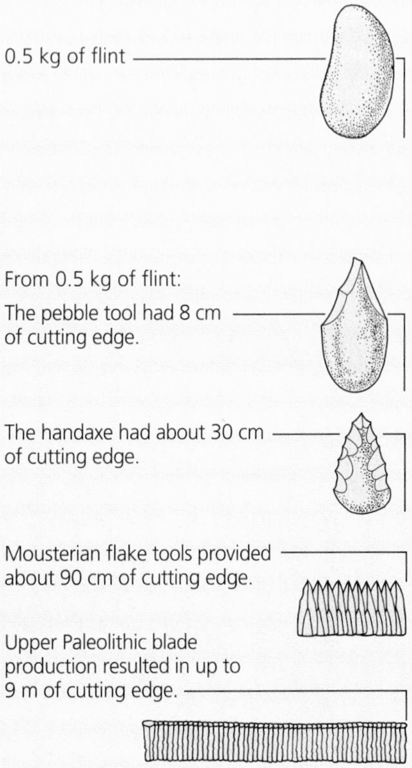

**Figure 3.7** A major trend through the Paleolithic: increasing efficiency in the production of cutting edge. Pebble tools, handaxes, flakes, and blades were likely produced from the same original piece of flint. Blade production provides an enormous increase in the amount of cutting edge available from the same amount of material.

An even earlier subdivision of the Paleolithic has been used for the earliest stone artifacts discovered in Africa. The Basal Paleolithic includes the pebble and flake tools of the Oldowan industry dating from around 2.6 m.y.a. until the appearance of handaxes. The Lower Paleolithic includes the Acheulean (ash-oo-LEE-an) assemblages generally associated with *Homo erectus*. Handaxes and flake tools characterize this time period (see "The Acheulean Handaxe," p. 99). The Lower Paleolithic thus extends from approximately 1.9 m.y.a. to the beginning of the Middle Paleolithic, about 200,000 years ago.

The Middle Paleolithic is associated with Neanderthals and other forms of early *Homo sapiens* and is characterized by a predominance of flake tools in artifact assemblages. In Europe and Southwest Asia, Middle Paleolithic assemblages are known as Mousterian. The Upper Paleolithic begins around 40,000 years ago with an emphasis on tools made of long, thin flakes of stone, known as blades, and on tools made from a number of other materials, including bone and antler (see "The Upper Paleolithic," Chapter 4, p. 123). The finale of the Upper Paleolithic generally coincides with the end of the Pleistocene, about 10,000 years ago.

Some of the major developments in the Paleolithic include the appearance of the first stone tools around 2.6 m.y.a., the controlled use of fire around 800,000 years ago, evidence for the hunting of large game by around 500,000 years ago, the first definite living structures perhaps 200,000 years ago, the intentional burial of the dead perhaps 100,000 years ago, the first art and decoration after 50,000 years ago, and the dispersal of human populations throughout the world by the end of the Pleistocene (Figure 3.8). Our human ancestors lived as hunter-gatherers throughout the Paleolithic, more than 99% of prehistory, successfully harvesting the wild foods of the land. Domestication—the planting of crops and the herding of animals—did not begin until the very end of the Paleolithic, around 8000 B.C.

What relationship, if any, exists between brain size and human technology?

Several important technological trends occurred during the Paleolithic, one of which was the increasing specialization of tools. The earliest stone artifacts were general-purpose tools—pebble tools, extremely simple in form. Over time, there was an increase in the kinds of tools and in the total number of kinds of tools in use. Efficiency in using stone also increased, as did the amount of cutting edge produced by flaking stone. For example, 0.5 kg (1 lb) of flint would produce about 8 cm (3 in) of cutting edge on an Oldowan pebble tool, about 30 cm (12 in) around the circumference on a handaxe from the Lower Paleolithic, and about 90 cm (30 in) of edge on the flake tools of the Middle Paleolithic. In the Upper Paleolithic, production of long, thin blades would result in almost 9 m (30 ft) of cutting edge.

During the Paleolithic, there was also an increase in the variety of materials used to make tools. Bone, antler,

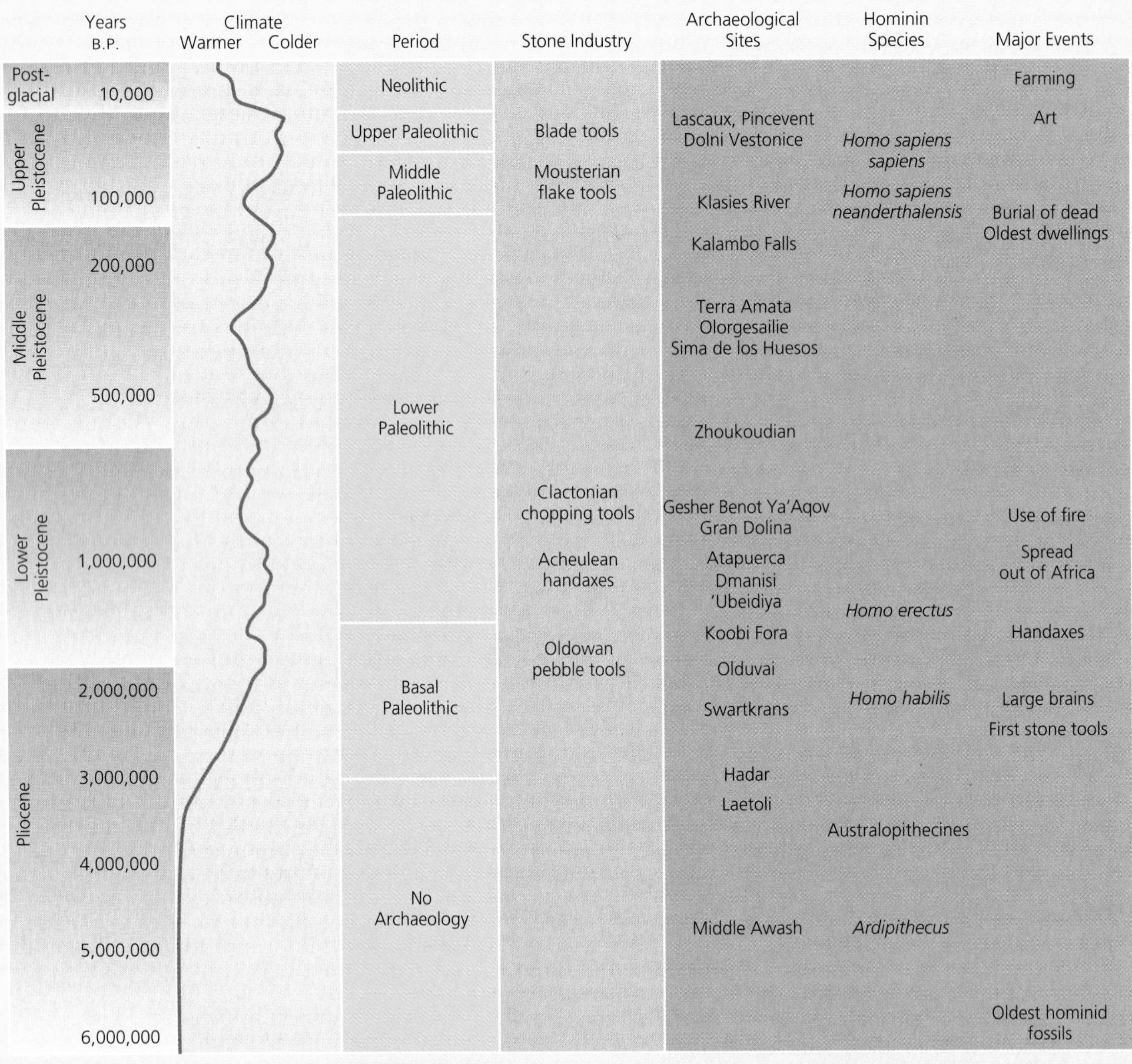


**Figure 3.8** The Pleistocene and the Paleolithic. This chart shows the major divisions of the Pleistocene and years before present, along with the major divisions of the Paleolithic, important stone industries, archaeological sites, hominin forms, and significant events.

*I tend to live in the past because most of my life is there.*

—Herb Caen

ivory, and wood were commonly used by the end of the period, although that evidence may be a result of better preservation at the more recent sites. The Paleolithic witnessed the achievement of humanness, a heritage that has been passed on to the inhabitants of the most recent 10,000 years of our species' past. The major developments in that recent past would not have been possible without the population expansion, the innovative technology, and the development of language, social relationships, and ritual that characterized the journey of our ancestors through the Paleolithic.

*Concept*

# Climate and Environment in the Pleistocene

## *Challenging conditions for human survival*

The Pleistocene, a geological epoch and the time of *Homo erectus,* began approximately 2 m.y.a. in a period characterized by active volcanoes, cooling temperatures, and the appearance of several modern species of animals. The earth's temperature had gradually been cooling for millions of years (Figure 3.9). Although the Pleistocene is also known as the Ice Age, there were, in fact, many ice ages, or glacials, as they are known. There were at least nine, and probably more, alternations between colder and warmer conditions, known as **glacials** and **interglacials,** during the Pleistocene.

These glacial episodes were first recognized in Europe. During the 1800s, two Swiss geologists, A. Penck and E. Brückner, identified four periods of glaciation in Europe from a series of Alpine deposits and river terraces. They named these glacial stages after local rivers—the Günz, the Mindel, the Riss, and the Würm—from oldest to most recent. The intervening warm periods were designated Günz/Mindel, Mindel/Riss, and Riss/Würm. However, subsequent research has demonstrated that in the past million years or so, there have been a larger number of pronounced swings from warmer to colder.

It may be surprising to learn that information about the dramatic changes in temperature and **glaciation** in the Pleistocene has come from underwater in the Caribbean Sea and from the ice cap in Greenland, where scientists have made deep corings of marine sediments and glacial ice, respectively. The small animal shells (foraminifera) that make up much of the sediment on the ocean floor contain oxygen isotopes in the carbonate of the shell. In Greenland, oxygen isotopes from the Pleistocene are preserved in the kilometer-thick layer of glacial ice that covers the huge island. **Oxygen isotope ratios** vary with the temperature of the ocean water or the atmosphere and can thus indicate temperature change over time. The amount of the $^{18}O$ isotope relative to the $^{16}O$ isotope decreases with increasing temperature. For the Pleistocene, alternations between warmer and cooler periods defined by oxygen isotopes have been numbered sequentially and are defined as isotope stages (Figure 3.10). These stages are sometimes used for the chronology of the Paleolithic. The figure shows these years before present, changes in isotopes and temperature, stage numbers, and divisions of the Pleistocene for the past 800,000 years.

It is not difficult to imagine the consequences of a sharp drop in temperature during the colder episodes of the Pleistocene. In parts of northern Canada today, temperatures are cool even in summer, with lows at night around 4.5°C (40°F). The last snowfall is often in June, and the first flakes of autumn come in September. A drop in average summer temperature in this area of about 5°C (8°F) would mean that not all the winter snow would

**Figure 3.9** Oxygen isotope ratios, a proxy for atmospheric temperature, from foraminifera in marine sediments during the Cenozoic, the past 70 million years of the earth's history. Notice the gradual decline in atmospheric temperature since the Eocene.

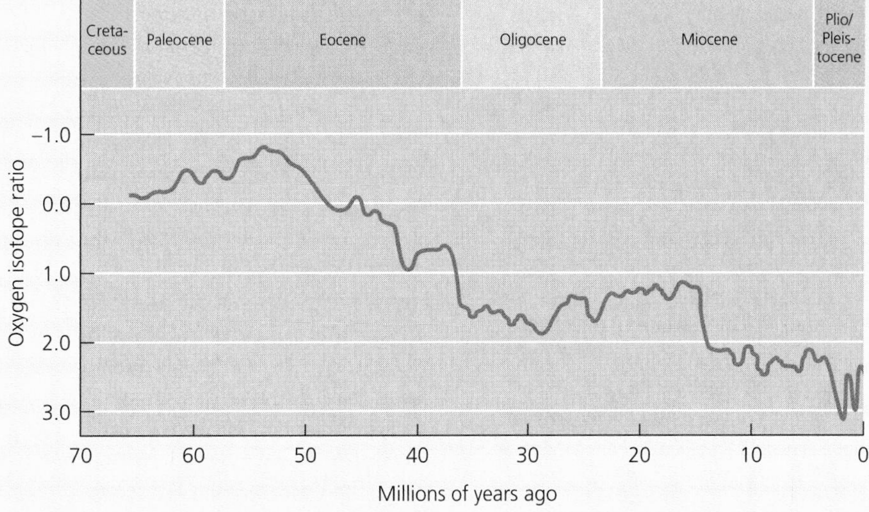

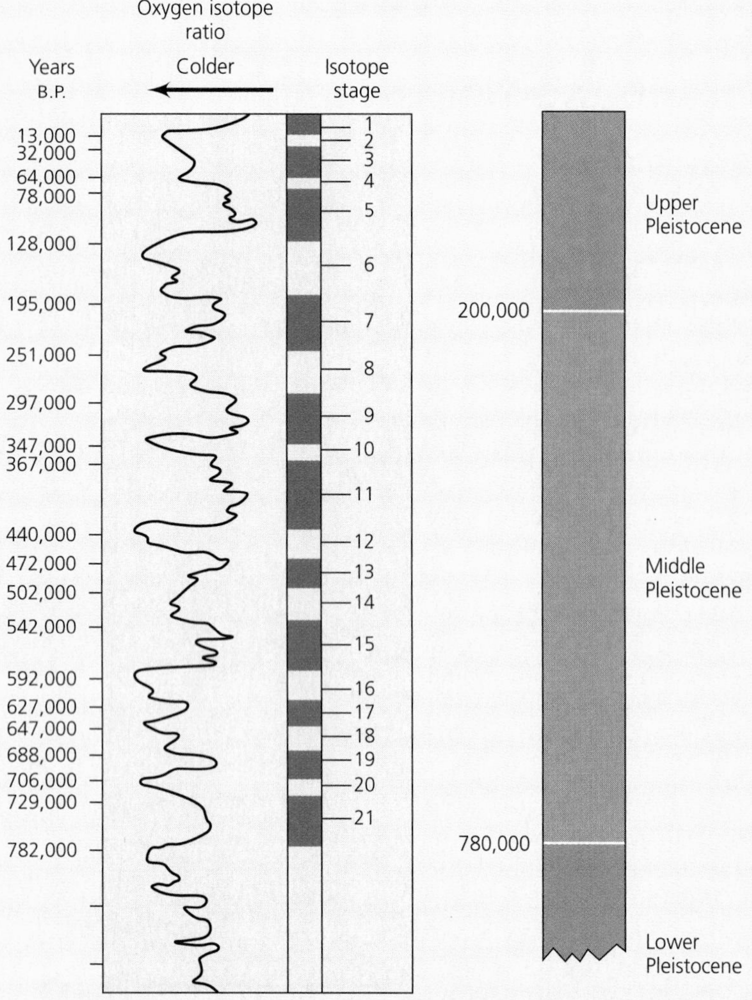


**Figure 3.10** Pleistocene glacial chronology based on oxygen isotope ratios in foraminifera in marine sediments. Notice the many oscillations between cold and warm phases over the past 800,000 years or so. (Data from Shackleton and Opdyke, 1973.)

**glacial** A cold episode of the Pleistocene; also called an ice age.

**interglacial** A warm period of the Pleistocene.

**glaciation** The expansion of continental glacial ice during a period of cold climate.

**oxygen isotope ratio** The ratio of different isotopes of oxygen in ocean water, varying with the temperature of the water.

melt each year; snow would fall later in summer and earlier in autumn. Even if these snowbanks increased by only a few centimeters each summer, they would grow substantially over the course of time. For example, just 10 cm (4 in) of snow every year for 10,000 years would build an enormous snowdrift over 1 km (0.6 mi) high.

The 5 trillion snowflakes it takes to cover a football field with a foot of wet snow weigh almost 550 tons. Ice forms under piles of accumulating snow. Its weight causes the mass of ice to begin to spread at the edges. In such a manner, huge sheets of ice expanded horizontally during the Pleistocene, as more and more snow and ice accumulated. It has been estimated that such ice sheets expanded across the landscape at a rate of as much as 100–150 m (350–500 ft) per year. In a thousand years, such a growing ice mass would cover a distance of 100 km (62 mi). In 20,000 years of accumulation, the ice could have spread 2000 km (1250 mi) from its original center.

Today, perhaps 10% of the land surface of the earth is covered by glaciers—in Antarctica; Greenland; northern Canada, Europe, and Asia; and high mountain regions. During the past million years, sheets of continental glaciers more than 5 km (3 mi) thick grew in the Northern Hemisphere. During the colder episodes of the Pleistocene, continental ice sheets expanded from these same areas to cover perhaps 30% of the land surface (Figure 3.11).

In North America, these ice masses filled most of Canada and extended into the United States as far south as what is now St. Louis, Missouri. In northern Europe, a similar sheet moved from the Baltic Sea basin to cover Scandinavia, northern Great Britain, parts of the Netherlands, northern Germany, Poland, and the northwestern part of the former Soviet Union. These sheets of ice acted like enormous bulldozers, grinding down the landscape as they advanced and depositing huge blankets of homogenized earth and rock, known as moraines, as they retreated. The weight of the ice also forced down the land surface, often to great depths. In Greenland today, for example, where the ice sheet is 2 km (1.3 mi) thick, the land surface resembles a very deep bowl, higher at the edges, where the ice is thinner. The land surface in the interior of Greenland is far below present sea level and one of the lowest spots on earth.

The masses of ice reduced the earth's liquid water reservoir, particularly the oceans. During the time of maximum cold, when water was frozen in huge continental sheets, the global sea level was lowered as much as 150 m (500 ft), completely changing the outlines of the continents and often creating connections between former islands and separate landmasses.

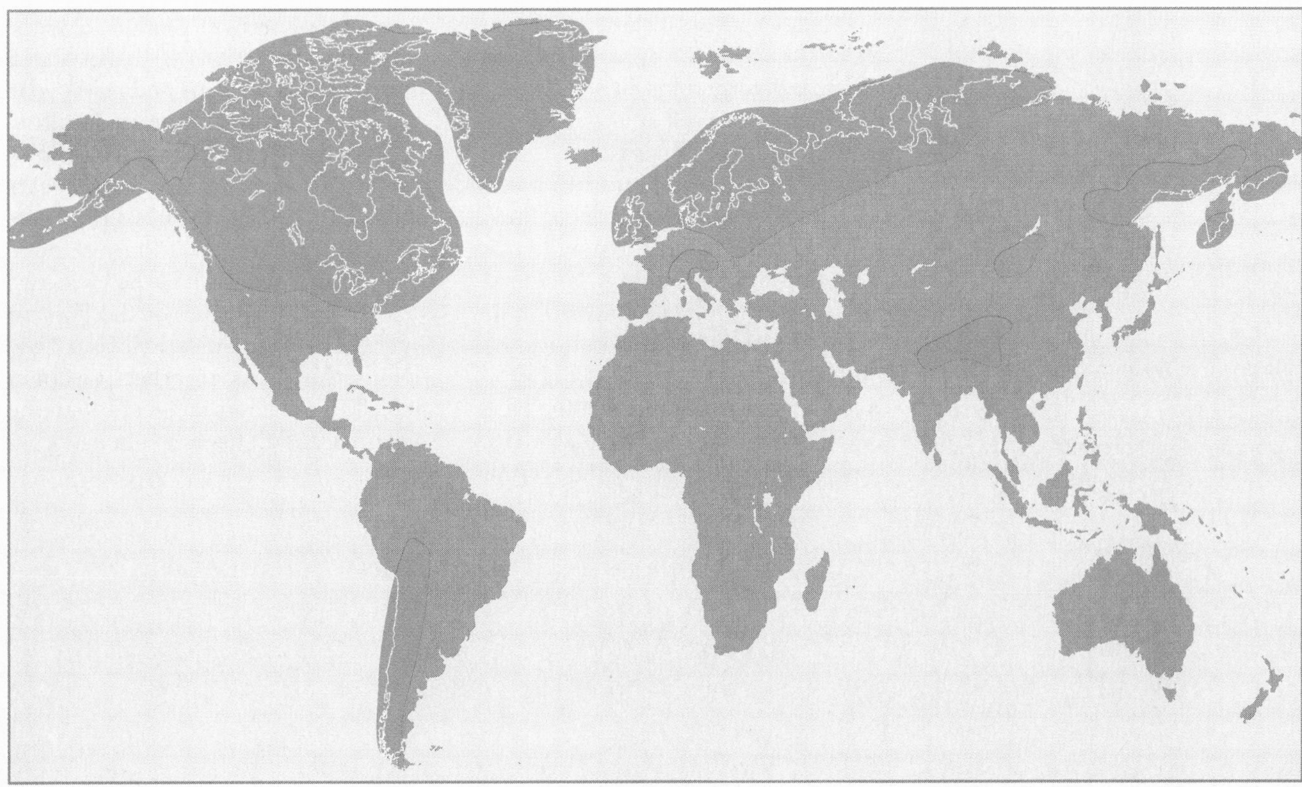

**Figure 3.11** The maximum distribution of continental glaciation during the colder periods of the Pleistocene. Ice sheets are more common in the Northern Hemisphere partly because there is much more land at the higher northern latitudes.

As the massive ice sheets melted at the end of the Pleistocene, two processes operated to change the shape of the continents. At the same time the melting ice refilled the seas and coastlines moved higher, the enormous weight of the ice sheets disappeared, removing a heavy burden from the land. The surface of the earth had been depressed by the weight of the ice (just as the center of Greenland is today). This surface began to come back, or rebound, as the ice disappeared. For example, the coast of Finland today is expanding at the astounding rate of several meters per century as the area recovers from the weight of the glacial ice.

The causes of Pleistocene climatic change and continental glaciation have been debated for many years. Volcanic plumes filling the air with ash and smoke and shading the earth or changes in the level of solar radiation were once thought to be responsible for the onset of the Pleistocene. Recent attention has been given to the role of mountain uplift in cooling the earth's climate. Walter Ruddiman and John Kutzbach have suggested that the uplift of the North American Rocky Mountains and the Himalayas of South Asia resulted in a global disruption of weather patterns and the onset of a cooler, drier climate.

Fluctuations in air and water temperature were not uncommon during the Pleistocene and are cyclical in nature. In the 1920s, Serbian mathematician Milutin Milankovitch argued that the variations in the earth's orbit changed climate in a cyclical fashion. Slight variation in the precession of the earth's axis and shifts in orbit eccentricity change the distribution and intensity of sunlight reaching the planet, like the changes in our seasons. Milankovitch predicted cycles of 100,000, 40,000, and 20,000 years for these climatic changes, based on his calculations of the earth's orbital variation. Such a cyclical pattern seems to fit the information on climatic change found in the oxygen isotope cores.

Thus, it appears that minor changes in factors such as the distance from the earth to the sun and the tilt of the earth's axis play a major role in the amount of sunlight reaching the earth, the atmospheric temperature, and ultimately the expansion and retreat of continental glaciation. This factor, now known as **Milankovitch forcing,** is considered to be the prime reason for the cycle of fluctuating temperatures that marks the Pleistocene. It is not at all clear that the glacial cycles of the Pleistocene have ended; we may now simply be witnessing one of the warmer intervals between fluctuations of glaciation and climatic change that occurred during the Pleistocene and repeatedly over the past several hundred million years of the earth's history. The end of the Pleistocene is dated to 10,000 years ago (8000 B.C.), when the last ice sheets retreated. The interval that we presently occupy is known as the Holocene (a.k.a. the Postglacial, or the Present Interglacial). The similarity of our present interglacial to an earlier one about 400,000 years ago suggests that the next glacial will begin in about 20,000 years.

**Milankovitch forcing** A term describing the phenomenon considered to be the prime reason for glacial fluctuations and climatic change.

Site

# Zhoukoudian

## *Bones of the dragon*

For millennia, many Chinese believed that fossil bones had medicinal and curative powers. Called dragon's teeth, such fossils were ground into powder and sold at apothecaries throughout the country. For more than a century, paleontologists and other natural scientists have visited such shops to look for the bones of new species and to learn about potential new fossil sites. In 1899, a European doctor in Beijing found an unusual fossil tooth at one such apothecary and identified it as an upper third molar of either human or ape origin. The tooth came from a place called Dragon Bone Hill, a large limestone ridge near the town of Zhoukoudian (joe-ko-tea-EN), 50 km (30 mi) southwest of Beijing (Figure 3.12). Before the doctor returned to Europe, he passed the tooth and the information on to a Swedish geologist, John Gunnar Andersson. Andersson and his friend Davidson Black, a Canadian anatomist, were convinced they could discover an early human fossil where the tooth had been found. Black persuaded the Rockefeller Foundation to sponsor excavations at the site. On the basis of two hominin teeth that were found, Black announced the discovery of *Sinanthropus pekinensis* (Chinese man of Peking) in 1927. Later that same year, the first skull was found, confirming Black's bold proclamation.

For 10 years, a large workforce essentially mined the deposits in the complex of caves at Zhoukoudian, removing over half a million tons of material in the quest for fossils (Figure 3.13). Almost 2000 days, more than 6 months each year, were spent blasting out the limestone and removing rock and sedimentary deposits over a

www.mhhe.com/priceip6e

For a Web-based activity on Zhoukoudian, see the Internet exercises on your online learning center.

**Figure 3.12** The location of the excavations at Dragon Bone Hill, Zhoukoudian.

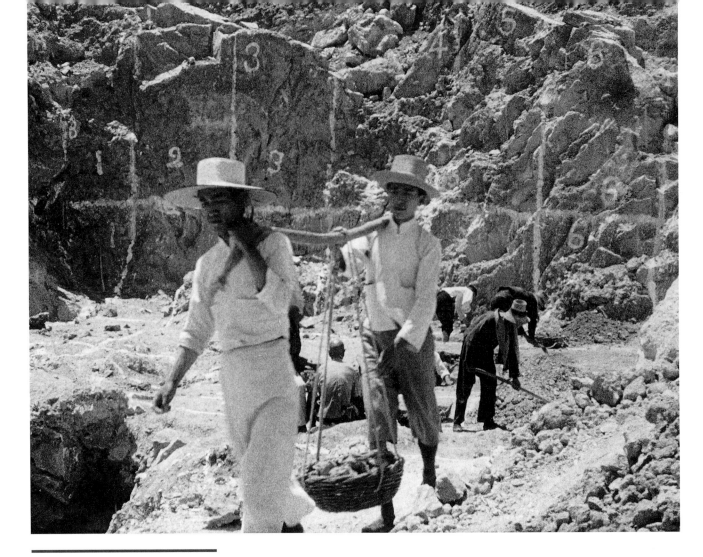

**Figure 3.13** Excavations in the lower levels at Zhoukoudian. An enormous amount of material was removed from the deposits at the site, the volume equivalent in size to a small building.

vertical distance of 55 m (180 ft), as high as a 17-story building. The large limestone chamber at the center of the Zhoukoudian caves is enormous, 140 m (450 ft) north to south, by 40 m (125 ft) east to west, by approximately 40 m (125 ft) high—the size of a supertanker. The deposits in this chamber were almost completely removed in the course of the excavation (Figure 3.14). The crude excavation methods and untrained labor meant that stone tools and other materials were often missed and that important information about the context of the deposits was not recorded.

In his report, Black described dense layers of ash, baked sediments, and charred bone resulting from fires in the cave (Figure 3.15). These materials were thought to be evidence of the places where people lived, made tools, built fires, ate, died, and left their bones. Over 20,000 stone tools, including flakes, scrapers, and choppers (but no handaxes), were found, made from quartz, sandstone, rock crystal, and flint (Figure 3.16). These materials do not occur naturally in limestone areas and must have been brought into the caves. The artifacts are generally very crude and irregular but do improve in quality toward the top of the deposits.

The abundant bones in the deposits come from both large and small species. Most of the large animal bones come from an extinct species of deer with enormous horns and from wild horses and giant boars, elephants, water buffaloes, hyenas, such carnivores as bears and saber-toothed tigers, and others—a total of 96 mammalian species. The presence of these animals indicates that the climate was somewhat warmer than it is today. Moreover,

**Figure 3.14** Entrance to the site of Zhoukoudian today.

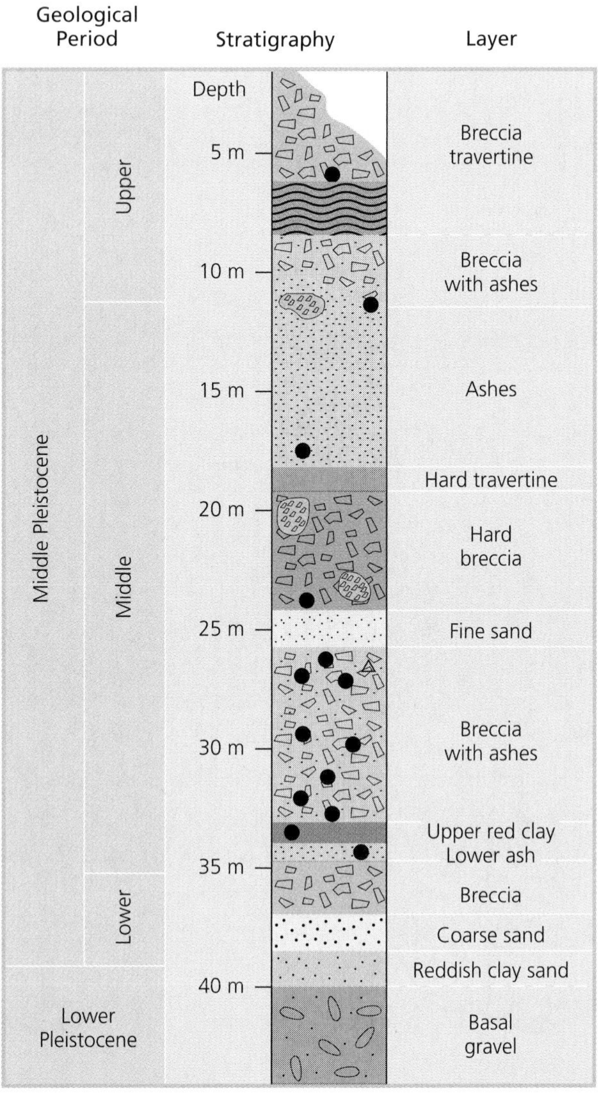


**Figure 3.15** The stratigraphy of 40 m (130 ft) of deposits at Zhoukoudian, showing the location of the *Homo erectus* skeletal remains.

the habitat requirements for these species suggest that the area around Zhoukoudian was a mosaic of forested hills, open plains, lakes, and rivers. The forest was likely dominated by pine, cedar, elm, hackberry, and the Chinese redbud tree. The charred seeds of hackberry fruits found in the deposits at Zhoukoudian led to the suggestion that plant foods such as these may have formed part of the diet of the human inhabitants.

By far the most important finds at Zhoukoudian were the remains of the early hominins, today designated *Homo erectus*. A total of 6 skullcaps (the face and the lower portion of the crania are missing), 12 skull fragments, 15 lower jaws, 157 teeth, 7 thighbones, 1 fragment of shinbone, 3 bones from the upper arm, 1 collarbone, and 1 wrist bone were recovered. As in the South African caves, hominin skulls are more common than other bones of the skeleton, partly because they are more resistant to destruction and partly because they are more readily recognized. These fragments come from adult males and females and from children.

An increase in brain size over time can be seen in the materials from Zhoukoudian. Skulls from the deeper part of the deposits have a cranial

Figure 3.16 Stone artifacts found at Zhoukoudian. These materials were largely flakes and small chopping tools. No handaxes were recorded at this site.

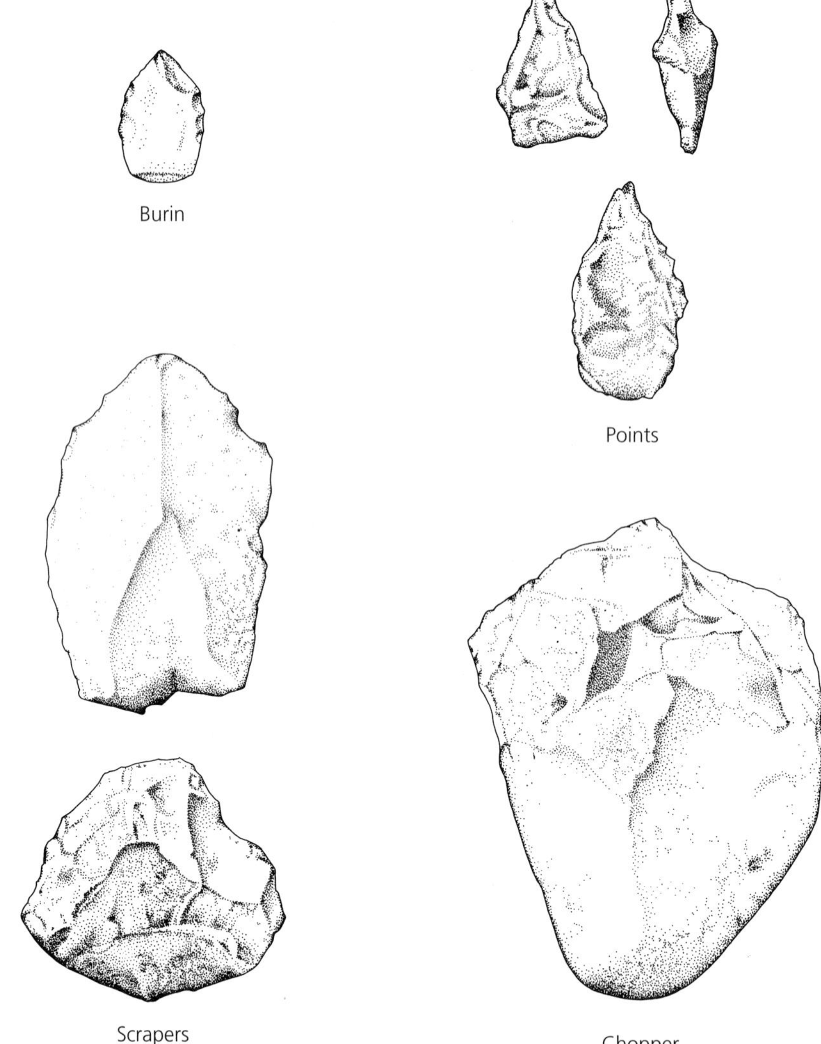


capacity of about 900 cc, whereas those from the upper levels are closer to 1100 cc on average, within the range of variation of modern humans.

The investigations conducted by Black, and since 1949 by Chinese archaeologists, have revealed 12 stratified layers in the deep deposits at Zhoukoudian (see Figure 3.15). The layers themselves date to at least 700,000 years ago at the bottom and to roughly 200,000 years ago at the top of the sequence.

Unfortunately, these important fossils have disappeared. The excavations at Zhoukoudian were closed in 1937 with the outbreak of war between Japan and China. A decision was made to move the fossils to the United States for safekeeping. They were packed carefully in crates and placed in the hands of a detachment of U.S. Marines. Somewhere between the consulate in Beijing and the port of departure from China, the fossils were lost or stolen. Today they may be still in China, in Japan, in the United States, or at the bottom of the Pacific—no one knows. Fortunately, plaster casts were made before the fossils were lost, so that there is at least some information on their size, shape, and important features. In addition, the more recent Chinese excavations since 1949 have uncovered a few more examples. Nevertheless, these priceless relics of some of our earliest ancestors would be a marvelous rediscovery.

# Concept

## The First Europeans

*An early date of arrival*

As we have seen, early hominins began to migrate out of Africa into Asia at the beginning of the Pleistocene, by at least 1.9 m.y.a. The earliest evidence for humans in Europe is now 1.2 million years old. If *Homo erectus* spread into Asia, why did they not move into Europe at the same time? The answer to this question may simply be that we don't yet have enough information, or it may relate to the geography of the European continent. New York City lies at the same latitude as Madrid and Rome. In fact, much of Europe is farther north than the U.S. border with Canada (Figure 3.17). Very cold climatic conditions would have prevailed in Europe during much of the last 1 million years of the Pleistocene, making large portions of the continent generally inhospitable to human occupation. Huge glaciers extended across the Pyrenees, the Alps, Scandinavia, and Britain during the Pleistocene. Permafrost tundra covered much of the central part of the continent during colder periods. Thus, the arctic and subarctic climate of Europe may have delayed human settlement until behavior and technology overcame this obstacle.

There are several very old archaeological sites in Europe. The earliest is in northern Spain, a remarkable 1.2-million-year-old site at Atapuerca, excavated since 1994 and described in the next section. Another early site has been found in Italy, at a place known as Isernia. A few simple stone tools and animal bones were found together in deeply buried lakeshore deposits underlying a volcanic ash that has been dated to 730,000 years ago using radiopotassium methods. Large animal species associated with the deposit are bison, rhinoceros, elephant, bear, hippo, pig, goat, and deer.

Other pieces of early humans have been found around the continent: a lower jaw from Mauer near Heidelberg and a crushed skull from Steinheim in Germany, a skull from Petralona in Greece, the facial front of a skull from Arago in France, and a skull from Swanscombe and a leg bone from Boxgrove in England (Figure 3.18). These European fossils date to the period after 600,000 years ago and appear slightly more modern than their *Homo erectus* neighbors in Asia. These remains have sometimes been referred to as Archaic *Homo sapiens*, but they are now designated as *Homo heidelbergensis*.

Why does large-game hunting play an important role in human survival?

**Figure 3.17** The map of Europe shows the locations and ages (in thousands of years) of some of the earliest archaeological sites mentioned in the text. Europe is superimposed over the United States to show the relationship of the two continents in size and latitude.

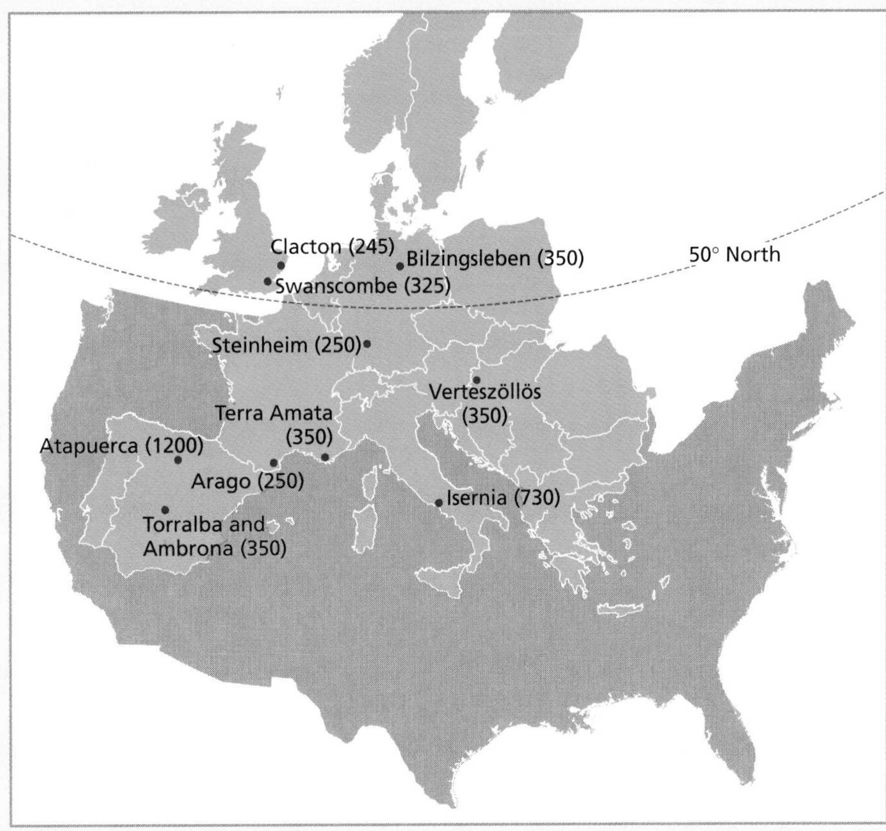

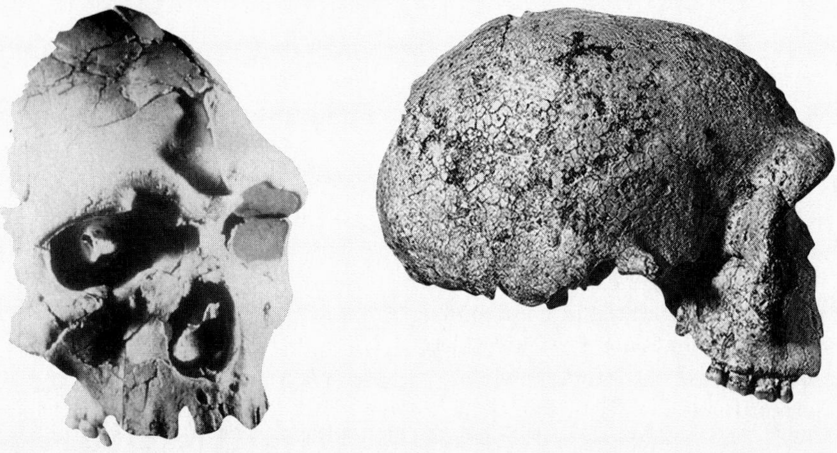

**Figure 3.18** Early hominin skulls in Europe: Steinheim (left) and Arago (right). Dating to 300,000–200,000 years B.P., these specimens likely represent an intermediate form between *Homo erectus* and fully modern *Homo sapiens.* Thus, they are now considered as *Homo heidelbergensis* and the ancestors of *Homo neanderthalensis.*

**Figure 3.19** Excavations at the site of Ambrona in central Spain, dating to 350,000 years B.P. The site documents the association of stone tools and the bones of extinct animals such as the woodland elephant. Notice the linear arrangement of bones and tusks.

A few other sites in Europe may be more than half a million years old, but reliable dates are rare. By 400,000 years ago, however, most of Europe had been occupied. Lower Paleolithic sites are found throughout the central and southern parts of the continent at places such as Bilzingsleben in Germany, Verteszöllös in Hungary, and Torralba and Ambrona in Spain.

Bilzingsleben lies in an area of natural mineral springs; human and animal bones and small stone tools were preserved in the hardened deposits of travertine around the springs. Isotopic dates for the site indicate an age between 400,000 and 300,000 years old, during an interglacial period. Human skull fragments were found in the deposits, along with numerous animal bones. A site very similar to Bilzingsleben exists in Hungary at Verteszöllös, roughly 50 km (30 mi) west of Budapest. Here again, the stone artifacts are curious because of their small size, probably the result of an absence of larger pieces of raw material in the area. Short cutting edges were produced on thousands of tiny pebbles, often only 2.5 cm (1 in) in diameter. Charcoal and burned animal bones document the use of fire at this site. As at Bilzingsleben, fragments of skull from early European hominins were found in the layers at Verteszöllös.

Some 150 km (100 mi) northeast of Madrid, a steep-sided valley cuts through a high plateau, creating one of the few routes between north and south in the region. During the Pleistocene, this valley almost certainly would have been an important path of migration for large animals moving between the north in summer and the south in winter. Two almost-identical sites, Torralba and Ambrona, are located in this valley, containing deposits of stone artifacts and the bones of extinct elephants, horses, deer, and other animals (Figure 3.19). The bones and stones accumulated here during a colder episode of the Pleistocene, probably during a glacial period, perhaps 350,000 years ago. The artifacts at the sites include objects made of stone, bone, ivory tusk, and wood. The stone artifacts belong to the early Acheulean; handaxes were made and used here, along with cleavers and a variety of other flake and core tools. Some of the stone used for making these artifacts came from tens of kilometers away.

# Atapuerca

## *Remains of the first Europeans, 1.2 million years B.P.*

The limestone hills of Atapuerca (ah-tah-PWER-ka), near the city of Burgos in northern Spain, hold a treasure trove for Paleolithic archaeologists. Human remains and artifacts from the Lower, Middle, and Upper Paleolithic are hidden in the many caves of this porous rock mass. Limestone is a soft rock, gradually dissolved by rain and groundwater, which cut channels, caves, and underground streams through the hills. The entrances to many of these caverns collapsed over time, closing and hiding the chambers and entombing the materials within. Then, in the 1890s, a railroad was built through the hills of Atapuerca. Because of the elevation and the need to maintain a reasonably level grade, several deep cuts, or trenches, were hacked through the limestone for the rail line. This railroad trench in fact exposed a number of caverns and chambers that had been hidden for millennia (Figure 3.20).

It was not until the 1970s, however, that prehistoric artifacts and bones were first found in these deposits and not until the 1990s that major excavations began to expose the richness of their contents (Figure 3.21). There are many interesting layers in the Atapuerca hills, but the two most important for the Paleolithic are known as Sima de los Huesos (SEE-ma day lohs

**www.mhhe.com/priceip6e**

For a Web-based activity on Atapuerca, see the Internet exercises on your online learning center.

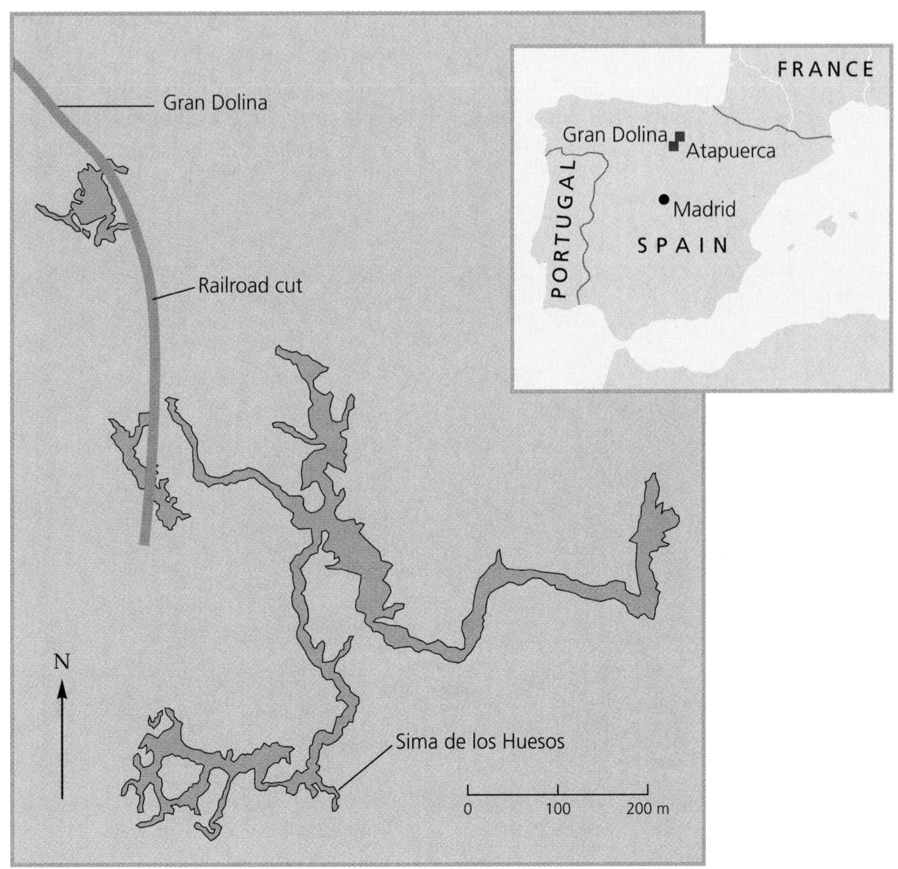


**Figure 3.20** A plan of the railroad cut and some of the large caves and chambers exposed in the Atapuerca hills. The locations of Gran Dolina and Sima de los Huesos are shown on this plan.

**Figure 3.21** Excavations at Gran Dolina in the Atapuerca railroad cut. The scaffolding is necessary to reach the deposits high on the side of the trench wall.

Do artistic reconstructions of the faces of past ancestors help or hinder our knowledge of their appearance?

WHEY-soss) and Gran Dolina (graan doe-LEEN-ah). The remains from Gran Dolina are immediately relevant to our discussion of *Homo erectus,* but the finds from Sima de los Huesos are equally fascinating and will be described briefly before we turn to Gran Dolina.

Sima de los Huesos or "pit of bones" is an extraordinary crevice deep in one of the largest caves in the Atapuerca region. The "pit" lies 55 m (175 ft) below ground and 500 m (1500 ft, or five football fields) from the nearest entrance to the cave. The pit is

**Figure 3.22** An artist's reconstruction of the 32 individuals placed in the "pit of bones" at Atapuerca, dating to more than 350,000 years ago.

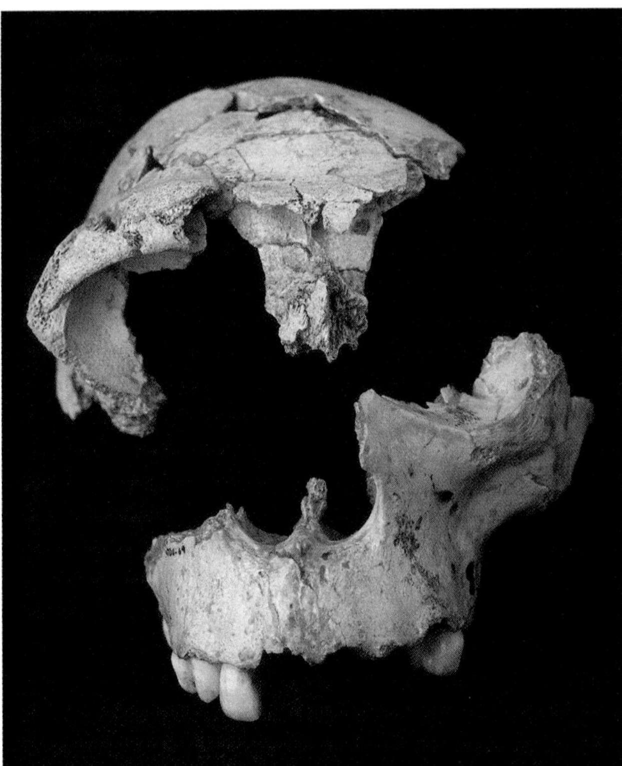

**Figure 3.23** The face of *Homo erectus*, one of the best-preserved skulls from Gran Dolina, dating to approximately 900,000 years ago—one of the earliest inhabitants of Europe.

"sock shaped," a small depression at the end of a sloping passage entered from a 13-m (40-ft) vertical shaft. Merely reaching this crevice is a difficult journey for the excavators. The passage is narrow and slippery, and part of the trip requires traversing a deep shaft. Only one or two individuals can work in the space that exists in this nook of the cave. The excavations, however difficult, have produced spectacular results and the largest set of human remains ever recovered from the Paleolithic. Parts of the skeletons of at least 32 individuals have been found (Figure 3.22). Nine are male, and 9 female; the sex of 14 could not be determined. The largest number, 11 individuals, were between ages 13 and 17. Four children were between ages 3 and 13. Only 4 people were over age 30 when they died, and no one had reached age 40. These individuals were of normal height; males averaged 1.75 m (5 ft, 9 in), females 1.7 m (5 ft, 7 in). The tallest person was 1.8 m (5 ft, 11 in) in height and weighed 90 kg (200 lb). The cause of death is unknown at present. The remains are an extraordinary sample of a human group living during the Lower Paleolithic.

What is most remarkable is that all these individuals were intentionally put into the pit. Their bodies were carried into the cave, through the difficult passage, and placed or dropped in the crevice. Perhaps this behavior foreshadows the practice of intentional burial of the dead that is first seen among Neanderthals in the Middle Paleolithic, some 300,000 years later.

Uranium-series dating of redeposited limestone at Sima de los Huesos produced an estimated age between 350,000 and 500,000 years. The human remains in Sima de los Huesos have been designated as *Homo heidelbergensis* and represent the ancestors of the Neanderthals we will discuss in the next chapter.

It is in regard to *Homo erectus*, however, that the finds from Gran Dolina are the most important and represent the oldest yet-discovered humans on the continent of Europe. It is intriguing that the earliest finds should be in the westernmost parts of Europe. The deposits at Gran Dolina originally accumulated at the entrance of a cave or rockshelter that has largely disappeared. The original entrance area was exposed when the deep railroad cut was made through the area. High scaffolding is necessary to reach the deposits where the excavations take place.

Does cannibalism indicate that there were food shortages in the Lower Paleolithic?

There are many layers at Gran Dolina, but an important one is Layer 6, which has been dated by magnetic reversal to approximately 900,000 years ago. This layer is one of the richest in the remains of the bones of more than 25 animal species, such as horse, deer, bison, rhinoceros, wild cat, hyena, and wolf. Among the bones have been found several hundred stone tools, for the most part simple pebble tools and flakes along with a few handaxes. Among the stone and the animal bones were also found some 90 human fossil fragments, representing at least four individuals. These bones belong to a form of *Homo erectus* (called *Homo antecessor* by the Spanish scientists) (Figure 3.23). These bones exhibit a pattern of breakage and of cutting and chopping marks from stone tools that clearly indicates that the humans who butchered the animals represented by the bones in the cave also butchered and must have consumed the humans. Gran Dolina documents the fact that the early Europeans were cannibals.

And the discoveries keep coming. In 2008, the archaeologists and paleoanthropologists working at Atapuerca announced a new and even older find. A portion of a human mandible, several stone tools, and broken animal bones were found in a deep layer in an area of the caves known as Sima del Elefante. Several methods were used to obtain an estimate of the date for this layer and the archaeological finds of 1.2 m.y.a., the oldest human remains yet found in Europe. Stay tuned; there will no doubt be more extraordinary discoveries from this remarkable site at Atapuerca.

# *Concept*

## Pleistocene Mammals

### *Prehistoric species now extinct*

Although the Pleistocene witnessed the appearance of a number of modern mammals (e.g., elephants, horses, and cattle), many other animals that existed then are now gone. In North America, a group of animals largely different from those we see today wandered across the cold and largely treeless regions—woolly mammoths, mastadons, ground sloths, caribou, giant beavers, saber-toothed tigers, bison, and horses (Figure 3.24). Most are now extinct. In Europe, woolly mammoths and woolly rhinoceroses, cave bears and cave lions and cave hyenas, giant deer and beavers, bison and aurochs (wild cattle) roamed over much of Europe during the colder periods of the Pleistocene. These species were generally much larger than their modern equivalents and are now extinct. The bones of these animals from archaeological sites give some indication of the species that were present in different parts of Europe.

The cave lion and the cave bear are generally well known because of the large number of their bones that have been found in the caverns and grottoes of Europe. The cave bear was enormous, at least the size of a modern Alaskan grizzly, with a very large head and huge canine teeth. The cave bear ranged over much of Europe, and many of this creature's bones have been found in caves at high elevations in the Alps. Tight crevices in the caves had been polished by the passage of bears over tens of thousands of years. Thousands of skeletons of cave bears that died during hibernation have been preserved. The Drachenhöhle in Austria is estimated to have contained the remains of over 30,000 bears.

**Figure 3.24** Notable among the mammals found in Pleistocene North America were beavers the size of a small bear, woolly mammoths, mastodons, sloths, saber-toothed tigers, bison, and horses. Many of these same species lived across the colder regions of Asia and Europe. Most are now extinct.

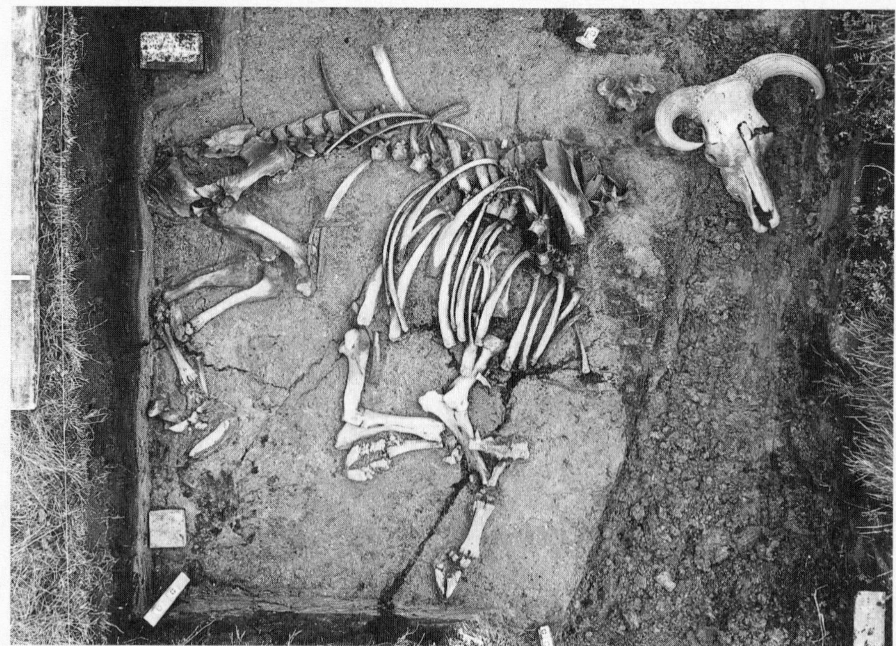

**Figure 3.25** Excavation of a large bull aurochs skeleton at Prejlerup in eastern Denmark. This animal escaped from its hunters but died from its wounds.

The woolly mammoth is also well known, both from the skeletal material that has been found and from a few examples of almost complete animals—soft parts, skin, and hair—found frozen in the permafrost of Siberia and Alaska. In Alaska, mammoth hairs still frozen in the ground sometimes clog the equipment of gold miners. This animal had a huge domed head, enormous curved ivory tusks, and humped shoulders. Standing approximately 3–4 m (10–13 ft) at the shoulder, it was covered with a short, woolly undercoat and long, hairy overcoat. The mammoth inhabited arctic steppe environments and consumed a diet of tundra grasses. This species ranged from western Europe across northern Asia and into North America during the late Pleistocene.

The giant Irish deer, from the bogs of Ireland and northern Europe, was known for its enormous antlers, as much as 4 m (13 ft) across. This animal was about the size of a North American moose, but it more closely resembled an elk. Wild cattle, known as aurochs, were common game animals during the warmer periods of the Pleistocene and survived until the middle of the nineteenth century A.D. (Figure 3.25). These animals were probably adapted to woodlands and were particularly common in the early Postglacial.

A number of these species disappeared around the end of the Pleistocene (Figure 3.26); mammoths, cave bears, and many large species were extinct by 11,000 B.C. (see "Pleistocene Extinction," Chapter 4, p. 151). The giant Irish deer may have survived around the Black Sea until 3000–2000 years ago, long after it had disappeared from the European continent. The last aurochs died in a game forest in Poland in A.D. 1627. The large-headed Prezwalski horse, depicted in Paleolithic cave paintings, still exists, in several European zoos. Other important Pleistocene species, such as reindeer, red deer, elk, musk ox, and brown bear, survive to the present and continue to exist at the edges of urban civilization.

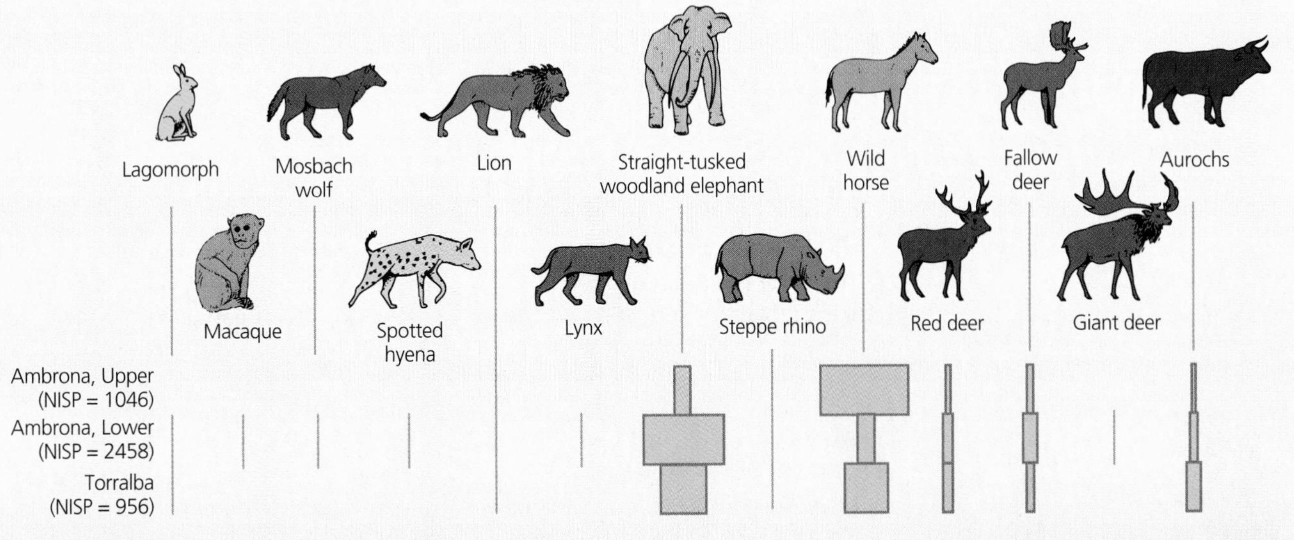


**Figure 3.26** Species of animals represented by the bones at the Spanish Lower Paleolithic sites of Torralba and Ambrona. The width of the bar for each site and level indicates the abundance of the species. Elephants and horses are by far the most common at these sites. "NISP" stands for the number of identifiable bones per species.

*Site*

# Kalambo Falls and Olorgesailie

## *East Africa 200,000 years ago*

**Figure 3.27** Wooden artifacts, including a club (left) and a sharpened object (right) from Kalambo Falls.

The Kalambo River flows peacefully through the plateau country of East Africa until its waters suddenly leap over the edge of the Rift Valley at the border of Tanzania and Zambia. There, the river falls over 250 m (800 ft) into a spectacular gorge close to the present shore of Lake Tanganyika. Deposits in the valley above the falls have provided one of the longest archaeological sequences anywhere in East Africa—or the world, for that matter. Over 200,000 years of successive human occupations are preserved in the water-lain deposits from the floods and backwaters of the river.

The site of Kalambo Falls was first discovered in 1953 by Desmond Clark, of the University of California at Berkeley, while he was examining a steeply eroded bank of the river. Preserved tree trunks and branches were present in the layers at the bottom of the bank, along with handaxes and cleavers of the Acheulean tradition in almost fresh condition (Figure 3.27). This lowest level, designated Bed I, is over 3 m (10 ft) thick and composed of alternating layers of white sand and dark clay.

Kalambo Falls is a very unusual site for two reasons. First, evidence for the use and consumption of plants is preserved at this early site; and second, evidence for meat-eating in the form of animal bones is not represented. The acidic sediments at the Kalambo site removed all traces of bone, but the waterlogged condition of the lower layers allowed the preservation of a variety of plant materials. Bed I contains several living floors from the late Acheulean period, along with a remarkable set of plant materials, including leaves, nuts, seeds, and fruits, and some of the oldest wooden objects in the world. A club, a smoothed and pointed piece, and other wooden objects shaped by human hands were recovered from the lowest Acheulean layers (Figure 3.28). Evidence for fire is also preserved in charred logs found on the living floors.

In contrast to Kalambo Falls, the site of Olorgesailie (o-lorg-a-SIGH-lee) in Kenya documents meat-eating in the Acheulean of Africa. The site was located along a sandy streambed at the edge of a former lake and contained over 400 handaxes and numerous animal bones. Much of the stone raw material for the handaxes came from nearby Mount Olorgesailie. Over a ton of lithic material was transported to the site, testimony to the importance of stone tools for these Acheulean groups.

Bone preservation was exceptionally good at Olorgesailie. Most of the animal bones come from at least 65 individuals of an extinct species of very large baboon, known as *Theropithecus*. All the skeletal elements of the baboons were represented, both large and small bones. There is strong evidence for one or more episodes of humans hunting baboons along the tree-lined stream banks at Olorgesailie. The two sites of Kalambo Falls and Olorgesailie together document the importance of both plants and animals in the diet of *Homo erectus*.

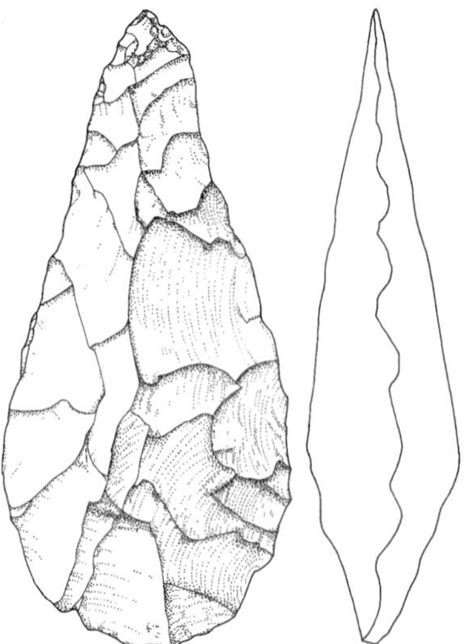

**Figure 3.28** An Acheulean handaxe from Kalambo Falls shown in front view and cross section.

Concept

# The Acheulean Handaxe

## *The Swiss Army knife of the Lower Paleolithic*

Although pebble tools do have a cutting edge, they are extremely simple and unwieldy. These basic tools changed, evolved, and improved over time as early hominins began to remove more and more flakes from the core of raw material, reshaping it and creating longer, straighter edges for cutting (Figure 3.29). When such a core tool assumes a distinctive teardrop shape—pointed at one end, rounded at the other, retouched to a desired size, shape, and heft—it is known as a **handaxe,** the signature tool of *Homo erectus.* The name comes originally from the French phrase *coup de poing* (axe wielded in the hand). But the handaxe is truly an all-purpose piece of equipment that was used for cutting, sawing, digging, bashing, and boring large holes, among other things.

The handaxe is, in fact, a more complex tool than it first appears. Its final form is a shape inside a piece of stone and in the mind of the maker; a cobble must be heavily modified for the handaxe to emerge. Moreover, the handaxe is symmetrical in outline, reflecting purpose, skill, and foresight in manufacture. Handaxes are often made from small cobbles 10–15 cm (4–6 in) long. A number of much larger examples, however, also exist, some more than 30 cm (1 ft) in length. The oldest Acheulean handaxes are known from the site of Konso-Gardula in southern Ethiopia and date to 1.9 m.y.a., in association with early *Homo erectus.*

The 700,000-year-old site of Kilombe in Kenya contains a fascinating collection of handaxes. Here, hundreds of these tools were discovered eroding out of the same geological layer. Remarkably, most of the handaxes are very similar in size and shape. Stone artifacts are made by a process of **reduction,** the removal of flakes from a core, and errors or mistakes cannot be erased. Nevertheless, the symmetry and relationship between length and width of the handaxes from Kilombe is striking. Small and large implements have the same length-to-width ratio, indicating the importance of the mental image the makers had of

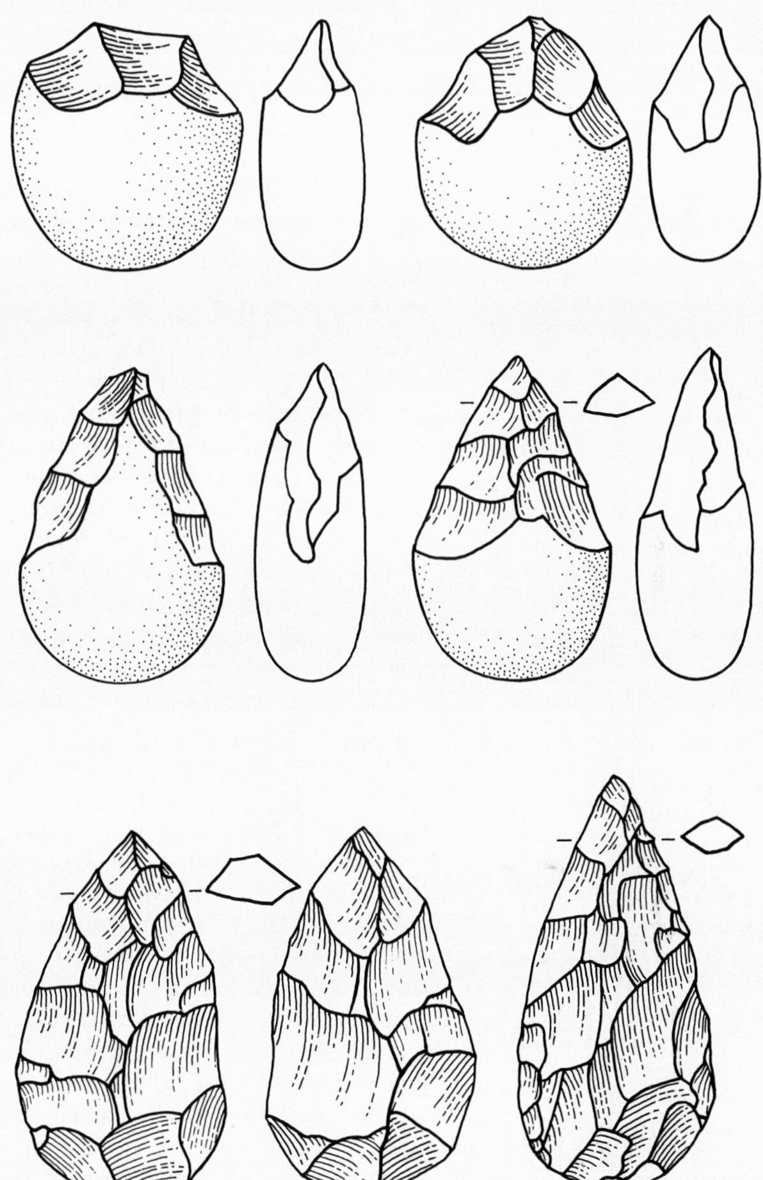

**Figure 3.29** The evolution of the handaxe, from simple pebble-tool forms through the removal of the sides and surface of the pebble. The elongated, teardrop shape is characteristic of the handaxe, giving the artifact one pointed end and one broad end.

*Man is a tool-using animal . . . without tools he is nothing, with tools he is all.*
—Thomas Carlyle (1795–1881)

what a handaxe should look like. The handaxes from Kilombe also document the skill the makers had in producing that image in stone.

Handaxes and associated tools are referred to as **Acheulean** artifacts, after the original find location at St. Acheul in northern France. Floods of meltwater at the end of each glacial period downcut the rivers of western Europe, creating a series of terraces in the river valleys. On those terraces during the nineteenth century, near the towns of Abbeville and St. Acheul, prehistorians collected these signature tools of the Lower Paleolithic. Objects on the higher, older terraces were crude handaxes, with irregular edges and heavy flake scars on their surface. Acheulean handaxes from the lower, younger terraces were more symmetrical with straighter edges. A stone-on-stone method, or **hard-hammer technique,** was used to make the more irregular tools of the early Acheulean. A **soft-hammer technique** was used in making the younger, more regular handaxes. Mallets of bone, antler, or even wood can be used to remove flakes from stone. Lighter, soft hammers are easier to control, and the flakes that are removed are both thinner and wider.

Acheulean assemblages include both handaxes and a variety of other tools, both heavy-duty pieces and smaller ones. **Cleavers**—handaxes with a broad, rather than pointed, leading edge—are also quite distinctive of the period. Other artifacts include a variety of flake tools such as scrapers, **burins** (stone tools used for gouging or engraving), and borers.

Fifty years ago, Harvard archaeologist Hallam Movius described the distribution of handaxes as limited to Africa, the southern two-thirds of Europe, and western Asia. More recent research, however, has expanded the known distribution of these tools; handaxes are now known from most of Africa, Asia, and Europe.

The term **Clactonian** refers to the nonhandaxe assemblages of the Lower Paleolithic. These assemblages represent what is called an evolved Oldowan series of artifacts, including simple pebble tools and flakes. The term is taken from the site of Clacton-on-Sea in England where this distinctive set of tools, with heavy choppers, notches, and denticulates (saw-toothed) but lacking handaxes, was found during the nineteenth century. Flake tools in these assemblages are generally blocky and irregular in shape. Clactonian assemblages lack the regularly shaped core and flake artifacts of the Acheulean. Clactonian tools appear to have been made quickly for special tasks.

The distinction between handaxe and nonhandaxe assemblages is of considerable interest to prehistorians, and its significance is still not clear. Mary Leakey found both kinds of assemblages, with and without handaxes, in the same levels of Bed II at Olduvai Gorge, suggesting that the differences in the assemblages are more likely due to the activities performed than to change over time. Research in England has documented the contemporaneity of Clactonian and Acheulean assemblages, so their differences do not seem to be related to one assemblage being earlier or later than the other. Some researchers have suggested that the differences between Clactonian and Acheulean were the result of the availability of raw material, handaxes being made only where good raw material could be found nearby. Nevertheless, the presence of both kinds of assemblages at Olduvai does not support such an interpretation. The actual reason for the presence or absence of handaxes on sites of the Lower Paleolithic has not been determined.

**handaxe** A large, teardrop-shaped stone tool bifacially flaked to a point at one end and a broader base at the other.

**reduction technique** In archaeology, a manufacturing process involving the removal (as opposed to the addition) of materials from a core that becomes the finished product.

**Acheulean** A major archaeological culture of the Lower Paleolithic, named after the site of St. Acheul in France.

**hard-hammer technique** A percussion technique for making stone tools by striking one stone, or core, with another stone, or hammer.

**soft-hammer technique** A flintknapping technique that involves the use of a hammer of bone, antler, or wood, rather than stone.

**cleaver** A tool with a broad leading edge.

**burin** A stone tool with right-angle edges used for planing and engraving.

**Clactonian** A term used for assemblages from the Lower Paleolithic, lacking handaxes and characterized by large flakes with heavy retouching and notches.

# *Images and Ideas*

## The End of the Lower Paleolithic

### Homo erectus *in the Old World*

*Homo erectus* appeared shortly after the beginning of the Pleistocene, around 1.9 m.y.a. These hominins invented the handaxe and other tools; controlled fire; spread the human lineage outside Africa for the first time, to many parts of Asia and Europe; and appear to have thrived during this time. This is all the more remarkable because the Pleistocene was a very difficult and challenging period, with major changes in climate, environment, sea level, and the basic conditions of human life.

It is essential to understand that during this time our ancestors began to exert their influence on their environment, to change the world around them. Clearly, the spread of early humans out of Africa was one of the most important developments in human prehistory. Following the initial appearance in southern and eastern Africa, the human species gradually increased in number and inhabited most of the more hospitable zones of the African continent. Population continued to expand, as did the geographic range of the species, and after almost 3 million years in Africa, groups of early humans began to move north toward Asia and Europe.

The move out of the tropics demanded solutions to new problems in northern regions, especially the cold weather and a shortage of edible plants. Groups that had survived easily in warm climates where roots, seeds, and nuts were often available had to find new and improved ways to stay warm and obtain enough food. Although an efficient cooling system for the tropics, sweat glands were of little help to furless humans in the chilly temperate reaches of the Old World. Almost certainly, fire, shelter, and clothing—if only in the form of animal skins wrapped around the body—were used by *Homo erectus* in the course of their northern expansion into the continents of Asia and Europe.

Fire must have been a major factor in the increasing success of human adaptation and the move into new, colder habitats. Recent evidence from the site of Gesher Benot Ya'Aqov in Israel has pushed back the earliest date for the intentional use of fire to around 800,000 years ago. Several types of wood were burned there, including willow, poplar, ash, and wild olive. Fire is used for light, warmth, protection, and cooking. Cooking with fire provides a number of advantages in addition to making food more tender and palatable. Cooking also improves the digestibility of many foods and destroys harmful toxins and microorganisms. Boiling removes juices and fats from plants and animals that are otherwise inedible. In general, the staple foods of humans are much more nutritionally rich than those of other large primates, who can subsist on leaves and fruit. Fire allows humans to make their food even more nutritional. Cooking changes the forms of starches, fats, and proteins and concentrates the nutrients in foods. High-nutrition diets were necessary for our human ancestors to meet the growing energy demands of their large brain.

For *Homo erectus,* cooking probably made it possible to add new foods to the diet. The use of marine resources also expanded the diet of some *H. erectus* groups, as fish and shellfish remains from the site of Terra Amata in France document. The seas are a very rich source of food, and one that must have been exploited in the Lower Paleolithic.

"Say, Thag ... wall of ice closer today?"

Figure 3.30 One of the remarkable, well-made spears of spruce wood from Schöningen, Germany, approximately 7 feet long and 400,000 years old.

Longer, colder winters in more northern latitudes also put a premium on successful predation. Meat was the primary source of sustenance during winter, when roots, nuts, leaves, and other edible plants were not available. Hunting became essential to the human way of life in colder climates. At least eight wooden spears have been found recently at the site of Schöningen in northern Germany dated to 400,000 years ago. The artifacts were found among abundant bone remains from butchered horses and several fire hearths (Figure 3.30). The spears have carved points and a length of 2.0–2.5 m (6.0–7.5 ft). The technology is impressive. The spears are made from the trunks of 30-year-old spruce trees, with the bark removed, and are sharpened at the base of the trunk, where the wood is hardest. The thickest and heaviest part of the carved shaft is about one-third of the distance from the spear point, as in a modern javelin. These weapons appear to have been designed for throwing. Such evidence indicates that the early Europeans were hunting large game by this time.

It is highly unlikely that many females burdened with infants and young children could successfully hunt regularly to provide their own food. By this time, a viable relationship between males and females, incorporating food-sharing as part of pair-bonding, necessarily emerged to ensure the continuance of the human lineage. Relationships between males and females and basic family structure must have been related to these essential, adaptive changes. These connections—individual to individual, male to female, parents to offspring, kin to kin, group to group—are critical links in the chain of human society and survival.

The **sexual division of labor** exemplifies the cooperative relationship between the sexes. Roles for males, faster and larger, as hunters and for females, with young children, as gatherers of wild plant foods emerged as an efficient, synergistic pattern for the maximization of biological capabilities. Sex, and maybe love, bonded males and females for food-sharing and reproduction; maternal instincts and extended childhoods bonded mothers to children and siblings to one another. We have no information on the precise nature of prehistoric male-female relationships—whether monogamous, several females to one male, or several males to one female. But the present universality of the human family suggests a substantial depth of time for this basic unit of society.

**sexual division of labor** The cooperative relationship between the sexes in hunter-gatherer groups involving different male and female task activity.

Almost certainly, some form of protofamily emerged among *Homo erectus* populations if not before. Pair-bonding may have helped ensure the survival of offspring, as males began to recognize individual children as their own. The incest taboo, another human universal, may well have arisen at the same time to promote and solidify relationships beyond the immediate group. Marriage or mating outside the family ensures alliances with other families and groups, reducing the potential for conflict. *Homo erectus,* as a creature of the Pleistocene, was a very successful member of our lineage, expanding out of Africa, taking the human species into Asia and Europe, and setting the stage for the next step in human evolution.

The evidence from the Lower Paleolithic essentially documents the appearance and spread of *Homo erectus* out of Africa and into Asia around 2 m.y.a. and then into Europe after 1 m.y.a. Discoveries at sites such as 'Ubeidiya and Dmanisi in Southwest Asia document the arrival of our ancestors at the crossroads of the Old World. Farther to the east, older investigations at Zhoukoudian evidence the arrival and activities of *erectus* groups in the east of Asia. The rigors of colder climate in much of Europe may have delayed the appearance of the first humans in this area by a million years. The first Europeans are not seen until after 1,000,000 B.P. in places such as Gran Dolina and Isernia, both in the Mediterranean part of the continent. The spears and animal prey from Schöningen boldly document our presence as big-game hunters. Back in Africa, the evidence from sites such as Kalambo Falls and Olorgesailie emphasizes our developing role as hunter-gatherers in the natural environment. Increasing brain size and more humanlike behaviors characterize the almost-2-million-year evolution of *Homo erectus.* Technology changed little during the Lower Paleolithic, but this time period took us from apelike to humanlike through the icy cauldron of the Pleistocene. The results of that transformation become much clearer with the arrival of *Homo sapiens,* described in the next chapter.

## DISCUSSION QUESTIONS

1. What are the major characteristics of the Lower Paleolithic period?
2. What dating techniques can be used to determine the age of fossils and artifacts from *Homo erectus* sites?
3. What are the major characteristics of the Pleistocene epoch, and what consequences did they have for human evolution?
4. What kinds of evidence did the first humans outside Africa leave behind?
5. Does the handaxe represent a conceptual or a technological advance?
6. What are some of the consequences of the domestication of fire for human survival?

**www.mhhe.com/priceip6e**

For more review material and study questions, see the self-quizzes on your online learning center.

## SUGGESTED READINGS

For Internet links related to this chapter, please visit our Web site at www.mhhe.com/priceip6e.

Carbonell, E., J. Castro, J. Pares, A. Perez-Gonzalez, G. Cuenca-Bescos, A. Olle, et al. (2008). The first hominin of Europe. *Nature* 452: 465–469. *A scientific report on the most recent finds of the oldest European.*

Gamble, C. 1999. *The Palaeolithic societies of Europe.* Cambridge: Cambridge University Press. *A summary of the European Paleolithic, including the first inhabitants.*

Klein, R. 1999. *The human career,* 2d ed. Chicago: University of Chicago Press. *Probably the most authoritative volume on the evolution of biology and culture in the Pleistocene.*

Larsen, C. S., R. M. Matter, and D. L. Cabo. 1998. *Human origins: The fossil record.* Longrove, IL: Waveland Press. *A very readable account of human evolution.*

Sutliffe, A. J. 1985. *On the track of Ice Age mammals.* Cambridge, MA: Harvard University Press. *A detailed study of the mammals of the Pleistocene.*

Tattersall, I., and J. H. Schwartz. 2001. *Extinct humans.* Boulder, CO: Westview. *How we know what we think we know about human evolution.*

# CHAPTER FOUR

**Figure 4.1** The Venus of Brassempouy, the small head of a woman carved in ivory, 3.65 cm high, ca. 25,000 years old, France.

# The Hunters

## Introduction
### The Rise of *Homo sapiens*

*Modern humans take the stage toward the end of the Pleistocene*

Figure 4.1 shows the face of an Upper Paleolithic woman, found in France, carved in ivory and dating to more than 20,000 years ago. It is one of the very few surviving portraits of early fully modern humans in the Pleistocene. It is a remarkable statement of the interests, abilities, and directions that human beings were exhibiting at that time.

Major changes in human behavior took place toward the end of the Pleistocene. For the first time, our ancestors began to exhibit behaviors that were more than just practical activities, beyond the basic necessities for survival. The genus and species *Homo sapiens* took the stage and became fully modern. In the Middle Paleolithic, those behaviors included burial of the dead, cannibalism, and nurturing of the weak and the elderly. By the end of the Pleistocene, our own species (*Homo sapiens sapiens*)—biologically indistinguishable from modern humans—had created art, invented many new tools, made tailored clothing, started counting, and spread to almost all parts of the world.

The evolution of *Homo sapiens* is the most important development of the later Pleistocene (Figure 4.2).As we have seen, *Homo erectus* was the first early human form found outside Africa. By 1.2 million years ago, *H. erectus* fossils are known in Europe and Asia; by 100,000 years ago, *H. sapiens* is present. *Erectus* became *sapiens* during that time. The earlier varieties of *Homo sapiens* are sometimes referred to as Archaic *Homo sapiens,* whereas more recent *Homo sapiens sapiens* are termed fully modern humans (FMH).

By 200,000 years ago, Europe and southwestern Asia were occupied by *Homo neanderthalensis* (or *Homo sapiens neanderthalensis* to some). Conventional wisdom today generally regards the Neanderthals as a rather specialized form that evolved from *Homo erectus* in the colder, more isolated areas of Europe (Figure 4.3). In the time of the Neanderthals, the Middle Paleolithic, new behaviors included burial of the dead, cannibalism, and nurturing of the weak and elderly.

The earliest fully modern humans have been found in East and South Africa. The earliest known example of *Homo sapiens* has been found at Kibish in southwestern Ethiopia, dating to 195,000 years ago. A new project at the Cape of Good Hope at the southern tip of Africa has provided remarkable new discoveries regarding our early fully modern human ancestors. The evidence from the caves around Pinnacle Point is not in the form of fossil skeletons but rather regards the behavior of these early *Homo sapiens.* Several finds—small stone tools, red ochre as a pigment, the earliest known collection and consumption of shellfish—point to new kinds of food, new tools that probably required hafting, and the use of powdered mineral as a pigment or preservative. These are firsts in the

**CHAPTER OUTLINE**

Figure 4.2 Human evolution in the Middle Pleistocene, 800,000–35,000 years ago. Current evidence suggests that *Homo erectus* expanded out of Africa into Asia sometime after 2 m.y.a. Fully modern human forms of *Homo sapiens sapiens* began to appear sometime after 200,000 years ago, again in Africa, moving to the Near East around 90,000 years ago and replacing the Neanderthals in Europe after 40,000 years ago.

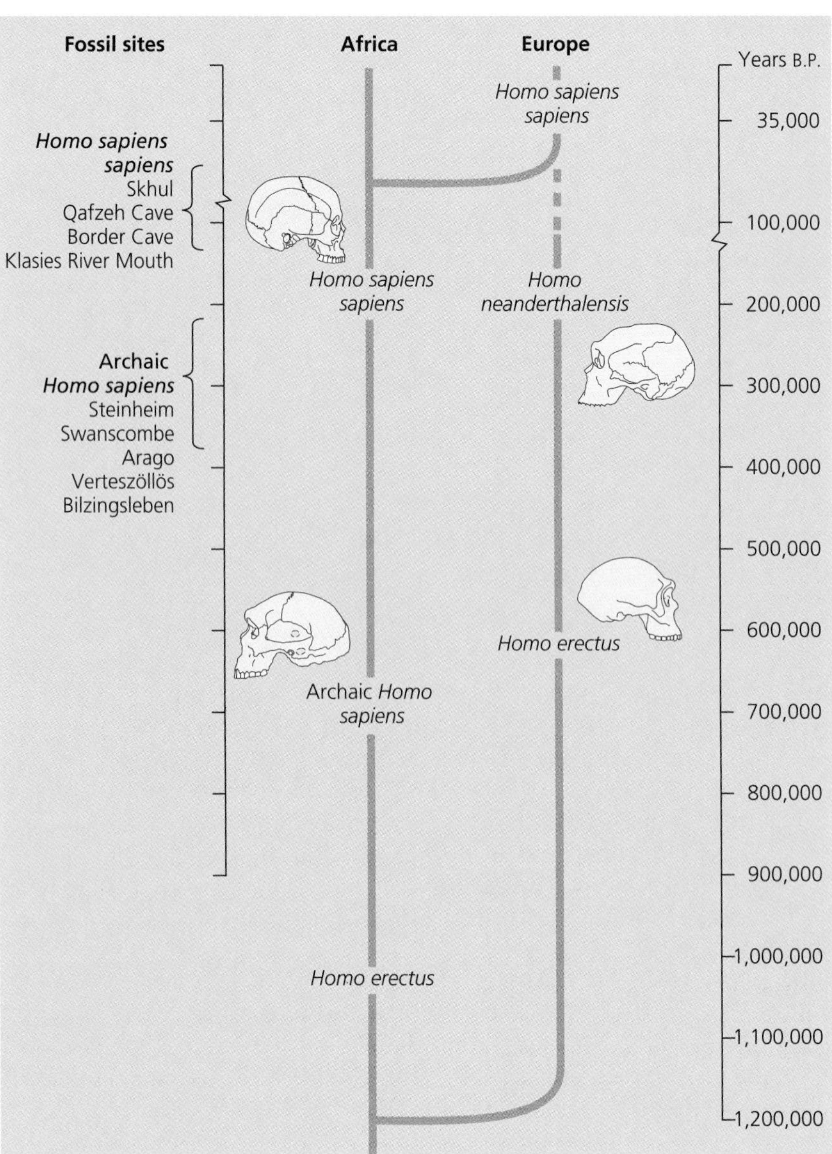


**www.mhhe.com/priceip6e**

For preview material for this chapter, see the comprehensive chapter outline and chapter objectives on your online learning center.

Figure 4.3 A computer reconstruction of a young Neanderthal male. Most noticeable is the long face.

archaeological record and likely point to the beginnings of the creative explosion witnessed more fully after 50,000 years ago.

Beginning around 50,000 years ago, fully modern humans replaced Neanderthals in southwestern Asia and then the rest of Asia and in Europe. The mechanism for this replacement is the subject of vigorous debate among archaeologists and physical anthropologists. The major question is whether fully modern humans evolved only in Africa and spread from there across Asia and Europe, or whether they evolved in many places through the flow of genetic material between different human populations. These two competing explanations are known as the Out of Africa theory and the Multiregional theory (Figure 4.4). Different lines of evidence, from genetics and from the human fossils themselves, can be used to evaluate these theories. Genetic evidence relies on mutation rates in individuals with slightly different DNA to estimate how long ago a common ancestor existed. Such estimates suggest 200,000–140,000 years ago as the date for a common ancestor for *Homo sapiens sapiens* and point to Africa as the place of origin (see "Modern and Ancient DNA," p. 114), and are close to the dates for the fossil evidence.

From both genetic and fossil evidence, then, it seems very likely that fully modern humans appeared initially in Africa, sometime around 200,000 years ago. These expanding groups of modern humans created a number of remarkable innovations in human culture. Human culture, in fact, changed more during the period shortly after 50,000 years ago than it had during the previous several million years.

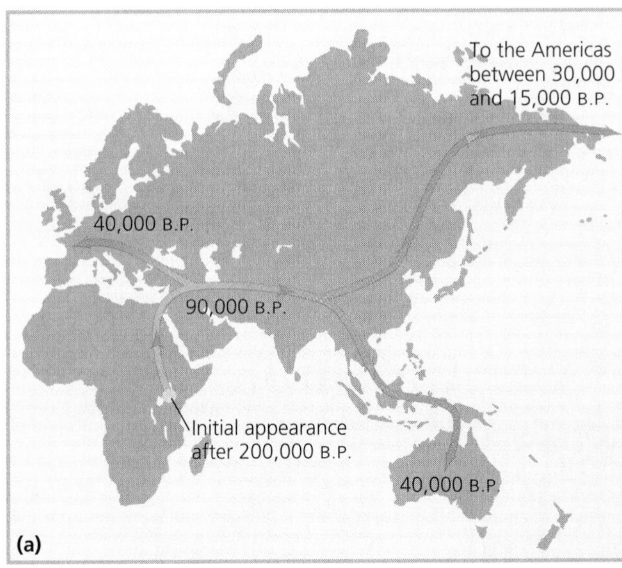


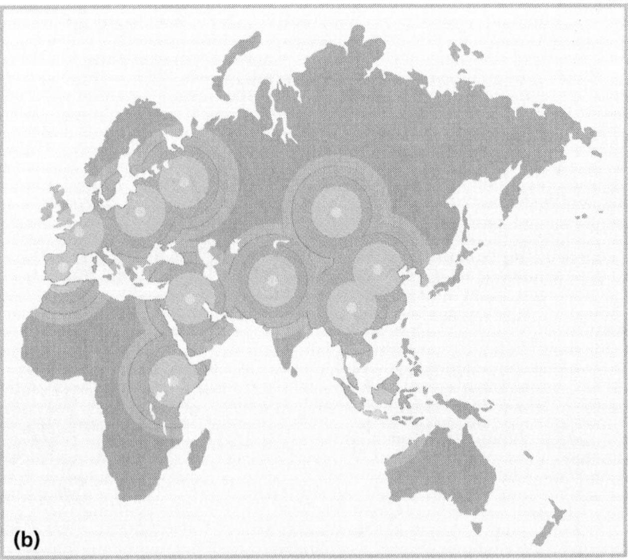


**Figure 4.4** The two major competing theories about the evolution of fully modern *Homo sapiens.* (a) The Out of Africa theory involves the evolution of *H. sapiens* from *H. erectus* in Africa and the spread of that species. (b) The Multiregional theory argues that *H. sapiens* evolved from *H. erectus* in several places and that interbreeding kept them similar. Most of the archaeological and genetic evidence supports the Out of Africa theory.

Richard Klein, of Stanford University, has listed some of the innovations that mark this time: the shaping of new materials such as bone, wood, shell, and ivory into tools; the transport or exchange of raw materials, such as flint, over long distances; great diversity and specialization in artifacts; and the first art. In Europe, this period is known as the Upper Paleolithic, dating from 40,000 to 10,000 years ago. In this same general time, modern humans spread into Australia and New Guinea (around 40,000 years ago) and into North and South America (perhaps 15,000 years ago). Klein and others have suggested that these innovations represent a major change in the organization of the human brain, an advance that may be related to the emergence of complex language skills (see "The Origins of Language," p. 109).

Other changes were taking place as well. A new line of evidence concerning the use of clothing in the Paleolithic comes from a surprising source: the genetic code of lice. There are two kinds of lice in this story—head lice, which live in the hair on the head and have been around for millions of years, and body lice, which live in clothing, not on the body, and are a relatively recent species. Using mutation rates in modern lice genes, Mark Stoneking and his associates estimated that the body louse first appeared between 72,000 and 42,000 years ago. Humans must have been wearing clothing at that time to provide a habitat for this new species.

As fully modern humans evolved in Africa, one assumes that their skin color was dark, pigmented by the genes for skin color as protection against the sun. As *Homo sapiens* migrated out of Africa into Asia and Europe, clothing would have become more important as protection against the rigors of Pleistocene winters. A recent study of a gene skin color suggests that the appearance of pale skin in European populations may be quite recent, perhaps only in the past 10,000 years.

This chapter tells the story of the Neanderthals and of the appearance, expansion, and spread of *Homo sapiens* to virtually all parts of the world, as evidenced at sites such as Klasies River Mouth in South Africa, the Neander Valley in Germany, Shanidar in northern Iraq, Dolni Vestonice in the Czech Republic, and Lascaux and Pincevent in France (Figure 4.5). The evidence from Lake Mungo in Australia and from Monte Verde, Lindenmeier, and Kennewick in the Americas documents the movement of humans to Australia and the New World during the past 40,000 years. (A useful distinction is often made between the Old World—Africa, Asia, and Europe—and the New World of North and South America. The New World is conventionally considered new because it was discovered by Europeans at a relatively late date.)

The Pleistocene and the Paleolithic came to an end some 10,000 years ago. The glaciers retreated as warmer temperatures prevailed, and our present epoch began. The Paleolithic closed as the human species on six continents began to adapt to the warmer conditions of the post-Pleistocene, or Postglacial, as it is also known.

**www.mhhe.com/priceip6e**

For a Web-based activity on the controversy surrounding the emergence of our species, see the Internet exercises on your online learning center.

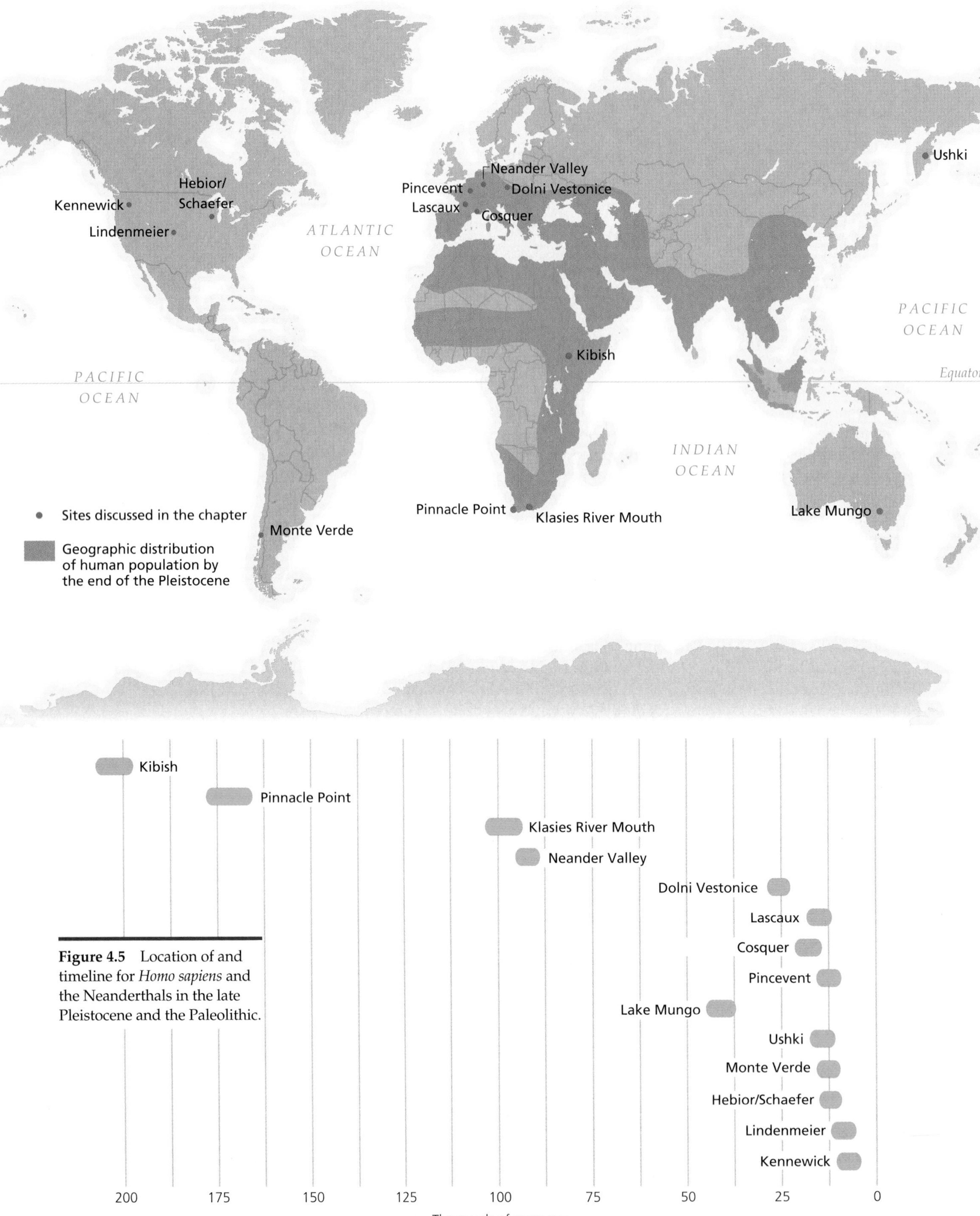


**Figure 4.5** Location of and timeline for *Homo sapiens* and the Neanderthals in the late Pleistocene and the Paleolithic.

Concept

# The Origins of Language

## Why *we first spoke may be more important than* when

The origin of human speech and language is one of the most fascinating aspects of human adaptation and evolution, yet perhaps the most difficult to explain. Modern languages contain hundreds of thousands of words. We use words to convey information about every aspect of our lives. Shakespeare's vocabulary is estimated to have been 24,000 words; a newspaper reporter uses approximately 6000 words; the average person on the street has a speaking vocabulary of some 3000 words.

We have a natural interest in when and where this ability to communicate with the spoken word originated. Language did not appear suddenly at some point in the past, without antecedents; it evolved gradually from the utterances and cries of early primates to its modern forms. On the one hand, the English language today is a huge complex of vocabulary, grammar, and structure, to which many new words are added each year. On the other hand, most animals make sounds. Monkeys vocalize to express emotion but do not have voluntary control over vocalization; for one thing, they lack the vocal apparatus humans have (Figure 4.6). Chimpanzees, however, have a repertoire of 20 or more vocalizations and gestures for expressing their needs. Although these apes can manipulate symbols, they are unable to connect more than two or three concepts in a single phrase. To understand the evolution of language from gestures and cries to its complexity today, we must appreciate the path of its development.

Studies of the physical remains of early humans provide substantial information about language use by early hominins. Discovery of the hyoid bone in a Neanderthal burial from Kebara Cave in Israel showed that it was no different from our own. The **hyoid bone** holds the muscles of the tongue to the throat. The similarity between the hyoid bone in Neanderthal and in modern-looking *Homo sapiens* suggests that speaking abilities would also have been similar.

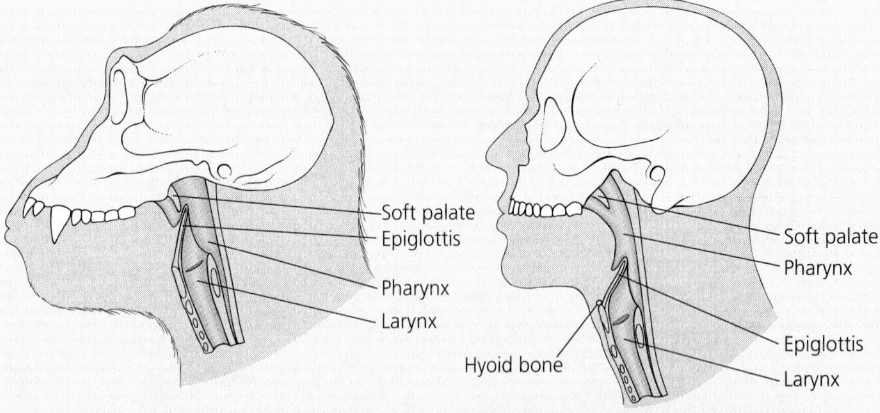


**Figure 4.6** The vocal apparatus of a chimpanzee (left) compared with that of a modern human (right). Notice the more complex vocal cords in humans. The human pharynx is more curved, is deeper in the throat, and produces a great variety of sounds.

**Endocasts** of the inside of the skull provide the only direct evidence of brain organization (Figure 4.7). The cerebrum, the upper portion of the brain, is primarily concerned with the complexities of behavior. This area is large and developed in higher primates. The size of the cerebrum, its convoluted surface, and the extent of wrinkling have increased over the course of evolution of the human species from our primate ancestors.

The organization of the cerebrum is critically important. In modern humans, the front of the brain is much larger than the back, and the sides of the brain are well developed, in contrast to the brains of chimpanzees and other apes. The two sides of our brain operate cooperatively to direct and control different aspects of our behavior and activities. This division in the organization and operation of the brain is called **lateralization.** One side of the brain controls language, and the other side regulates motor skills and perception. Lateralization is essential for language, because the processing of word

**hyoid bone** A delicate bone in the neck that anchors the tongue muscles in the throat.

**endocast** A copy or cast of the inside of a skull, reflecting the general shape and arrangement of the brain and its various parts.

**lateralization** The division of the human brain into two halves.

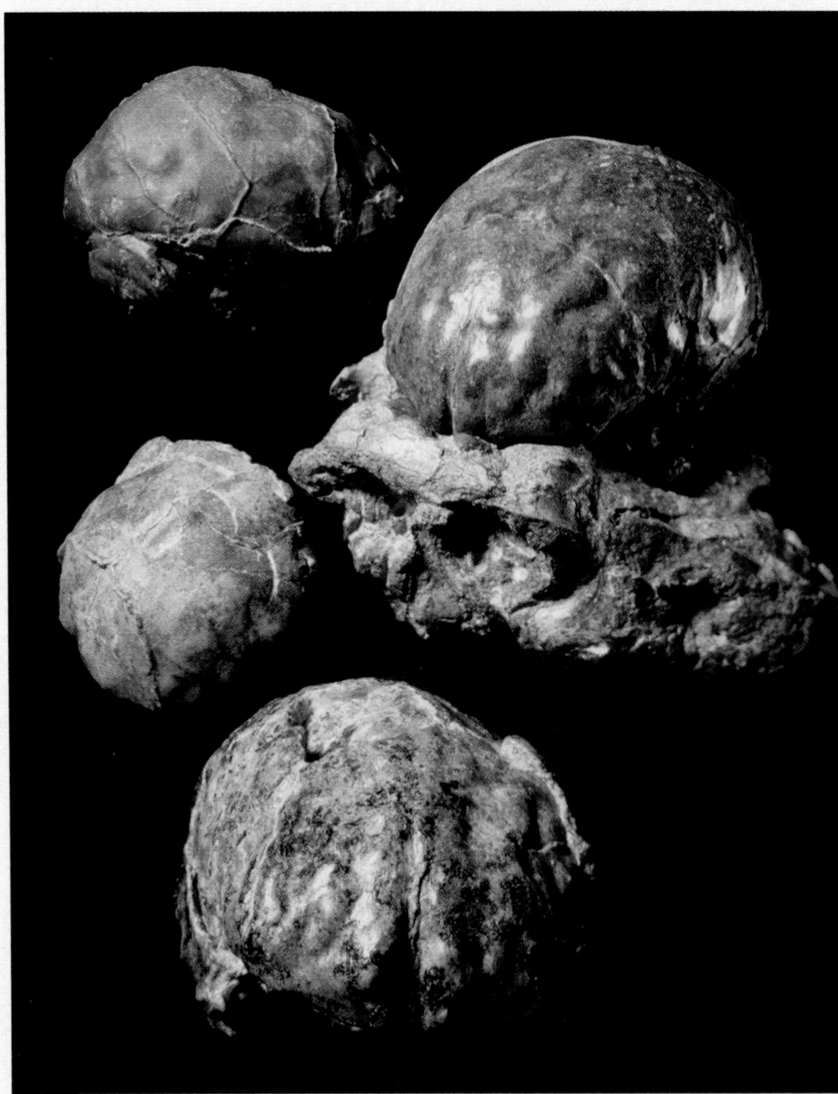

**Figure 4.7** Endocasts from South African australopithecines. Notice the details of the blood vessels and other features of the brain that have been preserved in the fossil casts.

strings must occur in close proximity in the nerve cells of the brain. Individuals with speech problems are probably sequencing words and controlling speech from both sides of the brain.

Studies by Ralph Holloway, of Columbia University, have shown that the pattern of lateralization in fossil endocasts goes back well into the Pleistocene and probably to australopithecines as well. Dean Falk, of the State University of New York, has also been involved in the study of endocasts, pointing out that Broca's area, a region of the brain involved in the control of language, is larger in *Homo habilis* than in their contemporaries, the australopithecines from East Africa.

Research on human use of language has recently turned to the hypoglossal nerve, which controls the movement of the tongue. This nerve is twice as thick in humans as in chimpanzees. This thick nerve began to appear around 500,000 years ago with larger-brained members of the genus *Homo*, and it may be at that point that more sophisticated language became possible. Other fossil evidence indicates that the necessary mouth and throat anatomy for a spoken language was not in place until 150,000 years ago. It is still not clear when language emerged or whether the process was gradual or sudden.

Certainly, many of the activities of our early Pleistocene ancestors would have required some form of communication. Food-sharing, social organization, and other distinctly human characteristics imply a system of verbal expression. These abilities must have evolved and expanded through time, as both brainpower permitted and need required.

One of the major unresolved issues in the development of language is the shift from a primitive language, like that of small children, to a syntactic one, with grammatical rules and structure. This development may be related in part to further changes in the human brain. Some linguists suggest that all the world's languages evolved from a common "mother tongue," and a few would even suggest a date of 100,000 years ago for this common language. Needless to say, this is highly speculative, but it does suggest that future research may provide more information on the development of human languages. One of the more striking developments in human prehistory was the "creative explosion" that occurred about 50,000 years ago, around the beginning of the Upper Paleolithic. The changes witnessed in this period may well be related to significant advances in our language abilities.

# The Klasies River Mouth Caves

## *One of the longest continuous sequences of human habitation in the world*

A series of caves cluster at the mouth of the Klasies (CLASS-ease) River where it empties into the Indian Ocean in South Africa (Figures 4.8 and 4.9). The caves were originally cut by wave action against the high sandstone and shale cliffs in this area at a time when sea level was higher than it is today. The caves and the sandy area in front of them were a hospitable place for human residence for more than 60,000 years, from 120,000 to about 60,000 years ago. Occupation remains were so abundant here that the accumulated debris in one of the caves had completely buried the opening of a lower cave. The attractions of the site for repeated residence included the shelter of the caves; the moderate climate; the immediate availability of marine foods such as shellfish, seals, and even beached whales; nearby fresh water; access to large and small mammals living along the river; and good-quality stone for toolmaking.

The 60,000 years of deposits are 20 m (65 ft) deep (the height of a 6-story building) and span the entire Middle Stone Age (MSA) of southern Africa (Table 4.1). (In Africa, the terms *Early, Middle,* and *Late Stone Age* are used to distinguish the archaeological divisions of the Paleolithic.) Although the deposits at the Klasies River Mouth are enormously deep, they accumulated at a rate of only 5–10 cm (2–4 in) every 100 years.

**Figure 4.8** Caves 3 and 4 at Klasies River Mouth, along the southern coast of South Africa.

**Figure 4.9** The Klasies River Mouth area coastline, showing the location of caves, artifacts, and resources.

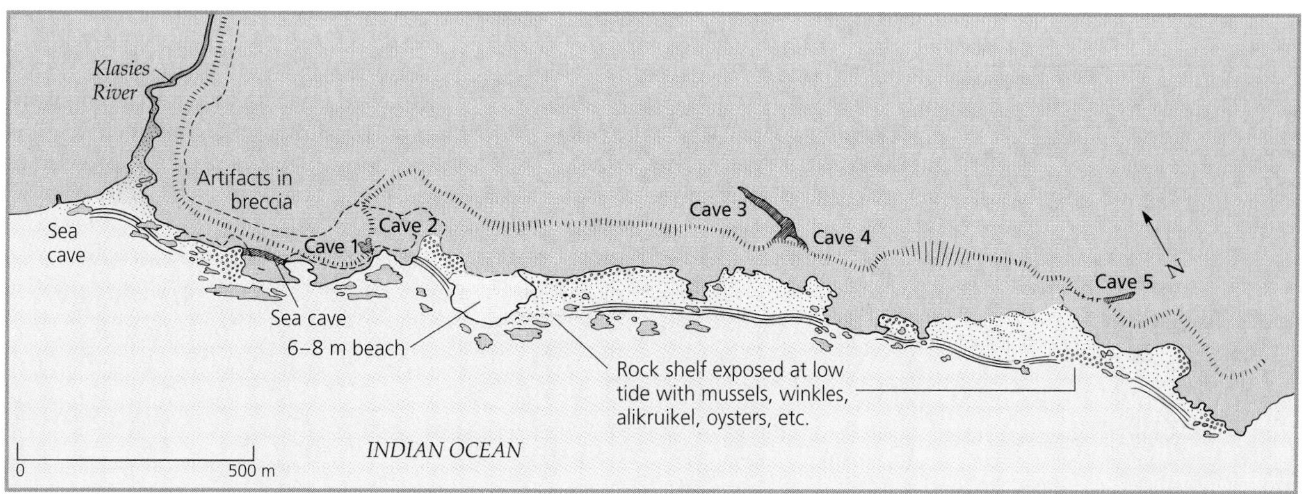

**TABLE 4.1 Sequence of Layers and Corresponding Changes in the Environment at Klasies River Mouth**

| *Age* | *Period* | *Deposits* | *Environment/Resources* |
|---|---|---|---|
| 10,000 B.P. | Later Stone Age | Sand with thin layers of silt and clay | Seacoast 60 km distant; some limpets |
| | No archaeology | | |
| 70,000 B.P. | Middle Stone Age III | Shell middens and sand | Cooler and wetter, drop in sea level; shellfish (mussels, turbot); open grasslands |
| | Middle Stone Age IIb | Shell middens and sand | |
| | Middle Stone Age IIa | Shell middens and sand; rubble and artifacts in cave | Cooler; increased forest and bush; marine species: seals, birds, dolphins, whales, limpets |
| 120,000 B.P. | Middle Stone Age I | Shell middens and sand | High sea level; temperate; mixed forest/grassland; seals, dolphins, penguins, shellfish (limpets and mussels) |

Dating these deposits is difficult. The lower layers are beyond the range of radiocarbon dating. Other dating techniques have been employed, including oxygen isotope ratios (see "Climate and Environment in the Pleistocene," Chapter 3, p. 81). Geological cores removed from deep ocean sediments contain microscopic shells that can be measured for water temperature. It is thus possible to construct graphs of changing water temperature extending hundreds of thousands of years into the past. It is also possible to measure the oxygen isotope ratio in shells found in archaeological sites. The shells in stratigraphic layers from the Klasies River Mouth (KRM) Caves were measured and the results compared with the ocean sediment curve for which the age was already known. This correlation and other dating methods—including electron spin resonance, uranium disequilibrium, and amino acid dating—suggest that the age of the MSA deposits extends from 120,000 to 60,000 years.

Excavations over a number of years by Ronald Singer and John Wymer, of the University of Chicago, and Hilary Deacon, of the University of Stellenbosch in South Africa, have exposed the buried occupation layers and revealed a number of pieces of evidence of major importance for understanding Old World prehistory. Fully modern humans (*Homo sapiens sapiens*) appeared here earlier than anywhere else in the world. A handful of fossil fragments from KRM and other sites in South Africa indicate that modern-looking humans were present in this area by 100,000 years ago. The human remains from Klasies are fragmentary and show breakage, cutmarks, and burning that suggest cannibalism.

Evidence from animal bones, studied by Richard Klein of Stanford University, documents a successful economy throughout the Middle Stone Age. A wide range of animal species is represented, and both large and small mammals were abundant (Figure 4.10). Porcupine, grysbok (a small antelope), eland (a large antelope), giant buffalo, rock hyrax (a small mammal), and the Cape fur seal were the most common. The site also records the early use of marine foods, evidenced by limpet and mollusk shells, and the bones of penguins and seals. The shells could have been collected all along the coast by wading at low tide. There are abundant carbonized organic remains in the deposits, and Deacon believes that these may represent roots and tubers that were collected and eaten by the inhabitants.

The faunal evidence from KRM can also be used to examine the hunting abilities of these Stone Age people in South Africa. Consider two possible patterns of death in a population of animals: (1) attritional, in which death is by natural causes, such as predation,

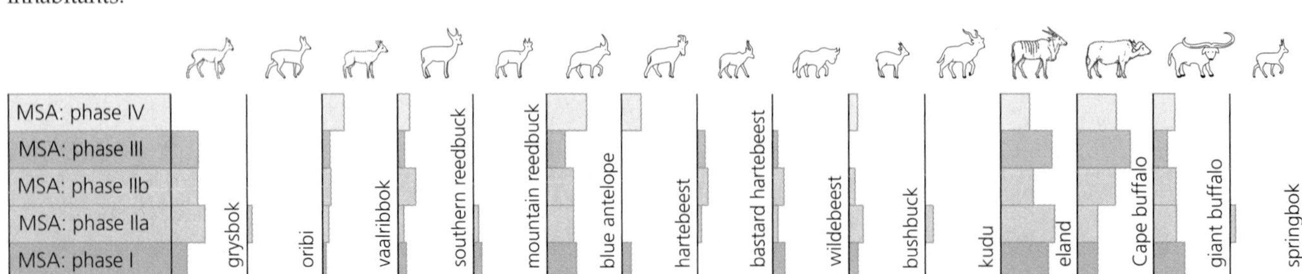


**Figure 4.10** Changing utilization of species over time at Klasies River Mouth documents the variety of species that were hunted by the inhabitants.

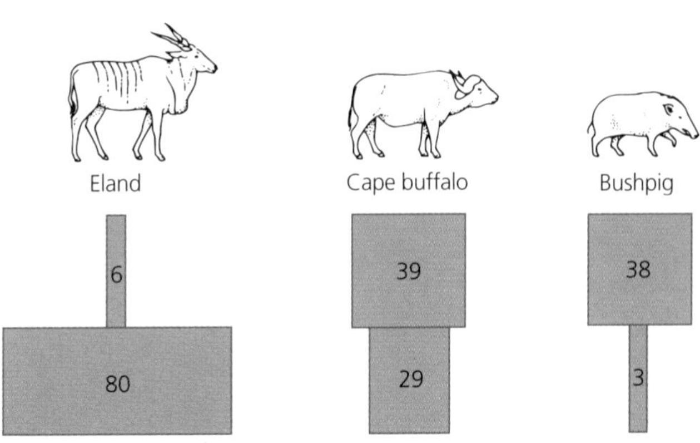


**Figure 4.11** The minimum number of eland, Cape buffalo, and bushpig at the sites of Klasies River Mouth and Nelson Bay Cave. Buffalo and bushpig are more difficult to hunt, and their abundance in the Holocene deposits of Nelson Bay Cave likely reflects the better technology of the more recent hunters.

disease, accident, and old age; and (2) catastrophic, in which a natural disaster, such as flood, epidemic, or mass hunting, simultaneously kills most of the members of the population. The catastrophic pattern would provide an almost complete picture of the ages and sexes of the living population, whereas an attritional pattern would be dominated by young and old animals, those more susceptible to predation and disease. Prime-age adults would be largely missing in the attritional pattern.

Comparison of the remains of two species of animals from KRM indicates that the eland, a large antelope, is represented by the catastrophic pattern, whereas the pattern for Cape buffalo is attritional. The eland is a relatively docile animal that can be driven into traps or falls by hunters, which probably explains the catastrophic death pattern. Cape buffalo are much more recalcitrant and dangerous. The high proportion of young in the pattern for the Cape buffalo was likely the result of selective hunting. Thus, animals that could be driven are represented by catastrophic death patterns, whereas more aggressive species were probably hunted individually with weapons. The higher number of elands at KRM, even though this species was much less common than the Cape buffalo in the environment, suggests that the MSA people were not particularly good hunters and that drives may have been more effective than stalking.

If we compare the remains of these two species from a younger site at nearby Nelson Bay Cave, dating to perhaps 10,000 years ago, we see that the death pattern for the buffalo is the same and that eland remains are very rare (Figure 4.11). This pattern suggests that the later groups were better hunters than their counterparts at the KRM caves. The argument is supported by evidence for bows and arrows at the time of the Nelson Bay Cave occupation.

On the other hand, Deacon believes that people of the Middle and the Late Stone Age were behaviorally similar, hunting smaller animals and both hunting and scavenging larger ones. Artifacts, hearths, bones, and shells are found in the oldest layers right next to the human skeletal remains dating to approximately 120,000 years ago. Shellfish, mostly brown mussel, were collected in quantity, and shell middens accumulated. One of the shell middens is approximately 5 m (16 ft) high and is as extensive as any Late Stone Age midden. This evidence is important because it shows regular shellfish collecting by the inhabitants and also systematic disposal of food refuse in localized heaps. This pattern suggests that people were living by the same rules for the use of space and cleanliness in both the Middle and the Late Stone Age.

Deacon points out that the large mammal bones and shell middens are the most obvious food remains. Remains of plant foods appear as carbonized materials around the hearths and indicate that plant gathering was also an important activity. It is this carbonized material that creates distinctive black horizons that are common features at the site. Deacon reports similar patterns of carbonized vegetation around the hearths of more recent inhabitants of South Africa. Deacon's perspective suggests that the general way of life in this area may not have changed from 100,000 years ago until the end of the Pleistocene.

*Concept*

# Modern and Ancient DNA

## *Archaeology and genes*

www.mhhe.com/priceip6e

For a Web-based activity on how the study of genetics impacts our understanding of modern human evolution, see the Internet exercises on your online learning center.

DNA (deoxyribonucleic acid) is the genetic material of all life. DNA is a long molecular chain of units called nucleotides, each composed of one of four base units (adenine, cytosine, guanine, or thymine). There are some 50,000 genes in the DNA of a human being. Genetic information is coded in a sequence of nucleotides in individual genes. Individual genes that determine the growth and characteristics of individuals are segments of DNA molecules. Molecules of DNA also have "intergenic" spaces between genes with no biological information that are important as markers for differences between individuals and between populations.

Two major types of studies, focused on either modern or ancient DNA, are being done to investigate the human past. Modern populations are studied to identify genetic differences and the time at which groups of people diverged in the past. These studies generally use DNA in blood or other cells. DNA studies of modern populations have been used to estimate the time of the first appearance of modern-looking humans and to examine the spread of Neolithic farmers into Europe, for example.

Evidence from genetic studies also provides some understanding of the point at which different animal species separated—for example, when humans became a species distinct from an apelike ancestor. Biological scientists have developed a "molecular clock" to estimate the number of years since different modern species separated from a common ancestor (Figure 4.12). The mechanism for this clock is the changes over time in the amino acids that make up DNA. Known as nucleotide substitutions, these changes are observed as

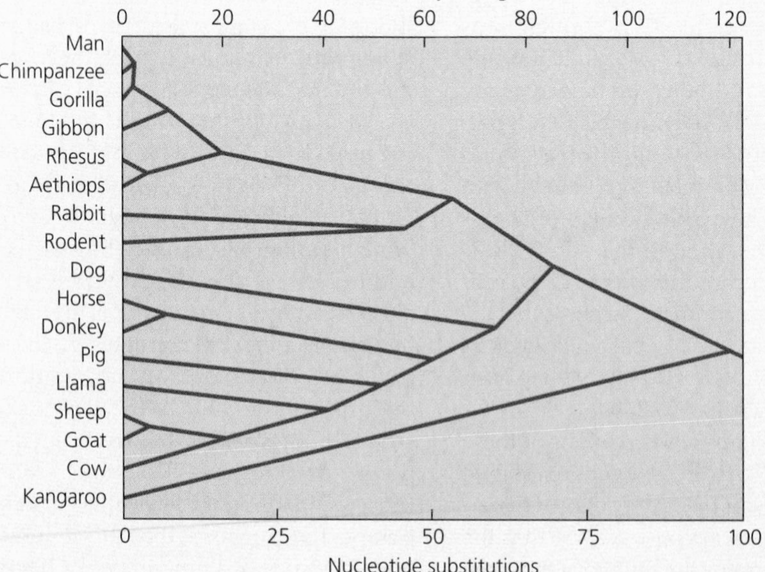


**Figure 4.12** Relative distances among various modern species as determined by nucleotide substitutions. The number of substitutions is shown at the bottom of the tree graph, and the estimated age of the divergence between two species and their common ancestor is shown at the top. For example, cows and dogs probably separated from a common ancestor around 70 m.y.a.

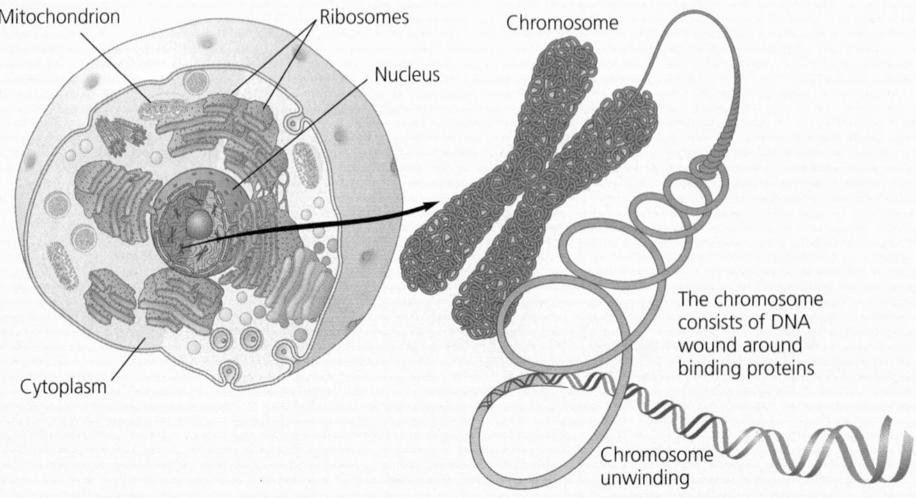


**Figure 4.13** DNA is found both in the nucleus (central core) of cells and in floating structures within the cell known as mitochondria.

mismatches in the genetic material of two species. The number of mismatches in the chromosomes of two species correlates closely with the evolutionary distance between the species and the amount of time they have been separate.

Our closest relatives are the chimpanzee and the gorilla. Comparison of amino acid sequences in humans, chimps, and gorillas indicates that the three species diverged between 5 and 4 m.y.a.—a date very close to that for the earliest fossil hominins.

There is also intriguing modern genetic evidence regarding the evolution of *Homo sapiens sapiens*. This evidence comes from studies of **mitochondrial DNA** (mtDNA), genetic material that is assumed to mutate at a relatively rapid and constant rate (Figure 4.13). Because this type of DNA is inherited directly through the maternal line, it provides a continuous trail back into the past. Graphing mutations in mtDNA results in a tree with the oldest changes as the trunk and more recent mutations as the branches. The number of mutations separating two individuals should be a function of how far back in time they shared a common maternal ancestor.

Analysis of this DNA from a number of women from around the world allows a map to be drawn of the spread of modern *Homo sapiens* after 200,000 years ago (Figure 4.14). On the basis of the number of accumulated mutations in the mtDNA, researchers concluded that *Homo sapiens* first appeared in southern Africa between 170,000 and 130,000 years ago. This is known as the "African Eve" hypothesis. Similar studies of the Y chromosome, present only in males, have indicated a similar date of divergence, around 200,000 years ago. These studies also suggest that modern humans moved out of Africa around 130,000 years ago, into Asia after 70,000 years ago, and into Europe after 50,000 years ago. Modern humans arrived in Australia after 40,000 years ago and came to the New World after 30,000 years ago.

The second kind of study involves **ancient DNA,** genetic material in the nucleus of cells extracted from the remains of ancient plants and animals.

**mitochondrial DNA** Genetic material in the mitochondria of human cells that mutates at a relatively constant rate.

**ancient DNA** Genetic material preserved in archaeological remains of bones and plants that can be studied for information about past genetic relationships.

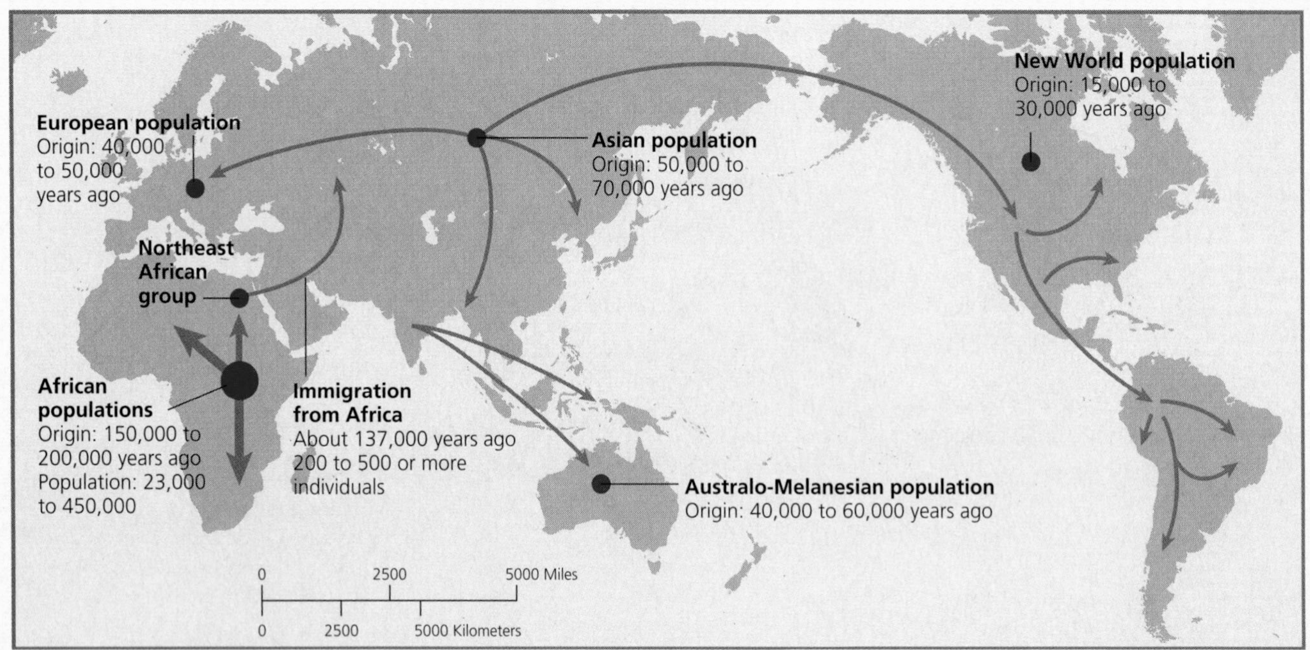


**Figure 4.14** Analysis of modern mitochondrial DNA provides a map of the origin and movement of modern humans from Africa across the continents of the Old and the New World.

Discovery of DNA preserved in prehistoric human bone was first reported in 1989. Since that time, numerous studies have looked for and found DNA in ancient materials. Samples from human bone, for example, can provide information on the sex or genealogy of an individual or on genetic relationships between populations and migration. In many cases, molecules in ancient DNA have been damaged by decay and degradation over time and are found often as short segments of the larger molecule. This breakdown of the molecule makes it more difficult, but not impossible, to reconstruct original genetic information.

Analysis of ancient DNA has been made possible by the development of the technique known as the polymerase chain reaction (PCR), which results in the cloning of large quantities of material for analysis even when only a very small sample is available—often the case with archaeological remains. Theoretically, even a single molecule, as well as badly degraded segments of molecules, can be analyzed with the help of the PCR technique.

Contamination is a significant problem. Since only small amounts of ancient DNA are present in samples, any contamination from living humans during excavation or laboratory analysis can mask or hide the prehistoric materials. Researchers must use great caution when removing and preparing samples for such analyses, and most researchers insist on duplication of their results in another laboratory.

# The Valley of the Neanderthals

## *Close relatives with strange habits*

In 1856, 3 years before Charles Darwin published his extraordinary treatise *On the Origin of Species,* proposing natural selection as a mechanism for evolution, pieces of an unusual skeleton were unearthed in a limestone cave in the valley of the Neander River, near Düsseldorf, Germany. Before this discovery, there had been no acceptance of human forms earlier than *Homo sapiens* and only limited awareness of a concept such as human evolution. Leading authorities first described the bones from the Neander Valley as those of a deceased Prussian soldier, a victim of Noah's flood, or a congenital idiot—but definitely not an early human ancestor. Gradually, however, more examples of these individuals came to light. In 1886, at the cave of Spy (pronounced "spee") in Belgium, two similar skeletons were discovered in association with early stone tools and the bones of extinct animals, clearly proving the antiquity of humans in Europe.

In 1913, French physical anthropologist Marcellin Boule published a study of an arthritic Neanderthal skeleton from the site of La Chapelle-aux-Saints (Figure 4.15). In this report, he described the finds from Europe as a new species, designated *Homo neanderthalensis.* Unfortunately, Boule did not acknowledge the discoveries of *Homo erectus* from Java and saw the Neanderthals as somewhere between ape and human. In Boule's own words (translated from the French), "The brutish appearance of this muscular and clumsy body, and of the heavy-jawed skull, declares the predominance of a purely vegetative or bestial kind over the functions of the mind" (1913). His work resulted in a view of Neanderthals as slow in wit, gait, and habit—an idea that continues in some quarters even today.

Gradually, however, as more *Homo erectus* and australopithecine specimens were reported and accepted into the family tree, Neanderthals came to be recognized as closer to modern humans. Today, they are usually classified as a member of our own genus but are distinguished at the species level, as *Homo neanderthalensis.*

**Figure 4.15** A Neanderthal skeleton from La Chapelle-aux-Saints, France, discovered early in the twentieth century. The femur and the vertebrae are deformed by arthritis. These remains led the scientist Marcellin Boule to describe Neanderthals as brutish and slow in wit, gait, and habit.

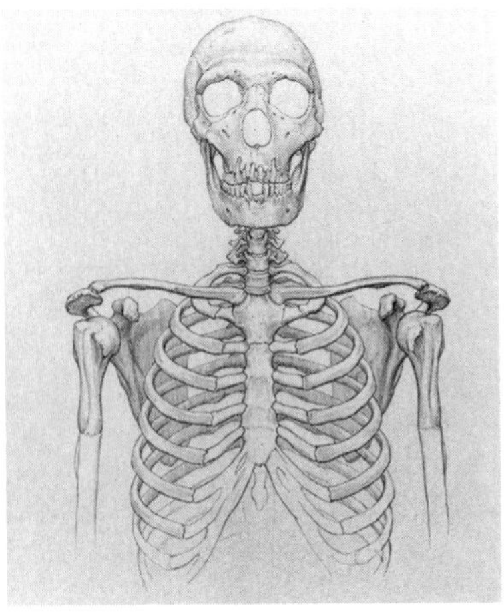

**TABLE 4.2 Major Characteristics of Neanderthals Compared with Modern Humans**

| *Trait* | Homo neanderthalensis | Homo sapiens sapiens |
|---|---|---|
| Forehead | Sloping | Vertical |
| Brow ridges | Moderate | Absent |
| Face | Slightly forward | Below forehead |
| Cranial capacity | 1450 cc | 1400 cc |
| Protrusion on back of skull | Present | Absent |
| Chin | Absent | Present |
| Appearance of skeleton | Robust | Gracile |

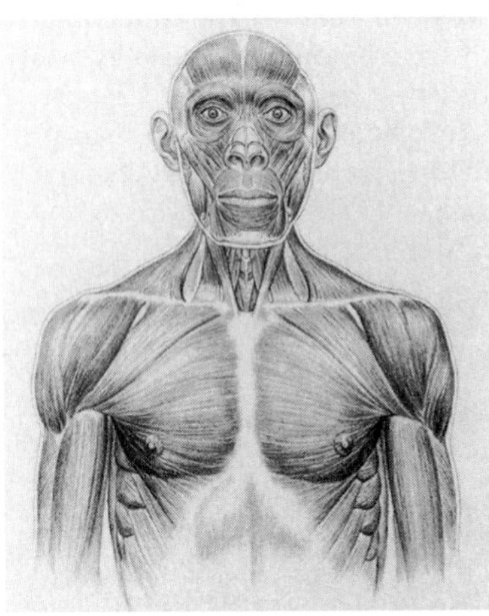

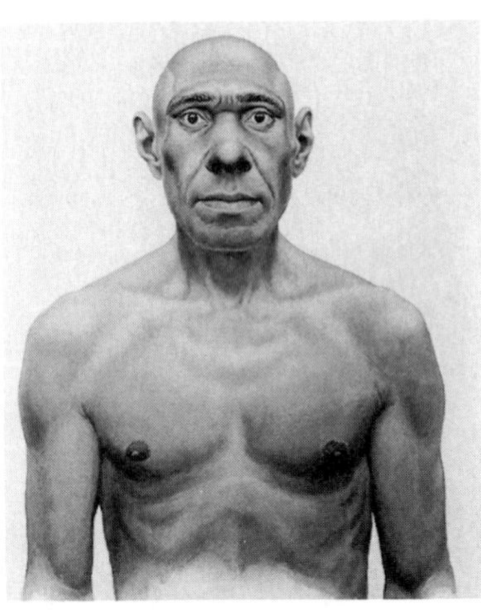

**Figure 4.16** A reconstruction of the soft tissue on a Neanderthal skeleton. Forensic scientists have studied the attachment of muscle, fat, and skin to the bones of the face and skull and are able to reconstruct a likeness of a deceased individual. Such skills have been applied to a Neanderthal, with the result shown here. Body hair was intentionally not added to the reconstruction, with the exception of the eyebrows.

Neanderthals were short and stocky, averaging about 1.5 m (5 ft) in height, with bowed limbs and large joints supporting a powerful physique (Figure 4.16; see also Figure 4.21). Fossil skeletons of Neanderthals are recognized today by several distinctive features in the skull and teeth (Table 4.2). The cranium is relatively low, and the face is long. Prominent **brow ridges**—bony protrusions above the eyes—and generally heavy bone structure give the skull a distinctive look (Figure 4.17). The face is large, the forehead slopes sharply backward, and the nose and the teeth sit farther forward than in any other hominin, giving the entire face an elongated appearance. This face is probably the result of a combination of factors, including adaptation to the cold. The average brain size of the Neanderthals is slightly larger than that of modern humans, probably a consequence of their heavier bone structure. A distinctive shelf or protrusion at the back of the Neanderthal skull is known as an **occipital bun.**

The front teeth are often heavily worn, even the deciduous teeth of young children, suggesting that they were used for grasping or heavy chewing. Intriguing small scratches often occur on the front teeth, usually running diagonally. These marks are thought to be the result of "stuff-and-cut" eating habits, in which a piece of meat was grasped in the teeth and a stone knife was used to cut off a bite-size piece at the lips. Occasionally the knife must have slipped and scratched the enamel of the front teeth. Most of the scratches run from upper right to lower left, although about 10% are in the opposite direction. Such evidence confirms that right- or left-handedness among humans was common by this time.

The skeleton of the Neanderthals differs somewhat from that of fully modern forms, although they had the same posture, dexterity, and mobility. Neanderthal bones are generally described as **robust;** they had heavier limb bones than fully modern humans, suggesting much greater muscular strength and a more powerful grip. This strength is also evident in the shoulder blades and neck, and on the back of the skull, where heavy muscle attachments are noticeable. Shoulder blade muscles would have provided the Neanderthals with strong, controlled downward movements for making stone tools or thrusting spears.

The robust appearance of the Neanderthals may be related to the strength and endurance required for long-distance travel over irregular terrain or to climate. Study of the Neanderthal body indicates that their stout shape is similar to that of the Eskimo, perhaps reflecting an adaptation to cold temperatures. Or perhaps Neanderthals had to be stronger to accomplish physically what fully modern humans accomplished with sophisticated tools. Neanderthal skeletons exhibit more traumatic damage, especially to the head and neck, from accident or violence than many modern populations, perhaps from close encounters with large game. The Neanderthals lived to their late thirties or mid-forties, a rather long life span in antiquity.

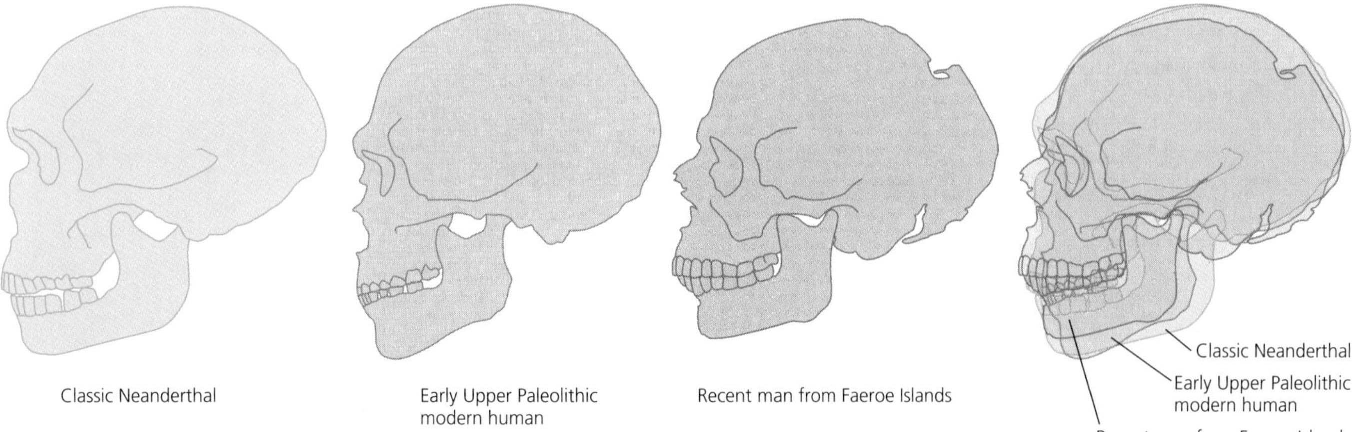


**Figure 4.17** Differences between the skulls of a Neanderthal (La Ferrassie A), an early fully modern individual from the Upper Paleolithic (Predmosti 3), and a recently deceased male *Homo sapiens sapiens* from northern Europe. The bulging forehead, the presence of a chin, reduced brow ridges, and the absence of a large protrusion on the back of the skull, known as an occipital bun, characterize modern humans.

(From *Athena Review*, Vol. 3, No. 2, p. 54, 2002. Image courtesy of Athena Review and C. Loring Brace.)

Neanderthal populations are generally associated with the manufacture of a variety of flake tools in groups of artifacts termed **Mousterian** (moose-TEER-e-an) assemblages, after the site of Le Moustier in France. The Mousterian belongs to the Middle Paleolithic, dating to approximately 120,000–40,000 years ago in Europe. Although handaxes continued to be made, large retouched flakes and **Levallois** pieces, from a technique for making thin flakes with a lot of cutting edge, are the major hallmarks of the period. Flakes were shaped into a variety of tools for more special purposes (Figure 4.18).

Neanderthal fossils and/or Mousterian assemblages are found primarily in Europe and southwestern Asia (Figure 4.19). The Neanderthals were large-game hunters. Isotopic studies of Neanderthal bones document a carnivorous diet. Their prey varied across Europe; reindeer were hunted primarily in the west, and mammoths were hunted in eastern regions. Neanderthals were apparently an indigenous adaptation in Europe, well adapted to the cold conditions of the Pleistocene. However, an extremely cold period around 75,000 years ago may have pushed some Neanderthal populations southeast into Southwest Asia and eastward into western Asia (see "The Fate of the Neanderthals," p. 121). The easternmost Mousterian sites are known from the Altai Mountains, around Lake Baikal and into western Mongolia.

Cultural innovations during this period include the first intentional

**Figure 4.18** Typical heavy flake tools from the European Mousterian.

**The fact that Neanderthals buried their dead is surprising to many people. What do you think this practice may have meant?**

*The past is a foreign country; they do things differently there.*

—L. P. Hartley

**brow ridge** That part of the skull above the eye orbits.

**occipital bun** A distinctive shelf or protrusion at the base of the skull; a feature usually associated with Neanderthals.

**robust** "Big-boned," heavy, thick-walled skeletal tissue. Robust early hominins had very large teeth.

**Mousterian** A term describing the stone tool assemblages of the Neanderthals during the Middle Paleolithic, named after the site of Le Moustier in France.

**Levallois** A technique for manufacturing large, thin flakes or points from a carefully prepared core.

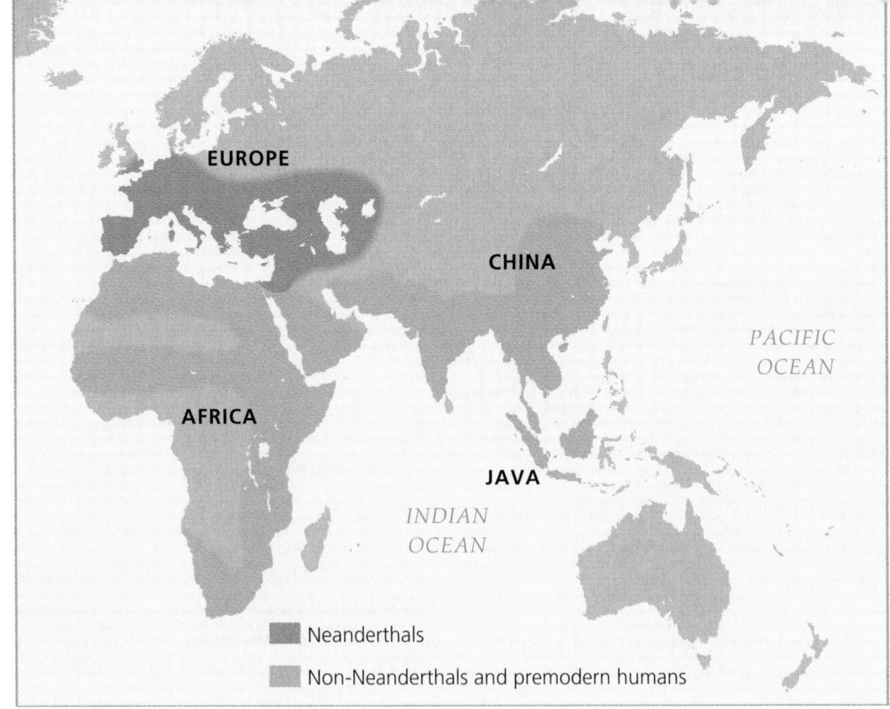


**Figure 4.19** The distribution of *Homo neanderthalensis* and Mousterian sites in Europe and the Near East. *Homo sapiens sapiens* were living in most of the rest of Asia and Africa during this time.

**Figure 4.20** An artist's speculative reconstruction of the Neanderthal burial ground at La Ferrassie, France. The graves of several infants and adults were uncovered here during the 1800s.

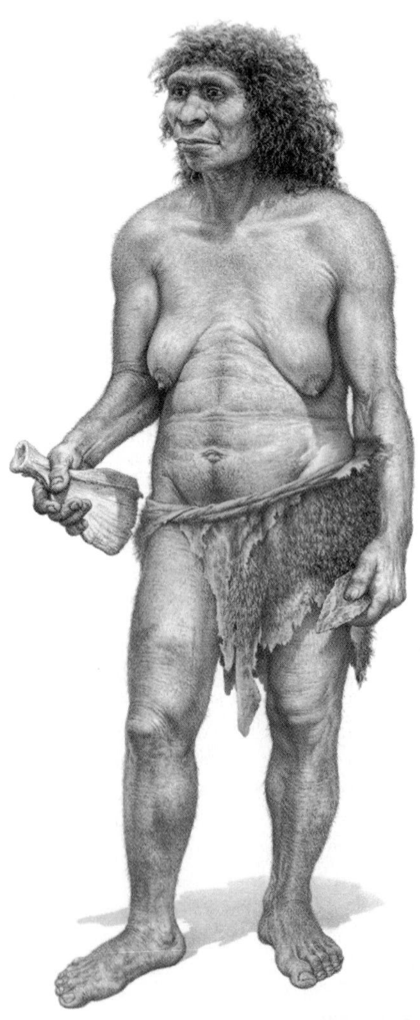

**Figure 4.21** An artist's reconstruction of a Neanderthal female.

burial of the dead in graves (Figure 4.20), sometimes accompanied by flowers, tools, or food. The presence of these materials in graves certainly implies concepts of death as sleep or of life after death.

More exotic practices emerge as well, difficult to understand or explain from our modern perspective. Several examples of broken and burned human bones have been found among the remains of other animals in deposits belonging to the Middle Paleolithic period. At the cave of Krapina in Croatia, the bones of at least 13 human individuals were found, along with those of various herbivores and other animals. The human bones had been burned, split to extract marrow, and treated like the bones of the animals that had provided meals for the occupants of this site. At the Grotte de l'Hortus in southwestern France, similar evidence of cannibalism was found. Heavily fragmented Neanderthal bones from at least 20 people were scattered among the numerous bones of small wild goats. Most of the human bones are skull and jaw fragments, and many of the individuals were over age 50. Whether such practices were rituals of consecration of the dead, or the bones were simply individuals from enemy groups that were added to the larder, is not known. It has also been argued that the bones may have been accidentally burned and broken by later inhabitants at the site.

Concept

## The Fate of the Neanderthals

### *A peaceful or violent end?*

Between approximately 45,000 and 25,000 years ago, Neanderthals became extinct and were replaced by fully modern humans in Europe and western Asia. The fate of the Neanderthals is open to question: Were they completely replaced by fully modern humans, perhaps violently, or did they interbreed and simply disappear in the mix? The evidence on this transition is quite different in Southwest Asia and in Europe.

Current evidence from newly dated sites in Southwest Asia suggests that the first fully modern humans appeared in this area as much as 100,000 years ago (Figure 4.22). At Qafzeh Cave and the site of Skhul in Israel (Figure 4.23), and elsewhere in Southwest Asia, the bones of *Homo sapiens sapiens* are found in layers with Mousterian tools, dating to 90,000 years ago. At other sites, such as Shanidar and Kebara, Neanderthal skeletons have been found dating to between 75,000 and 45,000 years ago. It is entirely possible that the Neanderthals found in Southwest Asia moved there from Europe during a period of intense cold. It appears that fully modern humans coexisted with Neanderthals in Southwest Asia until around 45,000 years ago. The earliest evidence for Upper Paleolithic technology comes from East Africa more than 50,000 years ago and includes bone tools and pendants, along with a standardized set of artifacts.

In Europe, the transition is less clear, and evidence for the first fully modern humans shows them appearing later. Neanderthals are first known in Europe by approximately 250,000 years ago, yet the earliest bones of fully modern humans do not appear in this area until after 40,000 years ago.

Recent evidence from new, calibrated AMS radiocarbon dates (see "Radiocarbon Dating," p. 145) has shown that the expansion of fully modern humans was faster than previously thought and that the period of their coexistence with Neanderthals was considerably shorter. Thus, *Homo sapiens sapiens* arrived in southeastern Europe from the Near East around 46,000 years ago and reached western Europe within 4000–5000 years. The Neanderthals may have been largely gone from Europe by 40,000 years ago, perhaps coinciding with the onset of one of the coldest periods of the Pleistocene, as well as the arrival of fully modern humans. Although there appear to have been some surviving populations of Neanderthals in some parts of Europe, for the most part

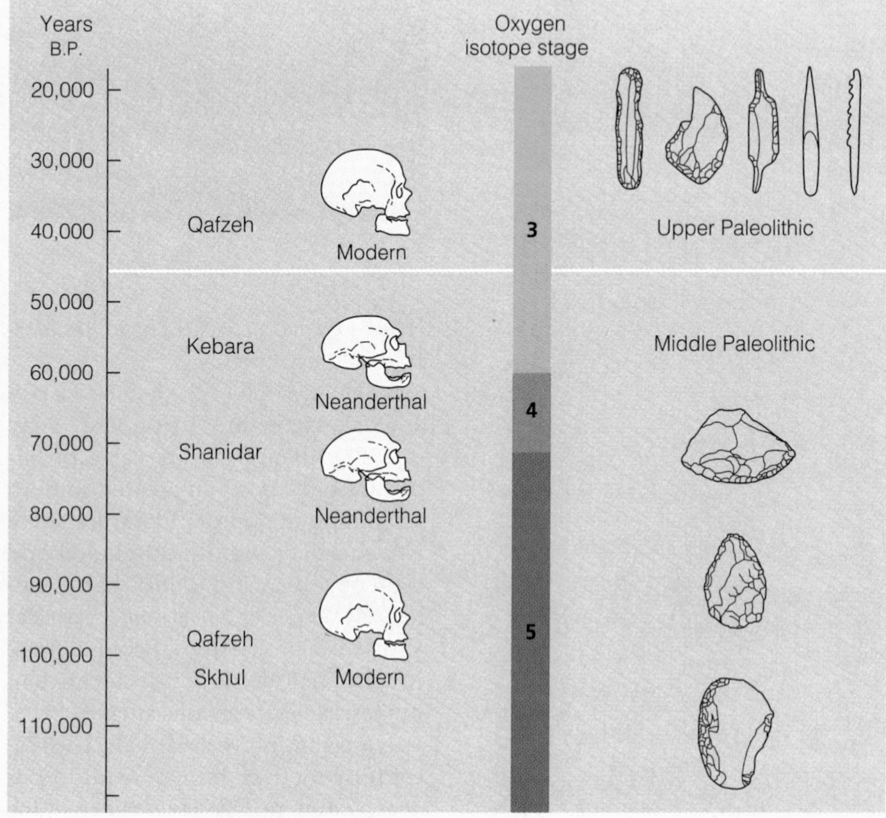


**Figure 4.22** The sequence of hominins from major sites in the Near East. This important evidence indicates that fully modern humans were present in this area by 100,000 years ago, before the Neanderthals. Neanderthals were probably forced out of Europe and into western Asia during an extreme period of cold. The Neanderthals in the Near Eastern sites date to between 70,000 and 45,000 years ago. Technological changes from Middle to Upper Paleolithic took place around 50,000 years ago and were not related to the human subspecies present.

**Figure 4.23** A view of the caves at Mount Carmel, Israel. The caves of Tabun and el-Wad are in the center of the photo. The site of Skhul is out of view to the left. Many of the Paleolithic sites in the Near East are found in similar caves that formed in the limestone geology of the region.

*Homo sapiens* replaced *Homo neanderthalensis* very quickly.

The question of the fate of the Neanderthals remains unsolved. Why did they disappear? Several possibilities have been suggested in both scientific and popular literature. Were Neanderthals simply conquered and slain by advancing groups of technologically superior *Homo sapiens sapiens*? Was it a major period of cold climate in Europe? Two recent discoveries of human skeletal remains suggest some interbreeding of Neanderthals. The oldest fully modern human skull in Europe, dating to 35,000 years ago at the cave of Oase in Romania, combines characteristics of modern humans and Neanderthals. A child burial at the cave of Lagar Velho in Portugal, dating to 24,500 years ago, has been described as the product of Neanderthal and modern mating. The long span of time between these two dates also suggests a very long period of contact between the two subspecies.

On the other hand, there is genetic evidence to the contrary. Did Neanderthals disappear into the gene pool of modern-looking humans as smaller numbers of Neanderthals interbred with larger numbers of *Homo sapiens sapiens*? Ancient DNA extracted from a newly excavated 40,000-year-old Neanderthal bone from Feldhofer Cave, Germany, and DNA from bones at several other places in Europe and western Asia suggests that there was little genetic relationship, and thus no mating, between the Neanderthals and the fully modern humans who replaced them (Figure 4.24). From this evidence, the end of the Neanderthals may have been more violent than romantic, or perhaps a combination of cold conditions and aggressive new neighbors. The jury is still out in this scientific trial.

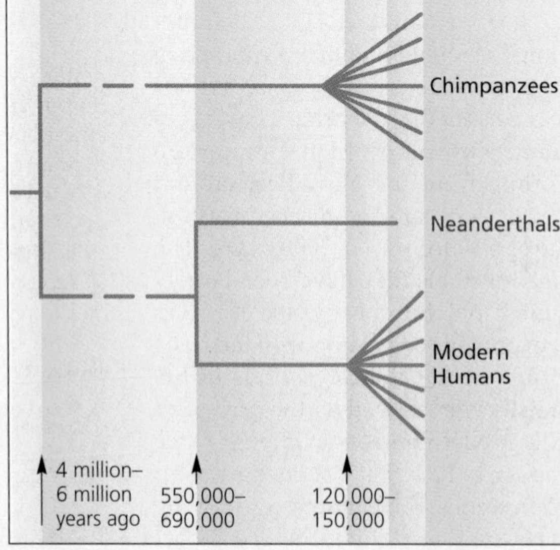


**Figure 4.24** A dendrogram of the genetic relationship between modern humans, Neanderthals, and chimpanzees, based on the study of ancient DNA in several European Neanderthals.

*Concept*

# The Upper Paleolithic

## *The arrival of* Homo sapiens sapiens

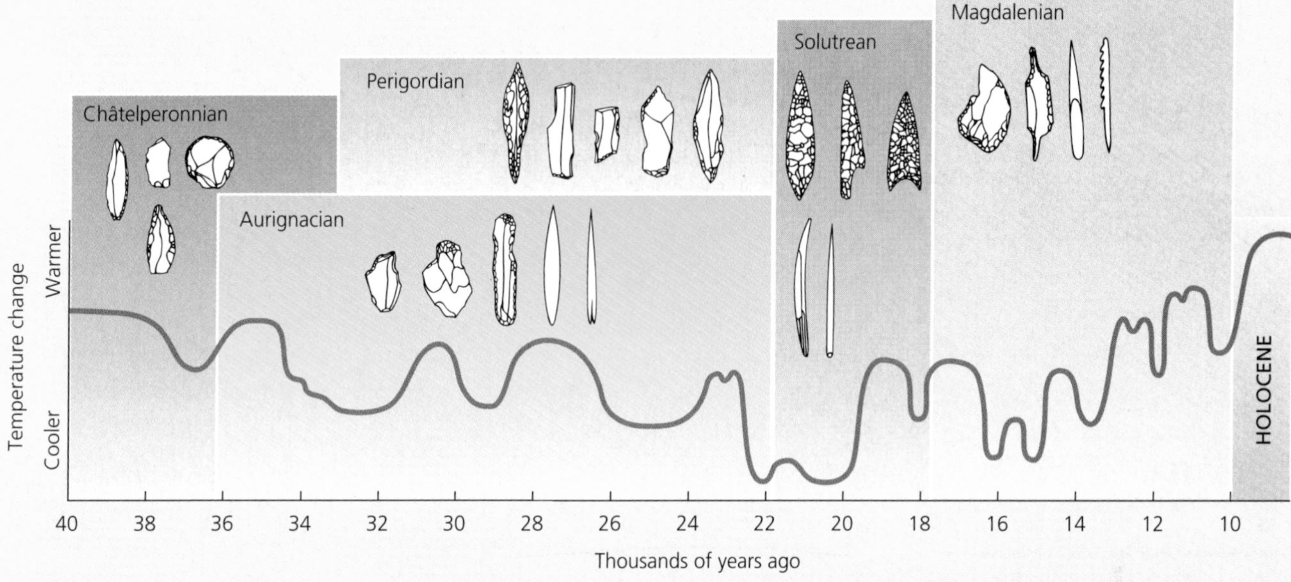


**Figure 4.25** A chart of the chronology, climatic changes, major cultural periods, and typical artifacts of the Upper Paleolithic. The differences between these European cultures were much greater during the Upper Paleolithic than during the Middle Paleolithic.

The Upper Paleolithic is characterized by a variety of innovations that developed over the last 40,000 years or so of the Pleistocene. These include the arrival of anatomically modern humans in Europe; the extensive use of stone blades; the widespread manufacture of a variety of objects from bone, antler, ivory, and wood; the invention of new equipment, such as the spearthrower and the bow and arrow; the domestication of the dog; and the appearance of art and decoration.

The Upper Paleolithic also represents an important phase in the geographic expansion of the human species. There were more sites in more places than ever before. Virtually all the earth's diverse environments, from tropical rain forest to arctic tundra, were inhabited during this period. Africa, Europe, and Asia were filled with groups of hunter-gatherers, and Australia and North and South America were colonized for the first time.

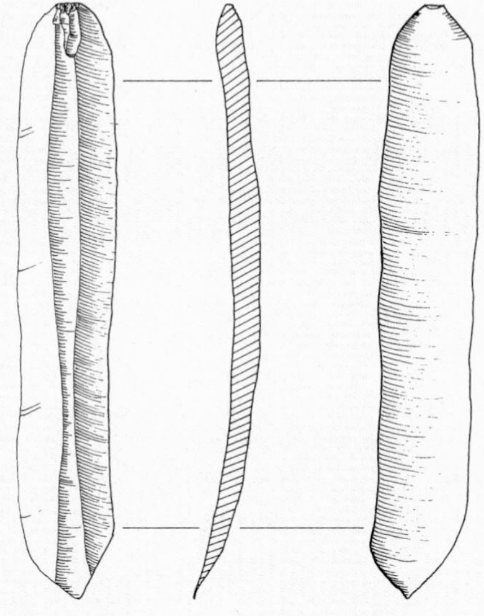

**Figure 4.26** Three views of a blade: a flake with a length at least twice its width.

What forces were at work making us more human? How did evolution select for more creative individuals?

**Figure 4.27** Upper Paleolithic manufacture of blades and blade tools. Blade manufacture is a kind of mass production of many elongated flakes. A pointed piece of bone or antler is struck with a hammerstone to remove the blade from the core using the indirect percussion technique.

**Figure 4.28** Blades as forms, or **blanks,** for making other tools. Increasing specialization in the function of tools was an important trend during the Paleolithic. This illustration shows some of the many types of tools that were made from blades.

The archaeological materials of this period are best known from Europe, especially from southwestern France, an important hub of archaeological activities during the twentieth century. In Europe, the Upper Paleolithic replaced the Middle Paleolithic after 40,000 years ago. Excavations over the past 100 years in the deep deposits of caves and rockshelters in this area have exposed layer upon layer of materials from the last part of the Pleistocene. These excavations and studies of the contents of the layers resulted in the recognition of a sequence of Upper Paleolithic subperiods, known as the Châtelperonnian, Aurignacian, Perigordian, Solutrean, and Magdalenian (Figure 4.25). In central and eastern Europe, the Upper Paleolithic remains are designated the Gravettian, roughly equivalent to the Perigordian in the west.

The earliest skeletal remains of *Homo sapiens sapiens* found in western Europe date to 42,000 years ago, following the appearance of blade tools and other distinctively Upper Paleolithic artifacts. These anatomically modern individuals were originally called Cro-Magnon, after the place in France where they were first discovered. In spite of this distinctive name, they were indistinguishable from fully modern humans. Lacking the robust frame, heavy brow ridges, and protruding jaw of the Neanderthals, the *H. sapiens sapiens* face sits almost directly under a bulging forehead. A chin reinforces the smaller, weaker jaw and its smaller teeth. Cranial capacity is fully modern, and there is no reason to assume that Cro-Magnons were intellectually different from us.

The material remains left by these Upper Paleolithic societies rein-

**Figure 4.29** Solutrean laurel leaf point produced by retouching and thinning the surface of the artifact.

force the idea that by this time our species had indeed arrived as creative creatures. Blade-manufacturing techniques and blade tools characterize the Upper Paleolithic. Stone **blades** are a special form of elongated flake, with a length at least twice its width and sharp, parallel cutting edges on both sides (Figure 4.26). Blades can be mass-produced in large quantities from a single nodule of flint, removed from a core in a fashion akin to peeling a carrot (Figure 4.27). Blades also provide a form, or **blank,** that can be shaped (retouched) into a number of different tools. Projectile points, burins, knives, drills, and scraping tools can all be made from a basic blade form (Figure 4.28).

Another distinctive aspect of Upper Paleolithic stone tool manufacture is the appearance of special flaking techniques during the Solutrean period, to make thin, beautiful, leaf-shaped points in several sizes (Figure 4.29). Some of these points were used for spears and some perhaps for arrows, while others may have served as knives. These tools are among the finest examples of the flintknapper's skill from the entire Paleolithic. At the end of the Solutrean, however, these flaking techniques largely disappeared from the craft of stone tool manufacture, not to be used again for thousands of years.

Many new kinds of tools—made of materials such as bone, wood, ivory, and antler—also distinguish the Upper Paleolithic. Spearthrowers, bows and arrows, eyed needles, harpoons, ropes, nets, oil lamps, torches, and many other things have been found. Hafting and composite tools, incorporating several different materials, were also introduced during the Upper Paleolithic. Resin and other adhesives, for example, were used to hold stone tools in bone or antler handles.

Spearthrowers provide an extension of the arm, enabling hunters to fling their darts with greater force and accuracy (Figure 4.30). A hunter with a spearthrower can kill a large animal such as a deer from a distance of 15 m (50 ft). Spearthrowers of bone, wood, or antler usually had three components: a handle, a balance weight, and a hook to hold the end of the spear. These spearthrowers were often elaborately decorated, with the carved figures of animals used for the weight (Figure 4.31). By the end of the Upper Paleolithic, the spearthrower was replaced by the bow and arrow as the primary hunting weapon. The bow provided an even more accurate means of delivering a long-distance, lethal blow to an animal.

Dogs were domesticated during the Upper Paleolithic, probably for the purpose of hunting. As temperatures warmed at the end of the Pleistocene and the European forests spread back across the continent, woodland species of animals became more common but less visible to the hunter. A strong sense of smell, lacking in a human hunter, to locate prey was well developed in his faithful canine companion.

**Figure 4.30** An artist's reconstruction of a spearthrower in action.

**blade** A special kind of elongated flake with two parallel sides and a length at least twice the width of the piece.

**blank** A basic form or preform from which various kinds of tools can be shaped.

**Figure 4.31** One end of a decorated spearthrower from the Upper Paleolithic in France. A carving of two embracing elks provides the balance weight.

Fine bone needles with small eyes document the manufacture of sewn clothing and other equipment from animal skins. Several categories of carved artifacts—buttons, gaming pieces, pendants, necklaces, and the like—marked a new concern with personal appearance, an expression of self, and the aesthetic embellishment of everyday objects. This development was closely related to the appearance of decorative art. Figurines, cave paintings, engravings, and myriad decorations of other objects reflect the creative explosion that characterized Upper Paleolithic achievement. There is also compelling evidence for a celebration of the seasons and an awareness of time in the archaeological remains from the Upper Paleolithic. Finally, the suggestion of counting systems and the beginning of a calendar of sorts—or at least a recording of the phases of the moon—may have appeared at this time (see "Symbols and Notation," p. 140).

# Dolni Vestonice

## *Mammoth hunters in eastern Europe*

The woolly mammoth of Pleistocene Europe was a magnificent creature. As seen in cave paintings and frozen remnants from Siberia, this animal had a huge domed head atop a massive body covered with long fur. The mammoth was roughly one-and-a-half times the size of a modern African elephant and must have been formidable prey for the late Pleistocene hunters of Europe. In addition to mammoths, herds of wild reindeer, horses, woolly rhinoceroses, and other species roamed the tundra of Europe. The mammoth, however, was the primary game in the east and provided the bulk of the diet for the inhabitants of this area. At one site in the Czech Republic, the remains of 800–900 mammoths have been uncovered.

The remains of the camps of these mammoth hunters were fortuitously buried under deep deposits of fine silt. This silt was originally picked up by the wind at the edges of the ice sheets, carried in the air across central Europe, and gradually deposited as blankets of sediment, known as **loess** (pronounced "luss"). Numerous prehistoric sites were slowly covered by this airborne dust; bone, ivory, and other materials have been well preserved in it. The major problem with such sites is simply finding them, because they are hidden under very deep deposits of loess.

Near the town of Dolni Vestonice (dol-NEE ves-toe-NEET-za), in the south-central part of the Czech Republic, the enormous bones of extinct mammoths were first uncovered in the course of quarrying loess soils for brickmaking (Figure 4.32). Although excavations were initially undertaken in 1924, the extent of the prehistoric occupation was not truly recognized until the commencement of the work that began in 1947 and continues today. Large horizontal excavations have removed the deep loess deposit covering the site and exposed a large area containing dwelling structures, mammoth bones, and many intriguing artifacts dating to about 25,000 years ago.

**Figure 4.32** Excavations at the site of Dolni Vestonice, uncovering the piles of mammoth bones on the south side of the site. Notice the deep layer of loess deposits above the level of excavation.

During the late Pleistocene, the area was one of tundra and permafrost, situated north of the treeline in Europe. Little wood was available, except possibly for small stands of willow and other species in sheltered valleys. Broad expanses of grass, moss, and lichen provided food for the herds

**loess** Wind-blown silt deposited in deep layers in certain parts of the Northern Hemisphere.

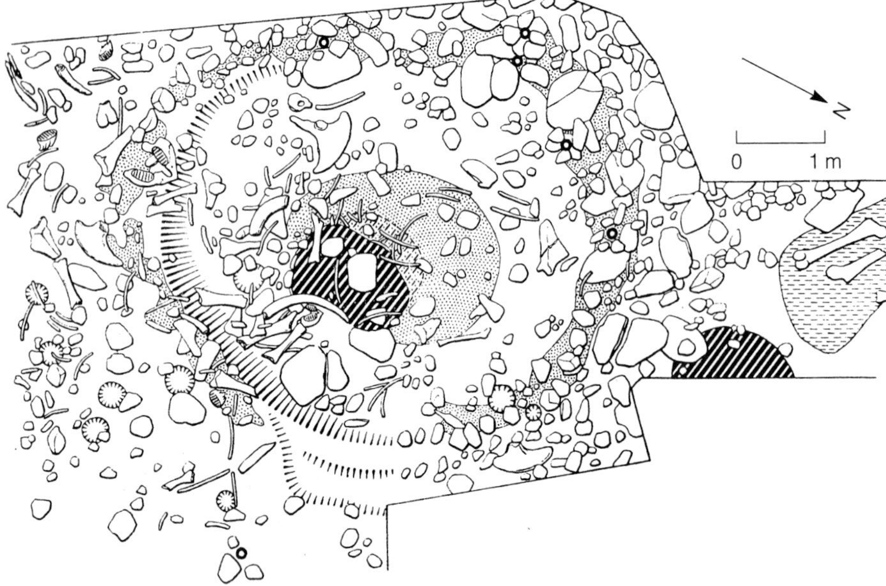


Figure 4.33 A residential structure from Dolni Vestonice showing the semisubterranean floor, with flat stones, fireplaces, and mammoth bones used for the framework. Postholes are indicated by small dark circles, and fireplaces are marked by black diagonal lines. The bone framework was likely covered with animal hides to complete the structure. The hut is approximately 6 m in diameter.

**solifluction** A phenomenon in which freezing and thawing of the ground results in slippage of the surface.

**red ochre** An iron mineral that occurs in nature, used by prehistoric peoples in powdered form as a pigment for tanning animal skins.

of mammoths, horses, and reindeer that were the predominant fauna of the area. The permafrost was responsible for large-scale movement of the ground surface, a phenomenon known as **solifluction.** Alternate freezing and thawing of the ground resulted in the disturbance of many of the remains at Dolni Vestonice. For this reason, it is somewhat difficult to interpret evidence from the site.

The highest layers in the deposits, containing a campsite, are still reasonably well preserved. This camp lay on a projecting tongue of land, along a local stream that becomes a bog just at the eastern edge of the site. Part of the site sits on a ridge, providing a good view of the valley of the nearby Dyje River. The effectiveness of the mammoth hunters is dramatically portrayed in the scatters of mammoth bones marking the boundaries of the settlement. The bones of at least 100 mammoths were piled up in an area measuring 12 × 45 m (40 × 140 ft). Stone tools and broken bones suggest that this was a zone where animals, or parts of animals, were butchered and where skins may have been cleaned and prepared. Other piles of bones were found throughout the settlement, often sorted according to kind of bone, presumably for use as fuel and raw material for construction. Fires were lit on some of these bone piles, as evidenced by ash, perhaps as a defense against predatory animals.

Stones, earth, wooden posts, and mammoth bones were used in the construction of structures at the site (Figure 4.33). The first structure to be uncovered was a very large oval, 9 × 15 m (30 × 50 ft), with five regularly spaced fireplaces inside. The size of the structure, about half a tennis court, and its contents suggested to the excavators that this was an open windbreak, without a ceiling, rather than a roofed structure, and that it was occupied primarily during summer. The wall posts were supported with limestone blocks and were likely covered with animal hides. At least three roofed huts have been found in this area. These structures are partially dug into the loess; they contain one or two hearths and have numerous large mammoth bones on top of the floor. These bones are probably the remains of the framework for the roof, which would have collapsed onto the floor of the structure after the site was abandoned.

In an open area near the center of the compound was a large hearth, almost 1 m (3 ft) deep and several meters (about 10 ft) across, which may have been a common, central fire for the community. In the ashes of this fire, an ivory carving of a female figure, called the Venus of Vestonice, was found (see "Portable Art," p. 136).

Another structure, uncovered in 1951, was found some 80 m (250 ft) along the stream to the west of the main concentration (Figure 4.34). This structure was smaller, 6 m (20 ft) in diameter, and very unusual. The floor of the hut had been dug into the loess slope to level it and to provide more protection against the elements. Limestone blocks were placed against the excavated slope to buttress the wall. Posts were also supported by these blocks at the front of the hut. Hollow bird bones were found inside; they were cut at the ends and may have functioned as musical instruments. In the center of the hut was an ovenlike fireplace with a domed clay structure raised around it. The oven was made of fire-hardened earth and ground

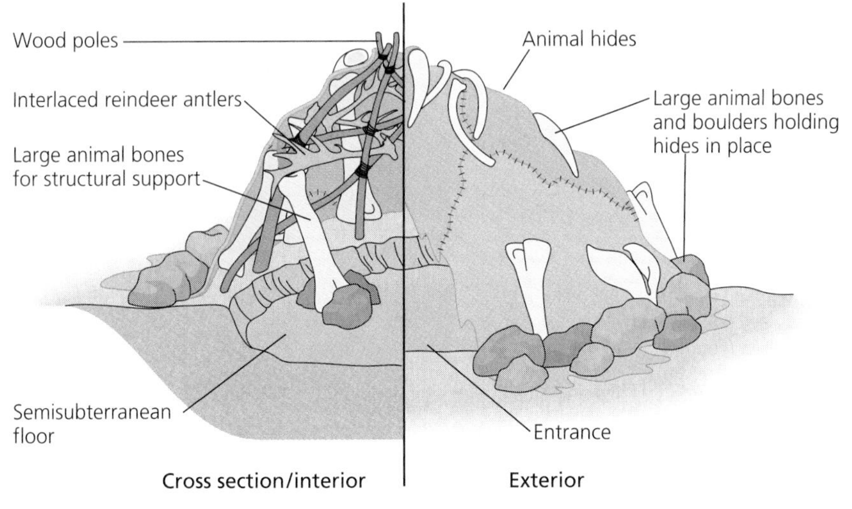


**Figure 4.34** A reconstruction of a mammoth-bone structure from the 18,000-year-old site of Mal'ta in south-central Russia, which may closely resemble the structures at Dolni Vestonice. Bones and animal skins were used as construction materials.

**Figure 4.35** An ivory carving of a mammoth from Vogelherd, Germany (8.8 cm long).

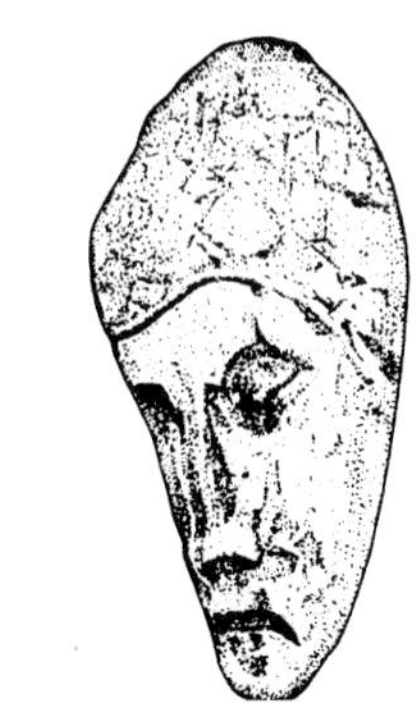

**Figure 4.36** The head of a woman with an asymmetrical face, carved in ivory (4.6 cm high).

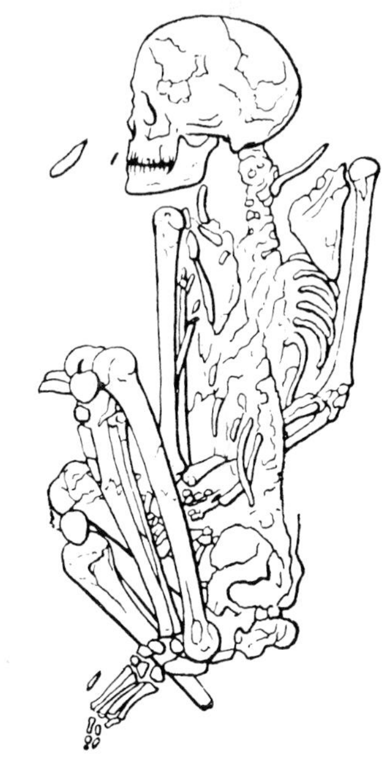

**Figure 4.37** The buried skeleton of an elderly female from Dolni Vestonice. The bones of the left side of the face revealed congenital nerve damage, probably resulting in an asymmetrical facial expression. The woman was buried under two mammoth shoulder blades, and the bones of an arctic fox were found next to her in the grave.

limestone. In the deep pile of ashes and waste that stood on the floor of the hut were found more than 2300 small clay figurines that must have been fired in the oven. This is the earliest example of the use of fired clay in the world, some 15,000 years before the invention of pottery. The figurines consisted of heads, feet, and other fragments of animal effigies and fired lumps of clay. Even the fingerprints of the maker were preserved in some of the pieces.

The depth and extent of deposits at Dolni Vestonice, along with the presence of both summer and winter huts, suggest that this site may have been occupied throughout the year. The remarkable artifacts and other materials found at the site confirm the impression that this is an unusual site indeed. Flint tools at the site belong to the Gravettian, the Upper Paleolithic of eastern Europe. Tools are made from narrow blades in the form of points, knives, burins, and others. There are also numerous tools made from mammoth bone and ivory: awls, needles, knives, spearpoints, lances, and digging implements. Ornaments in the form of pendants, necklaces, headbands, and the like are made of carved bone, ivory, and shell. Some of the shells were from the Mediterranean Sea, several hundred kilometers to the south, indicating either travel or trade. Other objects carved of antler or ivory, or made of baked clay, have no clear practical purpose and probably served as ritual objects in the ceremonies that took place at the site (Figure 4.35).

Perhaps the most remarkable finds may involve two representations of the same individual. Excavations in 1936 uncovered a small ivory plaque about 4.6 cm (1.8 in) high, with a crudely incised human face portrayed on it. The face is asymmetrical, with the left eye and the left half of the lip somewhat lower than the right. A second carved ivory head was found in 1948 in the open summer hut. This three-dimensional head also portrays an individual, and the left side of the face is somewhat distorted and asymmetrical (Figure 4.36). Finally, a burial was excavated in 1949, discovered beneath two huge shoulder blades from a mammoth. The skeleton belonged to a woman and was covered with **red ochre,** and a flint point was buried near her head (Figure 4.37). A study of the facial bones of this individual showed that she suffered from partial paralysis of the left side of her face. It seems entirely possible that the two faces carved in ivory are representations of the person in the grave.

# The Cave of Lascaux

*A monument to human creativity*

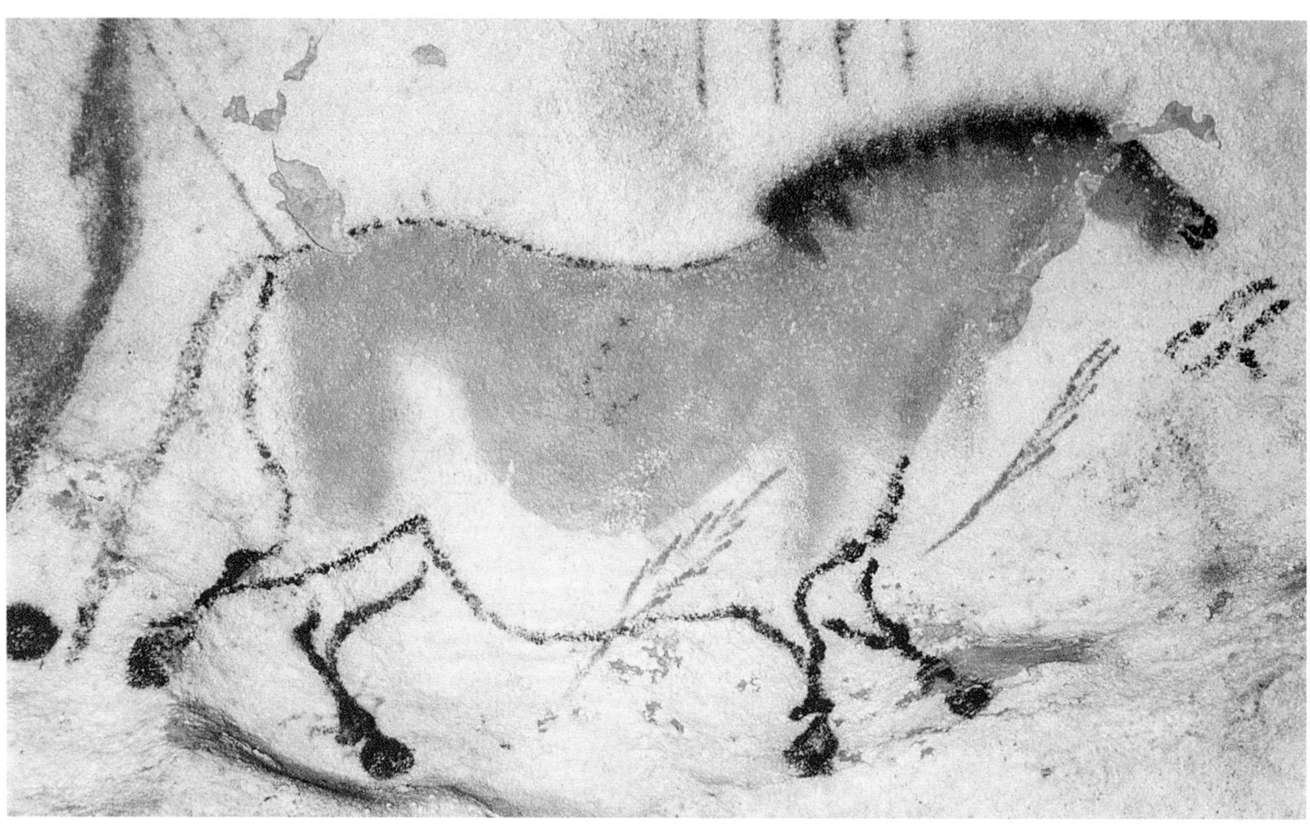

**Figure 4.38** The Upper Paleolithic cave of Lascaux in southwestern France contains many paintings of a variety of animals. This running horse is depicted in two colors along with two feathered darts or plants.

Nestled in the lovely countryside of southwestern France, the Vezere (VEZ-air) River runs past some of the most important Paleolithic sites in the world. This area, known as the Perigord (pear-e-GORE), is a prehistorian's dream. The spectacular landscape contains not only hundreds of important archaeological sites but also the kitchens and cellars of many superb French chefs. The limestone plateau is dissected by numerous streams and rivers that have carved high cliffs along the courses of the valleys. These cliffs contain caves and rockshelters, which provided residence for generations of Paleolithic groups.

Over time, the entrances to many of these caves have collapsed and hidden the caverns completely. The cave of Lascaux (lahss-CO) was discovered by chance in 1940 when a young boy noticed a hole in the ground where a pine tree had been uprooted by the wind. After dropping some rocks into the hole, he and several friends slid down the opening and into a cave, which we now know contains the most important collection of Upper Paleolithic art in the world (Figure 4.38). Lascaux had been sealed for perhaps 15,000 years, the outside world completely unaware of the splendor it held.

After World War II, the cave was opened as an underground museum. For two decades, it was one of the major tourist attractions in France, receiving as many as 1000 visitors a day. Unfortunately, the flow of tourists changed the environment of the cave

www.mhhe.com/priceip6e

For a Web-based activity on some of the best examples of cave art in the world, see the Internet exercises on your online learning center.

dramatically, raising the temperature and humidity and bringing in dust. These changes caused the growth of a fungus on the walls that began to cover and eventually flake off parts of the paintings. The cave was closed in 1963, and efforts were begun to halt the spread of the fungus, remove it, and preserve the paintings for posterity. The problem was fixed, but the cave has not been reopened to the public. Instead, the French government built a duplicate of the cave, Lascaux II, where tourists can view copies of the beautiful animal paintings that grace the walls of the original galleries.

The artwork of the Upper Paleolithic can be divided into two major categories: (1) **mural art**—paintings and engravings on the walls of caves—and (2) **portable art**—carvings, figurines, and other shaped or decorated pieces that can be moved from place to place. Upper Paleolithic mural art is found primarily in France and Spain (Figure 4.39), although ancient examples have also been found in South Africa and Australia. Portable art is found throughout Europe and much of the rest of the Old World. Although Upper Paleolithic mural art was also painted at cave entrances and along cliff faces and rock outcroppings, only deep inside the caves of France and Spain has it survived the erosive forces of nature.

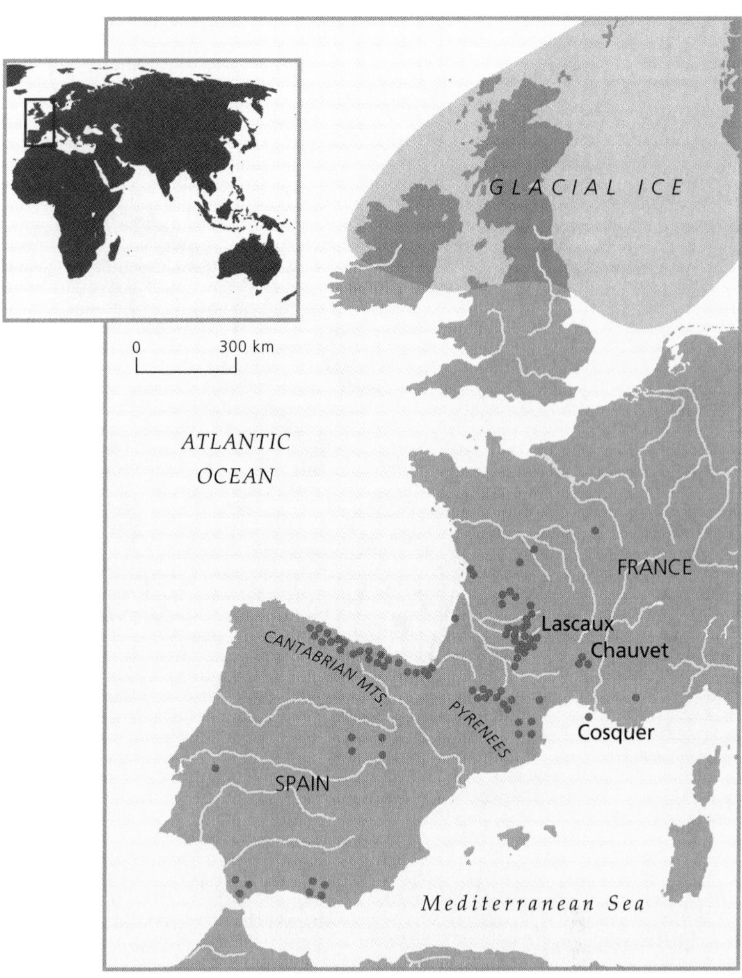


**Figure 4.39** Locations of the western European painted cave sites. The painted caves are primarily in the Perigord region of southwestern France, in the Pyrenees mountains between France and Spain, and in the Cantabrian Mountains of northern Spain, as indicated by dots on the map. The map also shows the extent of continental glaciation in northern Europe during the coldest period of the Upper Paleolithic.

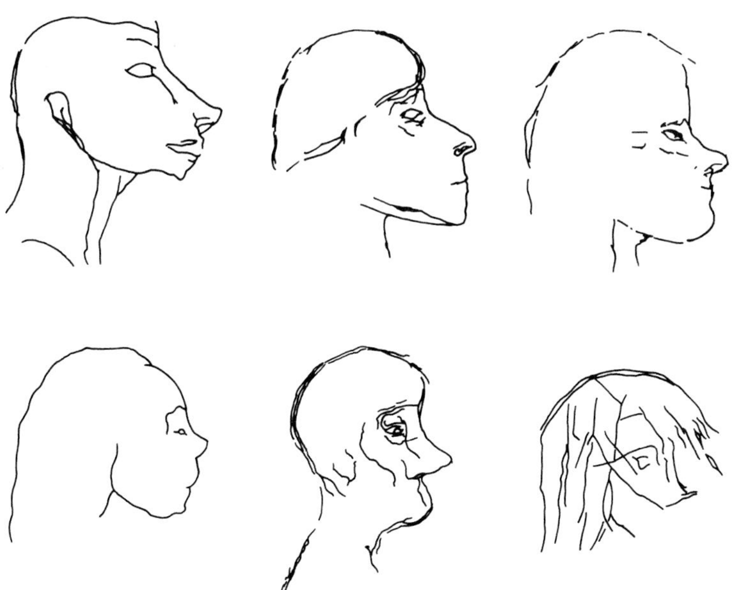

**Figure 4.40** Some of the human heads engraved on the walls of the cave at La Vache.

**mural art** Painting, engraving, and sculpting on the walls of caves, shelters, and cliffs.

**portable art** Decorated materials that can be moved or carried.

**Figure 4.41** Three depictions on the walls of the cave of Les Trois Frères, France, showing humans in animal costume. These individuals may be dancers, sorcerers, or hunters.

Many of the new aspects of the Upper Paleolithic are related to depictions of nature, especially the animal world. Why would it have been important to make images of these creatures?

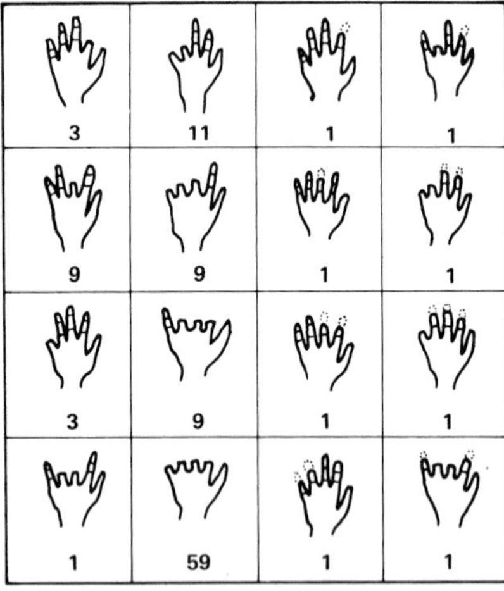


**Figure 4.42** The number and kinds of hand depictions appearing on the walls of the Upper Paleolithic cave of Gargas in France. Note the many missing fingers and digits.

The cave interiors were not living areas; they were visited only briefly by the artists and other members of society. The paintings are almost exclusively of animals; humans are only rarely represented. Human figures are depicted more commonly in engravings, both on cave walls and in portable objects (Figure 4.40). Some of the engravings of humans seem to show men wearing the skins and heads of animals (Figure 4.41). These individuals may have been dancers, participants in some ceremony, or camouflaged hunters. Single human hands are outlined on many of the cave walls. Curiously, they are often depicted without knuckles or even entire fingers. For example, at the cave of Gargas in the French Pyrenees, all but 10 of 217 hand paintings have missing fingers (Figure 4.42). These hands may be simple signatures or graffiti but their exact meaning is unknown.

The cave paintings themselves are rendered in outline and often colored in monochrome or polychrome. Animals are most often depicted in profile. The paintings are sometimes located high on the ceilings in the darkest areas of the caves; light and some form of scaffolding would have been needed to paint in these places. Pieces of rope and pine torches have been found in some caves, along with simple oil lamps made of stone bowls. Over 150 fragments of such lamps have been recovered at Lascaux.

The paintings must have had a great impact viewed in the light of a flickering torch by awed individuals deep in the earth's interior. The cave art is, by and large, carefully planned and skillfully executed, capturing both the movement and the power of the animals that are rendered. It is not graffiti, nor is it hastily sketched. The quality of the paintings is often such that we must assume there were recognized artists in the societies of the Upper Paleolithic.

Most of the paintings at Lascaux date to around 17,000 years ago, during the Magdalenian period. The art is dated from fragments of paints and other artifacts found in archaeological layers of known age in the cave. The paints were a blend of mineral pigments mixed with cave water, and the chewed end of a stick or pieces of hair or fur were used to tamp the paint onto the walls. The common colors in the paintings are black (charcoal and manganese oxide), yellow and red (iron oxides and clay), and occasionally white (clay and calcite).

Lascaux is a lengthy, narrow chamber a little longer than a football field. In spite of its relatively small size, more than 600 paintings and 1500 engravings grace the walls of the cave, making it the most decorated of the magnificent painted caves in Spain and France (Figure 4.43).

The opening of the cave leads into a large chamber, some 20 m (65 ft) long, filled with huge animal paintings. Four large bulls, up to 5 m (16 ft) long, stride across the ceiling. In the adjacent halls and passageways, hundreds of paintings depict bison, deer, horses, wild cattle, and other animals. Very specific characteristics, such as spring molting, are shown in some of the paintings. Animals are often depicted as pregnant or with their meaty haunches exaggerated. In several instances, feathered

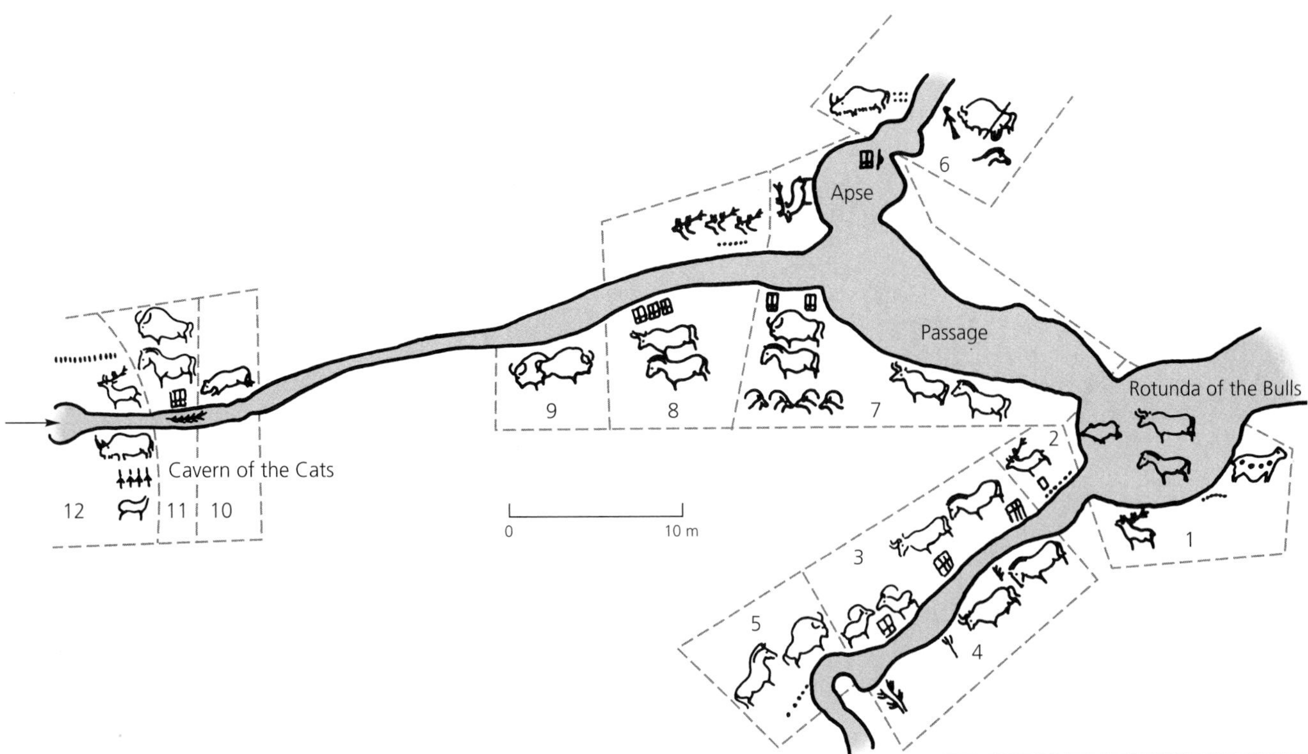


Figure 4.43 The distribution of animals and designs at Lascaux. The numbers indicate major areas of art in the cave. Large prey animals tend to be in the major galleries of the caves; carnivores and other depictions are in less-accessible areas.

darts are heading toward the animals. Certain abstract patterns also appear either in isolation or in association with animals. Rows of dots and multicolor checkerboard patterns are painted at various places in the cave.

Most of the paintings show one animal or a group of animals; there is little attempt at scenery or storytelling. Many of the paintings are superimposed over older ones, with little apparent regard for the previous work of other artists. Large herbivores, which provided much of the meat for Upper Paleolithic hunter-gatherers, most frequently appear in large chambers and open areas in the caves. Curiously, however, the most important game animal at this time, the reindeer, appears only once at Lascaux. Such dangerous animals as carnivores, bears, and rhinoceroses more often are found in the deep recesses of the cave and far-removed crevices.

One of the most remarkable paintings is found in a narrow, 5-m (16-ft) shaft off to the side in the cave (Figure 4.44). At the bottom of this shaft, a large woolly rhino with raised tail faces to the left, a series of dots near its hindquarters. Across a small crevice appears a striking scene of beast and man, the only human figure painted in the cave. A beautiful multicolor bison on the right is mortally wounded, its entrails spilled by a spear. The dying animal is either down on the ground or charging the human figure on the left. This figure, obviously male, is shown in mere outline, depicted with a birdlike face. On the ground nearby lies a long object with several barbs, perhaps a spearthrower, and a bird with a single long leg, possibly an important symbol. Is this painting a memorial to a hunter, a member of the bird clan or totem, killed by the bison? Does the rhino play a role in the scene? Such questions point out the difficulties involved in trying to read the minds of prehistoric people. We can speculate about, but we cannot know, what was intended by these paintings.

There are several schools of thought on the meaning of the cave paintings from the Upper Paleolithic. An apparent emphasis on pregnant animals has often been interpreted to represent a concern with fertility and the bounty of nature, reflecting an awareness of the

**Figure 4.44** Man and bison at Lascaux. This painting represents one of the very few examples of storytelling in the art of Lascaux, and it is the only painting of a human in the cave. The depiction is at the bottom of a deep, narrow shaft and has four elements: a detailed color drawing of a bison mortally wounded by a spear, a black outline of a male human with a birdlike face, a bird on a stick beneath the human figure, and a spearthrower with hook and handle lying on the ground beneath the man. The painting is subject to various interpretations, ranging from a memorial to the death of a kinsman to the depiction of an Upper Paleolithic myth.

*No matter how many caves one has explored, no matter how magnificent or crude or abstract the figures, it always comes with a catch of breath. It may be a bull or a bison drawn larger than life or an engraved horse no bigger than your little finger. It may appear high in a fissure or down close to the floor, on wide exposed surfaces for all to see or in private crawl-in places, painted bare red or black outline or in rich polychrome, starkly grand or delicate in a low key—a variety of locations and styles, and yet all part of a single tradition that endured for some twenty millenniums.*

—John Pfeiffer (1982)

importance of reproduction and the replenishment of the herds on which these people depended for food. Other scholars, pointing to the exaggerated hips and haunches of the animals and spears in flight, argue for a concern with the hunting of animals for meat. Hunting rites and ritual killings of animals before a hunt might magically help ensure success in the quest for food.

A few prehistorians suggest that the cave paintings were simply "art for art's sake," a means for artists to express themselves and to change the way their fellow humans saw the world. Still others suggest that the painted caves were primitive temples, sanctuaries for ceremony and ritual, such as the initiation of the young into society. Huge animals flickering in the light of torches and lamps deep within the bowels of the earth would have provided a breathtaking experience for the uninitiated. Footprints preserved in the muddy floors of painted caves in France indicate that people of all sizes walked in the cave. Margaret Conkey, of the University of California at Berkeley, argues that these caves may have served as a focus of social activity for large groups of people. She suggests that the caves may have been a permanent symbol on the landscape and a place for the ceremonies and rituals associated with the aggregation of several different groups of hunter-gatherers.

More than 200 painted caves have been discovered in France over the past 100 years. In the past decades, several major new art sites have been revealed (Figure 4.45). The cave of Chauvet (SHOW-vay) was found in a tributary of the Rhône River in the south of France in 1995, containing more than 300 paintings and engravings. The site was discovered by French spelunkers who cleared a small hole at the surface and climbed down 9 m (30 ft) into a great chamber. The cave is at least five times larger than Lascaux. There are several groupings of animals, including bears and rhinos, on the walls, in addition to a number of solitary animals. New radiocarbon dating of some of the art in the cave places it at 36,000 years old, making these some of the oldest known paintings in the world (see "Radiocarbon Dating," p. 145).

Another important cave, Cosquer (KOS-care), was found underwater by divers off the Mediterranean coast of France, near Marseilles, in 1992. Swimming through the long, narrow opening of this cave, divers entered dry chambers containing the untouched remains of Upper Paleolithic people, footprints, lamps, torches, hearths, and the like, along with many extraordinary paintings. Rising sea levels at the end of the last glaciation submerged the entrance of the cave. The opening of this cave, now almost 40 m (120 ft) below sea level, was along the shore during the Upper Paleolithic, when the sea level was lower. A number of the paintings reflect the proximity of the Mediterranean shore, depicting seals and seabirds such as the great auk. Most of the art in the cave dates to around 18,500 B.P.

The magnificent art of the Upper Paleolithic represents an initial awakening of the creative spirit, an explosion of our aesthetic senses. Such a transformation may also signify major changes in the minds of Upper Paleolithic people and/or in the way they viewed the world and organized their lives and their society.

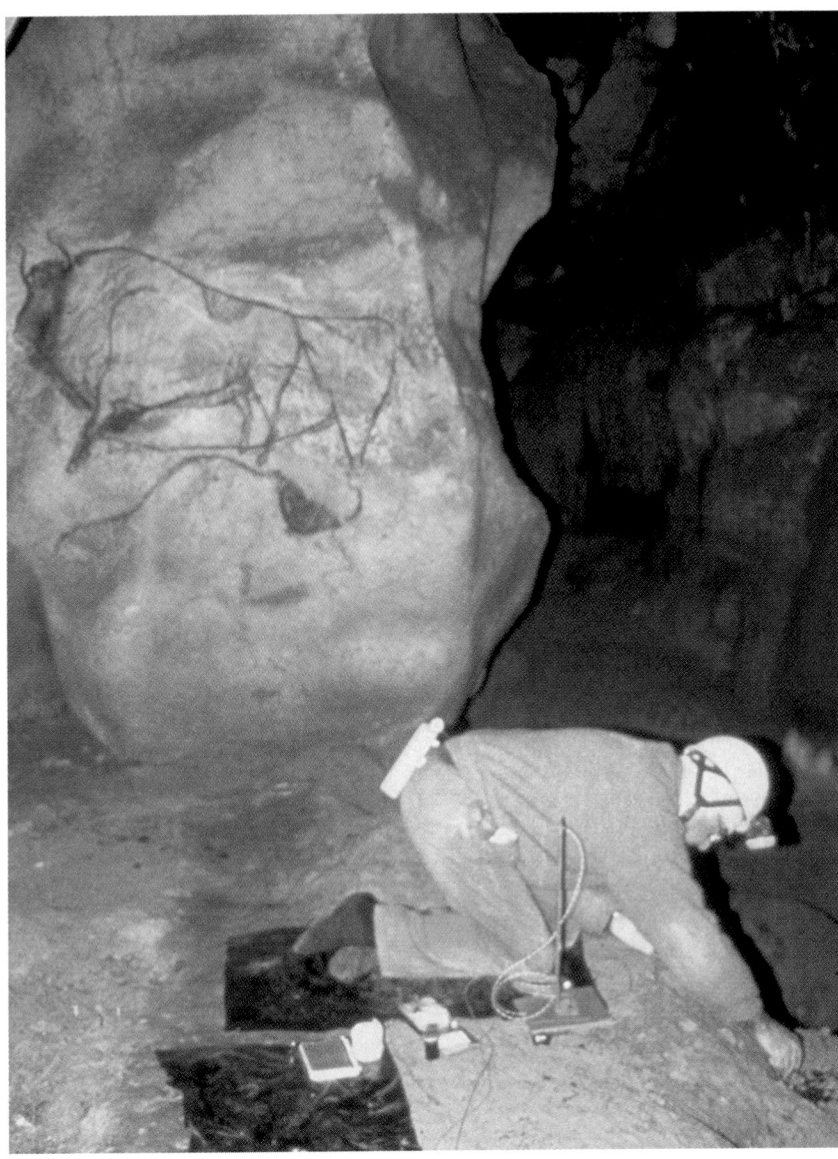

**Figure 4.45** Cave paintings cover the walls at the site of Vallon-Pont-d'Arc, discovered recently in southern France.

*"Does it strike anyone as weird that none of the great painters have been men?"*

# Concept

## Portable Art

*A sense of design and beauty*

The aesthetic sense that appeared during the Upper Paleolithic with the arrival of fully modern humans was expressed in a variety of forms. Carving, sculpting, and molding of various materials, including clay, antler, wood, ivory, and stone, is evidenced throughout this period (Figure 4.46). The decoration of artifacts and other objects occurred throughout the Upper Paleolithic beginning about 35,000 years ago. There is remarkably little evidence for the nonpractical modification of equipment and utensils before the appearance of *Homo sapiens sapiens* in Europe. Only a handful of decorated objects have been found in Middle Paleolithic contexts.

Beginning in the Aurignacian some 35,000 years ago, however, bone be-

**Figure 4.46** Examples of Upper Paleolithic decoration of bone, antler, ivory, and wood objects. Such decoration was applied to a variety of pieces, some utilitarian and others more symbolic.

came a common material for human use, modification, and decoration. For example, a variety of bone points date to this early period. Initially simple and plain, such points had become heavily barbed and decorated by the end of the Upper Paleolithic. At the same time, carved bone and antler figurines of both humans and animals began to appear in the archaeological record.

Perhaps the most spectacular portable objects from the Upper Paleolithic are the "Venus figurines." These small sculptures appeared throughout most of Europe during a brief time around 25,000 years ago. The figures were engraved in relief on the walls of caves; carved in the round from ivory, wood, and stone such as steatite; and modeled in clay. The female characteristics of these statuettes are usually exaggerated: breasts, hips, buttocks, and thighs are very large; the head, arms, hands, legs, and feet are shown only schematically (Figure 4.47). The pubic triangle is sometimes outlined; one figurine has a detailed vulva. Some of the figurines appear to be pregnant, and others are displayed holding a horn, perhaps a cornucopia or horn of plenty, to imply fertility, bounty, and reproduction.

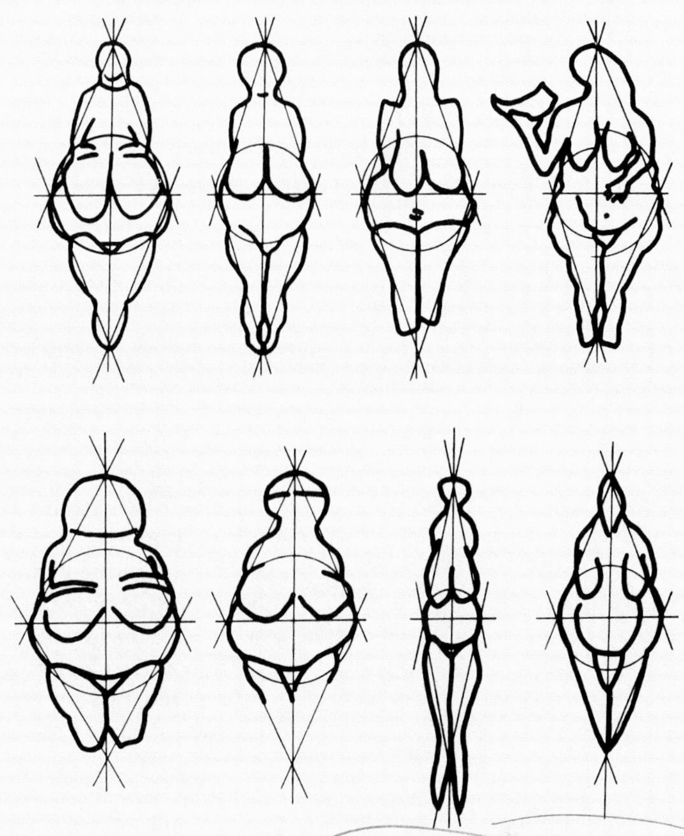

**Figure 4.47** Venus figurines in various shapes and sizes. The individual holding the horn or cornucopia (top row, far right) supports the interpretation of these figures as symbols of fertility, nature's bounty, or "Mother Earth."

Probably 80% of the prehistoric art known today comes from the last stage of the Upper Paleolithic, the Magdalenian. Objects with a short life were decorated in a cursory fashion, whereas more important pieces with a longer life expectancy were heavily ornamented. Spearthrowers were decorated elaborately, with carved animals serving as the counterweight and end-hook. Engraved bone was common, and such portable art was often painted as well. Body adornments, including necklaces, bracelets, and pendants, also appeared in the Magdalenian.

Portable art was more common in the larger settlements than in smaller ones. This pattern suggests a connection between art and the ritual activities that likely occurred when larger groups of people came together. Hunter-gatherers commonly aggregated in a larger group at a certain time each year to exchange raw materials and learn new information, to find mates, and to celebrate important events, such as marriage and initiation into adulthood. Rituals and ceremonies provided a common bond in both the physical and psychic realms; dance, trance, and the reaffirmation of common beliefs were important aspects of such gatherings. Decorations in the form of masks, face and body painting, costumes, and the like were probably used during such ceremonial occasions (see "Contemporary Hunter-Gatherers," Chapter 5, p. 194).

One of the more intriguing features of becoming fully modern is the evidence for jewelry and self-adornment. Artifacts such as beads, pendants, and decorated batons suggest that individuals were distinct, that egos were emerging. Why is such behavior an important part of being human?

Site

# Pincevent

## *Brief stops by reindeer hunters in the Upper Paleolithic*

Several shallow fords on the Seine River in northern France were important crossing points for migrating reindeer herds when tundra and permafrost covered northwestern Europe at the end of the Pleistocene. The sandy banks and bars of the Seine and other rivers were the sites of the camps of Magdalenian reindeer hunters approximately 12,000 years ago. In the vicinity of Paris, the Seine may lie near the northern end of what was a major route of reindeer migration at the close of the Pleistocene, with herds moving north each spring from the south of France.

Scatters of stone, bone, antler, hearthstones, and charcoal mark these ephemeral summer encampments of reindeer hunters. A number of such sites, including one called Pincevent (PONCE-von), were quickly buried and extremely well preserved (Figure 4.48). The archaeological remains are found in thin layers of clay, deposited when the river flooded annually. The river floods must have been gentle, because there is little disturbance of the materials. Several artifacts were found standing upright, and two crushed bird eggs remained at the site.

At Pincevent, at least four levels with archaeological remains have been recognized, extending over an area of 2 ha (5 acres), larger than a soccer field. Excavations, originally directed by A. Leroi-Gourhan and M. Brezillon, began in 1964 and continue today. The excavators intentionally exposed broad horizontal areas of the site, leaving features, artifacts, and bones in place. In this way, entire "living floors" could be seen and the pattern of discarded materials studied to determine where people slept, cooked, made tools, and so on. The excavators also made latex rubber casts of many areas, which were then painted to reconstruct and permanently preserve the archaeological remains.

The concentrations of materials average 60–70 sq m (650–750 sq ft), about one-half of one side of a tennis court, and they probably represent single tents or structures as the residence and focus of activity of a few hunters. Each concentration contains 20,000–30,000 stone artifacts and other materials. Stone blades, a major product at these sites, had a variety of purposes. At the nearby site of Etiolles, extremely long blades were produced, some more than 80 cm (30 in) long, from large nodules of raw material weighing 40 kg (90 lb) or more. The

**Figure 4.48** Two hearths at Pincevent, France, with the distribution of stones and bones deposited here some 12,000 years ago. All these objects lie where they were discarded by the Upper Paleolithic hunters.

blades from these nodules were as long as 50 cm (20 in). The absence of wear marks on the edges of some of these blades suggests they had not been used and were being stockpiled for some later purpose.

At Pincevent, one of the most important areas excavated to date is in Layer IV. This area contains 94,000 kg (200,000 lb) of flint artifacts, the skeletal remains of at least 43 reindeer, fire-cracked rock, ochre, and several shallow pits and fireplaces (Figure 4.49). Red ochre stains are concentrated around three large fireplaces. The excavators suggest that activities were centered on three contemporary huts, each with an associated fireplace (Figure 4.50). Each hut contained a central zone for actual living space and surrounding zones of domestic activities and refuse disposal. The intensity of activity decreased with distance from the hearths. Small piles of waste materials from stone tool manufacture lie on one side of the hearths, finished tools and red ochre on the other.

Near one of the hearths is a large stone that was likely the seat of a flint-worker. Most of the flint was available in the immediate area of the site. A few pieces, however, came from some distance, confirming the mobility of the hunters who stopped here. Reconstruction or refitting of the pieces removed from the flint nodules provides a good indication of how tools were made. Moreover, pieces that are missing and not found at the site provide evidence of which tools were carried elsewhere. Finally, the scattered locations of pieces that fit together indicate how the tools and waste materials were moved about at the site.

Most of the reindeer at the site were killed and butchered during summer. The distribution of bones on the living floor is similar to that of the flint debris. Larger bones were at the periphery; smaller pieces and smaller fragments were found near the fireplaces. The bones from a meal were apparently tossed away from the hearth. Small fragments of antler were found near the hearths, but larger pieces were discarded at the edge of the activity zone. Most antler working was apparently done at this periphery. The lack of sweeping or cleaning of the living area suggests that the occupation at Pincevent was very brief.

Lewis Binford, of Southern Methodist University, has questioned the existence of actual tents or structures at Pincevent, arguing that the distribution of materials observed in arcs of debris around the hearths could just as easily have happened without tents or huts present. There is no definitive evidence that the hunters built shelters on the site. Binford also argues that all the materials around the two largest hearths could have resulted from one or two individuals working and shifting position in response to wind direction. Binford based his suggestions on observations of Eskimo hunters in Alaska and the manner in which they moved away from the smoke of a fire on a windy day.

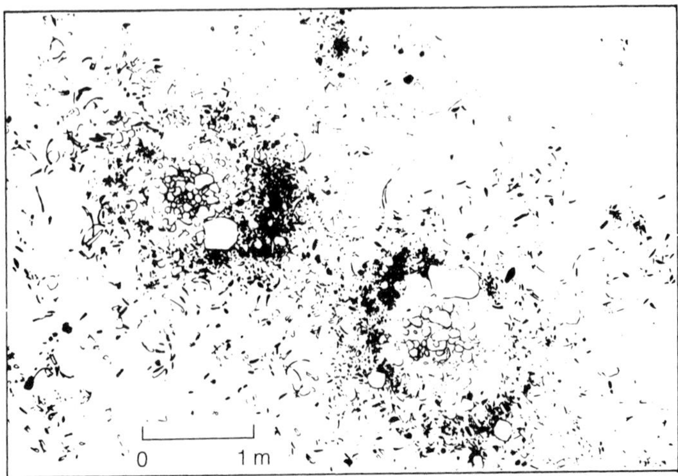


**Figure 4.49** The distribution of stones and bones around two hearths at Pincevent. The large stones were used for sitting during stone tool manufacture; the scatters of lithic debris were produced as a result.

**Figure 4.50** Reconstruction of a possible hut around one of the Pincevent hearths: (a) concentration of artifacts, (b) hearth.

Concept

## Symbols and Notation

### *Evidence of seasonal awareness, numbers, and phases of the moon*

Some of the many decorated objects from the Upper Paleolithic contain unusual images that are not easy to understand. These designs are carved into the polished surface of bone using pointed stone tools. The motifs that often occur together suggest that specific concepts were being depicted.

One example is a bone knife from the French site of La Vache (la VASH). The design on one side of this piece has two animal heads—a doe and an ibex—wavy lines that may represent water, and three plants. The other side of the knife shows the head of a bison in autumn rut, four plant motifs that may be pine branches, a drooping stem, and three seeds or nuts. Alexander Marshack (1918–2004) suggested that the two sides of the knife are intended to convey images of spring and fall, in recognition of the seasons and their distinctive characteristics.

Other bone artifacts have unusual combinations of notches and patterns of dots that are more difficult to comprehend. One example of such an object comes from the cave of La Vache and dates to about 14,000 years ago. The polished fragment of long bone, about 15 cm (6 in) long, is decorated at the base with one entire horse and the head of another (Figure 4.51). About 10 pointed lines are drawn into the complete horse, perhaps symbolically representing the hunt. When the bone with the horses broke, it was reused to flake flint tools; later, elaborate sets of marks were added in a series of rows on both sides of the bone above the horses.

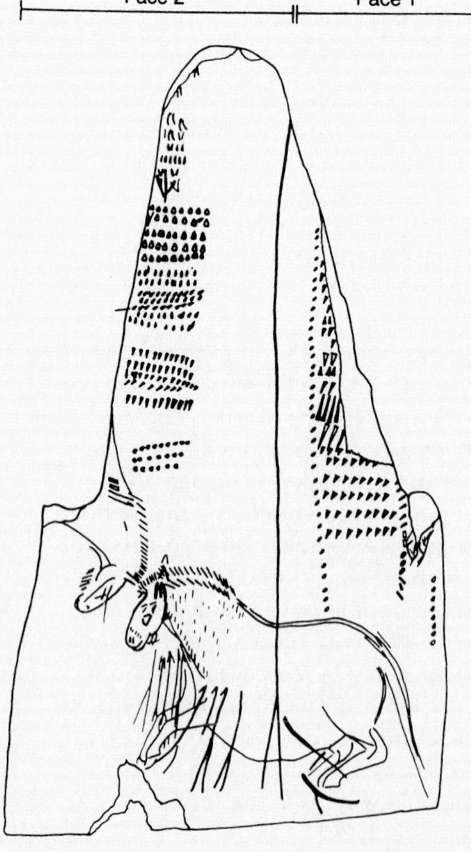


**Figure 4.51** An engraved bone piece from the site of La Vache, France. Two horses appear at the bottom of the piece, one with a number of arrows drawn into the animal. The repeated sets of tally marks, usually in groups of 8–10, were made with different stone tools, suggesting that something was being counted or recorded over time.

Marshack had undertaken detailed, microscopic studies of these objects to determine how the notches and dots were placed on the bone. He was able to distinguish both the type of pointed tool that made the marks and the order in which at least some of the marks were made. For example, at least four tools were used to carve the arrows in the horse on the La Vache bone; the tally marks all occur in sets or blocks, each of which was made with a different tool in a slightly different shape. The number and pattern of the marks suggest that they were added over a period of time. On other decorated bones from the Upper Paleolithic, Marshack observed marks in groups of 30 or 31. The number 7 also seems to regularly define groups of marks on other objects. Although such marks on bones have been considered decoration, they could signify some kind of tally, counting a series

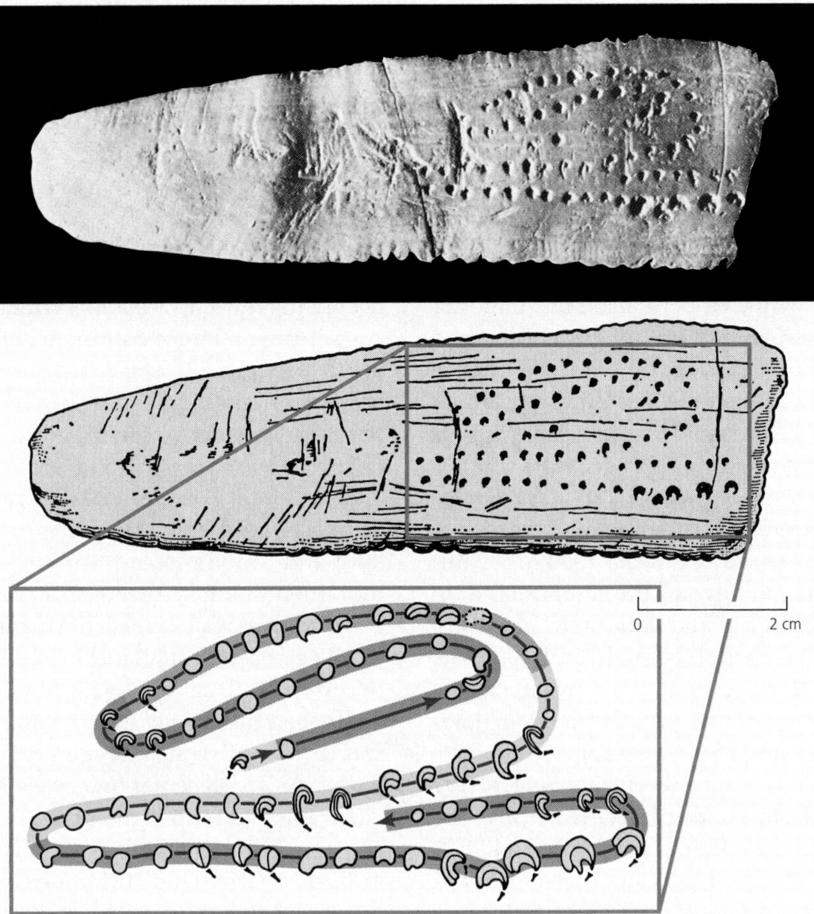


Figure 4.52 The 32,000-year-old bone plaque from Abri Blanchard, France (top), with the area of engravings shown in detail (bottom). Marshack suggests that these marks record the phases of the moon. The different shapes and colors on the drawing of the piece indicate marks made by various stone tools, perhaps indicating the passage of time.

of events, or perhaps the number of hunting kills.

Possibly the most intriguing decorated bone object yet found is from the site of Abri Blanchard in France. A flat, irregular rectangle, this bone has no animal or figure engravings, but rather a series of carved and engraved notches and marks (Figure 4.52). The 80 notches cover about half the edge of the object, and the marks form a semicircular pattern of two parallel lines on the flat surface. Microscopic examination indicates that at least 24 tools were used to make the 69 marks on the surface of this bone. Marshack believed that these marks record the phases of the moon. The shape of the marks changes with the moon's phases, over a period of about 6 months.

Marshack argued that our Upper Paleolithic forebears were noting the passage of time, reckoning the year according to the seasons and a lunar calendar. Marshack's discoveries are controversial, but the idea that Upper Paleolithic people were capable of counting and notation, as well as symbolic representation, does not seem farfetched, in light of the other evidence of their creativity and accomplishments.

Site

# Lake Mungo, Australia

## *The spread of* Homo sapiens sapiens

Although it may seem strange to find Australia in the middle of this discussion of the Upper Paleolithic, there are several important things to be learned from a consideration of the evidence from the Land Down Under. Australia was colonized by *Homo sapiens sapiens* around 40,000 years ago. Rafts or boats of some kind were likely used. These first emigrants somehow crossed a body of water at least 100 km (65 mi) wide, far beyond the sight of land, to reach the island continent. There are archaeological sites at least 20,000 years old in all corners of the continent; the oldest, on the Upper Swan River, dates to around 38,000 years ago.

At this time, during one of the coldest periods of the Pleistocene, sea level was as much as 150 m (400 ft) lower than it is today. The continental shelves were exposed, and land bridges connected several areas formerly separated by the sea. Australia was connected to New Guinea and Tasmania, constituting a larger continent called Sahul (Figure 4.53). The Sahul Strait, a body of water that today is several thousand meters (more than a mile) deep, lay between Australia and Asia. At that time, Southeast Asia was a bridge of land connecting the mainland and Indonesia and Borneo. The first inhabitants crossed this deep, wide body of water to reach Australia.

The absence of a land bridge between Australia and mainland Asia is evidenced by the fact that the animal species in the two areas are so very different. Asian placental mammals and Australian marsupial mammals have not been in contact in the past several million years. This difference was originally noted by British naturalist

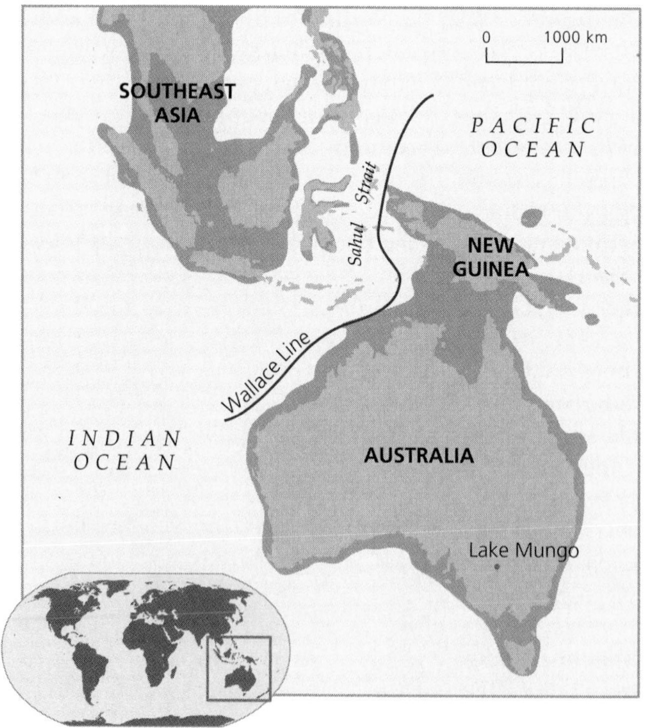


**Figure 4.53** Australia and Southeast Asia during the colder periods of the Pleistocene. At that time, sea level was as much as 150 m lower than it is today, and much of the continental shelf was exposed as dry land. The outlines of the continents changed considerably, and many of today's islands became part of the mainland. Australia and New Guinea joined together but were never part of Southeast Asia. One of the deepest bodies of water in the world, the Sahul Strait, would have always been sea. Thus, the early inhabitants of Australia would have crossed a large body of water to reach the continent. The Wallace Line (red line) marks the divide between Asian and Australian animal species.

Alfred Russel Wallace, a contemporary of Darwin's, and the term *Wallace Line* is used to designate the divide between the two distinct groups of animal species.

Some of the oldest sites in Australia lie along the margins of dry lakebeds in the southeastern part of the country, an area known as Lake Mungo. Sites at Lake Mungo contain hearths and shells dating to around 32,000 years ago. This area would have contained a series of lakes with fertile shorelines in the period of initial occupation, when rainfall was higher than it is today. The sites were discovered in 1968 by a geologist who found human bones buried in a sand dune that was at least 20,000 years old. The bones appeared to have been buried at a time when the dune was active on the shore of a former lake.

Further examination of the area around the bones on the dune revealed a series of stone artifacts and several patches of charcoal, which must have been the locations of hearths. Most of the hearths contained fish and mammal bones. Bird bones, eggshells, and shells from freshwater mollusks were also found in a few fireplaces. Other sites around the fossil lakeshore have revealed concentrations of shellfish, burned areas with charcoal and fired clay lumps, probably used as cooking stones. The material culture of these early inhabitants included both bone tools and stone tools, with a large number of heavy core and pebble artifacts.

Several burials have been found, one of which, the remains of a woman 20–25 years old, is the oldest example of cremation yet known in the world. Other remains include another female and a male. Red ochre was used in some of the graves to cover a portion of the remains. All these individuals are *Homo sapiens sapiens* and document the presence of fully modern humans in the eastern part of Eurasia, several thousand years before their appearance in Europe.

These early inhabitants rapidly occupied all of Australia, as indicated by the spread of radiocarbon dates across the continent. Some of the oldest rock art and wall paintings in the world are known from Australia (Figure 4.54). What is almost equally remarkable, however, is how little change took place here over thousands of years. Foraging was apparently a very successful and stable activity in prehistoric Australia. Hunter-gatherers arrived here almost 40,000 years ago, and they were still present when Captain Cook "discovered" the continent 200 years ago.

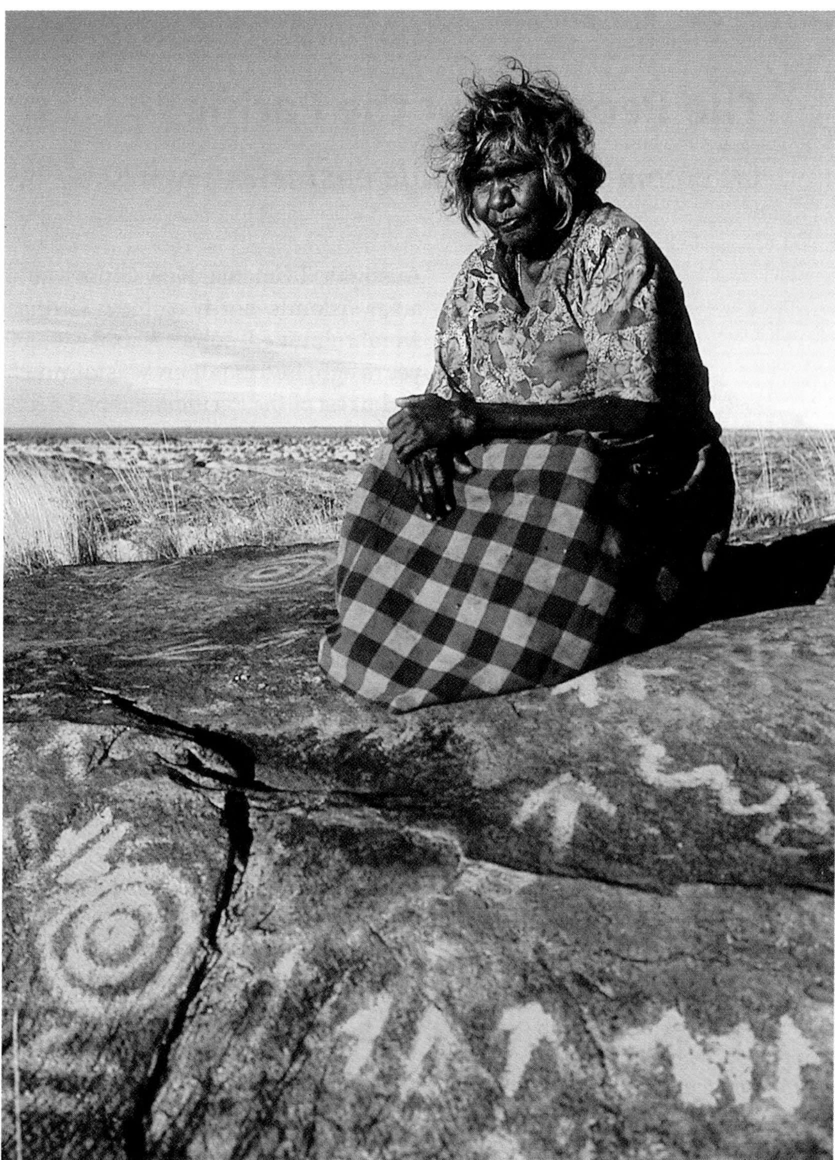

**Figure 4.54** Australian Aborigine art begins to appear about the same time as Upper Paleolithic art in Europe. This photo shows petroglyphs (carvings on stone).

Site

# Monte Verde

*Early hunter-gatherers in South America*

Figure 4.69 Monte Verde, 1983: a general view of the site and field laboratory. Excavation trenches can be seen running perpendicular to the creek in the lower right of the photograph. The buildings in the center of the photograph are part of the excavation headquarters.

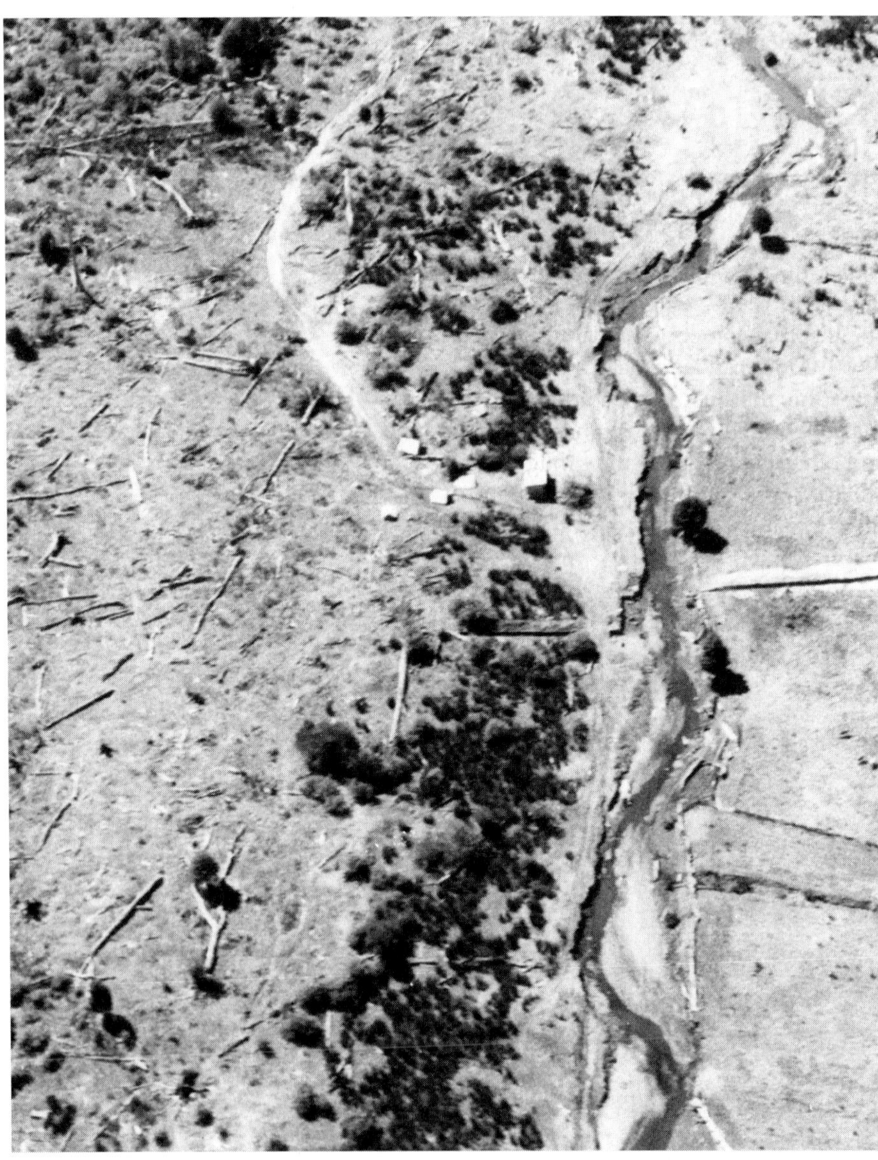

Traces of human groups in the Americas before 12,000 years ago are almost nonexistent. There are only a few examples of archaeological sites in the New World that contain both definite evidence of an early human presence and reliable radiocarbon dates. In many instances, sites that were candidates for very early human occupation have been discounted because of contaminated carbon samples or questionable stone artifacts.

The best examples of human occupation sites before 10,000 B.C. are in South America, rather than nearer the original point of entry across the Bering Strait. Monte Verde (MON-tay VER-day) is a 13,000-year-old residential site in the cool, forested region of northern Chile (Figure 4.69). The site was discovered in 1976 by Tom Dillehay, of the University of Kentucky. While surveying in the area, he discovered bone and stone artifacts in a shallow, swampy area—a peat bog—along Chinchihuapi Creek, a small, slow stream that drains this part of the rain forest of southern Chile. The site lies along the sandy banks on either side of the creek (Figure 4.70).

Excavations since the original discovery have uncovered a number of remarkable and unexpected finds for such an early site. Excellent conditions of preservation resulted in the recovery of plant remains and numerous wooden objects, along with stone flakes and broken animal bones. Wood is rare at most archaeological sites, but it was preserved in the bog at Monte Verde. Apparently, the bog developed during or shortly after the abandonment of the site and quickly enclosed all the remaining materials in a mantle of peat. Peat provides a waterlogged, oxygen-free environment where such objects can be preserved.

The timber and earthen foundations of perhaps 12 living structures were recovered in excavations (Figure 4.71). The rectangular foundations, made of logs and planks held in place with stakes of a different kind of wood, enclose rooms 3–4 m (10–13 ft) long on each side. Posts were placed along the foundation timbers and supported a framework of saplings, which may have

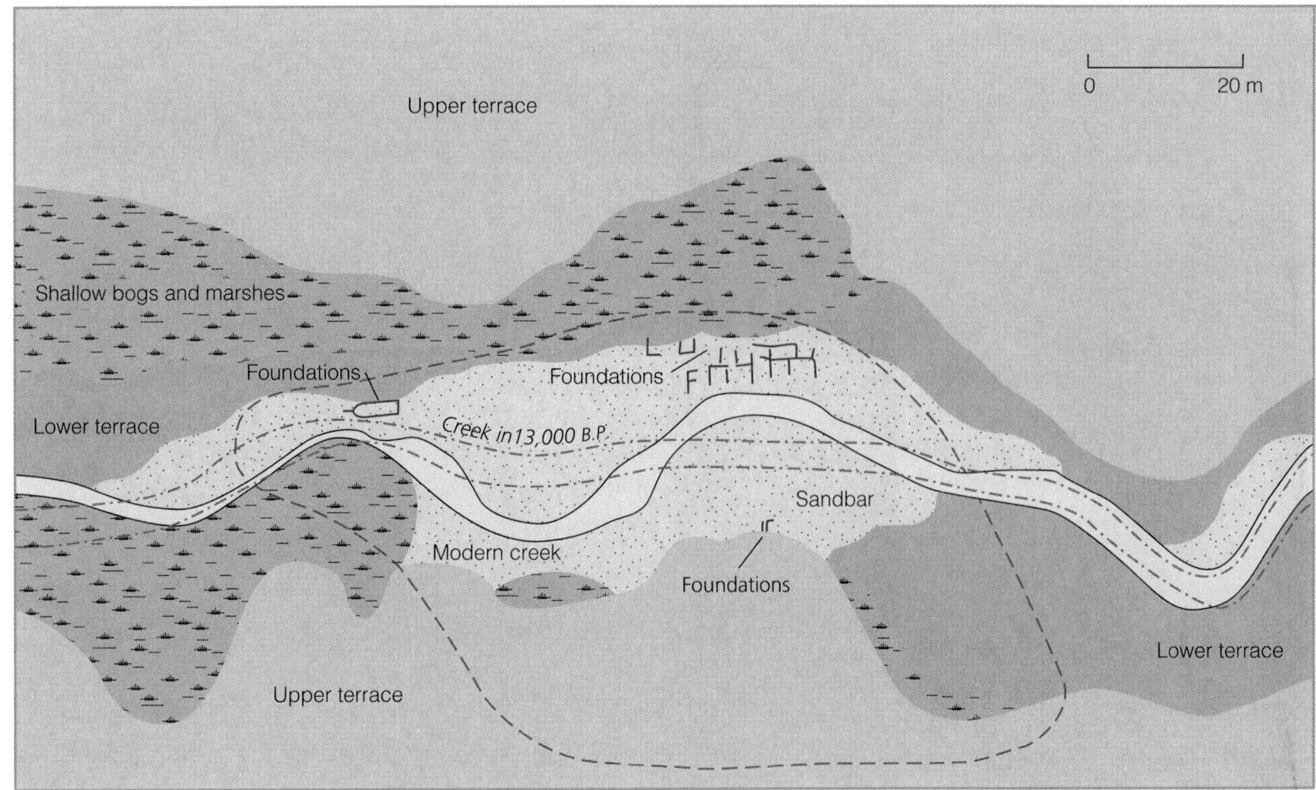


**Figure 4.70** The location and plan of the Monte Verde site. The settlement lay on both sides of the creek, covering an area of approximately 7000 m$^2$, as indicated by the dashed line. Foundations are outlined where they have been located.

been covered with animal skins. Small pieces of what may be animal hide were preserved next to the timber foundation. Two large hearths and a number of shallow clay basins provided fireplaces for the inhabitants of these huts. Even a child's footprint was found preserved in the hardened clay of the basin of one of the small fireplaces.

Many of the artifacts at the site were found inside the structures. Wooden artifacts include digging sticks, tool handles, spears, and a mortar or basin, in addition to the material used for construction. Several kinds of stone tools, both flaked and ground, were found. No stone projectile points were made here, but evidence of other weapons was uncovered. Spherical stones with an encircling groove were probably bola stones, a South American throwing weapon with three leather thongs weighted at each end. The bola is thrown in a spinning fashion, and the stone weights wrap the thongs around the prey. Other stone balls without grooves were likely used in a sling as heavy projectiles.

To the west of the living floors was a single, more substantial, rounded structure with a pointed end and a foundation of sand and gravel. The bases of wooden posts at the edge of the foundation mark the walls of the structure; a kind of yard or patio was marked off with branches near the entrance. Mastodon bones, animal skins, stone and wooden tools, salt, and the remains of several types of plants were found in this area.

The arrangement of these structures over an area of roughly 70 × 100 m (220 × 400 ft, about the size of a soccer field) suggests a well-organized community. Dillehay estimates that the site was occupied for perhaps a year by 20–30 people. The occupants of Monte Verde apparently relied primarily on plants and large animals for their livelihood. Most of the bones came from mastodons (a close but extinct relative of the elephant and the mammoth), a type of llama, amphibians, reptiles, and birds. Plant remains at the site are from species that ripen throughout the year, suggesting that this was a

Figure 4.71 Excavated structures at Monte Verde. The photo shows the remains of wooden hut foundations.

year-round settlement. The wetlands (marshes, bogs, and streams) of the Monte Verde area are a very rich environment, and many edible plants grow there today.

The plant remains document extensive gathering of the local vegetation. A total of 42 edible species of plants have been identified from the site. Most of the evidence is from tubers and roots that were preserved, including the wild potato. This is the oldest evidence anywhere for the potato, which was later domesticated in the Andes Mountains. The products of other plants, including seeds, berries, nuts, and fruits, were also recovered during the excavations. The number of grinding stones at the site points to the importance of plants in the diet at Monte Verde. Herbaceous plants were found, which today are used for medicinal, rather than nutritional, purposes. A chewed cud from two kinds of seaweed and the leaf of a tree was perhaps medicinal. Exotic objects, including several of the plant species, beach-rolled pebbles, quartz, and bitumen (an adhesive tar), were also brought to the site from the Pacific coast about 25 km (15 mi) to the south.

Why did it take so long for our ancestors to reach the New World?

The evidence from Monte Verde contradicts most traditional views of the peopling of the Americas. The radiocarbon date of 11,000 B.C. for this site in South America documents the fact that early Asians crossed the Bering Strait before 13,000 years ago.

The information from Monte Verde has forced a reconsideration of our interpretation of the earliest inhabitants of the New World, because it is in direct contrast to what has been observed at most sites where preservation is not nearly as good. Paleoindian sites normally contain small concentrations of stone artifacts, sometimes in association with the bones of large, extinct animals. Paleoindians are thought to have lived primarily as small, mobile groups of big-game hunters. The evidence for permanent residence at Monte Verde is in direct contrast to Paleoindian occupations elsewhere. The organic materials indicate the importance of plants, as well as animals, in the diet at that time. The existence of wood and wooden tools, more common at Monte Verde than stone artifacts, provides an intriguing look at the organic component of tools and equipment rarely seen in the archaeological record.

Site

# Lindenmeier

## *Late Pleistocene hunters in Colorado*

Lindenmeier, located in northern Colorado at an elevation of 2000 m (6500 ft) in the foothills of the Rocky Mountains, lies at the intersection of three major environmental zones: the eastern slope of the Rockies, the Colorado Piedmont, and the High Plains (Figure 4.72). Gullies cutting through sedimentary deposits in this area washed out and exposed the buried bones of large bison and large spearpoints. The local ranchers, who discovered these remains in 1924, wrote to the Smithsonian Institution in Washington, DC, to inform them of the site's existence.

In 1934, Frank Roberts, of the Smithsonian, was sent to investigate the site. Roberts wanted to document the association of hunters and extinct animals in the past. Early sites in North America were almost unknown at the time. Roberts' excavations at Lindenmeier continued each year from 1934 through 1940. The field crew spent almost 600 days on the excavations, opening over 1800 sq m (almost half an acre) in the process and digging deeply into the buried archaeological deposits (Figure 4.73). This project eventually uncovered one of the largest Paleoindian sites in the New World. Roberts' careful excavations and recording procedures allowed the final results of his original investigations to be published by others after his death.

Radiocarbon dates from the site place the occupation of Lindenmeier at 9000 B.C., just before the end of the Pleistocene. The climate at that time was less arid and cooler than it is today. The local environment at the site was more wooded, with stands of juniper and pine. Fragments of charcoal from these species were recovered from fireplaces at Lindenmeier. Ground cover would have been heavier, with thick grasses over much of the area. The area around the site can be envisioned as a lush meadow watered by an active spring, which attracted both animals and their predators. The spring, adjacent to the site, must have been the reason this spot was selected as a campsite.

More than 15,000 animal bones were recovered in the excavations. Twelve species were represented at Lindenmeier, including wolf, coyote, fox, hare, rabbit, turtle, deer, antelope, and bison; they inhabited all three

**Figure 4.72** The site of Lindenmeier (at the juncture of the arrows) located between the plains and the piedmont in eastern Colorado.

Figure 4.73 The 1937 Smithsonian Institution excavations at the site of Lindenmeier.

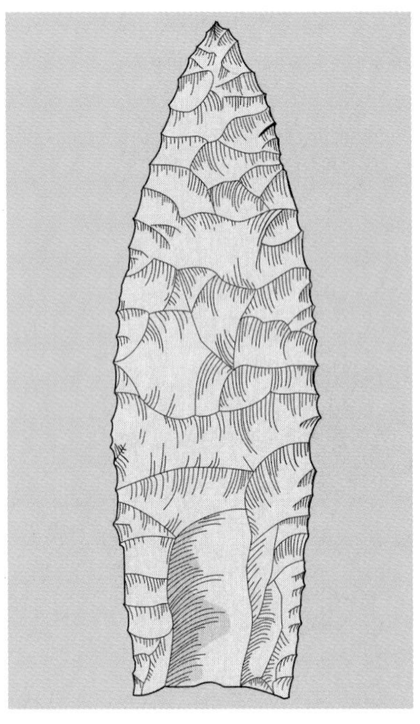

Figure 4.74 A Folsom Paleoindian point.

pressure flaking A technique for producing stone artifacts by removing flakes from a stone core by pressing with a pointed implement.

environments near the site. Antelope, wolf, and fox are native to the Rocky Mountains and the piedmont; bison, coyote, and jackrabbit are common in the High Plains. The bison was by far the most common animal represented at the site and must have provided most of the meat consumed there. This was a now-extinct form of bison, a huge animal some 2 m (6.5 ft) at the shoulder. In all likelihood, the Folsom hunters cooperated to drive these animals into blind canyons and other traps where they could more easily be killed.

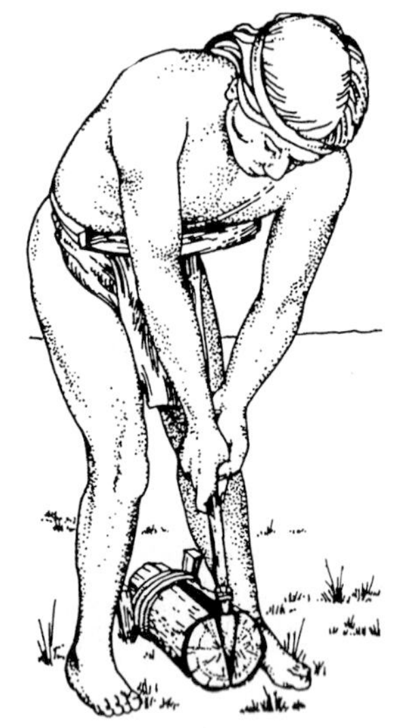

Figure 4.75 A Paleoindian flintknapper removing the flute from a Paleoindian point. A chest crutch is used to apply pressure to remove the flake from the base of the point. This flute, or channel, facilitates hafting.

More than 50,000 stone artifacts have been counted from the excavated areas at Lindenmeier. Approximately 5000 of these stone pieces and 70 bones were shaped into finished tools. The bone tools included needles and simple pointed pieces. In addition, a number of bone pieces decorated with notches and engraved lines, and several bone beads, were excavated.

More than 600 projectile points were recovered, including almost 250 Folsom points (Figure 4.74). These Paleoindian spear tips are slender, bifacially worked stone points, shaped carefully on all surfaces by **pressure flaking.** To finish the point, a single long flake, or flute, is removed from the base of each side as a channel to facilitate hafting to a wooden spear shaft. This fluting flake was probably removed by pressure using a chest crutch and vise (Figure 4.75). Paleoindian points are often found with the skeletons of big game animals such as giant bison, mastodon, and mammoth. Often broken points were either resharpened or reworked into other tools, such as scrapers and knives. The repair of broken equipment was one of the characteristic activities at these campsites.

Fifteen distinct concentrations of archaeological materials were observed in the excavations at Lindenmeier. Two groups of these concentrations, designated Area I and Area II, deserve special attention. Were these two collections of artifacts and bones left by the same group on separate visits or by two distinct groups, perhaps there at the same time? Careful measurements of the Folsom points in the two concentrations indicated two sizes. The points in one area were, on average, slightly smaller than, and fashioned in a different manner from, those in the other area. These differences suggest that two different groups of people were responsible for the two concentrations.

Further evidence for the differences between the two areas comes from the original sources for the obsidian found at the site. **Obsidian** is a type of natural glass produced by volcanic eruptions and is highly prized for making stone tools. Sources for obsidian are limited in number and size. The obsidian in Area I came from New Mexico, and the material in Area II came from the north, near Yellowstone National Park in Wyoming. Lindenmeier thus seems to provide evidence of two or more different social groups that came together, perhaps to cooperate in bison hunting, for a brief time some 11,000 years ago.

**obsidian** Translucent, gray-to-black or green, glasslike rock from molten sand.

Site

# Kennewick Man

*An early American*

In recent decades, our picture of the first inhabitants of the New World has changed dramatically because of the discovery of a number of new sites and skeletons. One of the most important of these finds is the human skeleton found near Kennewick in the state of Washington. The Kennewick material has provided major lessons in both archaeology and human relations.

Spectators at a boat race on the Columbia River in 1996 came across a human skull washing out close to the riverbank near the town of Kennewick, Washington. Over the next month, many other bones were found, and by the end of August that year, a radiocarbon date of 7500 B.C. revealed that Kennewick was one of the earliest human skeletons in the New World.

The discovery of Kennewick caused a major controversy about the ownership of the remains. Native American groups in the region wanted to rebury an ancient ancestor. Scientists wanted to study this early and unusual skeleton. This important matter was in the courts for years, and eventually, it was decided to let the scientists study Kennewick man in detail. The ethical debate surrounding this human skeleton is discussed in more detail in Chapter 12.

The original study of the Kennewick remains led the investigator, James Chatters, to conclude that they were probably from a more recent European descent because of the very good preservation of the bone, an absence of distinctive Native American features, and the location of an early European homestead near the site (Figure 4.76). However, Chatters subsequently noticed a stone projectile point, embedded in the pelvis of this individual, of a type known to be at least 4500 years old in the Pacific Northwest of North America.

Further examination of the Kennewick man revealed that his body had been intentionally placed in a grave on his back with his arms at his sides and his palms down. The skeleton was very well preserved, and all the teeth were intact in the jaw. The man was somewhat older, age 40–55, slender, and tall (around 173 cm; 5 ft, 7 in). He had endured a number of injuries in his lifetime, including a compound fracture of the rib cage and significant damage to his left shoulder, in addition to the projectile point in his pelvis. The cause of death could not be determined since all the observed injuries had healed. Analysis of amino acids and carbon and nitrogen isotopes in the bone revealed that fish was a substantial component of his diet.

This skeleton of a male individual is important not only because of its antiquity but also because of the unusual nature of the remains. The questions raised by the unusual features of the skull demand further investigation to better understand the original inhabitants of the Americas.

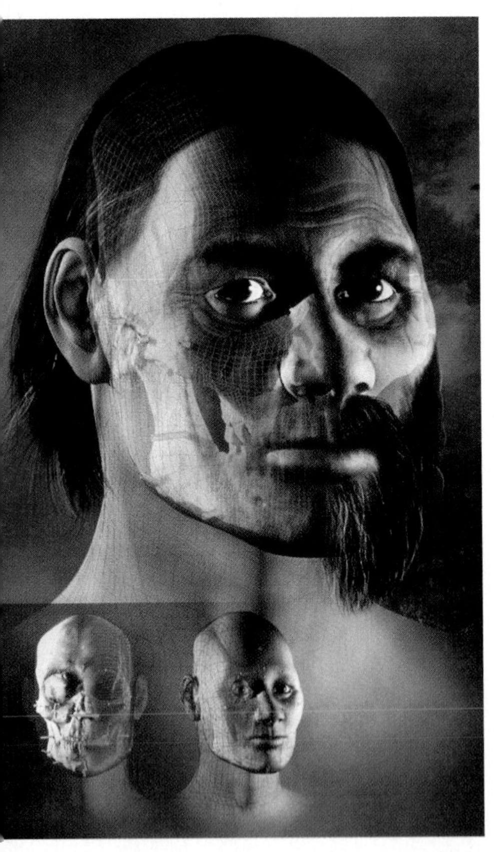

**Figure 4.76** The Kennewick skull, and the artistic reconstruction of the face.

# Images and Ideas
## The End of the Paleolithic

**Figure 4.77** A highly romanticized 1870 engraving of the noble savages of the Paleolithic.

The story of the Paleolithic is a remarkable saga—an evolutionary journey from primate to human. The major changes that occurred in human biology and culture made us essentially what we are today. We began more than 4 million years ago as chimpanzee-like primates living in open grassland environments of subtropical Africa. The climate was mild, plants grew year-round, and large predators killed and ate many animals, leaving behind bits of meat and bone marrow for hungry hominins. Sharpened edges of stone helped remove the meat, and other stones cracked the heavy bones. Biologically—lacking claws, big teeth, and speed—early humans were ill-equipped to defend themselves or their young from the predators of the plains. As social beings, however, with safety in numbers, they may have been able to drive away those ferocious carnivores.

The early hominin adaptation was a successful one that spread over most of Africa by about 2 million years ago. Brain size almost doubled during this period, and faces underwent dramatic changes. The handaxe was invented—a marvelous, multipurpose tool sculpted from a slab of stone. As hominin numbers and adaptive success increased, early humans began to move out of the African cradle into Eurasia, where a cooler, more temperate climate challenged ingenuity. The mysterious force of fire was controlled during this time for heat, light, and cooking, becoming a new ally in the continuing battle with nature. Plants were not available during the northern winters, and survival came to depend more on the hominins' abilities as hunters.

By 100,000 years ago, our ancestors had occupied much of the Old World, including the cold tundras of Pleistocene Europe and Asia. The human brain reached modern size. New tools and ideas prevailed against the harsh environment. Life became something more than eating, sleeping, and reproducing. Burial of the dead and care of the handicapped and injured illustrate a concern for fellow hominins. A cultlike preoccupation with cave bears and some evidence for cannibalism suggest a concern with the supernatural; ritual and ceremony achieved a place in hominin activities.

The Upper Paleolithic was the culmination of many trends—in biology and culture, in language and communication, in ritual and ideology, in social organization, in art and design, in settlement and technology—that had begun several million years earlier. Evolution brought humanity to our modern form, *Homo sapiens sapiens*. New continents were explored; Australia, North America, and South America were colonized. More kinds of implements were made from a wider variety of materials than ever before. Bows, boats, buttons, fishhooks, lamps, needles, nets, spearthrowers, and many other items were produced for the first time during this period. The dog was domesticated as a faithful hunting companion and occasional source of food. Caves and many artifacts were decorated with paintings, carvings, and engravings, as an awareness of art and design developed in the human consciousness (Figure 4.77). Sites from the Upper Paleolithic were larger and more common than those from previous periods. From almost any perspective, this period of the Upper Paleolithic represents a dramatic change in human behavior, almost certainly associated with changes in the organization of the brain or in the use of language, or both. Essentially modern behavior appeared following this transformation, and the rapid change from hominin to human, from archaic to modern, from the past to the present had begun.

The end of the Paleolithic was likely the apogee of hunter-gatherer adaptations. Successful groups of foragers lived and increased in almost all the environments on Earth. It was, in fact, this expansion in numbers that was partly responsible for the end of a hunter-gatherer way of life. Increasing populations required new and more productive sources of foods. The bounty of the land, the wild plants and animals of nature, simply were not enough to feed everyone. Experiments to increase the available amount of food were necessary. The story of the domestication of plants and animals and the beginning of the Neolithic is the subject of Chapter 6. Chapter 5 describes events after the end of the Pleistocene, leading to the beginnings of agriculture.

## DISCUSSION QUESTIONS

1. What caused the disappearance of Neanderthals in western Eurasia?
2. The Upper Paleolithic has been described as a time when human creativity expanded enormously. What kinds of evidence document these changes?
3. What are the major changes that mark the end of the Pleistocene and the Paleolithic?
4. Where did the first fully modern humans come from, and where did they go?
5. The arrival of the first Americans is one of the more controversial subjects in archaeology today. What is your impression, based on the available evidence?

**www.mhhe.com/priceip6e**

For more review material and study questions, see the self-quizzes on your online learning center.

## SUGGESTED READINGS

For Internet links related to this chapter, please visit our Web site at www.mhhe.com/priceip6e.

Bahn, P., and J. Vertut. 1997. *Journey through the Ice Age: Art and architecture.* Berkeley and Los Angeles: University of California Press. *Breathtaking photographs of the creative explosion.*

Bonnichsen, R., ed. 2004. *Who were the first Americans?* Corvallis, OR: Center for the Study of the First Americans. *The latest evidence from the artifactual and skeletal remains of the original inhabitants of the Americas.*

Clottes, J. 2008. *Cave art.* London: Phaidon Press. *A new view on the making of cave paintings.*

Fagan, B. 1987. *The great journey.* London: Thames & Hudson. *A very readable account of the arrival of the first Americans.*

Findlayson, C. 2004. *Neanderthals and modern humans: An ecological and evolutionary perspective.* Cambridge: Cambridge University Press. *An up-to-date review of the evidence for Neanderthal extinction and the role of modern humans.*

Harvati, K., and T. Harrison, eds. 2007. *Neanderthals revisited: New approaches and perspectives.* New York: Springer.

Hoffecker, J. F., W. R. Powers, and T. Goebel. 1993. The colonization of Beringia and the peopling of the New World. *Science* 259:46–53. *A technical synthesis of the evidence from northern North America and Asia.*

Klein, R. 2002. *The dawn of human culture.* New York: Wiley. *A new view of what it means to be fully human.*

Lewis-Williams, D. 2002. *The mind in the cave: Consciousness and the origins of art.* London: Thames & Hudson. *A recent consideration of the explanations for cave art with new insights from the ethnographic record.*

Lieberman, P. 1991. *Uniquely human: The evolution of speech, thought, and selfless behavior.* Cambridge, MA: Harvard University Press. *The evolution of language and other very human behaviors.*

Meltzer, D. J. 2009. *First peoples in a new world: Colonizing Ice Age America.* Berkeley: University of California Press. *The latest evidence on the colonization of North and South America.*

Mulvaney, J., and J. Kamminga. 1999. *The prehistory of Australia.* Washington, DC: Smithsonian Institution Press. *The latest summary of Australian archaeology.*

Schrenk, F. 2008. *The Neanderthals.* London: Routledge.

Tattersall, I. 1999. *The last Neanderthal: The rise, success, and mysterious extinction of our closest human relatives.* Boulder, CO: Westview Press. *A good summary of the Neanderthal question.*

Thomas, D. H. 2000. *Skull wars: Kennewick Man, archaeology, and the battle for Native American identity.* New York: Basic Books. *An examination of the Kennewick lawsuit and the ongoing conflict between Native American tribes and the scientific community over who owns the rights to archaeological finds.*

White, R. 1986. *Dark caves, bright visions: Life in Ice Age Europe.* New York: American Museum of Natural History. *A wonderfully illustrated volume on the art, both cave paintings and portable objects, of the Upper Paleolithic.*

# CHAPTER FIVE

**Figure 5.1** Burial of mother and infant son from Mesolithic Denmark, 5000 B.C.

# Postglacial Foragers

## Introduction
### The World after 8000 B.C.

*New solutions to changing environments*

Figure 5.1 shows a photograph of a double burial from the Stone Age cemetery at Vedbaek, north of Copenhagen, Denmark. The burial belongs to the Mesolithic period, dating to around 5000 B.C. There are a number of remarkable graves in this cemetery. This particular burial is of a mother and infant child. The 18-year-old mother's head rests on a bundle of tooth pendants that would have decorated a hide blanket or a piece of clothing. The newborn was buried next to his mother with a stone knife at his waist, like all the males in the cemetery. The child's body was placed on the wing of a swan. An artist's reconstruction of this grave can be found on page 173.

These remarkable graves also point to the rapid developments that were taking place in human society. The pace of change had increased dramatically over time. For example, there were more innovations in artifacts and behavior during the Upper Paleolithic than in all the preceding periods. A number of major changes also took place at the end of the Pleistocene, beginning around 11,000 years ago. Large-game hunting, an adaptation that had characterized human prehistory for much of the Middle and Upper Paleolithic, began to decline as certain large-animal species became extinct and environments changed in response to warming climatic conditions. Human diet became more diversified and included more plant and animal species.

This chapter examines the early part of the Postglacial period. In a few areas—Southwest Asia, the Far East, and parts of the Americas—plant and animal domestication appeared in the early Postglacial and began to alter the long-standing hunting-and-gathering pattern of human subsistence. These origins of agriculture are discussed in Chapter 6. In other places, hunter-gatherers continued their way of life, adapting to the changing environmental conditions of the Holocene. The term **hunter-gatherers** refers to human groups (also known as foragers) who use only the wild, natural resources of the earth, hunting animals, fishing, and collecting plants, nuts, seeds, shellfish, and other foods for their sustenance. Although different terms are used in the Old World and the New World for this period—Archaic in the New World and Mesolithic in the Old World—the basic way of life was very similar.

The term **Mesolithic,** or Middle Stone Age, designates the period between the end of the Pleistocene and the beginnings of agriculture in Europe, North Africa, and parts of Asia. Only in the past 30 years has the significance of the early Postglacial period been recognized. Since the beginning of the 1800s, the Upper

#### CHAPTER OUTLINE



**www.mhhe.com/priceip6e**

For preview material for this chapter, see the comprehensive chapter outline and chapter objectives on your online learning center.

"A word of advice, Durk: It's the Mesolithic. we've domesticated the dog, we're using stone tools, and no one's naked anymore."




Paleolithic and the Neolithic have been acknowledged as important episodes in human prehistory. The Mesolithic, however, was thought to have been a period of cultural degeneration, occurring between the time of the spectacular cave paintings of the late Paleolithic and that of the farming communities of the Neolithic. Today, however, the Mesolithic is recognized as a time of intensification in human activities and organization (Figure 5.2).

In their adaptations, these hunter-gatherer societies were similar to other groups in Africa, eastern Asia, and North and South America, consuming a wide range of wild plant and animal species and using a highly specialized technology. An incredible range of fishing gear, including nets, weirs, hooks, and harpoons, was developed during this period. Ground stone artifacts appear as axes, celts, plant-processing equipment, and other tools. Projectile weapons were equipped with a variety of tips made of bone, wood, antler, or stone.

In those areas of Europe where bone and other organic materials have been preserved, artifacts are often decorated with fine, geometric designs. Cemeteries that are sometimes present at Mesolithic sites suggest more sedentary occupations. An example of a Mesolithic settlement discussed in this chapter is found in Denmark, where excavations at Vedbaek have exposed a cemetery and settlement dating to about 5000 B.C. Information from this site provides a good picture of early Postglacial hunter-gatherers.

In South and East Africa, the term *Late Stone Age* is used to refer to the artifacts and the encampments of Holocene hunter-gatherers. Although most studies focus on the earlier periods of human prehistory in Africa, new findings from Elands Bay Cave on the west coast of South Africa provide some indication of the way of life of these groups shortly before the introduction of herding and farming.

The similarity of Postglacial adaptations in many parts of the world is remarkable. What is responsible for this pattern?

In Japan, the period between the beginning of the Holocene and the introduction of rice cultivation is known as the Jomon. Thousands of settlements were occupied during this time, and these food-collecting peoples created very sophisticated pottery. In fact, some of the earliest ceramics in the world were made in Japan approximately 12,000 years ago. Sannai Maruyama in northern Japan is a remarkable example of a Jomon settlement around 5500 years ago.

In North America, the Paleoindian period of big-game hunting ended approximately 9000 years ago, about the same time many species of big game became extinct. The period between 6000 and 1000 B.C. is known as the **Archaic** and is very similar to the Mesolithic in Eurasia. Human groups began to exploit a broad spectrum of food sources. Many new sorts of subsistence pursuits seem to have begun at this time. Ground stone tools such as mortars and grinding stones have been found at some Archaic sites, indicating an increasing reliance on plant foods. Exotic materials in some regions document an increase in long-distance trade for obsidian, copper, and shell. The date for the end of the Archaic varies in different areas of North America. In some regions, such as the West Coast, the basin and range landscapes of what is now the western United States, and the subarctic and arctic reaches of Canada and Alaska, hunting and gathering persisted up to and beyond European contact. In other areas, such as the southwestern United States (Arizona, Colorado, New Mexico, Utah) and the major river valleys of the midwestern and southeastern United States, a more sedentary way of life involving the use of cultivated plants, or **cultigens,** began as early as 1000–500 B.C., and

**hunter-gatherer** A hunter of large wild animals and gatherer of wild plants, seafood, and small animals, as opposed to farmers and food producers.

**Mesolithic** The period of time of hunter-gatherers in Europe, North Africa, and parts of Asia between the end of the Pleistocene and the introduction of farming; the Middle Stone Age.

**Archaic** The term used for the early Holocene in the New World, from approximately 6000 B.C. to 1500–1000 B.C.

**cultigen** A cultivated plant.

perhaps even earlier. In fact, recent evidence from plant genetics suggests that the domesticated gourd was carried into the Americas by some of the early settlers almost 10,000 years ago.

Great diversity in Archaic adaptations was also seen in eastern North America, with major emphasis on fishing, hunting, and plant and nut collecting. Archaic sites such as Carrier Mills in southern Illinois document adaptations typical of this area. Settlements were often located along lakes, rivers, and coastlines to take advantage of aquatic resources. Piles of freshwater mussel shells, the remains of prehistoric meals, are enormous; some examples up to 0.5 km (600 yd) long, 100 m (300 ft) wide, and 8 m (25 ft) high are found along major rivers in the southeastern United States. Along the Atlantic seaboard, huge shell middens also accumulated, documenting the importance of marine foods in the diet of the hunter-gatherers of New England and the East Coast. In the Great Lakes region, native copper from the Lake Superior region was used extensively by peoples of the Old Copper culture. Copper knives, spearpoints, and various pendants and jewelry were cold-hammered from nuggets of native copper (Figure 5.3).

Archaic sites in the Great Plains document a major focus on bison hunting. Sites in the dry, desert West contain artifacts and organic materials that indicate an emphasis on both plant foods and hunting for subsistence. Groups in the Great Basin collected numerous seeds and nuts and hunted antelope and small game such as rabbits. The location of the sites discussed in this chapter, as well as the timeline for these places, is shown in Figure 5.4.

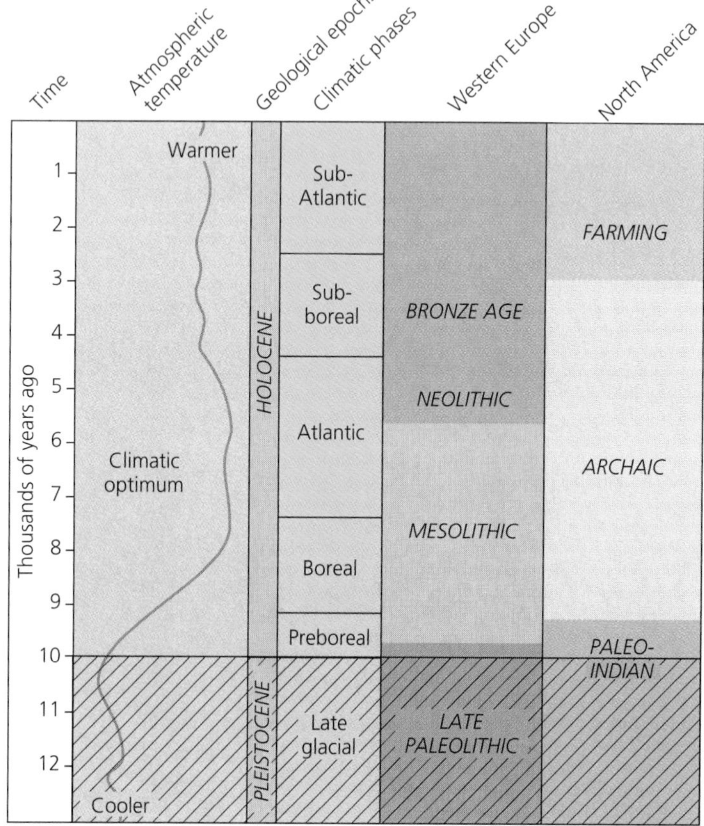


**Figure 5.2** The climate, geology, and archaeological sequence in Europe and North America during the past 12,000 years. The end of the Pleistocene is shaded.

**Figure 5.3** Artifacts from the Old Copper Archaic culture in the midwestern United States. The longest spear point is approximately 15 cm (6 in) long.

We have been hunters for much of our past. Does that behavior have consequences today?

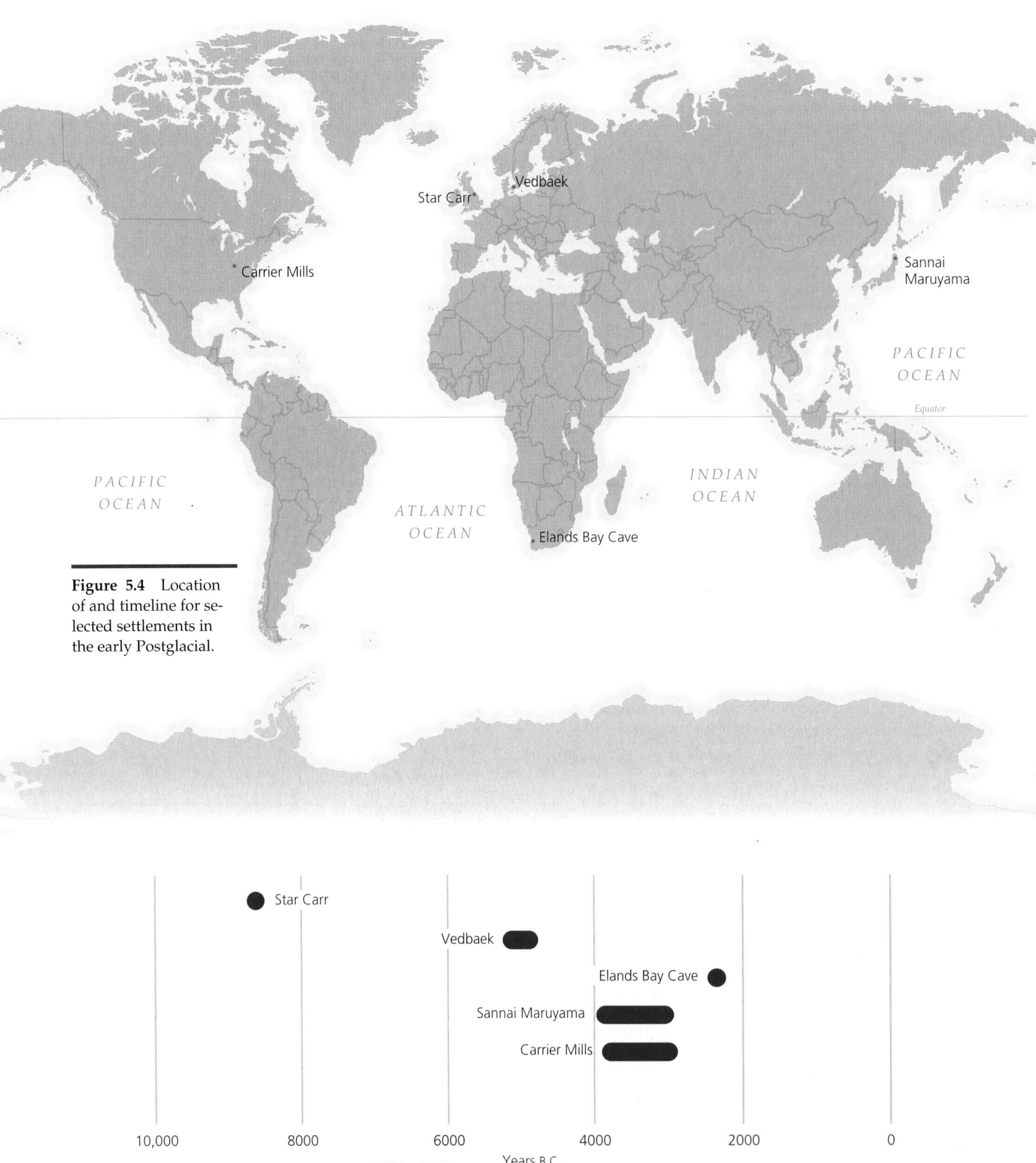


**Figure 5.4** Location of and timeline for selected settlements in the early Postglacial.

*Concept*

# The Postglacial Environment of Europe

## *The conditions of the Present Interglacial*

Although the basic topography of the earth has not changed significantly since the end of the Pleistocene, the environment itself has undergone dramatic modifications in vegetation, fauna, and sea level. A marked shift in climate at the end of the Pleistocene was largely responsible for such environmental changes (Figure 5.5). Dramatic deviations from modern conditions are clear. Europe was as much as 8°C (20°F) colder during the ice ages some 18,000 years ago than it is today, and warmer than at present by 1–2°C (2–5°F) around 7000 years ago, during the early Postglacial.

One of the results of the increasing temperatures at the close of the Pleistocene was the melting of continental ice sheets and a consequent rise in the level of the oceans. During the maximum cold period of the last glaciation, around 18,000 years ago, the sea was as much as 125 m (400 ft) below its present level. A gradual rise in the level of the oceans began after 16,000 years ago and continued during the early Postglacial (Figure 5.6). The rate of increase was variable, but a rise of as much as 1 m (3.3 ft) per century occurred during the period of maximum warming. The rising Postglacial seas did not reach present beaches until sometime after 5000 years ago.

The higher sea levels of the Postglacial transformed the outline of the continents. Australia separated from New Guinea and Tasmania. The peninsula of Indonesia broke up into islands. The Bering Land Bridge was submerged and filled by the Bering Strait. The east coast of North America moved west by more than 100 km (60 mi) in some areas. The British Isles separated from the European continent as

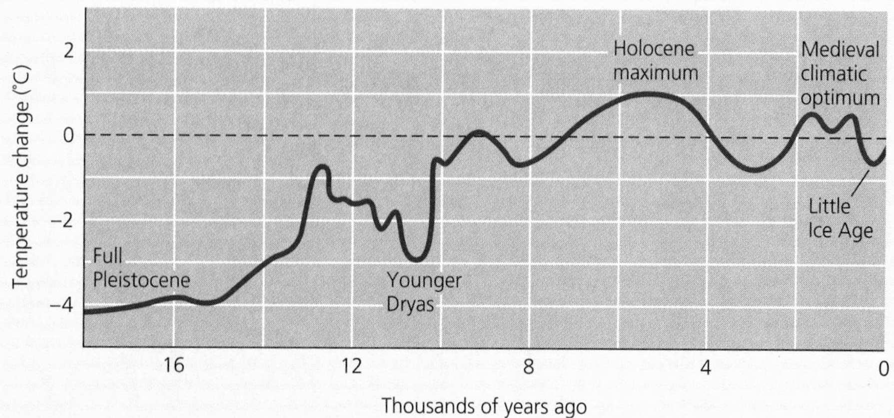


**Figure 5.5** Average temperature increased dramatically from the late Pleistocene into the Holocene. The dotted line at 0°C represents the average temperature today.

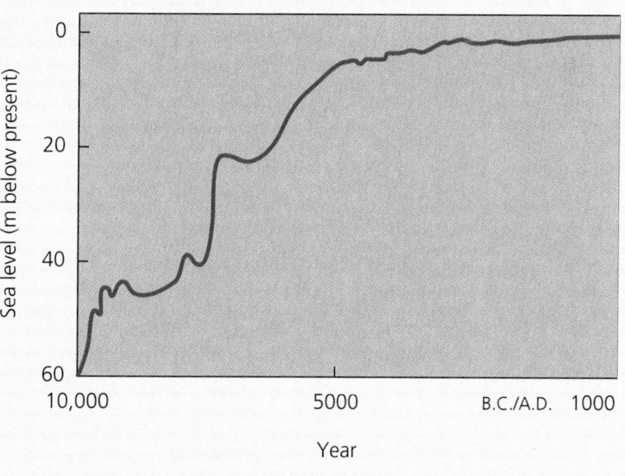


**Figure 5.6** Changes in sea level over the past 12,000 years. Holocene sea levels reached modern coastlines only in the past few thousand years.

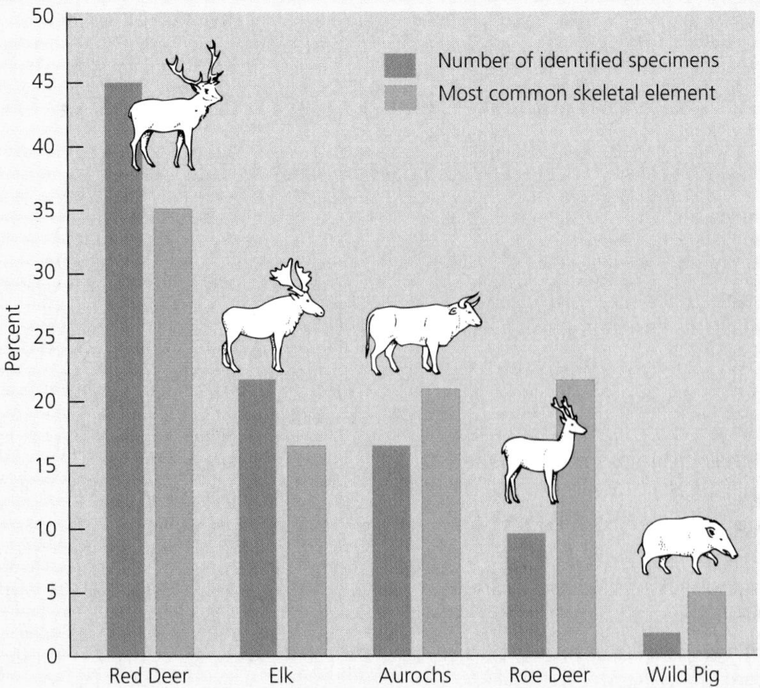


**Figure 5.7** Animals represented in the bones at the Mesolithic site of Star Carr in England, and the estimated weight of their meat. Notice that although the bones of roe deer are the second most common, the meat from this animal provides only a small part of the diet. Aurochs contribute the largest portion of animal protein.

the English Channel was flooded by rising seas.

The forest history of Europe emphasizes the complexity of vegetational development through the end of the Pleistocene and during the early Holocene. Many of the plant species that disappeared during glacial conditions in the north survived along the southern coasts of Europe. Late Pleistocene deciduous forests were restricted primarily to southwestern Europe; hazel, oak, and elm survived in western France and northern Spain. Following the close of the Pleistocene, deciduous forests spread through most of western Europe, with the exception of small areas of Mediterranean forest in southern Italy, southern France, northeastern Spain, and the islands of the western Mediterranean.

Along with those dramatic changes in climate and vegetation, there were pronounced changes in animal life. The large migratory herds of reindeer, mammoth, horse, and other game that roamed the tundra disappeared, either moving to the north where ice sheets previously existed or becoming extinct. In their place came the more recent species of European mammals adapted to the forest: the European elk (the same animal as the North American moose), the aurochs (wild cattle), the European red deer (the same animal as the North American elk), the wild boar, and the small roe deer. Those species made up the bulk of the terrestrial animal diet of Mesolithic hunters in Europe (Figure 5.7).

# Site

## Vedbaek

### *Prehistoric communities in Mesolithic Denmark*

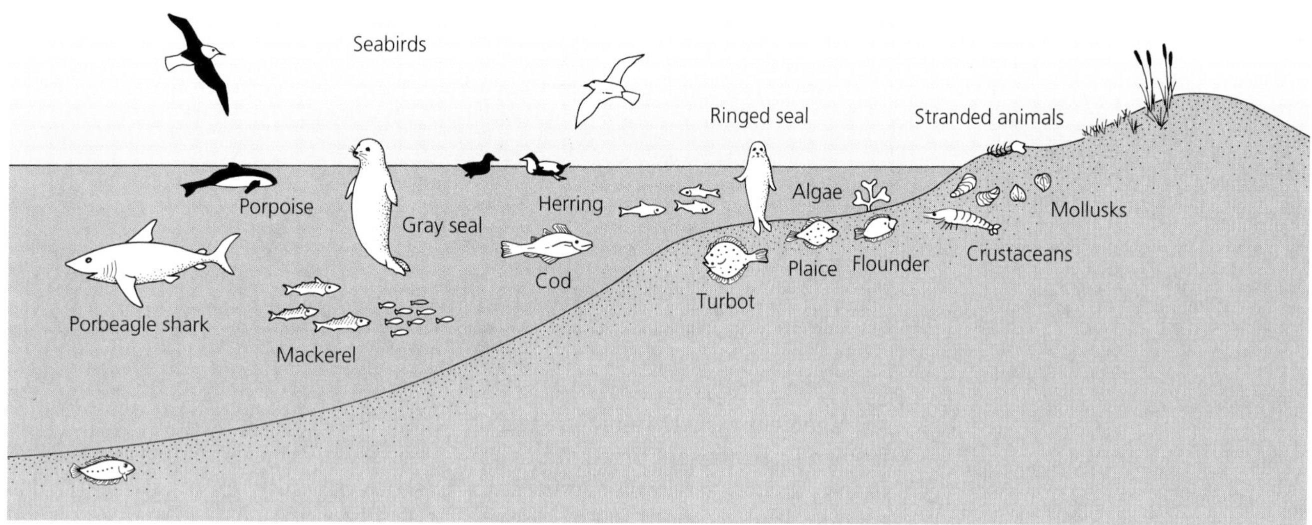


**Figure 5.8** A variety of marine foods were consumed by the inhabitants of Vedbaek. Some of those species and their preferred habitats are indicated here.

Denmark and the rest of Scandinavia have been occupied only briefly in the scale of prehistoric time, essentially since the close of the Pleistocene and the retreat of the ice sheets from northern Europe. At that time, as temperatures rose, the tundra gave way to open woodlands of birch and pine, and eventually to a mixed forest of lime, oak, elm, and other deciduous trees. These forests were occupied initially by herbivores such as aurochs and European elk, followed soon after by wild pig, the European red deer, roe deer, and many small mammals and birds. Inhabiting the streams and lakes were large numbers and varieties of fish. The inlets and islands of the seas around southern Scandinavia would have offered a rich source of food and were the locations of human settlement during the later Mesolithic. Wild animals and plants from the land, sea, and air were the focus of their hunting-and-gathering activities. The inland forests were probably quite dense, supporting little wildlife.

By 7000 years ago, there had been a dramatic shift in human social

**Figure 5.9** Excavations at Vaenget Nord. The excavators removed the topsoil, leaving the Mesolithic artifacts in place to map their location and distribution.

Figure 5.10 The plan of the Vedbaek site after excavation, showing specific activity areas and features. The site was located on a small island.

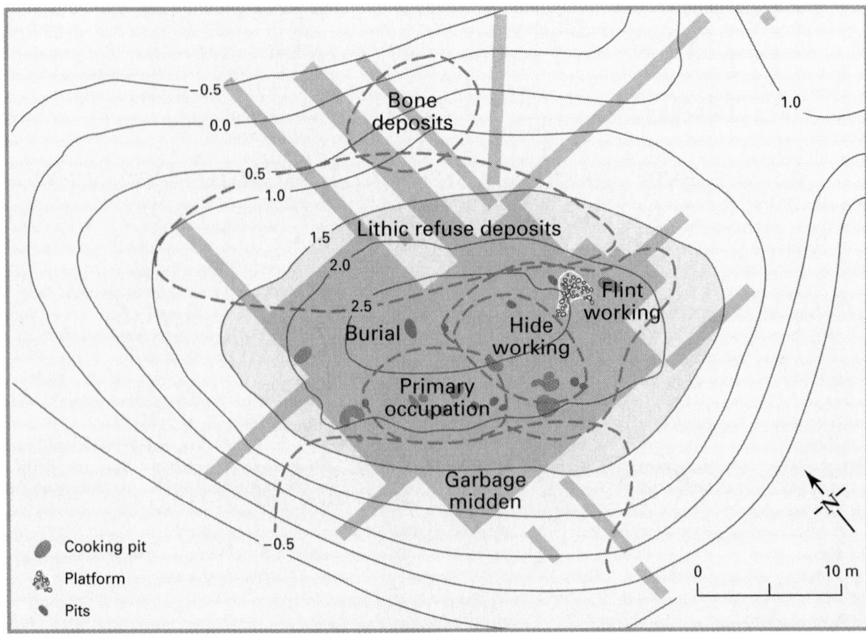


arrangements in this area from the first small, scattered groups of inland, tundra-dwelling reindeer hunters to concentrations of more sedentary societies along the coastlines. These groups expanded their resource base, eating fish, seals, porpoises, small whales, oysters, mussels, clams, and the like (Figure 5.8). Settlements became more permanent, and the dead began to be buried in cemeteries.

**www.mhhe.com/priceip6e**

For a Web-based activity on an archaeological excavation in Norway, see the Internet exercises on your online learning center.

An example of such a situation can be seen at an important archaeological area near the town of Vedbaek (vay-BEK) near Copenhagen, Denmark (Figures 5.9 and 5.10). Following the retreat of the ice, the Vedbaek Valley contained a freshwater system of lakes and streams. Warming trends continued, and rising sea level filled the mouth of the valley sometime around 5500 B.C., creating a brackish inlet. The shallow waters around the shoreline and islands of the inlet were covered with stands of reeds and sea grass. Over time, the inlet filled up with deposits of reeds, leaves, and other organic materials, becoming the layer of peat that it is today.

In 1975, a Mesolithic graveyard was discovered here during the construction of a new school (Figure 5.11). The cemetery is radiocarbon-dated to approximately 4800 B.C. and contains the graves of at least 22 males and females of various ages. All the individuals in the burials were fully extended, with one slightly curled-up exception. Powdered red ochre was found in many of the graves. Racks of red-deer antler were placed with elderly individuals; males were buried with flint knives; females often were interred with jewelry made of shell and animal teeth.

In one grave, a newborn infant was found buried on the wing of a swan next to his mother (Figure 5.12). The infant was buried with a flint knife, as were all the males in the cemetery. The mother's head had been placed on a cushion of material such as an animal skin that was elaborately decorated with ornaments of snail shells and deer teeth. Similar materials were found around her waist, suggesting a skirt or costume of some kind. The cemetery also contained rather dramatic evidence for conflict among the groups occupying northern Europe at that time. The simultaneous burial of three individuals in a single grave—an adult male with a lethal bone point in his throat, an adult female, and a child—suggests both the violent death of all three and the existence of a nuclear family (Figure 5.13).

Since the discovery of the cemetery, Vedbaek has been the focus of in-

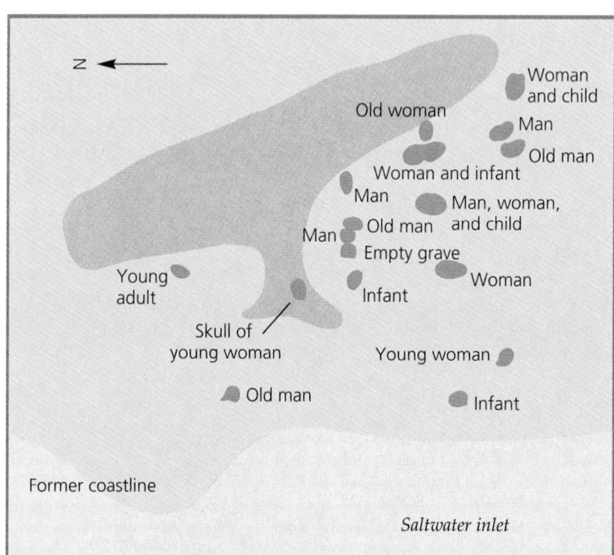


**Figure 5.11** The Mesolithic cemetery at Vedbaek, near the coastline of the former inlet. The darker area is the location of the construction activities that resulted in the discovery of the burials.

tensive investigations. More than 50 archaeological sites have been located around the shore of the inlet, and excavations have been undertaken at several of these places. Some 60 species of fish, reptiles, birds, and mammals have been identified in the bone remains from these sites. These species come from every environment—the forest, streams, lakes, wetlands, the inlet, the sound, and the sea. Terrestrial animals are predominantly red deer, roe deer, and wild pig. Marine foods, however, provided a major portion of the diet; fish and seal bones are very common at the sites.

Mesolithic sites in northern Europe were usually located on the shore, emphasizing the importance of the sea. Distinct zones of artifact deposition can be seen at such sites. The actual living floor on dry land is characterized by the presence of hearths, pits, construction stone, and some artifacts. Stone tools and other artifacts are generally small, suggesting that larger refuse may have been swept up and tossed or discarded elsewhere. Organic materials such as bone and plant remains generally do not survive on the surface of the ground in temperate climates.

A second zone of refuse, originally discarded in the water next to the settlement, can be recognized in the layers adjacent to the occupation floor. Larger materials in this zone are well preserved, including stone, bone, antler, and sometimes wooden artifacts. Because much of the shoreline of the Vedbaek inlet was occupied during the Mesolithic, this second zone often contains a vertical stratigraphy of tools and other debris. This information has been used to construct a detailed chronology for the area. Changes in artifact types and manufacturing methods can be traced through time.

Repeated residence at the same location, however, tends to smear and obscure information about the horizontal arrangement of the prehistoric settlement, the locations of structures and associated hearths and pits. For that reason, an excavation was organized to uncover a settlement of brief occupation, where horizontal patterns

**Figure 5.12** An artist's interpretation of the mother and infant burial at Vedbaek. A photo of their grave opens this chapter.

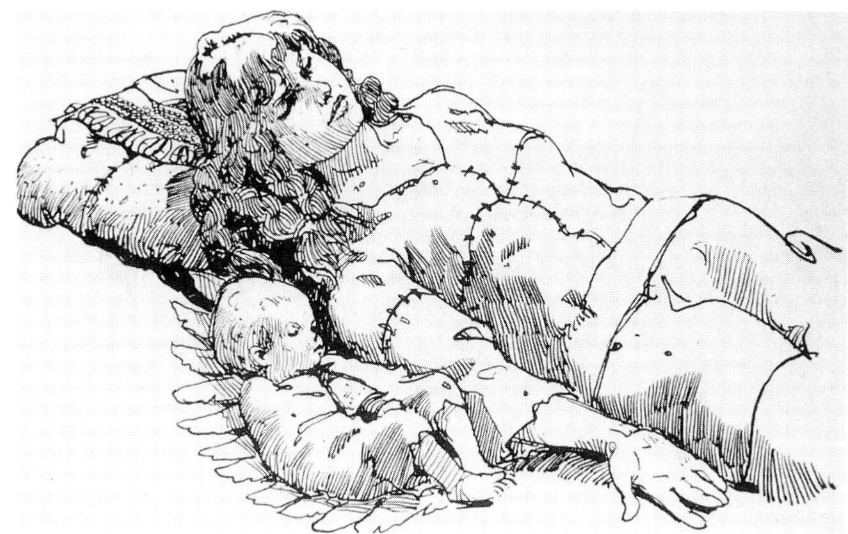

**Figure 5.13** The burial of an adult male, a small child, and an adult female from Vedbaek. Notice the lethal bone point in the throat of the male and the cluster of animal teeth on the chest of the female.

of the use of living space might be examined. Several factors pointed to a site called Vaenget Nord (VING-it nord). Today, the location of this site is marked by a grove of birch trees growing on a slight rise in the landscape. The rise had been a small island during the period when an inlet of the sea filled the Vedbaek valley around 7500 years ago. The island was flooded and eventually submerged by rising sea level shortly after that date. Thus, the period when it could have been a platform for human occupation was limited. The age of the artifacts and radiocarbon dates reinforce these impressions. Excavations revealed that the number of artifacts per square meter was lower at this site than at the heavily used shoreline sites.

Major excavations by teams of Danish and American archaeologists began in 1980 and concluded in 1983. The excavation strategy was twofold. Narrow trenches were cut into the deep marine deposits along the former shore of the island to reveal the refuse zone. Broad horizontal units were opened on the surface of the island to expose the living floor and the distribution of artifacts, pits, fireplaces, and other items.

The surface sediments of the island are light sandy clays. The darker traces of past human activities such as digging, fire building, and the placement of posts are often retained in this light soil. On top of this natural surface of the island is a layer of cultural materials, made up of ash and charcoal, organic refuse, and the like. The thickness of this layer varies across the top of the island and is deeper along the sloping shoreline.

In two areas at the southern and eastern margins of the island, large boulders had been fractured into numerous

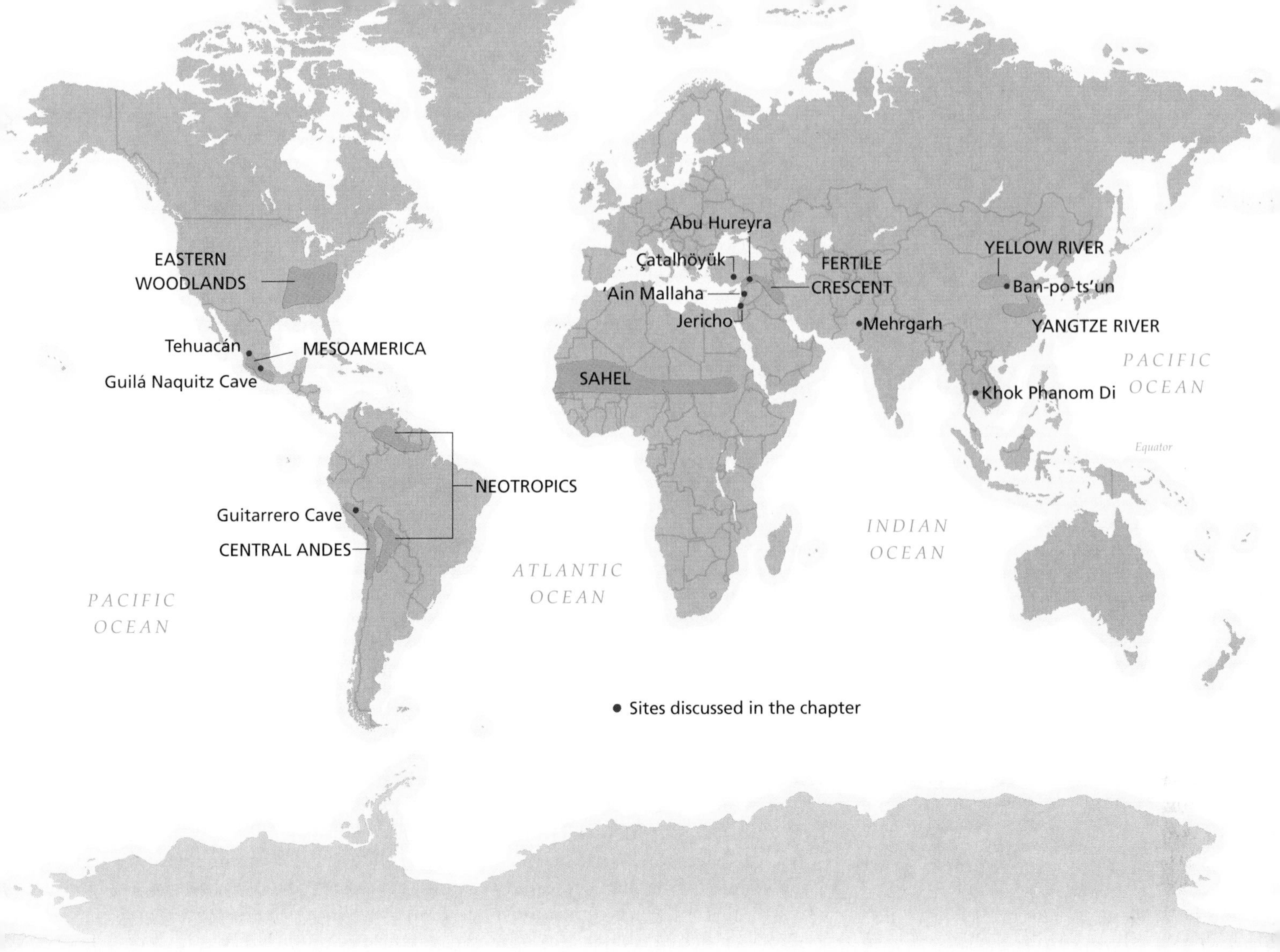

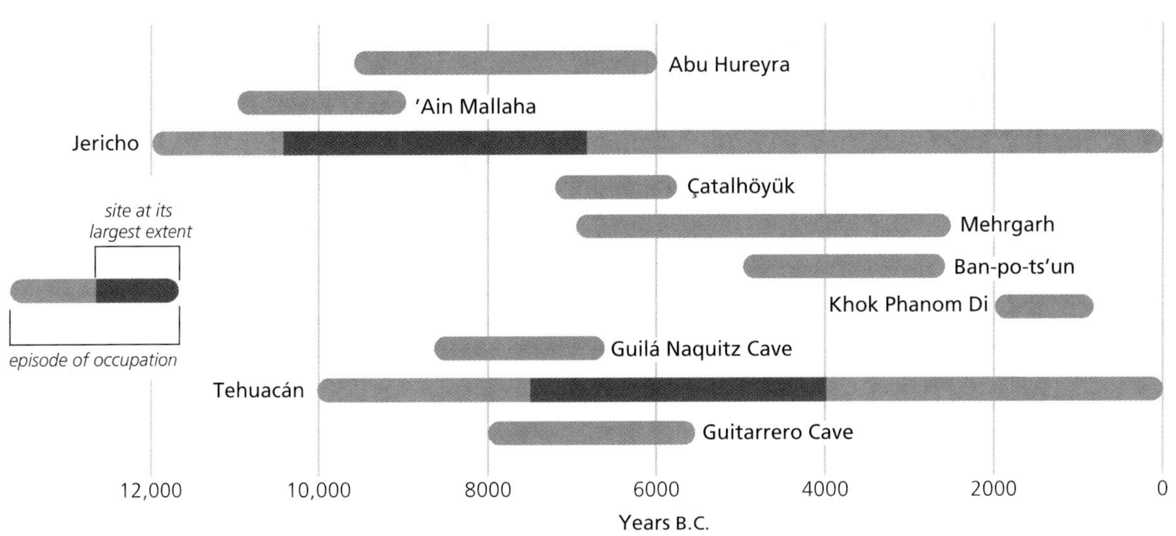


**Figure 6.5** Location of and timeline for primary centers of domestication.

**Figure 6.6** Images of maize production from the Codex Florentino.

In addition to those major centers of domestication, other areas witnessed the beginnings of horticulture or agriculture shortly after the end of the Pleistocene. Recent evidence suggests that agriculture was practiced very early in New Guinea. Radiocarbon dates from a digging stick found in what appear to be ancient agricultural fields indicate a date of around 7000 B.C. These fields were probably used for fruit and tuber crops such as yams. In eastern North America, several local plants such as marsh elder and goosefoot (*Chenopodium*) were domesticated by 1500 B.C., long before the introduction of corn from Mexico (see also "Agriculture in Native North America," p. 258). Clearly, there was a trend toward domestication and agriculture on a global scale at the beginning of the Holocene.

Following a discussion of various explanations for the origins of agriculture, this chapter traces the beginnings of farming in the different centers that have been identified. Because of the better quantity and higher quality of archaeological information from Southwest Asia, much of the discussion focuses on that area. Many geographic terms have been used to designate the area, including *Near East, Middle East,* and *Southwest Asia. Near East* refers to the Arabic countries of North Africa and southwestern Asia. The Middle East and Southwest Asia have similar boundaries, but the term *Middle East* reflects the view from Europe. Hence, *Southwest Asia* is the best way to describe the region.

In Southwest Asia, we examine one site from before the transition to agriculture—'Ain Mallaha—and two early Neolithic communities—Abu Hureyra and Jericho—to see the changes that took place. Çatalhöyük, an enormous early Neolithic settlement, documents the consequences of the Neolithic revolution in terms of completely new ways of inhabiting the world. From Southwest Asia, the tour goes to South Asia and the site of Mehrgarh, an early Neolithic community in Pakistan. In East Asia, the sites of Ban-po-ts'un in northern China and Khok Phanom Di in coastal Thailand provide some sense of the Neolithic in that part of the world. There are at least three primary centers of domestication in the New World as well, in Mesoamerica, South America, and North America. The important early sites of Guilá Naquitz and in the Tehuacán Valley provide evidence of early plant domestication in Mexico. Excavations at Guitarrero Cave, high in the Andes, give us a glimpse of the process of domestication in South America.

The summary section, "Images and Ideas," considers the spread of agriculture from those primary centers, like the ripples spreading from a pebble thrown into a pond, to areas where domesticates were introduced from other places. Subsequent chapters explore the expansion of agriculture into Europe and parts of North America. We also discuss how this major change in human subsistence revolutionized economies, social organization, settlement, and ideology. Human society was never again the same after the beginnings of domestication. Even societies that continued to hunt and gather after the Neolithic were dramatically, and often drastically, affected by neighboring farmers.

Concept

# Explaining the Origins of Agriculture

## *The how and why of farming*

It is remarkable that the process of domesticating plants and animals appears to have taken place separately and independently in a number of areas at about the same time. Read it again: The almost simultaneous appearance of domesticated plants and animals around the globe between roughly 10,000 and 5000 years ago is astounding. Given the long prehistory of our species, why should the transition to agriculture happen within such a brief period, a few thousand years in a span of over 6 million years of human existence? An important and dramatic shift in the trajectory of cultural evolution demands explanation. But such answers are hard to find.

Views on and evidence for the origins of agriculture continue to be revised and updated. We can best understand ideas about the origins of agriculture from a historical perspective, considering the early theories first. Hypothetical explanations of why domestication occurred include the oasis hypothesis, the natural habitat hypothesis, the population pressure hypothesis, the edge hypothesis, and the social hypothesis. A consideration of these ideas also reveals much about the nature of archaeology and archaeologists. Theories about the origins of agriculture have often focused on the earliest evidence from Southwest Asia and, for that reason, may not be appropriate to all places where early domestication actually occurred.

During the first half of the twentieth century, the best information on early farming villages came from riverine areas or oases with springs in North Africa and Southwest Asia—along the Nile River in Egypt or at Jericho in the Jordan Valley, for example. At that time, the end of the Pleistocene was thought to have been a period of increasing warmth and dryness in the earth's climate. Researchers reasoned that because the ice ages were cold and wet, they should have ended with higher temperatures and less precipitation. Given that view of past climate, logic suggested that areas such as Southwest Asia, a dry region to begin with, would have witnessed a period of aridity at the end of the Pleistocene when vegetation grew only around limited water sources. The **oasis hypothesis** suggested a circumstance in which plants, animals, and humans would have clustered in confined areas near water. V. Gordon Childe, one proponent of this idea, argued that the only solution to the competition for food in these situations would have been for humans to domesticate and control the animals and the plants. In this sense, domestication emerged as a symbiotic relationship for the purpose of human survival.

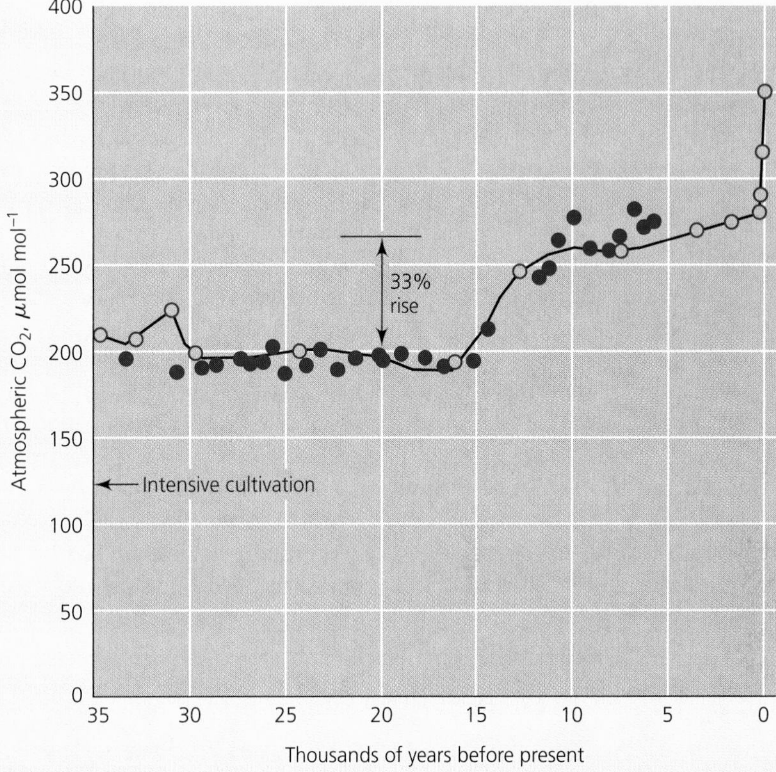


**Figure 6.7** A graph of carbon dioxide levels in the atmosphere for the past 35,000 years. Note particularly the big increase between 15,000 and 10,000 years ago and then again in recent decades.

**oasis hypothesis** The theory that domestication began as a symbiotic relationship between humans, plants, and animals at oases during the desiccation of Southwest Asia at the end of the Pleistocene.

*The conditions of incipient desiccation . . . would provide the stimulus towards the adoption of a food-producing economy. Enforced concentration by the banks of streams and shrinking springs would entail an intensive search for means of nourishment. Animals and men would be herded together in oases that were becoming increasingly isolated by desert tracts. Such enforced juxtaposition might promote that sort of symbiosis between man and beast implied by the word domestication.*

—V. Gordon Childe (1951)

*The food-producing revolution seems to have occurred as the culmination of the ever increasing cultural differentiation and specialization of human communities. Around 8000 B.C., the inhabitants of the Fertile Crescent had come to know their habitat so well that they were beginning to domesticate the plants and animals they had been hunting and gathering.*

—Robert Braidwood (1960)

**natural habitat hypothesis** The theory that the earliest domesticates appeared in the area that their wild ancestors inhabited.

**population pressure hypothesis** The theory that population increase in Southwest Asia upset the balance between people and food, forcing people to turn to agriculture as a way to produce more food.

**edge hypothesis** The theory that the need for more food was initially felt at the margins of the natural habitat of the ancestors of domesticated plants and animals; a revised version of the population pressure hypothesis.

More recently, detailed information on climate change has come from a most unlikely place—the glaciers of Greenland. Deep corings of the ice sheets there have provided a layered record of changes in temperature and other aspects of climate for the past 100,000 years and more. One of the very interesting results of this research was the documentation of a 33% increase in atmospheric carbon dioxide at the end of the Pleistocene (Sage, 1995) (Figure 6.7). Higher levels of $CO_2$ would foster the expansion of temperate species such as grasses, which include many of the ancestors of the major domesticated species. The full implications of such changes in the atmosphere are not yet clear, but the changes may have played a role in the transition from hunting to farming.

During the 1940s and 1950s, however, new evidence indicated that there had been no major climate changes in Southwest Asia at the close of the Pleistocene—no crisis during which life would have concentrated at oases. The new information forced a reconsideration of the origins of agriculture. The late Robert Braidwood pointed out—in his **natural habitat hypothesis**—that the earliest domesticates therefore should appear where their wild ancestors lived. That area, the "hilly flanks" of the Fertile Crescent in Southwest Asia, should be the focus of investigations. Braidwood and a large team of researchers excavated at the site of Jarmo in northern Iraq. The evidence from this early farming village supported his hypothesis that domestication did indeed begin in the natural habitat. Braidwood did not offer a specific reason as to why domestication occurred, other than to point out that technology and culture were ready by the end of the Pleistocene, that humans were familiar with the species that were to be domesticated. At that time, archaeologists and others considered farming to be a highly desirable and welcome invention, providing security and leisure time for prehistoric peoples. Once human societies had recognized the possibilities of domestication, they would have immediately started farming.

Lewis Binford, of Southern Methodist University, challenged those ideas in the 1960s and proposed the **population pressure hypothesis.** Binford argued that farming was backbreaking, time-consuming, and labor-intensive. Citing studies of living hunter-gatherers, he pointed out that they spent only a few hours a day obtaining food; the rest of their time was for visiting, talking, gambling, and otherwise enjoying life. Even in very marginal areas, such as the Kalahari Desert of South Africa, food collecting is a successful adaptation, and people rarely starve. Binford argued, therefore, that human groups would not have become farmers unless they had no other choice, that the origin of agriculture was not a fortuitous discovery but a last resort.

Binford made his point by positing an equilibrium between people and food, a balance that could be upset by either a decline in available food or an increase in the number of people. Since climatic and environmental changes appeared to be minimal in Southwest Asia, Binford thought it must have been increased population size that upset the balance. Population pressure was thus introduced as a causal agent for the origins of agriculture: More people required more food. The best solution to the problem was domestication, which provided a higher yield of food per acre of land. At the same time, however, agricultural intensification required more labor to extract the food.

Binford further suggested that the effects of population pressure would have been felt most strongly not in the core of the natural habitat zone, where dense stands of wild wheat and large herds of wild sheep and goats were available, but at the margins, where wild foods were less abundant. This theory, incorporating ideas about population pressure and the margins of the Fertile Crescent, has become known as the **edge hypothesis.**

Binford's concern with population was elaborated by Mark Cohen, of the State University of New York–Plattsburgh. Cohen argued for an inherent tendency for growth in human population, a pattern responsible for the initial spread of the human species out of Africa, the colonization of Asia and Europe, and eventually colonization of the Americas as well. After about 10,000 B.C., according to Cohen, all the habitable areas of the planet were occupied, and population continued to grow. At that time, there was an increase in the use of less desirable resources in many areas. Land snails, shellfish, birds, and many new plant species were added to the human diet around the end of the Pleistocene. Cohen argued that the only way for a very successful, but rapidly increasing, species to cope with declining resources was for them to begin to cultivate the land and domesticate its inhabitants, rather than simply to collect the wild produce. Domestication for Cohen was a solution to problems of overpopulation on a global scale.

Others, arguing that the transition to farming and food storage and surplus cannot be understood simply in terms of environment and population, have developed **social hypotheses** to explain the origins of agriculture. Barbara Bender, of the University of London, and Brian Hayden, of Simon Fraser University, for example, have suggested that the success of food production may lie more in the ability of certain individuals to accumulate a surplus of food and to transform that surplus into more valued items, such as rare stones and metals. From this perspective, agriculture was the means by which social inequality emerged and egalitarian societies became hierarchical.

There are several other useful theories about why human societies adopted agriculture at the end of the Pleistocene. Geographer Carl Sauer suggested that agriculture began in the hilly tropics of Southeast Asia, where sedentary groups with knowledge of the rich plant life of the forest might have domesticated plants for poisons and fibers. Botanist David Rindos has argued that domestication was a process of interaction between humans and plants, evolving together into a more beneficial symbiotic relationship.

In a fascinating book titled *Birth of the Gods and the Origins of Agriculture,* French archaeologist Jacques Cauvin argues that the important changes associated with the "Neolithic revolution" were more cultural than economic. That is, the transition to farming involved concepts and ideas as much as or more than cultivating and herding. Specifically, he suggested that domestication was preceded by the emergence of new religious practices and symbolic behavior (Figure 6.8). The transformation of hunter-gatherers that allowed them to view their habitat in a different way also promoted the more active exploitation of that environment.

Some problems with all these theories can be seen in a brief consideration of the evidence from Southwest Asia. The earliest agricultural villages, places such as Abu Hureyra and Jericho, were indeed located at the margins of the natural habitat. Attempts to artificially reproduce stands of wild wheat there may have resulted in

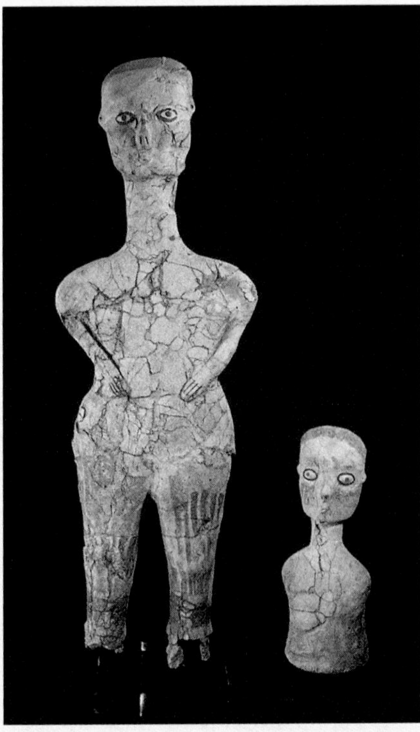

**Figure 6.8** Two statues of plaster found with several others at the site of 'Ain Ghazal in Jordan. The eyes are cowrie shells set in bitumen. The taller statue is 90 cm (about 3 ft) high. Such figures likely reflect changing religious beliefs in the Neolithic.

*Change in the demographic structure of a region which brings about the impingement of one group on the territory of another would also upset an established equilibrium system, and might serve to increase the population density of a region beyond the carrying capacity of the natural environment. Under these conditions, manipulation of the natural environment in order to increase its productivity would be highly advantageous.*

—Lewis Binford (1968)

*Technology and demography have been given too much importance in the explanation of agricultural origins; social structure too little. . . . Food production is a question of techniques; agriculture is a question of commitment. . . . Commitment is not primarily a question of technology but of changing social relations. This account has chosen to emphasize the social properties of gatherer-hunter systems; to show how alliance structures, and the individuals operating within these structures, make demands on the economic productivity of the system; how demography and technology are products of social structure rather than independent variables.*

—Barbara Bender (1978)

**social hypothesis** The theory that domestication allowed certain individuals to accumulate food surplus and to transform those foods into more valued items, such as rare stones or metals, and even social alliances.

**Non Sequitur** by Wiley

*By approximately 11,000 or 12,000 years ago, hunters and gatherers, living on a limited range of preferred foods, had by natural population increase and concomitant territorial expansion fully occupied those portions of the globe which could support their lifestyle with reasonable ease. By that time, in fact, they had already found it necessary in many areas to broaden the range of wild resources used for food in order to feed growing populations. I suggest that after that time, with territorial expansion becoming increasingly difficult and unattractive as a means of adjusting to growing population, they were forced to eat more and more unpalatable foods, and in particular to concentrate on foods of low trophic level and high density.*

—Mark Cohen (1977)

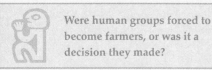

Were human groups forced to become farmers, or was it a decision they made?

**sedentism** Living in permanent, year-round contexts, such as villages.

domestication. However, human populations were not particularly large just before agriculture. Several sites show signs of abandonment in the levels beneath those layers that contain the first domesticated plants. The most recent climatic evidence indicates that there was, in fact, a period of slightly cooler and moister temperatures in Southwest Asia at the end of the Pleistocene, which may have greatly expanded the geographic range of wild wheats and barley, making them available to more human groups and fostering the process of domestication. In combination with the evidence for changes in $CO_2$ at that time, the possibility becomes intriguing. At the same time, however, these species were present in North Africa and parts of Southwest Asia during the Pleistocene and were not domesticated. Other factors were at work.

Some theories may seem reasonable in one of the primary centers of domestication but not in another. The sequence of events in two areas is of particular interest here. In Southwest Asia, permanent settlements are known from 11,000 B.C., before the presence of direct evidence for domesticated plants or animals. Cultivated plants appeared about 9000 B.C.; animals were probably not herded until perhaps 8500 B.C. Pottery did not come into general use until around 7500 B.C. In Mesoamerica, however, the archaeological sequence reveals that domesticated plants first appeared around 5000 B.C., followed by pottery and then permanent villages several thousand years later. Domesticated animals were never important in this area. The differences in these two areas indicate that **sedentism** and cultivation are not totally dependent on each other. It is also clear that domesticated animals are not a part of the equation in all areas.

Because of the difficulties in trying to excavate phenomena such as social relations and population pressure, many of the current theories are hard to evaluate. Any adequate explanation of the agricultural transformation should deal not only with *how* it all began but also with *why* it happened rather suddenly. Population and climatic change certainly play a role in cultural evolution, but we cannot yet say precisely why plants and animals began to be domesticated shortly after the end of the Pleistocene.

The how and the why of the Neolithic transition remain among the more intriguing questions in human prehistory. Simply put, there is, as yet, no single accepted general theory for the origins of agriculture. No common pattern of development is apparent in the various areas where domestication first took place. At the same time, of course, the evidence we have is still scanty and limited. This chapter examines the origins of agriculture in more detail in the several primary centers where it first appeared: Southwest Asia, East Asia, Mexico, and South America, as well as Africa and eastern North America.

# 'Ain Mallaha

## *Pre-Neolithic developments in Southwest Asia*

Discussions about the origins of agriculture often focus on Southwest Asia, for several reasons: (1) The earliest evidence for plant domestication from anywhere in the world is found here, (2) there is a reasonable amount of information available from excavations and other studies, and (3) Southwest Asia is often considered the "cradle of Western civilization."

To better understand the origins of agriculture in this region, it is useful to look at human settlements that preceded domesticated plants and animals. The period just before agriculture, roughly 11,000–9000 B.C., is referred to as the Natufian. Most of the evidence for this period comes from the **Levant,** a mountainous region in the eastern Mediterranean. The period was characterized by an increase in the number of sites, and therefore people, coinciding with a period of more rainfall and abundant vegetation. The natural habitat was rich in wild plants and animals, resources that supported permanently settled communities before any evidence of domestication.

The Natufian site of 'Ain Mallaha (ein ma-LA-ha) lies beside a natural spring on a hillside overlooking the swamps of Lake Huleh in the upper Jordan Valley of Israel (see Figure 6.12). 'Ain Mallaha was one of the earliest villages anywhere in the world, dating to 11,000–9000 B.C. The entire settlement covered an open area of about 2000 $m^2$ (½ acre, the size of a large hockey rink), with a population estimated at 200–300 people. Excavations between 1955 and 1973 by Jean Perrot, of the French Archaeological Mission in Jerusalem, uncovered three successive layers with the remains of permanent villages. Each layer contained a number of round houses, ranging from 3 to 8 m (10 to 25 ft) in diameter (Figure 6.9). House entrances faced downhill toward the water.

**Figure 6.9** Excavations at 'Ain Mallaha exposing burials under the house floors.

The remarkable architecture consists of large substantial houses with stone foundations standing to a height of almost 1 m (3 ft). Wooden center posts may have supported conical roofs. Stone-lined square or oval hearths and bins were found in the center of the rooms or against the walls. **Mortars** and **querns**—grinding tools and surfaces for preparing grain—were occasionally set into the floor (Figure 6.10). Although the structures were built close together, the community had a centrally located open area with round storage pits.

The ground stone artifacts include plates, bowls, mortars, and pestles, indicating a need for containers at this time (Figure 6.11). Several objects are decorated with elaborate geometric designs. Carved limestone figurines of a human body, a human face, and a tortoise also were found. The flaked stone industry is rich, with more than 50,000 pieces. The bone tools include awls, skewers, needles, and fishhooks.

The animal bones found at the site come from wild pig, three kinds of deer, wild goat, wild cattle, wild horse, and

**Levant** A mountainous region paralleling the eastern shore of the Mediterranean, including parts of the countries of Turkey, Syria, Lebanon, and Israel.

**mortar** A bowl-shaped grinding tool, used with a wood or stone pestle for grinding various materials.

**quern** A stone grinding surface for preparing grains and other plant foods and for grinding other materials.

**gazelle** One of several species of small to medium swift and graceful antelopes native to Asia and Africa.

**net-sinker** A small weight attached to fishing nets.

Figure 6.10 Two circular houses at 'Ain Mallaha. These structures have rock wall foundations and often contain grinding equipment, storage bins, and pits. Burials were often placed in abandoned storage pits.

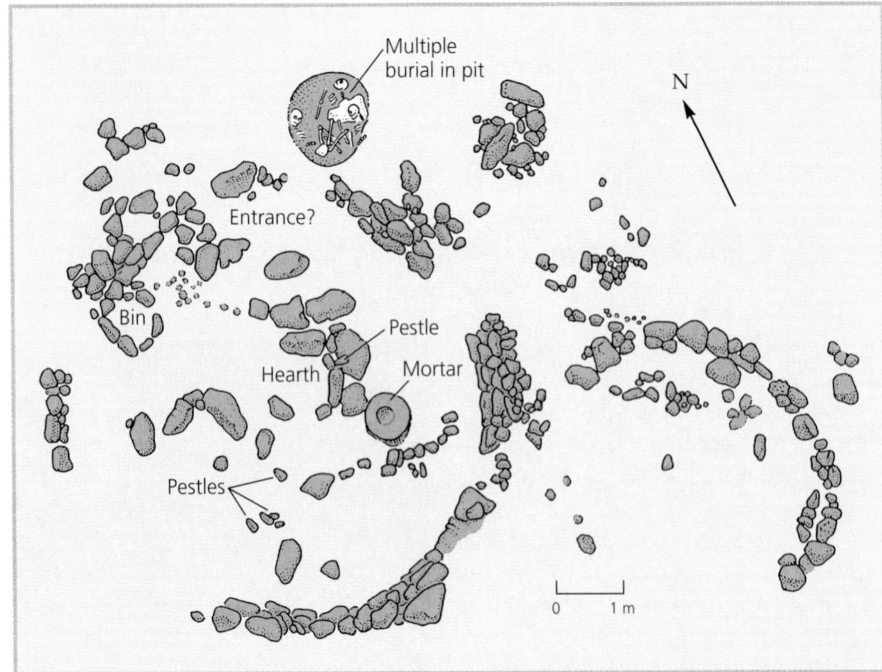


Figure 6.11 Various artifacts from 'Ain Mallaha. a–j: chipped stone tools; k–m, o: ground stone tools; n: a mortar; p–r: ground stone containers.

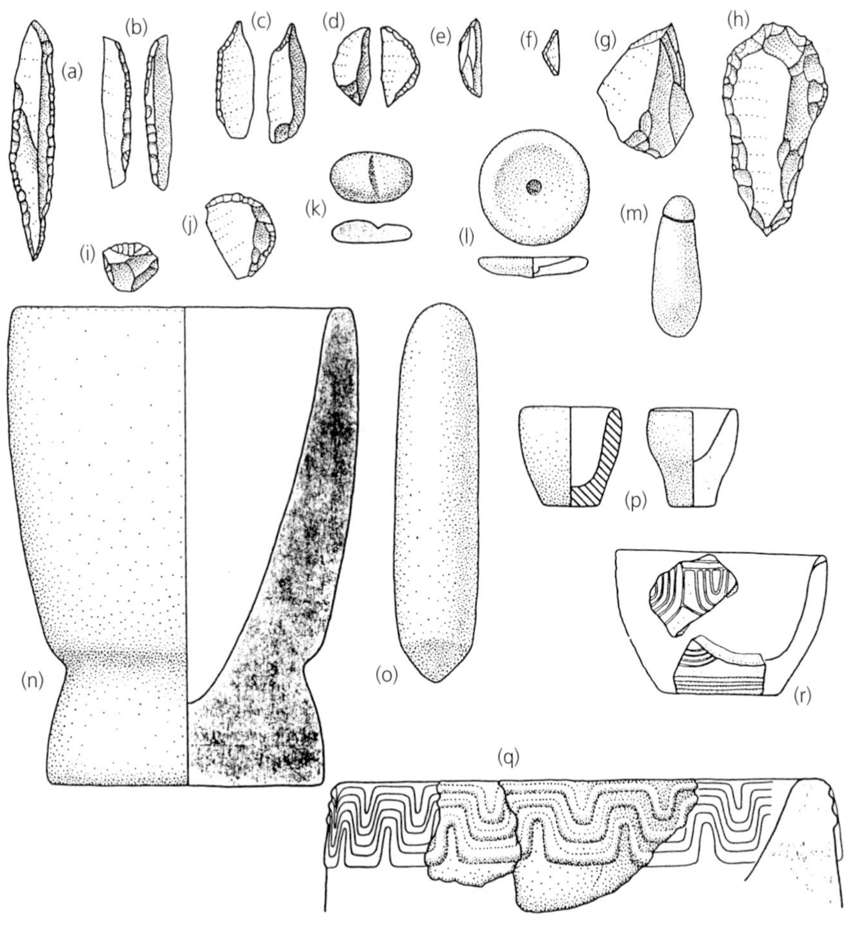


**sickle** A tool for cutting the stalks of cereals, especially wheat. Prehistoric sickles were usually stone blades set in a wood or antler handle.

gazelle. **Gazelle** is the most common game animal at sites of this period. Bird, fish, tortoise, and shellfish remains also were found. The lake was clearly an important resource for these people, as indicated by the fish and shellfish remains, along with **net-sinkers.** The high incidence of decay in the teeth of individuals buried at 'Ain Mallaha suggests that carbohydrates from cereals or other plants were consumed in quantity. Wild barley and almonds were found charred in excavations, and it is clear from the abundance of **sickle** blades and other plant-processing equipment that wild cereals played an important role in the diet.

Two kinds of burials were found at 'Ain Mallaha: (1) individual interments, including child and infant burials beneath stone slabs under the house floors; and (2) collective burials in pits, either intact or as secondary reburials after soft tissue had disappeared. Most of the 89 graves were found outside the houses. Abandoned storage pits were often reused for burial purposes. Many graves contained red ochre, and limestone slabs covered several of the simple graves. Four horns from gazelle were found in one grave, and in another, an old woman was buried with a puppy. Shells from the Mediterranean and rare greenstone beads or pendants from Syria or Jordan were occasionally placed with the burials, but grave goods were generally rare.

*Concept*

# Wheat, Barley, Pigs, Goats, and Sheep

## *The appearance of the first farmers in Southwest Asia at the end of the Pleistocene*

Southwest Asia is a fascinating region. Perhaps too well known today for the political problems that beset it, the area also was the home of the earliest domesticated plants and animals, as well as some of the world's first civilizations. Southwest Asia is an enormous triangle of land, approximately the size of the contiguous United States. The area is bounded on the west by Turkey and the Mediterranean, on the south by Saudi Arabia and the Indian Ocean, on the north by the Black and Caspian seas, and on the east by Afghanistan, at the edge of South Asia.

Southwest Asia is a series of contrasts. Some of the highest and lowest places in the world are found there, along with both rain forest and arid desert. Snow-capped mountains are visible from scorching-hot wastelands. Water is an important resource; arable land with fertile soil is scarce. The environment of this area can be visualized as a series of bands, driest in the south and moistest in the north. Arabia is largely sand and desert; Mesopotamia, the classic region between the Tigris and Euphrates rivers, is too dry for farming unless some form of irrigation is used. Mesopotamia has nothing to do with the origins of agriculture.

Most plants cannot survive in areas with less than 300 mm (1 ft) of rain each year. The line showing this 300-mm rainfall isobar stretches along an arc of mountains. The Zagros Mountains of western Iran, the Taurus Mountains of southern Turkey, and the highlands of the Levant along the eastern Mediterranean shore form a region where more rain falls and a variety of plants grow in abundance. The area is known as the **Fertile Crescent,** a name that reflects the variety of plants and animals that became the basic staples of many agricultural societies (Figure 6.12). This region is the natural habitat of many of the wild ancestors of the first species of plants and animals to be domesticated at the end of the Pleistocene—the wild wheats and barleys; the wild legumes; and the wild sheep, goats, pigs, and cattle that began to be exploited in large numbers at the time of the first agriculture.

Some 20,000 years ago, a series of developments began in Southwest Asia that set the stage for village farming. Climatic conditions during this period are not completely understood, but some general patterns are known. Around 18,000 B.C., global temperatures were about 6°C (10°F) cooler than they are today. A warming trend began about 14,000 B.C. and increased to a maximum temperature around 4000 B.C. Climate at the very beginning of the Neolithic, 11,000 years ago, was somewhat variable. Precipitation changes were not dramatic, but in an arid area, minor changes in rainfall can have a significant impact on vegetation. Rainfall was lowest during periods of maximum cooling around 18,000 B.C. As temperature and precipitation increased, the forest zone expanded in Southwest Asia, and the number of species was greater than it is today. After about 8000 B.C., however, continuing increases in temperature likely resulted in more evaporation, so that effective precipitation began to decline and the forest cover shrank.

Within this climatic and environmental context, a gradual change from a broad-spectrum diet, focusing on the many wild species of the region, to a diet that concentrated on a few domesticated plants and animals can be seen. In the late Paleolithic, after 20,000 years ago, groups of hunter-gatherers lived in small, seasonal camps throughout the area. Although they exploited a range of resources, they focused on

**Fertile Crescent** An upland zone in Southwest Asia that runs from the Levant to the Zagros Mountains.

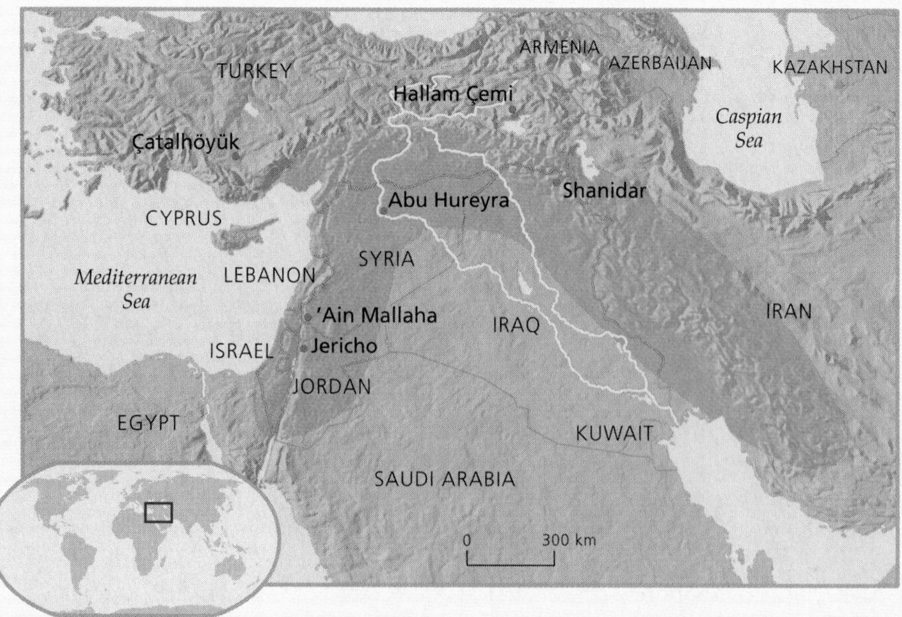


**Figure 6.12** Locations of Southwest Asian sites mentioned in the chapter. The shaded area marks the Fertile Crescent.

animals such as the gazelle. Plant foods are not common in the sites from this period.

In the period just preceding the Neolithic, there was more intense utilization of plant foods. Particularly noticeable is the range of equipment for processing plants: sickle blades and grinding stones, along with storage pits and roasting areas for preparing wild wheat. Sites were often located in areas of cultivable land, but such settlements depended on wild cereals, as evidenced in the remains of wild wheat and barley. These same locations were occupied during the Neolithic, too, probably because of the quantity or quality of arable land. Hunting continued, and more immature animals were killed, including gazelles and wild goats.

Between 9000 and 8000 B.C., changes in the size, shape, and structure of several cereals indicate that they had been domesticated. The archaeological data from Jericho and Abu Hureyra (A-boo hoo-RAY-rah), for example, mark this transition. The Neolithic, defined by the appearance of domesticated plants, began at that time. The earliest known domesticated cereal, rye, has been dated to 10,000 B.C. at the site of Abu Hureyra in Syria. In fact, eight or nine "founder" plants were domesticated during the period 9000–7000 B.C., including three cereals—emmer wheat, einkorn wheat, and barley—and four or five pulses—lentils, peas, bitter vetch, chickpeas, and maybe fava beans. (Pulses are the edible seeds of leguminous plants, such as peas and beans.) Flax also was domesticated during this period and probably was used for oil and fiber; linen is made from the fibers of the flax plant. The first evidence for domestication of these founder plants comes from the same areas in which their wild ancestral stock is common. For example, genetic analysis has identified the original homeland of einkorn's (a primitive wheat) wild ancestor in southeastern Turkey. The archaeological evidence can tell us when and where, but not why and how. The transition to the Neolithic was marked not by abrupt changes but by increasing emphasis on patterns that appeared during the Natufian.

The number and the size of prehistoric communities expanded greatly during the early Neolithic, as populations apparently concentrated in settlements. The first towns appeared. Major changes in human diet, and probably in the organization of society as well, began to take place. Some of the first domesticated animals are from Hallam Çemi, a very early Neolithic site in eastern Turkey, dating to around 9000 B.C. Excavated by Michael Rosenberg, of the University of Delaware, the site was a village of small, round houses and one larger, nondomestic building with a centrally located feasting area. The food remains at the site include wild sheep and goats, along with various nuts and wild legumes. Wild cereals were not an important part of the diet. About 10% of the animal bones came from pigs. Evidence for the domestication of these pigs is seen in the sex and age of death of the animals. Most of the bones were from young female animals. It appears that the inhabitants were selecting suckling pigs to eat, supporting the argument that these animals were controlled, or herded. In addition, the teeth of the pigs at Hallam Çemi are smaller than those of their wild relatives.

Some of the more interesting recent discoveries come from the island of Cyprus in the eastern Mediterranean. Cyprus lies more than 60 km (40 mi) from the coast of the Near East. Nevertheless, early Neolithic farmers had sailed here from the mainland by 8000 B.C. Even more remarkably, they brought a number of domestic and wild animal species with them to populate the island. Red deer were not present on the island of Cyprus prior to this time, strongly suggesting that the waterborne farmers brought this animal with them. The farmers also introduced cattle and sheep and goats along with a number of crop plants originally domesticated in the Near East. Finally, they appear to have brought their pets. The earliest known domestic cat skeleton has been found buried next to a human grave from a settlement dating to 7300 B.C. Cats may have been domesticated to control the mice that were attracted to the stored grain of the farming villages.

By 7500 B.C., domesticated sheep and goats had made their first appearance in the Levant, and a number of changes in architecture had occurred. Pottery was invented in Southwest Asia around 7500 B.C. to serve as easily produced, waterproof containers. These dishes were probably used for holding liquids, for cooking a gruel made from wheat and barley (bread was a somewhat later invention), and for storing materials. The complete Neolithic package of domesticates, village architecture, and pottery was thus in place shortly before 7000 B.C., as the Neolithic revolution began to spread to Europe and Africa.

**Was the adoption of agriculture almost instantaneous in human prehistory?**

Site

# Abu Hureyra

*Hunter-gatherers and early farmers in northern Syria*

www.mhhe.com/priceip6e

For a Web-based activity on Abu Hureyra, see the Internet exercises on your online learning center.

In 1974, the site of Abu Hureyra in northern Syria was submerged beneath the waters behind a new dam on the Euphrates River. Fortunately, in 1972 and 1973, before the water level in the reservoir rose and flooded the area, rescue excavations uncovered parts of this site, one of the largest early Postglacial communities in Southwest Asia. Excavations were conducted by A. M. T. Moore, of the University of Rochester, and his colleagues.

The **tell**—an accumulated mound of occupation debris—covered 11.5 ha (about 30 acres), with deposits from the Natufian and the early Neolithic up to 8 m (25 ft) high in some places. One million cubic meters (1.3 million cubic yards) of earth were removed during the excavations. The primary component of the tell was the decayed mud walls of the generations of houses that were built there, along with the artifacts and food remains left behind by the inhabitants. The layers indicated an uninterrupted occupation of the mound from approximately 10,500 B.C. to 6000 B.C., through the Natufian and the Neolithic periods in Southwest Asia. Abu Hureyra thus contains one of the best available records of the changes that took place as farming and herding first began (Figure 6.13).

The mound lies at the edge of the Euphrates River, with the river floodplain on one side and dry, level steppe on the other. The area today receives approximately 200 mm (8 in) of rainfall per year; cultivation is difficult without irrigation. During the Natufian occupation of the site, however, the climate was warmer and wetter. An open forest of oak and pistachio trees grew on the steppes nearby, with dense stands of wild grasses among the trees. These grasses, probably no more than 1–2 km (about 1 mi) distant, included wild wheats, rye, and various pulses (lentils and legumes).

**tell** A mound composed of mud bricks and refuse, accumulated as a result of human activity.

The Mesolithic settlement was located on the northern side of the tell, adjacent to the Euphrates River. The settlement may originally have been placed here along the migration route of the gazelle herds. These animals were killed in great numbers during the spring migration. The settlement consisted of small, circular pit dwellings dug into the original ground surface. These structures had a framework of wooden posts supporting the wall and roof. Almost 1 m (3 ft) of debris accumulated during this first phase of occupation, between approximately 10,500 and 9000 B.C. The population of the site is estimated to have been between 200 and 300 at that time.

Clearly, the bulk of their food came from the wild plants, some of which were staples. The plant remains at the site indicate a year-round occupation in both the Mesolithic and the Neolithic periods. The excavators used sophisticated techniques at Abu Hureyra to recover more than 500 liters (140 gallons) of plant remains from the site. From the Natufian levels, there was evidence for wild lentils, hackberry fruit, caper berries, and nuts from the turpentine tree, related to pistachios. Most intriguing, however, were the remains of wild wheat, barley, and rye.

Around 10,000 B.C., the climate became cooler and drier and the nearby stands of wild cereals and other plants retreated more than 100 km (62.5 mi) to the higher elevations of the Fertile Crescent. Fruits and seeds of drought-sensitive plants from an oak–pistachio open woodland disappeared at Abu Hureyra. Then wild lentils and other legumes declined. Local vegetation around the site appears to have changed from moist, woodland steppe to dry, treeless steppe. Wild wheats continued to be consumed at the site even though their habitat in the area had been eliminated. The excavators believe that the Natufian inhabitants practiced plant husbandry of wild cereals before changes in the glume and rachis brought about by domestication were evident.

Significantly, the earliest known domesticated plant, rye, appeared at that time. Grinding stones and milling equipment also point to the importance of cereals in the diet during that period. Experiments by Gordon Hillman, of the University of London, were designed to estimate the amount of time needed for wild cereals to change to the domesticated variety through the process of cultivating and harvesting the wild seeds and replanting them. This study indicated that the domestication of the plants could have taken place within a period of less than 300 years, perhaps no more than 25 years.

Shortly after the initial domestication of rye and the probable cultivation of wild wheats, lentils and legumes reappeared in the deposits and increased. By 8500 B.C., the range of domesticated plants included rye, lentils and large-seeded legumes, and domesticated wheats. Clearly, plant domestication began in the Natufian period at Abu Hureyra, perhaps in response to the disappearance of the wild stands of these important foods.

Two tons of animal bone, antler, and shell also were removed during the excavations. Shells from river mussels, fish bones, and bone fishhooks indicate that the inhabitants obtained food from the Euphrates River, as well as from the surrounding hills. Gazelle bones dominate the lower layers at Abu Hureyra and constitute 80% of all animal bones from the Mesolithic and early Neolithic periods. By the beginning of the Neolithic, however, sheep and goats had been domesticated and were being herded. After 7500 B.C., the number of gazelle bones dropped sharply, and sheep and goats became much more important in the diet (Figure 6.14). During the subsequent phases of the Neolithic at Abu Hureyra, domesticated cattle and pigs were added to the larder.

Abu Hureyra grew quickly to become the largest community of its day,

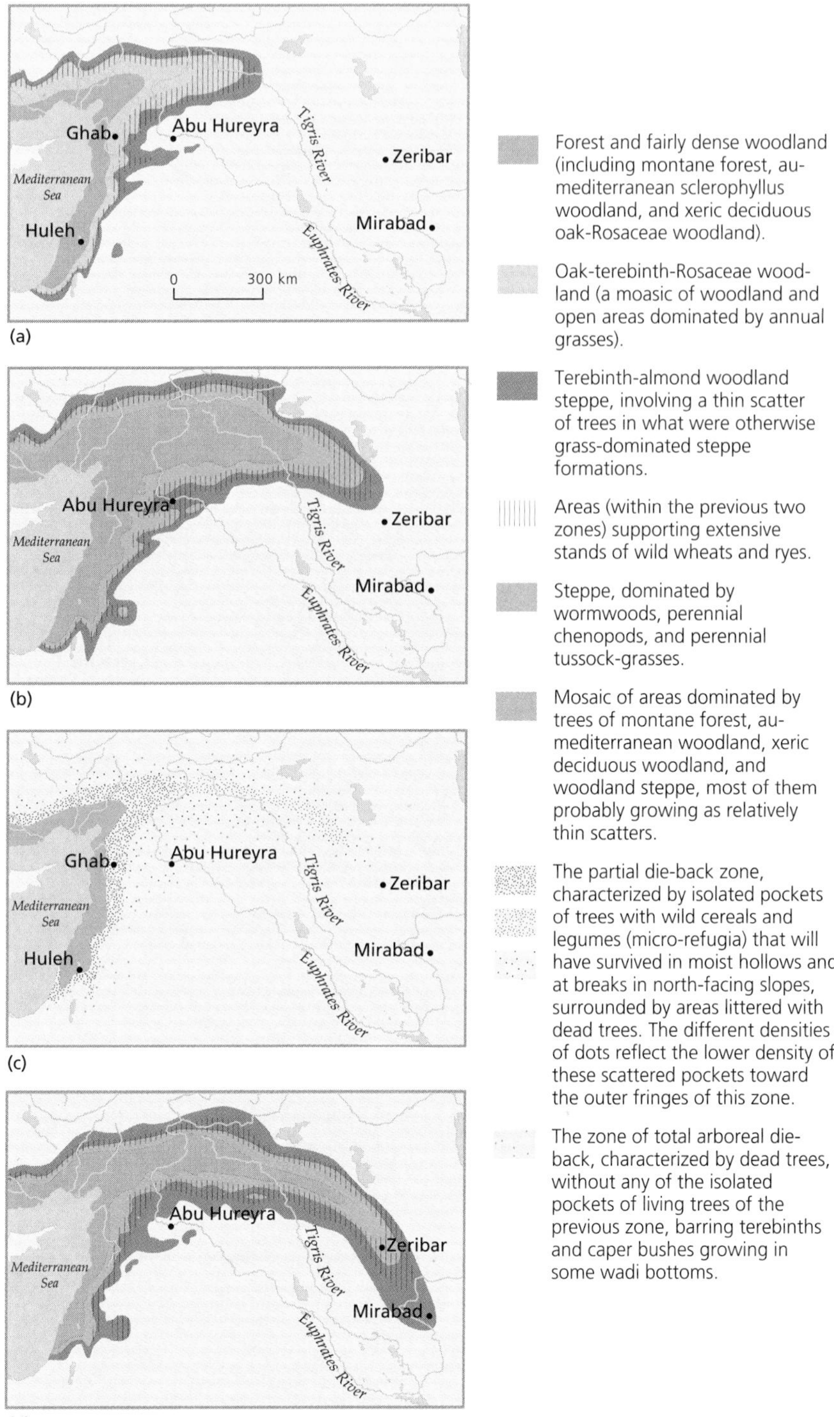


**Figure 6.13** The landscape of Southwest Asia at the end of the Pleistocene. These four maps show a sequence of changing vegetation for four periods of the late Pleistocene and early Holocene. Note particularly the changes at Abu Hureyra, where the vegetation goes from (a) grass steppe, to (b) lightly forested with wild wheats and ryes during an episode of cooler and wetter conditions around 12,000 years ago, and then reverts to (c, d) dry grass steppe. These changes may have important implications for the domestication of plants. The four named locations (Huleh, Ghab, Zeribar, and Mirabad) are sites where environmental data for this reconstruction were obtained.

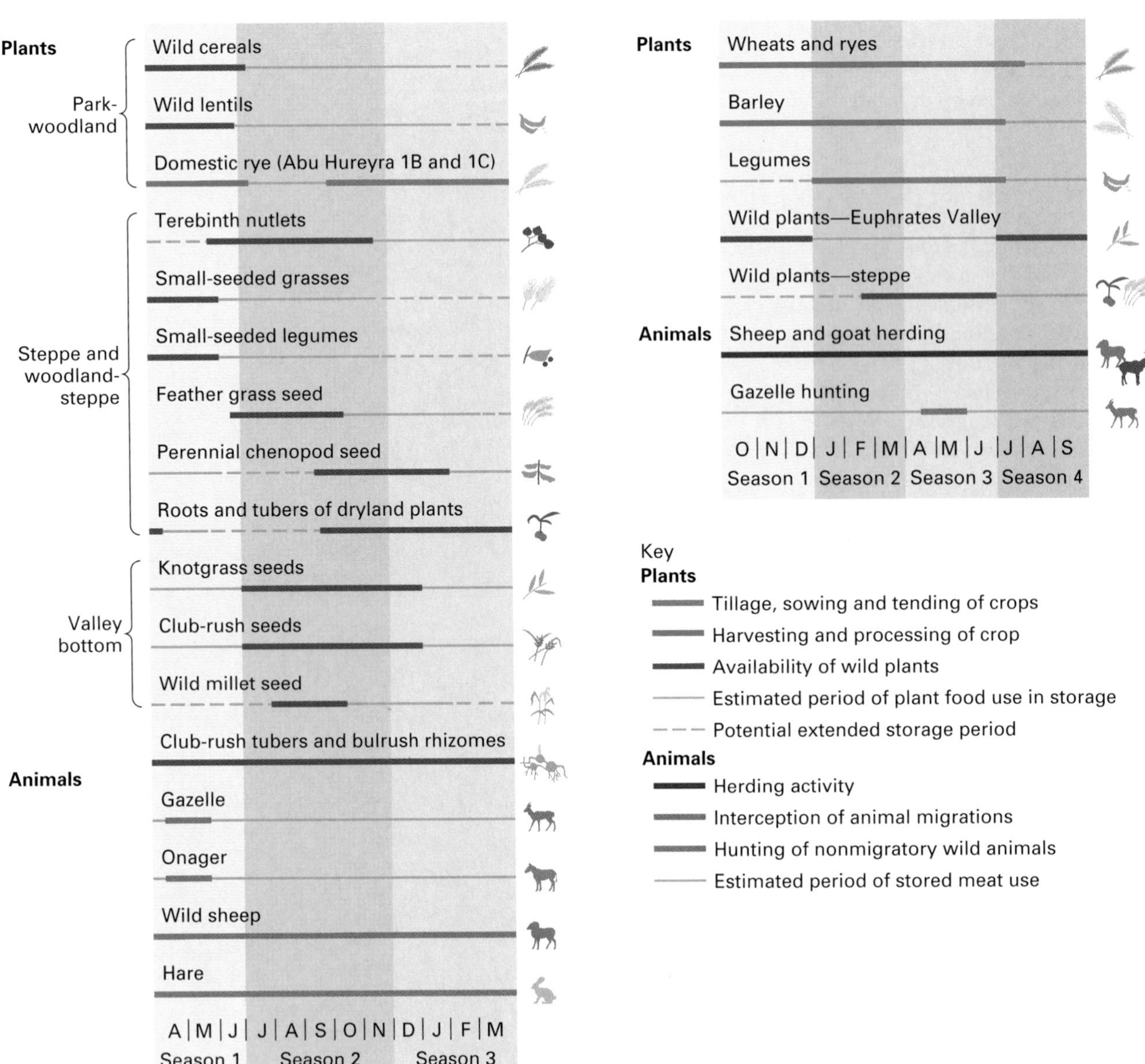


**Figure 6.14** The seasonal availability and use of plants and animals at Abu Hureyra during the pre-Neolithic and the Neolithic. During Abu Hureyra 1, ca. 12,000 years ago, there were no domesticated plants or animals, and a wide variety of species contributed to the diet during all seasons of the year. In the Early Neolithic (Abu Hureyra 2A), ca. 10,500 years ago, domesticated plants and herded sheep and goats played an important role in subsistence. Wild plants remained important, and the seasonal hunting of wild gazelle continued to supplement the food provided by herds of domestic sheep and goats. In later periods, the wild species declined in importance.

with 2000–3000 inhabitants in an area of about 11.5 ha (30 acres). Houses were rectangular, with mud-brick walls that were plastered and whitewashed (Figure 6.15). Plaster also was used to make heavy rectangular containers. Clay was used for beads and figurines, but pottery was not present in this level of the site. The importance of this community is documented by the quantity and variety of exotic materials that arrived there through trade and exchange: cowrie shells from the Mediterranean or Red Sea, turquoise from the Sinai Peninsula, and obsidian, malachite, agate, jadeite, and serpen-

| TABLE 6.1 Changes in Environment, Economy, and Settlement Types at Abu Hureyra | | | | | |
|---|---|---|---|---|---|
| *Years* B.C. | *Period* | *Environment* | *Economy* | *Settlement* | *Other Sites* |
| 6000<br>6300 | | | Mixed farming cereals, legumes, sheep, goats, cattle, pigs | 7 ha clustered mud-brick houses | |
| 7500 | Neolithic | | Cereal and legume cultivation, sheep and goat husbandry | > 16 ha clustered mud-brick houses | Çatalhöyük |
| 8500 | | Decline in gazelle | Cereal and legume cultivation, plant gathering, gazelle hunting, domesticated sheep and goats | 8 ha clustered mud-brick houses | Asikli |
| 9000 | Intermediate | | Cereal and legume cultivation, plant gathering, gazelle hunting | Huts | Jericho, 'Ain Ghazal |
| 9500 | | Cooler and drier; retreat of forest; dry, open steppe | Wild einkorn wheat out of habitat. Domestication of rye, plant gathering, gazelle hunting | Timber and reed huts | 'Ain Mallaha, Jericho, Hallam Çemi |
| 10,000 | Natufian | Younger Dryas | | | |
| 10,500 | | Open, rolling steppe and grassland with nearby park woodland of oak and pistachio, wild cereals and legumes | Gathering wild plants, hunting gazelle | Pit dwellings | |

tine from the mountains of Turkey. These rare stones were made into large, thin "butterfly" beads, often found in burials. Table 6.1 summarizes the various changes at Abu Hureyra from 10,500 B.C. to 6000 B.C.

By 6000 B.C., Abu Hureyra had been abandoned. A similar pattern is seen at other Neolithic sites in the Levant at that time. It seems likely that increasingly arid conditions reduced agricultural productivity and made herding a more viable enterprise. It may be at that time that nomadic herding became the dominant mode of life, much like that of the pastoralists who still roam parts of Southwest Asia with their herds of sheep and goats.

The evidence from Abu Hureyra indicates that cultivation began in ancient Southwest Asia in a small, sedentary village of hunter-gatherers around 10,000 years ago during a period of environmental change. The disappearance of the habitat for wild species coincided with the early domestication of rye and eventual cultivation of wheat, lentils, and legumes. But the transition from dependence on wild, gathered foods and hunted animals to domesticated varieties took 2500 years. Not all families were initially involved in farming, and the number increased over time. The first sheep and goat husbandry appeared around 8500 B.C., followed by that of cattle and pigs. The general sequence involves settlement in villages, followed by plant cultivation and subsequent animal herding. This pattern of a gradual transition from food collection to production is typical in most parts of the world.

**Figure 6.15** An artist's reconstruction of houses from the early Neolithic in Southwest Asia. These houses had rock wall foundations with walls and roofs of timber and reeds covered with mud. In areas lacking rock, such as Abu Hureyra, the foundations were made of mud brick.

Concept

## Archaeobotany

*The study of prehistoric plant remains*

Preserved plants in archaeological sites are rare unless the remains have been carbonized, generally through burning or oxidation. Such burned plant materials can sometimes be obtained through a process called **flotation.** Excavated sediments are poured into a container of water (Figure 6.16), and the lighter, carbonized plant remains float to the top (Figures 6.17 and 6.18). In addition to the kinds of plants used, the major issues in **archaeobotany** (the study of the prehistoric use of plants) include the contribution of plants to the diet, medicinal uses, and domestication—the origins of agriculture.

The archaeobotany of Southwest Asia is of particular interest because of the evidence for early domestication in this area (Table 6.2). Two varieties of wheat (emmer and einkorn), two-row barley, rye, oats, lentils, peas, chickpeas, and other plants were originally cultivated in Southwest Asia. The wild forms of these species are still common today, as they were in the past. Wild emmer wheat has a restricted distribution in the southern Levant. Wild einkorn wheat is relatively widespread in the northern and eastern sections of this region. Wild barley grows throughout the Fertile Crescent. All these wild grasses grow well in disturbed ground around human settlements. Einkorn was probably domesticated in southern Turkey, and emmer may have been first cultivated in the Jordan Valley.

Agronomist Jack Harlan, of the University of Illinois, participating in an archaeological project in southern Turkey in the 1960s, experimented to find out just how much food was available from wild wheat. Dense stands of wild einkorn wheat grow on the slopes of the mountains in that area. This wild wheat is more nutritious than the hard winter red wheats grown in the United States today. Harvesting when the wheat was ripe, Harlan collected more than 1 kg (2 lb) of cereal grain per hour with his hands and even more with a sickle. He estimated that a family of four could harvest enough grain in 3 weeks to provide food for an entire year. If this wild wheat was so abundant and nutritious, why was wheat domesticated? The answer probably lies in the fact that wild wheats do not grow everywhere in Southwest Asia, so some communities may have transplanted the wild form into new environments.

Although artifactual evidence for the use of plants (e.g., sickles, milling stones, storage pits, and roasting areas) exists in a number of areas, domesticated varieties cannot be distinguished from wild types without actual plant parts or grain impressions in clay bricks or pottery. Archaeobotanist Gordon

| TABLE 6.2 Common Food Plants in Early Neolithic Southwest Asia |
|---|
| Einkorn wheat, wild and domesticated forms |
| Emmer wheat, wild and domesticated forms |
| Rye, wild and domesticated forms |
| Barley, wild and domesticated forms |
| Chickpeas, domesticated form |
| Field peas, domesticated form |
| Lentils, wild and domesticated forms |
| Common vetch |
| Bitter vetch |
| Horse bean |
| Grape, wild and domesticated forms |
| Caper |
| Prosopis (mesquite) |
| Fig |
| Hackberry |
| Turpentine tree |
| Wild pistachio |

Hillman, of the University of London, studied wild einkorn and observed that simple harvesting had no major impact on the genetic structure of the wheat. Only when specifically selective harvesting and other cultivation techniques were applied could changes in the morphology of the seeds be noted. Such a pattern suggests that certain characteristics of domesticated wheat and barley, which show definite morphological differences from the wild ancestral forms, must have been intentionally selected. Results from Hillman's experimental studies suggest that the change from wild to domesticated wheat may have occurred in a brief period, perhaps 200 years or less.

According to Hans Helbaek, an archaeobotanist who worked on the issue of plant domestication, the most important characteristic of a domesticated species is the loss of natural seeding ability. The plant comes to depend on human intervention to reproduce. This change also permits humans to select the characteristics of those plants to be sown and reproduced, leading to preferred characteristics. Another major change in domesticated plants is the human removal of plants from their

**Figure 6.16** A Dausman flotation machine in use. Water in the tank is used to separate lighter plant remains from soil and other sediments. The archaeologist uses a hose to spray some of the recovered materials.

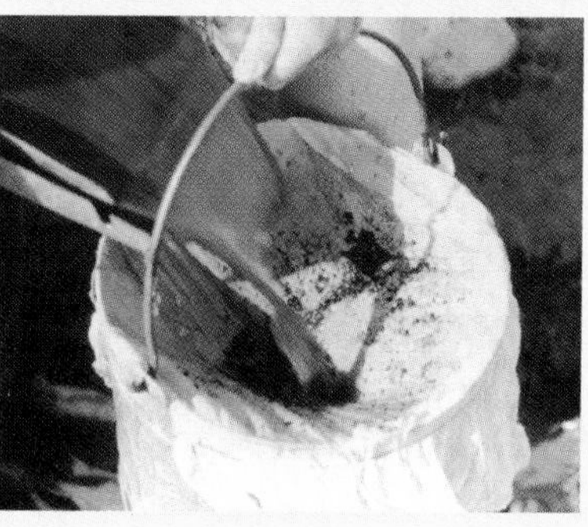

**Figure 6.17** In this photo, the charred seeds and charcoal separated by flotation are being captured in a cheesecloth sieve.

**Figure 6.18** An assortment of seeds and other plant remains from an archaeological site.

**flotation** A technique for the recovery of plant remains from archaeological sites. Sediments or pit contents are poured into water or heavy liquid; the lighter, carbonized plant remains float to the top for recovery, while the heavier sediments and other materials fall to the bottom.

**archaeobotany (**or **paleoethnobotany)** The study of plant remains from archaeological sites.

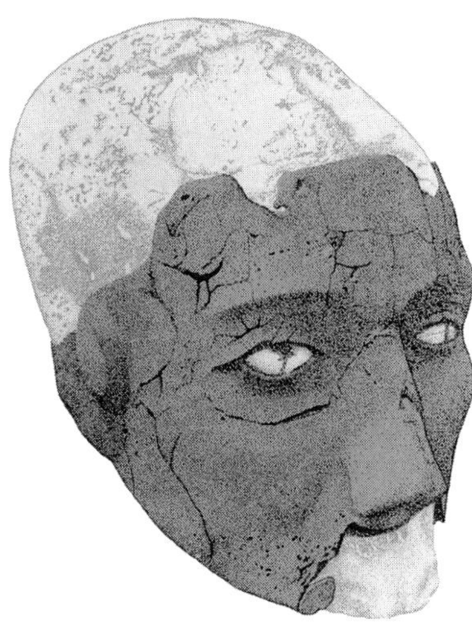

**Figure 6.21** A plastered and painted skull from Jericho. The plaster remodeling of the features of human heads is found at several early Neolithic sites in Southwest Asia and may reflect an increasing reverence for ancestors.

275 m (900 ft) below sea level. The mound itself was abandoned sometime before A.D. 1, as settlement spread to the surrounding low area.

The biblical connection has made Jericho a place of major interest and importance for archaeologists in Southwest Asia. Today, the tell resembles the surface of the moon. Craters and trenches mark the excavations of many archaeological projects that have explored these accumulated layers since 1873. British archaeologist Dame Kathleen Kenyon exposed a number of levels beneath biblical Jericho containing remains from the Bronze Age, the Neolithic, and the Mesolithic.

Evidence from the early Neolithic (8500–7600 B.C.) at the bottom of the tell is of interest here. Because the mound is so deep, these lowest levels could be reached only by narrow trenches. The residential structures and artifacts exposed in Kenyon's excavations were similar to those from other Southwest Asian sites from this period. Closely packed round houses contained interior hearths and grinding equipment.

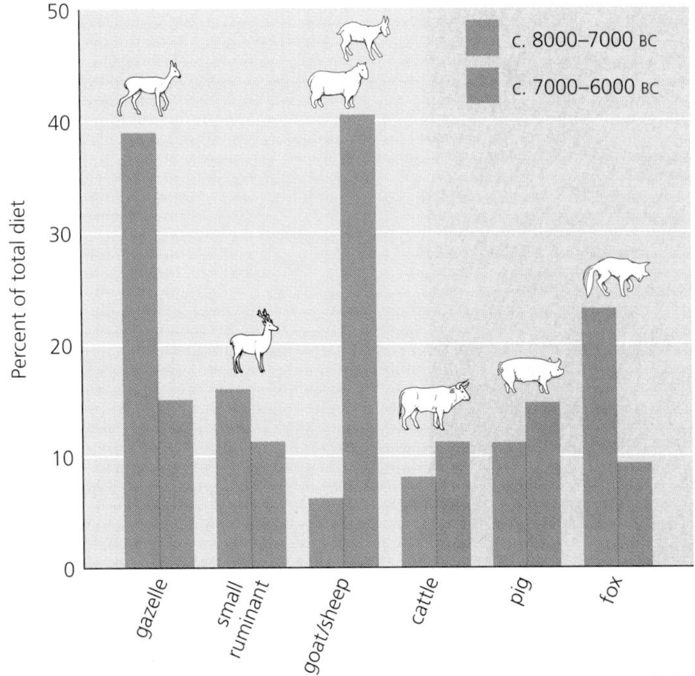


**Figure 6.22** Changes in the consumption of animals between 8000 and 6000 B.C. at Jericho. Notice especially the shift from wild gazelle to domesticated sheep and goat.

Headless burials were uncovered in the houses at Jericho; skulls were found separated from the skeletons (Figure 6.21). Kenyon estimated that the early Neolithic community at Jericho had a population of 600 people.

Gazelle bones were abundant in the lowest layers at Jericho. This important game animal probably was exploited by large drives that captured a number of animals simultaneously. Aurochs, wild boars, and foxes also were eaten. Many animals present in the surrounding hills were not hunted, including wild goats, oryx, hartebeest, and wild camels. In later periods, gazelles declined in importance, replaced by sheep and goats (Figure 6.22). The presence of equipment for processing grain (sickles and grinding stones) and storage suggests that cereals were important in the lowest levels. In the slightly higher early Neolithic layers, these cereals were domesticated and probably cultivated in the fertile soil of the Jericho oasis.

The inhabitants of early Neolithic Jericho traded various items over long distances. Materials such as salt, tar, and sulfur came from the area around the Dead Sea. Turquoise was brought from the Sinai Peninsula, cowrie shells from the Red Sea, obsidian from Turkey, and greenstone from Jordan. The reasons for such exchange probably lie in the importance of contacts with neighboring communities and in the accumulation of status items for some portion of the community.

Long-distance exchange and expansion appear to have been hallmarks of the early Neolithic, probably reflecting the success of early agriculture and associated economic systems. Evidence for the spread of domesticates, architecture, and other components of the prepottery Neolithic seen at Jericho and elsewhere in the Levant appears on the island of Cyprus shortly before 8000 B.C. The colonists brought domestic cattle and wild deer with them to the island, traveling at least 80 km (50 mi) across open waters of the eastern Mediterranean.

Most remarkable of Kenyon's discoveries from this period was a large stone tower (Figure 6.23), wall, and ditch, which appeared to encircle the site. These structures were built at the beginning of the eighth millennium B.C. The wall itself is 1.8 m (6 ft) thick at the base, narrowing to 1.1 m (3.5 ft) at the top, and stands 3.6 m (12 ft) high today, buried under the accumulated deposits of Jericho. The rubble-filled stone tower also was completely buried, at a height of 8.2 m (27 ft). The tower was built inside the wall and has a diameter of 9 m (30 ft) at the base. An interior staircase with 22 steps leads from the bottom to the top. In front of the wall is a deep ditch, which added greatly to the height of the total structure. The ditch is 2 m (6.5 ft) deep and 8.5 m (28 ft) wide, cut into the bedrock under the site. Such a construction project would have been a major undertaking by a small community in the eighth millennium B.C. The tower and wall were abandoned by 7300 B.C. and rapidly disappeared under the accumulating layers of the tell.

The significance of these structures has been the focus of discussion and debate. Kenyon suggested that the tell was completely encircled by the wall and ditch, with towers placed at regular intervals. However, only one tower was exposed in the excavations, and the wall was not found on the southern, lower, side of the mound. Numerous unanswered questions have arisen regarding the nature of the enemy, the materials to be protected, the location of the tower *inside* the wall, the reason for its abandonment, and the size of the population. Comparable fortifications are not seen at other early Neolithic sites in Southwest Asia, and a massive defensive structure seems out of place.

Ofer Bar-Yosef, of Harvard University, examined the evidence for fortifications at Jericho and found it lacking. Bar-Yosef interprets the wall and ditch as a defense against nature rather than against humans (Figure 6.24). In this arid region, flash floods are common, and each rainfall moves a great deal of sand and silt from higher ground to lower areas. Such erosion and deposition would have been aggravated by land clearing and the removal of trees and shrubs by the inhabitants at the site. Sediments may have accumulated on the upslope side of the tell of Jericho and at other early Neolithic sites.

To counteract this rapid accumulation of sediments at the edge of their community, the residents of Jericho, Bar-Yosef argues, built the wall and dug the ditch to hold back the sediments. The rock-cut ditch at Jericho filled with water-transported sediments shortly after it was dug. The wall was thickest in the middle portion, where the sediment accumulation was heaviest. The large tower inside the wall is another matter. Bar-Yosef has noted the excellent preservation of the tower to its total height in the tell. He argues that there was likely a mud-brick structure on top of the stone tower, a building for communal storage or religious activities that made the tower a very special place in the settlement. The tower thus may represent an early shrine or temple for the community, a concept that was later transformed into the monumental ziggurats of the Mesopotamian states.

Around 7500 B.C., major changes in the architecture, artifacts, and animals occurred at Jericho. Houses became square, constructed with what have been described as "hog-backed" bricks—large, cigar-shaped mud bricks with a herringbone pattern of thumbprints on the top. Domesticated animals became important at that time; sheep and goats constituted almost half of the animal bones, along with a few wild cattle and pigs, gradually replacing the gazelle. Pigs and cattle were possibly in the process of change, because their bones were slightly smaller than those of the wild forms but not as small as those of the domesticated forms.

**Figure 6.23** The tell at Jericho. Excavations have exposed a circular stone tower.

**Figure 6.24** The tower, wall, and rock-cut ditch at Jericho.

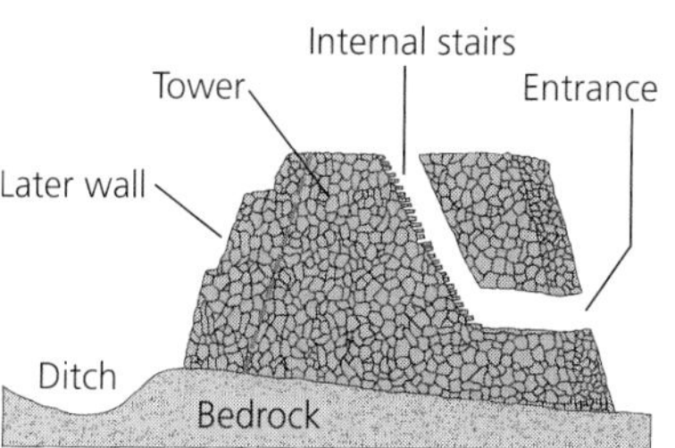

Concept

# Archaeozoology

## *The study of animal remains*

Why were plants and animals domesticated about the same time?

The companion of paleoethnobotany, **archaeozoology** focuses on the hard body parts of animals that survive—bone, teeth, antler, ivory, scales, and shell. Studying these materials, archaeozoologists attempt to answer questions about whether animals were hunted or scavenged, how animals were butchered, how much meat contributed to the diet, and the process of domestication.

Archaeozoologists are trained to identify the genus or species of an animal from small fragments of bone, as well as the age and sex of the animals, how the animal was butchered and the bone was broken, and how many individual animals are represented in the bone assemblage. Fracture patterns in long bones may reveal intentional breakage for removing marrow. An analysis of cutmarks on bone may provide information on butchering techniques.

The study of animal domestication is also an important part of archaeozoology. Four major criteria are used to look for domesticates: geographic evidence, abundance, morphological changes, and herd demographics. Geographic evidence involves discovery of animal species outside their natural habitat and presumes human involvement. However, environments changed dramatically in the past, as did the geographic distribution of animal species. Thus geography is a difficult criterion to use. Increases in the abundance of a species in the layers at a site are often taken to indicate domestication, but again this evidence is not particularly reliable. Numbers of animals may increase for a variety of reasons, including environmental change and increased hunting.

Herded animals show certain morphological changes in size and body parts that provide direct evidence for domestication. Domesticated species are generally smaller than their wild ancestors. The shape of the horns often changes in the domestic form, and the microscopic structure of bone under-

**www.mhhe.com/priceip6e**

For a Web-based activity on archaeozoology, see the Internet exercises on your online learning center.

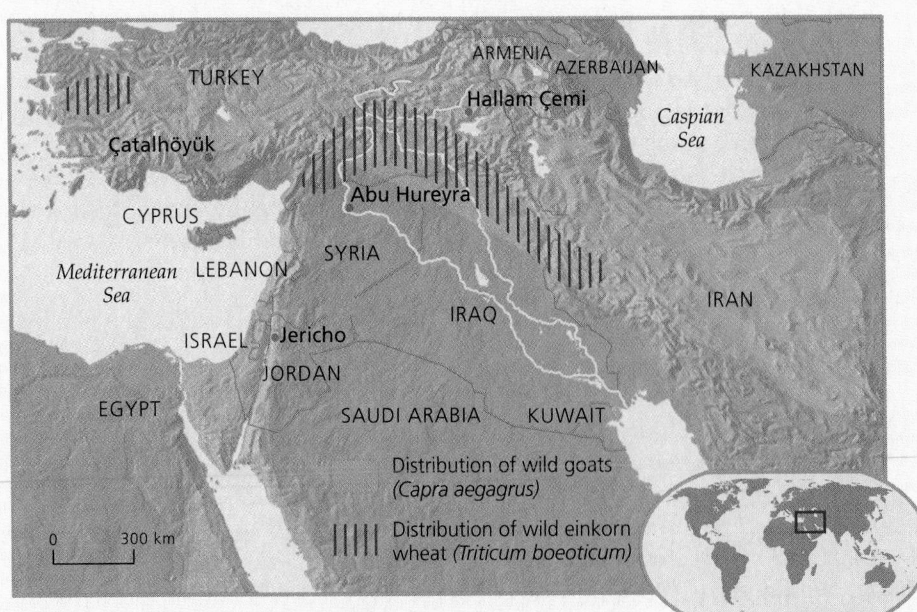


**Figure 6.25** The distribution of wild einkorn wheat (*Triticum boeoticum*) and of wild goats (*Capra aegagrus*) in Southwest Asia and Egypt is indicated by the shaded areas.

**archaeozoology** The study of animal remains from archaeological sites.

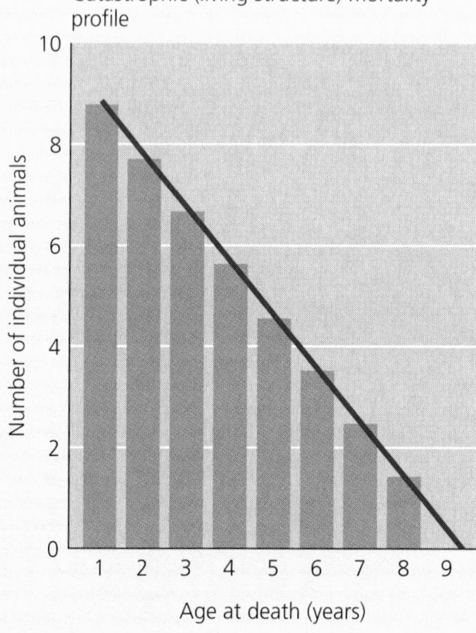


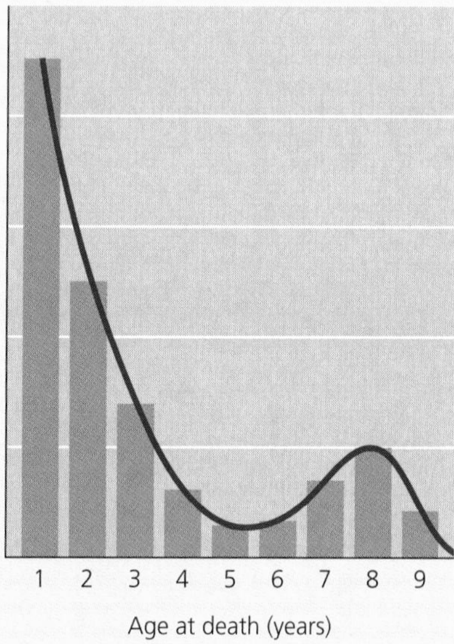


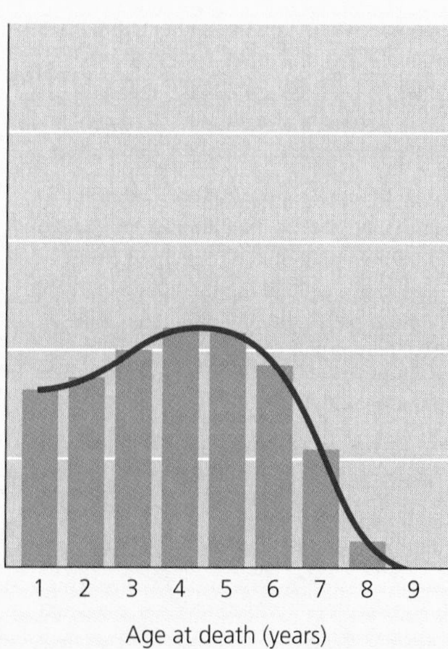


**Figure 6.26** Three hypothetical age profiles for animal populations used by archaeozoologists to look for indications of human control and domestication. A catastrophic pattern would reflect that all the animals in the herd died at the same time. An attritional pattern is the normal life-and-death cycle for an animal herd in which very young and very old animals are more likely to die. The prime-dominated mortality curve is the pattern that appears when humans eat a predominance of young males, a common herding practice. Females and a few older males are kept for the reproduction of the herd.

goes modification in domestic animals. Other traits may be selected by herders to increase the yield of milk, wool, or meat. However, because such biological change takes many generations and requires physical separation between wild and domestic animals, the earliest stages of domestication may not have been recorded in the bones and horns that remain (Table 6.3).

Brian Hesse, of the University of Alabama–Birmingham, and Melinda Zeder, of the Smithsonian Institution, have used herd demographics to document early animal domestication in Southwest Asia (Figure 6.26). They estimated the age and the sex of animals that had been killed at prefarming sites in the Zagros Mountains of western Iran and used this information to study whether hunting or herding was practiced. The basic principle relies on the fact that herded animals are slaughtered when the herder decides; for most species, this means that the average age of death for domesticated animals is younger than for wild animals. Hunted animals are killed in chance encounters, and the proportion of adults is higher in such situations.

The ages of animals are most frequently determined by an assessment of tooth eruption and wear, along with information about changes in bone. All the known sites in the Zagros Mountains before 10,000 years ago show similar slaughter patterns for sheep, goats, and red deer; bone assemblages contain primarily adult animals, indicating that all were hunted in the wild. However, a number of sites contain assemblages after 10,000 years ago that are dominated by the bones of younger animals. In each case, the younger groups are sheep or goats, proportionally higher than in a normal wild herd.

At Abu Hureyra, a study of the bones of wild gazelles and domesticated goats and sheep has provided new information on the process of animal domestication (Figure 6.27). Around 11,000 years ago, the site was occupied by prefarming hunter-gatherers who hunted gazelles in large numbers. The gazelle bones and teeth include the remains of many young animals. The teeth, in particular, indicate that both newborns and yearlings were common in the faunal assemblage, along with adults of all ages. This pattern of newborns, yearlings, and adults, and the absence of animals of ages in between, indicates that most of the animals were killed during the same time each year, shortly after the calving period in late April and early May. These hunters were taking entire herds of gazelles as the animals migrated north

Figure 6.27 Changes in animal species at Abu Hureyra, Syria, between 9000 and 6000 B.C. The width of the bars indicates the relative abundance of the species. The most pronounced change is the decrease in gazelles and the increase in sheep and goats between 6500 and 6000 B.C. There was an absence of human occupation at this site between 8000 and 7500 B.C.

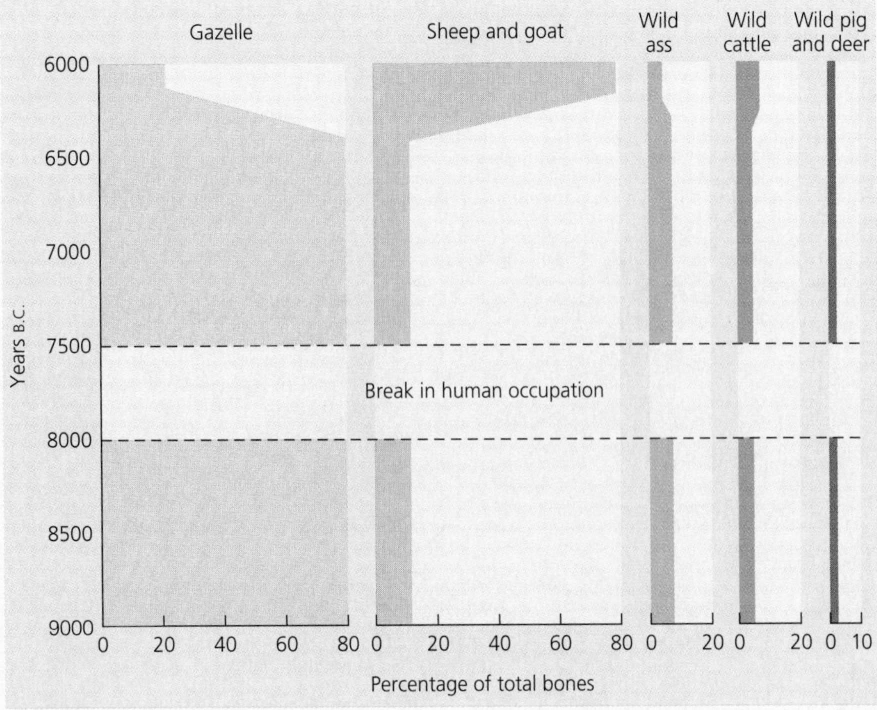


during early summer. They probably used a technique that would drive an entire herd into an enclosure or series of pitfalls, where all the animals could be killed. These hunters were so effective that the number of gazelles in the area dropped dramatically, to less than 20% of all the animals at the site, by 7500 B.C.

Goat and sheep domestication may have been a solution to the problem of decreasing numbers of gazelles. Sheep and goats were slaughtered throughout the year, in contrast to the seasonal hunting of gazelles at Abu Hureyra. Goat and sheep bones constituted about 10% of the faunal assemblages until 7500 B.C., after which they very rapidly became the predominant component, at almost 80%. This period was about 1500 years after plant domestication had been initiated at the site; wheats and barley at that point provided a significant portion of the diet. It also was some 3500 years after the initial occupation of the site, documenting the sequential stages of sedentism, plant cultivation, and animal domestication typical of Southwest Asia. Such information suggests a very complex picture of animal and plant domestication in Southwest Asia at the end of the Pleistocene.

| TABLE 6.3 Important Animal Species in Neolithic Southwest Asia |
|---|
| Gazelle |
| Goat, wild and domesticated forms |
| Sheep, wild and domesticated forms |
| Roe deer |
| Fallow deer |
| Cattle, wild and domesticated forms |
| Pig, wild and domesticated forms |
| Onager |
| Bear |
| Jackal |
| Hare |
| Wildcat |

# Çatalhöyük

*The first city, central Turkey*

Large communities began to appear shortly after the domestication of plants and animals in Southwest Asia. By 8000 B.C., 'Ain Ghazal and Jericho had populations in the hundreds, sizably larger than those in pre-agricultural settlements. And by 7250 B.C. the first "city" had appeared at the site of Çatalhöyük (sha-TAL-who-YUK) in central Turkey (Figure 6.28).

The tell of Çatalhöyük is huge, 600 m (1900 ft) long, 350 m (1000 feet) wide, and almost 20 m (65 ft) high (Figure 6.29). This massive mound of houses, garbage, and burials accumulated within a period of little more than 1000 years and was abandoned around 6000 B.C. At least twice as large as early Neolithic Jericho, covering 13 ha (32 acres), Çatalhöyük was a large settlement of perhaps as many as 2000 families—on the order of 10,000 people.

The original excavations at this ancient settlement were conducted by James Mellaart, of the University of London, during the 1960s. Several

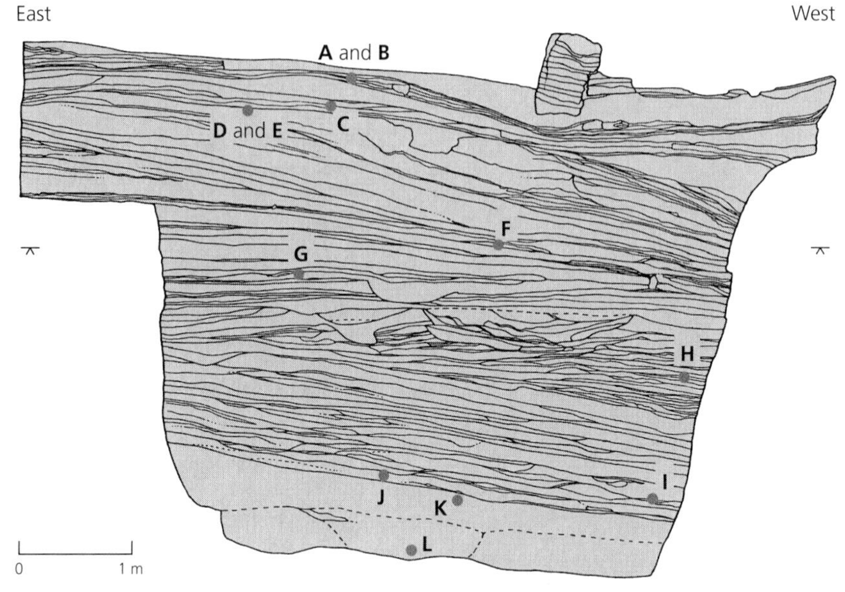


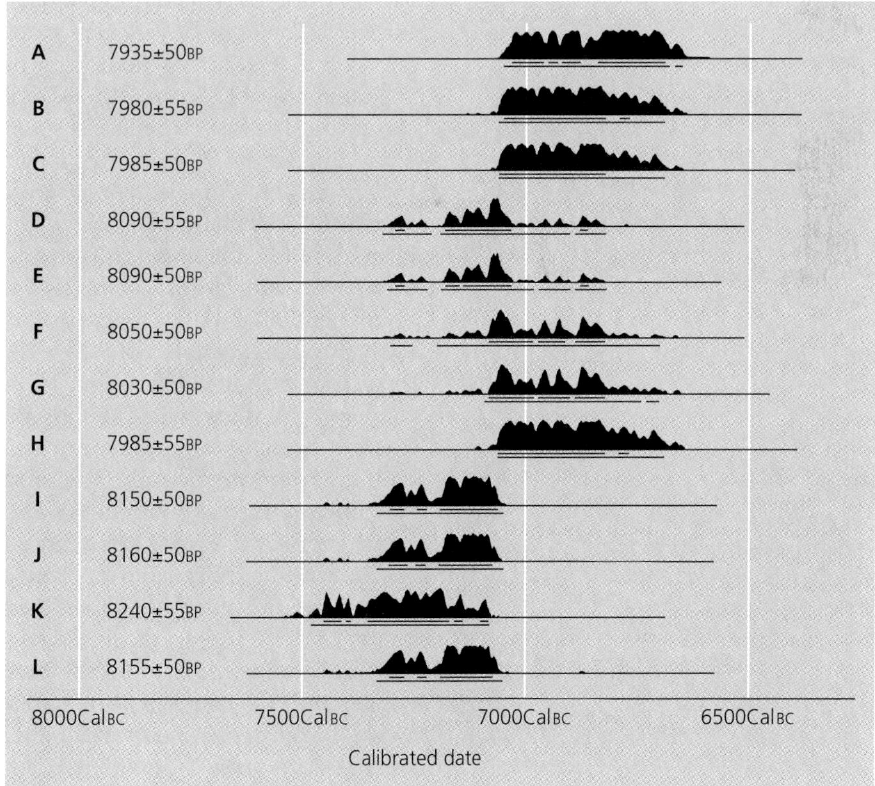


**Figure 6.28** Stratigraphy (top) and radiocarbon dates (bottom) from a deep-sounding at Çatalhöyük. The section drawing shows 4 m of the complex stratigraphy and the location of the radiocarbon samples. The graph of AMS radiocarbon dates shows the probability curves for the age of each sample. The center of each line of hills is a good estimate for the age of the sample. The dates indicate that the oldest occupation at Çatalhöyük was around 7250 B.C.

**Figure 6.29** An aerial view of the Neolithic mound of Çatalhöyük. Paths on top of the mound lead from the excavation headquarters to major excavation areas.

What role does sedentism play in the transition to agriculture?

seasons of fieldwork at the site exposed numerous walls and floors of rooms and houses. Houses were built closely together in one, two, or three stories around small courtyards (Figure 6.30). The houses were very similar, with a rectangular floor plan of approximately 25 sq m (30 sq yd), about the size of a large living room today. The houses were divided into a living area and a smaller storage area. Furniture—benches, sleeping platforms, ovens, cupboards, and storage bins—was built into the house. The houses had no doors, and access was likely through their flat roofs.

A number of burials also were found in the houses at Çatalhöyük. These burials of men, women, and children were under the floors and sleeping platforms (Figure 6.31). The bodies appear to have been exposed for some time before burial. Grave goods with the burials included jewelry such as necklaces, armlets, wristlets, and anklets of stone or shell, copper and lead beads, and weapons. A few burials contained rare objects such as stone vessels, ceremonial daggers, obsidian mirrors, polished maceheads, cosmetics, and metal beads and rings.

One of the remarkable things from the first excavations at Çatalhöyük was the large number of the structures, perhaps 20%, that appeared to have been shrines (Figure 6.32). The walls of these shrines are elaborately decorated, sculpted, and painted with a variety of remarkable figures and designs, including vultures, bulls, wild cats, and humans. Some of the paintings show women giving birth to bulls; others depict hunting scenes or vultures with headless humans in their talons. One of the paintings portrays an erupting volcano with a large settlement at its base. In addition, a number of sculptures and figurines have been excavated (Figure 6.33).

New excavations in the 1990s exposed more of the site and investigated in more detail the purpose and function of the various structures. These excavations, directed by Ian Hodder of Stanford University, suggest that households used their space for both domestic and ritual purposes and that the shrines may simply have been more elaborate households.

Two or three generations of a family were often buried under the house floor. The first burials in the houses were infants and young children; later

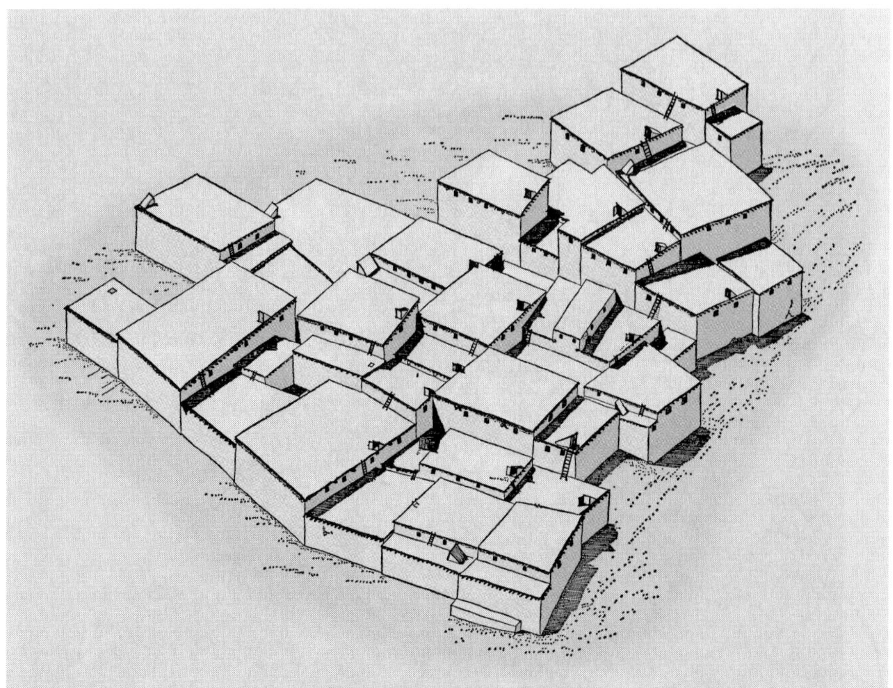

**Figure 6.30** An artist's reconstruction of complex architecture at Çatalhöyük, showing the closely packed, multistory buildings of timber and mud brick. This view reconstructs only a small part of the settlement.

burials were older adults. This pattern suggests a family life cycle represented in the burials. Houses may have been destroyed after the family had died. The paintings and sculptures on the walls of the houses are likely associated with the burials and may have been added to commemorate the deceased. David Lewis-Williams, of the University of Witwatersrand, South Africa, has described the artwork as a symbolic membrane connecting the living to the spirit world.

Analysis of the animal bones and plant remains has provided much new information about the site. The inhabitants depended heavily on wild flora and fauna. Important plants in the diet included domesticated wheat and barley, wild tubers and grasses, lentils, and fruits and nuts such as acorns, pistachios, crab apples, and hackberries. Cattle were an important part of subsistence at the site, but it is not yet certain if they were domesticated. Domesticated sheep and other species also were killed and eaten. There are no indications of differences in status, represented by wealth or surplus, among the houses. Çatalhöyük appears in many ways to have been a huge village of farmers rather than a complex and varied city.

Çatalhöyük was clearly a prosperous center, however, probably because of its control of the obsidian trade. **Obsidian** is produced by volcanoes; molten silica sometimes flows out of a volcanic core and hardens into this stone, which was highly sought by prehistoric makers of stone tools. Obsidian, like glass and flint, fractures easily and regularly, creating very sharp edges.

In the past, obsidian was often traded or exchanged over long distances—hundreds of kilometers or more. It is available from only a few places, limited by proximity to volcanic mountains and the chance formation of a silica flow. Most sources for obsidian are known because they are rare and the material is unusual. It also is possible to fingerprint different flows of obsidian through minor differences in the chemical composition of the material, which is specific to each source, allowing pieces found elsewhere to be traced to the places where they originated.

Agriculture quickly changes the way human society looks archaeologically. What are some of those changes?

**obsidian** Translucent, gray-to-black or green, glasslike rock from molten sand.

*Site*

# Mehrgarh

## *New evidence for the early Neolithic in South Asia*

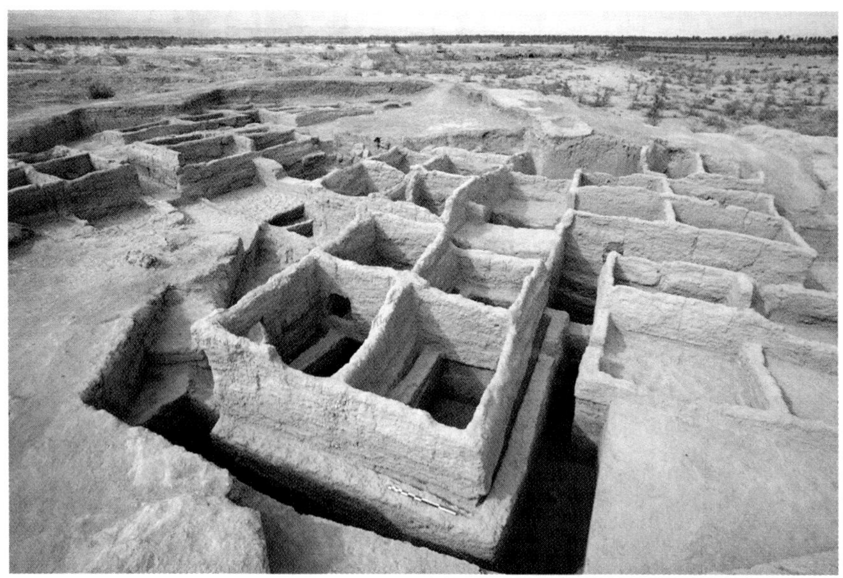

**Figure 6.34** Multiroom, rectangular structures uncovered during excavations at Mehrgarh.

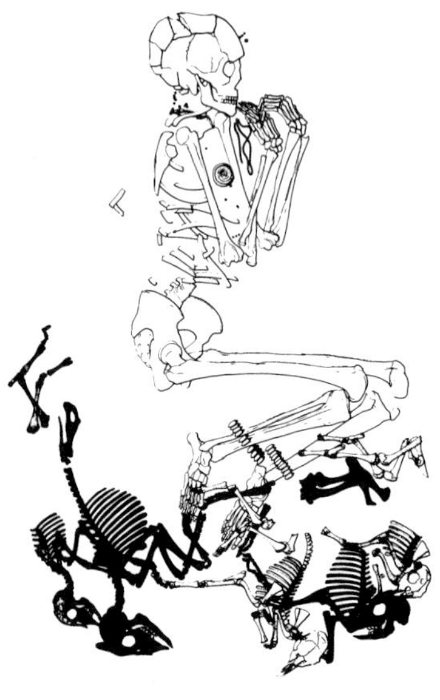

**Figure 6.35** A grave from an early level at Mehrgarh containing an adult male buried with several body ornaments and five young goats.

The Indus civilization, one of the world's early urban societies, emerged in South Asia, the subcontinent now composed of India, Pakistan, Bangladesh, and Nepal. The largest communities of this ancient civilization—the cities of Harappa, Mohenjo-daro, and others—were centered on the Indus River system in Pakistan. Until the 1970s, however, little was known about the antecedents of this ancient society. In the late 1960s, it was suggested that plant and animal domestication did not reach the subcontinent of South Asia until after 4000 B.C. The prevailing opinion was that migrants from the west, who made metals and wheel-thrown pottery, brought an agricultural way of life to South Asia just a few centuries before the rise of the Indus civilization.

More recent archaeological findings, however, have revealed an older, more indigenous picture of agricultural origins in the Indus River drainage. One key for this new perspective has come from a long-term research program, conducted by the French Archaeological Mission and the Pakistani Department of Archaeology, at the site of Mehrgarh (meh-her-GAR), located in the Kachi Plain about 200 km (120 mi) northwest of the Indus River. The site is also interesting because of its location immediately below the Bolan Pass, which cuts through the mountains that connect the Indus River Valley with highland Baluchistan and Iran (Southwest Asia).

In 1974, the first fieldwork at Mehrgarh, by Jean-François Jarrige and his colleagues, focused on a small mound. At that time, however, older pottery was collected over an area of several hundred hectares adjacent to the mound. Large-scale excavations in this area have yielded a sequence of deposits dating to the seventh millennium B.C. The earliest occupation level at Mehrgarh lacked pottery, although clay was used to make bricks for the construction of substantial, multiroom, quadrangular structures (Figure 6.34) and **anthropomorphic** figurines. A count of plant impressions in the mud bricks by Lorenzo Costantini found that barley was the most abundant cultigen in this early level. This barley had several distinctive local characteristics and may not have been completely domesticated. Other cereals grown at that time include smaller amounts of einkorn wheat, emmer wheat, and a kind of bread wheat. Whereas the wheats appear to have been imports from the west, it remains unclear whether barley was as well.

As in the early Neolithic sites of Southwest Asia, gazelle was the most abundant of the wild animal species, which included sheep, goat, cattle, swamp deer, and a large South Asian antelope. Some goats have been identified anatomically as domesticated. In each of two burials from an early level of the occupation, five young goats were placed at the foot of an adult male, whose body was covered with red ochre (Figure 6.35). These early graves also contained a diverse combination of body ornaments made from exotic materials such as seashell, turquoise, and **lapis lazuli.**

After 6000 B.C., important subsistence shifts occurred at Mehrgarh, and the first ceramic vessels began to be used. Richard Meadow, of Harvard University, has noted a reduction in the body size of the goats, sheep, and humped zebu cattle (*Bos indicus*) at the site, which he interprets as evidence for domestication. The relative abundance of wild species decreased, and the proportion of cattle bones increased greatly, suggesting that cattle husbandry may have begun about the same time at Mehrgarh as in sites to the west (Figure 6.36). Therefore, whereas sheep and goats may have been brought to Mehrgarh already tamed or domesticated, archaeological as well as recent genetic evidence suggests that local humped cattle were indigenous to South Asia.

Between 6000 and 4000 B.C., domesticated barley, well adapted to floodplain irrigation, was the predominant cultigen. Charred seeds of the plumlike jujube fruit (*Zizyphus jujuba*) and date pits (*Phoenix dactylifera*) also have been recovered. Cotton seeds were found with wheat and barley grains after 5000 B.C., the earliest date for cotton in the world.

At that time, Mehrgarh was a well-planned community composed of compartmentalized, mud-brick structures that served primarily as storage rooms. Features found in other parts of the settlement include circular fireplaces, containing burnt rocks for **stone boiling,** with bone and other debris nearby. These areas may have been used for large-scale food processing or cooking, or some other kind of communal activity.

Both specialized craft production and extensive long-distance trade, so evident at the major centers of the later Indus civilization, had clear antecedents millennia earlier at Mehrgarh. By 4000 B.C., the community had spread over tens of hectares and included specialized centers where fine ceramic ware was made. For roughly the next 1500 years, Mehrgarh was an important craft center. Wheel-thrown pottery was mass-produced, and beads of lapis lazuli, turquoise, and carnelian were perforated with cylindrical drill bits made of **jasper** and rotated by a **bow-drill.** Fragments of crucibles used to melt copper also were found at Mehrgarh.

The archaeology at Mehrgarh, along with recent studies at other contemporary sites, has revised South Asian prehistory. No longer can we envision the inhabitants of the Indus River drainage as simple recipients of inventions from the west. Nor can we attribute the rise of the Indus civilization after 2600 B.C. to the diffusion of ideas from Mesopotamia. We now recognize a sequence in South Asia that documents a pre-pottery Neolithic phase and the indigenous domestication of humped zebu cattle, along with the development of highly specialized local craft industries.

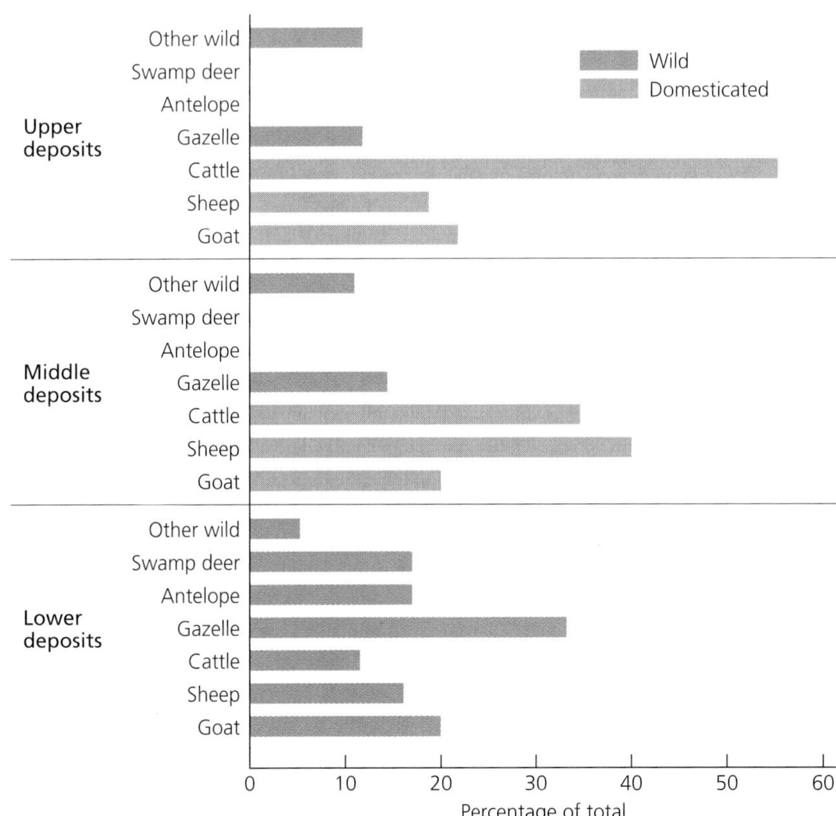


**Figure 6.36** The transition from hunting to herding at Mehrgarh. In the lower deposits, all the species present are wild, including gazelle (*Gazella*), goat (*Capra*), sheep (*Ovis*), cattle (*Bos*), antelope (*Boselaphus*), and swamp deer (*Cervus*). After 6000 B.C. (middle deposits), the reduced size of cattle, goat, and sheep bones at Mehrgarh indicates that these animals were domesticated. After the Neolithic (upper deposits), domesticated cattle were dominant.

**anthropomorphic** Having human form or attributes.

**lapis lazuli** A semiprecious stone of deep blue color.

**stone boiling** The process of heating stones in a fire and then adding them to containers to boil water or cook other foods.

**jasper** A high-quality flint, often highly colored.

**bow-drill** A device for perforating beads or other small objects, in which a bow is used to rotate the shaft of the bit.

# Ban-po-ts'un

*A Neolithic village in northern China*

Botanists have long recognized that many Chinese food plants were indigenous to the region. Prior to the last half century, however, archaeologists believed that the "idea" of agriculture, along with the knowledge for domesticating animals and making pottery, had diffused to the rich soil of the middle Huang (Yellow) River Valley in northern China from elsewhere. Before 1960, the few known Neolithic sites with their characteristic black-and-red pottery were assigned to the Yangshao culture and presumed to date to around 3000 B.C. The general view that products from Southwest Asia arrived in China about that time was supported by the presence of small amounts of foreign domesticates, such as wheat and barley, at known Yangshao sites, along with larger quantities of a locally domesticated grain (millet) and domesticated pigs.

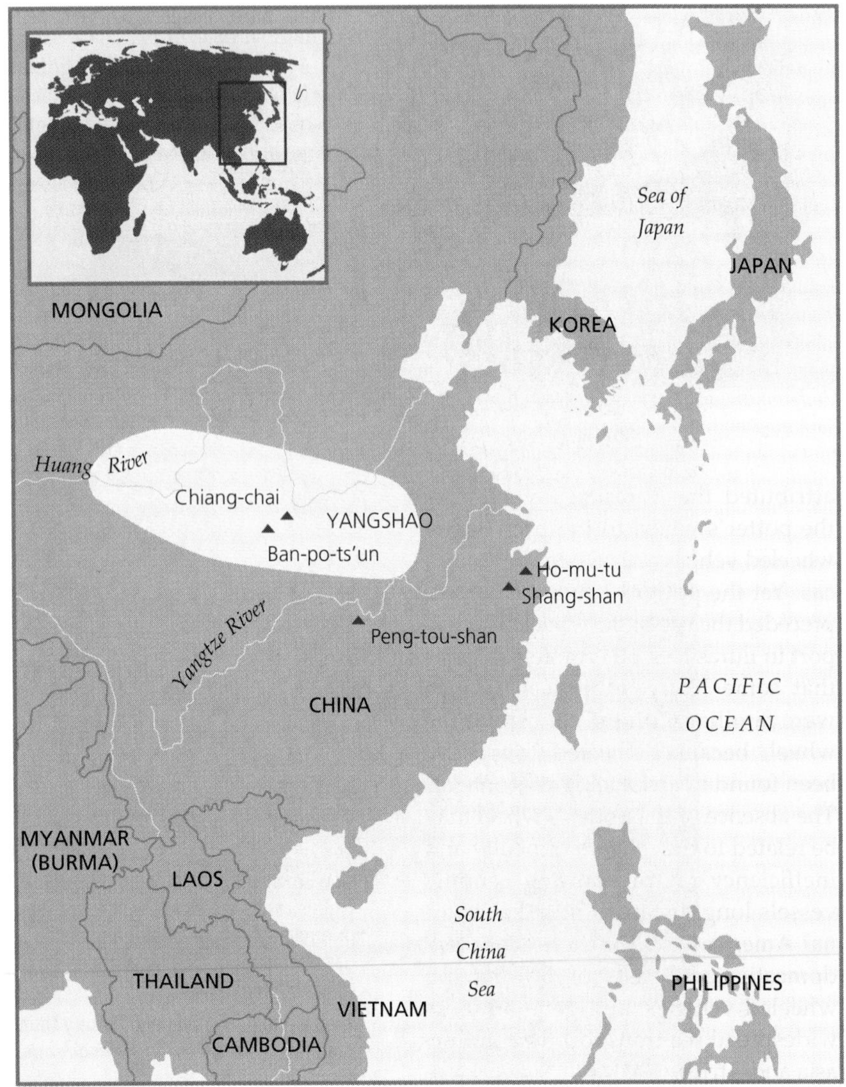


**Figure 6.40** Location of Ban-po-ts´un and other sites mentioned in the text. The distribution of Yangshao sites is shown in yellow.

In the past 40 years, however, information about the Chinese Neolithic has undergone a major transformation. Thousands of new Neolithic sites have recently been discovered in various areas of the country. Dozens of these sites have been excavated, and several earlier sites have been recorded (Figure 6.40). Early Neolithic sites in North China with millet and pigs have now been dated to the sixth millennium B.C., and the age for some Yangshao sites has been pushed back to 5000 B.C. Equally significant has been the discovery of Neolithic sites, such as Peng-tou-shan, Shang-shan, and Ho-mu-tu in South China, that predate 6000–5000 B.C. At these more southerly sites, the staple food plant was rice, not millet. Charred husks of domesticated rice from Shang-shan, a small sedentary village in the lower Yangtze River valley, have been dated to 8000 B.C. The origin of agriculture now appears to have been an indigenous process in North and South China, since in both areas local cultigens have been found to be more abundant and earlier than exotic domesticates.

The best-known Chinese Neolithic site, Ban-po-ts'un (ban-POT-sun), is not the oldest but rather the first to have been excavated extensively. (Work was completed between 1953 and 1955.) Located on a loess terrace about 9 m (30 ft) above a tributary of the Huang River near the city of Xian, Ban-po-ts'un covers 5–7 ha (12.5–17.5 acres). Roughly 100 houses, some circular and others square, were surrounded by a defensive and drainage ditch (Figure 6.41). Many of these structures were excavated, and the evidence indicates that the occupation at Ban-po was long and continuous. In one instance, five superimposed house floors were uncovered.

Many of the houses were semisubterranean, 3–5 m (10–16 ft) in diameter, with floors roughly a meter below the ground surface. Each house had timber beams that rested on stone bases, supporting a steeply pitched thatched roof. Floors and interior walls were plastered with clay and straw. One or two circular or pear-shaped fire pits, modeled in clay, were situated at the center of most of the dwellings. Storage pits and animal pens were interspersed among the houses at the center of the settlement.

At Ban-po, the principal crop was millet (*Setaria italica*), which was cultivated in the rich, soft-textured loess soils that surround the village. Such agricultural tools as bone hoes, polished stone adzes, axes, knives, and digging-stick weights were abundant at the site. Chestnuts, hazelnuts, and pine nuts supplemented the grain diet. The inhabitants of Ban-po-ts'un grew **hemp,** probably for use as a fiber. Silk production is suggested by a neatly sliced silkworm cocoon that was recovered. Numerous **spindle whorls,** for spinning thread, and bone needles also were found. Impressions of cloth, as well as baskets and mats, provide more evidence of weaving.

Pigs and dogs were the principal domesticated animals, although cattle, sheep, and goats also were utilized. Bone and quartz arrow points, bone fishhooks, and net-sinkers all were present, along with plentiful bones of several varieties of deer. Thus hunting and fishing contributed to the diet at Ban-po.

Ban-po-ts'un has yielded more than 500,000 pieces of pottery. Six pottery **kilns** were recovered beyond the ditch at the east side of the settlement, outside the residential zone (Figure 6.42). Most of the vessels were handmade into a distinctive redware. Whereas cooking pots tended to be coarse and gritty, water vessels and food-serving bowls were made of a finer clay. Cord-marking was the most common surface decoration, although basket, textile, and fingernail impressions also were used. The black-painted **geomorphic** and **zoomorphic** Yangshao designs were applied primarily to bowls and jars (Figure 6.43).

The inhabitants of Ban-po were buried in one of two ways. Infants and small children were placed in large redware pottery jars and interred near the houses. The cemetery for adults was located outside the enclosing ditch at the north end of the settlement, where corpses were placed in pits 2 m (6.5 ft) deep and arranged in rows. With very few exceptions, each individual was buried separately in an extended position. Ceramic vessels

**Figure 6.41** An artist's reconstruction of houses at Ban-po-ts'un. Circular structures are believed to have housed a single family; the larger, square structure is thought to have been a communal clan house.

**hemp** A tall annual plant whose tough fibers are used to make coarse fabrics and ropes.

**spindle whorl** A cam or balance wheel on a shaft or spindle for spinning yarn or thread from wool, cotton, or other material; usually made of clay.

**kiln** A furnace or oven for baking or drying objects, especially for firing pottery.

**geomorphic** Having the form or attributes of surface features of the earth or other celestial bodies.

**zoomorphic** Having animal form or attributes.

Site

# Khok Phanom Di

*The documentation of the spread of rice into Southeast Asia*

www.mhhe.com/priceip6e

For a Web-based activity on Khok Phanom Di, see the Internet exercises on your online learning center.

In 1952, geographer Carl Sauer proposed that the cradle for the world's earliest agriculture should lie in mainland Southeast Asia, rather than in Southwest Asia, as most scholars still believed. Sauer thought that the highly diverse, tropical, and riverine environments of Southeast Asia would have provided a superb locale for the fishing and farming way of life that he surmised would constitute the earliest stage in the transition to agriculture. Like the Russian botanist Nikolai Ivanovich Vavilov before him, Sauer was aware that the wild ancestors for a wide array of modern cultigens (root, tree, and seed crops) had been traced to Southeast Asia.

For over a decade, few prehistorians gave serious consideration to Sauer's ideas because of an absence of information to evaluate them. Moreover, his proposal did not conform to the traditional views of mainland Southeast Asia as a kind of cultural recipient or backwater area that obtained most technological advances from India or China. For Thailand, traditional archaeological reconstructions suggested that the earliest domesticates came from North China after 3000 B.C.

During the 1950s, the most relevant archaeological materials for tropical Southeast Asia belonged to the Hoabinhian complex, known from a series of limestone caves and shell middens. Because this complex was not well dated, the presence of cord-marked pottery with edge-ground stone axes in the upper deposits of several Hoabinhian sites was presumed to signal the introduction of agriculture from North China.

In the mid-1960s, Chester Gorman began a research project in the uplands

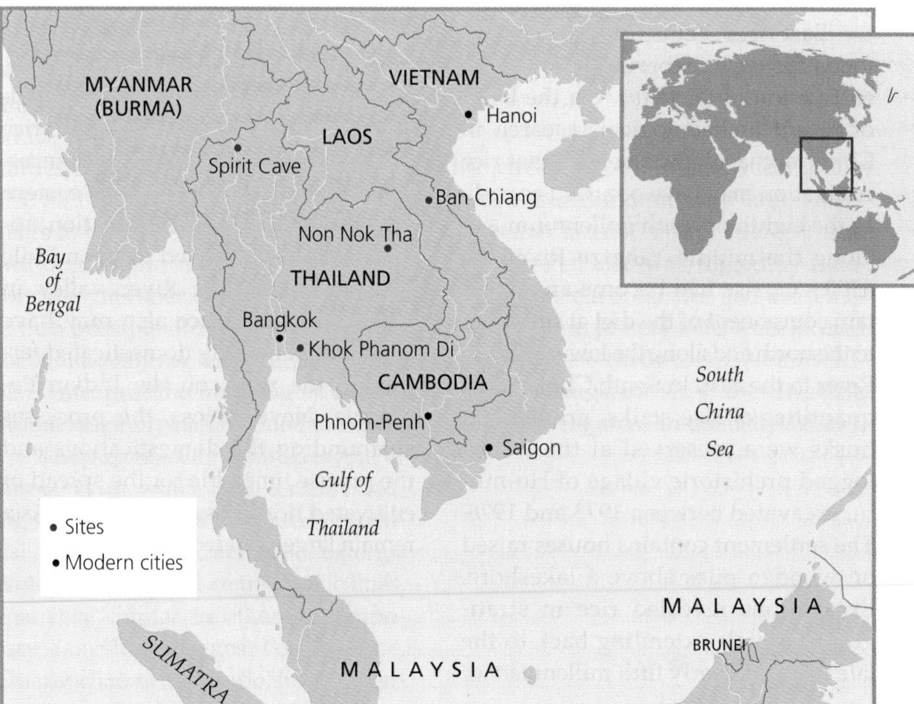


**Figure 6.45** Locations of the Southeast Asian sites mentioned in the text.

**temper** A nonplastic material (such as sand, shell, or fiber) that is added to clay to improve its workability and to reduce breakage during drying and firing.

of northern Thailand to elucidate the local Hoabinhian hunting-gathering pattern and to document the possible shift to plant cultivation. He began at Spirit Cave, in the rugged, hilly terrain near the Burmese border (Figure 6.45), where excavations revealed a stratigraphic sequence of two cultural levels. The lower deposits, dating from 9000 to 5500 B.C., contained standard Hoabinhian chipped stone artifacts and grinding stones. Polished adzes, cord-marked and burnished pottery, and polished slate knives, similar to tools used to harvest rice in Java today, were found in the upper soil layers, which have been dated by accelerator mass spectrometry (AMS) to the second millennium B.C. The most unexpected findings, however, resulted from the careful study of plant remains.

The first archaeologist to carefully sieve the excavated soil from a Hoabinhian site, Gorman found a great variety of seeds, shells, husks, and other plant parts. Food plants such as butternut, almonds, cucumbers, water chestnuts, a few beans, and peppers were recovered, as were remains of the stimulant betel nut, candlenuts (probably used for lighting), and the bottle gourd, a probable container. None of the recovered plant species differs significantly from its wild prototype, indicating that the plants were not domesticated. Nonetheless, a wide variety of plants was intensively utilized, possibly involving the tending or fostering of some species.

Significantly, the remains of rice were absent at Spirit Cave. Yet rice has been recovered at other sites broadly contemporaneous with the later occupation of Spirit Cave. At Non Nok Tha, a habitation mound in the lower northeastern part of Thailand, clear impressions and carbonized remnants of rice chaff were found in potsherds. Apparently, the ancient potters, like their modern counterparts, mixed the plant materials into their clay as a fiber **temper** to improve the workability of the clay and to reduce breakage. In spite of disagreements over whether the rice was domesticated, analyses by Charles Higham, of the University of Otago, New Zealand, of the animal remains from Non Nok Tha, and contemporary levels at the more northerly site of Ban Chiang, have revealed an increasing reliance on domesticated animals—cattle, pigs, chickens, and dogs—at these sites. Yet hunting and gathering also continued to be important for subsistence.

Cultivated rice has been recovered at Khok Phanom Di (COKE fa-nome DEE), which translates from Thai as "Good Mound." This coastal site, a 5-ha (12.3-acre) mound that rises 12 m (39 ft) above the surrounding floodplain in a rich estuarine setting near the Gulf of Siam, was occupied between 2000 and 1500 B.C. (Figure 6.46). The first settlers may have been attracted by the broad estuary, its inexhaustible supply of food, abundant potting clay, and a river that facilitated exchange with other regions. Most of the artifacts recovered from the earliest layers relate to fishing and the manufacture of ceramic vessels (Figure 6.47). Recovered bones from animals known to inhabit the nearby mangrove swamps, such as macaques and pigs, reveal hunting activities. The saltwater estuary was not conducive to rice cultivation, so Higham believes that the earliest rice at the site was obtained from inland farming communities by exchange. The coastal inhabitants of Khok Phanom Di also exchanged for exotic ornaments made from shell, ivory, and slate. Hoes and harvesting knives made from shells found in later levels indicate that rice was cultivated late in the occupation of the site. Dog, the only domesticated animal present at the site, also was found in the later levels.

**Figure 6.46** The site of Khok Phanom Di is the large, tree-covered mound on the horizon. The site, surrounded by the flat floodplain of the Bang Pakong River, lies 22 km (14 mi) from the present shore of the Gulf of Siam.

**Figure 6.47** Excavations at Khok Phanom Di have revealed a 7-m-(23-ft)-deep sequence of occupations spanning 500 years from approximately 2000 B.C.

**Figure 6.48** "The Princess" of Khok Phanom Di. This woman in her mid-thirties was interred wearing a garment that had been embroidered with more than 120,000 small shell disc beads. She wore a necklace of 1000 I-shaped shell beads and a shell bracelet on her left arm. Two large shell discs were placed on her shoulders.

The inhabitants of Khok Phanom Di invested significant energy in mortuary ritual. Excavations into the site's mound exposed over 150 graves. Many of the bodies were covered with red ochre, wrapped in shrouds, or placed on wooden **biers.** Grave offerings included well-made pottery that was brilliantly burnished and incised with complex designs, shell beads, and bangles fashioned from fish vertebrae. An especially rich grave, sometimes referred to as "The Princess," was accompanied by thousands of small shell beads, richly ornamented black pottery vessels, a clay anvil, and a potter's kit that included two burnishing stones (Figure 6.48). The remains lay under a pile of clay cylinders that once had been destined to become pottery vessels. The nature and richness of the burial goods have been interpreted as evidence that the woman was a potter of high status. Yet individuals thought to be her descendants were interred with few grave offerings, suggesting that status may have been achieved through personal endeavor and was not entirely determined at birth or ascribed.

The burials at Khok Phanom Di reveal significant social differences in a sedentary community of hunter-gatherer-cultivators in a rich estuarine setting who exchanged with newly established inland farming communities. Although rice was not originally domesticated at Khok Phanom Di (more likely to the north in South China), the presence of cultivated rice there documents its arrival in Southeast Asia by the second millennium B.C.

In recent decades, knowledge about the early Holocene in Southeast Asia has expanded significantly. We have learned that the broad-spectrum Hoabinhian complex extended more deeply into the past than had been previously believed and that plant tending may have contributed importantly to the diet. A more dramatic transition occurred during the past several millennia B.C. with the introduction of cultivated rice, as seen at Khok Phanom Di. At other settled villages, such as Non Nok Tha and Ban Chiang, the inhabitants lived in houses built on piles or wooden stilts, buried their dead in low mounds, and made socketed spearpoints and adzes as well as adornments of bronze. The appearance of these objects in northeastern Thailand around 1500 B.C. is significant in that they represent some of the world's earliest known bronzeworking, or **metallurgy.** More than 800 metal ornaments and weapons were uncovered at Ban Chiang, and many more were found at Non Nok Tha. At these later settlements, rice agriculture and domesticated animals constituted the bulk of the diet.

Although much has been learned, many questions remain. We cannot evaluate the importance of indigenous tropical domesticates, such as yam and taro, because these root crops preserve so poorly in the archaeological record. The specifics of rice adoption remain a bit sketchy, although recent research places the original hearth for this key grain in South China. Consequently, although Sauer's hypothesis for indigenous Southeast Asian plant domestication may eventually hold for certain tropical roots, fruits, and tubers, concerted archaeological studies over the past decades now indicate that the region's staple grain—rice—was probably introduced into the region from South China.

**bier** A stand on which a coffin or a corpse is placed.

**metallurgy** The art of separating metals from their ores.

Site

# Guilá Naquitz Cave

## *A preceramic seasonal campsite in Mexico*

Kent V. Flannery spent the day before Christmas of 1964 in the foothills of the eastern Valley of Oaxaca, in southern Mexico, searching for the best site to study agricultural origins in Mexico. Having just completed several seasons of fieldwork as the faunal analyst on Richard MacNeish's interdisciplinary team in arid Tehuacán 150 km (90 mi) to the north (see "Tehuacán," p. 250), Flannery wanted to see what form early agriculture might have taken in a more humid valley with greater farming potential (Figure 6.49). On that December day, Flannery found a preceramic occupation at Cueva Blanca, a site that, he says, more than any other launched his Valley of Oaxaca Human Ecology project (Figure 6.50).

On Christmas day, heartened by the previous day's finds, Flannery began to prepare a research proposal. A year later, with support from the Smithsonian Research Foundation, he returned to Oaxaca. On January 26, 1966, less than a week after beginning a reconnaissance of caves in the area, he found a rockshelter with lots of chipped stone debris and half of a projectile point on the ground surface. This small overhang, named Guilá Naquitz (ghee-LA nah-KEETS), which means "white cliff" in the native Zapotec language of Oaxaca, was subsequently excavated (Figure 6.51).

At Guilá Naquitz, Flannery and his field crew carefully peeled away the layers of preceramic occupations dating to 8750–6670 B.C. On the basis of careful retrieval and analysis of the floral, faunal, and artifactual remains found in the cave strata, Flannery suggested that the shelter of Guilá Naquitz was occupied seasonally between August and December by small groups, or **microbands,** perhaps composed of a series of nuclear families. As in the rest of the Mexican highlands at that time, the ancient inhabitants of Oaxaca were mobile, living in several different

*We have indicated that the research problem we chose for ourselves at Guilá Naquitz was to develop a model that would not only deal with some of the underlying and more universal aspects of early domestication but also tie that process into the specific cultural pattern for the Valley of Oaxaca.*
—Kent V. Flannery (1986)

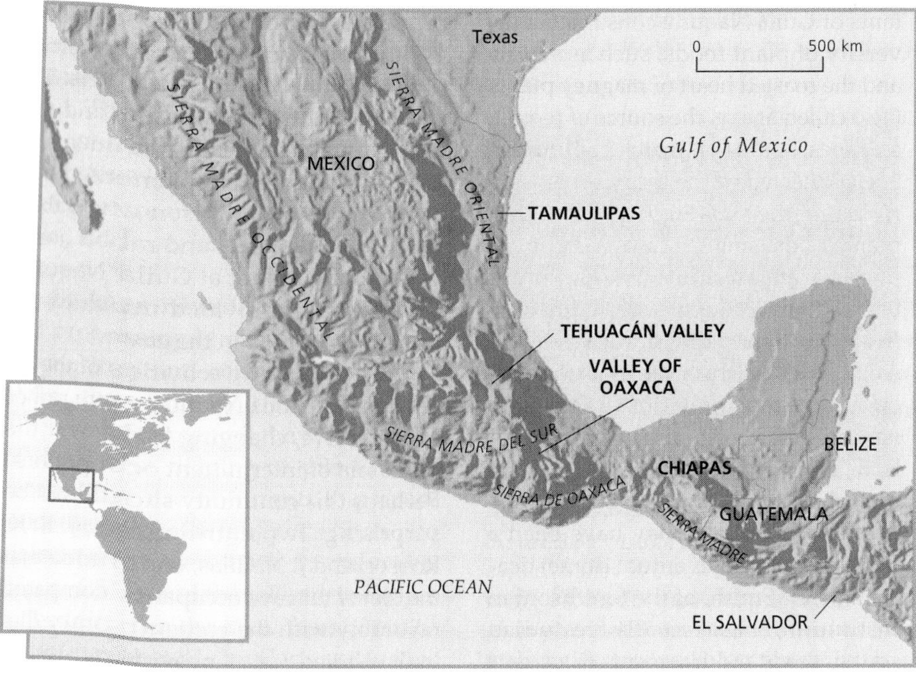


**Figure 6.49** Regions of Mesoamerica mentioned in the text where evidence of early agriculture has been recovered.

**microband** A small family group of hunter-gatherers.

similar to maize than the other geographic subpopulations of this plant. In fact, recent genetic analysis by Doebley and his colleagues suggests that a small number of single-gene changes could account for the transformation of these annual teosintes into maize. The Balsas drainage, largely unknown archaeologically, may be a promising area for pursuing the initial domestication of maize.

To date, archaeological findings have supplemented but not resolved these debates. Archaeological deposits at Guilá Naquitz, dating to the seventh or eighth millennium B.C., contained bean and squash seeds and grains of *Zea* pollen. Yet we do not know whether the pollen came from maize or teosinte, or how the pollen was transported into the cave. Today, teosinte often grows in the same fields with beans, squash, and maize. Teosinte is a weedy pioneer that thrives in disturbed areas such as seasonally wet streambeds and abandoned campsites. Although teosinte can be neither popped nor ground into flour as easily as maize, the wild plant is occasionally eaten as a low-choice or "starvation" food in times of need. Young teosinte ears could have been eaten for their sugary taste. Seasonally, stems of the plant may have been (and are still) chewed, because the pith stores so much sugar.

According to Richard MacNeish's Tehuacán research, the earliest domesticated corn remains appear in cave deposits dating to the end of the sixth millennium B.C. The original dating of these Tehuacán cave strata was accom-

**Figure 6.56** Archaeological corncobs recovered during excavations of Tehuacán cave strata document the increasing size of the maize ears through time.

plished through the conventional radiocarbon analysis of charcoal samples.

Two decades ago, the early dates for Tehuacán maize were questioned, based on subsequent direct radiocarbon accelerator dating of the early maize cobs themselves. Accelerator mass spectrometry enables researchers to count individual carbon-14 atoms, rather than relying on the conventional counting of radioactive disintegrations (see "Radiocarbon Dating," Chapter 4, p. 145). As a result, they can handle much smaller samples. Recent analysis dates the early Tehuacán maize to the mid-third millennium B.C., several thousand years more recent than previously thought. The new AMS dates therefore provide a new date for the arrival of maize in the Tehuacán Valley. Nevertheless, at the same time, pieces of maize cob from strata at Guilá Naquitz have been dated to approximately 4200 B.C., indicating that maize domestication may well have occurred to the west of Tehuacán, possibly in the Balsas.

On the basis of these new AMS dates from the valleys of Oaxaca and Tehuacán and other innovative analysis, it is clear that the highland Mesoamerican people who adopted maize were organized in small, seasonally mobile societies. These groups added corn to their way of life, perhaps as early as 10,000 years ago, without radically changing their social or economic behavior. Not surprisingly, this relatively primitive maize does not appear to have become an immediate preceramic dietary staple. Although we cannot directly determine the role of human selection in the evolution of these early ears, later deposits and contexts from the Tehuacán Valley reveal a record of increasing cob size, from the earliest tiny cobs to the much larger and more productive ears (with bigger kernels and more seed rows) grown today (Figures 6.56 and 6.57). The important role of human selection in this latter process is evident.

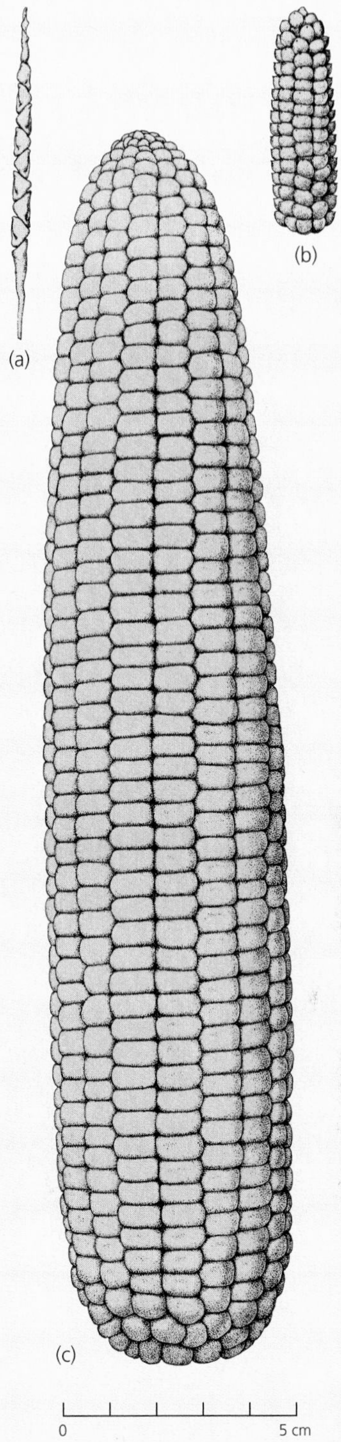

(a)
(b)
(c)
0
5 cm

**Figure 6.57** The role of human selection in the domestication of corn is evident in the increasing size of the cob: (a) teosinte, (b) early maize, and (c) modern maize, all drawn to the same scale.

Site

# Tehuacán

*The evolution of early maize*

**Figure 6.58** Excavated units in Coxcatlán Cave in Tehuacán show its stratigraphy.

**Mesoamerica** The region consisting of central and southern Mexico, Guatemala, Belize, El Salvador, and the western parts of Honduras and Nicaragua that was the focus of complex, hierarchical states at the time of Spanish contact.

In the early 1960s, when Richard MacNeish began his fieldwork in the highland Tehuacán (tay-wa-CON) Valley in Puebla, Mexico, little was known about either the preceramic occupation of **Mesoamerica** or the beginnings of agriculture in the Americas. Before MacNeish's work, Mesoamerica was theorized to be a hearth of early agriculture. Yet no archaeological evidence existed to support that hypothesis.

MacNeish chose to search for the origins of maize (*Zea mays*) in the relatively small Tehuacán Valley for two reasons. First, because of the region's dryness, preservation was unusually good. Preliminary excavations unearthed fragments of basketry and plant materials in limestone cave deposits. Second, MacNeish already had recovered tiny 5000-year-old corncobs in caves in both the northeastern Mexican state of Tamaulipas and the southern state of Chiapas. He reasoned that the earliest domesticated *Zea* should be still older and would be found in a highland region such as Tehuacán, located between Tamaulipas and Chiapas.

MacNeish designed his Tehuacán research to examine two critical ques-

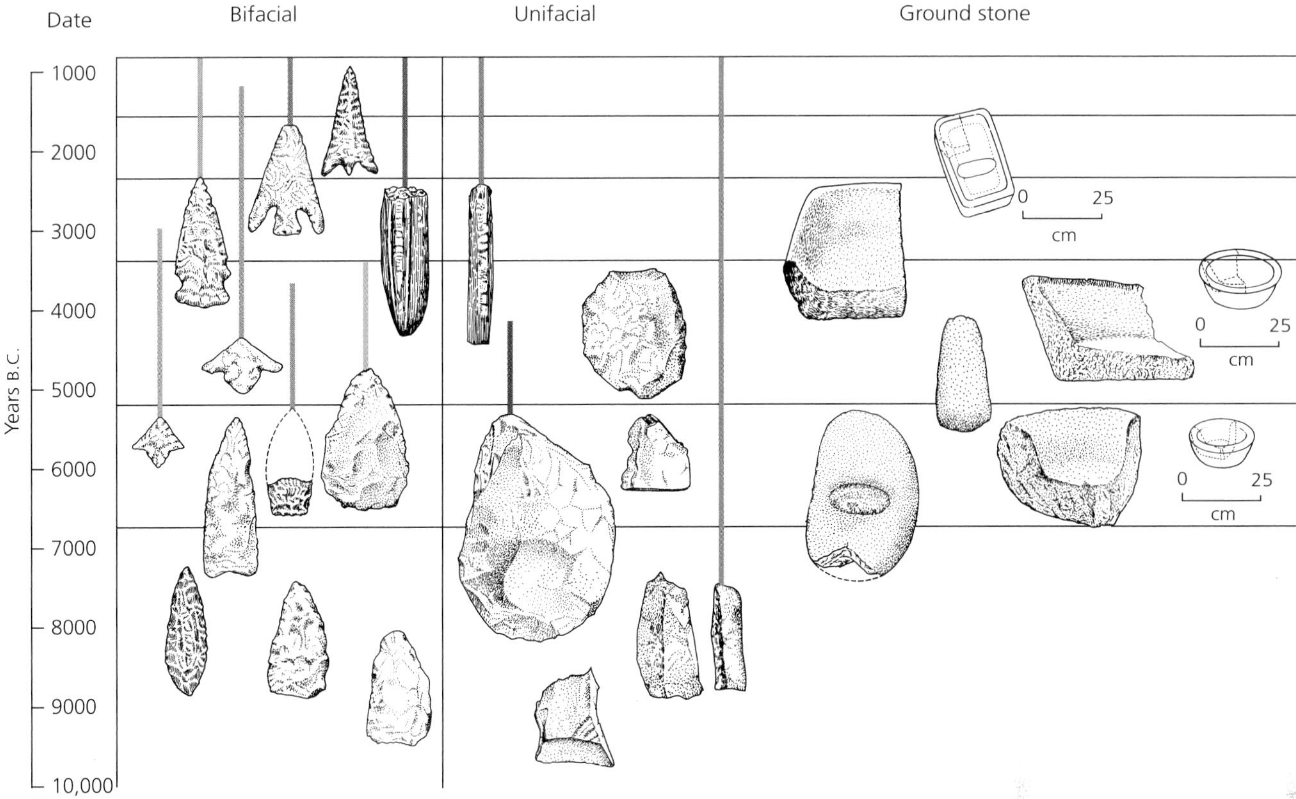


Figure 6.59 Changes in the flaked and ground stone industry in Tehuacán, 10,000–1000 B.C.

tions: (1) What led to the domestication of maize? (2) How did these changes lay the foundation for later Mesoamerican civilization? He undertook a large survey that located more than 450 prehispanic sites over the 1500 sq km (575 sq mi) of the valley and excavated at a series of 12 cave and open-air deposits, including Coxcatlán Cave (Figure 6.58). Controlled stratigraphic excavations, combined with a large number of radiocarbon dates, enabled MacNeish to reconstruct an unbroken 12,000-year sequence of occupation, at that time the longest recorded in the Americas. For the first time, a picture of early presedentary, preceramic society in Mesoamerica could be sketched, using both artifacts and the plant and animal remains preserved in dry caves of Tehuacán (Figure 6.59).

During the preceramic era, according to MacNeish, the few people of the Tehuacán Valley lived in microbands that dispersed periodically. Some camps accommodated only a single nuclear family, while others sheltered much larger groups. The plant and animal remains recovered from preceramic sites in Tehuacán's diverse topographic zones led to the recognition that the **seasonality** of resource availability and the **scheduling** of resource extraction were critically important in determining the annual regime. More specifically, the early inhabitants of Tehuacán scheduled their seasonal movements across the highland region, from the riverbanks to the foothills to the mountains, to coincide with the periodic availability of local plant and animal species.

For most of the preceramic era, such game as rabbits and deer supplemented plants in the diet. During the May–October rainy season, edible plants were more abundant, and a diversity of seeds, cactus fruits, and berries were exploited, in addition to the bountiful seedpods of the mesquite tree. Rabbits, rodents, lizards, and other small animals were consumed at this time of year, when the size of human groups

*From a personal point of view, and closely connected with satisfying my innate curiosity, has been the thrill of discovery of art and artifact and the fact that these objects have remained unknown to anyone until my little trowel or paintbrush uncovered them—often after long periods of searching for these new and thrilling finds. I have been doing archaeology now for over forty years but the thrill is still there and I feel that this thrill should happen to anyone and everyone.*

—Richard MacNeish (1978)

**seasonality** The changing availability of resources according to the different seasons of the year.

**scheduling** The process of arranging the extraction of resources according to their availability and the demands of competing subsistence activities.

Figure 6.60 Changes in diet and farming strategies in the Tehuacán Valley, 6000 B.C.–A.D. 1000.

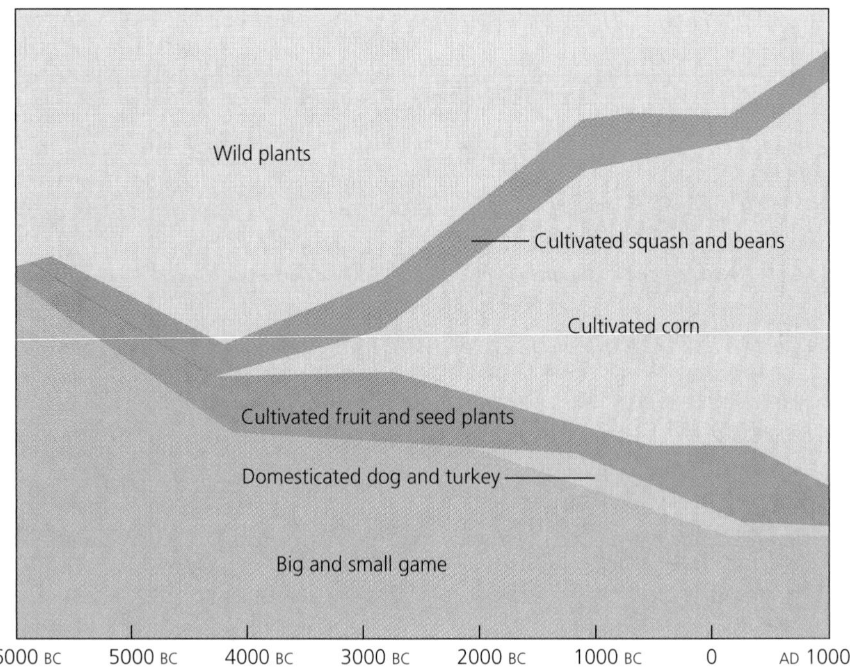


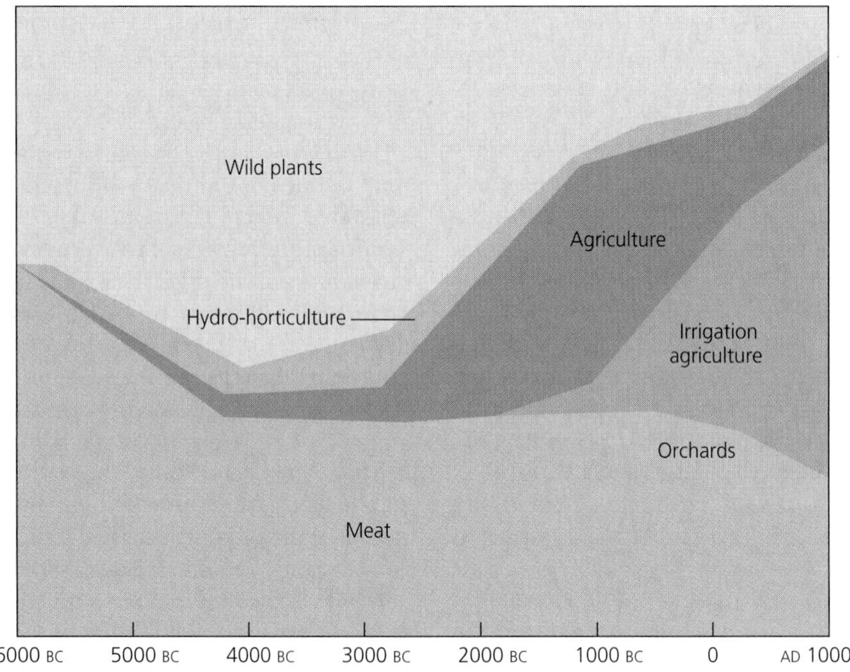

was generally larger. Although some fruits were still available in the early part of the dry season (November and December), cactus leaves and deer apparently were the staples during the dry spells that lasted from January to April.

Although this way of life persisted for at least 6400 years, from about 8000 to 1600 B.C., several important dietary changes did take place. A wild ancestor of the domesticated squash was used by roughly 8000 years ago, probably as a container or for its protein-rich seeds. Thereafter during this 6400-year period, domesticated varieties of squash and maize appeared. These early maize ears were small (about the size of an index finger) and contained no more than eight rows of kernels (see Figure 6.56). These early domesticated plants did not immediately provide a large portion of the diet, which still was based primarily on wild plants and animals. Thus these initial experiments in plant domestication occurred among a population that was largely mobile and remained so for thousands of years.

Somewhat enigmatically, the bone chemistry assay of human bones from the Tehuacán excavations provides a rather different picture for the period after 5000 B.C. (see "Bone Chemistry and Prehistoric Subsistence," Chapter 5, p. 176). These studies indicate a smaller amount of meat in the diet than is seen in the archaeological deposits, as well as a greater role for either early cultigens or wild ***setaria*** grass, the seeds of which were present but not recovered in abundance in the archaeological record (Figure 6.60). Yet the relative importance of meat inferred from archaeological deposits is not very surprising, given that bone generally preserves better in ancient deposits than do smaller plant materials.

In addition to the gradual increase in the overall proportion of both wild and domesticated plant foods in the diet, the Tehuacán sequence reveals an increase in population and a decrease in residential mobility. Based on the size and number of sites known from the preceramic phases, the total population density for the Tehuacán Valley, though low, appears to have increased severalfold during this period. Although the earliest sedentary villages in Tehuacán did not occur until 4000–3000 years ago, the length of site occupation increased, and the size of sites grew during the preceding millennia. A single circular pithouse, the earliest known in Mesoamerica, was found in a 5000-year-old level at an open-air site in the region. Later preceramic occupations also tend to have more storage features.

There is little question that MacNeish's Tehuacán research has revolutionized our knowledge of early Mesoamerica, as well as our understanding of the diversity of situations in which early agriculture developed. In the Tehuacán Valley, the first experiments toward plant domestication occurred among people who remained residentially mobile for thousands of years, a sequence that is very different from what has been long known for early farming in Southwest Asia.

The wild ancestors of the major Mesoamerican cultigens—maize, beans, and squash—were all highland plants. Thus it is not surprising that the earliest archaeological evidence for Mesoamerican agriculture has been found in highland valleys such as Tehuacán and Oaxaca. The dry caves in these upland valleys are recognized for their superb archaeological preservation. Yet some of Mesoamerica's earliest sedentary villages were established in the lowlands, where the highland cultigens eventually were incorporated into a coastal subsistence economy that also included marine resources and lowland plants.

How and why has AMS dating of archaeological samples revolutionized our perspective on early agriculture?

***setaria*** A wild grass with edible seeds.

# Guitarrero Cave

## *The origins of domestication in the high Andes*

**Figure 6.61** The location of Guitarrero Cave in the mountains of northern Peru.

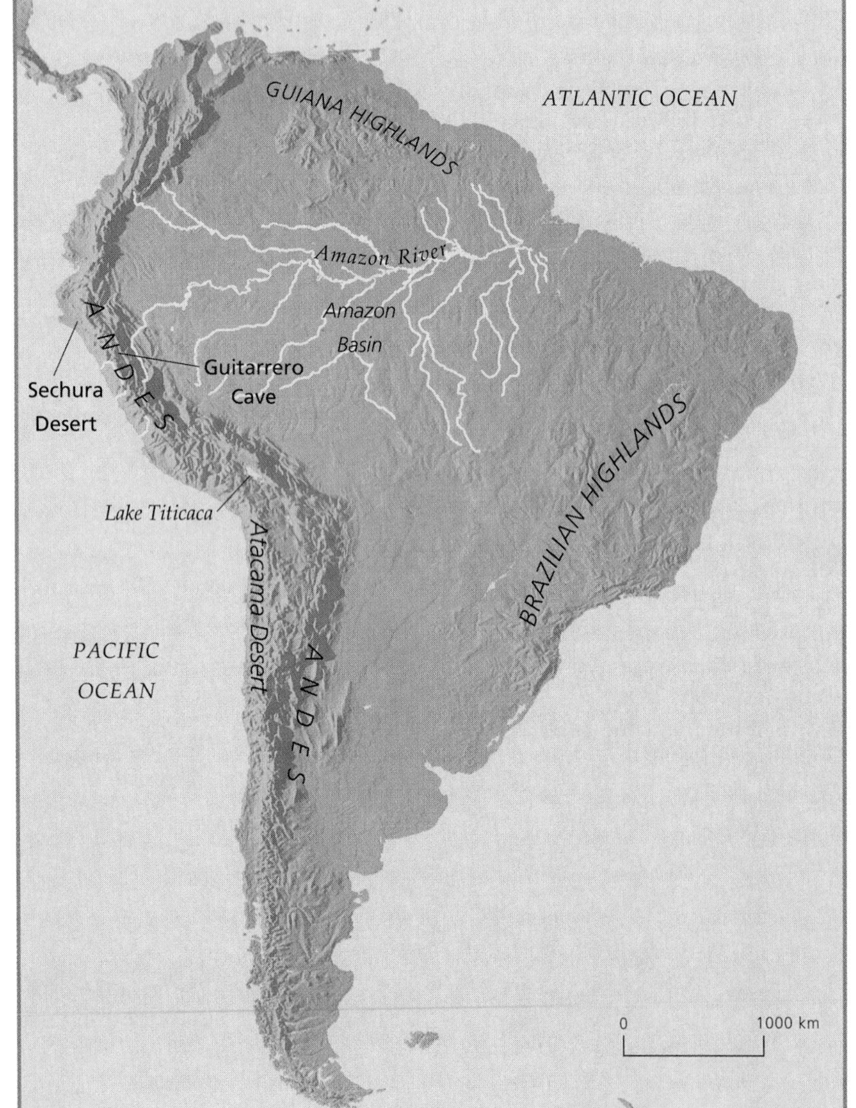


A century before the arrival of the Spanish in the sixteenth century A.D., prehispanic America's largest empire was in place along the western side of South America (see Chapter 9). This political domain stretched from the Inca capital of Cuzco, in Peru's southern highlands, down into Chile and northwestern Argentina and up through Ecuador. It encompassed high Andean mountain slopes, Pacific coastal deserts, and the western fringes of the Amazonian tropics. The Inca established a network of roads and trails to move people and goods across these diverse topographic zones.

Thousands of years before the beginnings of Inca expansion, the earliest steps toward agriculture were taken in this part of South America, where the high Andes are sandwiched by a coastal desert and a tropical rain forest. Although roads were not yet built, communication between these environments was critical to the beginnings of Andean domestication. By 10,000–8000 years ago, Amazonian plants had been introduced into the Andes. After 6000 B.C., morphologically wild plants and animals from the rain forest and mountains were present at sites established along the Pacific. Yet the earliest indications for cultivation and domestication appear in the mountains.

As mentioned in the earlier discussion of Monte Verde, human groups first arrived in South America as mobile hunters and gatherers, using stone implements and eating a variety of foods (see "Monte Verde," Chapter 4, p. 154). They spread rapidly across the continent. Although earlier sites have been reported, archaeologists have a much more complete understanding of the past 10,000–12,000 years in the Andean highlands. One of the important sites for the early period is Guitarrero (gheeta-RARE-o) Cave, a large natural rockshelter at 2580 m (8500 ft) above sea level in the mountains of northern Peru (Figure 6.61). First occupied more than 10,000 years ago, Guitarrero Cave served as a campsite for thousands of years, accumulating a valuable record of the beginnings of domestication in the Andes (Figure 6.62).

Thomas F. Lynch, of Cornell University, directed excavations in the

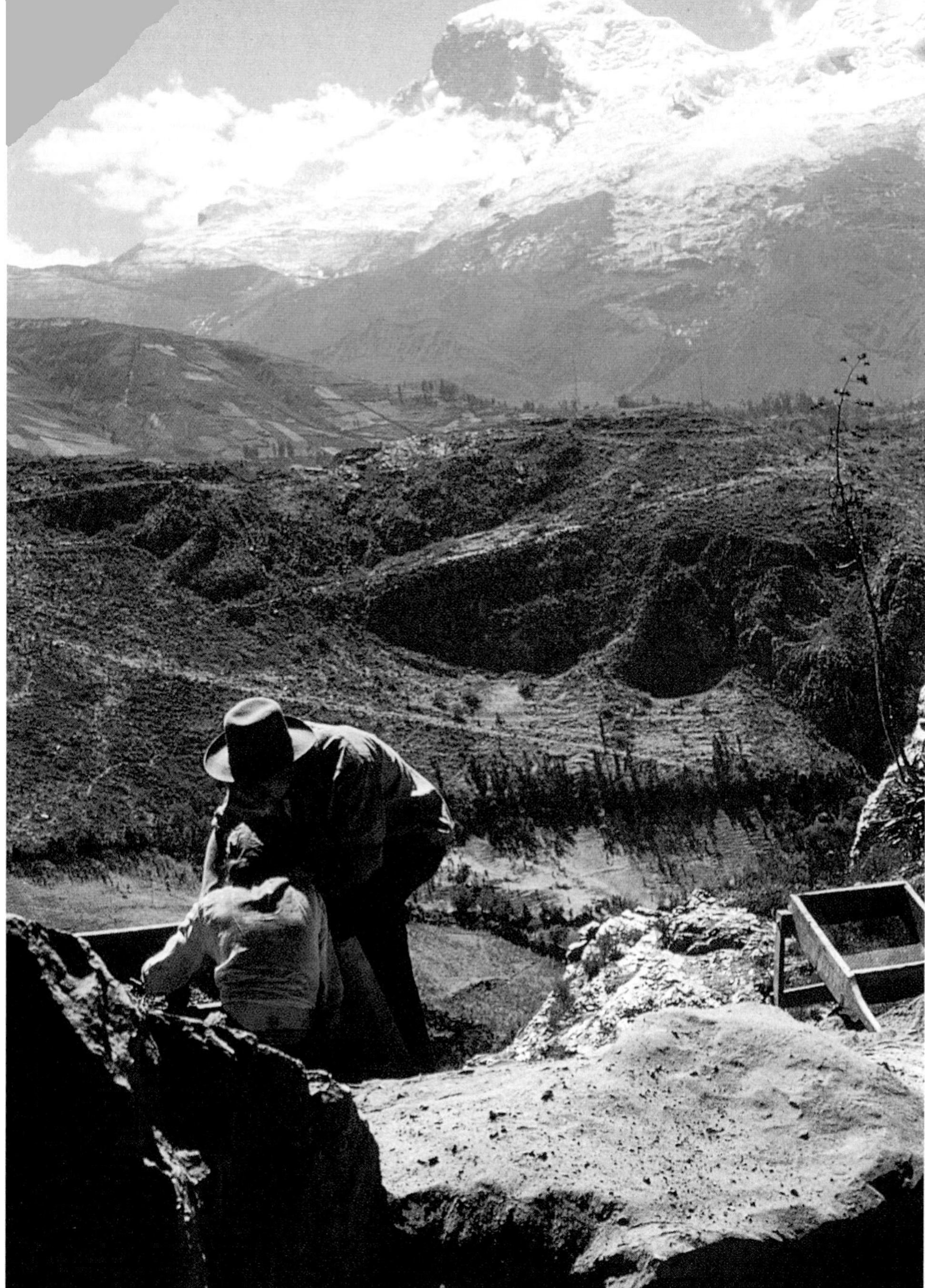

**Figure 6.62** A view of the Andes from Guitarrero Cave, a large natural rockshelter situated 2.5 km above sea level in the mountains of northern Peru. The site was first used by Native Americans more than 10,000 years ago and contains a valuable record of the beginnings of domestication in the South American highlands.

cave during the late 1960s (Figure 6.63). The dry highland cave environment preserved many organic materials, and polished bone knives, fragments of gourd bowls, cordage, basketry, and textiles were recovered (Figure 6.64). C. Earle Smith noted that the total bulk of the inedible fibrous plants was roughly equivalent to that of the food plant remains at the site, suggesting that the Andean utilization of fibers and textiles had a very early origin (Figure 6.65). The basic twining, or finger-weaving, technique, used to create many of the textiles at Guitarrero Cave, is clearly an important step toward the elaborate techniques used for later prehispanic Andean fabrics.

Organic remains also revealed continuity in another important Andean cultural pattern: communication and exchange between different environmental areas. Guitarrero Cave, on the western slope of the Andes, sits in the middle of three principal environmental zones. The high-altitude shelter

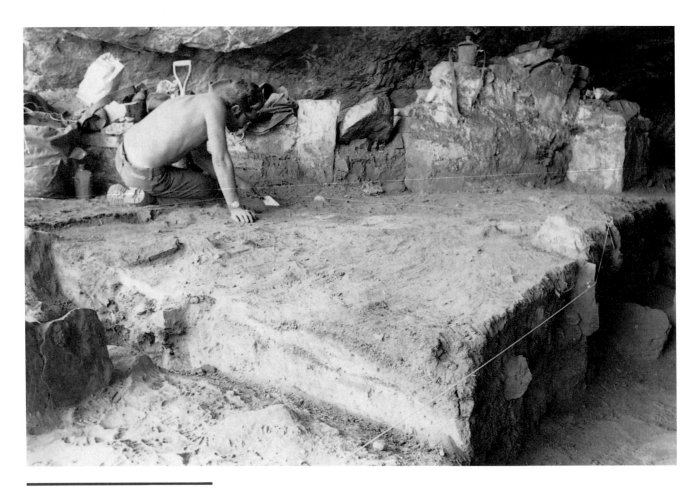

Figure 6.63 Excavating the early Archaic deposits at Guitarrero Cave.

**Figure 6.64** Early Archaic flint scraper wrapped in deer hide and cord recovered from Guitarrero Cave.

faces the exceedingly dry, narrow Pacific coastal zone. To the east, over the Andes, are the wetter, tropical eastern slopes, or ***montaña*** zone, which grades down to the Amazon jungle. The presence of lima beans, a plant native to the Amazon Basin, in archaeological levels dated to roughly 8000 years ago, reveals both the antiquity of pan-Andean connections, at least in an indirect, down-the-line fashion (passing from person to person, group to group over long distances), and the origins of cultivation in South America.

As with the lima bean, many wild ancestors of the major South American domesticated plants, including manioc, peanut, guava, and coca, were native to the eastern side of the Andes. Yet because of the poor archaeological preservation in the *montaña* zone, we know little about the first stages in the process of cultivation and domestication. Other root crops, such as the potato, are indigenous to the mountain

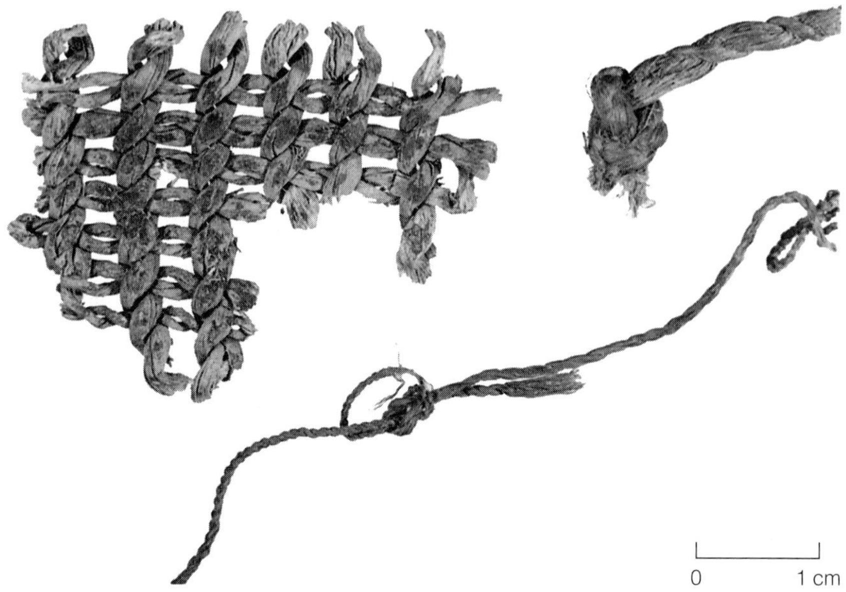

0 1 cm

**Figure 6.65** Basket fragments recovered from Guitarrero Cave.

zone. Unfortunately, efforts to learn the origins of root crops are hampered because these plants reproduce asexually (see "The First Farmers," p. 199). Ten thousand years ago, Andean **tubers** and **rhizomes** were prime sources of carbohydrates for the occupants of Guitarrero Cave. Yet these plants may have been wild, collected from higher elevations.

As in highland Mesoamerica, the first steps toward cultivation and domestication in the Andean highlands resulted in few immediate changes in society. In both regions, the preceramic era was characterized for thousands of years by continued mobility and a rather resilient diet. At Guitarrero Cave, the earliest inhabitants relied for generations on a variety of tubers, rhizomes, and squash for carbohydrates; several kinds of beans for plant protein; and wild fruits, along with a variety of chili peppers, for minerals and vitamins.

Analysis of the faunal remains from Guitarrero by Elizabeth Wing, of the University of Florida, indicates that deer, camelids, rabbits, and a range of small animal and bird species were hunted. Wing observed a steady decline in the number of deer bones and an increase in those of camelids through time, a pattern also seen at other Andean sites from this time and particularly at sites in the higher grassland, or ***puna,*** region. In the Andes, the increase in camelid remains is only part of the evidence for manipulation and eventual domestication (for both meat and wool) of the larger llama and the smaller alpaca. The larger llama also served as a pack animal, carrying goods across the Andes. Another Andean species, the guinea pig, also was domesticated for meat but was not abundant at Guitarrero Cave.

***montaña*** (Spanish) Mountain, specifically referring to the wet, tropical slopes of the Amazonian Andes.

**tuber** A fleshy, usually oblong or rounded outgrowth (such as the potato) of a subterranean stem or root of a plant.

**rhizome** An edible, rootlike subterranean plant stem.

***puna*** (Spanish) High grassland plateaus in the Peruvian Andes.

Concept

## Agriculture in Native North America

### *Indigenous plant domestication before the spread of maize*

By the time Europeans arrived in the Americas, the maize plant had spread far to the north and south. Its arrival in Central and South America followed the plant's initial domestication in highland Mesoamerica. Yet until recently, the exact timing of the plant's introduction to the south had been a matter of considerable conjecture. The recent AMS dating of maize starch grains that were extracted from charred residue on ceramic cooking vessels has now placed domesticated maize in Ecuador by around 3000 B.C. In South America, maize supplemented a range of other agricultural plants that were indigenously domesticated.

The history of maize in the Americas north of Mexico is somewhat clearer. Maize reached the Southwest by 2100 B.C., and from there it apparently was carried across the Great Plains and arrived in the Eastern Woodlands by approximately 200 B.C.–A.D. 200. Although the timing of maize's North American arrival is now better established, the role of the exotic domesticates in the beginnings of North American agriculture is still a matter of discussion. Formerly, most scholars postulated that agriculture in eastern North America began in response to the diffusion of exotic domesticated plants (specifically, squash) from the south, but that view is beginning to be challenged in the face of mounting archaeological and genetic evidence.

Based on excavations at a range of sites in eastern North America, from Ohio to Arkansas, archaeologists have found that native North American seed plants were domesticated in riverine floodplain settings as early as 2500–1500 B.C. The plants include chenopod (*Chenopodium berlandieri,* also known as goosefoot or chia), sunflower (*Helianthus annuus*), and marsh elder (*Iva annua,* var. *macrocarpa*). In each case, botanical studies have shown that the domesticated varieties have larger (Figure 6.66) and morphologically different seeds than the wild ancestors (Figure 6.67). As in Mesoamerica and South America, these domesticated seed plants were incorporated into the diet of mobile peoples, who also exploited a range of wild foods.

Although AMS dates on the maize found in eastern North American caves have consistently placed the arrival of this Mesoamerican plant well after the domestication of native North American seed plants, the picture is a bit fuzzier for squash (*Cucurbita pepo*). Small carbonized pieces of squash rind were recovered in flotation samples collected at river valley sites in Illinois

**Figure 6.66** The seeds of domesticated marsh elder, sunflower, and squash (top to bottom, on the right) are larger than those of their wild ancestors (on the left). Larger seeds germinate faster and produce plants that grow more quickly, resulting in greater quantities of food. Selection in the past for larger seeds was an important part of the domestication process of these seed plants.

and Kentucky. These fragments yielded direct AMS dates of roughly 5000–3500 B.C. Though *C. pepo* does include some wild gourds, it is best known for its rich variety of domesticated squashes and pumpkins. Researchers also documented its domestication in highland Mexico around 8000–7000 B.C. The archaeological contexts that produced these early pieces of rind were outside the current range of the Texas wild gourd, another *Cucurbita* species that grows in eastern Texas. An obvious initial conclusion was that domesticated squash was introduced to eastern North America, along with the notion of agriculture, well before the cultivation of native plants.

This first scenario has been challenged by an alternative viewpoint suggesting that *C. pepo* was independently domesticated twice from different ancestral populations of wild gourds. It was domesticated in Mexico and then later in eastern North America around 2500 B.C. (around the same time the indigenous seed plants were domesticated). All the early eastern North American *Cucurbita* rind samples are thin and likely came from wild gourds. Early seeds from these plants also are small, within the range of wild gourds. The earliest morphological marker, larger seed size, of *Cucurbita* domestication in eastern North America did not appear until 2500–2300 B.C. These interpretations are supported by the findings of botanist Deena Decker-Walters, of Texas A&M University. Her biochemical analyses of *C. pepo* have revealed that the species is composed of two developmental lineages, one from Mexico and the other from eastern North America. This view has recently been supported by the discovery of wild squash in the Ozarks of Missouri and Arkansas. This Ozark gourd occupies the same floodplain niche inhabited by two of the seed plants (goosefoot and marsh elder) that were indigenously domesticated in the East.

On the basis of these recent findings, researchers believe that the early squash rind found in eastern North America was probably from a native plant. Consequently, agriculture appears to have occurred indigenously in this North American region, well before the diffusion of the concept or any plant from Mexico.

**Figure 6.67** The compaction of seeds is a good indicator of domestication. In the wild *Chenopodium* plant known as lamb's-quarters, on the right, seeds are distributed in numerous small clusters. On the left, in contrast, the seeds of a domesticated *Chenopodium* plant are tightly compacted at the top of the main stem.

## *Images and Ideas*

# The Spread of Agriculture

*The success and consequences of food production*

*The question "why farm?" strikes most of us modern humans as silly. Of course it is better to grow wheat and cows than to forage for roots and snails. But in reality, that perspective is flawed by hindsight.*

—Jared Diamond (2002)

Different concepts and methods are used by researchers who study the Paleolithic and those who investigate agricultural societies. Paleolithic archaeologists tend to excavate in natural stratigraphic levels, often in caves, paying careful attention to the distributions of bone and stone materials. Researchers focused on later agricultural peoples concentrate more on the stratigraphic levels revealed in the architectural remains of past structures, such as temples and houses, and they must analyze pottery and metalwork as well as stone and bone. Because pre-Neolithic sites have fewer artifacts and are often deeply buried, systematic regional surveys, which find and map archaeological remains visible on the land surface, are rarely as practical or as useful for the specialist in the Pleistocene as they are for many archaeologists who study later periods.

These differences in archaeological perceptions and practices reflect real changes in the nature of the archaeological record that began 10,000–3000 years ago in many (though not all) areas of the world. In most regions, Paleolithic sites tend to be small, thin scatters of lithic materials, reflecting generally lower populations and the tendency for occupations to involve fewer people over shorter periods of time. The low artifactual densities and the general absence of substantial structures at prefarming sites also suggest greater residential mobility.

In many regions, the presence of residential and civic architecture and cemeteries at archaeological sites is unique to prehistoric farming societies. In addition, whereas the artifacts of the Paleolithic—spearpoints, knives, and scrapers—tended to be largely for capturing energy (food), "facilities," or materials (stone bowls, ceramic containers) and features (pits) to store energy became much more important in later eras. Kent Flannery aptly noted that there are more storage facilities at 'Ain Mallaha alone than are known from all earlier Southwest Asian sites, indicating a sudden transition to residential stability, with its implied social and economic adjustments.

The archaeological record reveals that a more sedentary way of life, plant and animal domestication, and pottery were not adopted simultaneously, nor did those changes occur in a single or uniform sequence in all regions. For example, sedentary villages preceded any evidence for plant domestication in Southwest Asia, whereas the domestication of maize, beans, and squash occurred before the earliest Mesoamerican villages. Furthermore, although the Mesoamerican combination of beans and corn provides a complete protein source, as well as adequate calories, some of the other staple grains (barley and rice) are high in carbohydrates but low in protein. In addition, the domestication of animals clearly was a much more significant part of the Neolithic transition in the Old World than in the Americas. Many of the regions of early, indigenous domestication were relatively arid (Southwest Asia and highland Mexico). Yet that was not the case in either South China or the riverine settings of eastern North America.

Given the varied climatic, demographic, and cultural conditions of the early Holocene, the successful adoption and rapid spread of food production clearly was a widespread phenomenon. In regions where indigenous resources were not domesticated, exotic cultigens and animals often were quickly introduced and adopted. Once domesticated, wheat and barley were transmitted rapidly to the Nile Valley, many parts of Europe, and North China as a supplement to millet. In the river valleys of eastern North America, maize from Mexico

Figure 6.69 Some major African food crops (left to right): yam, finger millet, and sorghum.

was incorporated into local agricultural complexes that included different combinations of oily seed plants, such as marsh elder and goosefoot.

The Neolithic transition apparently was an even more complex mosaic in sub-Saharan Africa. Imported sheep and goats were introduced from Southwest Asia into diverse economies that locally domesticated more than a dozen plant species, including finger millet (Ethiopia and northern Uganda), sorghum (Lake Chad to the Nile), African rice (middle delta of the Niger), tiny-seeded teff (Ethiopia), and yams (West Africa) (Figure 6.69). Whereas domesticated sheep and goats clearly were foreign, the origins of domesticated cattle in sub-Saharan Africa are less certain; they either were exotic or were domesticated independently in northern Africa, where they were present by the fifth millennium B.C. As in Japan, where ceramics preceded food production, pottery vessels were found at sites occupied by semisedentary fisher-foragers from the fifth and sixth millennia B.C. in the Sudan, as well as along the margins of now-dry lakebeds south of the Sahara Desert.

The beginnings of cultivation also are being unraveled in the islands of the Pacific, where the transition from foraging to farming clearly was more gradual, with few stark or immediate shifts in lifeway. On the basis of recent studies by Tim Denham, of Flinders University in Adelaide, Australia, and his colleagues at the Kuk Swamp site in the highlands of New Guinea, it appears possible that the banana may have been cultivated as early as 7000 years ago.

From a global perspective, food production emerged over the past 12,000 years, broadly coincident with major cultural changes that have shaped the course of recent human history, along with significant climatic and sea-level shifts. Just as the Neolithic creates a divide in the archaeological record and among archaeologists, the beginnings of domestication are generally (although not always) linked in time with more permanent or sedentary communities, changing social and political relationships, larger and denser populations, new technologies, and shifting networks of exchange and communication. The complexity of these relationships and their diversity from region to region make it difficult to decipher the exact causes for prehistoric changes. Yet archaeologists have developed some ideas by studying contemporary peoples, particularly those who have recently shifted from a mobile hunting-and-gathering way of life to more sedentary and agricultural pursuits.

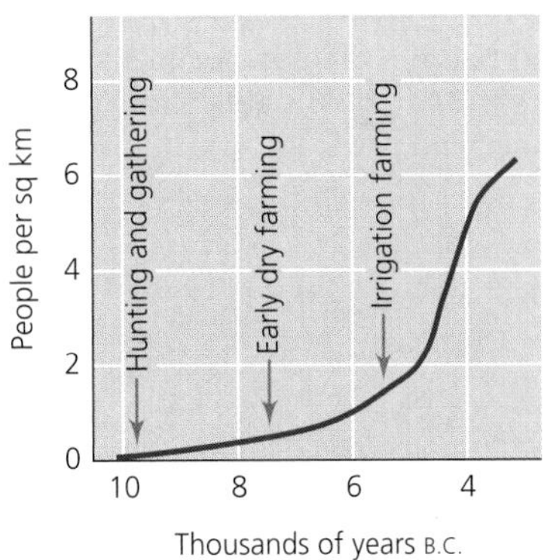


**Figure 6.70** Population densities associated with different subsistence strategies.

During the Pleistocene, human populations grew at a slow pace (Figure 6.70). If modern hunter-gatherer populations are a reliable guide, a few individuals may have separated from parent groups when resources were exhausted or when disputes became common. In larger campsites, the latter could have been a potential problem, because as the population grows, the number of interactions between individuals increases even more rapidly. By the end of the Pleistocene, with the peopling of most of the continents (albeit at low densities), fissioning would have become less of an option for many groups. This pattern may partially account for observed late Pleistocene–early Holocene increases in local population densities, residential stability, greater reliance on lower-quality foods, and decreases in social group territory sizes.

Over the past 10,000 years, the earth's population has doubled 10 times, from less than 10 million people to more than 6.7 billion. Following the end of the Pleistocene, the more rapid rates of demographic growth may have related in part to changing patterns of child rearing and diet. Recently settled hunter-gatherers often witness a reduction in birth spacing. A mobile way of life limits the number of infants a family group can transport and hence care for at any one time. Intensive exercise and prolonged breast-feeding have been suggested as factors that temporarily diminish a woman's fertility. With increased sedentism, storage, and domestication, both the frequency of intensive female activity and the length of the nursing cycle may have decreased. Contemporary hunter-gatherers tend to breast-feed for 2–6 years because of the frequent absence or unreliability of soft weaning foods. The storable, staple cereal grains provide such an alternative food to mother's milk. In certain regions, animal milk also could be substituted.

*Soil erosion, desertification, water pollution and soil degradation are intimately related to agriculture in terms of both the past and the present; they are not phenomena of the twentieth century.*

—Antoinette Mannion (1999)

More productive and storable food resources may have permitted larger communities and denser populations, yet a series of organizational changes often occurred at roughly the same time. For long-term maintenance and survival, larger communities would have required new mechanisms for integration, cooperation, the resolution of disputes, and decision making. Kin relationships are severely tested when decisions must be made for groups of several hundred. Increased evidence for burials, ritual objects (e.g., figurines), nonresidential structures, more formal patterns of exchange, and in some cases more unequal access to goods and labor would seem to signal these very significant changes in social and political relationships. Some of these new organizational forms were hierarchical, with more permanent, formal leadership roles instituted above the remainder of the population. Such leaders or decision makers, in turn, may have fostered greater concentrations of resources and labor, leading to intensified production and even larger communities.

The transition to agriculture and sedentism occurred at the onset of a rapid succession of changes that have culminated in our modern world. The pace of these recent changes is truly remarkable when viewed from the perspective of all of human history. Although neither domestication nor sedentism alone is necessary and sufficient to explain the formation of early cities and ancient states, both permanent communities and food production are critical elements of those very significant, later developments.

## DISCUSSION QUESTIONS

1. Where are the six cradles of agriculture around the world?
2. What are the most important of the early domesticated plants and animals?
3. Discuss the different kinds of natural environments in which early domestication took place.
4. Australia is one of the few places within the limits of cultivation where agriculture did not spread. Why might that be?

www.mhhe.com/priceip6e

For more review material and study questions, see the self-quizzes on your online learning center.

5. Compare the process of change from foraging to farming in Southwest Asia and highland Mesoamerica.
6. Compare and contrast the role of social, environmental, and demographic factors in the emergence of agriculture in different areas of the world.
7. Discuss how and why human lives tended to change with the advent of sedentary settlements.
8. What are the long-term implications of the origins of agriculture in regard to contemporary concerns about the environment, natural resources, and ecological diversity?

## SUGGESTED READINGS

For Internet links related to this chapter, please visit our Web site at www.mhhe.com/priceip6e.


Bellwood, P. 2005. *First farmers: The origins of agricultural societies.* Malden, MA: Blackwell. *A comparative study of the origins and dispersal of agricultural communities.*

Cauvin, J. 2000. *The birth of the gods and the origins of agriculture.* Cambridge: Cambridge University Press. *A new perspective on the beginnings of domestication, focusing on conceptual changes, translated from the French.*

Clutton-Brock, J. 1999. *A natural history of domesticated animals.* Cambridge: Cambridge University Press. *A detailed compendium of recent information on the domestication of animals.*

Cohen, M. 1977. *The food crisis in prehistory.* New Haven, CT: Yale University Press. *A comprehensive indictment of global population increase as the cause of the domestication of plants and animals.*

Flannery, K. V., ed. 1986. *Guilá Naquitz: Archaic foraging and early agriculture in Oaxaca, Mexico.* New York: Academic Press. *A detailed report on an important preceramic settlement in highland Oaxaca in the distinctive style of Flannery.*

Harris, D. R., and G. C. Hillman, eds. 1989. *Foraging and farming: The evolution of plant exploitation.* London: Unwin Hyman. *A volume of papers on early agriculture, presenting evidence from around the world.*

Hodder, I. 2006. *The leopard's tale: Revealing the mysteries of Çatalhöyük.* New York: Thames & Hudson. *A first-hand description of the recent finds at Çatalhöyük.*

Price, T. D., and A. B. Gebauer, eds. 1995. *Last hunters–first farmers: New perspectives on the transition to agriculture.* Santa Fe, NM: School for American Research. *A series of papers dealing specifically with the question of cause in regard to the origins and spread of agriculture.*

Smith, B. D. 1998. *The emergence of agriculture.* New York: Scientific American Library. *A well-illustrated and up-to-date summary of agricultural beginnings worldwide.*

Zeder, M. A., D. Bradley, E. Emshwiller, and B. D. Smith, eds. 2006. *Documenting domestication: New genetic and archaeological paradigms.* Berkeley: University of California Press. *A collection of scientific papers dealing with the most recent evidence for early domestication.*

Zohary, D., and M. Hopf. 2001. *Domestication of plants in the Old World: The origin and spread of cultivated plants in West Asia, Europe, and the Nile Valley,* 3rd ed. Oxford: Oxford University Press. *A botanical tour of the first domesticated plants in Asia, Europe, and Africa.*

# CHAPTER SEVEN

**Figure 7.1** Monks Mound towers over the surrounding terrain at the site of Cahokia in southern Illinois. This immense earthen mound, which was constructed in stages, beginning in the tenth century A.D., is the largest prehistoric structure in what was to later become the United States.

# Native North Americans

## Introduction

### The Diversity of Native American Life

*Hunter-gatherers, farmers, and chiefs*

www.mhhe.com/priceip6e

For preview material for this chapter, see the comprehensive chapter outline and chapter objectives on your online learning center.

CHAPTER OUTLINE



The towering Monks Mound that dominates the ancient site of Cahokia in southern Illinois was by far the largest earthen feature built north of Mexico by Native American peoples (Figure 7.1). Yet it was only one of many such mounds and earthworks that dotted the landscape of eastern North America before the arrival of Europeans roughly 500 years ago. Nevertheless, by the time of the American Revolution, these landscape features had been largely destroyed or were ignored by most Euro-Americans, and those colonists who did take note questioned their historical connection to the indigenous populace who had inhabited North America for millennia.

Interestingly, it was Thomas Jefferson, the third president of the United States, who played an early role in reestablishing the evidential link between North American earthworks and indigenous Native American peoples. Jefferson's late-eighteenth-century exploration of an earthen mound near Charlottesville, Virginia, was the first stratigraphic study of a North American earthen feature, and he accurately described how that feature served as the repository for a significant number of burials. Although Jefferson did not immediately connect the mound to Native Americans, he eventually did so. Through this scientific contribution, Thomas Jefferson can be considered a father of American archaeology as well as the principal father of the Declaration of Independence.

On the twelfth of October in 1492, when Columbus landed on a small island in the Caribbean, roughly 40 million Native Americans resided in the Western Hemisphere. These peoples spoke about 400 mutually unintelligible languages, compared with the more than 2500 languages that were spoken in the Eastern Hemisphere. Yet the diversity of the "spoken tongues" is impressive, considering that the landmass of North and South America is less than half the size of Eurasia and Africa. One important factor influencing linguistic divergence is time, and hominids have lived for only thousands of years in the Western Hemisphere compared with millions of years in the Eastern Hemisphere. At the time of European contact, the populations of the Western Hemisphere were diverse in many ways other than language. Some peoples were incorporated into the great empire of the Inca in the Peruvian Andes; others paid tribute to the rulers of Aztec Tenochtitlán in the Basin of Mexico. Yet not all Native American peoples were as socially and

www.mhhe.com/priceip6e

For a Web-based activity on the Native American Graves Protection and Repatriation Act, see the Internet exercises on your online learning center.

economically stratified as the Inca and the Aztecs. Although some Mississippian lords in eastern North America may have received tribute from surrounding populations, the sociopolitical formations in what is now the eastern United States were not as complex as those farther south. More egalitarian hunter-gatherers lived in the Arctic and sub-Arctic, on the Plains, in desert areas of the western United States and Mexico, and at the tip of South America.

The Americas were first colonized by hunter-gatherers who either crossed the broad Bering land bridge or traveled from Asia to the Americas by boat. Initially, their way of life was highly mobile. In western North America, the colonists relied in part on the hunting of large herd animals; the subsistence regime in eastern North America was generally more diversified. In much of the Americas, a long Archaic period followed the millennia (the Paleoindian period) during which several species of large herd animals that were important food sources became extinct. (See "Beringia" and "Lindenmeier," in Chapter 4, for a discussion of the Paleoindian period and "Carrier Hills," in Chapter 5, for a discussion of the Archaic.)

During the Archaic, regional populations diversified their subsistence pursuits, each concentrating on a distinct set of local resources, hunting a wide range of animals, and gathering a variety of wild plants. In the later Archaic period, cultigens were added to the diet. In midwestern North America, local seed plants were domesticated during the Archaic before the arrival of the exotic domesticates (see "Agriculture in Native North America," Chapter 6, p. 258). In certain other parts of what is now the United States, the earliest domesticated plants appear to have been imports from highland Mesoamerica. These plants—such as maize (corn), certain varieties of squash, and gourds—were domesticated initially in the south and then traded to the north in a down-the-line fashion, reaching the American Southwest. Yet in most of North America, the introduction (or local domestication) of these agricultural plants generally did not promote immediate or drastic shifts in dietary composition or residential mobility. In certain areas, such as the coastal Southeast, the increasing exploitation of riverine and marine life, in conjunction with hunting and gathering, led to increasing residential stability even before cultigens were incorporated into the diet.

Native American lifeways also were diverse at the time of the European arrival, although no populations in the continental United States lived in urban communities as dense as those in the Basin of Mexico (discussed in Chapter 8). In the desert West, mobile hunting-and-gathering lifeways persisted until historic times. Yet in parts of the Southeast, the Midwest, the Northwest Coast, California, and the Southwest, a variety of more hierarchical political formations developed during the later precontact period. These institutions were diverse, distributed mosaically, and often short-lived in any specific locality or region. Although an increasing reliance on maize was one key factor in the development of nonegalitarian social systems in the Southeast, the Midwest, and the Southwest, such institutions were established in portions of the West Coast and in peninsular Florida in the context of sedentary hunting and gathering. Other late precontact populations incorporated the plant into their diet but remained more egalitarian and more mobile.

Up to now, we have referred to **prehistory** as the time before the appearance of written records. In North America, the prehistoric era extends into the second millennium A.D. and ends with the arrival of populations from Europe, Asia, and Africa, who carried writing to this part of the world. The historic period begins between the sixteenth and eighteenth centuries A.D., with the specific timing varying by region, depending on the pace of European conquest and expansion. The study of the fragmentary and/or scanty historic records written by both native peoples and Europeans is called **ethnohistory.**

**prehistory** In general, the human past; specifically, the time before the appearance of written records.

**ethnohistory** The study of ancient (often non-Western) cultures using evidence from documentary sources and oral traditions, and often supplemented with archaeological data.

In this chapter, eight North American sites are discussed (Figure 7.2). Although Mexico is geographically part of North America, the peoples who lived in most of that land area are culturally part of Mesoamerica and are discussed in Chapter 8. In time, they span the late Archaic (Poverty Point) to the era of European contact (the Draper site and Ozette). These sites—ranging from the southern Arizona desert (Snaketown) to the floodplains of the middle Mississippi (Cahokia) to the arid lands of the Colorado Plateau (Chaco Canyon)—capture some, but certainly not all, of the tremendous variability characteristic of the later prehistory of native North America. In fact, in focusing on the above sites, as well as Hopewell (Ohio) and Moundville (Alabama), we have selected rather elaborate ancient settlements, many of which have attracted archaeological attention for decades. Many of these sites are much larger and were occupied far longer than the average prehistoric North American settlement; hence, they are relatively well known. Native Americans also lived in small communities and utilized many temporary camps, but such sites are generally less well known and therefore are not featured here.

Poverty Point (Louisiana) is one of the few late Archaic period sites north of Mexico where monumental earthworks were constructed. Poverty Point exemplifies certain late Archaic trends in the southeastern United States: decreasing mobility, experimentation with fired clay, and an emerging role for cultivated plants in the diet. Over the next centuries, those trends became increasingly important in several areas outside the Southeast as well. For example, roughly coincident with the decline of Poverty Point in the middle of the last millennium B.C., the **Adena** (ah-DEEN-ah) complex developed in the Ohio River Valley. Adena sites tend to be associated with earthen burial mounds, larger and more elaborate assemblages of grave offerings, rudimentary cultivation (of food plants as well as tobacco), and friable (soft, porous) pottery. Mobile lifeways still may have been common, but the presence of circular houses and/or ceremonial structures, as well as the increasing abundance of pottery, suggests greater residential stability at Adena sites relative to earlier occupations in the region. In many ways, the Adena complex was directly ancestral to later Hopewell sites in southern Ohio (and surrounding states). The Hopewell site, one of the richest of these settlements, was excavated on the farm of M. C. Hopewell in the early 1890s to provide artifacts for an anthropological exhibit at the 1893 World's Columbian Exposition in Chicago.

The unequal distribution of grave offerings at Hopewell sites may be evidence of social differentiation, but it is not clear how marked those distinctions were or whether they were inherited. A similar debate concerns the nature of social organization at Poverty Point. However, by the end of the first millennium A.D., on the floodplains of the Mississippi, such inherited social distinctions appear to have been well entrenched, at least at the Cahokia site in East St. Louis, Illinois. This ancient settlement, which contains the largest precontact pyramid built north of Mexico, includes ample indications of unequal access to wealth and power. Cahokia was one of the largest and most impressive **Mississippian** centers. Increasing reliance on corn farming at Cahokia is part of a trend found at later prehistoric sites across the eastern United States, although many Mississippian peoples continued to hunt, gather, and fish as a supplement to farming.

Moundville, overlooking the Black Warrior River in Alabama, was one of several important later Mississippian centers (along with Etowah [EH-toe-wah] in Georgia). Although these two centers are well known, in part because of their monumental mound complexes and the elaborate artifacts recovered during excavations, they were not entirely typical of corn-farming peoples of the late prehistoric period who resided in what is today the eastern United States. Archaeological findings, as well as the accounts from early European explorations into the Southeast, indicate that many indigenous peoples lived in smaller, dispersed communities and were organized in less hierarchical social formations than are evident at great centers such as Moundville and Etowah.

**Adena** A burial mound complex that developed in the Ohio River Valley toward the end of the last millennium B.C.

**Mississippian** The collective name applied to the agricultural societies that inhabited portions of the eastern United States approximately A.D. 800–1700. Mississippian peoples constructed earthen platform mounds and shared certain basic cultural conventions.

*The first Americans north of Mexico have figured as little more than a few stereotyped and contradictory images in most accounts of the New World. They are generally regarded as savages with no past and no future, sparsely inhabiting a continent, and childlike both in their generosity—"selling" Manhattan Island for $24 worth of "trinkets"—and in their ferocity—scalping the victims in battle. In the West they have been seen as a jumble of opposites, as the earlier "only good Indian is a dead Indian" attitude has given way to a latter-day Hollywood "good Indian" peacemaker juxtaposed against the "bad Indian" fighter. Only most recently can a "good" Indian fight for his people's independence. Contemporary Indians are seen as a beaten people on reservations, sharing in a general "culture of poverty," a curiosity for passing tourists, while the notion persists, despite census figures to the contrary, that Indians are "vanishing" as a racial and sociocultural entity.*

—Eleanor B. Leacock (1971)

The late prehistoric groups of the Northeast and southern Canada also appear to have been organized less hierarchically. Their villages, which were composed of multifamily **longhouses,** lacked the monumental constructions that were found at Moundville and Cahokia. The Draper site, a large Iroquoian village in southern Ontario, was almost completely excavated and thus provides a good picture of the village plan and community organization in the Great Lakes region just before European contact.

One difference between the maize-farming peoples of the late prehistoric eastern United States and those in the West is the greater reliance on water control (irrigation) in the latter area. In the dry, changeable climate of the southwestern United States, rainfall farming would have been a risky endeavor at best. This distinction is clearly indicated in the discussion of the **Hohokam** of the Sonoran Desert of southern Arizona. Snaketown, an early Hohokam community between Phoenix and Tucson, was for a long time the only example of an Arizona desert village. However, spurred by the contemporary construction boom in the region, additional archaeological fieldwork at other sites has supplemented and broadened our understanding of these early villagers, documenting their evolution from local hunting-and-gathering peoples. Nevertheless, Snaketown remains a key site in the region. Early-twentieth-century scholars postulated that the Hohokam migrated from Mexico; such explanations are no longer necessary to account for the transition to sedentary farming communities.

The emergence of the Hohokam tradition during the first millennium A.D. occurred with the rise of two other southwestern cultural traditions, the **Mogollon** and the **Ancestral Pueblo.** Although these traditions were not completely discrete, they do help characterize the great cultural variation that marked the prehistoric southwestern United States. For the most part, the indigenous peoples of the Southwest lived in small, dispersed communities; therefore, it is not surprising to find so much diversity in diet, ceramic styles, and even residential and nonresidential construction.

Periodically, the peoples of the American Southwest clustered into larger and more hierarchically organized multicommunity social networks. In general, these times of nucleation were short-lived and spatially localized. At Chaco Canyon on New Mexico's dry Colorado Plateau, the period around A.D. 900 witnessed the beginning of perhaps the most spectacular of such episodes. Although this buildup of construction and population nucleation was relatively brief, it left an impressive record.

Although the focus of this chapter is on the agricultural inhabitants of indigenous North America, we also examine the late prehistoric coastal village of Ozette in Washington. As early as 500 B.C., ranked social distinctions may have developed among certain hunter-gatherer populations in the Pacific Northwest. Although Ozette dates much later, the village's destruction and burial by a mudslide resulted in unusually good archaeological preservation. As a result, it provides a clearer picture of Northwest Coast hunter-gatherers than can be gained from earlier sites in the area.

In "Images and Ideas" (p. 317), we briefly discuss the changing Euro-American perspective on North American Indian sites. The archaeology of North America is extremely important because it provides a historical context for, and helps establish the rich heritage of, Native American peoples—the first inhabitants of the United States. We also raise the important issue of ethnographic analogy and discuss the less-than-perfect fit often found between ethnohistoric accounts and the archaeological record.

**longhouse** A wooden structure that is considerably longer than it is wide and served as a communal dwelling.

**Hohokam** One of three major cultural traditions of the American Southwest during late prehistoric times. The Hohokam were centered in the deserts of southern Arizona.

**Mogollon** One of three major cultural traditions of the American Southwest during late prehistoric times. The Mogollon were centered in the mountainous areas of southeastern Arizona and southwestern New Mexico.

**Ancestral Pueblo** One of three major cultural traditions of the American Southwest during late prehistoric times. The Ancestral Pueblo were centered in the northern Southwest, on the high plateau of the Four Corners region.

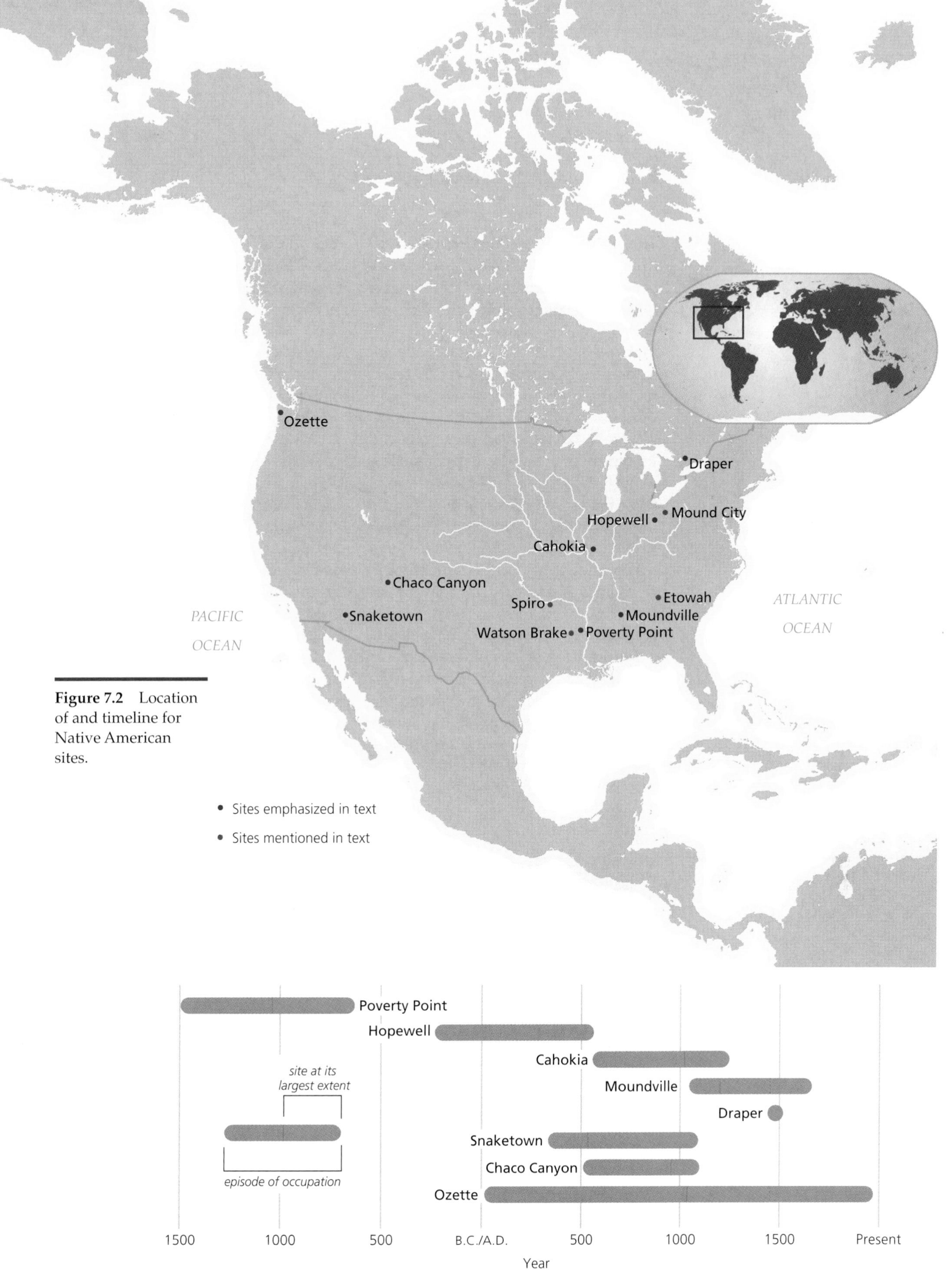


**Figure 7.2** Location of and timeline for Native American sites.

Site

# Poverty Point

## *Ancient earthworks in southeastern North America*

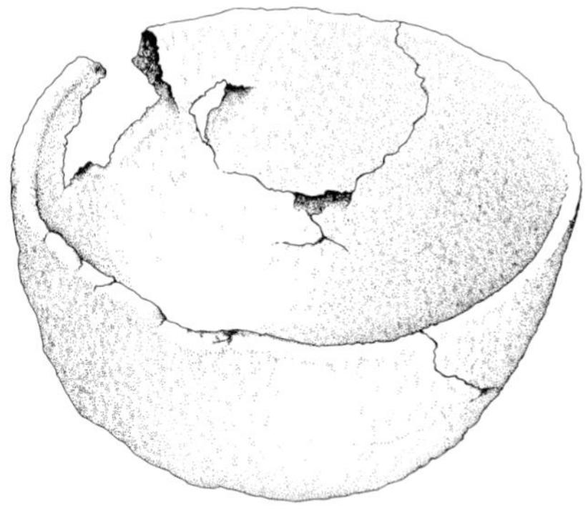

**Figure 7.3** New implements found at some late Archaic sites include simple, fiber-tempered pottery bowls.

The early Archaic hunter-gatherers of the southeastern United States lived in small, impermanent camps and followed a seasonal pattern of life based on a broad spectrum of plant and animal foods. The most important resources included nuts, acorns, berries, and roots and animal species such as deer, elk, bear, fox, wolf, squirrel, raccoon, opossum, beaver, otter, freshwater mussel, fish, turkey, and migratory waterfowl. By the middle of the Archaic period, around 4000 B.C., population growth contributed to reduced residential mobility and the increasing differentiation of local cultural traditions. In coastal and riverine settings, the Archaic foragers often returned to the same location year after year in scheduled seasonal rounds to exploit localized and predictable resources. For example, deep Archaic shell middens that have been excavated along the lower Tennessee River represent the accumulated refuse of small communities that occupied these same sites repeatedly at the time of the year when shellfish were abundant.

By 1500 B.C., before the end of the Archaic period, several plant species were cultivated in the midwestern and southeastern United States, but foraging remained the dominant subsistence strategy. One of the first crops grown, gourds were used largely as containers. Their seeds are edible, and it appears that a reliance on this part of the plant increased over time. Other plants associated with domestication included marsh elder, goosefoot (*Chenopodium*), and indigenous varieties of squash. New tools, including heavy ground stone implements for grinding seeds, were added to the simple portable toolkits of earlier Archaic groups. There also was an increase in food storage, and at some sites, a fairly simple and friable fiber-tempered pottery, in which fibrous plant inclusions were mixed with the clay, was made (Figure 7.3). Stone containers of carved **steatite** (soapstone) and sandstone are found

**Figure 7.4** Aerial view of Poverty Point, showing the C-shaped earthen embankments on the west bank of the Macon Bayou.

**steatite** Soapstone, a variety of talc with a soapy or greasy feel, often used to make containers or carved ornaments.

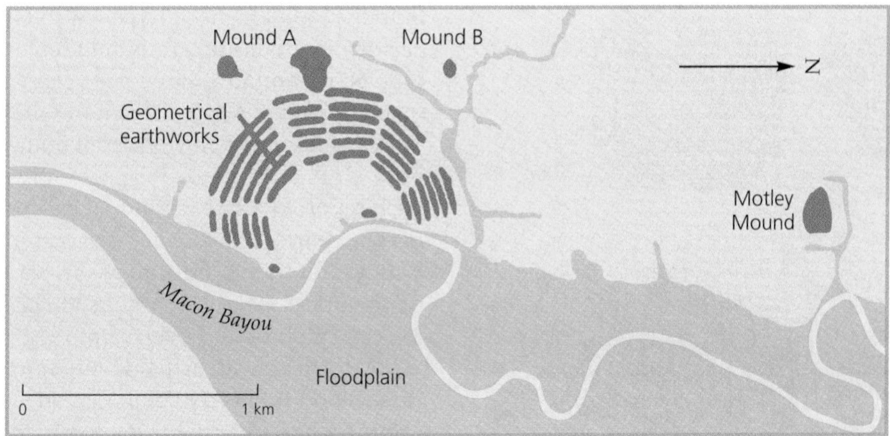


**Figure 7.5** A plan of the earthworks and other structures at Poverty Point. The two largest structures, Motley Mound and Mound A, were constructed of basket-loaded dirt; some researchers believe they may have represented birds.

as well. An increasing reliance on domesticated plants (as well as other riverine resources), in conjunction with the use of less portable tools, signals a change to greater residential stability.

Monumental constructions were not frequently built during the Archaic period. Out of hundreds of contemporary sites, there are only about two dozen Middle/Late Archaic settlements with small mound complexes in the lower Mississippi Valley. These sites typically have one or two conical mounds measuring between 1 m (3 ft) and 5 m (16 ft) high. The largest and most securely dated is the Watson Brake site in northeastern Louisiana. Constructed before 3000 B.C., the site's 11 mounds, from 1 m (3 ft) to 7.5 m (25 ft) high, are connected by low earthen ridges to enclose an oval-shaped area of approximately 8 ha (20 acres). The plant and animal remains recovered at the site indicate that Watson Brake was occupied seasonally. Although no evidence of domesticated plants has been recovered, the Archaic hunter-gatherers who constructed the site were already collecting the wild ancestors of several plants that were later domesticated. Excavation has revealed few clues about the purpose of the mounds and enclosure at Watson Brake.

A later, much larger complex of great earthworks, involving the movement of as much as 750,000 cu m of earth, was constructed between 1600 and 1200 B.C. at Poverty Point in northeastern Louisiana (Figure 7.4). In spite of increasing evidence of an Archaic mound-building tradition in the lower Mississippi Valley, the large-scale construction at Poverty Point continues to dwarf contemporaneous Late Archaic settlements in North America. The monumental construction at Poverty Point provides additional evidence for a more sedentary residential pattern and emergence of greater social differentiation than was present elsewhere in eastern North America at that time.

Poverty Point is located on the Macon Ridge overlooking the Macon Bayou and the floodplain of the Mississippi River. A portion of the site has been eroded by recent stream action; nevertheless, what remains is impressive. The main complex at Poverty Point is a set of six concentric earthen ridges that form a large semicircle, the outer one of which measures 1.2 km (0.75 mi) in diameter (Figure 7.5). The ridges are spaced approximately 45 m (150 ft) apart, and each one is composed of a series of separate smaller ridges, averaging 2 m (6 ft) high and 24 m (80 ft) wide. The presence of numerous **post molds** or postholes, soil stains indicating the past placement of wooden posts, as well as hearths and pits, indicates that the ridgetops were used as living surfaces. The level area encircled by earthen embankments is close to 14 ha (35 acres) and contains a central plaza that likely was used for ritual activities.

To the west of these earthworks sits a large mound more than 21 m (70 ft) high and 200 m (655 ft) long. A long

**post mold** The circular remains, often just a dark stain in the soil, of a wooden post that formed part of the frame of prehistoric structures. Also called a posthole.

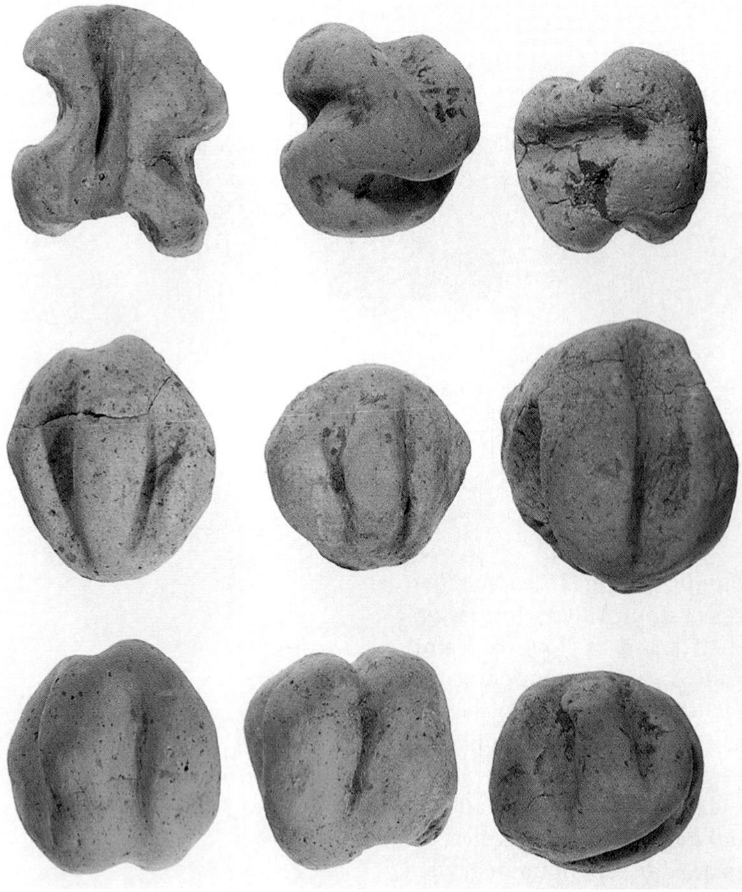

**Figure 7.6** Examples of small baked clay objects found at Poverty Point and elsewhere in the lower Mississippi Valley. Used for cooking in earth ovens, distinct shapes have different thermal properties, which may have permitted some control over temperatures.

**equinox** A time when the sun crosses the plane of the equator, making night and day the same length all over the earth, occurring about March 21 and September 22.

**chert** A dull-colored, subtranslucent rock resembling flint that was often used for making flaked stone tools.

**galena** A common heavy mineral that is the principal ore of lead.

**hematite** A common heavy mineral that is the principal ore of iron.

**slate** A fine-grained rock with a dull, dark bluish-gray color that tends to split along parallel cleavage planes, often producing thin plates or sheets.

**jasper** A high-quality flint, often highly colored, often used as a raw material for the manufacture of stone tools, beads, and other ornaments.

**lapidary** Of or related to the practice of working or cutting precious or semiprecious stones, usually for ornamental use.

ramp descends from the mound and faces the semicircular complex. From the mound, it is possible to view the vernal and autumnal **equinoxes** across the center of the earthworks; it is not clear, however, whether this alignment was intentional. A small conical mound lies about 0.5 km (0.3 mi) north of the large mound. Another large mound, similar in form to the tall ramped mound, is 2 km (1.2 mi) away. Gully erosion down the sides of the large mounds has revealed that they were built with basketloads of clay fill.

The early population of Poverty Point is not well established, although the earliest excavators of the site, James Ford and C. H. Webb, estimated that several hundred houses may have been occupied. Other estimates range as high as several thousand people. Smaller settlements, which lacked earthen mounds and contained fewer than 60 inhabitants, have been found up to 15 km (9 mi) away from the site. Similar settlement clusters, containing both large and small sites, also have been reported along tributary streams in other parts of the lower Mississippi Valley. Yet none of the associated earthworks is nearly as large as the impressive mounds at Poverty Point.

Most sites with artifacts similar to those found at Poverty Point occur in locations where riverine resources were available. The presence of stone adzes or hoes (some of which are well worn) originally led some researchers to suggest that cultivation may have been practiced on the floodplains. Yet ethnobotanical studies have not revealed a significant presence of cultigens. Of the indigenous eastern North American domesticates, squash is most abundant. But nuts, acorns, deer, and fish seem to have constituted equal or greater portions of the diet than cultivated plants. The stone adzes (or hoes) may have been used for clearing vegetation or perhaps as digging tools for constructing the earthworks.

At Poverty Point, hunting, fishing, and gathering were important means of subsistence. Very little pottery, except for some nonlocal ware, has been found. However, thousands of small baked clay objects have been recovered. Most of these fired concretions, sometimes referred to as Poverty Point objects, are smaller than a baseball and were made in a variety of forms, including balls, cylinders, and odd finger-squeezed shapes (Figure 7.6). These baked clay forms are thought to have served for cooking in earth ovens in place of rocks, which are scarce in the alluvial areas of the lower Mississippi. In this method of cooking, the clay objects were placed in pits, with fires built on top of them. Once they were heated, food was placed in the pit and roasted by the heat radiated from the clay objects.

Large quantities of such ornamental objects as polished beads, pendants, and effigies were manufactured at Poverty Point, even though little stone is found on the marshy coastal plain where the site is situated (Figure 7.7). Flints and **cherts,** dull-colored rocks resembling flint, were imported from the north, and steatite from the Appalachians. Other imported stone included **galena** (lead ore), **hematite, slate,** and **jasper** (a high-quality flint). Poverty Point was strategically located between the sources of some of these materials and the more heavily inhabited areas to the south.

A well-developed **lapidary** (stone-working) industry is one of the key features that distinguishes Poverty Point and surrounding sites. At some sites, distinctive microblade drills were manufactured and used to perforate stone and bone artifacts (Figure 7.8). The distribution of stone debris and finished artifacts indicates that this craft was to some degree specialized, in the sense that different communities and specific sectors within larger sites (such as Poverty Point) engaged in the manufacture of different kinds of goods. Thus the finished items as well as the raw materials probably were exchanged over great distances throughout the Southeast.

Poverty Point and the specific cultural tradition associated with the site began to decline and change around 700 B.C., just as mound building increased dramatically in the Ohio Valley to the northeast. In these northern woodland areas, the construction of burial mounds implies an increasing preoccupation with death and mortuary ritual. Common practices included cremation and the placement of exotic objects with the dead. Ornaments made of marine shell, unsmelted native copper, jasper, slate, and greenstone occurred with greater frequency in these contexts. Throughout the woodlands of the eastern United States, ceramic containers became more prevalent during the last centuries B.C. The cultivation of squash and local weedy plants, which still were not staples, also became more important. These developments were foreshadowed at Poverty Point, but centuries elapsed before northeastern Louisiana again saw the scale of monumental earthen construction evident in the region at the end of the Archaic.

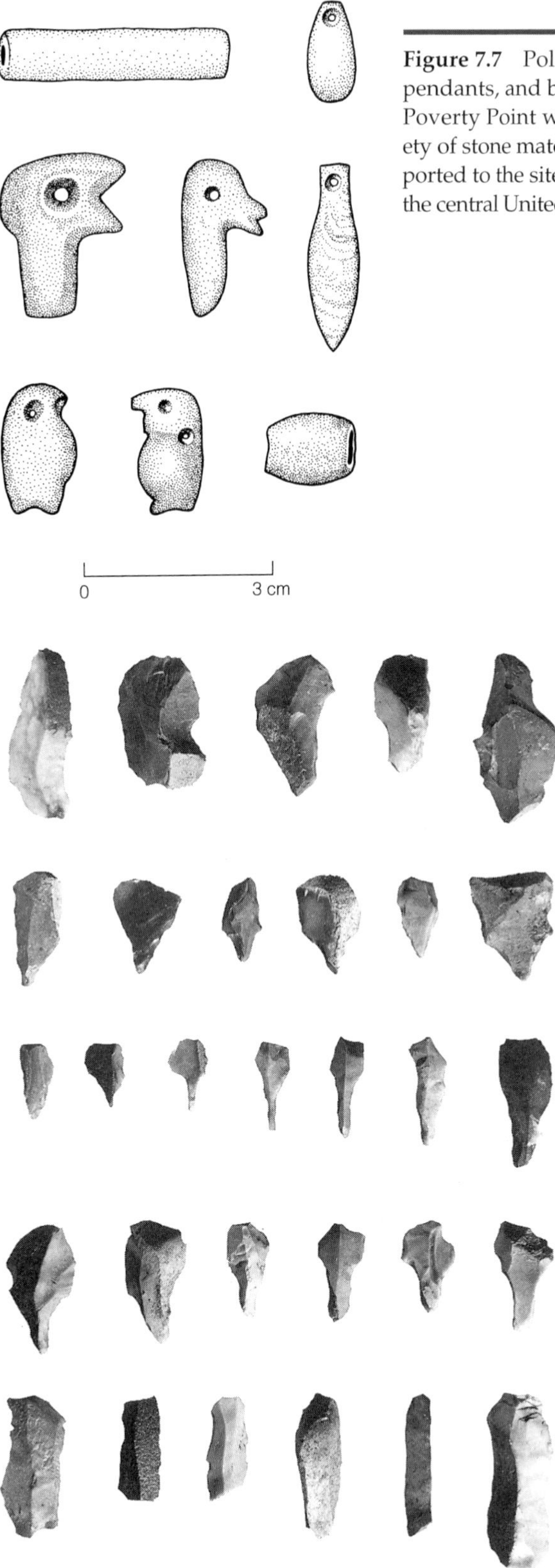


**Figure 7.7** Polished stone beads, pendants, and bird effigies from Poverty Point were made from a variety of stone materials that were imported to the site from many parts of the central United States.

**Figure 7.8** Flint tools from Poverty Point, including microblade drills (three middle rows) that were used to perforate stone and bone artifacts. Almost 30,000 of these flint microtools have been recovered at Poverty Point alone.

*Site*

# Hopewell

## *Prehistoric artisans and mound builders*

www.mhhe.com/priceip6e

For a Web-based activity on Adena culture, see the Internet exercises on your online learning center.

In eastern North America, marsh elder and goosefoot may have been domesticated as early as 2000–1500 B.C., but it was not until the end of the Archaic that some prehistoric peoples in the region increasingly relied on the harvesting of these and other native plants. At archaeological sites dating before 500 B.C., the scarcity of seeds of these early domesticates suggests that these plants mainly served to buffer temporary shortages and were not yet true staples; hunting and gathering continued to provide the primary dietary resources. Nevertheless, many of these local cultigens, which produced a variety of seeds, had the advantage of being easily stored. Indigenous varieties of squash also may have been cultivated initially for their seeds rather than their flesh.

These early Archaic experiments in cultivation laid the foundation for later developments, such as Hopewell in the Midwest (100 B.C.–A.D. 400). After 500–200 B.C., native cultigens became increasingly important at many sites in eastern North America. Nevertheless, food production did not completely replace hunting-and-gathering economies. Foraging remained an important part of survival; Hopewell subsistence also included a variety of wild plants and animals, including seeds, nuts, deer, turkeys, and fish. By around A.D. 100, maize was introduced into eastern North America from the West (possibly from the American Southwest, which in turn received the plant from highland Mexico, where it was originally domesticated). Yet after its appearance, maize remained a minor crop for more than 500 years in eastern North America.

About the time of the decline of Poverty Point in the lower Mississippi

**Figure 7.9** An artist's reconstruction of two stages in Hopewell burial mound construction. Cremation and burial occurred in a sacred enclosure that was later covered by a mound of earth.

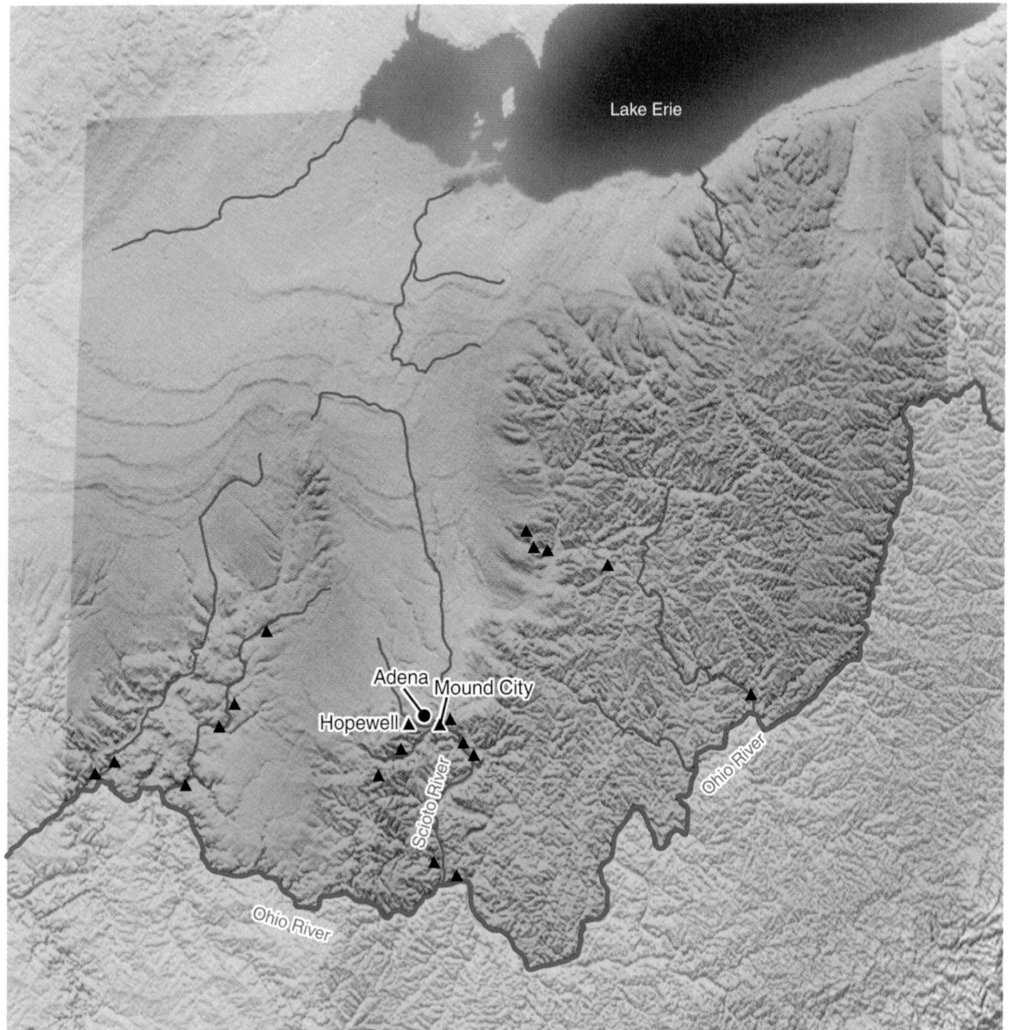


**Figure 7.10** Location of Hopewell sites and other burial mound sites. Hopewell materials are found throughout the Midwest, but the focus was southern Ohio.
Source: Bradley Lepper, *Ohio Archaeology: An Illustrated Chronicle of Ohio Ancient American Indian Cultures.* Orange Frazer Press, p. 112.

Valley, mound building and long-distance exchange intensified to the north in the Ohio River Valley. Elaborate earthworks—some as large as 100 m (330 ft) or more in diameter—were constructed in the shape of circles, squares, and pentagons. These earthen features appear to have been sacred enclosures rather than defensive works, perhaps serving to affirm and strengthen group cohesion and to establish the link between a local group and its social territory.

During the last centuries B.C., the construction of burial mounds became an important part of mortuary activities throughout the midwestern United States (Figure 7.9). Early burial mounds contained up to three individuals in a log tomb. Cremations often were found in simpler graves. The unequal distribution of grave goods suggests that social distinctions were marked at death in some (though not all) societies in the eastern United States. The more elaborate graves often contained greater quantities of highly crafted and exotic grave goods that possibly served as markers of rank. These items included **gorgets,** circular ornaments that were flat or convex on one side and concave on the other; axes, bracelets, beads, and rings made from copper imported from northern Michigan; carved tablets, some with abstract zoomorphic designs depicting birds of prey; and tubular pipes for smoking.

The Hopewell tradition first appeared in Illinois around 100 B.C.

**gorget** A circular ornament, flat or convex on one side and concave on the other, usually worn over the chest.

Figure 7.11 A plan of the earthworks at the Hopewell site. Within the large rectangular embankment, or Great Enclosure, were smaller earthworks, including a circle and a D-shaped feature surrounding the largest mound at the site.

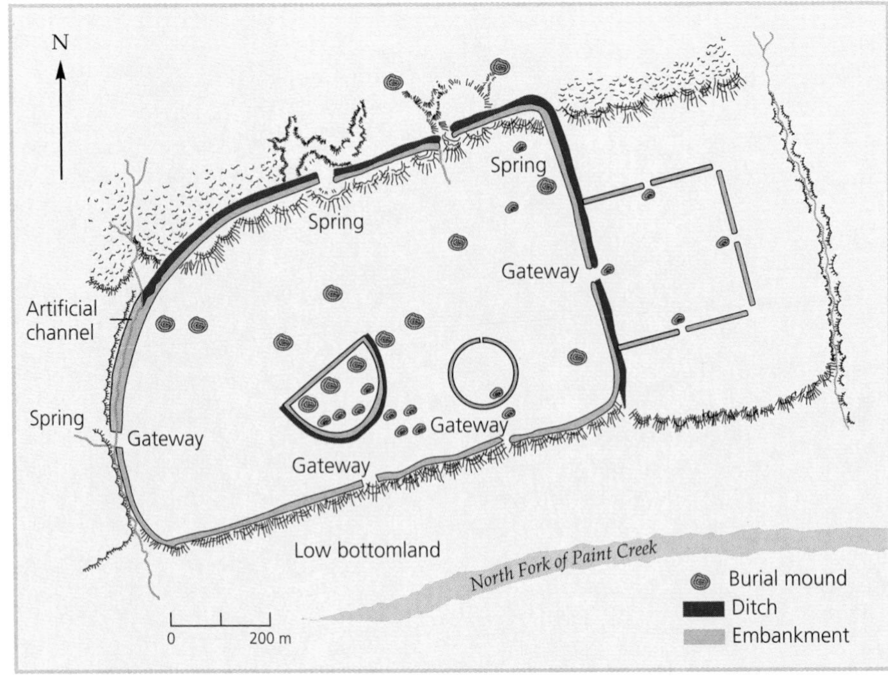


Material objects associated with this tradition quickly spread as far as upper Wisconsin, Louisiana, and New York, although the core of the phenomenon remained in the Midwest. The Hopewell tradition was not a single cultural group or society; rather, it was an exchange system for goods and information that connected distinct local populations. The complex trade network that defined this tradition has been referred to as the **Hopewell Interaction Sphere.** Goods that entered the network came from across the continent, including copper from the upper Great Lakes region and Georgia, obsidian and grizzly bear teeth from Yellowstone, chipped stone from Minnesota and North Dakota, galena from Illinois and Wisconsin, shell and shark teeth from the Gulf Coast, silver nuggets from Ontario, and **mica** and quartz crystals from the Appalachian Mountains.

Although goods entered the Hopewell Interaction Sphere from a wide area, the focus was the Scioto River Valley in the south-central part of Ohio (Figure 7.10). Monumental mounds and extensive geometric earthworks were erected there between 100 B.C. and A.D. 400. House structures and village debris occur both within and outside the walls of these impressive earthworks. The Hopewell site in Ross County, Ohio, covered 45 ha (110 acres) and contained at least 40 mounds (Figure 7.11). Most of these mounds were small, dome-shaped structures, but one mound was 9 m (30 ft) high, 152 m (500 ft) long, and 55 m (180 ft) wide, and contained over 250 burials, as well as concentrations of grave offerings. Another Hopewell burial mound complex at Mound City, Ohio, has at least 24 mounds inside a large square enclosure covering 5.2 ha (13 acres). Not all the mounds at the Ohio Hopewell sites contain burials; some are **effigy** mounds alone.

Ohio Hopewell graves contain many objects made from unsmelted native copper, such as earspools, gorgets, beads, pendants, and **panpipes** (primitive wind instruments). Heavy sheets of copper were used to make breastplates, and large copper nuggets were fashioned into axes, adzes, **celts** (Figure 7.12), and awls. Sheets of mica were cut into serpents, human hands, heads, swastikas, and bird talons (Figure 7.13). Other items found in the graves include flint tools, imported conch and other shells, teeth from alligators and sharks, turtle shells, and grizzly bear canines. A certain kind of fine pottery was cre-

**Hopewell Interaction Sphere** A complex network involving the exchange of goods and information that connected distinct local populations in the midwestern United States from approximately 100 B.C. to A.D. 400.

**mica** A colored or transparent mineral silicate that readily separates into very thin sheets.

**effigy** A representation or image of a person or an animal.

**panpipe** A wind instrument consisting of bound sets of short pipes in graduated lengths.

**celt** An implement shaped like a chisel or an axe; may be made of stone or metal.

ated to be used only as grave offerings. Charms were made from galena and quartz crystals. Carved stone pipes were one of the most important trade items (Figure 7.14). These pipes feature an animal effigy (beaver, frog, bird, bear, and even human) on top of a rectangular platform. The bowl of the pipe was positioned in the animal's back, and the smoke was drawn through a hole exiting at the end of the platform.

Several of the most elaborate Ohio Hopewell sites were excavated prior to 1900, before the use of modern equipment or contemporary standards of archaeological data recovery. Consequently, few of these contexts are well dated. The early excavators concentrated on the mounds where "museum pieces" could be recovered. As a result, Hopewell is known largely from these features and their contents. Less is known about Hopewell community patterns. Although many settlements were small and occupied seasonally, larger, more nucleated settlements in major river valleys were inhabited year-round.

Because most of the earlier excavations were in burial mounds, some archaeologists initially thought the elaborate artifacts that were recovered represented a ritual burial cult. Yet the subsequent discovery of some of these same items in domestic settings indicates that they were more likely status-specific objects that functioned in various civic-ceremonial contexts and eventually were deposited with the dead. The nature and quantities of burial goods may reflect the accomplishments and status of individuals during their lives. Only rarely were children interred with unusually large amounts of grave offerings. The Hopewell groups appear to have been organized in a number of socially differentiated polities or societies in which people reached high status principally through their individual achievements, and less through an established structure of inherited ranks.

In general, it is very difficult to reconstruct the religion, ideological beliefs, or ceremonial activities of prehistoric peoples because written records are unavailable. Yet Robert L. Hall, emeritus professor at the University

**Figure 7.12** A copper celt. Large copper nuggets from the shores of Lake Superior were worked into a variety of forms, in addition to celts.

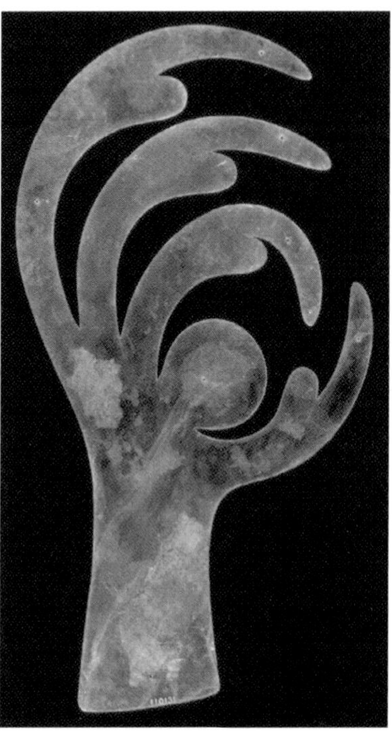

**Figure 7.13** A mica sheet that was fashioned into a large effigy of an eagle talon, 28 cm high.

**Figure 7.14** A platform pipe in the shape of a panther. The steatite pipe is 16 cm long. Smoke was drawn through the platform below the animal's hind legs.

of Illinois–Chicago, focusing on the symbolic importance of the famous Hopewell platform pipes, provides one potentially promising example. Drawing an analogy with postcontact customs of eastern native North Americans, Hall argues that peace pipe ceremonialism served to mediate interaction over very great distances. European explorers and traders observed that violence was absolutely forbidden among the Native Americans when the pipe was being passed. Curiously, at the time of European contact, almost all smoking pipes were in the form of weapons, such as arrows. The pipes were thus thought of as ritual weapons, and during peace pipe mediations, the participants were sometimes considered to be "fighting with words."

Hall suggests that the Hopewell platform pipes also may have been ritual weapons. These earlier pipes were made in the form of the most common Hopewell weapon, the **atlatl** (AT-lat-ul), or spearthrower. (The bow and arrow were not in use in Ohio at that time.) According to Hall's interpretation, these Hopewell effigy pipes were not simply just one of many items that were exchanged; they also were part of the mechanism of exchange itself. According to Hall, ritual "peace pipe diplomacy" served to reduce regional differences and to promote communication and friendly contact between the disparate groups involved in the Hopewell Interaction Sphere. The Hopewell pipes were prominent items in elaborate burials, most likely because of their importance to leaders who were involved in mediation, intergroup relations, and exchange.

**atlatl** A spearthrower, or wooden shaft, used to propel a spear or dart.

The Hopewell Interaction Sphere began to decline after A.D. 400. Its demise undoubtedly was related to the disruption of the trade network, but we do not know exactly what factors prompted this breakdown. One explanation is that competition in rich river bottoms between emergent slash-and-burn horticulturalists, relying increasingly on maize, led to greater competition between communities. Such frictions may have caused the closing of regional boundaries. In a few cases, dispersed settlements were replaced with small nucleated villages (enclosed by ditches or walls) located in defensive positions on blufftops. The exchange of luxury goods linked the interaction sphere. Once the complex trade network was broken, either because artisans could not obtain the resources they needed or because warfare and competition disrupted alliances, the repercussions were felt throughout the regional system.

# Concept

## The Archaeology of Exchange

### *A perspective on ancient economies*

Most—if not all—human societies engage in the exchange of goods and information, both within their own population and with other groups. Yet the volume and the mechanisms of those transactions vary greatly. Prehistorically, many communities produced most of the items they required for subsistence and survival, only occasionally exchanging an ornament or food with neighboring peoples. Other villages and societies included many specialist producers who depended on trade for their livelihood.

Much ancient trade involved simple barter or **reciprocity,** face-to-face exchanges between known participants, such as kin or trading partners. In such small-scale exchanges, the giver assumed that a trade good or gift would be returned in the future. In the ancient Near East, pastoral herders traded mutton to sedentary farmers in exchange for grain.

Other ancient trade networks were more centralized and included "nodal" individuals (like a Polynesian chief) or central institutions (such as the Inca state) that controlled the movement, or **redistribution,** of certain goods. Items were collected from peripheral communities by a central authority, which then redistributed all or part of what was collected. In certain cases, redistribution primarily served to balance out environmental or economic differences between participating communities. Often, such systems allowed central authorities to accumulate large surpluses, since they would return only part of what was collected. Centrally stored goods could be amassed for military campaigns, construction projects, or the relief of local emergencies and natural disasters. Today, the U.S. federal income tax system acts as a very large and complex redistributive network.

Although reciprocity and redistribution were the most common mechanisms of exchange in the past, some ancient societies were involved in market transactions. For example, as we will see in Chapter 8, the market was particularly important in prehispanic Mexico. The principles of supply and

Can researchers use the study of the archaeological record to distinguish reciprocal exchange from reciprocity? If so, how might this be accomplished?

Figure 7.15 A large obsidian blade from the Hopewell site.

**reciprocity** The exchange of goods between known participants, involving simple barter and face-to-face exchanges.

**redistribution** The accumulation and dispersal of goods through a centralized agency, individual, or institution.

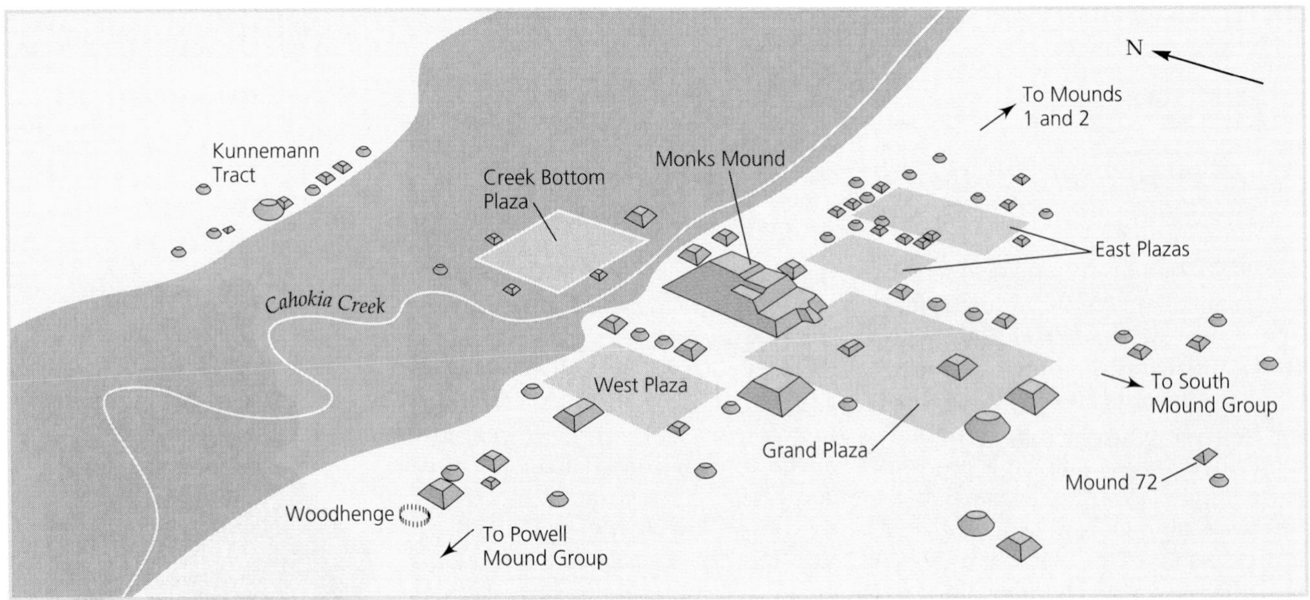


**Figure 7.18** A plan of Cahokia, showing the dispersal of mounds and plazas across the central area of the site. The mounds occur in a variety of shapes and sizes, reflecting their different functions.

of the site was not carried out until the 1920s, by Warren Moorehead under the auspices of the Illinois State Museum and the University of Illinois. This work confirmed that the mounds were humanmade, rather than just erosional remnants. Also in the 1920s, the first aerial photographs of Cahokia, and probably some of the earliest shots of an archaeological site in the United States, were taken. Today, Cahokia is designated a **UNESCO World Heritage Site,** and the central part is protected, but each year the expansion of subdivisions and highways continues to destroy outlying portions of this ancient settlement. During the past few decades, many of the archaeological projects at Cahokia have been salvage operations designed to recover as much information as possible before the destruction of a portion of the site.

Fully agricultural inhabitants first settled in the Cahokia area between A.D. 600 and 800. Small hamlets and villages consisted of small houses constructed in shallow rectangular basins. Several distinct villages were dispersed on the terrain that later was to become Cahokia. By A.D. 900, the population in the region had expanded, and a hierarchy of settlements had emerged. The larger communities or towns contained 100–150 people. These sites often included a series of flat-topped platform mounds that served as the foundations for temples, other public structures, or elite residences. Frequently, the platform mounds were arranged around rectangular open plazas. Not long after, sites often were fortified with defensive **palisades,** barricades that enclosed the plazas and other nonresidential features. Houses generally were erected both inside and outside the palisades. Many of the towns were planned settlements, with rectangular single-family houses arranged in an orderly manner around the central plaza.

At its peak between A.D. 1050 and 1250, Cahokia was the largest prehistoric civic-ceremonial center north of Mexico (Figure 7.18). The site encompasses more than 100 earthen mounds in an area of approximately 13 sq km (5 sq mi) and may have had a population as high as 10,000 to 20,000, although population estimates for the site vary widely. The central part of Cahokia consists of a large plaza surrounded by the giant Monks Mound and 16 other earthen platforms (Figure 7.19). This entire "downtown" area covered more than 80 ha (200 acres)

**UNESCO World Heritage Site** A property considered by the World Heritage Committee to have outstanding universal value. UNESCO (United Nations Educational, Scientific and Cultural Organization) encourages the protection and preservation of cultural and natural heritage that is considered to be of outstanding value to humanity.

**palisade** A fence of posts or stakes erected around a settlement for defensive purposes.

and was surrounded by an elaborate and massive wall. The wall served defensive purposes, since it included screened entrances and bastions. Yet it also may have been used to limit access to the central portion of the site. The people residing within the palisaded area undoubtedly were the highest-ranked individuals in the community. People of lesser status had their own houses, public buildings, and burial mound areas outside this central portion of the site.

Monks Mound, the largest prehistoric structure in the United States, consisted of four platforms, with a large public structure and some related smaller structures and walls located on the summit (see "Monumental Architecture," p. 287). The other mounds at the site occur in a variety of shapes. Conical mounds were probably used as burial mounds. Linear "ridgetop marker" mounds situated at the edges of Cahokia may have served to delineate the limits of the site. The most common mounds are large square platforms, several of which had two levels, such as Mound 42, a rectangular platform mound with a smaller mound on one corner. Excavations have revealed the presence of wood and postholes on top of several platforms, which are assumed to have served as sites for ceremonial structures. Also within the site area are features called **woodhenges,** demarcated by large upright timbers that once had been arranged in a circle. By sighting along certain marker posts, one can observe the annual sequence of the **solstices** and the equinoxes; woodhenge features may have served as solar observatories.

Excavations by Melvin Fowler, emeritus professor at the University of Wisconsin–Milwaukee, at Cahokia's Mound 72 have uncovered a series of burials that date between A.D. 1050 and the early 1100s. In all, there were six burial episodes, involving at least 261 individuals (118 of whom are thought to have been retainer sacrifices), and each episode resulted in the expansion

**Figure 7.19** An artist's reconstruction of Monks Mound and the central, walled part of Cahokia at its peak, around A.D. 1150.

What indicators might archaeologists use to find evidence of past warfare?

**woodhenge** A circular feature demarcated by large upright timbers, probably used by prehistoric groups as astronomical observatories.

**solstice** The time of year when the sun is at its greatest distance from the equator, occurring about June 21 and December 22.

**cache** A collection of artifacts, often buried or associated with constructed features, that has been deliberately stored for future use.

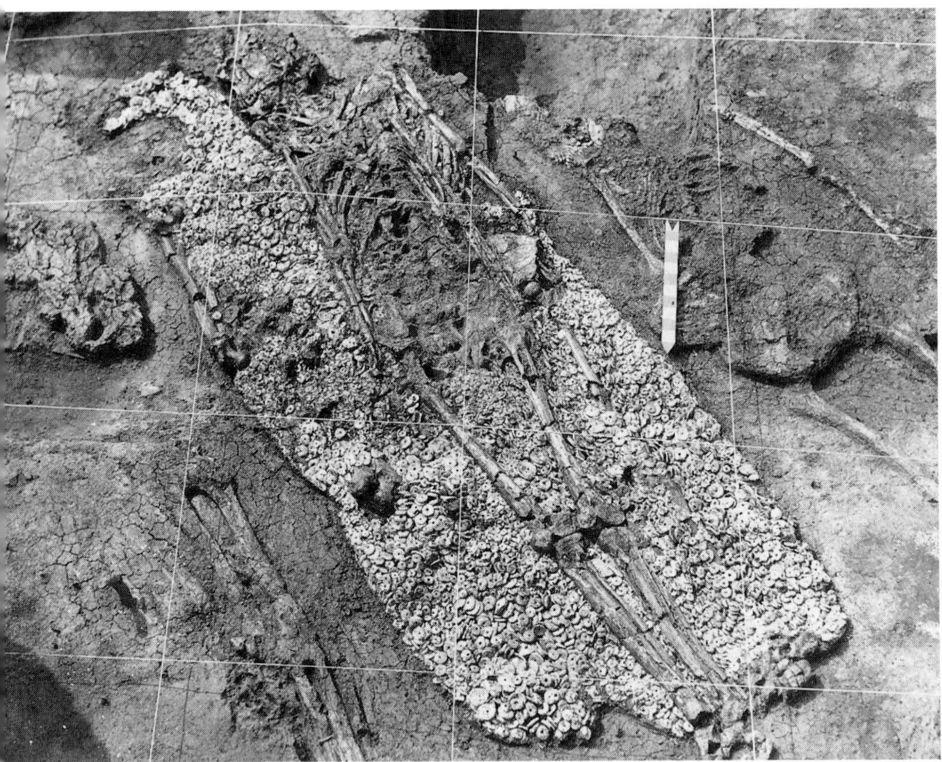

Figure 7.20 The skeleton of a man lying on a burial platform made of thousands of drilled shell beads. The burial is from Mound 72.

Figure 7.21 A Cahokia pottery vessel decorated with a sophisticated spiral scroll design. This tall vase stands 23 cm high.

of the mound as prior burials were covered over. During one of the first episodes, a **cache** of offerings, including pottery vessels, projectile points, and shell beads, was placed in a pit. In a subsequent episode, a pit containing more than 50 young women and a platform with 4 young men, who had been beheaded and behanded, were added. The closeness in age of the women argues against their having died from disease or some common disaster. Along with the 4 men, they appear to have been sacrificial victims who were dispatched to accompany powerful chiefs after death. One burial contained a possible chief who was laid out on a litter composed of thousands of drilled shell beads and surrounded by offerings (Figure 7.20). Near this figure were 6 individuals with elaborate grave goods, including rolled sheet copper, mica slabs, polished stones, and caches of arrowheads. The complexity of the Mound 72 burial sequence, the sacrifices, and the grave goods document elaborate burial ceremonialism and marked social differentiation at Cahokia.

Cahokia was a great center that grew rapidly to dominate the floodplain for miles around. At its height, it contained a disproportionate amount of elaborate public architecture compared with the settlements in its surrounding hinterland. The artisanship and diversity of the goods present in burial and domestic contexts at Cahokia were unmatched at the smaller settlements (Figure 7.21). In addition, there is every reason to believe that Cahokia was well planned and that its construction required the control of a reasonably large, organized labor force. Cahokia appears to have been at the pinnacle of a hierarchically organized and complex social system that was centered on the rich American Bottom for several centuries.

After A.D. 1250, Cahokia continued to be occupied, but many of the site's mounds fell into disuse. Population at the site and throughout the American Bottom was greatly diminished as people moved into surrounding uplands. The decline of Cahokia and some nearby settlements may have been related to the growing importance of other large Mississippian centers, such as Moundville in Alabama, that redirected channels of exchange, alliance, and communication. At the same time, the great buildup at Cahokia could have precipitated degradation of the local environment.

Whatever led to the transition, the period after A.D. 1250 was dominated by a series of important Mississippian centers that were dispersed across the southeastern United States. Archaeological findings suggest that each of these sites was smaller and less monumental than Cahokia had been. The archaeological record on this point dovetails with early documentary accounts from the period of first white contact. The earliest European travelers in the southeastern United States encountered a number of chiefs, temple mounds, and hierarchically organized societies, but none of the reported centers matched the size or monumentality of Cahokia.

*Concept*

# Monumental Architecture

## *Monks Mound at Cahokia*

Monumental construction is characteristic of complex societies. Some of the most famous structures of the ancient world are the Egyptian pyramids and the massive architecture and pyramids along the Street of the Dead in Teotihuacan, Mexico. Although large-scale constructions were erected by most ancient civilizations, the specific activities associated with these massive edifices vary from structure to structure and region to region. Some large-scale architecture served primarily to commemorate the dead, and other structures served as platforms for temples or high-status residences. In certain cases, massive architectural features (elaborate tombs or gigantic palaces) were built to confirm and glorify the power of a specific ruling individual or family, but in other places, great public structures or plazas were built to hold more corporate political and ritual functions in which a larger segment of society participated. Of course, many monumental buildings served multiple functions. The study of ancient architecture allows archaeologists to identify the political and ceremonial activities carried out by peoples in the past. In some cases, the examination of ancient buildings has enabled archaeologists to estimate the size of the labor force that was required to construct them.

The largest prehistoric structure in North America (north of Mexico) is Monks Mound at Cahokia (Figure 7.22). This immense earthen mound, located at the center of Cahokia, was 30 m (or 98 ft) high, as tall as a 10-story building, and larger than a city block (316 m long × 241 m wide, or 1036 × 790 ft). Covering 6.5 ha (16 acres), it contained about 731,000 cu m (25,810,000 cu ft) of earth, or the equivalent of seven modern oil tankers. Monks Mound was erected in as many as 14 stages, beginning early in the tenth century A.D. The last level, the summit on which large public buildings were built, dates to the middle of the twelfth century.

In 1809, a land claim of 160 ha (400 acres), including Monks Mound, was assigned to Nicholas Jarrot, who donated this area to a group of Trappist monks. The monks, who established a monastery, gardened on the first terrace of the largest mound and built their settlement on a small mound nearby. They abandoned the site only 4 years later because of disease and hardship, but it is from this brief occupation that the largest mound at the site is now known as Monks Mound. In 1831, Amos Hill moved onto the property and built his house on the summit of Monks Mound. The area was under private ownership until 1923, when it was turned into a state park.

The form of Monks Mound is unique; it consists of four terraces or platforms. The lowest, or first, terrace extends across the south end of the structure and stands approximately 11 m (36 ft) above the surrounding ground surface. A projection that appears to have been a ramp leading to the ground is situated near the center of the southern end of the terrace. The southwest corner of this terrace is slightly higher than the rest. Excavations have shown that large public buildings were erected in this area; it likely was an important focal point for the Cahokia community around A.D. 1100. These public buildings were later covered over by another platform mound that also had a public structure on top of it. This platform mound was rebuilt several times. Later, a ridge was

*As a product of social effort, patterns of public architecture may communicate the nature and scale of social order.*

—Jerry Moore (1996)

**Figure 7.22** Monks Mound at Cahokia as it appeared in 1892, looking north. The base is approximately 300 m north to south, more than 210 m east to west, and 30 m above the surrounding fields at the highest point.

constructed connecting this platform with the main mass of Monks Mound to the northeast. Around A.D. 1700, Native Americans returned to the site and buried several individuals in this part of the mound.

The second terrace, extending from the first terrace back toward the northwest corner of the mound, actually consists of two flat-topped platforms at an elevation of 19 m (62 ft). These platforms were built sometime after A.D. 1250. The third and fourth terraces, situated in the northeast part of the structure, form the highest points of the mound.

The uniqueness and size of Monks Mound attest to its function as a symbol of civic-ceremonial power. Yet to many archaeologists, Monks Mound is more than a sacred place where annual ceremonies probably took place. The identification of ramps and stairways on the mound suggests that access to the apex of the mound, which stood far above the surrounding floodplain, was restricted, possibly limited to a small segment of Cahokia's population. Its monumentality provides an indication of the large amount of labor needed for its construction. Yet how many households were involved in this work effort and how much labor each domestic unit contributed remains an issue of debate.

Finally, Monks Mound, still visible today for miles around, also was the focal point of a powerful polity, a place where Cahokia's rulers surely must have displayed their political influence for many to witness. In fact, Cahokia remained the largest population center ever to exist north of the Rio Grande until the eighteenth century.

# Moundville

## *A late Mississippian center in Alabama*

Major changes in subsistence, material culture, and settlement patterns took place in the southeastern United States after A.D. 700. As with groups living on the Mississippi River bottomlands, corn became more important in the diet. Shell-tempered pottery appeared—a technological breakthrough that made possible the construction of larger, more durable ceramic vessels. Although most settlements in the Southeast remained small, a few larger communities with several small pyramidal earthen mounds arranged around an open plaza were established. While none of these sites yet approached the size and complexity of Cahokia, the presence of residences on the tops of some of the mounds, which were continuously rebuilt, enlarged, and inhabited for generations, suggests that a more stable or institutionalized form of elite status (perhaps inherited leadership positions) had developed in portions of the Southeast.

Although the shift to maize did not occur simultaneously throughout the area, large quantities of maize were grown in much of the Southeast by A.D. 1200. Wild plants and animals continued to be important sources of food, but maize agriculture (supplemented by beans and squash) was the economic foundation of these complex societies. The social and political hierarchies of this period were manifested in public architecture, as civic-ceremonial centers proliferated across the region. One of the largest of these centers was Moundville, a Mississippian community located on a bluff overlooking the Black Warrior River in west-central Alabama (Figure 7.23).

Most Mississippian settlements were linked by political, economic, and social ties into larger regional polities (political organizations) that varied greatly in size and complexity. Some were small and simple, each consisting of a single center and its immediate hinterland. Others were much larger, consisting of major centers, minor centers, and villages. The larger polities, which may have had several levels of chiefs, did not emerge until after A.D. 1200. Many of the groups actually consisted of semiautonomous polities linked together by alliances. Such formations, or confederations, were constantly subject to fragmentation and realignment, especially as distance from the paramount center increased.

Relationships between communities also were maintained through exchange. Such materials as copper, marine shell, mica, galena, fluorite, and bauxite were moved over great distances in both raw and finished form. At Moundville, nonlocal materials were abundant, including marine shell from the Florida Gulf Coast, copper from the Great Lakes, pottery from many areas of the Southeast, galena from Missouri, and finished ceremonial objects from Tennessee and the Spiro site in Oklahoma. Most of the artifacts made from these exotic materials tend to be associated with rich burials at Moundville, suggesting they were traded through elite channels. More domestic items, such as salt and chipped stone, probably were traded through reciprocal transactions at the household level.

One of the more striking features at Moundville and other large Mississippian centers is the presence of an art style known broadly as the **Southeastern Ceremonial Complex,** also called the Southern Cult (Figure 7.24). It was not really a cult but a network of interaction, exchange, and shared information that crossed regional and local boundaries. Yet the specific iconographic motifs that were used varied

*The European colonization and conquest was a disaster to Indian societies. Among the most effective introductions were epidemic diseases, which reached the interior much faster than direct intervention.*

—James B. Griffin (1967)

**Southeastern Ceremonial Complex** A network of interaction, exchange, and shared information present over much of the southeastern (and parts of the midwestern) United States from around A.D. 1200 until the early 1500s; also previously referred to as the Southern Cult.

**Figure 7.23** Mississippian sites were concentrated on the wide floodplains of the Mississippi River and its major tributaries. Although there were thousands of Mississippian mounds in the southeastern United States, few of them remain today.

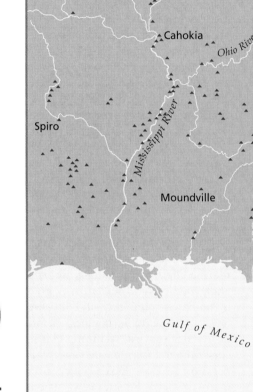

**Figure 7.24** A black pottery vessel with bird effigy found at Moundville, 16 cm high. Birds and serpents figured prominently in the iconography of the Southeastern Ceremonial Complex.

across space and over time. Items belonging to this complex have been found from Mississippi to Minnesota, and from Oklahoma to the Atlantic Coast, although they are most abundant at certain sites in the Southeast. Such **motifs** as human hands with an eye in the palm, sunbursts, weeping eyes, and human skull-and-bones are elements of this style (Figure 7.25). They appear on polished black shell-tempered pottery, are embossed on pendants made from Lake Superior copper, and are incised on imported Gulf conch shells. The most famous Mississippian cult objects are the so-called effigy jars that are decorated with human faces, some with signs of face painting or tattoos. Others represent sacrificial victims, with eyes closed and mouths sewn shut. Often the effigies are shown weeping, possibly denoting a connection between tears, rain, and water in Mississippian cosmology. Some of the common motifs—wind, fire, sun, and human sacrifice—seem to share certain thematic elements with Mesoamerica, although the basis for this similarity has not been established. The greatest concentrations of Southeastern Ceremonial Complex objects occur in temple mounds at some of the major late Mississippian sites, suggesting that these goods had political and symbolic importance.

Because of its large size, Moundville has long attracted public atten-

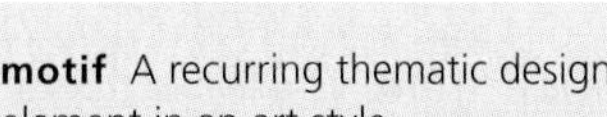

**motif** A recurring thematic design element in an art style.

**charnel house** A house in which the bodies of the dead are placed.

tion. In 1840, Thomas Maxwell, a local planter and merchant, excavated in one mound, noted the stylistic similarities with Mesoamerica, and concluded that the site was an outpost of the Aztec empire. Several small-scale investigations of the site were made by the Smithsonian Institution during the latter part of the century, but the first large-scale excavations were not carried out until 1905–1906 by Clarence B. Moore. Excavating both the platform mounds and village areas, Moore uncovered over 800 burials, many accompanied by pottery vessels and other artifacts of shell, copper, and stone. The second major episode of excavation was carried out by the Alabama Museum of Natural History. From 1929 through 1941, 4.5 ha (11 acres) of the site surface were opened, and the excavations yielded over 2000 burials, 75 structures, and many other finds. More recent work has concentrated on understanding the chronological sequence at the site. In all, excavations at Moundville have yielded more than 3000 burials and over 1 million artifacts.

Based on recent studies, the history of Moundville is divisible into three episodes. Moundville was occupied initially around A.D. 1050. At first, the site contained only two small mounds and was one of several small ceremonial centers in the region. The burials from this period indicate some signs of marked, possibly inherited, social differentiation, though not to the extent found for later occupations. As noted above, this initial episode of growth was associated with a rapid intensification of maize farming.

By A.D. 1200, a marked period of growth and political centralization had occurred at a time when Cahokia was already in decline. Moundville grew to over 75 ha (185 acres), and at least 30 pyramidal mounds were built around a large 32-ha (79-acre) plaza (Figure 7.26). Around A.D. 1300 the character of Moundville shifted again. The overall population declined, yet the site was still occupied by a higher-status segment of the population. Moundville continued to be an important political and religious center and remained a locus for mortuary activities.

The mounds at Moundville were large, flat-topped earthen structures constructed to elevate temples or the dwellings of important individuals above the surrounding landscape. The mounds were built in stages, probably as part of community rituals. The two major mounds, the largest of which was 17.3 m (58 ft) high and covered more than 0.8 ha (2 acres) at its base, were located within the plaza at the center of the site along the north-south axis. The 18 earthworks surrounding the plaza are arranged into pairs of one large and one small mound. The small mounds usually include burials; the larger earthen structures do not (Figure 7.27).

In the northeast corner of the site, the dwellings were larger and more complex than in other parts of Moundville. Broken artifacts that correspond to items found in the higher-status burials also are found in this probable elite residential area. **Charnel houses** and a sweat house are located along the margins of the plaza. Commoner residential areas were placed at greater distances from the eastern, southern, and western sides of the plaza. At its height, Moundville is estimated to have been occupied by a few thousand people.

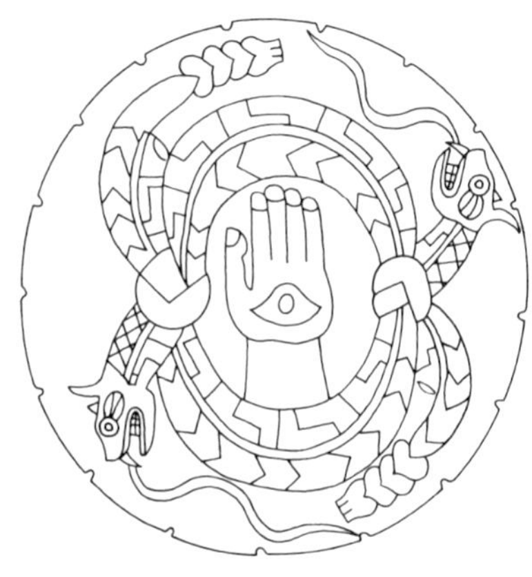

**Figure 7.25** An engraved sandstone palette from Moundville, with the eye-in-palm motif circled by two horned rattlesnakes (diameter about 31.9 cm).

**Figure 7.26** An artist's rendering of Moundville as it may have appeared at its height of occupation.

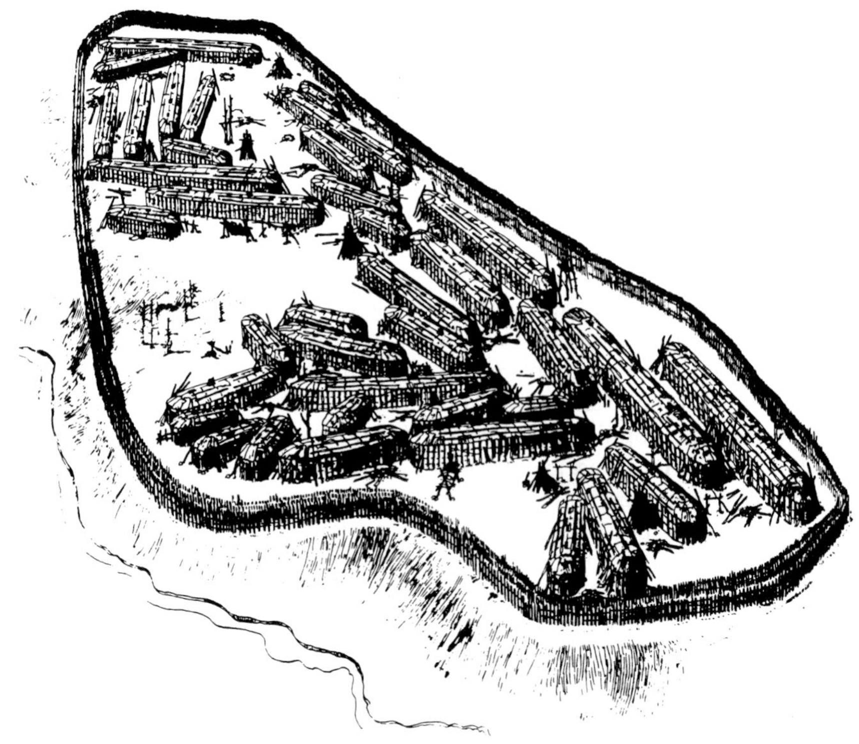

**Figure 7.29** An artist's reconstruction of the main palisaded village and enclosed longhouses at the Draper site, after the village had undergone its final expansion.

areas, settlement pattern studies suggest that these larger villages were formed through the nucleation of several smaller communities. In these larger villages, the alignment of houses was usually much more formal than in the earlier, smaller settlements.

Excavations at the Draper site, located 35 km (22 mi) northeast of Toronto, have provided a wealth of information on village organization in the late prehistoric period. Most of the settlement was excavated as part of a salvage operation initiated before the construction of a new Toronto airport. An unusually large village for late prehistoric Ontario, the site is particularly important because almost the entire settlement was excavated. The high cost of modern archaeological excavation makes it very rare for more than a small portion of a site to be examined carefully. Yet in a few cases—Draper being one—the opportunity to excavate a large segment of the original village provides an unusually detailed picture of community plan, changes in settlement size over time, and house-to-house variation.

The Draper site is one of more than 15 Iroquoian villages in the Duffin drainage, located in the white pine–hardwood forest region of southern Ontario. The settlement was inhabited between A.D. 1450 and 1500. This relatively short occupation is not unusual for southern Ontario, where most villages were resituated every 25–50 years, usually to new locations only 3–5 km (2–3 mi) away. Many factors have been proposed to account for these frequent relocations, including infestation of the wood-and-thatch longhouses by insects, soil exhaustion or weed competition (which would have prompted the clearing of forest for new agricultural fields), depletion of wood (for construction and firewood) and game, and community realignments resulting from disputes and other social stresses.

The Draper site was composed of three spatially discrete areas of occupation: the main palisaded village (Figure 7.29), a small group of seven houses located 50 m (160 ft) south of the main village, and a lone structure (Structure 42) located on a small knoll 80 m (260 ft) to the southwest. At different times in its occupation, the main village was surrounded by three or four palisade rows (each composed of wooden posts or beams). William Finlayson, who super-

**sweat bath** A hut or other space heated by steam that is created by pouring water over hot stones.

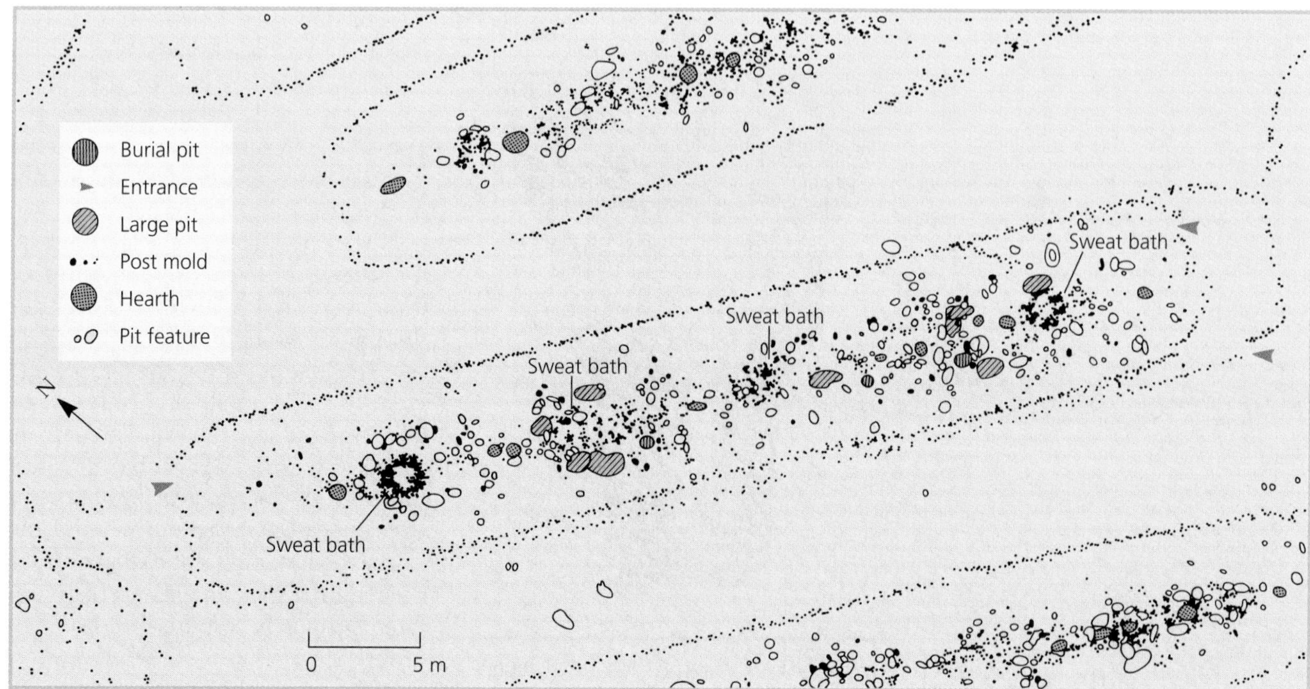


**Figure 7.30** Excavated longhouses at the Draper site, showing the distribution of sweat baths, hearths, burial pits, and other pit features. The longhouses are clearly outlined by post molds. Other post molds also are present inside the houses.

vised the principal excavations in 1975 and 1978, believes the settlement was planned with defensive considerations in mind.

The site began as a 1.2-ha (3-acre) village of seven to nine longhouses (accommodating roughly 400 people). All the houses were built well back from the palisades. These first houses were arranged in two clusters, with the houses in each cluster laid out according to similar compass orientations. Each set of houses may have represented a distinct social unit, perhaps a lineage or clan segment.

All the longhouses had a relatively similar set of internal features, including **sweat baths,** cooking hearths, pits (some of which were burials), storage cubicles, and benches (2–2.5 m, or 6.5–8 ft, wide), which were placed along the house walls (Figure 7.30). Each nuclear family in the longhouse is thought to have had its own cooking and sleeping area. The sweat baths were less abundant and were probably used in a more communal fashion. According to ethnohistoric accounts of the Huron, the Iroquoian tribal group considered to be the descendants of the people at the Draper site, sweat baths usually were taken by groups of men to prevent disease. Before the bath, the stones were heated in a large fire, then removed and put in a pile in the center of the lodge. Sticks were arranged at waist height around the pile and then bent at the top, leaving enough space between the sticks and the rocks for naked men sitting with their knees raised in front of their stomach. When the men were in position, the whole bath was covered with large pieces of bark and skins to prevent air from escaping. While in the bath, the men would often sing. These sweat-bath rituals are thought to have had an important integrative function for a group of people who resided in very close quarters.

In the first Draper village, one longhouse had several characteristics suggesting a special function. This large structure had one of the highest densities of wall posts and sweat baths. It also had the greatest average distance between hearths, indicating that each family group had more space than other longhouse occupants. In addition, a special hearth was placed at one end of this somewhat unusual residential structure. Finlayson suggests that this large longhouse may have been occupied by a

**Figure 7.31** This effigy pipe bowl is one of thousands of clay pipe fragments that were recovered during excavations at the Draper site. Smoking pipes played an important role in Iroquoian council meetings.

community or kin-group leader or village chief. Such special structures may have been used for council meetings, community feasts, and ceremonies (Figure 7.31).

The Draper village underwent five expansions, eventually reaching a maximum population of 1800–2000 people. Before abandonment, the village was 3.4 ha (8.5 acres) in size. During each expansion episode, between three and nine houses were built. The houses often were added in clusters, with the houses having similar orientations. The additions may represent new kin segments that moved into the site. Over time, an increasing amount of space was devoted to nonhouse use; with each expansion, the houses, or clusters of houses, were positioned to create new plazas. The plazas may have served as places for village ceremonies and social activities. Such integrative events may have increased in importance as the community grew. Two of the houses that were added during these expansions are thought by Finlayson to have been leaders' houses.

Two rectangular structures that abutted the palisade also were added. These buildings have been interpreted as houses set aside for visitors. According to ethnohistoric accounts, visitors were assigned to special cabins so that they could be closely monitored; they were not allowed to wander through the community.

The longhouses in the Draper site were 14.5–75.1 m (48–247 ft) long and 6.7–7.9 m (22–26 ft) wide. The narrow range of widths was probably determined by the mechanical limitations of the construction procedures and the available material (wood). In contrast, the length variation was probably related primarily to household or kin-group size.

The seven houses in the south field were smaller than those in the main village. They had a low density of pits and sweat baths, suggesting a shorter occupation. The presence of only a partial palisade, possibly used as a windbreak, suggests less concern for defense. Perhaps the occupants of this southern area moved inside the larger palisaded village when sieges occurred. Structure 42, also outside the main village, appears to have been a special-purpose structure, although its specific function remains little understood. Fragments of human bone were found on the surface before its excavation, but further study has not yet revealed additional signs of a burial area.

The late precontact Iroquoian villages in the Great Lakes region were not organized as hierarchically as the larger, contemporaneous Mississippian polities in the Southeast. In the latter, labor was amassed to construct large pyramid mounds at central settlements. These focal settlements differed in size and function from the many smaller villages that also constituted the settlement system. In contrast, the differences between the Draper site and surrounding settlements were not substantial. Although Draper was somewhat larger than its neighbors, the construction remains and material items at the site were basically similar to those found at surrounding communities.

Because of the tremendous changes that occurred in Native American lifeways as a result of direct European contact (and sometimes before, since the spread of disease and trade goods often preceded actual face-to-face relations), the early European historical accounts present a sketchy and sometimes inaccurate picture of the late precontact period. This potential disparity between archaeological and historical records is especially troublesome in areas where major settlements, such as the large Hohokam villages of the Arizona desert, were apparently abandoned sometime before European contact (see "Snaketown," p. 300). In such cases, the native peoples that the Europeans first encountered were not necessarily the direct descendants of earlier native populations, whose communities have been found by archaeologists. In other areas, the direct sequence between the historic and prehistoric peoples is somewhat clearer, such as for the Iroquoian groups of the Northeast. In these cases, historical information can more readily be used to test and support interpretations derived from archaeological data. Nevertheless, the careful researcher must be prepared to recognize diversity and changes in the archaeological and historical records.

For example, in the Great Lakes region, indirect contacts spread trade goods and disease vectors to most areas before direct meetings between native peoples and Europeans took place. In fact, some scholars have argued that the large-scale Iroquoian alliances and confederacies, which at times joined up to 25 villages and are well documented in the early historical accounts, may have been formed in response to contact period processes. Such large linkages appear not to have been in place prehistorically. New trade demands and land pressures may have prompted the formation of new political structures. Warfare and trade certainly were important prehistorically in the Great Lakes region, but after European contact, they took on new forms. Scholars, such as those studying the Iroquoian peoples, who can use and compare archaeological and historical sources as partially independent records, stand the best chance of unraveling the multifaceted and often destructive processes that surrounded European arrival in the Americas and the effects of these processes on the native peoples.

Site

# Snaketown

*A desert village in the American Southwest*

**Figure 7.32** Mano resting on a well-used metate.

**metate** The stone basin, often trough-shaped, or lower part of a stone-milling assembly for grinding maize or other foods.

**mano** The handheld part of a stone-milling assembly for grinding maize or other foods.

**wattle and daub** A building technique that uses a framework of poles, interspersed with smaller poles and twigs; the wooden frame is plastered with mud or a mud mixture. This building technique also was employed in the Southeast and other parts of the world.

Despite its often arid and unforgiving landscape, the American Southwest has a rich archaeological past. The region was first populated around 9000 B.C. by hunter-gatherers who hunted big-game species, such as mammoth and giant bison. These early inhabitants had highly mobile food-collecting strategies and manufactured sophisticated tools for hunting and butchering game and for processing hides, wood, and bone. Their remains occur primarily as small, ephemeral kill and butchering sites characterized by animal bones and flaked stone implements. By 5500 B.C., big-game hunting had declined in importance, and emphasis shifted to smaller animals and a variety of local plant resources. In southeastern Arizona and southwestern New Mexico, these wild foods included yucca, cactus leaves and fruits, and sunflower seeds.

After 2100 B.C., maize was introduced into the area from Mexico. Along with other early southwestern cultigens (beans, squash, and bottle gourds), maize had a long history of cultivation in Mexico before its appearance in the Southwest. Eventually, maize became the most important cultivated crop in the Southwest. However, for 1000 years following its introduction, most peoples of the Southwest relied surprisingly little on maize or any other exotic domesticate, and many groups retained a primarily hunting-and-gathering subsistence regime.

The earliest villages in the Southwest appeared in the desert river valleys of southern Arizona during the Late Archaic period (middle of the last millennium B.C.). This more sedentary existence was marked by circular foundation pits, storage facilities, crude plainware pottery jars and bowls, jewelry made from marine shells, and maize farming. By the end of the Late Archaic, agricultural villages dotted the landscape throughout the American Southwest, coexisting in some areas with groups who continued more traditional foraging practices and nomadic lifeways. In the more northerly, cooler parts of the Southwest, farming was relatively risky. Perhaps that is part of the reason many early villages were positioned defensively and generally included storage facilities. In the hot Sonoran Desert of southern Arizona, crop production was more secure (as long as sufficient water was available), villages were situated more in the open, and no specialized storerooms were constructed. The presence of basketry containers, along with **metates,** grinding stones, and **manos,** companion handstones—for grinding corn or seeds—is indicative of a more settled existence in that area (Figure 7.32).

The early villages of the Southwest shared certain general characteristics. The earliest permanent dwellings were pithouses, structures in which the lower parts of the walls were actually the earthen sides of a shallow pit (Figure 7.33). The top part of the walls consisted of a framework of poles, interlaced with small twigs and then completely covered with mud on the exterior, a construction technique known as **wattle and daub.** Settlements often contained only two or three pithouses. In contrast, larger villages usually had one or more community, or special-function, structures in addition to pithouses.

Although the earliest ceramics in the Southwest were plainwares (without decoration), distinct regional variations soon developed. During the early centuries of the first millennium A.D., the three major cultural traditions of the prehistoric Southwest began to emerge: Hohokam (ho-ho-KHAM) in the deserts of southern Arizona; Ancestral Pueblo on the high plateaus of the Four Corners region (northern Arizona and New Mexico, southwestern Colorado, and southeastern Utah); and Mogollon (muh-ghee-YOWN) along the Mogollon Rim (in east-central Arizona) and in the mountains of southeastern Arizona and southwestern New Mexico. Each tradition eventually developed its own pattern of settlement and land use, architecture, community organization, and craft specialization. The discussion here of Snaketown (Hohokam) and in the next section on Chaco Canyon (Ancestral Pueblo) highlights the diversity of Native American life in the prehistoric Southwest.

The Hohokam lived in the lower Sonoran Desert region of southern Arizona and adjacent Chihuahua and Sonora in northern Mexico. The area is basin-and-range country, composed of numerous more or less parallel mountain ranges rising 300–1070 m (1000–3500 ft) above the intervening basins. The desert area of southern Arizona receives less rain than the high plateaus of the Four Corners region and is intensely hot in the summer. The land supports a rich natural flora of shrubs and cacti (saguaro, barrel, cholla, and prickly pear); mesquite and other trees and shrubs grow in the washes. Yet because of the somewhat unpredictable rainfall, irrigation is necessary in many areas for reliable maize farming.

After A.D. 1, a large Hohokam community called Snaketown was settled in the Phoenix Basin, a broad, low alluvial region where southern Arizona's two major rivers, the Salt and the Gila, come together (Figure 7.34). Snaketown is situated on an upper river terrace about 1 km (0.6 mi) from the Gila River at an elevation of 360 m (1175 ft). According to the late Emil Haury, who excavated at Snaketown in 1934–1935 and again in 1964–1965, good agricultural land, a river that could be tapped for irrigation, and a high water table were important features determining Snaketown's location.

The largest of the early Hohokam pithouse villages, Snaketown may have had as many as 100 residents soon after its foundation. The early habitation levels included only residential pithouses; no public buildings were constructed. However, David R. Wilcox, of the Museum of Northern Arizona, has suggested that even early in its occupational history the site may have had a central plaza area. Maize was a dietary staple, although such wild plant foods as mesquite, maguey, saguaro, and cholla also were important.

By A.D. 600, the number of Hohokam villages had increased markedly, and the Phoenix Basin became the most densely populated area in southern Arizona. Many villages, including Snaketown, grew. At some sites, **ball courts** and platform mounds were erected (see "The Mesoamerican Ballgame," Chapter 8, p. 356). One of the most impressive of these oval Hohokam ball courts was constructed at Snaketown (Figure 7.35). Rubber balls, also found at Snaketown, suggest that certain aspects of the Hohokam ballgame may have been similar to the game played in Mexico. Hohokam platform mounds, usually low and rectangular, were made of earth and **adobe** and topped with caliche (calcium carbonate) or adobe plaster. Ceremonial structures may have been positioned on the tops of these mounds. Both platform mounds and ball courts were generally erected at larger Hohokam sites, such as Snaketown. These sites may have served as political-ritual centers for the populations of smaller surrounding settlements that lacked such nondomestic structures.

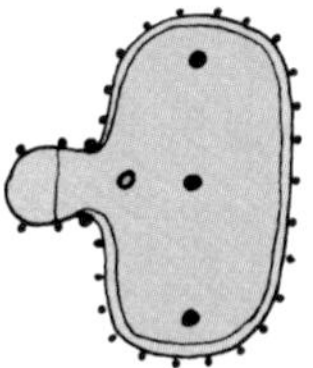

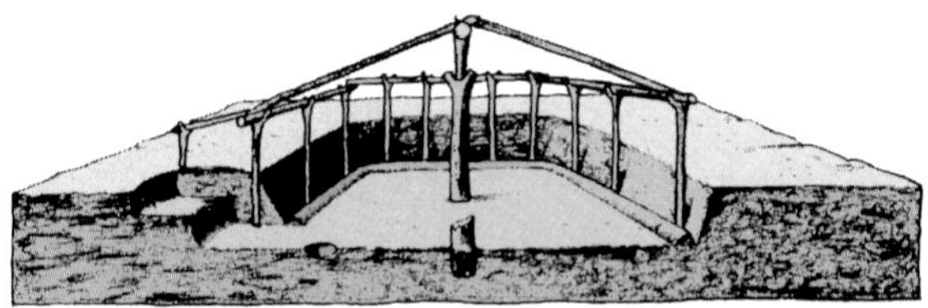

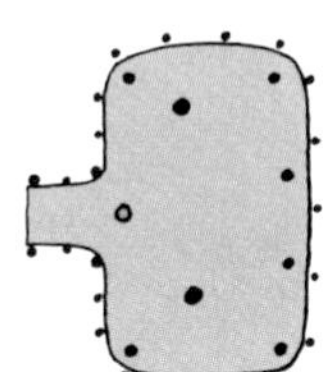

**Figure 7.33** Two examples of pithouses from Snaketown. The roof and wall constructions are postulated, in part, on the distribution of post molds found in the houses.

**ball court** A prehispanic structure that was the site of ritual ballgames.

**adobe** A mud mixture used to make sun-dried bricks for buildings in arid areas.

Site

# Chaco Canyon

*A prehistoric regional center in the American Southwest*

**www.mhhe.com/priceip6e**

For a Web-based activity on the disappearance of Ancestral Pueblo culture, see the Internet exercises on your online learning center.

The Four Corners region of the Southwest—the junction of Arizona, New Mexico, Colorado, and Utah—is dominated by an extensive highland (elevation above 1500 m, 5000 ft) called the Colorado Plateau. The plateau is drained by the Colorado River and its tributaries, which have cut a complex topography of mesas, buttes, valleys, and canyons into the landscape. Located in a remote part of northwestern New Mexico, Chaco Canyon is one of the largest of these erosion features (Figure 7.41).

Chaco (CHAH-ko) Canyon, 15 km (9 mi) long, has a sandy bottom and little permanent water. The bleak environment lacks trees and experiences dramatic temperature extremes. Rainfall, characterized by infrequent summer cloudbursts that cause washes to fill temporarily with water, is marginal for farming. Today the area is seldom used for agriculture, but once it was a center of prehistoric settlement and long-distance exchange. The Native Americans depended on rainfall for **floodwater farming,** in which they channeled seasonal runoff to agricultural fields, to supplement the water supply.

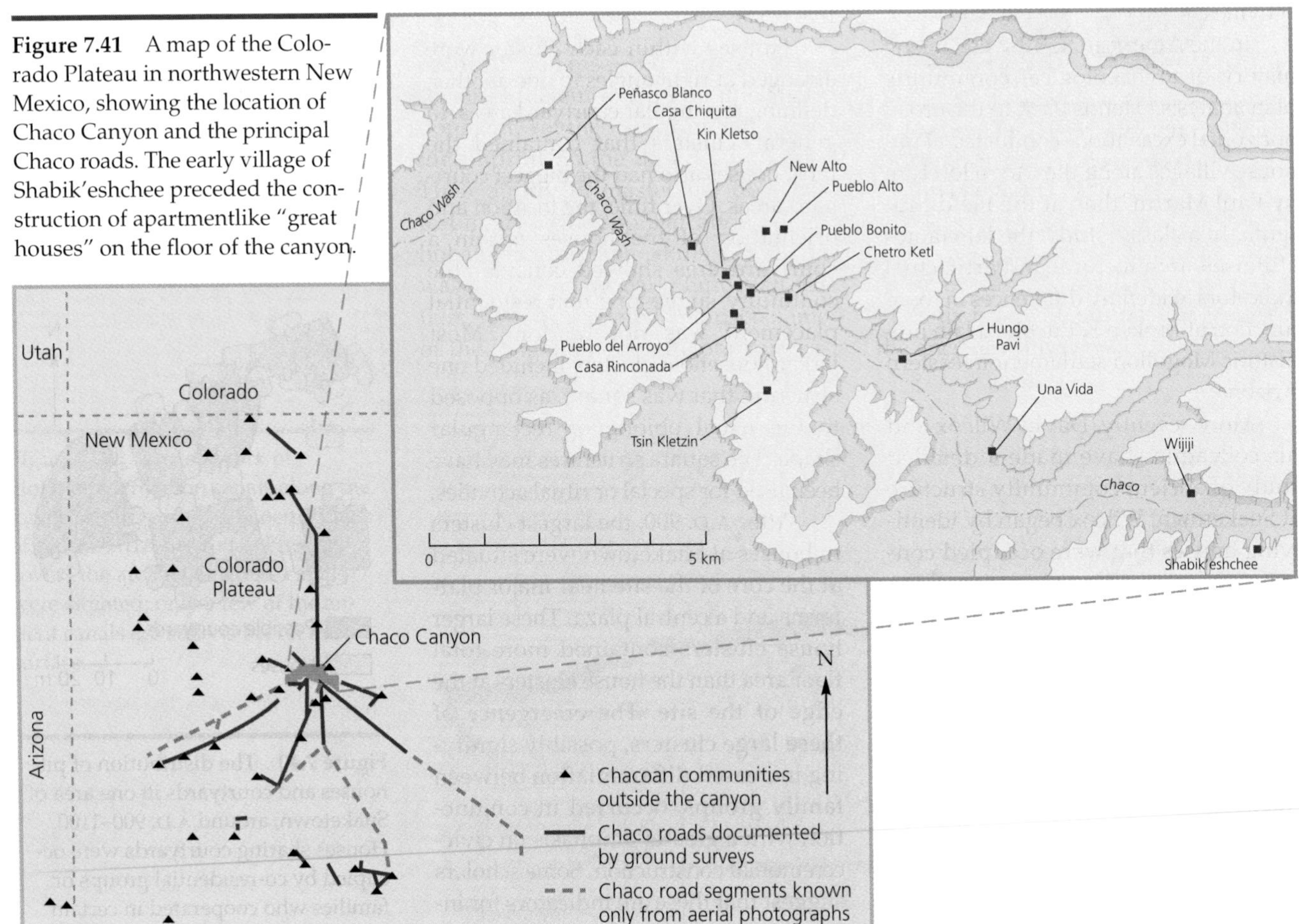


**Figure 7.41** A map of the Colorado Plateau in northwestern New Mexico, showing the location of Chaco Canyon and the principal Chaco roads. The early village of Shabik'eshchee preceded the construction of apartmentlike "great houses" on the floor of the canyon.

**Figure 7.42** Chetro Ketl, one of the great houses built on the floor of Chaco Canyon. For the most part, the large pueblo of Chetro Ketl was constructed during the late tenth and early eleventh centuries A.D. The outer rooms, which faced the courtyard, were used primarily for residential activities; the inner rooms were used for storage.

Several of the most spectacular ruins anywhere in the Southwest are located in Chaco Canyon. Although brief reports of these ruins extend back to the mid-seventeenth century when military forces from Spanish outposts entered the area, the first substantial accounts were not published until 1850. At that time, James Simpson, an officer in the Army Topographical Engineers, was sent to the canyon area to investigate claims that the Navajo were harassing isolated farms and ranchos (settlements consisting of only a few houses). Simpson was overwhelmed by the massive walls, which still stood three to four stories high and formed complexes of contiguous rooms (Figure 7.42). He described and measured many of the prehistoric structures, and many other curious visitors soon followed. In 1906, Chaco Canyon was made a national monument to protect the ruins from destruction by treasure hunters and vandals.

The continuity of past and present Native American groups in the Southwest is most evident between the prehistoric Ancestral Pueblo and the contemporary Pueblo Indians. Many Pueblo peoples consider the Colorado Plateau to be their traditional homeland. *Ancestral Pueblo* is now the term used for one of the major prehistoric southwestern cultural traditions that developed out of the hunting-and-gathering adaptation around 2000 years ago. Before that time, temporary campsites and kill sites were present on the Chaco Plateau, but not in the canyon itself. The first sedentary Ancestral Pueblo sites date to around A.D. 100, located on mesas away from the bottomlands of the canyon, possibly for reasons of defense. Most of these sites contained 5–10 shallow pithouses. Over the next several centuries, the diet at most Ancestral Pueblo sites showed an increasing reliance on domesticated corn, beans, and squash. Yet the collecting of pine, or piñon, nuts and the hunting of cottontail and jackrabbits, deer, antelope, and Rocky Mountain bighorn sheep remained important.

By the middle of the first millennium A.D., villages, which may have been inhabited year-round, were located on the floor of Chaco Canyon. Once the canyon was occupied, its population grew, and though small sites remained common, some larger communities, with 50–100 pithouses, were established.

**floodwater farming** A method of farming that recovers floodwater and diverts it to selected fields to supplement the water supply.

**Figure 7.43** A small kiva with a central fire pit and masonry walls.

**Figure 7.44** A black-on-white Ancestral Pueblo pottery vessel. This pitcher, 17.4 cm high, is decorated with characteristic geometric designs and hatching.

**kiva** A semisubterranean ceremonial room found at sites throughout the American Southwest.

**pueblo** A stone-masonry complex of adjoining rooms found in the American Southwest.

**dendrochronology** The study of the annual growth rings of trees as a dating technique to build chronologies.

**Kivas,** semisubterranean ceremonial rooms, were constructed at some sites (Figure 7.43), and the distinctive black-on-white Ancestral Pueblo pottery first appeared (Figure 7.44).

Shabik'eshchee (shuh-BIK-eh-she) is an early village in the Chaco region. Occupied between A.D. 550 and 750, the settlement had as many as 68 pit dwellings, a large kiva, numerous outdoor storage pits, and two large refuse heaps. Nevertheless, it is not clear that all these features were occupied or used simultaneously.

At Shabik'eshchee, the sides of the pithouses were lined with stone slabs and coated with mud plaster. The roofs were supported by four posts topped with crossbeams. The upper walls of the houses were formed by leaning poles and sticks against the crossbeams to the ground surface outside the excavated pit. The walls were coated with a mixture of mud, twigs, and bark. One entered the house through a small antechamber. Inside the main chamber of the house was a centrally located hearth. The kiva was larger than the pithouses, and unlike the pithouses, the interior kiva walls were encircled by a low bench.

Sometime after A.D. 700, aboveground rectangular rooms of adobe or roughly layered masonry were constructed on the Colorado Plateau. At first these structures may have been used for storage, while pithouses continued to serve as dwellings. In later communities, pithouses were used largely as kivas, while most dwellings were of adobe bricks and placed aboveground. The Ancestral Pueblo were the first in the Southwest to build compact villages of contiguous rectangular rooms, with different areas for habitation, storage, and ceremonial activities. For the most part, these later communities were situated at lower elevations, closer to the bottomlands, perhaps reflecting an increasing reliance on agricultural resources.

After A.D. 850, there was a considerable shift in settlement patterns as population congregated in larger, apartmentlike **pueblos,** stone-masonry complexes of adjoining rooms. Clusters of adjacent rooms served as the residences for separate families or lineages. Chaco Canyon supported at least nine large towns, or "great houses," of several hundred rooms each, plus hundreds of smaller villages of 10–20 rooms each. The towns were large, multistory complexes, standing as high as four stories at the back wall, and averaging 288 rooms, some of which were large with high ceilings. The towns appear to have been built according to a preconceived plan, and there was a high degree of quality and uniformity in masonry styles. Each town also had at least one "great kiva." Placed in interior courtyards, these large kivas had a central ceremonial role in community activities. Many smaller kivas were located elsewhere in the towns and most likely served as ceremonial chambers for the various kin or family units that made up the site population. These larger sites served as local centers for resource redistribution, long-distance trade, and ceremonial activities.

The largest and most impressive town, Pueblo Bonito, covers more than 1 ha. It is a huge, D-shaped complex composed of over 600 rooms arranged in several stories (Figure 7.45). When Pueblo Bonito was at its height, as many as 500–1000 people may have resided there, although archaeologists disagree on the number of rooms that were residential in character and the proportion of the rooms that were occupied contemporaneously. Situated at the base of a 30-m (100-ft) mesa on the north side of the canyon, the pueblo is protected by the steep cliffs of the canyon.

The occupation of Pueblo Bonito has been precisely dated using **dendrochronology,** the study of the annual growth rings of trees as a dating technique to build chronologies (Figure 7.46). This highly precise technique, pioneered by A. E. Douglass more than 60 years ago, is based on the recognition that certain trees produced distinctive ring sequences in response to shifts in temperature and precipitation. Based on the work of Douglass and his successors, a continuous tree-ring chronology for the Colorado Plateau has been projected back more

Figure 7.45 Pueblo Bonito. The circular features are kivas. Interior rooms were used for storage, and outer rooms facing the courtyards served as living quarters.

than a thousand years. Tree-ring dates obtained from preserved wooden beams at Chaco Canyon place the earliest building at Pueblo Bonito at A.D. 861; town construction apparently was finished by A.D. 1115.

At Pueblo Bonito, the masonry consisted of layers of stone covering an interior core of rock and adobe rubble. The room walls were faced with adobe plaster. The rooms surrounded central courtyards. The outer rooms, which had doors and windows facing onto the courtyard, served as living quarters, and interior rooms were used for storage. The most elevated rooms were at the back of the complex along its outer rim. These back rooms included one great kiva and several smaller ones. This great kiva, the largest in the community, measured 20 m (65 ft) in diameter and was encircled by a wide masonry bench.

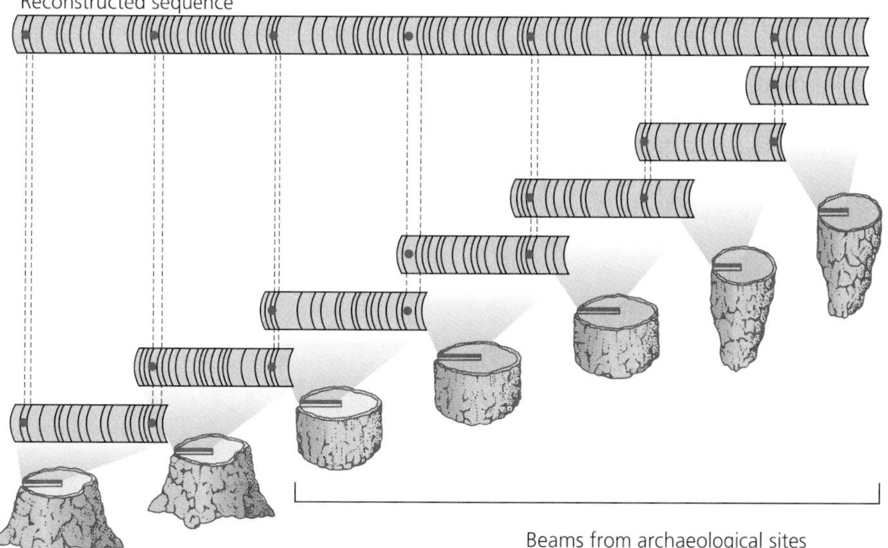


Figure 7.46 Dendrochronology. The matching of tree rings from a modern tree with a known cutting date to those of progressively older tree samples results in a long sequence of distinctive tree-ring patterns that can be used to date beams from archaeological sites.

*The many questions that remain unanswered about the Chacoan regional system signify both the accomplishments and the challenges of Southwestern archaeologists interested in the problem of sociopolitical development. After nearly a century of survey and excavation throughout Chaco Canyon and the San Juan Basin, investigators have . . . conclude[d] that the Chacoan regional system was hierarchically organized. This conclusion has prompted three major questions . . . : How did this complex system develop? What kinds of relationships existed among its different components . . . ? Why did the system collapse?*

—Jill Neitzel (1989)

From A.D. 1020 to 1100, the Chacoan system peaked in population and spatial size. Much of the population of the northern Southwest participated in the regional trading network centered at Chaco Canyon. Throughout this network, which covered at least 53,000 sq km (20,500 sq mi), there were at least 125 planned towns with distinctive Chacoan architecture. Settlements were linked by a complex of roads radiating from the canyon, built in straight lines, not contoured to the topography, with ramps and stairways ascending the cliffs. Some were lined with masonry curbs, and some were up to 9 m (30 ft) wide, leading to sites up to 190 km (120 mi) away.

Chacoan towns evidently had the capability of mobilizing large labor parties for construction. Timber was cut from forests up to 90 km (56 mi) away. Imported turquoise was worked in Chaco Canyon; some scholars have suggested it functioned as a medium of exchange. Such exotic goods as **jet,** turquoise, shell bracelets, iron pyrite mosaics, conch shell trumpets, ornamental copper bells, and **macaw** feathers are found more frequently at the large central town sites than at smaller villages. Social differentiation and some form of hierarchical leadership appear to have been in place, although the systems do not seem to have focused on special individuals. The nature of Chaco's political formations remains a matter of stimulating archaeological discussion despite the many years of productive multidisciplinary research conducted in the canyon and surrounding area.

The Chaco regional system was disrupted in the early 1100s. The population declined, although complete abandonment of the canyon did not occur for almost 200 years. The demographic collapse in the canyon coincided with population increases in other parts of the Colorado Plateau, including surrounding upland regions. In some areas, villages shifted to well-protected, defensive locations, such as the sheltered cliffs at Mesa Verde in southwestern Colorado. Defense was a likely motive in the resettlement of some Ancestral Pueblo villages, and this pattern may reflect an era of political instability that followed the collapse of the Chacoan centers.

In roughly A.D. 1300, the Colorado Plateau region went through another major restructuring, and many Pueblo sites were again abandoned. When Europeans arrived in the Southwest, only a small number of large Ancestral Pueblo settlements remained. Whether these episodes of dispersal and reorganization (first at Chaco and later in other parts of the Ancestral Pueblo region) were triggered by climate change, environmental degradation, shifting trade connections, changing political alliances, or other factors remains a matter of conjecture and discussion. Although the causes of these abandonments are still debated, the construction and maintenance of Pueblo Bonito, a structure that was the largest apartment building erected in the United States before the nineteenth century, in a dry, desolate canyon, remains a powerful testament to the ingenuity of the Native Americans who lived there.

**jet** A compact, black coal that can be highly polished; used to make beads, jewelry, and other decorative objects.

**macaw** Any of several varieties of parrots from Mexico and Central and South America that were prized for their colorful feathers.

# Ozette

*A prehistoric Northwest Coast whaling village*

The Pacific Coast of Oregon, Washington, and British Columbia is an environmentally rich area where land and sea hold a wealth of natural resources. The sea and the rivers contain mollusks and many species of fish, including salmon, halibut, cod, and herring. Sea mammals—such as seal, sea lion, otter, porpoise, and whale—thrive in the offshore waters. Waterfowl can be found along the shore, and farther inland there are deer, elk, bear, and smaller animals. The area has a heavy forest cover of fir, spruce, cedar, and some deciduous trees. Although vegetable foods are less plentiful, many species of berries abound.

The earliest known inhabitants of the Pacific Northwest were mobile hunter-gatherers who moved into the area before 8000 B.C. At first, coastal foods did not constitute a major portion of the diet, but by 2000–3000 B.C., the accumulation of large shell middens at several sites indicates an increasing use of the readily available marine shellfish. Over the past 2000 years, subsistence patterns have continued to emphasize the exploitation of fish, shellfish, and sea mammals, supplemented by land mammals and birds. Such plant foods as berries, roots, and bulbs were not staples, but they were available during lean times of the year.

In later prehistory, the peoples of the Pacific Northwest were specialized hunter-gatherers who lived in permanent villages and developed large food surpluses by exploiting a variety of fish species. Although subsistence was based on wild resources, many of these societies had specialists in hunting, fishing, curing, and toolmaking. Large, permanent settlements of several hundred people appeared by A.D. 1000, despite the absence of agriculture. The abundance of giant cedar trees provided plentiful material for building houses and making dugout canoes. The natural wealth of the environment and the range of available foods allowed for the production of surplus goods and ornate material items, such as decorative wood carvings, including **totem poles,** carved boxes, canoes, and masks, as well as cedar bark baskets and textiles. Canoes made long-distance travel possible, facilitating the gathering of seasonal resources, the hunting of sea mammals, and the maintenance of far-reaching social networks.

Social ranking appeared on the Northwest Coast by 500 B.C. At the time of European contact, all individuals in some Pacific Coast societies were ranked into a series of relatively higher and lower statuses, according to both heredity and wealth. There were chiefs and slaves and, in between, craftspeople, hunters, and fisherfolk. Most respected of all were the whale hunters. Whaling could be undertaken only by

**Figure 7.47** Ozette Village, located on the outer coast of the Olympic Peninsula. Excavations of the village were situated near the beach on the left side of this photograph.

**totem pole** A pole or post that has been carved and painted with totems or figures, such as animals, that serve as the emblems of clans or families.

**Figure 7.48** A carved wooden box from Ozette. The wet conditions at the site preserved objects of wood and fiber that usually do not preserve well in archaeological contexts.

men from wealthy families; it was a hereditary right. Only chiefs possessed the necessary wealth to build whaling canoes, to outfit them, and to assemble the crew. Hunting whales in these large, oceangoing canoes was very dangerous. Bringing home one whale brought enormous prestige to a family, in addition to vast amounts of food.

One well-known Pacific Northwest settlement, Ozette (oh-ZEHT), is located on the coast of Washington's Olympic Peninsula at Cape Alava, the westernmost point of the contiguous 48 states (Figure 7.47). Because the cape juts out into the Pacific Ocean, Ozette is close to the migration routes of a variety of whales, including gray, humpback, and sperm whales. The shoreline is a crescent-shaped beach protected by points of land, an offshore reef, and small islands. Abundant sea resources and a rich forest behind the beach made the cape an attractive location for prehistoric Native American groups. People settled in the area over 2000 years ago, and eventually Ozette grew into a major whaling village. Ozette is unique in that it was one of a few major whaling villages south of Alaska. Two other sites, south of Ozette on the coast, are located near quiet bays. Their long, straight beaches are washed by a rolling surf, making canoe travel much more difficult than at Ozette. In addition, sea mammals pass too far offshore to be worth hunting. As a consequence, those two sites show less reliance on ocean resources. Rather, the inhabitants focused on the land and bay resources, such as deer, elk, harbor seals, and salmon, in addition to oysters, mussels, and clams.

The village of Ozette stretched for almost a mile along the coast and had a maximum population of roughly 800 people. It is thought to have been a major settlement of the Makah Indians, a group that still resides on the Olympic Peninsula today. Although the population of Ozette declined after Europeans began to settle in the area during the mid-nineteenth century, it continued to be occupied until the late 1920s. Today, there are few surface remnants of the village left. Richard Daugherty, formerly of Washington State University, began excavations at the site in the late 1960s when told of native accounts of mudslides that were believed to have periodically buried parts of the site. However, the actual discovery of the buried village area occurred accidentally after a violent winter storm in 1970. The harsh waves of the storm eroded sections of a bank and exposed a number of timbers, baskets, boxes, paddles, and other wooden artifacts, which were discovered by hikers. That spring, Daugherty began excavation of the buried houses.

Part of Ozette has been preserved by a massive mudslide that buried five houses around A.D. 1500. Because the heavy layer of clay sealed the houses and kept out oxygen, perishable artifacts of wood and fiber, which normally do not preserve well in the wet environment of the Northwest Coast, could be recovered (Figure 7.48). Since the village was occupied at the time of the mudslide, the excavated material

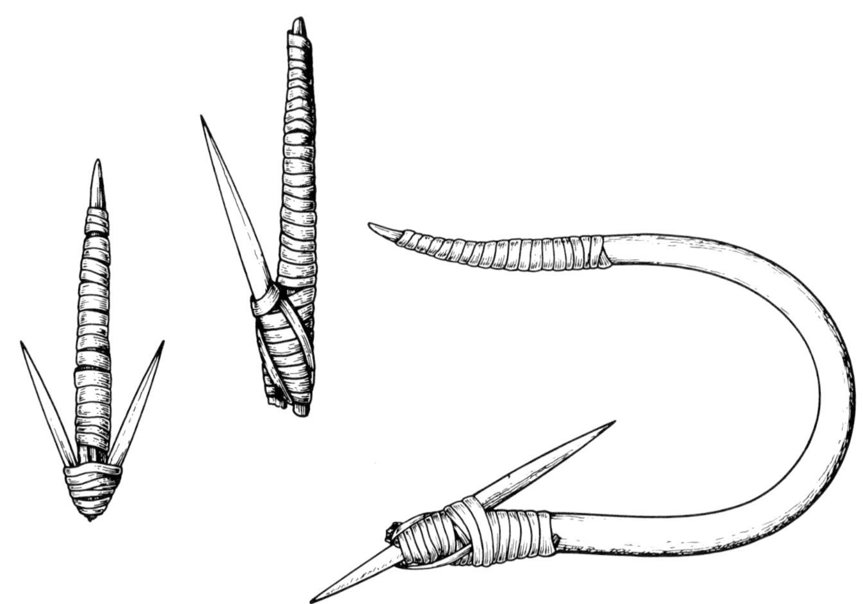

Figure 7.49 Examples of fishhooks made from bone and wrapped with bark. The abundance of fishhooks and points recovered during excavations at Ozette is an indication of the importance of marine resources to the site's inhabitants.

represents the entire range of wooden artifacts that were used by a Northwest Coast household. In addition to the wooden planks and posts of the houses, the excavators recovered baskets, mats, hats, **tumplines**, halibut hook shanks, arrow shafts, harpoons, finely carved wooden clubs and combs, box fragments, bowls, wood wedges, and a variety of fishhooks and barbed fish points (used on the end of a spear to stab fish in the water) (Figure 7.49). To date, over 60,000 artifacts have been recovered.

As a result of the region's abundant rainfall and high groundwater, Ozette is water-saturated, like many other sites on the Northwest Coast. This condition has made normal excavation procedures difficult. When trowels and shovels were used, as they are on most excavations, they sliced through and gouged the fragile wood and fiber. To deal with this problem, a method called **wet-site excavation** was developed. With this technique, water is pumped through garden hoses and sprayed onto the deposits to remove the dirt and expose the archaeological materials. Excavators use high water pressure to remove the heavy clay deposits and low pressure to remove dirt from more fragile artifacts. This procedure works well because the water pressure can be adjusted continually to expose an artifact without dislocating or destroying it. By using a very fine spray, excavators can carefully reveal and remove even the remains of basketry and other fibers (Figure 7.50).

The excavated houses at Ozette were very large, some 20 m (60 ft) long and 10 m (33 ft) wide, about the size of a tennis court. They were constructed of cedar planks, some up to 0.5 m (1.5 ft) wide, supported by upright wooden posts, and held in place with twisted cedar twigs (Figure 7.51). Roof boards were overlapped to keep out the rain. Raised platforms ringed the inside walls and were used for sleeping and storage. Most of the recovered artifacts were found in association with these platforms. The existence of several hearths in each house suggests that these large structures were occupied by more than one nuclear family. In one house, the highest-ranking family apparently lived in the left-rear quarter; ceremonial gear and whaling harpoons were found there. In this area, a woven cedar bark hat, traditionally worn by individuals of high status in later times, also was recovered. In another house, wood chips associated with woodworking activities were found.

Excavations at Ozette have provided ample evidence for the extensive hunting of sea mammals. Whale bones were found in the earliest levels, indicating that the prestige and

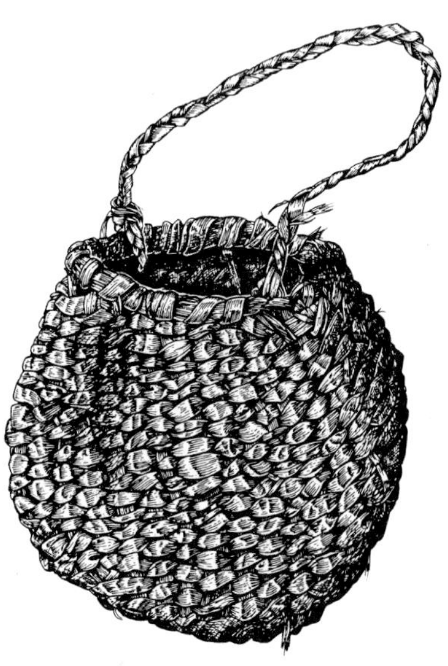

Figure 7.50 A basket woven of cedar bark. Cedar bark was used to make a range of baskets for collecting and storing food, textiles including blankets and conical rain hats, and sleeping mats.

**tumpline** A strap that is passed over the forehead or the chest to facilitate the transportation of a heavy load carried on the back.

**wet-site excavation** The technique of excavating waterlogged sites by pumping water through garden hoses to spray the dirt away and expose archaeological features and artifacts.

Figure 7.54 A carved, wooden potlatch mask from the nineteenth-century Northwest Coast.

The emergence of institutionalized social inequality was a fundamental human transition that apparently occurred relatively independently in many different places. Can you think of some reasons why? How did this important organizational change occur? How can different ideas about this transition be evaluated?

**potlatch** A large feast among Northwest Coast Native Americans that included the display and dispersal of accumulated wealth to the assembled guests.

grave offerings indicate the presence of powerful chiefs at these sites.

Chiefs also were present in some societies that did not practice agriculture. Most societies on the Northwest Coast were based on hunting and gathering. Their economies focused on a rich and diverse base of marine resources, which permitted the accumulation of surplus. These societies also had hierarchies of social rank. Only people from the highest-ranking families could become leaders.

Chiefs did not necessarily return all the produce they collected. This surplus often provided the resources to obtain exotic goods through trade. Much chiefly exchange involved the acquisition of high-status items that were either traded to establish new allies or loaned to attract followers. Often a chief's power was measured by the number of allies and dependents that could be mobilized for specific tasks.

Although chiefly positions were generally acquired through familial ties, personal achievements also were important. Among Northwest Coast Native American groups, only high-ranking individuals could attain the position of chief. But one's role as chief had to be validated continually; failure to do so resulted in a loss of status. One way chiefs validated their position was by publicly displaying their wealth and distributing their accumulated property. At the time of European contact in the Northwest, an elaborate ceremonialism had developed, based on the **potlatch,** a large feast that included the display and dispersal of accumulated wealth to assembled guests (Figure 7.54). The mere possession of wealth did not confer prestige. But by distributing the wealth, the chief created social debts and obligations that could be called in and used to bolster his position at a later date. A potlatch gave the host far greater prestige than selling or trading, but in economic terms, the result was relatively similar: the redistribution of goods. Politically, the quest for prestige gave momentum to the whole system; the more a chief gave away, the greater his status.

To date, most archaeological interpretations have emphasized the functional or managerial advantages, especially the mitigation of food crises, associated with the emergence of chiefs. Yet such arguments are incomplete; in many cases, the likelihood of major crop failures requiring chiefly intervention was low. The construction of complete explanations requires that archaeologists extend consideration beyond the benefits of chiefly societies to the political strategies of emergent leaders and the factors that allowed those strategies to work for the benefit of few at the expense of many.

# Images and Ideas

## The Clash of Worlds

### *Changing perspectives on native North Americans*

When European settlers and slaves from Africa first penetrated the Americas north of Mexico in the sixteenth, seventeenth, and eighteenth centuries, they observed huge earthen mounds at sites in the East that were no longer inhabited, as well as well-planned mud-brick ruins in the West. Blinded by the **ethnocentrism** of the era, many of the early explorers failed to recognize any of the obvious historical connections between the land's indigenous peoples and the impressive architectural features. Frequently, the Euro-American traders and adventurers speculated that the great earthworks and pueblos were remnants of earlier constructions built by Romans, Vikings, Celts, or people from imaginary lands, such as Atlantis. Few early explorers were willing to accept the possibility that the ruins were part of the heritage of Native American peoples, whose lands and resources they coveted. Sadly, such migrationist views are still all-too-frequently advanced (and may even attract occasional popular attention today), although they remain entirely without solid empirical support. (Some authors have gone so far as to postulate extraterrestrial contacts!) Fortunately, there were exceptions, such as Thomas Jefferson.

In the nineteenth century, a principal focus of early North American anthropology was the Native American, in the past as well as in the present. Information was collected from archaeological evidence, early historical accounts, and contemporary observations. Continuities in language, ritual, and material culture were emphasized in an effort to confirm the historical relationships between living indigenous peoples, past documentary records that described the aboriginal inhabitants of North America, and artifact inventories. Although many of the associations between present and past were reasoned and justified (laying the foundation for twentieth-century archaeology and anthropology), the absence of an adequate time scale (no absolute dating techniques were yet invented) contributed to the occasional overreliance on contemporary or historical records to interpret the archaeological past. Archaeology depends on inspirations, clues, analogies, and models from more recent times to help flesh out the past. Yet archaeologists studying the prehistory of North America, as well as other areas, should be prepared to recognize changes that occurred during prehistory and immediately thereafter. Prehistoric peoples may have had a way of life and organizational formations that were markedly different from those recorded in written texts.

Many studies have documented that the contact period, the sixteenth through eighteenth centuries, was a time of great change for most, if not all, native North American groups. In many areas, such as the Southeast, Native Americans not only were savaged in combat with the European invaders (such as the nine shiploads of *conquistadores,* led by Hernando de Soto, who landed on the coast of Florida in 1539) but also were vanquished by infectious, epidemic diseases (influenza, smallpox, measles, and whooping cough) introduced to the Americas. Because the aboriginal peoples had no immunity to these diseases, their effect often was calamitous, decimating the native populations. In many regions, the impact of disease may have been further intensified by social and economic dislocations occurring at the same time. Regardless of the specific causes, many Native American populations had been severely ravaged and disrupted in demographic size, subsistence, and sociopolitical organization when they first were encountered by more permanent settlers (and eventually anthropologists) during the seventeenth, eighteenth, and nineteenth centuries. As a consequence, anthropologists and

**ethnocentrism** Evaluating other groups or societies by standards that are relevant to the observer's culture.

archaeologists must be careful about relying too specifically on direct analogies between ethnohistoric, as well as early ethnographic, accounts and the deeper past that we see through archaeology. Nevertheless, many aspects of tradition, belief, and religion do show significant continuities between precontact and post-contact times.

*The history of European colonial expansion following the late 15th century is riddled with a multitude of curious and seemingly inexplicable encounters between native cultures and Europeans, which demand the conjoining of historical and anthropological methods.*
—Jeffrey L. Hantman (1990)

When the Europeans first arrived in North America, few, if any, sites as large as Cahokia in the Midwest or the pueblos of Chaco Canyon in the Southwest appear to have been inhabited, or were described. Yet this fact should not lead us to doubt the Native American heritage of these sites or force us to inhibit our interpretation of the past by assuming that the archaeological settlements were organized in exactly the same way as those of the ethnographically observed inhabitants of the respective regions.

Such variation should not be surprising, since diversity in both space and time seems to have been a key feature of the Native American way of life. In part, spatial variation may have been related to the great environmental differences that characterize the North American continent. At times, cultural changes may have been responses to documented episodes of climatic transitions. Yet such environmental factors alone cannot explain the range of prehistoric variability. Perhaps the smaller and less stratified social systems that occupied North America were generally more flexible and organizationally (and demographically) fluid than the more complex, hierarchical polities that developed in much of Middle and South America (see Chapters 8 and 9), as well as in a good portion of the Eastern Hemisphere (see Chapter 10). Such flexibility and fluidity also may help account for the great cultural diversity of the prehistoric North American peoples.

Although there still are gaps in our knowledge, anthropological archaeology has established that Native Americans inhabited vast tracts of North America for at least 12,000 years. It is clear that they adjusted to and modified the highly diverse environments of North America through a broad range of technological, social, and cultural behaviors and strategies. Archaeologists have documented that native lifeways changed over time, often gradually, but sometimes much more rapidly.

*The disadvantage of men not knowing the past is that they do not know the present. History is a hill or a high point of vantage, from which alone men see the town in which they live or the age in which they are living.*
—Gilbert K. Chesterton (1933)

In this chapter, we have reviewed key settlements, cultures, and lifeways of the native peoples who inhabited North America before the influx of peoples from the Eastern Hemisphere, or "Old World," during the latter half of the second millennium A.D. This chapter's discussions have drawn on more than a century of archaeological study, in conjunction with investigations in related fields. This research has illustrated how native North Americans thrived in locales as diverse as the deserts of southern Arizona, the woodlands of eastern North America, and the coast of the Pacific Northwest.

Our review also has highlighted how the prehistoric peoples of North America established a diverse array of hierarchical social formations. Some of these had clear hereditary chiefs, but others appear to have had forms of social differentiation that focused less on individual leaders or special personages (such as at Chaco Canyon during much of its history). Interestingly, although many kinds of hierarchical leadership developed in North America, the kinds of writing systems, institutionalized bureaucracies, and large urban centers that arose in many other regions had not materialized in this cultural region before 1492.

Nevertheless, similar to what archaeological findings have shown for humans around the globe, the behaviors and lifeways of native North Americans were far from entirely stable or unchanging. Both enduring traditions and significant transitions were key aspects of their long-term history even before the tragic disruptions that followed European contact. For this reason, it is important to recognize that archaeological data have a significant role to play in liberating and amplifying Native American history from an exclusive reliance on documentary sources, which are primarily products of Euro-American culture and pertain directly only to the end of the precontact era.

## DISCUSSION QUESTIONS

www.mhhe.com/priceip6e

For more review material and study questions, see the self-quizzes on your online learning center.

1. What are the major differences between reciprocity and redistribution? How might you distinguish these exchange practices archaeologically?
2. What other systems of exchange can you think of?
3. How can burial behavior be informative about the nature of social/economic organization in the past?
4. What are the major similarities or differences in the nature of settlement layout between the eastern Woodlands and the North American Southwest?
5. What do you think these similarities or differences can tell us about past social, political, and/or economic organization?
6. What is the nature of the relationship between chiefly organization, surplus production, and subsistence?
7. Why did Eurasian diseases have such a calamitous effect on indigenous Americans?

## SUGGESTED READINGS

For Internet links related to this chapter, please visit our Web site at www.mhhe.com/priceip6e.

Cordell, L. S. 1997. *Archaeology of the Southwest,* 2d ed. San Diego: Academic Press. *The best current synthesis of archaeology in the American Southwest.*

Crown, P. L., and W. J. Judge, eds. 1991. *Chaco and Hohokam: Prehistoric regional systems in the American Southwest.* Santa Fe, NM: School of American Research. *A scholarly compendium of papers that compare and contrast regional variation in southwestern prehistory.*

Fagan, B. 2005. *Ancient North America,* 4th ed. London: Thames & Hudson. *An amply illustrated synthesis of North American archaeology.*

Feder, K. L. 2001. *Frauds, myths, and mysteries: Science and pseudoscience in archaeology,* 4th ed. New York: McGraw-Hill. *An entertaining and informative exploration of fascinating frauds and genuine mysteries that relate to the human past.*

Gibbon, G., ed. 1998. *Archaeology of prehistoric Native America: An encyclopedia.* New York: Garland. *A comprehensive compendium of short essays concerning key topics and sites in North American archaeology.*

Neitzel, J. E., ed. 1999. *Great towns and regional polities in the prehistoric American Southwest and Southeast.* Albuquerque: University of New Mexico Press. *A series of scholarly essays that compare pre–European contact social formations in the North American Southwest and Southeast.*

# CHAPTER EIGHT

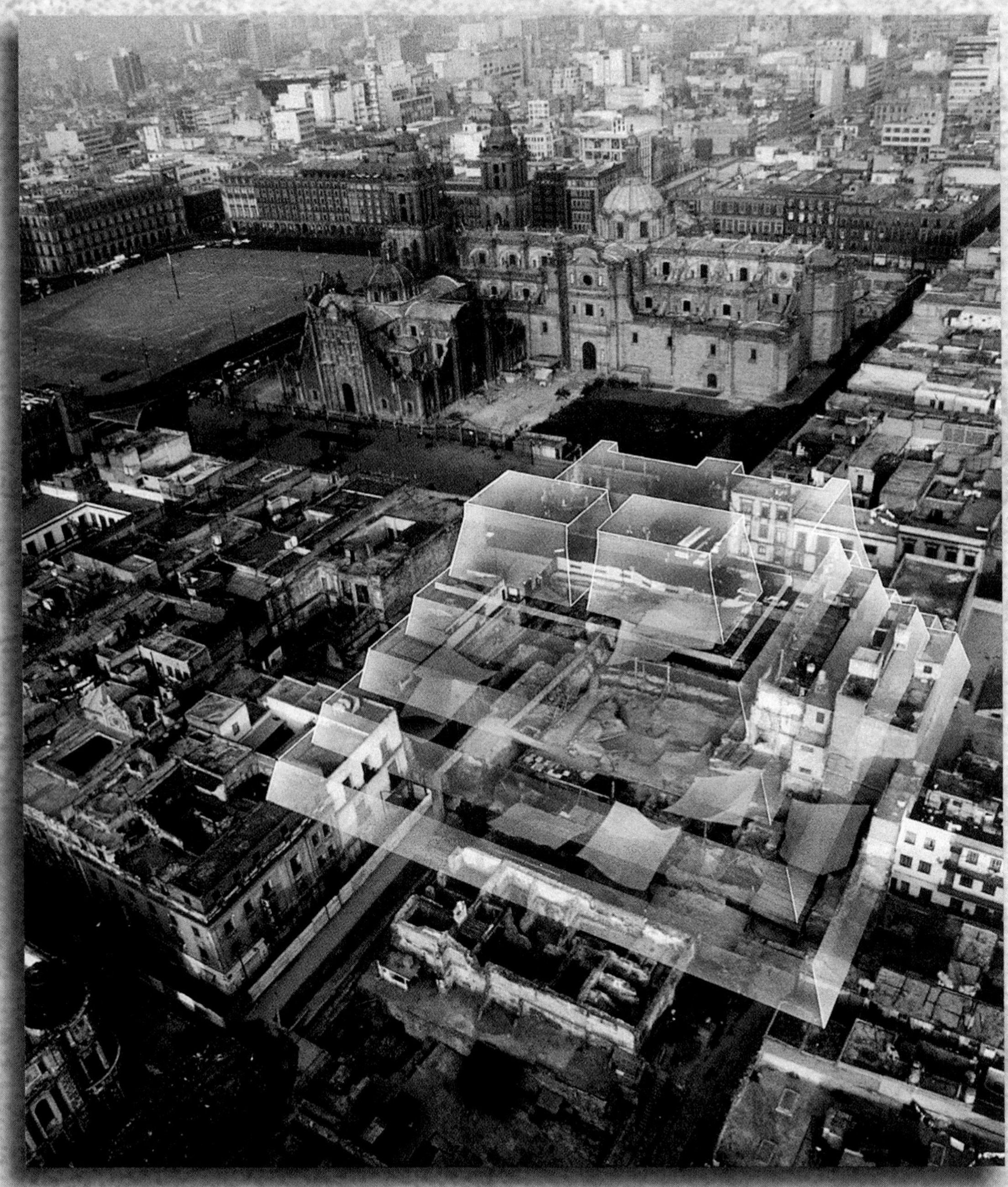

**Figure 8.1** Reconstruction of the Aztec Templo Mayor superimposed on the modern buildings in Mexico City that were constructed on top of the ruins of the razed temple.

# Ancient Mesoamerica

## *Introduction*

## Early State Development in Mesoamerica

*The Aztecs, the Maya, and their neighbors*

In the same year, 1492, that Christopher Columbus landed in the Caribbean, a boy is believed to have been born in a Spanish village, Medina del Campo, Castile. Decades later, that boy, Bernal Díaz, then a young man, traveled to Mexico in the company of Hernán Cortés, and later in life he recorded his memories. Díaz's written texts provide a gripping firsthand account of the clash of two great powers, sixteenth-century Spain and the Aztecs of central Mexico, a confrontation that led to the construction of the churches and government buildings of the conquering Spanish immediately on top of the ruins of the earlier Aztec temples and palaces (Figure 8.1).

Díaz's recollections of entering the Aztec island capital, Tenochtitlán, are particularly poignant:

> *(W)hen we saw so many cities and villages built in the water and other great towns on dry land and that straight and level causeway going towards Mexico, we were amazed and said that it was like the enchantments they tell of in (legend), on account of the great towers and cues and buildings rising from the water, and all built of masonry. (1956:190)*

Later, Bernal Díaz wrote of the great market in Tenochtitlán's sister city, Tlatelolco:

> *(W)e turned to look at the great market place and the crowds of people that were in it, some buying and others selling, so that the murmur and hum of their voices and words that they used could be heard more than a league [three miles] off. Some of the soldiers among us who had been in many parts of the world, in Constantinople, and all over Italy, and in Rome, said that so large a market place and so full of people, and so well regulated and arranged, they had never held before. (1956:218–219)*

These descriptions make it clear that the settlement patterns and economic organization of the late prehispanic Aztecs were rather different from any of the social formations that emerged north of Mexico before the arrival of Europeans. The Aztecs were a **state,** and through conquests of neighboring peoples and polities (some of whom were ethnically and linguistically very different), they had begun to establish an **empire.**

Archaeologists and other social scientists define a state as an internally specialized and hierarchically organized political formation that administers large

CHAPTER OUTLINE

www.mhhe.com/priceip6e

For preview material for this chapter, see the comprehensive chapter outline and chapter objectives on your online learning center.

and complex polities. States are associated with populations that are socially and economically stratified. In these societies, wealth, social status, and political power generally are inherited, whereas in unstratified societies, such advantages are most often achieved through personal skills and experience. Although some archaeologists have suggested that Cahokia, in the midwestern United States, was at the center of a short-lived state organization (see Chapter 7), most researchers argue that state formation in the Western Hemisphere did not occur north of Mexico before European contact.

Indigenous or pristine states—institutions that developed relatively free of significant external contact or outside influence—arose in Mesoamerica, South America, Southwest Asia, and China. The rise of these early polities, and several cases of secondary and tertiary state development, are presented in this chapter, as well as in Chapters 9 and 10. In this chapter (Mesoamerica) and Chapter 9 (South America), we take a more historical approach in surveying the complex processes surrounding the rise of civilizations in two areas of the Western Hemisphere. Although comparisons are made throughout, we adopt a more deliberately comparative perspective in Chapter 10, where we discuss early civilizations from several continents in the Eastern Hemisphere. Chapter 10 concludes with a discussion of some of the theories that have been advanced to explain state origins.

The first indigenous states were established in Southwest Asia during the fourth millennium B.C. For that reason, some of you may wish to review Chapter 10 before reading Chapters 8 and 9. Because so many of the theories about state origins were constructed with Southwest Asian cases in mind, we think it is helpful to consider these different explanations in Chapter 10 in conjunction with the examples from the Eastern Hemisphere. We also want to discuss these theoretical positions after we have considered the variability of early states. For that reason, we begin our discussion with Mesoamerica, drawing comparisons between the highland polities (such as Teotihuacan) and those of the Maya Lowlands. We then move to Andean South America in Chapter 9, where we consider some of the similarities and differences between the prehispanic Andean and Mesoamerican worlds. In Chapter 10, we offer a more global, synthetic perspective.

When Cortés and his Spanish *conquistadores* landed on the eastern coast of Mexico in A.D. 1519, they encountered a remarkably diverse landscape of cultures and environments. The terrain is a complex vertical mosaic of snow-capped volcanic peaks and arid highland valleys, lush tropical forests, "scrubby" plains, swampy lowlands and **estuaries,** and beautiful sand beaches. The climate ranges from the arctic cold of high mountain summits to the sweltering heat at sea level, and climatic and topographic variability results in a rich mosaic of animal and plant life. Before the 1519 arrival of the Spanish, Mesoamerica—which includes central and southern Mexico, the Yucatán peninsula, and the northern parts of Central America—was also a world of enormous linguistic and ethnic differences. The prehispanic inhabitants spoke many languages, employed a wide range of farming and water-control strategies, and inhabited towns and cities of diverse form and function.

Yet the peoples of Mesoamerica also shared a great deal, including a reliance on similar staple foods, widespread trade, and related religious systems. This shared ceremonial realm included a calendar, stepped pyramids, ritual sacrifice of blood, writing systems, and specific styles of dress. The dietary "trinity" of corn, beans, and squash (supplemented by avocados and chili peppers) provided a remarkably nutritious diet. Maize (corn) provides most of the essential amino acids for building protein; lysine, a missing ingredient, is present in beans. An enzyme in squash contributes to the digestion of the protein in beans. Maize extracts nitrogen from the earth in which it grows; beans release nitrogen back to the soil. Corn and squash are rich in carbohydrates and calories. Beans and the

**state** A form of government with an internally specialized and hierarchically organized decision-making apparatus. A state generally has three or more administrative levels.

**empire** A union of dispersed territories, colonies, states, and unrelated peoples under one sovereign rule.

**estuary** A low area along a coast where the wide mouth of a river meets the sea and the waters of the two mix.

avocado provide fat. The chili pepper, a regular condiment in Mesoamerican meals, is high in vitamins and aids in the digestion of high-cellulose foods.

As discussed in Chapter 6, corn, beans, and squash were domesticated by 6000–10,000 years ago in the highlands of Mexico, where the wild ancestors of these plants still grow side by side. These domesticated plants spread throughout Mesoamerica by 2000 B.C. At about that same time, perhaps a few centuries earlier, people began to make simple pottery in the shape of squashes and gourds. Yet it was not for centuries (roughly 1800–1500 B.C.) that we find the first permanent farming villages in this region. This pattern differs from what we saw in parts of North America (see Chapter 7), where some residential stability was present before reliance on domesticated plants. The sequence of development in highland Mesoamerica appears to be the domestication of plants, followed by the invention of ceramics, and then the emergence of village society. Once the indigenous peoples of Mesoamerica had adopted a sedentary farming lifeway, the advent of the region's earliest cities and states followed after roughly 1000 years. The Spanish conquest 2000 years later effectively terminated the indigenous rule of native Mesoamerican civilizations.

Information about those civilizations and their predecessors comes from a number of sources, including Spanish accounts, prehispanic texts, archaeology, and **ethnography.** The Spanish conquerors and priests kept diaries and descriptions of their impressions of this new world, which often incorporated the remembrances of indigenous confidants as well. These ethnohistoric sources provide an invaluable record of ancient Mesoamerican customs, beliefs, and individual histories at the time of European contact. However, they also provide an incomplete and often ethnocentric picture of the prehispanic past.

Scholars also derive information from the texts of the prehispanic peoples themselves. These records include both short accounts, written more than a millennium ago on stones, murals, and pottery, and a few later (and generally longer) books, or **codices.** The surviving codices date principally to the end of the prehispanic era. The religious zeal of the Spanish resulted in the destruction of much that was native, including the burning of many books, the razing of temples and palaces, and the destruction of the priesthood. Decipherment of the surviving written accounts, particularly those of the ancient Maya, has greatly enhanced our understanding of rituals, militarism, and rule in prehispanic Mesoamerican civilizations. The native texts are limited in scope and geographic coverage, however, and they reflect a bias toward the events in the lives of the literate elite and rulers.

Ethnographic studies of contemporary peoples in modern Mesoamerica provide information about the organization of agricultural systems and the survival of certain prehispanic customs. Nevertheless, the Spanish presence in Latin America effectively eliminated much of what was native through law, education, and religious doctrine.

Despite these historical and modern sources of information, archaeological research is essential for a basic understanding of the emergence of Mesoamerican cities and civilizations. More than a century of investigations in Mesoamerica has yielded significant findings. Major tomb and temple excavations have been conducted in lowland regions of Mesoamerica, where ancient Maya ruins sat virtually undisturbed from the time of their abandonment around A.D. 900 until their rediscovery in the nineteenth century. More recent studies have analyzed villages and their component houses (**household archaeology**) and the hinterlands of ancient cities, rather than exclusively temples and tombs, to understand the organization and operation of everyday life. In Mexico's Central and Southern Highlands, where archaeological preservation is generally good and ancient ruins are often visible on the present land surface, long-term, multistage archaeological excavation and settlement pattern survey programs have been implemented.

**ethnography** The study of human cultures through firsthand observation.

**codex** (plural **codices**) (Latin) A hand-painted book on bark paper or animal skins folded like a screen.

**household archaeology** The archaeological analysis of past houses and associated residential remains to learn about domestic life and activities.

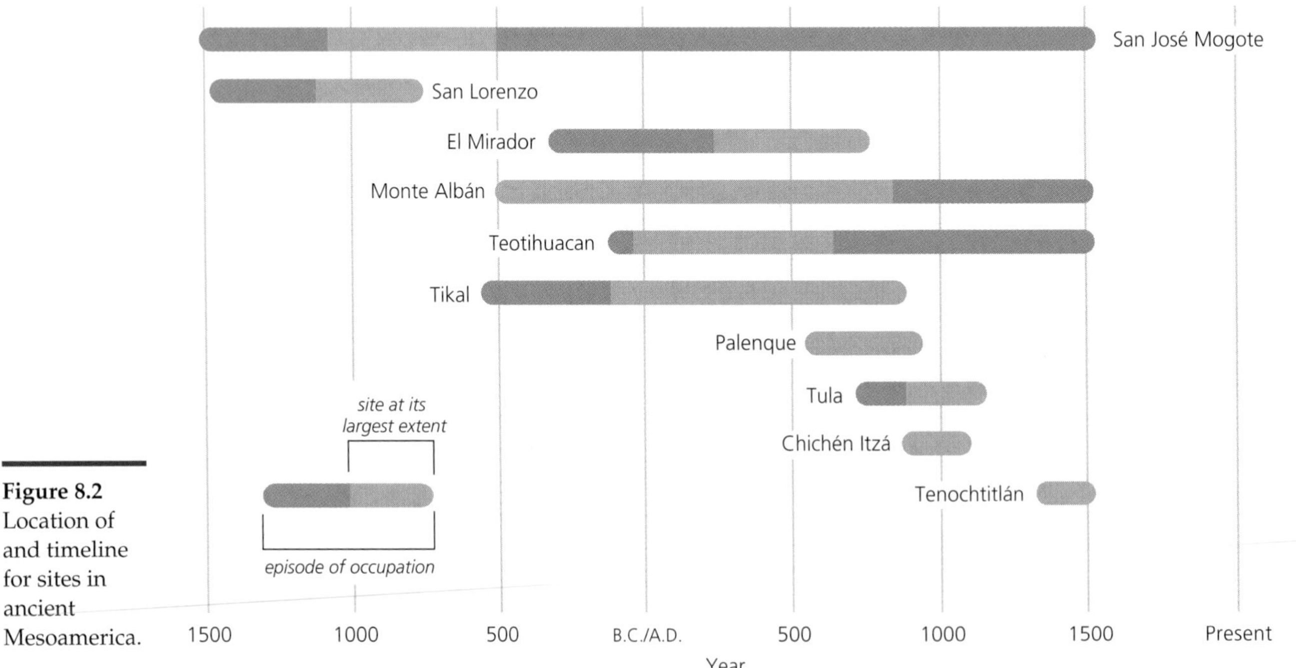
Gulf of Mexico
PACIFIC OCEAN
YUCATÁN
Chichén Itzá
Tulum
Calakmul
El Tajín
Tula
Tenochtitlán
Teotihuacan
Culcuilco
Tres Zapotes
Loma de la Coyotera
San José Mogote
Monte Albán
Gheo Shih
San Lorenzo
La Venta
Pomona
Tikal
El Mirador
Nakbe
Uaxactún
San Bartolo
San José
BELIZE
Caracol
Palenque
Yaxchilán
Siebal
GUATEMALA
Copán
HONDURAS
EL SALVADOR
NICARAGUA
Sites emphasized in text
Sites mentioned in text
Area of Mesoamerica
Modern international boundary
0
300 km
San José Mogote
San Lorenzo
El Mirador
Monte Albán
Teotihuacan
Tikal
Palenque
Tula
Chichén Itzá
Tenochtitlán
site at its largest extent
episode of occupation
1500
1000
500
B.C./A.D.
500
1000
1500
Present
Year

**Figure 8.2** Location of and timeline for sites in ancient Mesoamerica.

In Mesoamerica, the beginnings of sedentary village life mark the start of the Formative, or Preclassic, period. Studies at San José Mogote document this early stage of village living in highland Mesoamerica. The rapid transformation from simple village society to the construction of impressive ceremonial centers occurred precociously on Mexico's Gulf Coast. San Lorenzo is the earliest of these lowland centers and is roughly contemporaneous with Poverty Point in northeastern Louisiana (see Chapter 7). El Mirador is unusually large and spectacular for the Maya Lowlands, considering its early date.

Late in the Formative period, major urban centers were established in the highlands; hilltop Monte Albán in the Valley of Oaxaca and giant Teotihuacan in central Mexico illustrate this episode of development. By the beginning of the Classic period (ca. A.D. 200–300), Monte Albán and Teotihuacan grew significantly. The latter became one of the largest cities of the world at the time, even larger than Rome. Impressive centers, including Tikal and Palenque, also were built in the Maya Lowlands during the Classic era. Although the Classic Maya developed Mesoamerica's most sophisticated writing system, none of their centers equaled the population size of Teotihuacan.

Between A.D. 700 and 900, the Mesoamerican world underwent a sequence of upheavals and transitions that included the decline and depopulation of most extant centers. The succeeding Postclassic period was characterized by somewhat greater political fragmentation and fewer architecturally massive centers. Yet places like Tula, on Mesoamerica's northern frontier, and Chichén Itzá, in the northern Yucatán, did rise to power for several centuries. The greatest exception to this Postclassic pattern was Tenochtitlán, which during the last years before Spanish conquest became the largest city in the history of prehispanic Mesoamerica. Although the rulers of Tenochtitlán established a tributary domain that stretched as far as highland Guatemala, they were defeated by armies led by Cortés in less than 2 years.

In this chapter, our coverage emphasizes key large settlements that were the focal centers of prehispanic Mesoamerica (Figure 8.2). Yet it is crucial to understand that these centers often were linked through various mechanisms of exchange, interpersonal interaction, and shared systems of belief. Some of the longest-standing historical questions that remain for Mesoamericanist scholars to resolve concern the nature of the interactions between the Formative period Gulf Coast Olmec settlements and contemporaneous communities elsewhere in Mesoamerica and the kind of role that people from Teotihuacan, or influence from that central Mexican metropolis, may have had at Tikal and other Early Classic–period Maya centers. Another long-standing question concerns the nature and directionality of the connection between Tula and distant Chichén Itzá. Continued intellectual discoveries relating to these issues and others will only enhance the recognized richness of ancient Mesoamerican history.

Unlike most states in the Eastern Hemisphere, Mesoamerican civilizations rose and flourished without beasts of burden, wheeled transportation, or metal tools. Yet during the 30 centuries that elapsed between the establishment of village farming communities and the Spanish conquest, this prehispanic world was the scene of highly developed statecraft, major urban centers, magnificent artisanship, spectacular architecture, and large swamp and lakeshore reclamation projects. Mesoamerica thus provides a physically diverse and scientifically important natural laboratory for joining historical and archaeological methods to unravel and interpret societal continuity and change. Today the prehispanic history of Mesoamerica receives too little attention in the history books of Europe and most of North America. Through this research and associated discoveries, we hope to bring greater attention to this region and the great contributions it has made to humankind's heritage.

*Thus they have come to tell it,*
*thus they have come to record it in their narration,*
*and for us they have painted it in their codices,*
*the ancient men, the ancient women.*

*Thus in the future*
*never will it perish, never will it be forgotten,*
*always we will treasure it,*
*we, their children, their grandchildren,*
*brothers, great-grandchildren,*
*great-great-grandchildren, descendants,*
*we who carry their blood and their color,*
*we will tell it, we will pass it on*
*to those who do not yet live, who are yet to be born,*
*the children of the Mexicans, the children of the Tenochcans.*

—Fernando Alvarado Tezozomoc
(*Crónica Mexicáyotl*, 1609)

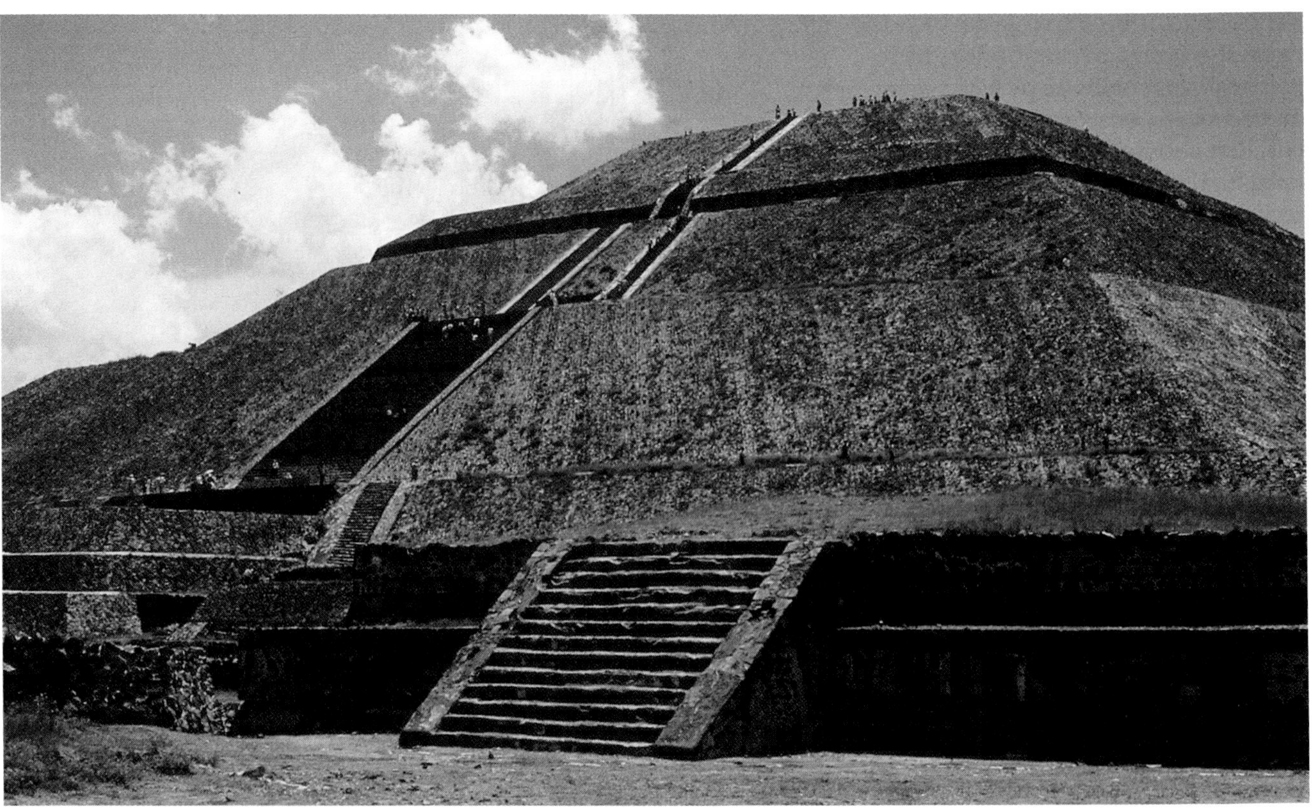

**Figure 8.32** The Pyramid of the Sun at Teotihuacan. The monumental pyramids at the site are among the largest structures ever built in the ancient Americas.

Some of the largest structures ever built in the ancient Americas were constructed at Teotihuacan. When and why are giant pyramids and monumental structures built?

The largest of the city's more than 5000 known structures, the Pyramid of the Sun and the Pyramid of the Moon dominate the surrounding landscape (Figures 8.32 and 8.33). The monumental Pyramid of the Sun was the largest structure ever built during a single construction episode in the ancient Americas. The structure stands 64 m (212 ft) high and measures roughly 213 m (700 ft) on a side. It contains 1 million cu m of fill (35 million cu ft), which was carried to the pyramid in basketloads. The cut-stone exteriors of these massive structures (as well as most other platforms at the site) are believed to have been faced with a thick, white plaster and painted red to enhance their visibility.

Hidden below the Pyramid of the Sun lies a cave. It runs 100 m (330 ft) from its mouth near the base of the pyramid stairway to a spot close to the center of the pyramid. The people of Teotihuacan must have used the cave, because ritual items were found within it, and in certain spots, the walls of the cave were reroofed. Caves were sacred in Mesoamerican religion, associated with the creation of the sun and the moon. Throughout Mesoamerica, important ritual activities were enacted in caves. Archaeologist Linda Manzanilla, of the National Autonomous University of Mexico (UNAM), has noted that the cave under the Pyramid of the Sun was just one of many at the site, and she has suggested that these tunnels and caverns were the source of virtually all the volcanic stone used to build Teotihuacan.

The residential pattern for the earliest years of Teotihuacan is not well known. However, a series of distinctive multihousehold residential units dating to the third century A.D. can be recognized. Some 2200 of these well-planned, single-story apartment compounds were eventually built. During the site's later history, these compounds were the principal kind of residential structure (Figure 8.34). The interiors of the compounds were divided into different apartments, each with rooms,

Figure 8.33 A view of the Pyramid of the Moon and the north end of the Avenue of the Dead from the top of the Pyramid of the Sun at Teotihuacan.

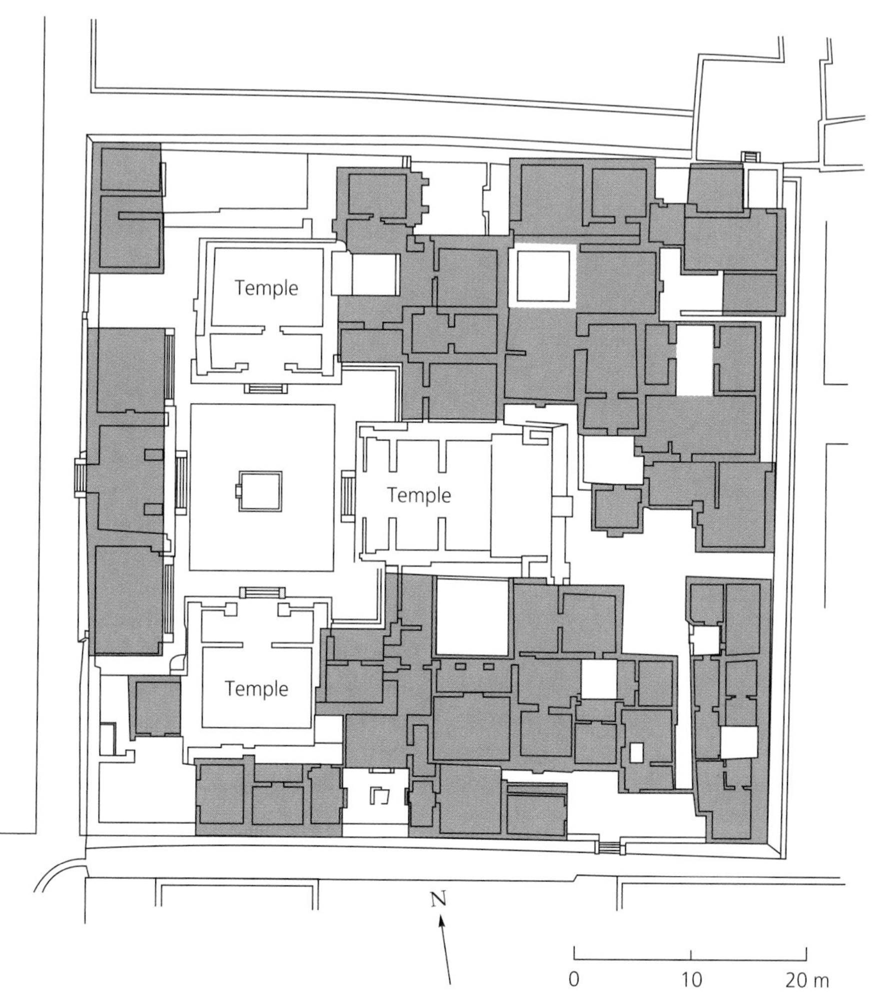


Figure 8.34 The plan of an apartment compound at Teotihuacan. The areas in color are roofed; the uncolored areas are open plazas or temples.

**Figure 8.35** Drawing of processional figures in mural at Teotihuacan.

patios, and passageways. The exteriors were surrounded by tall, windowless stone walls of cement and plaster. The compounds varied significantly in size. Millon estimates that the average structure housed about 60 people, while the larger ones held 100 or more.

From size, architectural differences, and the kinds of artifacts and wastes found at the compounds, it is clear that the occupants of these units varied in socioeconomic position. The groups that lived in the compounds were enduring. Many of the structures were rebuilt several times over several centuries, with little change in plan. The specific relationships that linked domestic units in a compound remain unknown. Spence's preliminary study of the skeletal materials led him to speculate that the males within one compound had fairly close biological ties, whereas the females did not. Such a pattern suggests a lineage or extended-family residence pattern that was **patrilocal,** in which females moved in with the family of the groom after marriage. Spence also has suggested that individuals within apartment compounds may have shared certain economic skills, such as working obsidian. Each compound had at least one temple or shrine, suggesting joint participation in ritual by the residents.

**patrilocal** Describing a residence pattern in which married couples live with or near the husband's family.

Certain neighborhoods at Teotihuacan were associated with foreign residents. The compound occupied by people from Oaxaca included a tomb with an inscribed stela bearing a glyph and number in the distinctive Oaxacan style. One ceramic urn came directly from the Valley of Oaxaca; other pottery vessels were made from local basin clays in the Oaxacan style. At least some of the foreign residents are assumed to have been merchants or traders.

In another neighborhood of Teotihuacan, the houses were built of adobe following the style of the Mesoamerican Gulf Coast. Teotihuacan was involved in trade relationships that extended as far as the Gulf Coast of Mexico, the Maya Lowlands, the Guatemalan highlands, and the deserts of northern Mexico. On Monte Albán's Main Plaza, carved stone monuments depict an important, yet apparently peaceful, meeting between an emissary wearing a costume from Teotihuacan and a Zapotec lord. Figures bearing symbols associated with central Mexico also are portrayed on stelae from Maya Tikal. Yet despite these long-distance exchange and diplomatic contacts, there is little evidence that Teotihuacan directly controlled much territory outside the Basin of Mexico. We also have no depiction, symbolic record, or even mortuary context that records an omnipotent ruler at Teotihuacan. In fact, mural art at the site often illustrates a line of well-dressed but similar figures in a procession (Figure 8.35).

Little is known about the decline of Teotihuacan in the seventh through tenth centuries A.D. The site was not abandoned, but its size decreased by more than half during this period. Militarism is a prominent theme in art during A.D. 650–750, although perimeter defensive walls were never constructed. Part of the city was burned in the seventh and eighth centuries; the fires appear to have started intermittently. The core of the city—the buildings along the Avenue of the Dead—was burned, as were temples, pyramids, and public buildings throughout the site. Millon has suggested that the conflagration was deliberate and ritually inspired, similar to the earlier desecration of the Olmec stone sculptures. In ancient Mesoamerica, the symbolic destruction of selected monuments or sacred structures was repeatedly associated with the decline and loss of power.

After A.D. 750, the enormous pyramids, the avenues and markets, and the memory of the Classic civilization were in decline. Centuries later, the Aztecs referred to the mounds of stone and broken walls as "the place of the gods." Today, Teotihuacan is one of the most important tourist attractions in Mexico. The magnificent Avenue of the Dead has been reopened and leads past the Pyramid of the Sun to the plaza and Pyramid of the Moon. The pyramids have been restored, and every year thousands climb them in awe of and admiration for the achievements of the ancient Mexicans.

*Most [artistic] scenes [at Teotihuacan] show human beings so loaded with clothing and insignia that faces and other body parts are barely visible. Emphasis is on acts rather than actors; on offices rather than office-holders. This, together with the multiplicity of identical scenes, suggests an ethos in which individuals were interchangeable and replaceable. . . . Supreme [Teotihuacan] political authority may not always have been strongly concentrated in a single person or lineage.*

—George L. Cowgill (1997)

*Concept*

## The Mesoamerican Ballgame

### *A ritual game with symbolic and political importance*

**Figure 8.36** The large I-shaped ball court on the Main Plaza at Monte Albán.

**Figure 8.37** A stone relief panel from the ball court at El Tajín.

The art historian Paul Kirchhoff drew up a list of cultural traits that generally defined the prehispanic societies of Mesoamerica and distinguished them from other large cultural regions in the New World, such as the Andean area in South America. Among the traits he used to define the boundaries of prehispanic Mesoamerica was a game played with a solid rubber ball. First reported in sixteenth-century Spanish accounts, the ballgame, ***tlachtli,*** was a team game played by somewhat different rules from place to place. Ceramic evidence suggests that some form of the ballgame was played in Mesoamerica as early as 1000 B.C., soon after the transition to village life. Ballplayers are depicted in clay figurines from central and western Mexico, as well as sites along the Gulf Coast. The pottery figures are shown wearing such playing gear as knee guards.

***tlachtli*** The Aztec word for their ritual ballgame.

Archaeological evidence also suggests that the ballgame was played in different ways during its history. For example, the Spanish chroniclers witnessed a game played on a court where stone rings were used as goals. Most ball courts from before A.D. 700 do not have such rings of stone. Small, shallow pits enclosed by four earthen retaining walls, known from San Lorenzo, may have served as early playing fields in the Olmec period. The earliest I-shaped ball courts with stone walls were not built until several centuries later (Figure 8.36). This more traditional form, often with sloping playing surfaces, has been found throughout Mesoamerica. (To compare the oval ball court of the U.S. Southwest, see "Snaketown," Chapter 7, p. 300.) The absence of a ball court at Teotihuacan is a mystery, since ballplaying is depicted on polychrome murals in one of the compounds. Ballplayer figurines also have been found at the site.

The Mesoamerican ballgame was not just for the sake of sport. Spanish chroniclers describe the sixteenth-century version as very rough, played with a ball weighing up to 11 kg (5 lb). In one version, the ball had to be kept in motion and could not be hit with hands or feet. Hips, knees, and elbows were used, and injuries were frequent. In prehispanic times, the game was associated with fertility, death, militarism, and sacrifice. At the site of El Tajín in Veracruz, a stone relief panel in the ball court graphically shows one player stretched over a sacrificial stone, while another is poised with a stone knife ready to be plunged into the chest of the victim (Figure 8.37). Sixteenth-century accounts also detail the sacrifice of defeated team members. Interestingly, the ball courts at the Maya site of Chichén Itzá and at the Aztec capital of Tenochtitlán were directly adjacent to the *tzompantli,* the skull rack where the heads of war captives were placed.

Site

# Tikal

## *A Maya city in the rain forest of Guatemala*

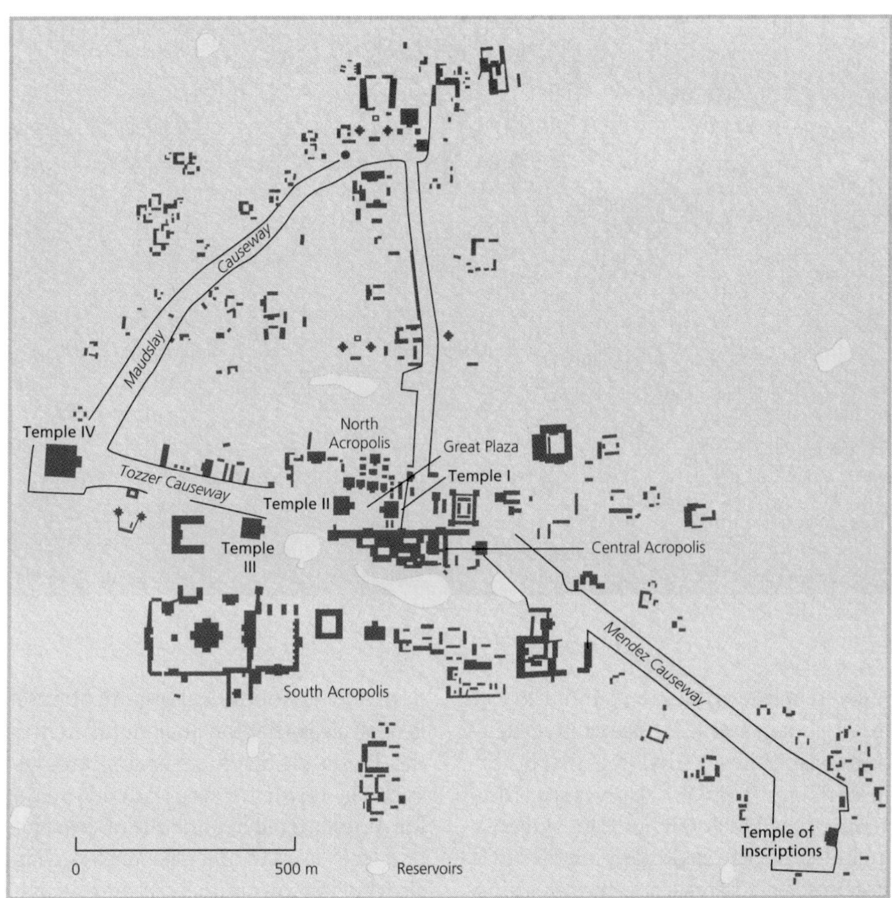


**Figure 8.38** A map of the core area of Tikal, showing the major buildings and causeways.

The first adventurers and antiquarians who discovered the overgrown ruins of Maya sites in the rain forests of the Petén assumed them to be the remains of ancient cities with large populations. Yet by the early 1900s, opinion had shifted to the belief that the ancient Maya resided in vacant ceremonial centers, inhabited only by small groups of priests. These individuals were purported to direct rural, peasant populations through periodic rituals at the centers. This shift in perspective, from urban to ceremonial, was the result of the concentration of archaeological investigations at the ceremonial cores of these sites, and of preconceived notions that tropical forests could not support urban centers. Researchers failed to recognize residential architecture, and they often neglected to look for houses outside the ceremonial cores of the sites. Moreover, since today the Maya practice slash-and-burn cultivation, it was assumed that the ancient Maya used the same technique. **Slash and burn** is a simple strategy that involves a cyclical process of field clearing, cultivation, and abandonment. Such extensive agriculture was not thought capable of supporting large urban enclaves or high population densities.

During the past three to four decades, however, new information has

**slash and burn** A type of farming in which the ground is cleared by cutting and burning the vegetation on the spot. The burned vegetation serves as a natural fertilizer. The field is farmed until yields decrease; then it is allowed to lie fallow.

**Figure 8.39** In this view of Tikal from the top of Temple IV, only the tallest buildings are visible above the dense rain forests of the Petén: Temple III in the center and Temples I and II to the left.

*Of all the New World states, it is perhaps the Maya that afford us the greatest opportunity for understanding the evolution, operation, and demise of a complex society. No other New World state offers us such a variety of complementary data sets, including eye-witness reports preserved as ethnohistorical documents, hieroglyphic texts that span some 600 years, regional settlement pattern data, linguistic reconstructions, subsistence data, and architectural evolution. The challenge remains for us to integrate all these lines of evidence, to highlight the differences and similarities among them, and to understand the Maya better by learning more about other Mesoamerican states.*

—Joyce Marcus (1983b)

revived an interpretation similar to the original one. Two decades of investigations at the site of Tikal (tee-CAHL) by researchers from the University Museum of the University of Pennsylvania included survey and mapping, excavation in selected areas, and the recording of carved stone monuments. The Tikal survey recorded thousands of small mounds in the thick forest vegetation. More common near the center of the site, the mounds decreased in number toward the periphery. A few of the mounds were excavated and found to be residential structures. At Tikal, the quantity of these residential structures demonstrated that the site had held a sizable population. Subsequent mapping of other Maya centers has indicated that the lowland population during the Maya Classic period, A.D. 250–900, was much larger than anyone suspected, considerably larger than it is today.

Once researchers recognized the population density of the ancient Maya, new questions were raised concerning agricultural subsistence, craft production, and sociopolitical organization. It is now clear that the ancient farmers of the lowlands used several strategies, such as terracing and ridged fields, for more intensive agricultural production (see "Wetland Fields," p. 363). Classic Maya communities apparently also had specific occupational groups, such as craftspeople, in addition to the groups of peasants and ruler-priests envisioned in the ceremonial center model.

The core of Tikal is situated on a series of low ridges standing roughly 50 m (165 ft) above two swampy areas (*bajos*) (Figure 8.38). Most of the great structures presently visible, clustered on the rises, date to the later part of the Classic period, the era of most pronounced construction activity at Tikal and in the Maya Lowlands in general. Yet excavations have revealed that many earlier buildings, some contemporaneous with the major Formative period occupation at El Mirador, were encased within the later structures.

For most of Tikal's history, the core of the city was the Great Plaza, although it did not dominate Tikal to the extent that the Main Plaza did at Monte Albán. In Tikal, this central open area, laid out before 100 B.C., extends for roughly 1 ha (2.5 acres) and was replastered four times. At the eastern end of the plaza, the Temple of the Great Jaguar (Temple I) rises to 45 m (150 ft), with its crowning **roof comb** peeking out above the tropical canopy of mahogany, cedar, and chicle (gum) trees (Figures 8.39 and 8.40). A large seated lord was originally painted in an array of colors on the face of the hollow comb. Temple I itself has three high, narrow rooms with carved wooden beams spanning its door frames. The innermost of these beams, or **lintels,** portrays a Maya lord towered over by a jaguar, which may serve as his protector. Temple I was dedicated in the Late Classic period to Jasaw Chan K'awiil I, the ruler whose sumptuous grave was found beneath its base and whose portrait is found on the lintels and roof comb. Directly across the plaza from Temple I lies the slightly shorter Temple II, probably dedicated to Jasaw's wife.

The north side of the plaza is framed by the North Acropolis, a huge, 100 × 80 m (325 × 260 ft) platform that was continually expanded between 200 B.C. and A.D. 550 (Figure 8.41). The University of Pennsylvania team, led by William Coe, intensively excavated this structure, discovering a rich succession of elaborate, elite tombs. Based on their findings, the North Acropolis appears to have been a burial place for a long sequence of Tikal's rulers.

South of the Great Plaza sits Tikal's greatest palace complex, the Central Acropolis. In total, this complex spreads over more than 1.6 ha (4 acres) and contains a maze of 42 multistory buildings with multiple rooms interspersed with internal courtyards. The elaboration of the room decorations, which included thronelike seats with armrests, implies that Tikal's lords and their retainers lived and conducted their activities here.

Other monumental buildings and important plazas are linked to the Great Plaza by broad, raised causeways called ***sacbes,*** or rain forest paths. The Tozzer Causeway (named for a renowned Mayanist) runs west from Temple II to one of the two tallest structures in the pre-Columbian world, Temple IV. Temple IV, some 70 m (230 ft) tall, was built in the middle of the eighth century A.D. by one of Tikal's last well-known rulers, Jasaw Chan K'awiil's son and successor, Yik'in Chan K'awiil, possibly to commemorate his father.

Tikal has a long history that is marked by two eras of powerful kings and monumental construction (see "Tikal's Monument Record," pp. 361–362). Following the decline of El Mirador at the end of the Formative period, new polities rose to power. Tikal, which was strategically situated to control

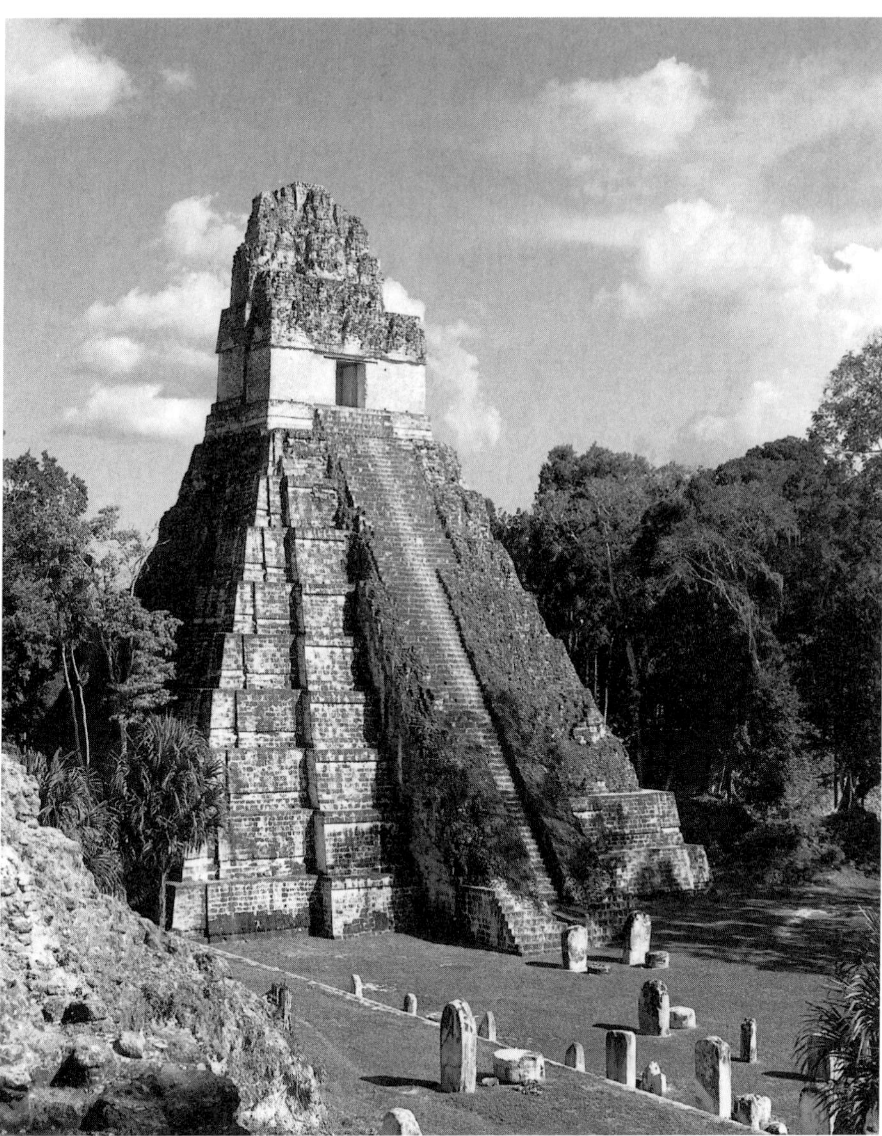

**Figure 8.40** The Temple of the Great Jaguar (Temple I).

**roof comb** An architectural feature, frequently carved with glyphs and figures, that is placed on the top of Mesoamerican temples.

**lintel** A horizontal beam of wood or stone that supports the wall above a doorway or window.

***sacbe*** The Maya word for a raised causeway constructed of stone blocks and paved with gravel and plaster.

**Figure 8.41** Monumental architectural structures in the North Acropolis at Tikal.

major inland trade routes, emerged as the largest and most important Early Classic city in the Maya region.

The first ruling dynasty at Tikal, which included several female rulers, exerted power over many of its neighbors, including nearby Uaxactún. Yet there was constant interpolity competition and shifting alliances among the rulers of a network of Maya centers. Tikal's principal rival, Calakmul (cah-lahk-MOOL), forged a series of alliances with nearby centers, including Caracol, and in the mid-500s A.D. defeated Tikal's ruler. For roughly the next 120 years, Calakmul, which equaled Tikal in size and monumental construction, and its political partners dominated the Maya region. There was little new construction at Tikal during that time, a sign of its fallen fortunes.

Jockeying for power, however, did not cease, and eventually, in A.D. 695, the Tikal king Jasaw Chan K'awiil I defeated Calakmul. For the next 100 years, during the reign of Jasaw and his successors in the Late Classic, monumental construction reached its peak at Tikal. Under Jasaw and his immediate successors, Tikal's central Twin Pyramid groups and the most massive **acropoli** were built, and the site grew to more than 120 sq km (45 sq mi). At its maximum size, bounded by the swampy *bajos* to the east and west and defensive earthworks to the north and south, the site is thought to have been occupied by 50,000–80,000 people.

Around A.D. 800, Tikal began to decline again, little construction was carried out, and few stelae were erected after that date. Whereas a large percentage of Tikal's excavated house mounds were occupied during the major episode of building, most of the habitation after A.D. 830 was restricted to the site core, and the total site population may have been only 10% of what it was 100 years before. A century or two later, this giant city was largely abandoned by humans and eventually reverted to forest.

**acropolis** (plural **acropoli**) (Greek) A raised complex of palaces and courtyards, especially in Mesoamerica and Greece.

# Concept

## Tikal's Monument Record

### *The rulers of Tikal*

Recent studies in Maya archaeology and **epigraphy** have demonstrated that Classic Maya society was not egalitarian but, instead, was hierarchically organized. The commemoration of the births, accessions, conquests, and deaths of important rulers was a major theme of their carved stone monuments.

One of the most important monuments at Tikal, known as Stela 29, exhibits the earliest known and well-provenienced inscriptions in the Maya Lowlands with a **Long Count** date of A.D. 292 (see "Writing and Calendars," p. 369). For archaeologists, Stela 29 is a rough marker for the beginning of the Maya Classic period, an era during which the Long Count was used on numerous Maya inscriptions (Figure 8.42). The end of the Classic period (A.D. 900) roughly coincides with the cessation of Long Count inscriptions. Stela 29 also includes the earliest **emblem glyph** (place name), a distinctive sign that identifies either a specific Maya center or the ruling lineage associated with that location.

In the Early Classic period, the importance of Tikal and its ruling lineage is indicated by the numerous dated monuments at the site. Although other Maya centers in the immediate vicinity of Tikal also asserted their importance and autonomy by erecting fourth-century A.D. monuments, Tikal and its neighbor Uaxactún (wah-shak-TOON) raised almost half of these early stelae. Stela 5 at Uaxactún, dating to A.D. 358, includes Tikal's emblem glyph, an indicator that the former site by that time may have been under Tikal's jurisdiction. Soon thereafter, several other Petén sites ceased erecting stelae, another signal that Tikal may have expanded its sovereignty early in the Classic period.

Precocious political development at Tikal and Uaxactún may have been related to the close ties that these centers developed with foreign elite. A stela erected in A.D. 378 at Uaxactún portrays a figure in non-Maya attire. Less than 2 years later, Tikal Stela 4 records the accession of a new ruler, Yax Nuun Ayiin I, who is posed facing front rather than in profile, as was typical of earlier Maya rulers. In pose and costume, Yax Nuun resembles Teotihuacan nobles, and the excavation of the tomb thought to have been his included objects suggesting a Teotihuacan connection.

This foreign link continued, although perhaps somewhat diminished, during the reign of Yax Nuun's heir, Siyaj Chan K'awiil II. The latter figure is portrayed on Tikal Stela 31, which commemorates the twentieth year of his rule (Figure 8.43). On the stela, Siyaj Chan appears in Maya regalia, flanked by two subordinate figures wearing outfits more indicative of the highlands. Their shields are adorned with the face of the central Mexican rain deity prominent at Teotihuacan. During and immediately after the reign of Siyaj Chan, Tikal's influence spread even farther in the lowlands, possibly stretching to distant Yaxchilán (yah-chee-LAHN), a Maya center on the Usumacinta River. Tikal's broad foreign ties and political importance may have stemmed from the site's location on land that lies between two major drainage systems, which linked the Gulf of Mexico with the Caribbean Sea, interconnecting the Maya Lowlands.

Early in the sixth century A.D., a stela at Yaxchilán displayed the site's own emblem glyph, which may imply that a greater degree of autonomy from Tikal had been secured. Tikal's declining influence was signaled by a construction slowdown and a long break, from A.D. 534 to 692, in the carving of dated stelae. During the first 59 years of this period, called the hiatus, monument erection practically ceased at many sites in the

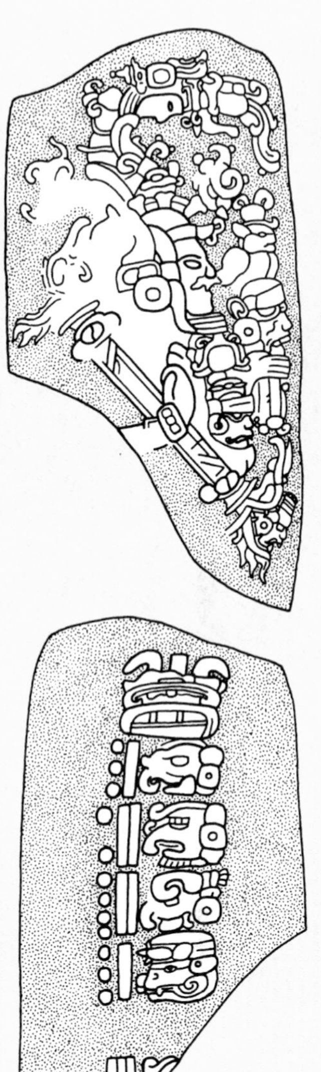

**Figure 8.42** Stela 29, with a richly dressed noble on one side of the monument and glyphs arranged in a single column on the other.

**epigraphy** The study of inscriptions.

**Figure 8.43** Stela 31, showing Siyaj Chan K'awaiil II flanked by two subordinate figures.

southern Maya Lowlands. Just before the hiatus, a Tikal ruler, Wak Chan K'awiil, was apparently defeated in battle by Caracol (car-ah-COAL), an ally of Calakmul. During the hiatus, even the tombs of the Tikal elite contained meager offerings compared with the exotic and sumptuous items buried earlier. Recent epigraphic breakthroughs stemming from the decipherment of glyphic texts from across the Maya Lowlands support archaeological indications that the power of Tikal's lords waned during this period. At the same time, another Maya center to the north, Calakmul, Tikal's principal rival, ascended to much greater influence.

But by A.D. 700, political fortunes appear to have shifted again. Late in the seventh century, the most extensive construction episode was begun at Tikal under the ruler Jasaw Chan K'awaiil I, who deliberately harkened back to powerful Siyaj Chan K'awaiil II. Clemency Coggins, of Boston University, has proposed that Jasaw's accession was timed to occur exactly 256 years after the inauguration of Siyaj.

The later Classic period was characterized by a series of politically competitive centers, including Tikal in the central Petén, Calakmul in the north, Palenque in the southwest, Yaxchilán along the Usumacinta, and Copán in the southeast. The specific fortunes of these centers, their interconnecting networks of alliance, and the overall degree of political consolidation in the Maya Lowlands appear to have vacillated over time. Yet during this era, stylistic and iconographic conventions were shared across the southern Maya Lowlands. A standardized lunar calendar was employed throughout the region for almost a century (A.D. 672–751). Monuments from various centers indicate that communications between the sites were fostered by elite intermarriage, as well as by military alliances. Archaeological findings suggest that exchange also was an important means of regional integration.

Whether the Late Classic period ruling lineage at Tikal ever developed the far-flung influence that Yax Nuun and Siyaj Chan apparently had achieved earlier remains a matter of scholarly debate. Although recent epigraphic findings indicate that the later lords of Tikal did extend their political influence over other Maya centers, those same texts seem to tell of increasing political fragmentation after A.D. 750. By the end of the eighth century A.D., construction at Tikal, and at many other major Maya centers, began to wane. In A.D. 889, the latest monument was erected at Tikal, and the last known Long Count date anywhere was carved in A.D. 909. Tikal's fate was only part of the significant demographic decline and political breakdown, the so-called Maya collapse, that characterized almost the entire central and southern lowlands during the ninth and tenth centuries.

**Long Count** The Classic Maya system of dating that records the total number of days elapsed from an initial date in the distant past (3114 B.C.). The system is based on multiples of 20.

**emblem glyph** A set of Maya hieroglyphs; generally, each emblem glyph is specific to a given Classic Maya city.

*Concept*

# Wetland Fields

## *Intensive agriculture in the Maya Lowlands*

Fifty years ago, most Mayanists believed that the ancient Maya relied entirely on the slash-and-burn farming practices used in Yucatán today. For example, in 1956, Sylvanus Morley and George Brainerd summarized the prevailing viewpoint as follows:

*Modern Maya agricultural practices are the same as they were three thousand years ago or more—a simple process of felling the forest, burning the dried trees and bush, planting, and changing the locations of the cornfields every few years. (p. 128)*

Yet during the past decades, with the completion of archaeological settlement surveys, a large number of sites have been mapped. Often these sites were found to have contained a greater residential population than expected, raising questions about Maya subsistence and population. Most notably, given the long fallow cycles required by slash-and-burn farming, how did the large Classic Maya populations sustain themselves?

Dennis Puleston, who surveyed outlying portions of Tikal, provided an alternative hypothesis. Noting the high spatial association between the ruins of Tikal house mounds and the distribution of **ramón** trees, Puleston suggested that the fruit of the ramón, eaten today as a dietary supplement, may have been a food staple in the past. Although Puleston may have overestimated the ancient dietary significance of ramón, more recent findings have supported his view that the ramón and other fruit trees were tended by the prehispanic Maya and probably contributed to their diet.

In 1969, Puleston, collaborating with geographer Alfred Siemens, discovered raised-field complexes during an aerial reconnaissance in the vicinity of a series of Maya sites along the Candelaria River in the state of Campeche. Subsequent aerial photographs, on-the-ground checks, and archaeological excavations confirmed that the observed patterns of raised fields and interdigitated canals were constructed before the Spanish conquest. Since the initial work of Siemens and Puleston, these agricultural features, which are similar in function to the prehispanic central Mexican ***chinampas,*** also have been noted in other parts of the Maya Lowlands (see "Tenochtitlán," p. 378).

Along the Hondo River in Belize, Puleston's excavations suggested that the prehispanic raised features were built up by piling floodplain sediments above the natural terrain (Figure 8.44). In other areas, canals were constructed to drain water from swampy and waterlogged zones. In both cases, cultivated fields were established above the high-water table, or floodplain, during the rainy season. Yet, if necessary, these raised or drained fields could receive water supplements from the intervening canals in the dry season. In addition, the periodic cleaning of the canals further raised and naturally fertilized the fields. Although these features could be laborious to construct, the returns were significant, allowing for a much more continuous output than that afforded by slash and burn. The canals within the raised-field systems also could have promoted fish cultivation and facilitated transport and communication. The Maya glyph signifying abundance was the water lily, a key natural floral component of the artificially constructed aquatic raised-field/canal environment.

Analyzed pollen samples from the silt of the ancient Hondo River canals have identified maize and cotton as crops grown in the raised-field complexes. Thus subsistence foods as well as nonfood plants were grown.

*I'm not particularly interested in ancient objects. This seemingly heretical statement for an archaeologist usually takes aback friends who believe that the best way to entertain me is to show me the local museum. On more than one occasion, I have had to explain that beautiful Classic Maya vases or finely carved jade pendants hold less interest to me—and to many of my colleagues—than the scientific investigation of ideas about why and how ancient cultures like the Maya developed.*

—Jeremy A. Sabloff (1990)

**ramón** A tree that grows abundantly in the tropical forests of the Maya Lowlands and bears an edible fruit, also called breadnut.

***chinampa*** (Spanish) An agricultural field created by swamp drainage or landfill operations along the edges of lakes.

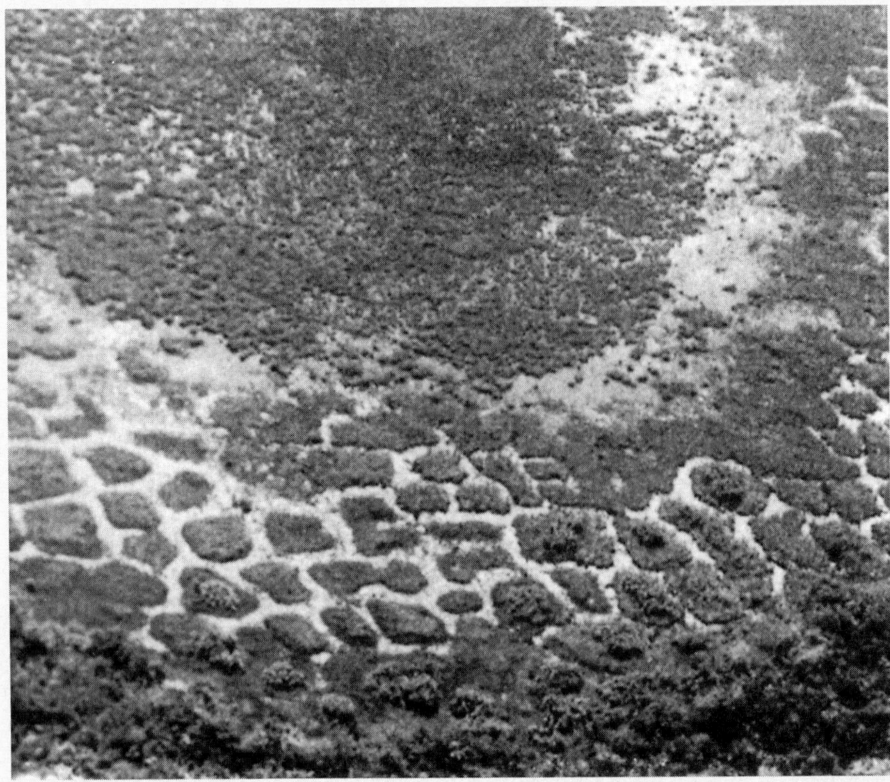

**Figure 8.44** An aerial view of a raised-field complex in Pulltrouser Swamp, Belize.

Significantly, radiocarbon dates from the Hondo River fields place the initial construction of this artificial landscape in the first millennium B.C., before significant population expansion in the Maya Lowlands.

Side-looking airborne radar (SLAR) has been used to locate huge areas of suspected raised-field complexes in a large portion of the Maya region. Yet most of these proposed field systems have not been checked on the ground. Several other linear patterns observed by SLAR reflect no more than natural soil formations. Thus the geographic extent of ancient Maya raised-field complexes remains unknown.

In several areas, the ancient Maya supplemented extensive slash-and-burn farming with the construction of artificial terrace systems. Evidence for these agricultural features, which converted otherwise unfarmable slopes into a patchwork of level plots, has been found both in western Belize and in the vicinity of the Bec River. Although doubts persist about the dating and distribution of Classic Maya agricultural systems, there is no longer any question that the Maya employed a great diversity of subsistence techniques, including a range of water management strategies and various kinds of intensive farming procedures.

*Indigenous knowledge systems of landscape management need to be studied and evaluated before they disappear forever. In cases where the prehistoric infrastructure has been completely abandoned, investigations using archaeology and agricultural experiments may be able to recover sufficient information on how these systems function. . . . Both contemporary and prehistoric systems may hold the clue to future rural development.*

—Clark L. Erickson (1992)

# Palenque

## *A Classic center at the edge of the Maya Lowlands*

The Maya and many other native groups in the Americas divided their physical realms into four quarters; each quarter was associated with specific colors, living things, and supernatural forces. Original Maya maps consistently place east at the top, suggesting that east was viewed as the dominant direction.

In A.D. 731, a stela was erected at the site of Copán (ko-PAHN), a large center in the southeastern part of the Maya Lowlands. This monument lists the place names of four major Maya centers, each associated with one of the four cardinal directions. Preceding this list is a clause that Joyce Marcus interprets as "four on high," or "divided into four quarters." It appears that the Maya associated each section of their world with an important place or center. Not surprisingly, the monument carvers at Copán associated their site with the foremost direction, east. Tikal was associated with the west, and Marcus has suggested that the emblem glyph associated with the south belonged to Calakmul. Palenque (pa-LEN-kay), a center at the western edge of the lowlands, was linked with the direction north. Although these directions did not correspond closely to the actual geography, the cosmological model, dividing the Maya world between a series of centers, did reflect the political fluidity of the Late Classic Maya realm. This is not to say that the lowland Maya world contained four autonomous centers in A.D. 731. Rather, some authority at Copán perceived these four centers to be of the greatest

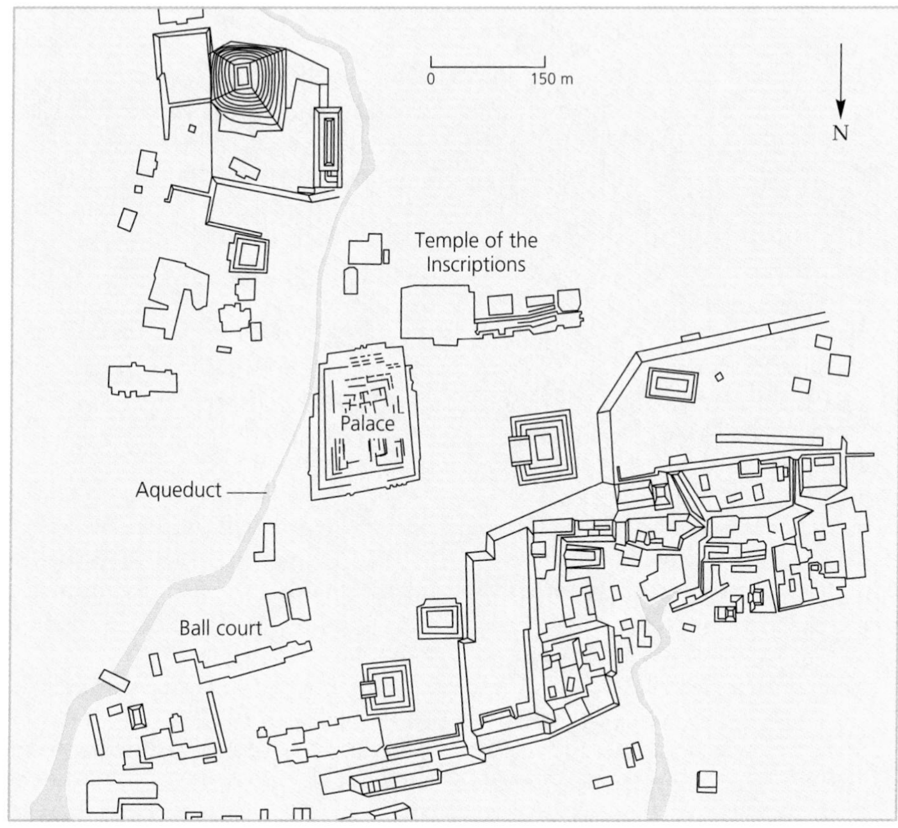


**Figure 8.45** A map of the principal buildings in the central part of Palenque.

**Figure 8.46** An artist's interpretation of the Temple of the Inscriptions, showing the staircase leading to Lord Pakal's tomb below.

importance. The listing of multiple centers speaks to the political fragmentation of the Classic period Maya world and the frequent rises and falls in political fortune of the Maya centers that were part of that landscape.

Palenque is situated on a series of rolling hills overlooking the vast Gulf Coast plain approximately 50 km (30 mi) from the Usumacinta River, in the state of Chiapas, Mexico. The site was occupied early in the Classic period but remained relatively small until the seventh century A.D. Following a military defeat of Palenque's ruler by Calakmul in A.D. 611, a major building boom was started by a powerful lord who, inscriptions indicate, came to power in A.D. 615 and may have been named K'inich Janaab' Pakal I ("shield"). During Pakal's rule, Palenque also grew in size and expanded its authority over the neighboring region. Palenque emerged as a major power, and the site's emblem glyph appeared. The major structures of the site today were begun after Pakal's accession (Figure 8.45).

Lord Pakal was buried in an elaborate tomb beneath the pyramid that supports the Temple of the Inscriptions (Figure 8.46). The tomb was discovered by Alberto Ruz Lhuiller (in 1949–1958). Several years later, after clearing a staircase that led deep under the pyramid, Ruz found a large stuccoed crypt. The huge stone coffin, or **sarcophagus,** was topped with a superbly carved lid depicting the dead ruler falling into the underworld (Figure 8.47). Beneath the lid were the remains of Pakal, wearing beads and a mosaic mask of jade, surrounded by other treasures (Figure 8.48).

Epigraphic studies of the stone lid of the sarcophagus and other inscriptions at Palenque have led to the reconstruction of the long dynastic history of the site. Pakal was succeeded directly

**sarcophagus** A stone coffin, usually decorated with sculpture and/or inscriptions.

by his son K'inich Kan Balam II, who in a relatively short reign continued the massive construction at the core of the site. Following Kan Balam's death early in the eighth century A.D., his brother Kan Joy Chitam II replaced him. During his rule, Palenque's realm reached its greatest extent. Kan Joy also expanded Palenque's so-called Palace structure by erecting an unusual four-story tower in veneration of his father (Figure 8.49). During winter solstices, the sun seems to set directly behind the Temple of the Inscriptions when viewed from the top of the Palace tower.

After the death of Kan Joy, the site and its inscriptions began to wane. A series of three rulers with brief and possibly broken reigns followed. The last recorded accession date of a ruler in Pakal's lineage was A.D. 764. The last Long Count date known from Palenque (corresponding to A.D. 799) occurs on an inscribed pottery vessel and records the accession of a ruler with a central Mexican–style name (non-Maya), suggesting that the site may have been taken over or influenced by foreigners late in the eighth century A.D. This ended a long recorded sequence of rule that included at least one female ruler.

Palenque was one of the earliest Maya centers to experience collapse. Monumental construction and the textual record waned during the latter half of the eighth century and ceased early in the ninth century. Pomona, a small former dependency of Palenque, displayed its own emblem glyph in A.D. 771, suggesting that it had achieved independence. Palenque was also one of the first sites to show increasing ties to Gulf Coast or central Mexican elements. In parts of the Classic Maya world, this external bond often was associated with the cessation of monumental building and the erection of stelae. On a stela that was raised at the site of Seibal (say-BALL) in A.D. 889, Palenque and Copán were no longer considered among the four primary centers of the Maya region. By then the realm of the Classic Maya had shrunk to little more than its former core around Tikal.

Although Palenque at its height was clearly part of the Classic Maya

**Figure 8.47** Inscriptions on the lid of Lord Pakal's coffin.

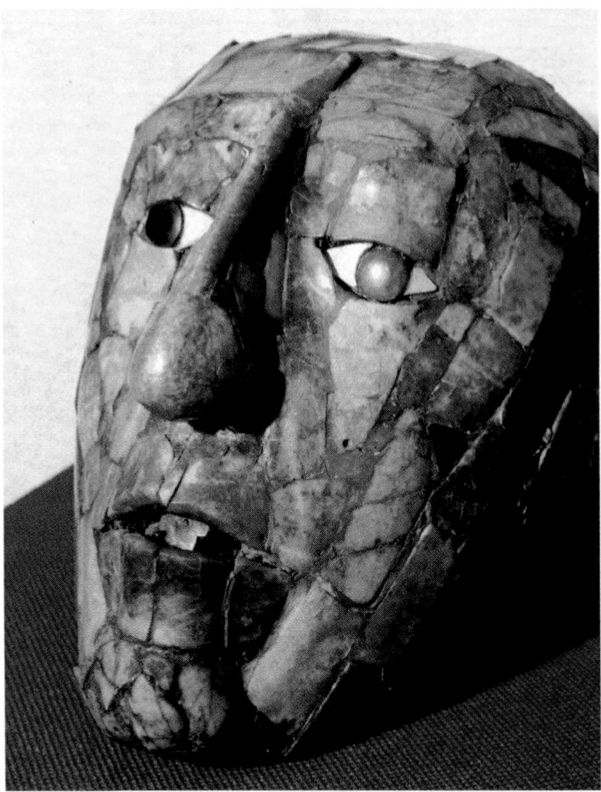

**Figure 8.48** The exquisite jade mask that was found in the sarcophagus, next to Lord Pakal's left shoulder.

cultural realm, the site's distinctive layout and architecture reflected its location at the western periphery of the lowlands. Compared with the imposing appearance and vertical thrust of the architecture at Tikal and other Classic Maya centers, Palenque's major structures were broader and more dispersed, giving the site's civic-ceremonial center a more horizontal flow. Palenque also lacked a corpus of freestanding sculptured monuments (stelae and altars). Instead, hieroglyphic inscriptions generally were written on stone panels or plaster and incorporated directly into buildings.

**Figure 8.49** The Palace at Palenque. The multiroom palace sits at the core of Palenque's complex of civic-ceremonial structures. The most distinguishing feature of the palace is a four-story tower, which provides a superb view of the city and the surrounding countryside.

Concept

# Writing and Calendars

## *The Maya numerical system and Calendar Round*

The earliest Mesoamerican writing appeared more than 2500 years ago, before the rise of the state or the existence of urban centers (see "Carved Stones and Early Writing," p. 341). Four different prehispanic Mesoamerican writing systems are known: the Maya, the Zapotec, the Mixtec (MEESH-tec), and the Aztec. Each appears to include a mixture of **pictographic, ideographic,** and **phonetic** elements. The Mixtec and the Aztec are known from late prehispanic texts written on prepared bark paper or deer skin; the older Zapotec system is preserved on inscriptions carved in stone. The Maya writing system has been preserved in late prehispanic folding books, as well as in a large body of texts on stone, pottery, and wall paintings (Figure 8.50). The Maya writing system is the best known of the four, and major breakthroughs in decipherment have come during the past two decades.

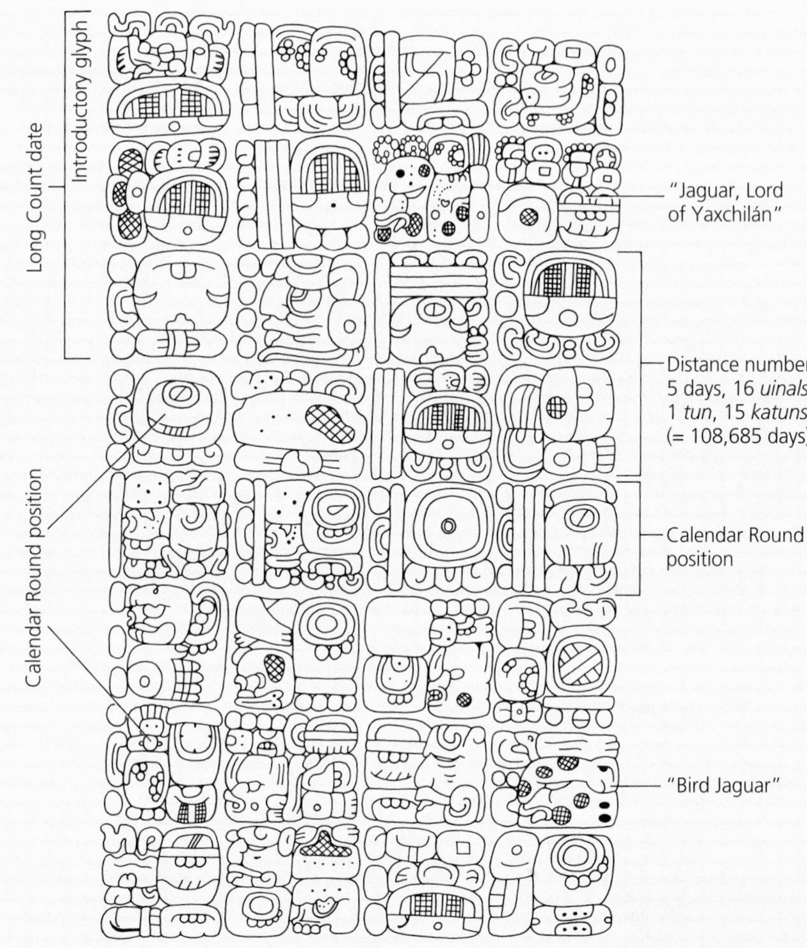


**Figure 8.50** An example of Maya hieroglyphs.

At first, the Classic (A.D. 250–900) Maya inscriptions were thought to relate exclusively to astronomy and calendrics, because these subjects constituted the first portions of the texts to be deciphered. Today, epigraphers recognize that the principal theme of Maya inscriptions is a political or dynastic one. As discussed earlier (see "Tikal's Monument Record," p. 361), scholars can now chart the military claims and political alliances of specific Maya rulers and compare these textual data with the archaeological and architectural record. Carved stones have been deciphered, which commemorate significant events—birth, autosacrifice, accession to rule, marriage, military victory, death—in the lives of the Maya lords and their kin. Often the text helps frame a stylized scene of the commemorated event. The blocky hieroglyphs are presented in double columns intended to be read from left to right and top to bottom. As with ancient Egyptian monuments, the messages are generally brief and composed largely of nouns and verbs.

Prehispanic texts are closely linked to the pre-Columbian calendar. Classic Maya inscriptions are distinguished by their frequent use of the Long Count calendar, a system capable of tracking extended cycles of time (Figure 8.51). Although the Maya did not invent the Long Count, they refined and used it to the greatest degree. The smallest Long Count unit is the day, or *kin.* The second Long Count unit, composed of 20 *kins,* is the *uinal.* The third unit, the *tun,* consists of 18 *uinals* or 360 *kins.*

**pictograph** A written or painted symbol that more or less portrays the represented object.

**ideograph** A written symbol that represents an abstract idea rather than the sound of a word or the pictorial symbol of an object (pictograph).

**phonetic** Pertaining to the sounds of speech.

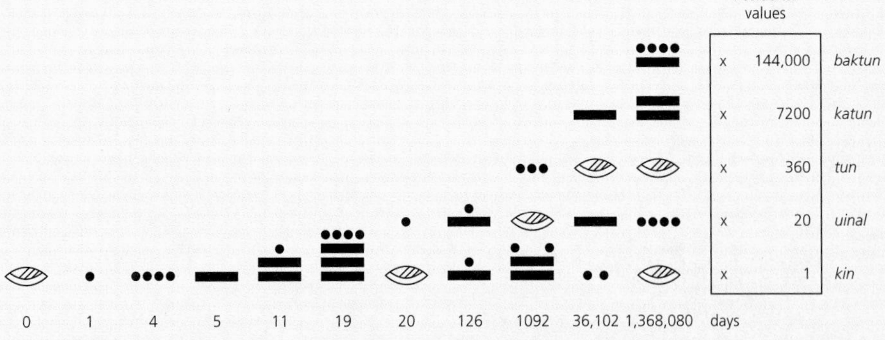


**Figure 8.51** The Maya numbering system and Long Count units. The base-20 system used only three symbols, the stylized shell for 0, a dot for 1, and a bar for 5. The numbers were arranged vertically (rather than horizontally, as in our Arabic numeration), with the lowest values at the bottom.

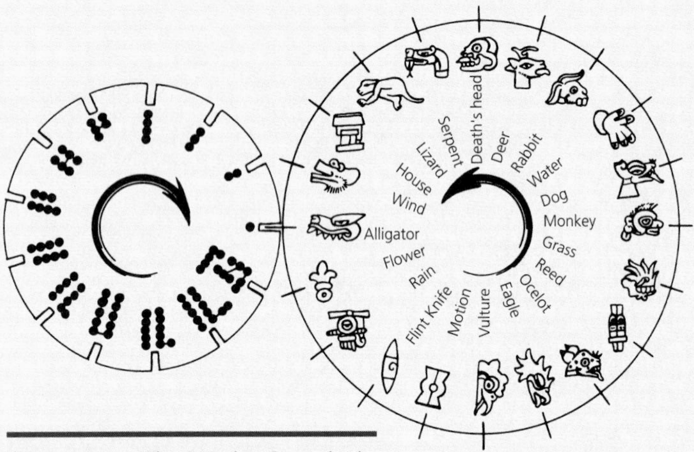


**Figure 8.52** The 260-day Sacred Almanac for the Aztecs. The 20 named days intermesh with the numbers 1–13.

Above this third cycle are the *katun* and the *baktun,* consisting of 20 and 400 *tuns,* respectively. In accord with all prehispanic Mesoamerican numeration systems, the Long Count had a vigesimal structure, one based on multiples of 20. The only adjustment necessary to approximate the solar year was a change in the third unit, or *tun,* from 20 to 18 *uinals.*

The Long Count system enables scholars to date precisely many of the Classic Maya inscriptions. Long Count dates were calculated by the Classic Maya and their Mesoamerican forebears, who established the system by adding the total amount of elapsed time to a base date from which they began their calendar. Until this starting point was calculated, Long Count dates could not be equated with our calendric system. Some scholarly disagreement still exists, but most researchers place the base date for the Long Count near the end of the fourth millennium B.C. (with 3114 B.C. the most widely accepted date).

Why do you think the Maya stopped using the Long Count calendar?

In addition to the Long Count, the Maya and other Mesoamerican peoples used the Calendar Round. The main element of this calendar was the Sacred Almanac, or 260-day count (Figure 8.52). Primarily religious and divinatory in function, the almanac can be visualized as having been composed of two integrated "cogged wheels," or cycles of numbers; one cycle of numbers ran from 1 to 13, and the other cycle consisted of 20 named days. In general, these named days were similar across Mesoamerica; however, some differences did occur from group to group. The combination of a number and a day name formed a unit that would not recur until 260 days had elapsed, at which point the cycle began again. The numbers were usually expressed in typical Mesoamerican bar-and-dot fashion, with a dot equivalent to 1 and a bar equivalent to 5.

A second element of the Calendar Round was the 365-day Vague Year. This year was divided into 18 "months" of 20 days each. An extra period of 5 days was added at the end of the year. Although the Classic Maya were aware that the tropical year actually was 365.25 days, they did not use a leap-year correction. The permutation of the Sacred Almanac and the Vague Year produced an 18,980-day Calendar Round that cycled back to its original start every 52 solar years.

The Maya believed that significant moments in time had their links with divinities and astrologically based auguries, and these associations were known and recorded. The Maya viewed time in a cyclical fashion. Points in time and the events assigned to them were not thought to be unique; the past, present, and future often could be woven together in prophecy and divination. Given the intricacy of Classic Maya writing and calendrics and their importance in the politico-religious sphere, it appears that this special knowledge was generally held by only a relatively small segment of the population.

# Tula

*Capital city of the Toltec*

When the fifteenth-century Aztec ruler Itzcoatl purged the state archives, burning older documentary records, he greatly limited our ability to reconstruct the late prehispanic history of central Mexico. Fortunately, some lists of rulers, called king lists, and other fragmentary accounts of the previous periods survived. In conjunction with archaeological discoveries, these records enable us to begin to understand events in the central highlands between the decline of Teotihuacan, beginning around A.D. 700–800, and the establishment of the Aztec city of Tenochtitlán in A.D. 1325.

Sixteenth-century Spanish clerics and men of letters, curious about prehispanic civilization, inquired about the native history of Mexico. Repeatedly, their Aztec informants attributed the origins of their society to a semi-legendary race known as the Toltecs (TOLL-tecs). According to these part-historical, part-mythical accounts, the Toltecs were great warriors but also peace-loving people. These mythic histories also describe the Toltecs as innovators, builders, and craftspeople, who cultivated giant ears of corn and colored cotton that did not have to be dyed. Their capital was supposedly an architectural masterpiece known as Tollan (toll-LAHN). The Aztecs traced their right to rule directly to their Toltec ancestry.

Like many such accounts, the origin myths of the Aztecs blended historical reality with fiction and distortion. Some of the stories did contain elements of truth, which enabled Mexican ethnohistorian Wigberto Jiménez Moreno to persuasively suggest that the Toltec capital was an actual place near the modern town of Tula de Allende (TOO-lah de ah-YEN-day), in the state of Hidalgo. Over the past decades, several archaeological projects at Tula have substantiated Jiménez Moreno's identification.

Tula is situated at the northern fringe of Mesoamerica, about 65 km (40 mi) northwest of modern Mexico City. The site had little significant occupation when Teotihuacan was partially burned and abandoned. The collapse of that great city, nearly coincident with the demise of monumental building at Monte Albán, marked a major transition in the highlands of

**www.mhhe.com/priceip6e**

For a Web-based activity on the Toltecs, see the Internet exercises on your online learning center.

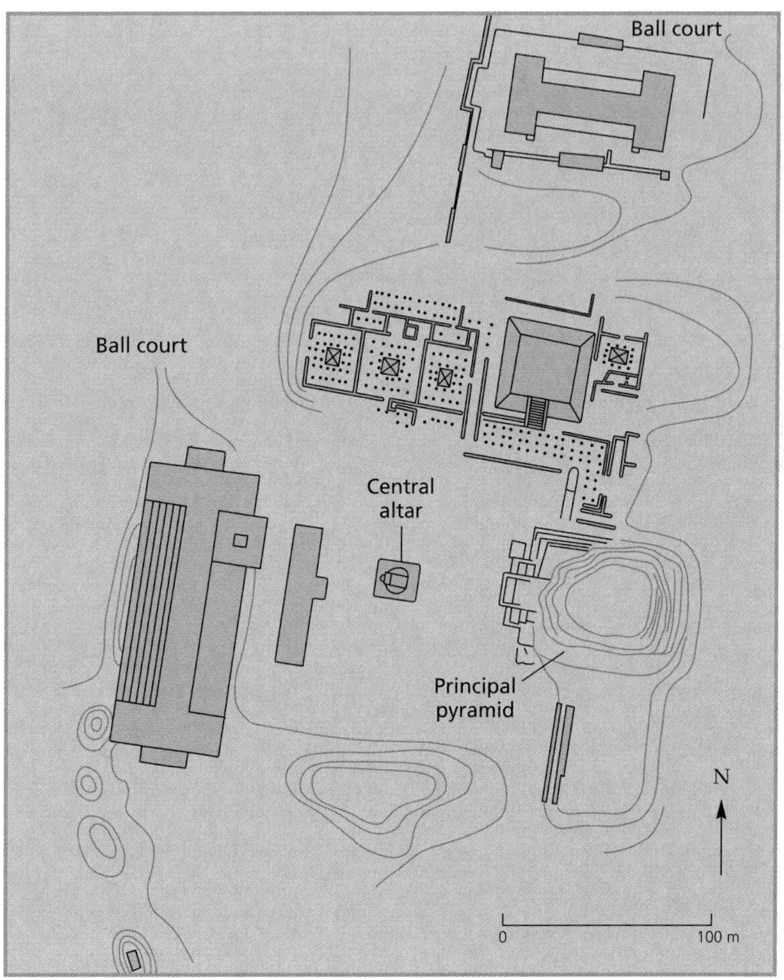


**Figure 8.53** A map of the major buildings in the central part of Tula.

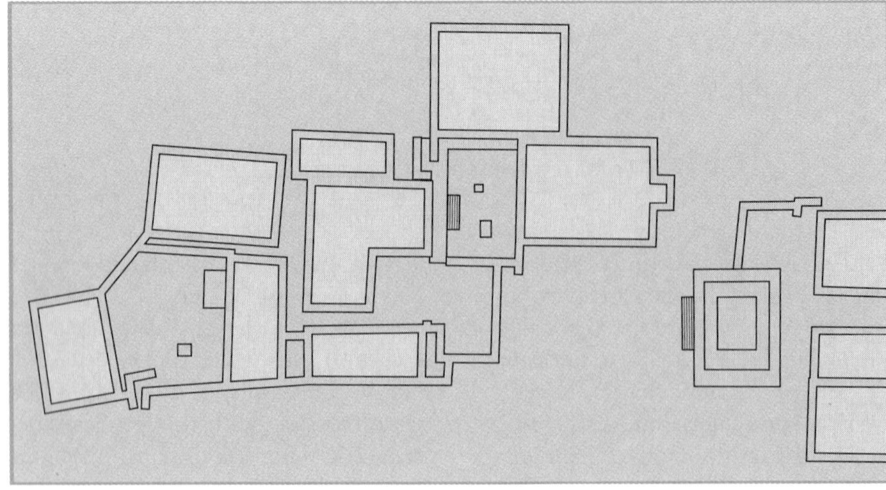

**Figure 8.54** An artist's reconstruction of a residential compound at Tula, showing covered living spaces and small open courtyards, or patios.

*After the fall of Teotihuacan, various warlike elites, flourishing different symbols of political legitimacy, appropriated the city's patrimony. These successor states contested one another's spoils and spread out in various directions in search of new horizons. For a brief time, the center of gravity within the Mesoamerican heartland shifted northward, apparently to Tula in Hidalgo, outside the Valley of Mexico. Tula became the capital of a Toltec domain, less an integrated "empire" than an epicenter of groups of warriors, traders, cultivators, and priests employing the Toltec name and symbols as charters for conquest and colonization.*
—Eric R. Wolf (1982)

**Atlantean column** A carved human figure serving as a decorative or supporting column.

Mexico. Following the fall of Teotihuacan, no single dominant community emerged in the Central Highlands to control the Basin of Mexico. Tula rose rapidly in this politically fragmented landscape.

Soon after A.D. 800, a substantial occupation was present at the site (Figure 8.53). Even at its height, Tula was considerably smaller than Teotihuacan or the later Aztec city of Tenochtitlán. Tula also lacks any evidence of urban planning outside its civic-ceremonial core. It reached its maximum size and its greatest influence between A.D. 950 and 1150: 13–16 sq km (5–6 sq mi) and about 40,000–60,000 people. The residential compounds at Tula are not as large as most of those at Teotihuacan, although they do appear to house more than a single nuclear family (Figure 8.54).

The major structures at the site, including two large ball courts, were built during this period. Although the monumental architecture at Tula was far less grandiose than at Teotihuacan, a series of squat but substantial temple pyramids were erected. The most impressive and best-known remains at Tula are the sculpted **Atlantean columns,** which stand 4.6 m (15 ft) high (Figure 8.55). The military theme depicted by these giant basalt figures is also evident in a series of carved stone relief panels showing jaguars, eagles eating hearts, and coyotes, all creatures perhaps associated with specific warrior groups in the city.

Trade, the procurement of raw materials, and craft production were very important economic activities at Tula, as they were at Teotihuacan and Tenochtitlán. Containers of travertine, a white sedimentary stone, were made at the site, and sixteenth-century accounts describe many other fine, high-status goods produced by the Toltec craftspeople. As at Teotihuacan, areas of heavy obsidian use and/or production have been recorded at Tula (Figure 8.56). Most of the obsidian was derived from the same source that furnished workshops at Teotihuacan. Tula borders on arid regions to the north, where little can be grown except maguey. This plant is an important source of fiber, needles, sap, and other products. In ancient Mesoamerica, maguey fibers were raw material for cloth, clothing, nets, and bags. The abundance of spindle whorls at Tula indicates that the spinning of these fibers into twine also was an important economic activity. The presence of pottery and marine shells from the Pacific Coast further documents the extent of exchange with peoples in northern and western Mexico.

Both historical and archaeological sources agree that Tula had lost much of its influence before A.D. 1200. Exca-

Figure 8.55 One of the large carved Atlantean columns at Tula.

vations at Tula by Mexican archaeologist Jorge Acosta revealed evidence of burning and disruption at all the major structures; however, the specific date of this destruction was not determined. A recent project by Richard Diehl found that Tula was at least partially abandoned by A.D. 1200, although the extent of the collapse is unknown. Diehl's study also recorded a sizable later Aztec occupation at Tula. Acosta found extensive evidence for late prehispanic looting in earlier monumental structures and even in the residential compounds. Colonial-era texts of the Spanish friar Bernardino de Sahagún allude to this looting, citing the removal of Toltec artifacts from the ground.

Various written accounts provide a more intriguing depiction of Tula's end, but their accuracy is unconfirmed. Although the accounts themselves are somewhat contradictory, the story ties the fall of Tula to a conflict between cosmic forces. The Mesoamerican cosmos was frequently symbolized as a duality. Quetzalcoatl, the representative of day, light, traditional religion, and good, was opposed to Tezcatlipoca, the embodiment of night, darkness, chicanery, and evil. In these accounts, Quetzalcoatl ("the feathered serpent"), or a ruler associated with him, is tricked, disgraced, and forced to leave the city, an event resulting in Tula's downfall.

Both archaeological and historical sources indicate that following the collapse, the Basin of Mexico and its northern fringes once again fragmented into a series of small polities, each controlling only its immediate vicinity. It was during this era of political decentralization that the Aztecs began their ascent to power.

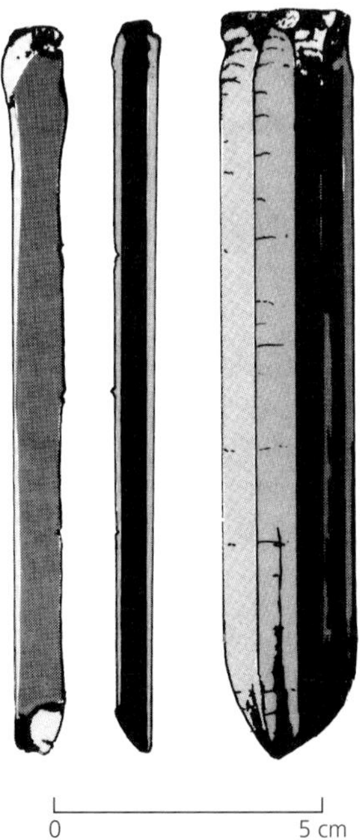


Figure 8.56 Two obsidian blades and an exhausted core from Tula.

Figure 8.60 The large ball court at Chichén Itzá. The Mesoamerican ballgame has a long history; however, the specific form and size of the courts varied across time and space.

figures surround a bowl-shaped impression at the navel, where sacrifices or offerings were placed.

Some archaeologists have suggested an actual central Mexican Toltec presence at Chichén Itzá on the basis of ancient legends that tell of the god Quetzalcoatl from Tula arriving in Yucatán in A.D. 987. This interpretation is supported, perhaps, by murals in a temple at Chichén Itzá depicting warriors (assumed to be Toltecs) arriving in canoes and doing battle with the local populace (Figure 8.63). Yet the same textual sources that tell of foreign invaders in Postclassic Yucatán note that they spoke a Mayan language, suggesting that they were not actually central Mexican Toltecs. Although the nature of the relationship between these two centers is still unresolved, recent interpretations favor a

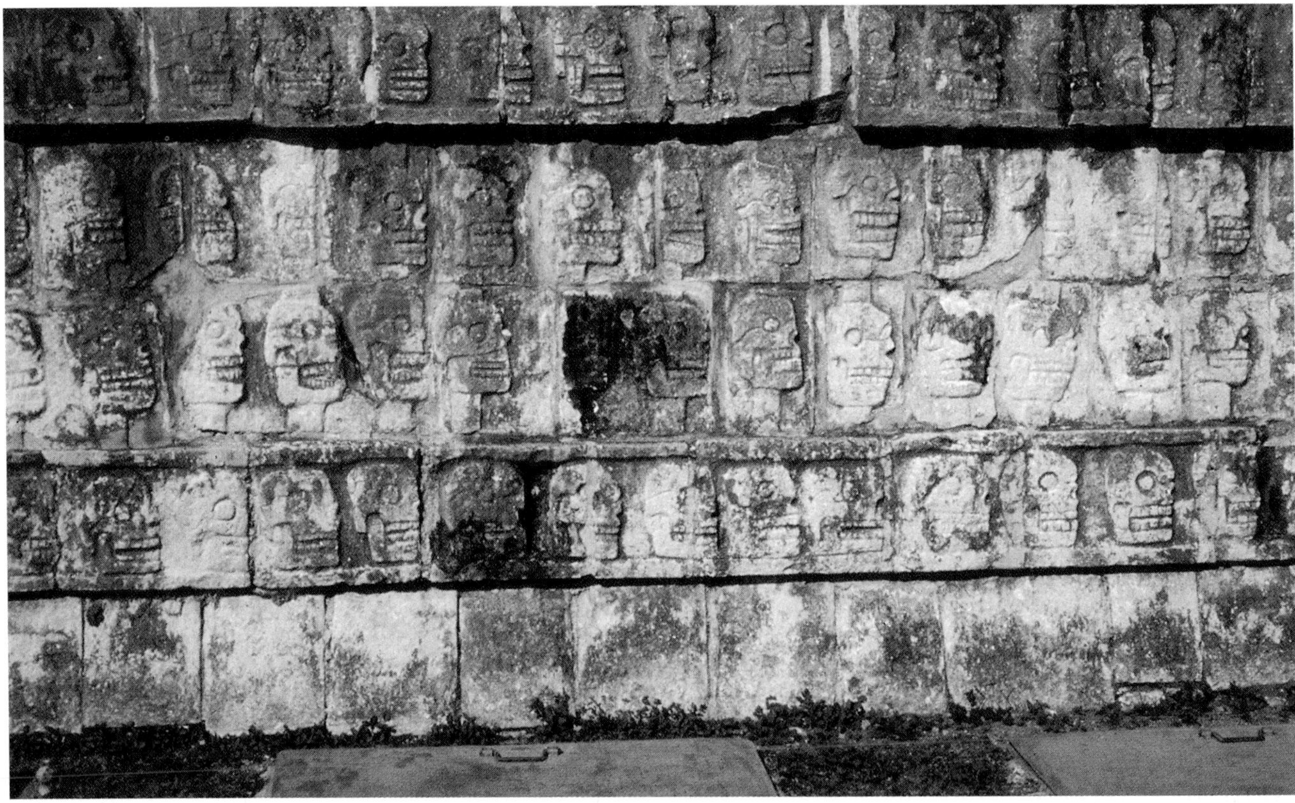

Figure 8.61 The *tzompantli* (carved skull rack) at Chichén Itzá depicts human skulls impaled on poles.

tually, they asked for the hand of the daughter of the ruler of Culhuacan to strengthen their bloodlines through marriage. Unfortunately, one of their gods, Huitzilopochtli, spoke to the Mexica priests and asked them to sacrifice the girl. The Culhua ruler, invited to a ceremony to dedicate his daughter as a goddess, instead found a Mexica priest dressed in the flayed skin of his offspring. His wrath again forced the Mexica to retreat.

At the start of their journey, the Mexica had been told by the same god that they would find an eagle perched atop a cactus plant to mark the end of their wanderings. Fleeing into the swamps of Lake Texcoco, one of the principal lakes of the basin, they found the eagle and cactus (a scene now immortalized on the flag of Mexico) on a nearby small, marshy island. The Mexica settled here and erected a temple for Huitzilopochtli. They named the settlement Tenochtitlán ("place of the fruit of the prickly pear cactus").

When Tenochtitlán was founded in A.D. 1325, the island lacked most construction materials (such as wood and stone), suffered periodic flooding, and was abundant only in insects. But the location offered several advantages. Water fowl and fish were plentiful, and the freshwater lakeshore was amenable to intensive *chinampa* agriculture (Figure 8.65). These farm plots, created by draining standing water and raising the surface of the swamp with soil and vegetation mats, became a major source of food production for the Aztecs. The little island was also in a prime location for controlling transportation in the basin. In ancient Mesoamerica, transport was exclusively by foot or canoe; there were neither beasts of burden nor wheeled vehicles (although toys with wheels were made). Water transport saved time and energy, especially when heavy loads were involved. Canoes plied the waters of the lake as the most efficient means of moving goods and materials between communities.

In the less than two centuries between its founding and the Spanish conquest, Tenochtitlán developed from a small island town to the largest and most powerful city in all of Mesoamerica. During its first century of existence (A.D. 1325–1428), the settlement was subordinate to more important basin centers. During this phase, the Aztec constructed *chinampas,* encouraged immigration to Tenochtitlán, and continued to gain renown for their mercenary skills. Their rulers strategically intermarried and allied themselves with more established elite in the region.

By 1428, Tenochtitlán was powerful enough to join with the petty states

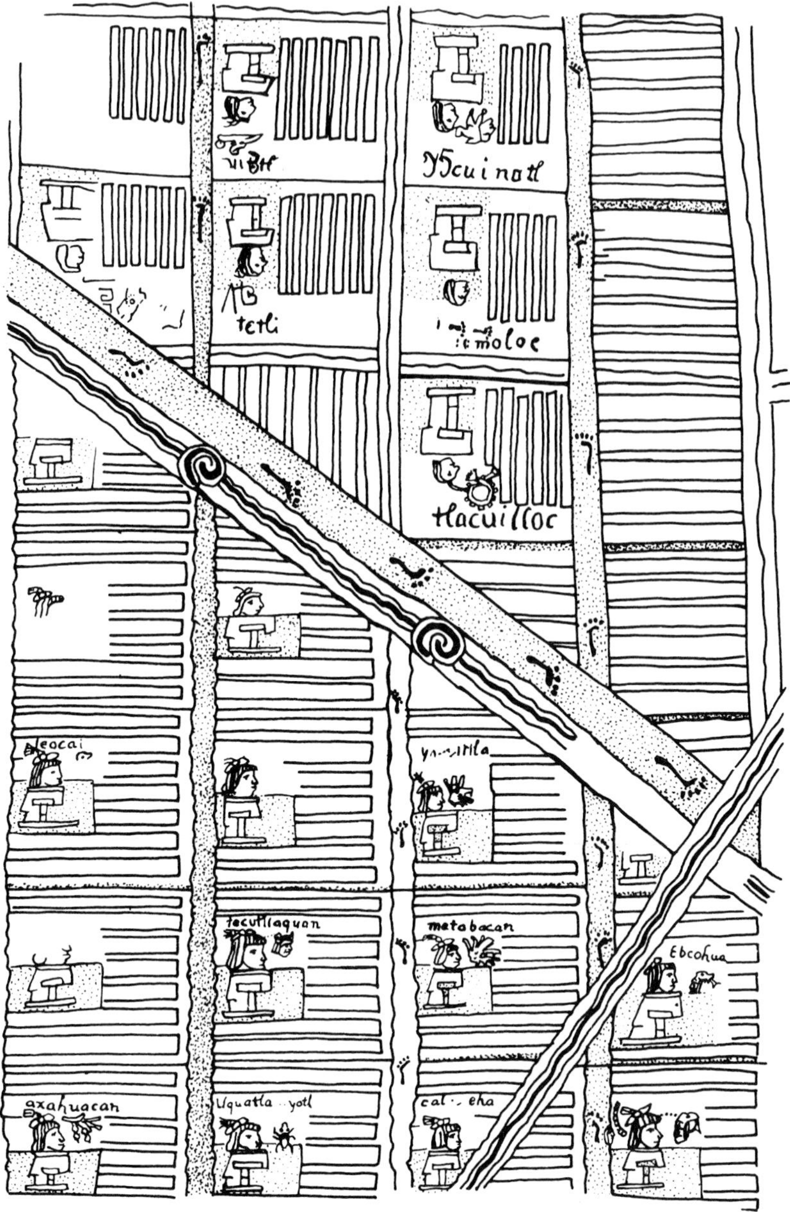


**Figure 8.65** Part of an early-sixteenth-century map of *chinampas* in Tenochtitlán. The *chinampas* are separated by water, and the houses of the owners, whose names are given in Spanish and Aztec hieroglyphs, are situated on squares of solid ground. Major canals are represented by wavy lines, and footprints indicate streets.

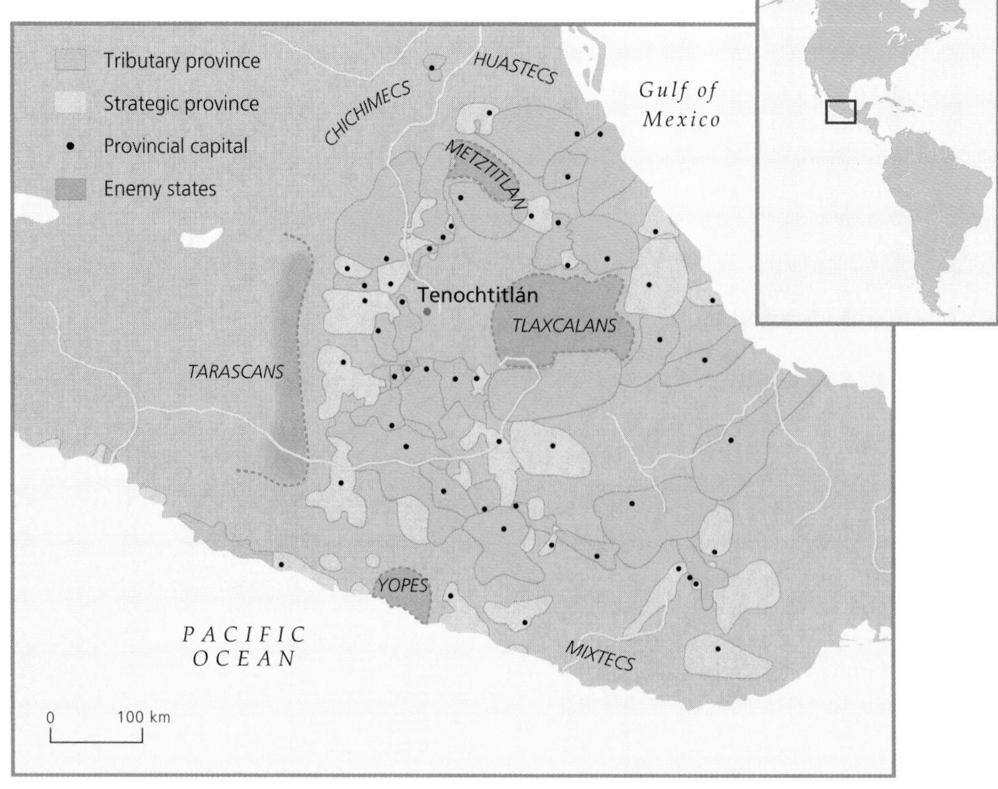


**Figure 8.66** The Triple Alliance controlled large parts of western Mesoamerica, although some groups were never defeated and maintained their independence.

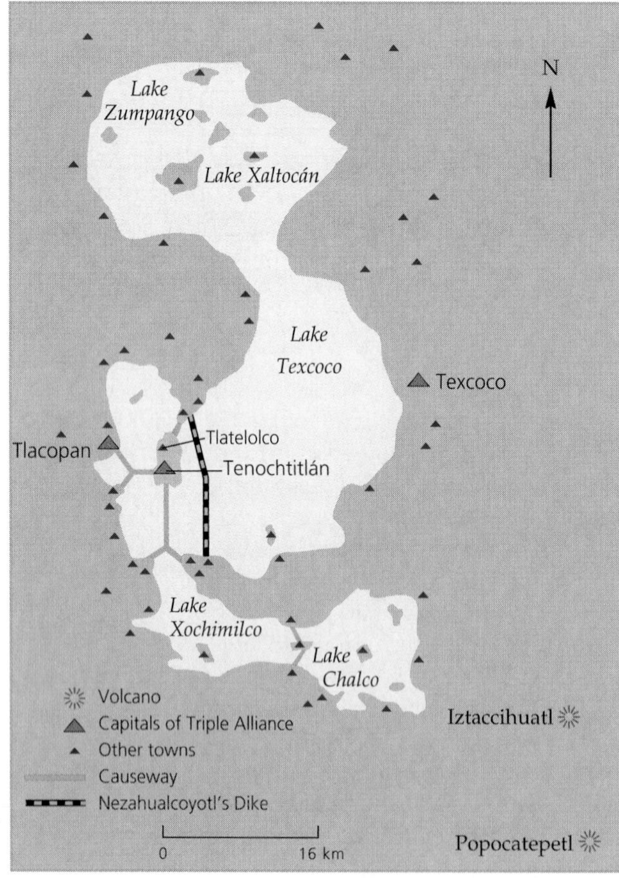


**Figure 8.67** The Basin of Mexico during Aztec times. Settled on an island in the southern part of the lake, Tenochtitlán was connected to the mainland by a series of causeways.

of Texcoco and Tlacopan (tlah-co-PAHN), forming a Triple Alliance that soon vaulted the Aztec capital to a supreme political position in the Basin of Mexico (Figure 8.66). In the years before the Spanish conquest, Tenochtitlán consolidated this political dominion while its armies defeated and demanded tribute from foreign polities across western Mesoamerica and as far away as Guatemala.

In 1473, Tenochtitlán defeated its neighbor city of Tlatelolco (tlah-tel-OL-co) and incorporated the latter, including its giant marketplace, into the metropolis. The dual city was linked to the mainland by three large causeways that ran from the lakeshore to the central ceremonial district of the capital (Figure 8.67). When the Spanish arrived, Tenochtitlán was a city of roughly 150,000–200,000 people. The Spanish leader Hernán Cortés was greatly impressed by the size and grandeur of Tenochtitlán, calling the Aztec city "another Venice."

Early Colonial period maps and accounts indicate that the basic residential unit at Tenochtitlán was smaller

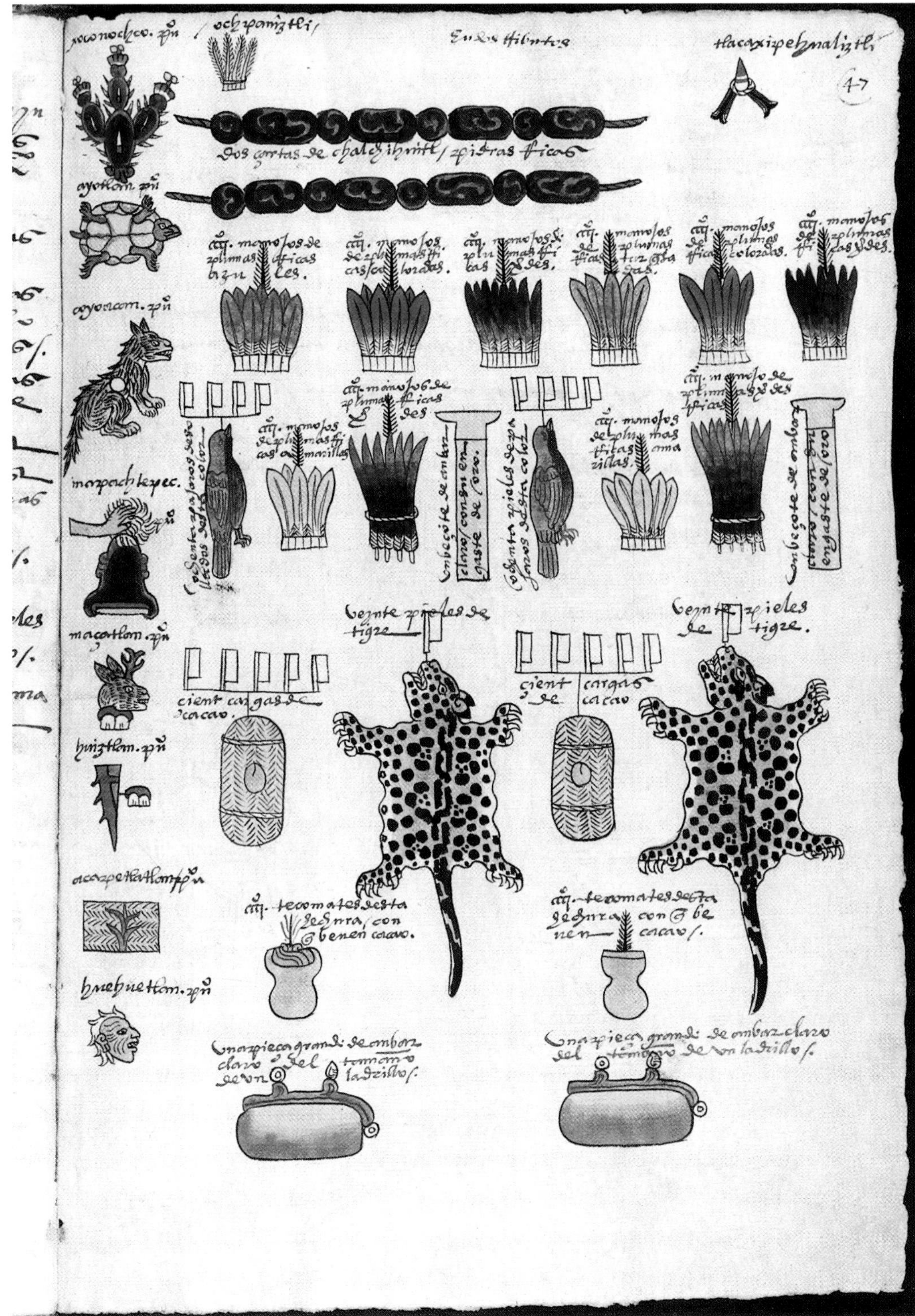

**Figure 8.68** A page from an ancient Mesoamerican codex. Aztec rulers of Mexico recorded the tribute they exacted from conquered peoples in books called codices. This page from the Codex Mendoza shows the name symbols of tributary towns and the kinds and amounts of tribute they owed.

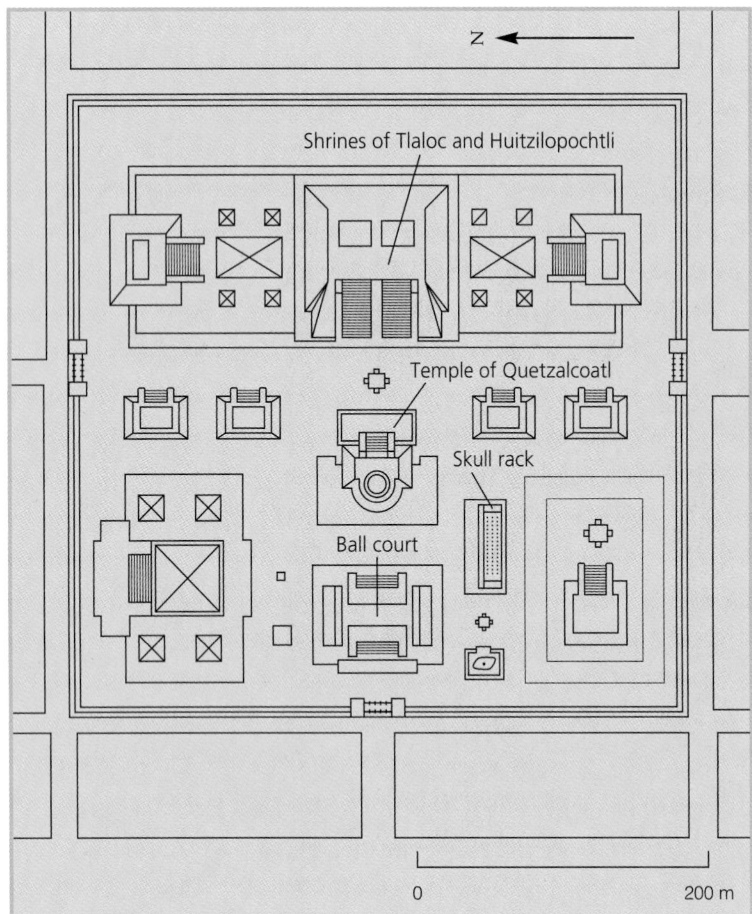


**Figure 8.69** The plan of the ceremonial core of Tenochtitlán. The shrines to Tlaloc and Huitzilpochtli sit atop the Templo Mayor.

than the apartment compounds at Teotihuacan. Most household compounds at Tenochtitlán were occupied by nuclear or joint families, each with its own direct access to the streets and canals of the city. Individual compounds were more easily differentiated, permitting public displays of status and wealth. In Aztec society, advances in social position could be achieved through military or economic successes.

Numerous craftspeople (including featherworkers, lapidaries, and reed-mat makers) were encouraged to settle in the city, adding to its importance as a commercial center. At that time, many women who were part of Aztec society engaged in some aspect of textile manufacture. The high volume of some finished goods in Tenochtitlán may have served to undermine local craft production at some outlying communities in the basin. Tenochtitlán also obtained large quantities of exotic resources and finished goods as tribute payments from defeated polities (Figure 8.68). In general, nearby polities gave foodstuffs, wood, woven mats, and heavier, more utilitarian items; more distant states sent rarer, more valuable goods. Captive states were typically instructed to send local materials. Other exotic goods were brought back to the city by the ***pochteca,*** an association of long-distance traders. The *pochteca* also returned to Tenochtitlán with valuable military or political information.

The Aztec tribute demands were heavy, and noncompliance was dealt with harshly. It is not surprising that Cortés' small band of adventurers received invaluable military and logistic support from Indian groups that despised the Aztecs. Obviously, Cortés and his few hundred men would not have defeated the Aztec armies as quickly and easily without this native assistance. Once victorious, the Spanish forced the conquered Indians to raze the ceremonial core of Tenochtitlán (Figure 8.69), replacing the temples and shrines with churches, government buildings, and palatial residences. Mexico City rapidly grew up over the ancient Aztec center. The upper level of the Templo Mayor was dismantled, and the materials were used to build Mexico City's Main Cathedral.

During the Colonial era, Spanish power in Mesoamerica was strengthened by occupation of the same place as the prior Aztec civic and sacred authority. Eventually, in response to several destructive floods, the once productive lakes were largely drained by the Spanish. The Colonial authorities could not adequately manipulate the complex networks of dikes and canals that had been built and used by the Aztecs. The dry lake bottom now serves as the soft foundation for Mexico's earthquake-prone capital.

***pochteca*** A privileged, hereditary guild of long-distance Aztec traders.

## Aztec Markets

*Cacao, currency, and "profit" in ancient Mexico*

**Figure 8.70** Aztec market scenes from the Codex Florentino. Top left: a produce market with neatly arranged wares; top right: King Ahuitzotl receiving shells, jaguar skins, plumage, jade, and cacao from the coast; bottom left: members of a slave family wearing bars across their necks as a sign of bondage; bottom right: a merchant from the coast bartering for cloth, gold ornaments, copper, obsidian tools, and maguey fiber rope from the highlands.

In today's market economies, people try to minimize costs and maximize returns to make a profit. Anthropologists distinguish this type of market endeavor from reciprocal and redistributive exchange networks (see "The Archaeology of Exchange," Chapter 7, p. 281). Reciprocity refers to face-to-face exchanges between known participants, such as relatives or trading partners, in which the specific return is not predefined (gift giving, for example). Redistribution is the accumulation and later dispersal of goods from a central place or by a central person (the income tax system, for example).

Aztec **marketing,** with its network of marketplaces, various currencies, and numerous participants, clearly fits within the conventional definition of a market system (Figure 8.70). The central market at Tlatelolco, Tenochtitlán's sister city, was the largest market in a network of centers that were situated across the Basin of Mexico.

The Tlatelolco market alone served 20,000–25,000 people on a normal day, and twice as many every fifth day, when it was the focus of a cycle of changing regional markets. Many exchanges in the market were made by bartering. Others were facilitated by accepted currencies. **Cacao** beans, used to make a favorite drink of the nobility, were the most common form of money, but large cotton cloaks, quills filled with gold dust, stone and shell beads, and copper beads and axes also were employed. Cacao beans, which in fact did grow on trees, were accepted in payment for either goods or labor. Their importance was such that the dishonest buyers and sellers tried to counterfeit cacao by filling the bark or skin of the beans with earth. These fake cacao beans were then adeptly sealed and mixed into piles with true beans, where they could be passed off as genuine. Both the existence of counterfeit beans and the presence of market judges to catch and punish dishonest merchants emphasize the importance of profit as a motive in this precapitalist society.

We know the Aztecs engaged in market exchange. Did other Mesoamerican groups also have markets? Do you think markets may have been present in Mesoamerica before the Aztecs?

**marketing** An exchange system that frequently involves currencies and generally extends beyond close kinsmen and a small group of trading partners. Market participants try to minimize their costs and maximize their returns to make a profit.

**cacao** A bean of the cacao tree, native to Mesoamerica; used to make chocolate. Cacao beans also were used as money by the Aztecs.

Concept

## Human Sacrifice and Cannibalism

*Divergent interpretations of ancient rites*

**Figure 8.71** A depiction of an Aztec ritual heart sacrifice from a sixteenth-century codex.

*Many lines of evidence confirm that human sacrifice was one of the most deeply rooted religious traditions of the Aztecs. However, it is clear that the Aztecs were not the only ancient peoples that carried out massacres in honor of their gods, and there is insufficient quantitative information to determine whether the Aztecs were the people who practiced human sacrifice most often. Indeed, sacred texts, literary works, historic documents, and especially evidence contributed by archaeology and physical anthropology, enable religious historians to determine that the practice of human sacrifice was common in most parts of the ancient world.*

—Alfredo López Austin and Leonardo López Luján (2008)

**cannibalism** The practice of eating human flesh.

No issue concerning ancient Mexico has attracted more attention and biting scholarly debate than human sacrifice and **cannibalism.** The Aztecs have frequently been portrayed in the popular press as violent, insatiable cannibals, practicing bloodthirsty and ghoulish acts (Figure 8.71). Ritual sacrifices have been documented archaeologically in early Mesopotamia, as well as in dynastic Egypt and ancient China. Human sacrifice has a very long history in prehispanic Mesoamerica, perhaps even dating back to the preceramic era in the Tehuacán Valley. Human sacrifice is depicted graphically in several Classic Maya inscriptions and is strongly suggested by the Oaxacan *danzante* stones. Ancient Mesoamerican societies also gave great ritual importance to blood. Both autosacrifice and the ritual offerings of blood are present in the archaeological and epigraphic evidence (Figure 8.72).

Why, then, are the Aztecs so closely linked to the practice of human sacrifice? Most likely it is because the custom was featured so prominently in Spanish descriptions of central Mexico. Whereas the Aztecs believed human sacrifice was a deeply religious practice, necessary for preserving the continuity of the universe, the Spanish Catholics saw it as the devil's work. Furthermore, the Europeans believed it their duty to abolish this behavior through conquest, conversion, and whatever means possible. The elimination of these customs, which horrified the Spanish, therefore became a rationale for achieving their envisioned destiny to rule New Spain. (It should be noted that, at the time, the Spanish themselves were not above ghoulish behavior; in Spain, people were burned at the stake, while in Mexico, many Indians were mistreated and massacred.)

Anthropologist William Arens, of the State University of New York at Stony Brook, argues that the Spanish were so interested in defaming the native inhabitants and justifying their conquests that their sixteenth-century accounts cannot be trusted. Arens questions whether cannibalism even existed among the Aztecs. Although the evidence for cannibalism is not as overwhelming as it is for large-scale sacrifice, independent accounts describe the consumption of sacrificed prisoners, particularly by warriors and members of the elite.

An alternative to Arens' explanation has been advanced by Michael Harner, who argues that the absence of domesticated animals and the large number of people in late prehispanic central Mexico necessitated enormous Aztec sacrifices to alleviate a dietary shortage of meat protein and fat through cannibalism. Harner's ecological interpretation, which lists cannibalism as the reason for enormous sacrifices, has met with little nutritional, economic, or historical support. Harner argues that some 250,000 people were sacrificed each year in central Mexico, whereas most scholars place the annual figure in the tens of thousands. Harner ignores the religious context of Mesoamerican sacrifice and symbolic blood offerings, which often occurred without cannibalism. Many of the Aztec sacrificial events, which elaborated and embellished these prior customs, were dedicatory, carried out as thanksgiving rituals, and involved no cannibalism.

The diet of the people of prehispanic Mexico probably was not deficient in either protein or fat. In combination, the dietary staples of maize and beans provide a complete protein source. Such staples were sent in tribute to Tenochtitlán from surrounding polities and distributed through the market system. In one sixteenth-century account, 32 different types of wild fowl, many of which were very fatty, were described as edible; several of these were noted as abundant. Fish and other lake flora and fauna, including high-protein algae that was made into a cheeselike delicacy, also were available, as were domesticated dog and turkey. Some agricultural fields, such as the *chinampas,* produced two or three crops annually.

If, as Harner implies, cannibalism provided the Aztecs with a major source of food, why were most sacrifices held immediately following the major harvest, when food was abundant? In addition, why was human flesh restricted to the warriors and elite, groups likely to have the most to eat anyway? During Cortés' long siege of Tenochtitlán, the inhabitants were starving, eating almost anything, even adobe and leather. Yet human bodies lay all around, untouched.

Aztec human sacrifice is more convincingly interpreted in its historical and symbolic context. The Aztec traditions are connected with earlier Mesoamerican customs of bloodletting, dedicatory offerings, and the sacrifice of war captives in ritual events. The embellishment of the practice of human sacrifice by the Aztecs would seem associated with their distinctly militaristic background. According to Aztec ideology, they were the people chosen to nourish the deities through human sacrifice, as a hedge against uncertainty and to maintain order in the universe. Since sacrificial victims were frequently (though not exclusively) prisoners or slaves, these beliefs may have motivated and fanaticized the Aztec military. The Aztecs conducted several kinds of sacrificial rituals—to bring rain, to commemorate temples, and as a kind of thanksgiving. Large sacrificial events also must have conveyed a powerful message about the strength and sanctity of Tenochtitlán to individuals both inside and outside the city.

**Figure 8.72** Two priests pierce their tongues and ears with thorns from the maguey plant in this drawing from a codex.

*Images and Ideas*

## The End of Prehispanic Civilizations in Mexico

### *The legacy of Mesoamerica's past*

People first set foot in Mesoamerica approximately 10,000–15,000 years ago. From their arrival until A.D. 1519, when the Spanish arrived, Mesoamerican societies developed and diversified independently of contacts with nonnative peoples. Over that period, a Mesoamerican world evolved, composed of diverse groups and polities connected through trade, warfare, intermarriage, and other long-distance contacts and communication. These peoples shared a common cultural background that was distinctively Mesoamerican. Sedentary villages emerged across Mesoamerica during the second millennium B.C., and cities and conquest states were first established in various regions after 500 B.C.

The study of ancient Mesoamerica, therefore, enables archaeologists to examine agricultural origins, the emergence of villages and institutionalized social inequality, and the rise and fall of early civilizations. It also permits the investigation of a large macroregion that, unlike portions of the Near East, was never politically controlled by a single empire. Even the powerful Aztec armies were unable to defeat and consolidate the nearby peoples of Tlaxcala or the west Mexican Tarascans. Although long-term change in Mesoamerica did not follow the same course as in Mesopotamia and China (Chapter 10), Europe (Chapter 11), or even South America (Chapter 9), there are many features of these sequences of change and transition that can be compared.

The prehistory of Mesoamerica is documented by a variety of sources of information, including both indigenous and sixteenth-century Spanish texts and archaeological studies. With recent breakthroughs in the decipherment of Classic Maya writing systems, scholars studying these lowland societies can now view the past from an indigenous perspective that is not available for other regions of the preconquest Americas. Alternatively, the Mesoamerican highlands are well suited to archaeological surveys. In the valleys of Tehuacán, Mexico, and Oaxaca, as well as in several other highland Mesoamerican zones, the regional perspective from such surveys supplements the more specific findings from careful excavations at individual sites. We have learned that the size and number of prehispanic settlements did not increase at a uniform rate during the prehispanic era and that the pattern of population change was somewhat different in each region.

**Figure 8.73** An example of a ceramic dog figurine with wheels (c. 15 cm tall).

The art and architectural ruins of ancient Mesoamerican societies have captured attention for centuries (Figure 8.73). Now, as we collect more information about their makers, archaeologists have become fascinated with economies, statecraft, religious systems, and other aspects of their lifeways. The diversity of ancient Mesoamerican cities in size and function is truly astounding. Thus Mesoamerica has become a fruitful domain for the study of early urbanism and the processes associated with the rise of ancient cities. Some Mesoamerican cities, such as Teotihuacan, were compact and laid out on a grid plan. Others were dispersed and positioned according to local topography, as in the Maya region during the Classic period. In Classic Maya cities and at Monte Albán, for example, the major thoroughfares were not strictly perpendicular to one another. Residential architecture also was far from uniform at major Mesoamerican cities. Craft manufacturing was central to ancient Teotihuacan, but it played a smaller role in other cities. Although exchange was an integrative mechanism that linked Mesoamerican cities with their hinterlands, marketing may have had an especially crucial role at Tenochtitlán.

In ancient Mesoamerica, the volume and magnitude of trade was limited by prehispanic transport. So one can only marvel at the mechanisms that allowed for the organization of tens (and even hundreds) of thousands of people. The longevity of cities such as Teotihuacan and rain-forest Tikal exemplify the effectiveness of the kin, ceremonial, and stately ties that integrated Mesoamerican polities. Such features as the calendar, the ballgame, certain symbols, sacrificial (blood) rituals, public architectural conventions, and astronomical knowledge were all part of key informational systems that were shared and communicated primarily by the elite, and seemingly central to the maintenance of both their position and societal continuity.

Yet the specific ways in which these symbols were used and the nature of Mesoamerican rulership were by no means uniform across time and space. Classic Maya rule emphasized specific lords, individuals like Palenque's Pakal and Tikal's Siyaj Chan, who were depicted on stelae in ornate costumes and were eventually buried in elaborate tombs accompanied by rich offerings. In contrast, we currently do not know the names of any of the rulers of ancient Teotihuacan, nor have elaborate burial displays been unearthed. Rule at Teotihuacan seems to have been less focused on specific individuals. Architectural emphasis was placed on large public spaces, such as inside the Ciudadela and the plaza in front of the Pyramid of the Moon. For the most part, mural art depicted ritual feasts and offerings, rather than glorifying the dynastic histories of specific kings. Although Teotihuacan undoubtedly had a ruling class, the strategies of rule and the mechanisms of societal integration were different from those of the Classic Maya. At the same time, whether we look at the Maya region, central Mexico, or Oaxaca, Classic- and Postclassic-period Mesoamerican states went through cycles of growth and decline, centralization and fragmentation.

The autonomy of ancient Mesoamerican societies ended in the sixteenth century with the arrival of the Spanish, but the ancestry and culture of the indigenous peoples has in large part survived, helping meld the contemporary lifeways of Mexico and Central America. The foods, artisanry, music, religion, and languages of these areas owe much to their prehispanic heritage. The demise of Aztec society, as well as that of their allies and enemies, has remarkable parallels to similar events farther south. In the northwestern quadrant of South America, the sixteenth-century Spanish clashed with a powerful indigenous Andean society, the Inca. Inca administration also had come to dominate a large cultural area, even larger than that dominated by the Aztecs. But they, too, were conquered by the arriving *conquistadores.* In the next chapter, we examine these Andean societies and the series of processes and events that culminated in the empire of the Inca.

*Does this mean that the Maya were then more advanced than their counterparts in, say, Europe? Social scientists flinch at this question, and with good reason. The Olmec, Maya, and other Mesoamerican societies were world pioneers in mathematics and astronomy—but they did not use the wheel. Amazingly, they had invented the wheel but did not employ it for any purpose other than children's toys. Those looking for a tale of cultural superiority can find it in zero; those looking for failure can find it in the wheel. Neither line of argument is useful, though. What is most important is that by 1000 A.D. Indians had expanded their Neolithic revolutions to create a panoply of diverse civilizations across the hemisphere.*

—Charles C. Mann (2005)

## DISCUSSION QUESTIONS

1. What are some similarities and differences in the settlement plans and residential architecture at Monte Albán, Teotihuacan, and Tikal? What might archaeologists learn from these differences and similarities?
2. How did the Classic Maya centers of Tikal and Palenque differ from later Chichén Itzá?
3. Were all states in indigenous Mesoamerica similar in organization? If so, explain. If not, how were they different?

**www.mhhe.com/priceip6e**

For more review material and study questions, see the self-quizzes on your online learning center.

## SUGGESTED READINGS

For Internet links related to this chapter, please visit our Web site at www.mhhe.com/priceip6e.


Blanton, R. E., S. A. Kowalewski, G. M. Feinman, and L. M. Finsten. 1993. *Ancient Mesoamerica: A comparison of change in three regions,* 2d ed. Cambridge: Cambridge University Press. *An analysis of long-term change in three Mesoamerican regions.*

Brumfiel, E. M., and G. M. Feinman, eds. 2008. *The Aztec world.* New York: Abrams. *A collection of essays by renowned Aztec scholars.*

Evans, S. T. 2004. *Ancient Mexico and Central America: Archaeology and culture history.* London: Thames & Hudson. *A recent overview of prehispanic Mesoamerica from first occupation through Spanish conquest.*

Flannery, K. V., ed. 1976. *The early Mesoamerican village.* New York: Academic Press. *A humorous, yet highly instructive, volume on ancient Mesoamerica that illustrates how archaeology should proceed at various scales of analysis to interpret the past.*

Flannery, K. V., and J. Marcus, eds. 1983. *The cloud people: Divergent evolution of the Zapotec and Mixtec civilizations.* New York: Academic Press. Reprint, Clinton Corners, NY: Percheron Press, 2003. *The synthetic overview for prehispanic Oaxaca.*

Sharer, R. J., and L. P. Traxler. 2006. *The ancient Maya,* 6th ed. Stanford, CA: Stanford University Press. *A classic text on the Maya.*

# CHAPTER NINE

**Figure 9.1** Gold bead in the form of a human head, 5.3 cm (2 in) high, from Tomb 3 at Sipán. This bead was part of a necklace (10 beads in all) that was placed near the neck of the principal individual in the tomb.

# South America

## The Inca and Their Predecessors

## Introduction

### Prehispanic South America

*The foundations and cycles of Andean states and empires*

In Peru (as in too many other places in the world), the tradition of pillaging ancient sites for priceless artifacts is an old one, extending back to Spanish conquerors, who, beginning in 1532, ransacked the Inca empire for gold, silver, and precious stones. Around midnight one evening in February 1987, Peruvian archaeologist Walter Alva, director of the Brüning Archaeological Museum in Lambayeque, Peru, was called by the local chief of police, who reported with urgency that there was something that Alva had to see. Looters had illegally tunneled into an earthen pyramid built by the ancient Moche (A.D. 100–700) at Sipán and exposed burials with associated metal, shell, and ceramic artifacts that the grave robbers intended for the international art market.

In response to the looting, Alva and his wife, Susana Meneses, began years of careful salvage excavations in this earthen mound at Sipán, scientifically investigating the richest tombs ever found in the Americas (Figure 9.1). Their excavations have made sense of these fabulous finds, placing them in a cultural context that could never have been achieved if the entire mound had been pillaged. In this chapter, the antecedents of the Moche, as well as the web of history that ran from the Moche to the Inca, are explored for this ancient Andean region.

When Christopher Columbus left Spain on the voyage that brought him to America, the largest empire in the world was Tawantinsuyu, the Inca empire. Much greater in size than any fifteenth- or twentieth-century European state, Tawantinsuyu ("land of four quarters") stretched over 984,000 sq km (380,000 sq mi), about the size of Washington, Oregon, Idaho, and Montana combined. The Inca controlled the most extensive political domain that has ever existed in the Southern Hemisphere. Cuzco, the capital of the realm, governed some 80 provinces that sprawled from Colombia in the north across the Andean highlands of Argentina, Bolivia, Peru, and Ecuador to Chile in the south.

From the Pacific Ocean, the Andes rise so abruptly that a mere sliver of flat coastal land separates the high mountains from the water. This coastal strip is one of the world's driest deserts. In the high Andes, where peaks rise to more than 6100 m (20,000 feet) above sea level (the highest peaks in North or South America), humans occupied the relatively flat basins and valleys, as well as the high grassland plateaus (*punas*). The eastern side of the mountains, called the *montaña,* is wet and heavily vegetated. Farther east lies the enormous drainage basin of the Amazon, composed of tropical forests and savannas. Feathers and many tropical plants were brought from the forest into the Andean and coastal zones.

**CHAPTER OUTLINE**

www.mhhe.com/priceip6e

For preview material for this chapter, see the comprehensive chapter outline and chapter objectives on your online learning center.

Our main focus in this chapter is Andean South America. The people of the Amazon rain forests and savannas had a unique and important prehistory as well. Yet because of the impenetrability of the lush environment, archaeologists and ethnohistorians still know much less about the latter area than about the more accessible coastal and mountain zones.

In 1948 and 1949, Betty Meggers and Clifford Evans, of the Smithsonian Institution, began preliminary investigations on Marajó Island at the mouth of the Amazon River. On this large island, 39,000 sq m (15,000 sq mi), huge earthworks were found, which Meggers and Evans interpreted as the remnants of a complex society that had moved to the island from the Andes, only to meet a rapid demise. At the time, this interpretation was well reasoned because the large scale of the earthworks was unexpected, given their absence in small, egalitarian, contemporary Amazonian Indian villages. Archaeological work on Marajó Island by Anna Roosevelt, of the University of Illinois at Chicago, and her colleagues has revised our perspective on Marajoara origins. Their research illustrates numerous continuities between modern Amazonian people and the earlier Marajoara occupation and documents a more-than-1000-year habitation sequence (400 B.C.–A.D. 1300) on the island. For example, Roosevelt found large, globular burial urns that were painted to represent crouching humans, decorated with multicolored, geometric patterns similar to the abstract drug visions illustrated by contemporary Amazonians. Marajoara art also has antecedents in earlier lowland styles, and the painting method is Amazonian (not Andean) in character. The physical affiliation of Marajoara skeletons is closer to Amazonian than to Andean people.

*The myth persists that in 1492 the Americas were a sparsely populated wilderness, "a world of barely perceptible human disturbance." There is substantial evidence, however, that the Native American landscape of the early sixteenth century was a humanized landscape almost everywhere. Populations were large. Forest composition had been modified, grasslands had been created, wildlife disrupted, and erosion was severe in places. Earthworks, roads, fields, and settlements were ubiquitous. With Indian depopulation in the wake of Old World disease, the environment recovered in many areas. A good argument can be made that the human presence was less visible in 1750 than it was in 1492.*
—William M. Denevan (1992)

At the same time, reanalysis of written accounts of sixteenth-century Spanish penetration into the Amazon, along with recent archaeological mapping and excavations, has led researchers to argue that many of the late prehistoric populations of this region lived in more permanent settlements that were more densely distributed than found for more contemporary settlements. The past settlements also were more hierarchically organized. Differences, such as the cessation of inherited positions of leadership, between pre-Columbian inhabitants and contemporary groups may owe much to the diseases brought by the Europeans.

Western South America contained the continent's first agricultural settlements (e.g., Guitarrero Cave), as well as its earliest sedentary communities. We examine the prehispanic peoples of this area, beginning with early monumental construction on the Peruvian coast and neighboring river valleys. We start with the early site of El Paraíso, a sedentary coastal community dating to before 2000 B.C., and conclude with the late prehispanic Inca sites of Cuzco, Machu Picchu, and Huánuco Pampa (Figure 9.2).

The prehistory of this part of South America is, in a general way, similar to that of Mesoamerica. In both areas, the earliest experiments with food production preceded the transition to sedentary village life. In South America, the first villages date to 3500 B.C., much earlier than in Mesoamerica. In both regions, however, these first sedentary communities were situated near the coast. Almost immediately, greater social differences and the first positions of leadership become evident in the archaeological record. In Mesoamerica, these changes occurred along with the development of an interregional style, the Olmec Horizon, represented in exotic and highly crafted items found in both the highlands and the lowlands. Between 900 and 200 B.C., a similar phenomenon, the Chavín style, was shared from the edges of the Amazon to the Pacific Coast. This style is named for the carvings found on a temple in the uplands of central Peru at Chavín de Huántar. In Peru, however, the spread of the Chavín style postdates the construction of truly monumental public architecture and the emergence of social differences at coastal sites that were contemporary with earlier El Paraíso.

In South America, the end of the last century B.C. was marked by the rise of major centers that became the core of states administering regional populations. We discuss Moche, on the north coast, and refer to the fantastic line drawings

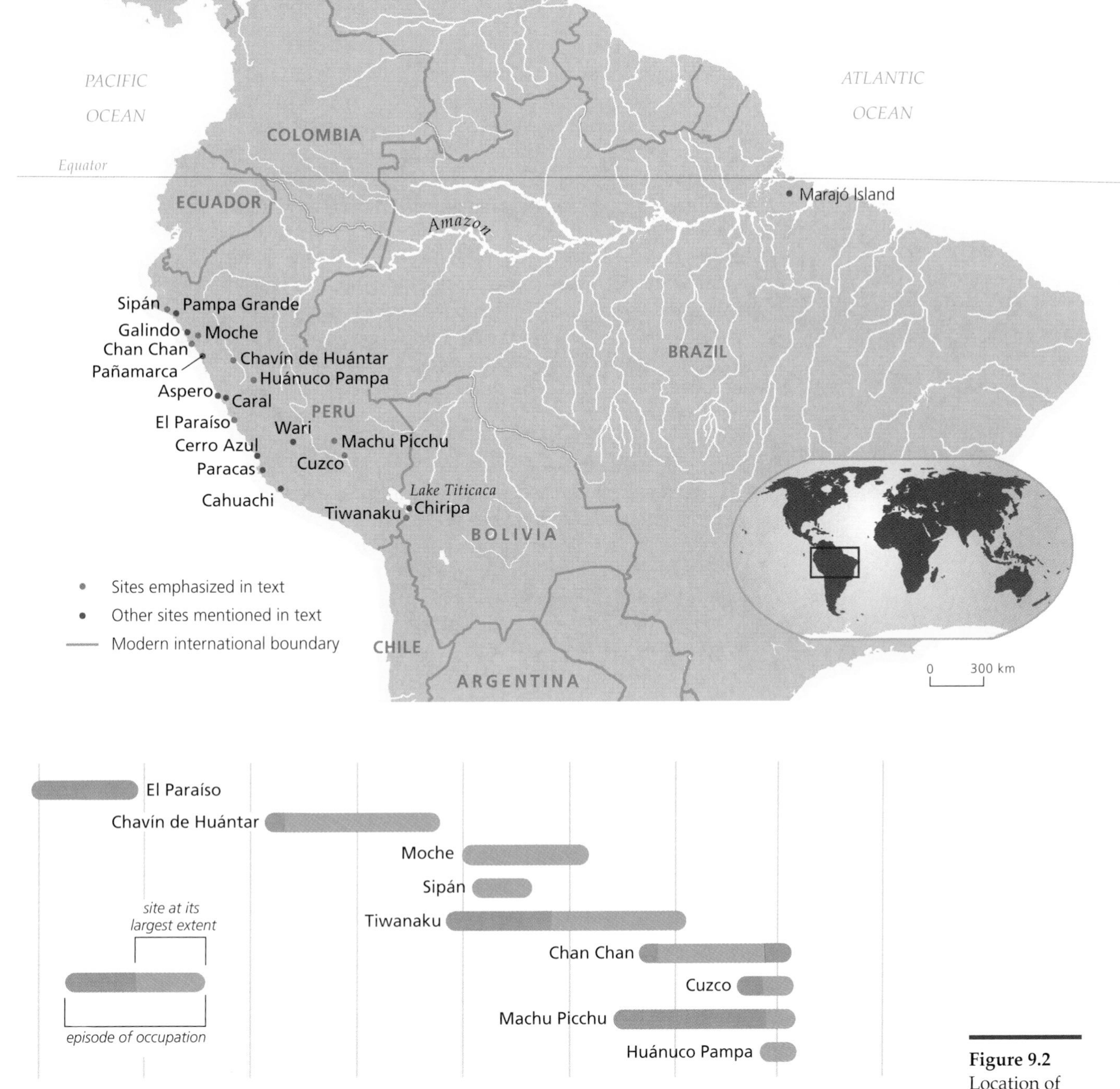


**Figure 9.2** Location of and timeline for South American sites.

constructed by the Nazca in the south. We also discuss the coastal site of Sipán, where spectacular Moche-era tombs were excavated. Later, Tiwanaku, a giant economic and religious center near the southern end of Lake Titicaca in Bolivia, began to incorporate larger areas outside its local region.

As with the Aztecs in the Central Highlands of Mexico, the end of the prehispanic era in South America was characterized by a powerful people, the Inca, whose rulers exacted tribute from a wide domain. Yet this much larger South American empire had clearer imperial predecessors, such as the Tiwanaku polity and the Chimú kingdom. After A.D. 1000, the latter, which was centered on the north coast at Chan Chan, consolidated a large, primarily coastal domain. This political sphere was eventually engulfed by the expansive Inca, who conquered the Chimú between A.D. 1462 and 1470. We examine the nature and organization of this Western Hemisphere empire by looking at Cuzco, the Inca capital, the famous high mountain settlement of Machu Picchu, and the provincial administrative center of Huánuco Pampa.

Although parallels can be drawn between the long prehispanic sequences in Mexico and Peru, there also were important differences. Most of the major Peruvian centers were shorter-lived than Mesoamerican sites such as San José Mogote, Monte Albán, and Teotihuacan, which were inhabited almost continuously for a millennium or more. The Andean world also seems to have lacked a core region like the Basin of Mexico, which dominated the larger landscape for much of the prehispanic era. In South America, the balance of power seems to have shifted repeatedly between the Pacific Coast and the rugged uplands. Likewise, at times, the core of the Andean world was positioned in the south (as at Inca Cuzco); at other times, the Andean world's most powerful centers lay in the north at Moche and Chan Chan.

Animal domestication was more important in South America, where a variety of camelids, in addition to guinea pigs, were tamed. Since only the turkey, the dog, and the honeybee were domesticated in Mesoamerica, long-distance land transport was conducted entirely by human bearers. In South America, the llama (a camelid), used also for wool and meat, served as a pack animal for loads up to 45 kg (100 lb), making land transportation considerably less costly than it was in Mesoamerica. Llamas, like the more efficient Eurasian beasts of burden, subsist on grasses and other foods that humans cannot digest.

The Inca built and maintained an extensive, often paved road system (with suspension cables, stone bridges, and a system of relay runners) that crossed almost the entire empire and was unmatched in Mesoamerica. Watercrafts, including giant trading canoes, were more developed in Middle America.

In Mesoamerica, a writing system developed more than 2000 years ago. Subsequently, it diversified, with several systems, particularly that of the Maya, becoming more complex (with relatively long texts). In contrast, to date no archaeological evidence for a traditional form of writing has been found in the prehispanic Andes. The Inca did possess an ingenious numerical apparatus, the ***quipu*** (knot), which was composed of a main horizontal cord from which a series of smaller strings hung. The *quipu* was used to record numbers, by tying knots at various intervals on these strings. The knots farthest from the main cord represent the smallest numbers. Recent studies of the *quipu* have proposed that it was used by the Inca to convey more information than just complex mathematical data. The color, placement, and nature of the various knots on *quipu* are now thought to have been used to record and transmit more intricate messages and information through a system of **binary-coded** sequences. Even without a traditional system of writing, the Inca were able to establish a larger and better integrated political system than ever existed in prehispanic Mesoamerica.

Although the written words left by the Maya and other Mesoamerican peoples are absent in the Andes, archaeologists working along the arid coast of Peru have the advantage of a quality of preservation unknown almost anywhere else. Standing adobe architecture frequently sits almost unscathed by the elements for centuries, even millennia. The recovery of large woven textiles is not unusual. Preservation can be so good that even fingernail clippings and human hair were found by Joyce Marcus using careful excavation procedures at coastal Cerro Azul, a site that postdates A.D. 1100. Marcus also found a series of mummified burials at Cerro Azul. Males generally were buried with fishing nets or slings (for hunting), and females were buried with an array of different weaving implements (including camelid bone tools, bobbins made of thorn, needles, and balls of various colored yarns).

South America provides another fascinating area for studying the emergence of an indigenous civilization. Only through archaeology can we hope to discover the remarkable similarities—as well as the all-important differences—that characterized these long cultural processes in various regions of the globe.

***quipu*** The Inca word for an elaborate knotted string device used by the Inca and other peoples in Peru for record keeping.

**binary-coded** A system of information storage or processing in two states (such as 0 and 1). Computers process immense amounts of information through the manipulation of such sequences.

Site

# El Paraíso

## *Settlement and monumentality on Peru's coast and adjacent river valleys*

The waters off the west coast of Peru are one of the world's richest fishing areas. A complex mixing of ocean currents provides an extraordinary source of marine foods. The shore of these abundant waters, however, is one of the world's driest deserts. The same cold waters that foster rich plankton and fish life also inhibit rainfall on the coast. This coastal zone, stretching from the shoreline to the foothills of the Andes, only rarely receives measurable quantities of precipitation. Short-lived torrential downpours occur only once or twice a decade. Rivers and streams carrying the snowmelt and rainfall from the Andes provide most of the surface water, cross-cutting the bleak coastal desert in an east-west direction. These waterways are in essence isolated verdant pockets along the arid coastline.

The desert coast of central Peru was first settled after 7000 B.C. by mobile groups who exploited a wide range of environmental zones. The Pacific Ocean was a source of fish and shellfish; deer, small mammals, and birds were hunted and wild plants collected in the coastal river valleys. The dry foothills of the western Andes become oases of scattered communities of vegetation, or ***lomas,*** between June and October (winter in the Southern Hemisphere). Here the early inhabitants ate deer and the edible seeds of grasses or sagelike plants. Grinding stones used in preparing these plant foods have been found in these areas.

After 5000 B.C., certain coastal populations relied increasingly on marine and plant products, including cultivated squash and tubers that had been introduced to the desert coast from the highlands. Peru's first permanent, year-round villages were established after 4000 B.C., more than 1000 years before the first Peruvian evidence for pottery.

**Figure 9.3** Main complex of platform mounds at Caral in the Supe Valley.

Based on recent research by Ruth Shady Solis, of the National University of San Marcos, Peru, preceramic sedentary settlements with monumental architecture were established around 3000 B.C. in several river valleys just inland from the coast. Caral is the largest and best known of these centers (Figure 9.3). Located in the Supe Valley, the settlement consists of a complex of six platform mounds, plazas, and residential buildings that cover 60 ha (150 acres). The large mounds were raised above the surrounding desert through a construction technique of placing ***shicra*** in the fill. Inside the ring of pyramids is a large sunken amphitheater. Regional surveys and test excavations by Jonathan Haas, of the Field Museum of Natural History in Chicago, and Winifred Creamer, of the University of Northern Illinois, have revealed other monumental settlements in the Supe and adjacent river valleys along a stretch of the Peruvian coast known as Norte Chico.

Other centers, perhaps slightly later in date, also were established on the coast. One of these sites, Aspero, at

***lomas*** (Spanish) Vegetation that is supported by fog in otherwise arid environments.

***shicra*** (Inca) Meshed bags containing rocks, used as fill in the construction of ancient Andean structures.

*Concept*

## The Nazca Geoglyphs

*Desert images*

**Figure 9.23** An aerial photograph of a monkey at Nazca.

On the south coast of Peru, the Nazca style developed from the earlier Paracas art around 200 B.C. Most Nazca ceramic art, renowned for brilliantly painted **polychrome** vessels with six or seven colors, comes from looted cemeteries, although a few large Nazca sites have been studied more systematically. Most notable is the site of Cahuachi (cah-WAH-chih) in the Nazca Valley, a large aggregation of adobe platforms, courts, and associated buildings that covers roughly 1 sq km (0.4 sq mi). Cahuachi, with a large 20-m (65-ft)-high stepped pyramid, was the largest center of its day in the Nazca region and may have had a role in the dispersal of the Nazca style to other valleys along the south coast.

Perhaps the most astonishing feature in the Nazca region of southern Peru is spread out over several hundred square kilometers (an area three to four times larger than Manhattan Island) in the desert between the Ingenio and Nazca River valleys. More than 1000 years ago, lines, geometric forms, and various figures were drawn on the desert surface by removing dark rock fragments to expose a light-colored underlying soil. The geometric shapes, mostly triangles and trapezoids, alone cover an amazing 360 ha (900 acres). The majority of the several dozen figures, the most famous of the Nazca **geoglyphs,** are animals, although several are plants and others are humanlike. The animals include birds, lizards, and fish, as well as a spider and a monkey (Figure 9.23). The latter, an inhabitant of the Amazon rain forest and not of the dry coast, is known to have been important in coastal religion and symbolism.

One of the myths about the Nazca geoglyphs is that they must be seen from the air to be appreciated. More recent studies indicate that they were meant to be viewed by people on the ground. Most of the lines and drawings are visible from the desert floor, and they can be seen even more clearly from either the low hills or the huge sand dunes that border the dry plain. Although the specific intentions of the original makers remain a matter of some debate, recent systematic research of the geoglyphs by Markus Reindel, of the German Archaeological Institute, and colleagues has revealed that the desert features were walked by the Nazca. As these lines and features were walked, the Nazca left small offerings in selected locations. Reindel suspects that the geoglyphs were part of a ritual landscape associated with water and fertility rites.

**polychrome** Multicolored; describing pottery that has been decorated with three or more colors.

**geoglyph** Ground markings, such as the lines and life-form representations found in the Nazca desert.

# Sipán

## *Clues to Moche ritual and politics*

Less than 200 km (124 mi) north of the pyramids of Moche is the fertile Lambayeque (lahm-bye-YEA-kay) Valley. Abundant water resources and rich, level farmland have combined to make this area highly suitable for intensive agriculture. At the center of the valley lies the small village of Sipán (see-PAHN), an agricultural community of approximately 1500 people, distinguished by the presence of ancient pyramids and cemeteries. The impressive Sipán pyramids are visible for miles, rising above the intensively farmed fields that today grow mostly sugarcane (Figure 9.24).

For decades, some of the farmers of Sipán have supplemented their agricultural income with sporadic looting from the rich archaeological resources in the region. The looters dig deep holes with picks and shovels and often find ceramic vessels or stone and shell beads, which they sell to the antiquities dealers who periodically pass through the region. Occasionally, the looters expose tombs containing objects of gold or silver, for which they receive much larger sums. Such occasional rich finds, and the periodically weak economy in the Lambayeque area, have helped keep this destructive tradition of looting alive. Over generations, some Sipán inhabitants have become adept at learning where to dig to recover the most valuable items and at avoiding the local police and government officials responsible for protecting archaeological resources.

At the end of 1986, the local looters, believing they had exhausted nearby cemeteries, focused their attention on the smallest of three Sipán pyramids. Working at night to avoid detection, they dug deep pits into the pyramid's core of solid mud bricks. For months, little was found. But on the night of February 16, 1987, they tunneled into one of the richest burial chambers ever looted, the royal tomb of a Moche ruler. Conflicting accounts make it difficult to know exactly what was removed, but several cloth sacks of priceless artifacts were undoubtedly carted away. Almost immediately, disputes arose over the distribution of the treasure, and one looter, displeased with his share, informed the police. The police went to Sipán, where they arrested some of the other participants and confiscated part of the plunder in their homes. They also notified Walter Alva, who had worked

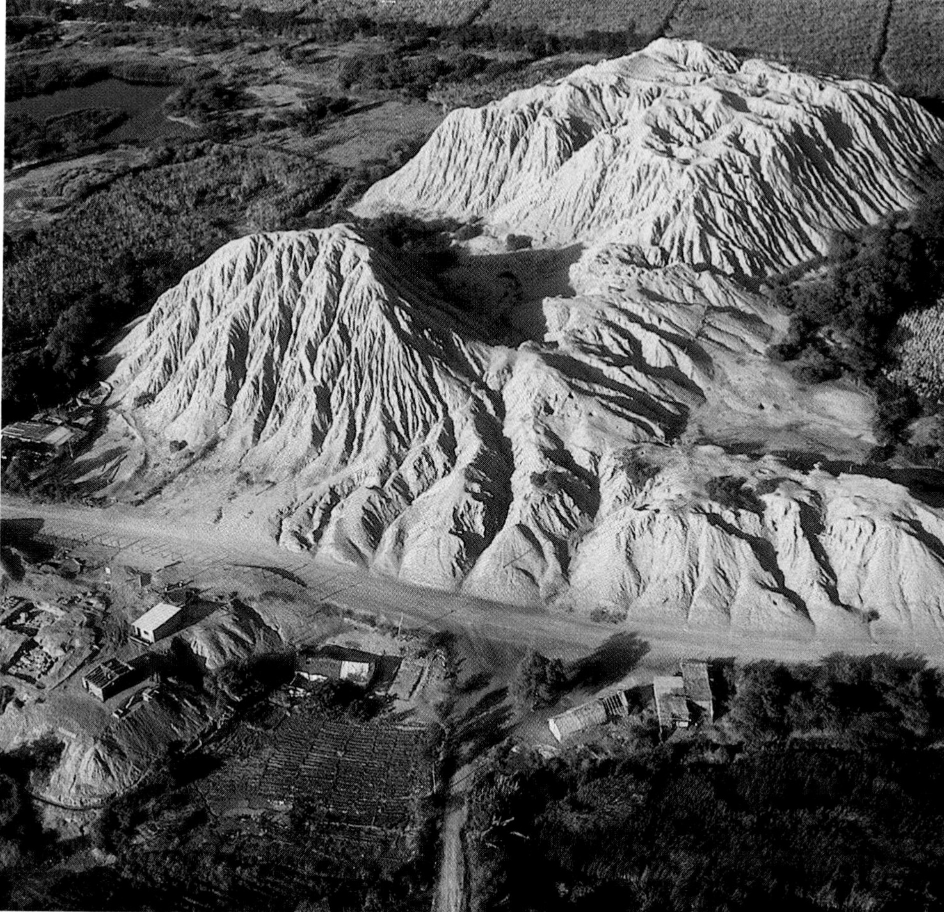

**Figure 9.24** An aerial view of the three pyramids at Sipán. The smallest pyramid, in the lower left, was the focus of looting and subsequent systematic excavation.

Figure 9.25 Excavations directed by Walter Alva in Tomb 1 in the summit of the smallest pyramid at Sipán.

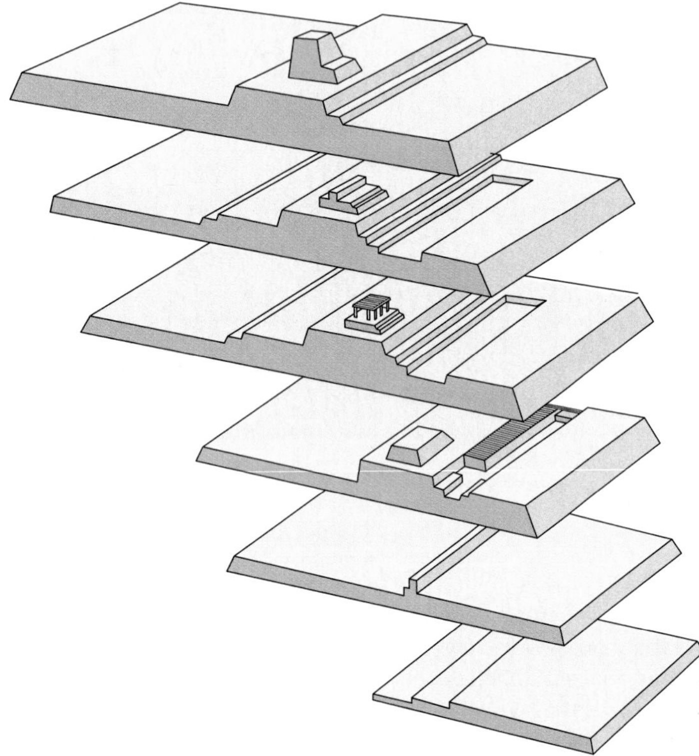

Figure 9.26 The six building episodes of the small pyramid at Sipán. The pyramid, beginning as a low platform, was enlarged during each episode of construction. The Old Lord of Sipán was buried in a tomb in the lowest level.

for years with the police in an effort to halt the looting.

Alva recognized the richness and scholarly significance of the finds, as well as the need to locate the tomb. In Sipán, word spread quickly about the discovered wealth, and many local residents flocked to the pyramids with window screens, kitchen utensils, and shovels to see what they could recover. Even after the police reached the scene, it took several hours to clear the pyramid of wealth seekers. From that point to the conclusion of the scientific excavations, the exposed pyramid had to be guarded 24 hours a day.

The damage to the funerary chamber was severe, from both the original grave robbers and those who later streamed to the site and ruthlessly hacked at the walls. Alva decided that an archaeological project should start immediately to investigate the pyramid before this important site was entirely destroyed. Although some of the looted finds were recovered that first night and a few items were confiscated later by the police, most of the plundered objects were never found. Instead, they were surreptitiously smuggled to Lima. From there, many items eventually were illegally transported to the

Figure 9.27 A large, gold, crescent-shaped headdress, 62.7 cm (24.7 in) wide, from Tomb 1 at Sipán.

art markets and private collections of Europe, the United States, and Japan.

Walter Alva, Christopher Donnan, and their colleagues immediately set to work on the Sipán pyramids (Figure 9.25). They mapped the complex, thereby determining the relationship between the smallest structure (now pitted) and the larger pyramids. Because the small mound was in greatest danger of further destruction, they concentrated their efforts there. Detailed architectural analysis of the areas exposed by the looters' trenches led to the discovery that the pyramid was built in six stages (Figure 9.26). In its earliest phase, thought to have been constructed during the first century A.D., the pyramid appears to have been only a low rectangular platform with two steps extending along its entire north side. Each subsequent building enlarged the pyramid, encapsulating the previous structure, with the final construction phase completed around A.D. 300.

The richness of the looted finds, as well as elaborate gold, silver, and ceramic artifacts recovered during the cleaning operation, prepared Alva and Donnan for the possibility that an important burial might be recovered. Before Sipán, the Moche burials with the most elaborate pieces generally had been looted rather than excavated scientifically. Yet the excavators could never have imagined that they would recover perhaps the richest burial ever found in the Western Hemisphere. Nor could they have known that their findings would help answer a key riddle about the ancient Moche. Were the repetitive scenes recognized in Moche art, such as the Sacrifice Ceremony (see p. 409), really enacted by the Moche people or purely mythic in nature?

Over months of painstaking effort, the Sipán excavations uncovered three

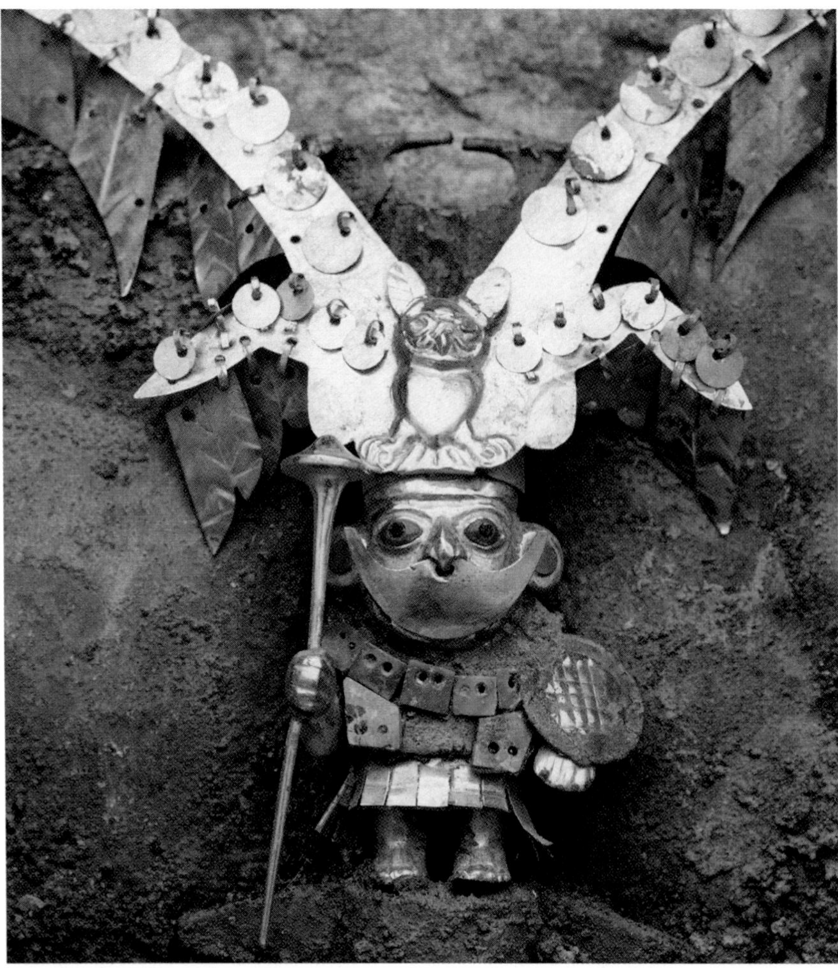

**Figure 9.28** A miniature figure from the tomb of the Old Lord at Sipán, holding a war club (5 cm, or 2 in, tall) and a shield. He wears a headdress of thinly hammered gold with an owl in the center and a gold nose ornament. Turquoise adorns his body, ears, and eyes.

The looting of archaeological sites is a major problem in many areas of the world. What do we lose in addition to the objects themselves?

**scepter** A staff or baton borne by a ruler as an emblem of his/her position and authority.

fabulous tombs. In each case, the central figure was elaborately costumed in exquisitely crafted gold and silver ornaments, as well as worked shell, gemstone, and metal finery of all kinds. In the two largest, most elaborate, and latest tombs—Tombs 1 and 2—the central figures had key costume elements that enabled the excavators to identify them as specific participants in the Sacrifice Ceremony. For example, the central rayed figure, referred to as the Warrior Priest, in the Presentation Theme often was depicted with paired backflaps, a crescent-shaped headdress piece, large circular ear decorations, a crescent nose ornament, and a pair of bells hanging from his belt (the large figure on the left in Figure 9.22). This individual is usually shown in military settings, accompanied by a dog, and often with a lamp-shaped **scepter** or war club. All these elements were excavated together in Tomb 1 at Sipán (Figure 9.27). Tomb 2 yielded an individual buried with many of the decorative and symbolic elements that have been linked to a second principal figure in the Sacrifice Ceremony, the Bird Priest (to the right of the Warrior Priest in Figure 9.22). The earliest of the three excavated tombs (Tomb 3) was neither as large nor as closely associated with the depictions of the Sacrifice Ceremony as the later two. Yet the central figure, called the Old Lord of Sipán by the site's excavators, was richly entombed with some elements of the Warrior Priest attire (Figure 9.28). It is possible that the Sacrifice Ceremony was less elaborate and stylized in earlier Moche times; artistic depictions of this event all postdate A.D. 300.

Amputated hands and feet were uncovered at Sipán. These sacrificial offerings would seem to indicate, not only that key participants in the Sacrifice Ceremony were buried in the pyramid, but also that the event itself was probably practiced on or near the pyramid.

The Sipán excavations provide a clearer understanding of Moche social and economic organization. Moche society was marked by greater differentials in wealth than previously believed. The elaborate costumes buried with these nobles would have demanded many highly skilled artisans to replenish the great objects of wealth that were buried. This burial custom helps contextualize the extraordinary artistic and technological achievements long associated with Moche craftworkers.

The royal tombs also have yielded significant clues about Moche art and religion. We now recognize that at least some of the art documents actual events enacted by real people. Although the treasures of the Sipán tombs seem priceless, of greater value is the exciting new cultural information they have provided, enabling us to develop a clearer picture of the Moche—one of the most fascinating civilizations of the ancient world.

# Tiwanaku

## *Bolivia's high-altitude ancient city*

When the Spanish chroniclers asked the Inca rulers about their origins, they were told that the genesis of the first Inca took place in the part of the realm called Collasuyu (coy-yah-SUE-you). This Inca origin myth may have developed from the belief in the sacred nature of Collasuyu's Lake Titicaca, the largest lake in South America. When the great king Pachakuti (A.D. 1438–1470) began the Inca imperial conquests, it is no coincidence that he moved first against polities on the shores of Lake Titicaca.

The first sedentary settlements south of Lake Titicaca, in what is today Bolivia, were established during the second millennium B.C. The inhabitants of

*[E]ven the great Emperor Inca Pachacuti was impressed by the stonework at the ruins of Tiwanaku in the late 15th century . . . the emperor ordered his engineers to learn the stone masonry techniques and use them in Cuzco. This account is most likely apocryphal but we can consider it the first recorded instance of the site being used for political purposes. Since at least this visit to the site by a conquering Inca emperor to the present day, Tiwanaku has stood at the center of some highly charged political, ideological, ethnic, and scientific debates.*

—Charles Stanish (2002)

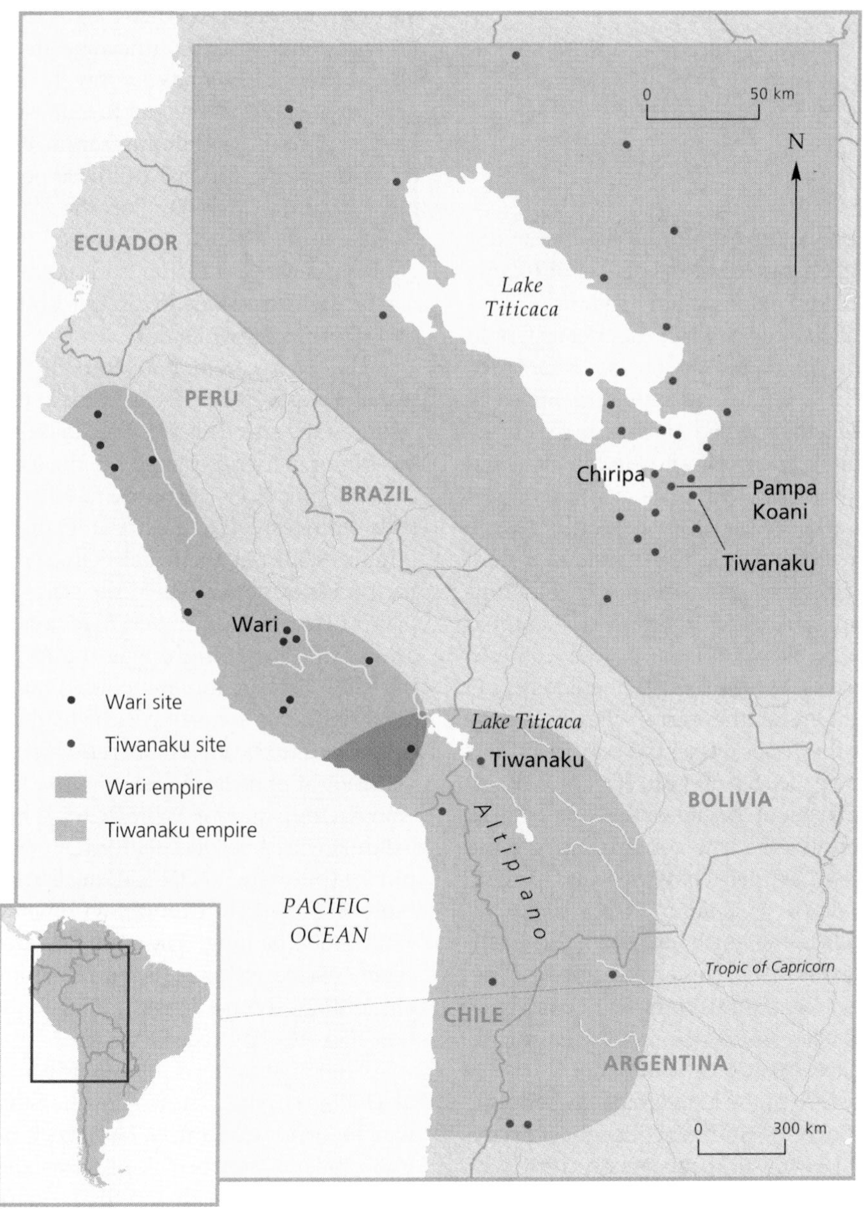


**Figure 9.29** Lake Titicaca and the domains of Tiwanaku and Wari.

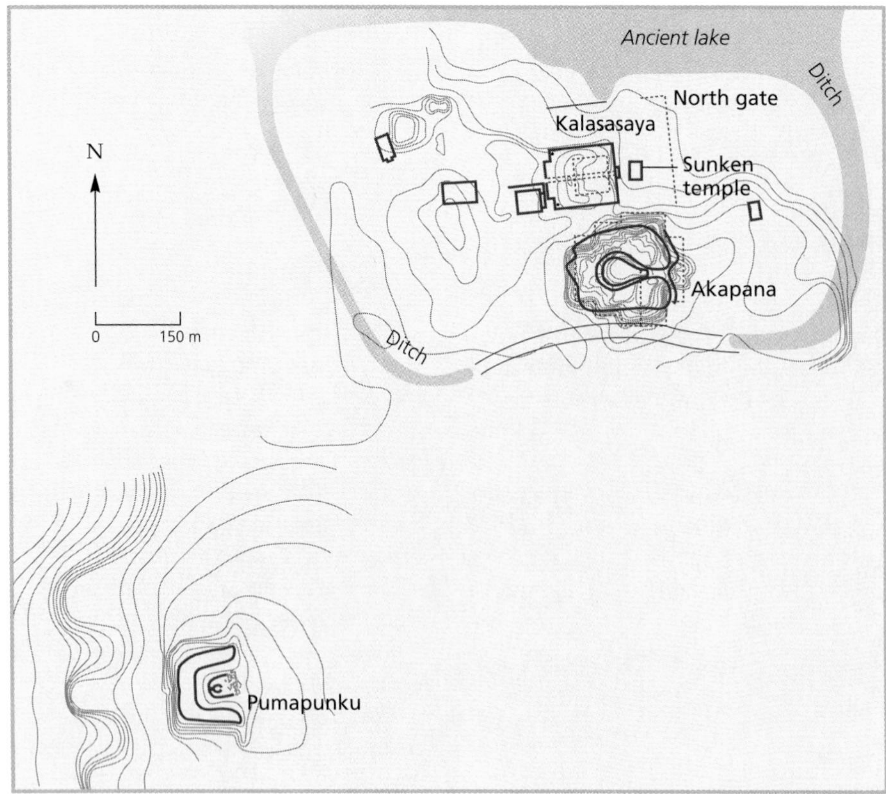


**Figure 9.30** The plan of the civic-ceremonial core of Tiwanaku.

**altiplano** (Spanish) The high-altitude plain between the eastern and western ridges of the Andes in Peru.

these early communities on the windswept high-altitude steppe, or **altiplano,** had a mixed agrarian economy in this zone that most North Americans would consider to be too elevated for agriculture. In the cold altiplano, the early villagers subsisted on a range of domesticated species adapted to the torrential rains of the wet season (November–May) as well as an extended dry season (April–October). The most important food resources were hardy tuberous plants like the potato, cold-adapted grains like quinoa, and such domesticated camelids as alpaca and llama.

One of the early villages on the southern shores of Lake Titicaca was Chiripa (cheer-EE-pah) (Figure 9.29). At the center of the site was a large artificial mound that was constructed around 900 B.C., largely contemporaneous with Chavín de Huántar in the Andean highlands to the north (although the site itself was first occupied centuries earlier). A series of subterranean houses were arranged around the mound. During recent excavations at the site, Christine Hastorf, of the University of California at Berkeley, and her colleagues discovered a semisubterranean structure (with a plaster floor), 200 meters south of the main mound, that dates to 800–750 B.C. This court, which measures approximately 11 × 13 m (36 × 43 ft), is one of the earliest known semisubterranean features in the region and presages the much larger sunken courts that occur later at Tiwanaku.

Around 800 B.C., a small settlement was founded 20 km (12 mi) south of Lake Titicaca, on the site that was to become the great city of Tiwanaku (tee-wah-NOK-u). Situated 3850 m (12,600 ft) above sea level in a small valley in the Bolivian altiplano, at more than twice the altitude of Denver, Colorado, Tiwanaku was one of the highest urban centers ever established. Monumental architectural construction began during the first centuries A.D., when the site rose to importance in the southern basin of Lake Titicaca. Tiwanaku grew to its greatest geographic size (more than 4 sq km, or 1.5 sq mi) and demographic extent (an estimated 25,000–40,000 people) around A.D. 400. For the next 600–800 years, the city dominated the entire Lake Titicaca region, and ceremonial art styles associated with the capital spread over a far wider area.

The civic-ceremonial core of Tiwanaku was a 20-ha (50-acre) area at the center of the site. This precinct, laid out according to a grid oriented to the four cardinal directions, included a series of truly impressive architectural features (Figure 9.30). Akapana (ah-kah-PAH-nah), an enormous stone-faced, stepped platform mound, 200 m (655 ft) on a side and 15 m (50 ft) high, was the most massive construction. It included huge blocks of stone, some of which weighed as much as 10,000 kg (11 tons) and had to be brought over land and water to Tiwanaku from quarries more than 100 km (62 mi) away. A second platform, Pumapunku (pu-mah-POON-ku), measured more than 5 m (16 ft) high, with walls 150 m (500 ft) long. Tiwanaku's civic-ceremonial core also included a complex of buildings, with a stone drainage system, that may have been a palace.

The most famous stone sculpture at Tiwanaku, the Gateway of the Sun, was incorporated into a large rectangular raised platform known as the Kalasasaya (kah-lah-sah-SIGH-yah).

**Figure 9.31** The Gateway of the Sun at Tiwanaku, shown here, broken in two, before it was excavated and the two halves were realigned. The central figure above the gate holds two scepters that end in the heads of condors.

The Gateway of the Sun, carved from a single huge stone block, portrays a central figure holding two scepters that end in the heads of condors (Figure 9.31). This individual is flanked by rows of winged attendants who each carry a condor scepter. The central character recalls a figure with two staffs, frequently shown in Chavín iconography. Inside the Kalasasaya are rectangular sunken courts (Figure 9.32). These architectural features, which may have been temple precincts, have a precedent at earlier Chiripa.

At Tiwanaku, the local altiplano economy of camelid pastoralism and the cultivation of hardy grains and tubers was supplemented by the reclamation for agriculture of waterlogged lands adjacent to Lake Titicaca. In addition, Tiwanaku maintained long-distance trade connections, establishing economic colonies in both the Pacific Coast zone to the west and the more tropical forested zones to the east. These earlier networks may have laid a foundation for the Inca to link the diverse and distant reaches of the Andean realm. Warm-region crops, such as maize and **coca,** were obtained, as were birds and medicinal herbs from the east and obsidian and coastal products, such as shell and dried fish, from the west. Trade connections were maintained by large llama caravans, which traveled throughout the Bolivian altiplano and to southern Peru and the Chilean coast.

Alan Kolata, of the University of Chicago, has studied agrarian reclamation on the Pampa Koani (pahm-pah ko-AH-nee), an area subject to frequent natural flooding on the southern border of Lake Titicaca. During the first millennium A.D., the waterlogged land was reclaimed through the construction of raised fields near the lake, by excavating the heavy Pampa soils on either side of the field surface and mounding the dirt in the center to form an earthen platform elevated above the seasonally high waters. Kolata found that some raised platforms were constructed more elaborately to enhance plant growth. In one field at the lakeshore, the platform consisted of a cobblestone base, covered by a thick clay stratum, superseded by three gravel layers and a rich layer of topsoil. In this ingenious structure, the clay, held in place by the cobblestones, prevented the brackish lake water from penetrating into the field from below, while fresh rainwater could percolate down to the roots of the crops from above.

During the latter half of the first millennium A.D., while Tiwanaku was the principal center in the southern Andes,

*On January 23, 2006, Evo Morales was formally inaugurated as Bolivia's new president in the capital city of La Paz. . . . But for many Bolivians, his "spiritual" inauguration the day before at the archaeological site of Tiwanaku represented the watershed moment in recent Bolivian political life. Evo Morales is the first indigenous president of Bolivia, and the first indigenous national leader in South America since the defeat of the Inca Empire by a small Spanish army almost 500 years ago.*

—David Kojan (2008)

**coca** A native Andean shrub whose dried leaves are chewed as stimulants.

**Figure 9.32** Cut-stone walls that line the sunken court of the Kalasasaya at Tiwanaku. The carved stelae and the anthropomorphic figures incorporated into the walls are part of Tiwanaku's powerful iconography.

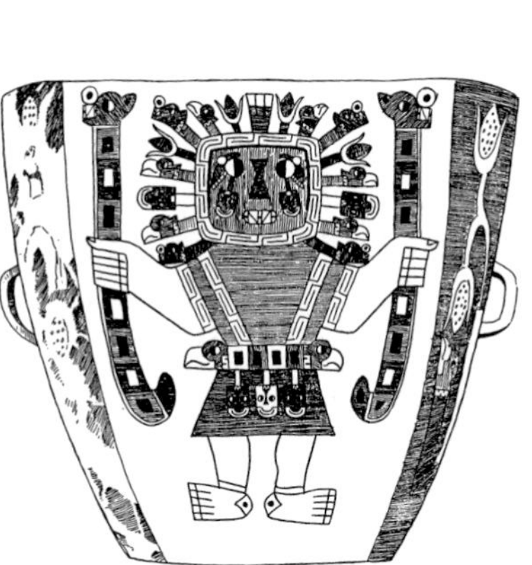

**Figure 9.33** A pottery vessel decorated with Tiwanaku/Wari stylistic elements.

the Peruvian highland site of Wari (WAR-ee) dominated the more northerly highland and coastal regions (see Figure 9.29). Andean archaeologists suggest that whereas Tiwanaku developed economic ties with its hinterland, Wari's control over the surrounding area was more militaristic. Wari's regional domination also was shorter, since that site lost its influence and was largely abandoned before the tenth century A.D. Although the artistic styles associated with Tiwanaku and Wari were similar, both of them featuring jaguars and raptors (birds of prey) (Figure 9.33), the specific relationship between the two centers remains unknown.

Soon after A.D. 1000, Tiwanaku's domination over the basin of Lake Titicaca began to wane. A number of smaller competing states emerged, each maintaining its own local sphere of influence until the middle of the fifteenth century A.D., when the Titicaca Basin was unified under Inca domination. The decline of Tiwanaku coincided with the abandonment of the raised fields of the Pampa Koani. The vast landscape of once-productive fields reverted to pasturage, a function they still serve today. Even the Inca did not reclaim the seasonally waterlogged Pampa lands that had once helped feed the population of Tiwanaku, focusing instead on the rocky mountain slopes above the plain. There, the Inca expanded the region's agricultural productivity by constructing terraces that transformed steep hillsides into arable farmland.

Although the specific causes of Tiwanaku's collapse have not been determined, we do know that several of the important organizational features associated with the later Inca empire can be traced to this earlier altiplano center. The widespread Tiwanaku iconographic style seems to presage the broad dissemination of Inca state art. Likewise, Tiwanaku's establishment of small economic colonies in diverse environmental settings augurs an Inca practice. Perhaps the Inca kings recognized the powerful influence of Tiwanaku on the later prehispanic Andean world when they traced their ancestry to the basin of Lake Titicaca. In so doing, the Inca rulers also were invoking the mystique of Tiwanaku's past grandeur to bolster their own efforts to reestablish a far-reaching Andean domain.

# Chan Chan

## *Desert city of the Chimú*

On the north coast of Peru, the seventh-century collapse of Moche coincided with a shift in political power. In the Moche Valley, occupation concentrated in the large settlement of Galindo (gah-LEAN-doh). Yet unlike at the Moche site with its huge adobe *huacas,* the nondomestic construction at Galindo was small. At the same time, a much larger settlement, Pampa Grande (pahm-pah GRAHN-day), with more elaborate architecture, was established in the Lambayeque Valley to the north (see Figure 9.20). Both Pampa Grande and Galindo were positioned in easily defendable locations from which they could control local irrigation systems. Thus, although the north coast was not conquered by Wari invaders from the south, that expansionist polity may have caused sufficient unrest to effect major shifts in population and power.

By approximately A.D. 800–900, a small settlement had been founded at the mouth of the Moche Valley at Chan Chan (CHAHN chahn). Although the exact extent of this early occupation has not been determined, it is clear the site grew rapidly in size and importance. By the middle of the fifteenth century, Chan Chan had become a sprawling coastal city, covering more than 20 sq km (8 sq mi). Chan Chan was also the capital of the Chimú (chee-MOO) state, which stretched 1000 km (620 mi) from southernmost Ecuador to central Peru (Figure 9.34).

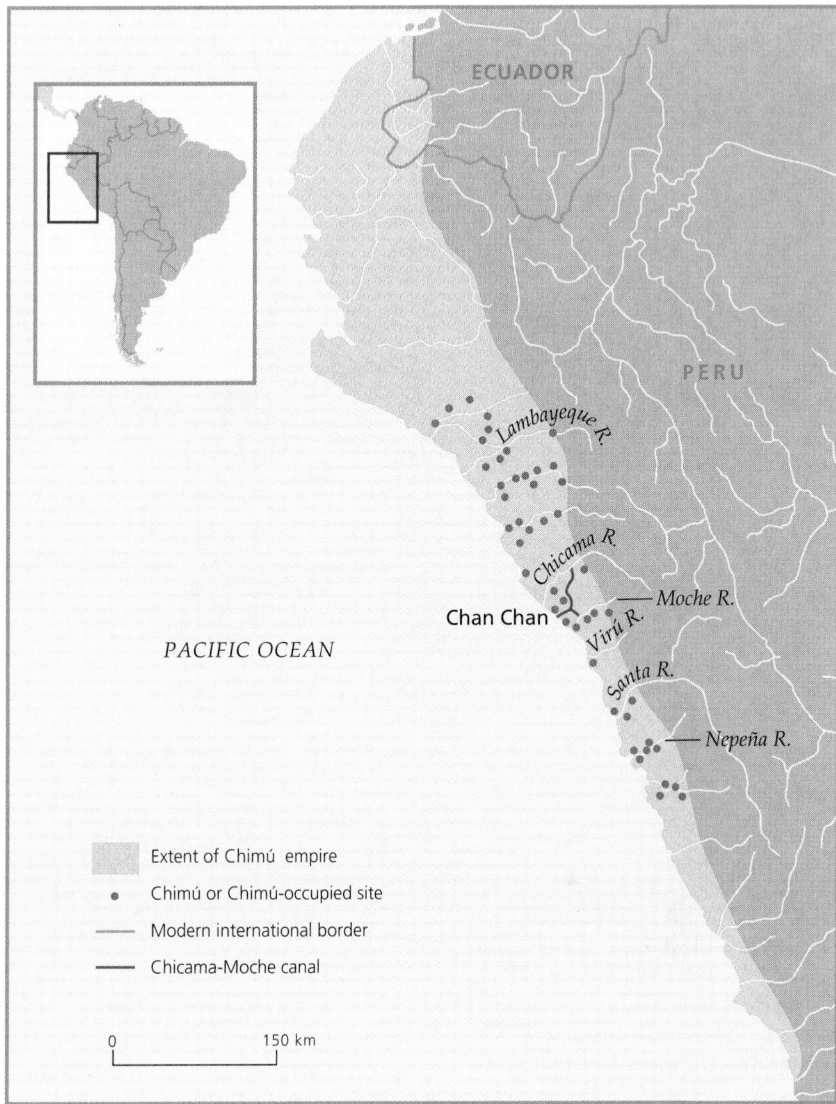


**Figure 9.34** The Chimú empire stretched along the Pacific Coast of South America from southern Ecuador to central Peru.

At its height in the mid-fifteenth century A.D., the civic-ceremonial core of Chan Chan covered roughly 6 sq km (2.3 sq mi, roughly twice the size of New York's Central Park). This central area was dominated by 10 rectilinear compounds, or *ciudadelas* (literally, "little cities"), each surrounded by high adobe walls (Figure 9.35). The nucleus of Chan Chan also included a large platform-court complex, as well as flat-topped mounds and numerous smaller monuments and structures; yet the most striking and massive features were the *ciudadelas,* many of which measured 200–600 m (650–1950 ft) on a side.

The *ciudadelas,* oriented roughly north-south, each had a single entrance through the north wall that opened onto a corridor leading to a broad court (Figure 9.36). A ramp

www.mhhe.com/priceip6e

For a Web-based activity on Chan Chan, see the Internet exercises on your online learning center.

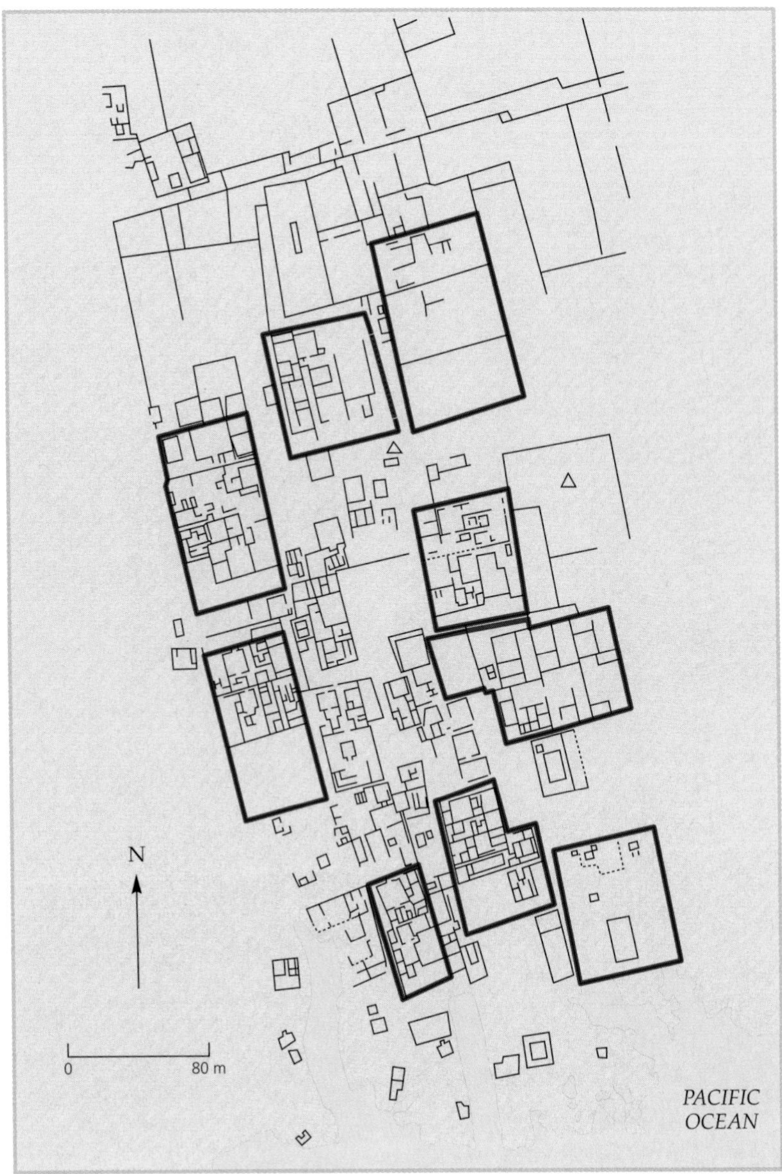


**Figure 9.35** The plan of central Chan Chan, which is dominated by the *ciudadelas.* The Rivero *ciudadela* is in the bottom center of the plan.

**split inheritance** An Andean practice by which the successor to the throne inherited only the office of the dead ruler; his junior kinsmen received the lands, palace, and personal wealth of the dead ruler.

sloped up to a long bench along the south wall of the court. Human corpses, probably buried when the compounds were constructed, were uncovered during excavations of these ramps. Each compound also included a multitude of storerooms, smaller courts, and living quarters (Figure 9.37). Usually the last structure built in each *ciudadela* was a burial platform, which presumably held the bodies of the family that occupied each of these mazelike compounds. Later records name ten Chimú kings, corresponding to the ten palatial compounds at Chan Chan. Geoffrey Conrad, of Indiana University, believes that each *ciudadela* was a particular king's residence and the administrative center for the Chimú kingdom. Following the death of the ruler, the compound became the mausoleum for the king, maintained by his living kinsmen. Conrad argues that the maintenance of a dead Chimú ruler's personal property by his heirs, who did not succeed him in office, was derived from a broader pan-Andean custom of ancestor worship. Upon succession, each new ruler built his own *ciudadela* to serve as headquarters and royal treasury.

Most of the inhabitants of Chan Chan resided outside these massive compounds in small structures composed of six to eight small rooms. During excavations in these quarters, few farming or fishing implements were found. Instead, the evidence for craft manufacture was abundant, including lapidary and woodworking tools, spinning and weaving implements, and the equipment for metalworking.

As at earlier Moche, most of the monumental construction at Chan Chan was built by a labor force from outside the center. Michael Moseley estimates that the population at Chan Chan remained relatively small, perhaps 25,000 people. In the city's hinterland, huge labor investments were made in agricultural intensification. Sophisticated hydraulic systems brought water to the land surrounding Chan Chan. The Chimú even constructed an intervalley canal designed to carry water to the Moche Valley from the Chicama River, 65 km (40 mi) away.

The development of the large irrigation networks around Chan Chan would seem to relate to the Andean practice of labor tribute (the *mit'a* system), as well as to the Chimú pattern of succession. According to one hypothesis, the Chimú, like the Inca, practiced a policy of **split inheritance,** by which the successor to the throne received the inherited office of the supreme leader, but the land, the palace, and the personal wealth of the dead ruler were left to a corporate group of other junior kinsmen. As a consequence, each new ruler had to raise his

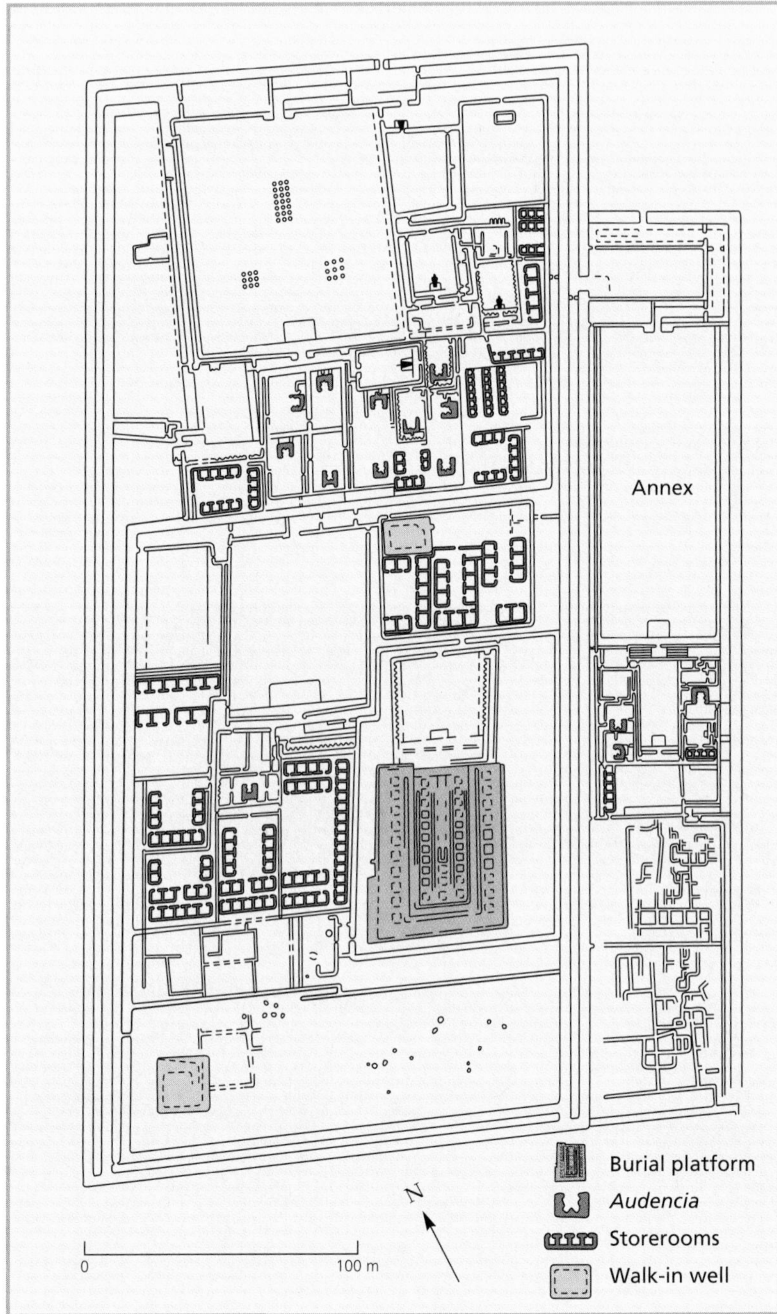


**Figure 9.36** The plan of the Rivero *ciudadela* at Chan Chan. The U-shaped structures, *audiencias*, may have been used by nobles holding audience with lower-status people. Each structure holds only one seated person, and each has its own court.

How did the built environment at Chan Chan compare with that of earlier Moche? What might these differences mean in terms of past behaviors?

own revenues to erect his residential compound and finance his reign. His principal resource was a large labor force that could be employed in monumental construction, agricultural intensification, road building, and militaristic ventures.

Between 1462 and 1470, the Chimú were in competition with the increasingly powerful Inca. By the end of the decade, this conflict had ended with the incorporation of the Chimú kingdom into the rapidly growing Inca empire. In this manner, the Inca were able to link their lands and road systems with those previously controlled by the Chimú. Curiously, Chimú artifacts were found more widely distributed after the Inca conquest than before, perhaps as a result of the emergence of new patterns of trade and taxation, or possibly because of the great admiration the Inca had for

**Figure 9.37** This U-shaped structure, or *audiencia,* at Chan Chan, with two large niches in each interior wall. Elaborate decorative carvings adorn the interior adobe walls of the *audiencia.*

**Figure 9.38** An aerial view of the western half of central Chan Chan. The large compound in the right foreground is the Rivero *ciudadela.*

Chimú craftspeople. For example, Chimú metalworkers were brought to the capital, Cuzco, to work for the Inca state.

Today the quiet desolation of the dry coastal environment is broken only by the nearly continuous howl of onshore winds. No one lives at Chan Chan, but the site is covered by a series of trails and paths that skirt the undulating tops of collapsed adobe ruins that were once the palaces of the Chimú kings (Figure 9.38). At dawn from a distance, the diffused, weak daylight makes it difficult even to distinguish the massive earthen walls of this once important city from the sky at the horizon.

# Cuzco and Machu Picchu

## *Highland Inca settlements*

As with the Aztecs of Mesoamerica, much of what we know about the Inca comes to us not from archaeology but through written documents, filtered through the eyes of European chroniclers, whose goals and experiences differed greatly from those of the Inca themselves. In 1532, a small band of Spaniards led by Francisco Pizarro came into contact with populations in the northern coastal valleys of Peru that were part of a giant centralized political domain called Tawantinsuyu (Figure 9.39). The capital of this great polity was Cuzco (KUSE-co), a city in the southern highlands. The highest-ranked leader was called Inca, son of the deity Inti (the Sun God) and descendant of a long line of heroic dynasties. At that time, the empire was in the midst of a severe crisis, provoked by a bitter rivalry between two brothers, Huascar and Atauhualpa. Although Atauhualpa eventually won the power struggle, his costly victory may have lost the empire; control of the Inca domain was soon in the hands of the Spanish.

According to legend, the rapid rise of the Inca began with hostilities between the inhabitants of Cuzco and the Chanca, a neighboring people. Fresh from military victories over several adjacent polities, the Chanca laid siege to Cuzco, forcing many of the inhabitants, including the reigning Inca, to flee to the surrounding hills. At Cuzco, a son of the Inca ruler, named Cusi Inca Yupanqui, was left to spearhead the final defense of the city. While waiting for the last Chanca onslaught, Cusi Inca Yupanqui had a vision in which he was told by a supernatural being that he would eventually rise to power and conquer many nations. Inspired by the apparition and buoyed by the support of new allies, Cuzco's defenders rallied to defeat the Chanca and drive them far from the Inca homeland. Cusi Inca Yupanqui was crowned Inca and renamed Pachakuti, "he who remakes the world." From that date, generally placed around A.D. 1440, Pachakuti is said to have initiated the dramatic series of conquests that culminated less than a century later in a huge empire that stretched over 4200 km (2600 mi) from north to south.

Inca imperial propaganda proclaimed that the Andean world was in a state of savagery before the rise of the Inca. This claim was obviously ethnocentric and fallacious. Clearly, the royal

**www.mhhe.com/priceip6e**

For a Web-based activity on a research expedition to find Inca mummies, see the Internet exercises on your online learning center.

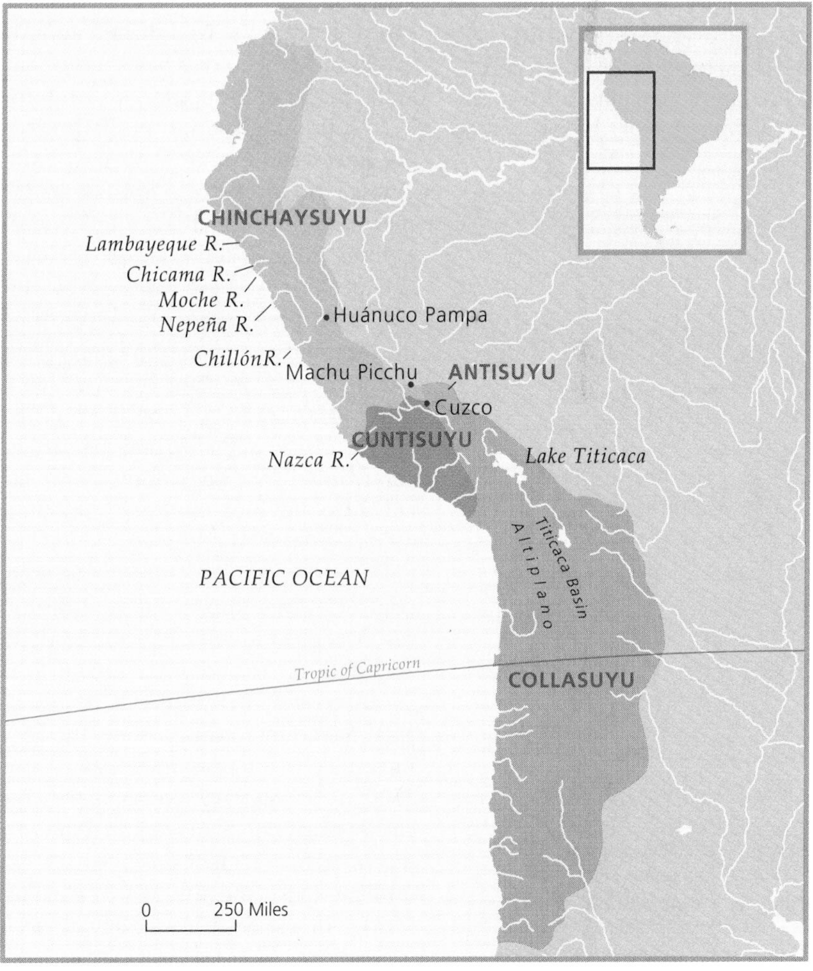


**Figure 9.39** The Inca empire (Tawantinsuyu) was divided into four quarters: Chinchaysuyu in the north, Antisuyu and Cuntisuyu in the center, and Collasuyu in the south.

Figure 9.40 The north face of the fortress of Sacsahuaman at Inca Cuzco, Peru. This edifice was constructed of huge stone blocks fitted together with great masonry skill. Some of these blocks weigh more than 100 metric tons. The fortress is perched atop a high hill that has a commanding view of Cuzco below.

families at Cuzco inherited administrative strategies and systems of legitimization from the rulers of earlier states, centered at Chan Chan and Tiwanaku. Archaeology has shown that at the outset of the second millennium A.D., following the fall of Tiwanaku, the southern highlands around Lake Titicaca did undergo an episode of decentralization in which many small polities fragmented a landscape that had previously been unified by the earlier altiplano center. In support of the legendary accounts, archaeological analyses indicate that by A.D. 1450, these autonomous competing polities of the Titicaca Basin had begun to come under Inca hegemony. Centered at Cuzco, the Inca rapidly established major ceremonial centers on islands in Lake Titicaca, not only to solidify their control of this important geographic resource, but also to legitimize their ancestral link to earlier Tiwanaku.

According to tradition, Cuzco was established by Manco Capac, the first Inca ruler, in a mountain valley nearly 3500 m (11,500 ft) above sea level. Yet earlier excavations in conjunction with recent archaeological surveys have established that the site was one of the largest in the region as early as A.D. 1000. Because Cuzco is relatively close to the equator, its climate is reasonably mild in spite of the high elevation. Cuzco remained a small community until it was rebuilt by the victorious Pachakuti. The Inca canalized and straightened several small rivers that cut through the settlement. Cuzco's most elaborate buildings, many of which were constructed entirely of finely hewn stone, were erected in the area between these rivers. An imposing fortress with massive masonry walls, the Sacsahuaman, was built on a steep hill above this central area, which was not fortified (Figure 9.40). Drawing on Inca sources, John Rowe, of the University of California, Berkeley, has suggested that Cuzco was intentionally laid out in the shape of a puma, with the fortress representing the animal's head and the intersection of the rivers serving as its tail (Figure 9.41). The area between the puma's front and back legs was paved with pebbles and served as a central ceremonial square.

The magnificent Temple of the Sun, the most important Inca structure in Cuzco, was built by Pachakuti at the site's center. The building's exterior walls, more than 50 m (160 ft) long per side, were decorated with a thick gold **frieze.** Entrances to the structure were covered with heavy gold plates, and the interior walls also were coated with gold. Early Spanish accounts describe a central patio or garden that included both natural and gold-crafted vegetation, including maize plants in which the ears, stalks, and leaves were all made of metal. The temple's principal sanctuary was dedicated to Inti. Inside the room were idols of gold and silver, as well as mummies of former Inca rulers and their wives.

Cuzco also contained other, smaller temples, in addition to public buildings and elite residences. Generally, these structures were built of cut stone, finished with such precision that the joints matched perfectly and mortar was not required. These architectural monuments, which required both great skill and significant labor power, were

**frieze** A decorative band or feature, commonly ornamented with sculpture, usually near the top of a wall.

erected by commoners as part of the *mit'a* system. Pachakuti also erected a special public building that served as a convent for Chosen Women, brought to the capital to weave the finest cloth and to participate in specific religious rituals.

As the nucleus of an empire, Cuzco was not a typical Inca city. Its principal function was administration, and many of its inhabitants were involved in civic-ceremonial activities: priests, nobles, military officers, architects, and servants. Most of the supporting commoner population resided in smaller communities in the surrounding valley. In these settlements, the structures were built of fieldstone and adobe rather than cut-stone blocks. A network of state storehouses and religious shrines also marked the well-planned terrain in the immediate vicinity of Cuzco.

The market in Cuzco was small and outside the center of the city. The peripheral nature of commercial activities at Cuzco reflects the administrative-elite character of the capital. However, it also indicates the nature of Inca economy, in which the state had a central role in the collection and redistribution of goods. Craftworkers and other specialists contributed labor to the imperial government, which thus took control of a wide range of craft items. Compared with the contemporary Aztec polity, private trade and marketing occurred at very low levels in the empire of the Inca.

The Spanish were greatly impressed by Cuzco, its stone architecture, and its treasure of precious metals. Before the arrival of the Europeans in 1532, the accumulation of wealth was fostered by an Inca regulation that forbade anyone to remove gold, silver, or fine cloth from the city, once it was inside. In 1535, Cuzco was systematically burned and largely destroyed by the Inca themselves, when they besieged a Spanish garrison. But because the conquering Spaniards reconstructed the city promptly, often using Inca builders, much of the prehispanic plan has endured. Solid Inca walls still provide the stone foundation for many later buildings. Even the remnants of the once-spectacular Temple of the Sun now stand as the base for the Church of Santo Domingo. Like modern Mexico City, lying above the ruins of ancient Aztec Tenochtitlán, Cuzco is undoubtedly one of the longest continuously occupied cities in the New World.

Today, the most famous archaeological site in Peru, and perhaps all of South America, is another Inca site, Machu Picchu (MA-chew PEE-chew). This site is dramatically situated on the eastern frontier of the Inca empire, and the ruins lie on a saddle between two mountain peaks, which tower over the site and overlook a large bend in the Urubamba River (Figure 9.42). Machu Picchu is a graphic reminder of the architectural grandeur of the Inca. Yet, in spite of its international popularity as

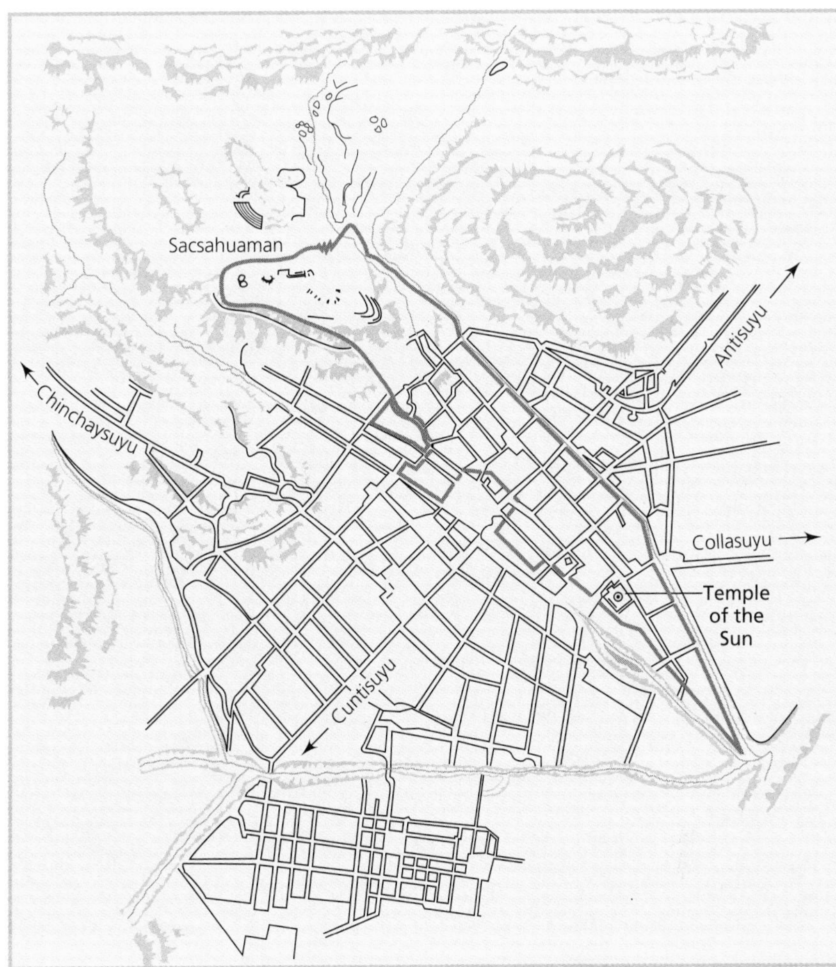


**Figure 9.41** The plan of Colonial period Cuzco, which was built on Inca remains. The fortress and walls of the Inca city are outlined as a stylized puma.

What contrasts can you draw between the political structures of the Aztecs and the Inca?

commoners. Thus in both regions, these peoples, with powerful government institutions and large population centers, also were characterized by a marked degree of social stratification.

Nevertheless, we know that personal attributes could be important even in highly stratified societies, such as the Inca, where great warriors or capable administrators could achieve noble status. With the Inca, this social mobility was necessary because their empire expanded so rapidly that there was a nearly constant need to fill administrative posts. Despite social mobility, however, the most powerful ruling positions could in principle be filled only by members of noble lineages. Inca emperors were believed to have ruled by divine right, claiming descent from the sun. Their power was absolute, checked only by the fear of revolt and past custom. Bloodlines were so important in later Inca times that the first wife of the Inca emperor was his full sister. Yet each emperor also had secondary wives, some of whom were the daughters of neighboring rulers.

Archaeological research provides the best avenue for understanding how the state and inherited social differences first emerged in human societies. Marked sociopolitical differences were not institutionalized in the earliest human societies, and they seem uncharacteristic of human populations with extensive hunting-and-gathering economies. Yet as we have seen in the Andes, inherited inequalities, social stratification, and the state developed long before European contact. Postconquest documentary records of the Spanish can never fully inform us about the ways in which social, political, and economic distinctions first emerged in the Andean world. Even in Mesoamerica, where written records have survived the ravages of time, the beginnings of social and political inequality predate the advent of writing. Many clues may exist at sites such as El Paraíso and Chavín de Huántar. Although they were not the capitals of urban states, these settlements also show indications of emergent inequities in power and wealth.

Ultimately, the solutions to these puzzles lie in the archaeological record, yet they will not be achieved quickly or easily. Questions about social inequality and the rise of states, as well as convincing explanations for the different historical pathways that we see for Mesoamerica and South America, are the kind of big, messy research issues that require mountains of carefully collected information, as well as brilliant, yet measured, inferences and ideas. Even then, each question probably has more than one answer or at least complex answers that interdigitate a multiplicity of factors. We can only hope to continue to make the kind of rapid progress in understanding our past that we have seen during the past few decades.

*People sometimes ask me, "Will archaeology survive in the twenty-first century?" If the dramatic discoveries and scientific achievements of the past 50 years are any guide, the answer must be a resounding yes.*

—Brian Fagan (1998)

Innovative excavations and a renewed dedication to regional settlement pattern surveys in the Andean region have increased our knowledge base. In this chapter, we have seen how scholars are just beginning to unravel the fascinating story of the emergence of hierarchical societies with monumental constructions on the dry Pacific Coast of Peru. These preceramic groups built large mounds and relied heavily on marine resources for their subsistence. Patterns of exchange and communication across diverse environments that later were to become integral to the Inca empire began at that time. Here we have traced the millennial cycles of transition from those early coastal societies through early states (such as the Moche) and larger polities (centered at Tiwanaku and Chan Chan) to the giant empire of the Inca, which broke apart in the face of the Spanish invasion and colonial conquest.

entrance and a pedestal in the center of the room. Signs of burning on the pedestal indicate that it may have been used for offerings. This possible temple suggests that the organizational capacity for the construction of minor public architecture was present; however, its small size reflects a much lower level of social complexity than in later times.

Yet the temple institution may have had antecedents that preceded the movement of populations into Mesopotamia's southern alluvium. An earlier T-shaped structure at Tell as-Sawwan, on the border between the northern plain and the southern alluvium, may have been a public building with functions similar to those of the later temple. In addition, a circular domed structure at Tepe Gawra, on the fringes of the northern plain, was found below a sequence of superimposed temples. At other northern Mesopotamian sites, similar circular structures, often joined to a rectangular entryway and thereby making a keyhole shape, have been found. These structures, or ***tholoi***, were distinct from the traditional rectangular dwellings and seem to have had a nonresidential purpose, perhaps related to ritual and storage.

Because the temple institution was a focal point of early civilizations in Southwest Asia, questions about its origin and antecedents are important for Southwest Asian prehistory. Yet there also are more general implications. If the temple emerged only in Sumer, its development may be linked to the increasing and necessary reliance on canal irrigation. Social theorists have long argued that the management of irrigation systems requires cooperation among farming populations to allocate water and maintain canals—a particular problem in Sumer, where the rivers carry and deposit great quantities of silt. Alternatively, if antecedents of the temple were established before the occupation of the southern Mesopotamian alluvium, perhaps the movement into Sumer became possible only once a central redistributive institution, such as the temple, was in place. Without that integrative institution, the agricultural hazards of flooding, drought, and dust storms could not have been overcome. In this scenario, irrigation management may have been responsible for the expansion and elaboration of the temple institution but not for its initiation. Likewise, another consequence of irrigation is that it tends to enhance disparities in agricultural productivity and hence land value. In Sumer, emerging inequalities in agrarian production may have fostered increasing economic stratification. Much more archaeological research is needed to address these issues adequately.

By 4500 B.C., the southern Mesopotamian alluvium was dotted with full-fledged towns and public buildings (Figure 10.4). Based on irrigation farming, the economy produced enough food to support a growing population, yielding a surplus that supported craft producers and decision makers. Eridu may have covered 10 ha (25 acres) by that time and had a population as large as several thousand people. The temple at Eridu was rebuilt numerous times and expanded so that it contained multiple altars and offering places (see Figure 10.7). The most elaborate residential dwellings were situated immediately around the temple at the center of the community; craftspeople and peasants lived at ever-increasing distances from the core of the settlement.

The development of the temple institution and the spread of canal irrigation were key features of the 'Ubaid period in Mesopotamia. This period was identified by a widespread monochrome pottery decorated with geometric designs (Figure 10.5). 'Ubaid times also were characterized by population growth and increases in craftwork. 'Ubaid pottery was made in a wider range of forms than the earlier Halafian ware. Yet it tended to be somewhat less decorated, and the different ceramic varieties were generally more uniformly distributed over space. Most of the 'Ubaid ceramics appear to have been made on a slow-turning potter's wheel, in use for the first time.

**Figure 10.5** Two examples of 'Ubaid pottery decorated with small rectilinear patterns. Other common designs include triangles, grids, and zigzag lines.

***tholoi*** Ancient Mesopotamian round structures that often were attached to a rectangular antechamber or annex, resulting in a keyhole shape.

Site

# Harappa and Mohenjo-daro

## *Urbanism and the rise of civilization in the Indus Valley*

www.mhhe.com/priceip6e

For a Web-based activity on Indus Valley civilization, see the Internet exercises on your online learning center.

The broad, fertile floodplains of the Indus and Ghaggar-Hakra rivers (the latter is now dry) and their tributaries, in what is now Pakistan, were the principal focus of the Indus Valley civilization, 2600–1900 B.C. Covering about 680,000 sq km (260,000 sq mi, roughly the size of Texas), this area is bordered by the Baluchistan Hills to the west, the Arabian Sea to the south, the Great Indian Desert to the east, and the majestic Himalayan Mountains to the north (Figure 10.15).

**Figure 10.15** The Indus area, with sites mentioned in the text.

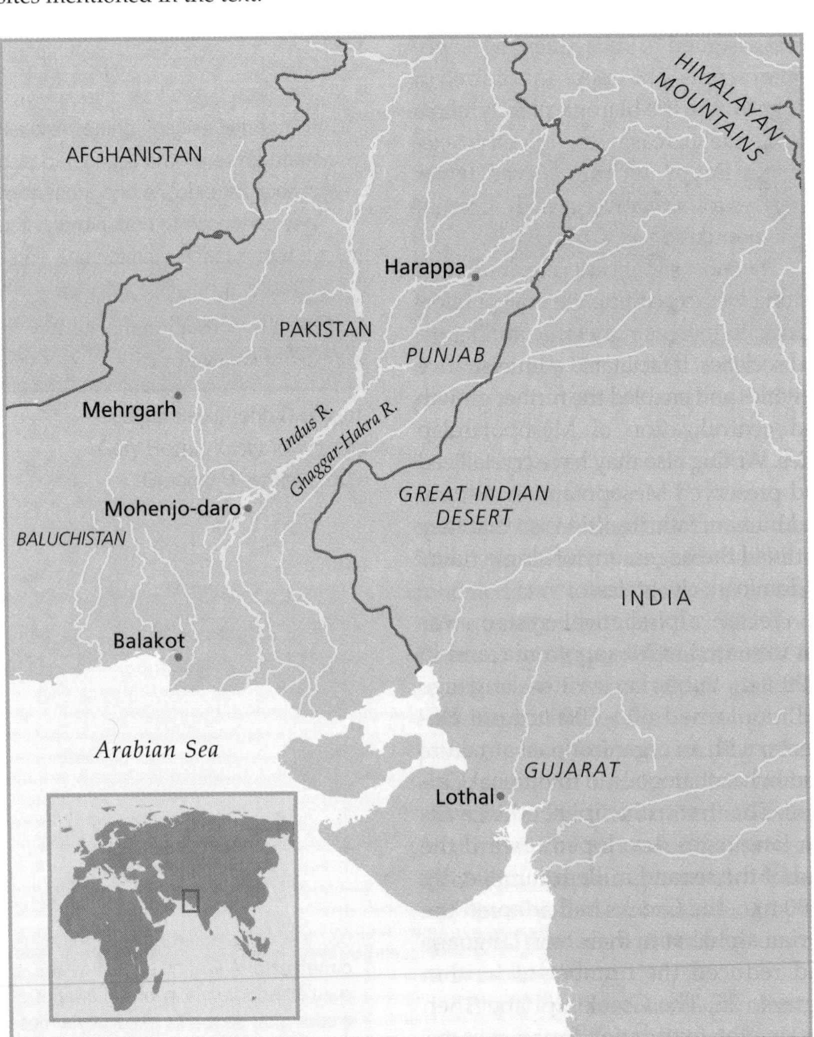


The earliest known sites in the riverine heartland of the Indus civilization date to the late fifth and early fourth millennia B.C., postdating earlier occupations such as Mehrgarh, 200 km (125 mi) to the west. These settlements, referred to as Early Harappan, were scattered across the plains in major agricultural areas or along important trade routes. Many of them exhibit artifacts and organizational features directly antecedent to the later sites, suggesting that the Indus Valley civilization had a long, local path of development. The Indus development does not appear to have been a simple consequence of stimuli from the ancient civilizations of Mesopotamia, a view held by previous generations of scholars.

The early Indus Valley settlements consisted of small, contiguous, rectangular mud-brick houses, some of which contained multiple rooms. The size of settlements varied, and a few included monumental construction. Some sites had massive mud-brick walls and neighborhoods laid out with north-south and east-west streets. Plow-based agriculture was practiced. Cattle, sheep, and goats were kept, but hunting and fishing remained important subsistence activities.

Craft technologies associated with later Indus civilization developed to a high degree at these pre-Indus settlements. Rings, bangles, beads, pins, axes, and celts were manufactured from copper and bronze. Fine stones were ground and polished into beads. Using kilns and the potter's wheel, craftspeople produced a variety of vessel forms, some of which were elaborate, such as serving dishes on stands. Much of the pottery was finely painted. Other important crafted items included terracotta figurines. By the late fourth millennium B.C., potter's marks were present, and seals were inscribed with various geometric symbols.

Indus Valley civilization, also called the Harappan tradition, was first identified by Sir John Marshall in 1921 at the site of Harappa (ha-RAP-ah) in the Punjab highlands in the upper Indus Valley. Although few systematic settlement pattern studies have been undertaken, 1500 Harappan sites have been reported. Few villages have been excavated, but most appear to be 1–5 ha (2.5–12.5 acres) in size and are located near rivers or streams. There are at least four large urban centers, the best known of which are Harappa and Mohenjo-daro (mo-HENGE-o-DAH-ro), roughly 500 km (310 mi) to the south in the lower Indus plain. The two sites, both of which have been the focus of major archaeological field studies, are surprisingly similar. Both towns are large, covering approximately 150–250 ha (370–620 acres), and contained populations of roughly 40,000–80,000 people. Both Mohenjo-daro and Harappa were built with massive mud-brick walls and platforms that raised the towns above the surrounding floodplains (Figure 10.16). Mohenjo-daro was rebuilt at least nine times.

Harappa and Mohenjo-daro consisted of several mounded sectors. Massive foundations of eroded mud-brick walls and traces of large brick gateways have been noted around the edges of these mounds. Both Harappa and Mohenjo-daro have a high rectangular mound on the west and other large mounds to the north, south, and east. Some of the most important public buildings associated with the Harappan tradition are located on the western, or tallest, mound at Mohenjo-daro. The major structures included a possible "granary," a "great bath," and a great hall ("college") almost 730 sq m (8100 sq ft) in size. Some scholars have argued that the granary (1000 sq m, or 11,000 sq ft, equivalent to an Olympic-size swimming pool) was erected over brick supports so that air could circulate under the stored grain. Others suggest that it was simply a public building with multiple rooms or the residence of a powerful merchant family. The Great Bath—12 × 7 m (39 × 23 ft) and 3 m (10 ft) deep, which may have been used for ceremonial ritual bathing—included eight small private bathrooms or changing cubicles (Figure 10.17). The bath itself was fed by a well, and its brickwork was sealed with waterproof bitumen or tar. The building was probably the first large water tank in the world.

Mohenjo-daro's other sectors were divided into blocks by streets, the broadest of which were about 10 m (33 ft) wide (Figure 10.18). Hundreds of houses lined the streets and alleys, some of which were paved with stone. Some of these structures had two stories and were made of baked mud

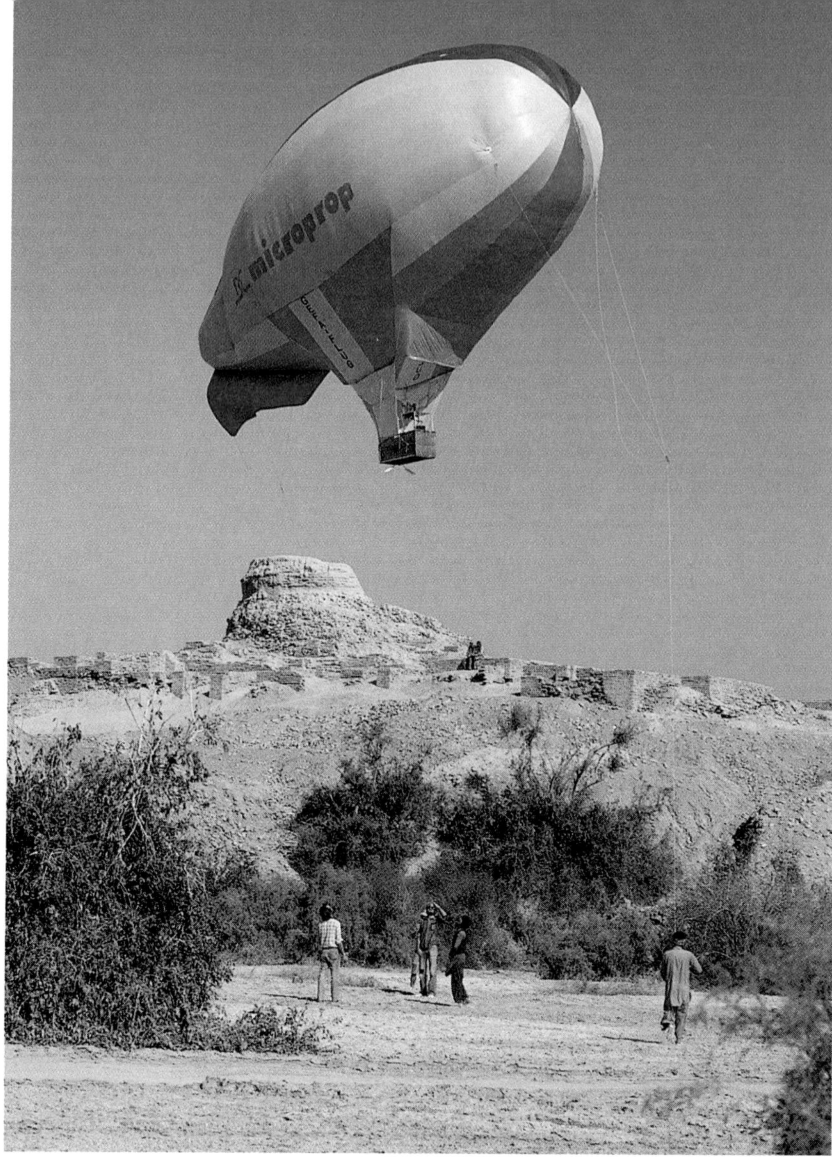


**Figure 10.16** The ruins of ancient Mohenjo-daro, a well-preserved center in the Indus Valley of modern Pakistan. Much of the site was built on a massive mud-brick platform, which raised the settlement over the wet alluvial plain below. The balloon above the site is used by archaeologists to view and photograph the ruins from the air.

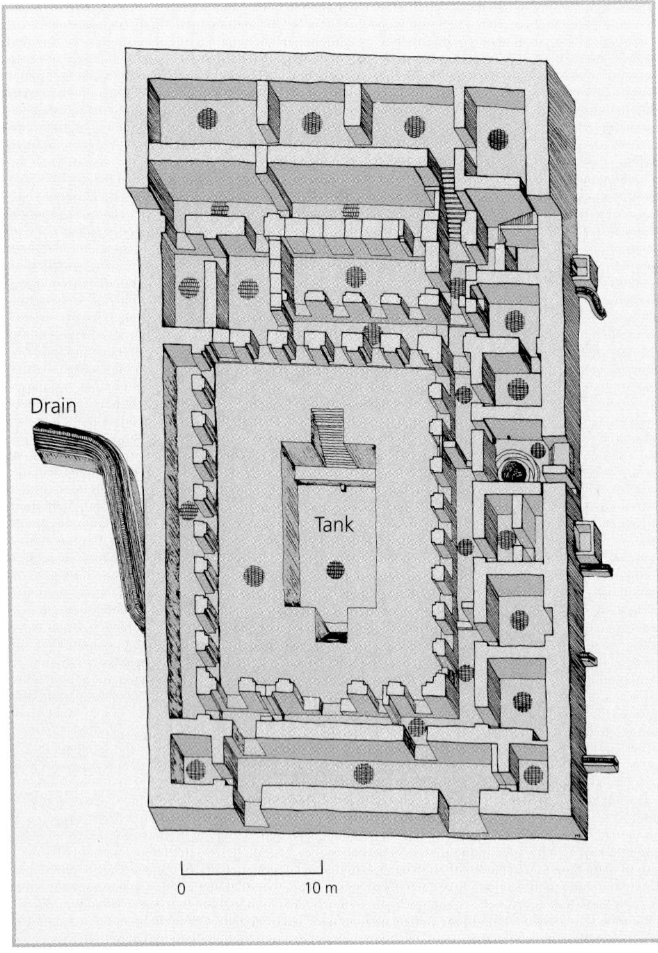


**Figure 10.17** The plan of the Great Bath at Mohenjo-daro.

bricks. (At smaller settlements, houses generally were built of sun-dried mud bricks.) At Mohenjo-daro, more spacious dwellings, perhaps for high-status individuals and merchants, were laid out around central courtyards. These residences had private bathing areas and toilets connected to a central drainage system built partially underground.

A striking feature of Harappan society is the extent of standardization, including a system of weights and measures. Precisely shaped pieces of chert or agate were used as counterweights in balances (Figure 10.19). Construction bricks had standard dimensions. Ceramic forms and ornamentation were remarkably similar at sites throughout the Indus system, although there was some regional variation and change over time.

**intaglio** An engraving in stone or other hard material that is depressed below the surface; an impression of the design produces an image in relief.

A considerable degree of occupational specialization characterized Indus society, and one's profession was probably an important factor in social differentiation. At the major urban centers, there were designated living and working quarters for beadmakers, coppersmiths, and weavers. Certain smaller sites were devoted almost entirely to a specific industry, craft, or trade, including beadmaking, shellworking, ceramic production, and coppersmithing. Metallurgy was well developed, and copper and bronze were used for a variety of tools and weapons. The availability of copper, lead, and silver within or close to Indus territory contributed to a greater use of metal tools than was evident in Mesopotamia.

There were significant differences between the Indus Valley and Mesopotamian civilizations. Although the Indus civilization covered a larger geographic area—650,000 sq km (260,000 sq mi)—it had a smaller number of major centers. Mesopotamia was composed of many city-states. The similarities between Harappa and Mohenjo-daro suggest that Indus centers were closely linked economically and culturally. The Indus civilization may have had a more equitable distribution of wealth than was the case in other early Eurasian societies. Exotic stones and metal were not restricted to large sites or to clearly elite contexts; considerable quantities of wealth have been recovered at even modest settlements. Indus material culture was simple compared with that of Mesopotamia; little representational or lavish art was constructed on a massive scale. Instead, one finds figurines, small sculptures, carvings on bone and ivory, decorated pottery, and **intaglio** figures on seals. Indus art is often in miniature.

The Indus elite engaged in fewer lavish public displays; they built no rich tombs, elaborate palaces, or fancy temples. But some mud-brick-lined tombs yielded more grave offerings (pottery, bronze mirrors, and a few beads) than the average burial. Nothing approaching the royal graves at Ur or the Egyptian tombs has yet been

Figure 10.18 The plan of streets and houses in one sector of Mohenjo-daro.

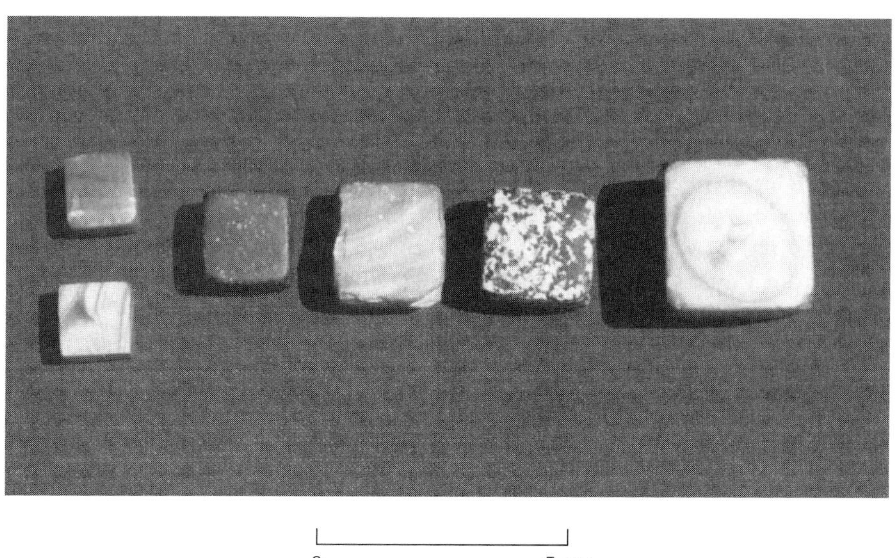


Figure 10.19 A collection of stone cubical weights from Harappa.

**Figure 10.20** A steatite figure of a ruler from Mohenjo-daro, standing 19 cm (7.4 in) high; such depictions of rulers are rare in Harappan civilization.

found in the Indus region. In fact, whatever rulers and elite the Harappans had remain anonymous. Individual conquests and accomplishments are not enumerated, and few portraits have been found. A steatite (soapstone) figure from Mohenjo-daro depicting a bearded man in an embroidered robe is a rare exception (Figure 10.20).

Indus settlements were closer to natural resources than Sumerian sites were. The large Harappan centers were connected with outlying rural communities and resource areas through complex trade networks. Both maritime and overland routes were used. Wheeled carts were drawn along regular caravan routes, and deep-sea vessels traveled the Persian Gulf and the Gulf of Oman. Long-distance exchanges moved seals, carnelian beads, and other miscellaneous items from the Indus region to the Persian Gulf, northern and southern Mesopotamia, Iran, and Afghanistan. Imports included lapis lazuli from Afghanistan, conch shells from Gujarat (western India), turquoise from northeastern Iran, carved **chlorite** bowls from the Iranian Plateau, and **serpentine** from central Asia. Few Mesopotamian items have been found in the Indus area. A possible explanation is that Mesopotamia exported mostly perishables or specific raw materials, such as barley, fruits, oil, and textiles.

A system of writing that was very different from the early Mesopotamian script developed in the Indus Valley. Over 4000 seals with Indus script have been found (Figure 10.21). Most inscriptions are short; no known inscription is longer than 21 signs, and the average text is only 5 or 6 signs. The lack of long texts has added to the difficulty of interpreting the Indus script. Over 400 symbols have been identified, yet none has been definitively deciphered. Inscriptions, including both writing and pictures, are found on small copper tablets and potsherds, but most are found on square seals of soapstone. Most seals had holes that allowed them to be strung and worn around the neck. The script seems to identify the owner of the seal or the official status of the bearer.

Many animals are depicted on the seals, including elephants, water buffalo, rhinoceroses, tigers, crocodiles, antelopes, bulls, and goats. Walter Fairservis, Jr., suggested that these animals may be totems or symbols representing specific kin groups; some seals depict processions with animal effigies being carried as standards. Each seal may thus identify its owner with a social group, which might help explain why similar scenes are repeated on multiple seals. One common theme is a figure seated in the yogic posture with

**chlorite** A kind of green stone that resembles mica.

**serpentine** A stone of dull green color that often has a mottled appearance.

**Figure 10.21** A Harappan seal with a bull in profile, a common motif on the seals; this medium-size square seal is 2.5 cm (1 in) high.

heels pressed under the groin. Surrounded by various animals, this individual wears a water buffalo–horned headdress. A second common scene is a **pipal tree** with various anthropomorphic and human figures. Some archaeologists have suggested that the figure with the headdress may be an early form of a deity that later came to be worshipped as Shiva, Lord of the Beasts, in Hinduism.

The Indus civilization began to decline around 1900 B.C. The major Harappan centers were greatly weakened, and the center of power shifted from the Indus to the Ganges River Valley to the east, where, after 600 B.C., large cities were built and state-level organizations formed. Archaeologists now think that the changes in the early part of the second millennium B.C. were not a complete collapse or population replacement, but rather the beginning of an episode of decentralization. Many elements of the earlier Harappan civilization were retained in these new settlements. The decline of the Indus civilization has been linked to the drying up of the ancient Ghaggar-Hakra River and the breakdown of the Indus system of exchange. Traditional views that proposed an Aryan invasion from the northwest are no longer supported.

The persistence of many aspects and traditions of the Indus civilization into more recent times is startling. Ceremonial bathing, ritual burning, specific body positions (such as the yogic position) on seals, the important symbolic roles of bulls and elephants, decorative arrangements of multiple bangles and necklaces (evident from graves and realistic figurines), and certain distinctive headgear—all are important attributes of ancient Harappan society that remain at the heart of contemporary Hinduism. The standard Harappan unit of weight, equivalent to 14 g (0.5 oz), continued in use at South Asian bazaars and markets into the nineteenth century. Although ancient Harappa and Mohenjo-daro lie in ruins today, the civilization of which they were a part has left an extremely important legacy.

Compare and contrast the Indus Valley and Mesopotamian civilizations. What are some of the major differences between these two early civilizations?

**pipal tree** A species of fig tree on the South Asian subcontinent that has had sacred significance for many cultures and religions throughout the region for thousands of years.

*Concept*

## Economic Specialization

### *Shellworking in the Indus civilization*

*Craft goods were extraordinarily important in the production and maintenance of ancient chiefdoms and states. In addition to basic domestic functions, they were used in almost all social, political, and ritual activities. Understanding the context and organization of their production is integral to a full understanding of daily life, political economy, and the role of material objects in social and political relations.*
—Cathy L. Costin (2004)

**division of labor** The differentiation of economic roles in a specific sociopolitical context.

With population growth, more densely packed communities, and increasing political complexity, household self-sufficiency becomes difficult, if not impossible, to sustain. Gaining access to all the resources that a family requires becomes difficult. As more tasks become specialized (a **division of labor**), people exchange what they produce for other goods and services through markets and trade networks. In some societies, the taxing or control of markets or exchange networks is an important source of power.

Today when we think of craft production or the specialized manufacture of goods for exchange, we often presume that such activities occur in nondomestic workshops or factories. Yet in many regions of the world, preindustrial economic specialization was largely situated in residential contexts or houses. Over the past few decades, archaeological investigations have devoted increasing attention to identifying the material indicators of craft manufacture, as well as the context of the locations where that production was situated and the volumes at which such craft products were made.

Exchange and craft production appear to have been key features of Indus Valley society. Complex internal trade networks connected the major urban centers of the Indus civilization with rural agricultural and resource areas. Evidence from Mohenjo-daro suggests that the large Indus cities included craft areas that served as the living and working quarters for specialists. Some crafts, such as the working of shell, stone, pottery, and metal, may have developed into hereditary occupations.

Shellworking, an important Indus craft, was undertaken by specialists. The earliest use of shell was limited to simple ornaments that were made by perforating natural shells. Later, during the time of the Indus civilization, shell use increased to include a variety of such decorative, utilitarian, and ritual objects as ornaments (bangles, rings, beads, pendants, and large perforated disks), utensils (ladles), inlay pieces, and other special objects.

According to J. Mark Kenoyer, of the University of Wisconsin–Madison, each of the workshops at Mohenjo-daro specialized in producing different shell items. For example, one area apparently produced mostly inlay pieces. Shell workshops similar to those at Mohenjo-daro were present at Harappa and other urban centers. But at Harappa, there was less variety in shell species and fewer shell artifacts in general, because of its location further inland. At the site of Lothal, on the coast of the Arabian Sea, shell workshops also produced a variety of shell objects.

Another major shell site, at Balakot, on the coast near Karachi, Pakistan, specialized in shell bangles, beads, and smaller objects. The site has workshop areas with stone grinders and hammers, bangles in various stages of manufacture, and unworked shell. One type of shell was cut with a specialized bronze saw. Metal tools were expensive and, at most sites, only craftworkers who were supported or controlled by more affluent individuals had access to metal tools. Most of the bangles were made by an alternative chipping and grinding process that used stone tools (Figure 10.22). Regardless of the method of manufacture, the resulting bangles at Balakot were almost identical. Even though Indus sites specialized in different types of finished products, a single standardized manufacturing technology and certain decorative conventions often were employed across the region.

Although certain shell items were purely decorative, the function of other

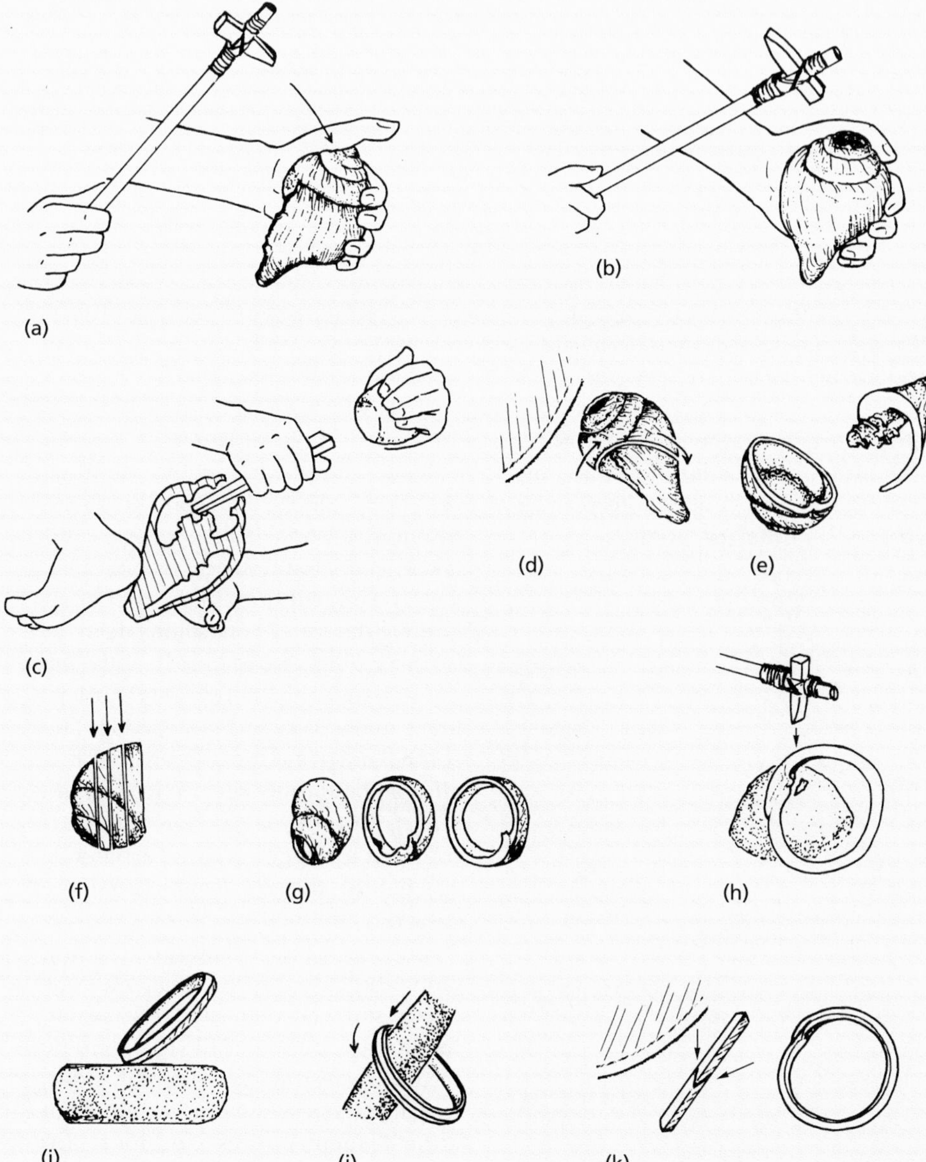


**Figure 10.22** The manufacturing process from large whole shell to finished bangles. The process begins with the preliminary chipping of the shell and the removal of the internal columella (a–c) and continues with sawing the body of the shell into thin circles (d–g), finishing the edges of the shell blanks (h–j), and incising the final bangle (k).

Indus shell artifacts remains a mystery. Recent excavations at the cemetery area in Harappa have found many adult women with shell bangles on their left arms. These arm bracelets may have been a symbol of ethnic identity or a signifier of a specific marriage status. Shell bangles are still used for various social and ritual functions across the South Asian subcontinent. Through historical accounts, the antiquity of finely crafted shell objects (and their ritual functions) can be traced back to 600 B.C. It seems reasonable to deduce that some of these social and ritual uses may have their ultimate roots in the practices of the Indus civilization.

# Hierakonpolis

*The emergence of the Egyptian civilization*

In spite of the general popularity of Egyptian archaeology, we know surprisingly little about early Egypt, particularly before the rise of early states and the first written documents. What we do know about Egypt suggests that this civilization along the Nile River was different in its long-term history from the ancient civilizations that developed in other parts of the world. For example, Egypt was relatively centralized for almost 2500 years, with only one major episode of political fragmentation, 2200–2000 B.C.

Egyptian civilization centered on the Nile Valley, a long oasis surrounded by desert (Figure 10.23). The Nile flows to the north and the Mediterranean Sea, more than 6400 km (4000 mi) from its source in the swamps and lakes of equatorial Africa. Its final 1300 km (800 mi) cut through Egypt before fanning out into an enormous delta. In Lower Egypt, an area of rich cultivable floodplains to the north, the river valley is up to 20 km (12.5 mi) wide. The south, known as Upper Egypt, has less alluvial land (only several kilometers wide), forming a narrow strip surrounded by jagged rock escarpments.

Before the construction of the Aswan Dam, near the First Cataract (rapids), in the 1960s, annual flooding along the Nile was common, and tons of rich soil were deposited. As a result, the floodplain of the Nile is extremely fertile. Because of sparse rainfall today, irrigation is necessary for farming, but annual temperatures are ideal for the cultivation of a wide range of crops. Staple crops are legumes, barley, onions, cucumbers, melons, and figs. Other plants include rushes and reeds used for making baskets, flax for linens, and **papyrus** for cordage and paper. As in the past, today the area also supports sheep, goats, pigs, cattle, ducks, geese, fish, turtles, crocodiles, hippopotamuses, and other game animals. Although the surrounding deserts provide very little in the way of food, they are rich in building stone and minerals, including copper, gold, and silver.

The floods along the Nile were more predictable and easier to control

**Figure 10.23** The Nile Valley in Egypt, with sites of Upper and Lower Egypt mentioned in the text.

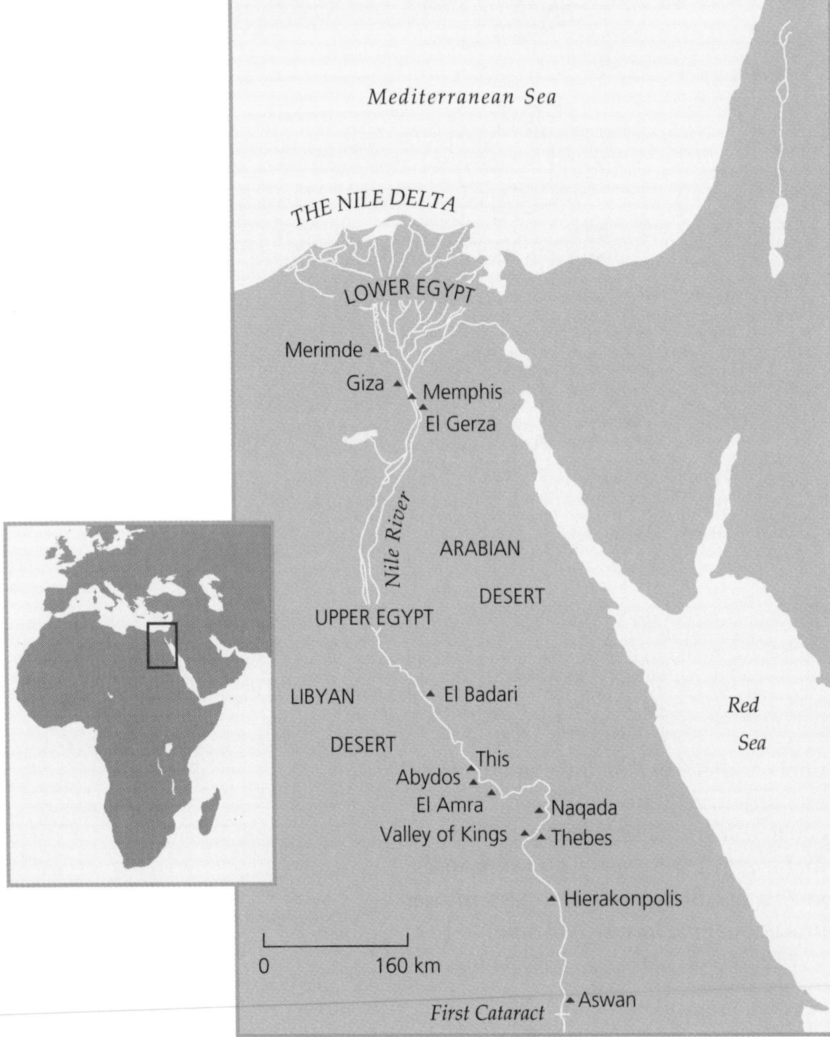

than those of the Tigris and Euphrates rivers in Mesopotamia. The Egyptians could very easily modify natural basins on the floor of the Nile Valley to retain floodwater for their crops. Higher levees along the river provided dry locations for settlements.

No definite sedentary villages have been found in the Nile Valley before the sixth millennium B.C., when nomadic cattle herders and farmers began to settle in the area. Before 6000 B.C., the Nile Valley was occupied by groups of hunter-gatherers who followed an annual round in which they hunted along the margins of the desert for wild cattle, gazelles, and birds during part of the year and took fowl and fish at other times. The presence of grinding stones indicates that wild grains also were an important food item.

Soon after 5000 B.C., food production was established in the Nile Valley. The early farming settlements raised Southwest Asian domesticates: wheat, barley, sheep, and goats. Most of what is known about predynastic Egypt comes from the south, where there has been less deposition to bury sites. Yet it is possible that sedentism actually occurred earlier in the more fertile north. One floodplain settlement near the Nile Delta, Merimde, dating to as early as 4900 B.C., consisted of a cluster of semisubterranean, oval houses with roofs of sticks and mud. The inhabitants used stone axes, knives, and flint arrowheads. Grains were stored in ceramic jars, baskets, and pits. Circular, clay-lined threshing floors also have been reported.

The earliest occupations in the south (roughly contemporary with those in the north) are called Badarian, after the best-known settlement of El Badari in Upper Egypt. Badarian settlements consisted of clusters of skin tents or small huts. Many of the dead were buried carefully in oval or rectangular pits roofed over with sticks or mats. Utensils and food were commonly placed in the burials. Other grave offerings included rectangular stone palettes (or tablets), ivory spoons, and small ivory or stone vases, all of which have been associated with the preparation and use of green face paint. These items are all common components of the predynastic burial assemblages. The Badarian focus on grave features and the accompanying goods may have been at the root of the later Egyptian emphasis on burial custom.

In the south, materials associated with the Amratian tradition (3800–3500 B.C.) are frequently found directly above Badarian levels. The name Amratian was derived from the site of El Amra near Abydos in Upper Egypt. Although the Amratian materials seem to reflect direct continuity with the earlier Badarian, the latter period is characterized by the appearance of more developed craft industries (particularly pottery, alabaster, and basalt) and a larger number and more widespread distribution of settlements. Copperworking, which may have been initiated in the Badarian, also gained in importance. Amratian metalworkers used copper to make pins, flat axes, awls, and daggers. Scholars do not agree on the origins of Egyptian metallurgy. Many argue that it was introduced from Southwest Asia, whereas others, pointing to earlier metalworking in Upper than in Lower Egypt, suggest that it may have been an indigenous accomplishment.

During the Amratian period, at least three important centers emerged in southern Egypt: Naqada, This (near Abydos), and Hierakonpolis (HIGH-ra-KON-po-lis). The best known of these, Hierakonpolis, had an estimated population of several thousand people. The Greek name for this settlement, which means "city of the hawk," comes from the falcon-headed Egyptian god Horus of the city Nekhen, the Egyptian name for this ancient center. Most of the site's inhabitants lived in rectangular, semisubterranean houses of mud bricks and thatch. The more important artisans and traders lived in larger houses in separate compounds. Near the site was a large cemetery with part of the burial area reserved for

**papyrus** A tall marsh plant, or reed, of the Nile Valley that the ancient Egyptians cut into strips and pressed into a kind of paper to write on.

**Figure 10.24** The ceremonial macehead found at Hierakonpolis, shown reconstructed here. The scorpion in front of the face of the principal individual, who wears the white crown of Upper Egypt, identifies him as King Scorpion, the predecessor of Egypt's first pharaoh.

**porphyry** An igneous rock with visible quartz or feldspar crystals embedded in a finer-grained base.

elaborate tombs. Although not as spectacular as later ones in Egypt, these tombs are impressive. The early tombs were constructed by cutting rectangular holes into the terrace of a dry streambed. The size and contents of the tombs varied, perhaps reflecting status and prestige. One grave, measuring 2.4 × 1.5 m (8 × 5 ft) and 1.8 m (6 ft) deep, contained baskets, fine pottery, rope, flint arrowheads, and wooden arrow shafts. Unfortunately, the grave was looted in later times, and the most valuable goods may have been stolen. A second grave contained scraps of papyrus paper and a disk-shaped macehead made of polished green-and-white **porphyry.** Maceheads, which were mounted on wooden staffs called maces, were recognized in Egypt as a sign of authority (Figure 10.24). The presence of the macehead at Hierakonpolis indicates that the process of political development already may have been well under way. Similar polished, hard-stone maceheads have been found at several other contemporaneous sites, possibly indicating the presence of several small, competing political units.

Hierakonpolis also was the center of a very large pottery industry. At least 15 Amratian kilns have been identified, the largest of which covered over 1000 sq m (0.25 acre). Two distinct types of pottery were made: a coarse ware for everyday household or industrial use and a fine, untempered ware for grave offerings. The kilns appear to have been part of one well-organized complex, in that each kiln was used for the firing of a different kind of pottery. The large kilns must have produced far more than was needed locally. Michael Hoffman postulated that the people in charge of pottery production acquired considerable economic power.

During the subsequent Gerzean period (3500–3100 B.C.), named after El Gerza in the north, craft activities, including pottery production, metallurgy, and the manufacture of stone bowls from very hard materials such as diorite and basalt, appear to have been carried out on an even larger scale. The use of copper artifacts, which were now cast as well as hammered, increased. Gold also was worked at this time, and some luxury items were wrapped in gold foil. Trade with Southwest Asia intensified in volume. Some of the pottery of this period was painted in Southwest Asian style, in dark red on a buff background. Foreign motifs also were incorporated into the local decorative tradition.

Gerzean remains have been found in Upper and Lower Egypt, possibly indicating greater integration between the two areas. Yet important differences in ceramic styles and burial customs continued to distinguish Upper and Lower Egypt. On carved palettes and other art, key individuals are depicted wearing distinctive headgear or crowns. These crowns vary from one area of Egypt to another (Figure 10.25), suggesting that several different polities may have developed along the Nile.

During Gerzean times, social and economic inequalities, evident from tomb size, grave design, and burial inclusions, increased markedly. One macehead found at Hierakonpolis, with a scorpion on it, has been identified as belonging to King Scorpion, the predecessor of Egypt's first pharaoh (see Figure 10.24). Hierakonpolis, whose location shifted slightly closer to the Nile, was one of the largest known settlements, with 5 ha (12.5 acres) of occupation, including large nonresidential structures such as palaces and temples.

Written records and stone monuments indicate that the incidence of warfare increased at that time, with local kings trying to gain control over adjacent kingdoms. Among the competing kings, it is thought to have been Narmer from Hierakonpolis who finally succeeded in unifying Egypt into one kingdom around 3100 B.C. As Egypt's first pharaoh, Narmer founded a dynasty (3100–2890 B.C.) and a political structure that lasted for nearly 3000 years.

The unification of Upper and Lower Egypt was recorded for posterity on a 64-cm (25-in) carved stone palette discovered by English archaeologists in 1898 at Hierakonpolis (Figure 10.26). One side of the tablet depicts Narmer, the leader of Upper Egypt, wearing the white crown of Upper Egypt and holding his symbolic mace. The other side shows him wearing the red crown of Lower Egypt. Both sides include scenes of the king in battle.

The Egyptian state was far larger and more complex than any city-state in Mesopotamia. The nature of rule also was much different in Egypt than in Mesopotamia. In Egypt, the royal court centralized power and wealth, and this consolidation is evident in the concentration of resources in the mortuary complexes of the kings. The relative stability of Egyptian rule diminished some of the insecurity that in Mesopotamia led to the construction of great walled complexes around nucleated urban centers. In Egypt, continuity with earlier occupations is apparent in such contexts as stoneworking, death rituals, and the use of the macehead as a symbol of rule.

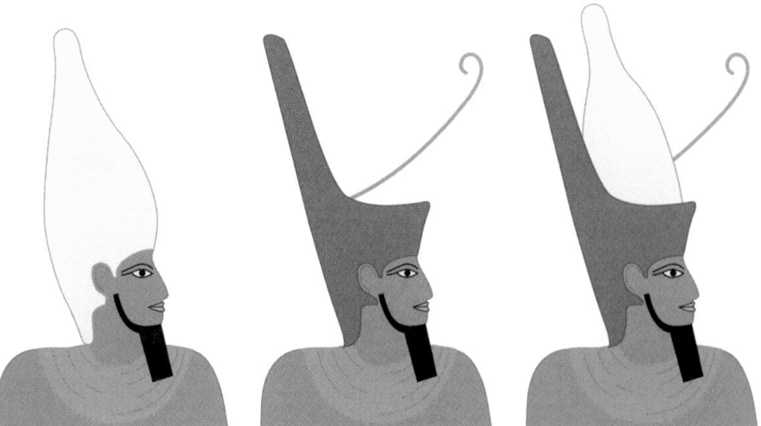

**Figure 10.25** The Egyptian crowns: the white crown of Upper Egypt (left), the red crown of Lower Egypt (center), and the double crown of unified Egypt (right).

The unification of Egypt was closely timed with the earliest hieroglyphic writing. Although writing first developed in Mesopotamia, the Egyptians devised their own script, which is very different from writing in Southwest Asia. Egyptian hieroglyphs consist of both pictographic and phonetic (vocal sounds) elements, written on papyrus, carved on stone as part of public buildings, or painted on wood or clay (Figure 10.27). Egyptian writing was more concerned with rule and kinship than with economic transactions. The deeds and accomplishments of leaders were recorded, and this may have had a role in the consolidation of power in the hands of a limited few.

The widespread adoption of irrigation agriculture also coincided with the unification of Egypt. Ancient Egyptian irrigation practices were very simple, such as modifying natural basins to serve as reservoirs for floodwater. Yet the large surpluses that these techniques permitted clearly were necessary to support the opulent lifestyles and mortuary rituals of the emergent pharaohs.

**Figure 10.26** Narmer's carved stone palette. One side (left) depicts Egypt's first pharaoh wearing the white crown of Upper Egypt and posturing over a defeated enemy in the presence of the falcon god Horus. On the other side (right), he wears the red crown of Lower Egypt and marches in a victory procession to view decapitated prisoners.

Scarab beetle (*kheper*) means "to become" or "to evolve"

The ankh, a cross with a looped top, means "life" or "to live"

Scepter (*was*), a forked staff topped with an animal's head, refers to "power"

**Figure 10.27** Some frequently used Egyptian hieroglyphs

Concept

# The Cemetery at Hierakonpolis

## *Steps toward the unification of Egypt*

The earliest tombs in Egypt were small wooden graves in which the dead were buried with utensils and food to sustain them in the afterworld. In late predynastic Egypt (the fourth millennium B.C.), more elaborate tombs were constructed for the burial of elite members of society. These graves contained a variety of goods, including beautiful pottery, baskets, braided leather rope, painted reed arrow shafts, flint arrowheads, pieces of papyrus, and maceheads.

The architectural styles of tomb construction differed in Lower Egypt and Upper Egypt (Figure 10.28). In the royal **necropolis** at Hierakonpolis, these differences were utilized symbolically by Narmer or his immediate predecessors. Constructed at the end of the fourth millennium B.C., the cemetery was arranged, according to Michael Hoffman, who excavated at the site, to represent the union of Upper and Lower Egypt, and perhaps to legitimize the military conquest of Lower Egypt by the Upper Egyptian rulers.

Tombs in the style of Lower Egypt were constructed at the downstream end of a **wadi,** which represented the downstream end of the Nile, or Lower Egypt. These tombs were lined with mud bricks, over which were placed large, painted wood and reed structures. Low reed fences surrounded the tombs. The burials occurred in groups of three, four, and five, suggesting that rulers were buried with other family members or members of their court. A fragmented wooden bed was found in one tomb. It was finely carved, with two legs crafted to resemble a bull's legs—a forerunner of the furniture in King Tutankhamen's tomb.

At the opposite end of the necropolis, or upstream with respect to the wadi, was a stone tomb in the architectural style of Upper Egypt. This stone feature is surrounded by apparently similar tombs that have yet to be excavated. Cut into subsoil bedrock, the excavated tomb was a long, narrow trench with an L-shaped hole cut into the middle of the floor. There was no superstructure associated with it. Surrounding this stone tomb were animal burials, including the remains of hippopotamuses, elephants, crocodiles, baboons, cattle, goats, sheep, and dogs. Some of the animals were mummified and probably had civic-ceremonial significance. In Dynastic times, the Egyptians used various animals as godlike symbols of the different **nomes** (provinces) that constituted the Egyptian state. Some of these same animal symbols are portrayed atop standards on Narmer's stone palette. In accordance with the rest of the cemetery, it seems possible that the animal burials also followed a symbolic orientation. For example, the easternmost tomb had six baboons, animals that ancient Egyptians associated with the rising sun.

Hoffman proposed that this desert necropolis presages key attributes of the Egyptian state. These features include the use of the royal death cult and an associated cemetery area as national symbols, the division of the state into the symbolic halves of Upper and Lower Egypt, and the incorporation of conquered polities and peoples through ritual as well as military means. In contrast to the neighboring polities of Southwest Asia, political integration in Dynastic Egypt was tied less directly to specific fortified towns and was linked more closely to elite lineages and cemetery and temple complexes. The roots of that civic-ceremonial organization appear to have extended to Hierakonpolis.

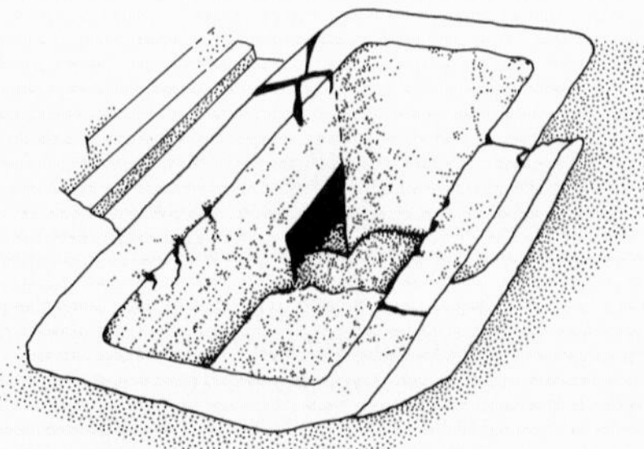


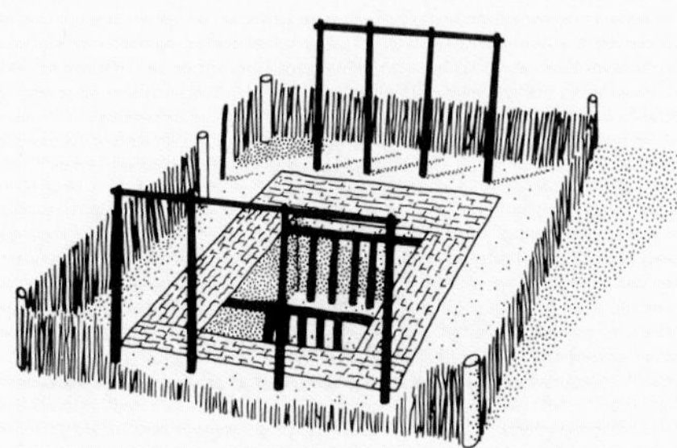


**Figure 10.28** The two tomb styles of Lower Egypt (bottom) and Upper Egypt (top).

**necropolis** (Greek) Cemetery.

**wadi** (Arabic) A dry streambed.

**nome** A geographic province incorporated within the ancient Egyptian state.

# Giza and Dynastic Egypt

*Pyramids and pharaohs*

www.mhhe.com/priceip6e

For a Web-based activity on the mummification and funerary practices of the ancient Egyptians, see the Internet exercises on your online learning center.

By 3100 B.C., Upper and Lower Egypt unified into one state when Narmer, Egypt's first pharaoh, conquered the northern delta. Narmer moved the capital from Hierakonpolis, in Upper Egypt, to Memphis, at the junction of Upper and Lower Egypt, where the Nile Valley spreads out into the broad delta. Memphis remained the political center of Egypt for 1500 years. Although the Nile Valley around Memphis was not a particularly rich agricultural area, the city was strategically positioned for riverine communication between southern and northern Egypt.

The symbol of the pharaoh was the double crown of Upper and Lower Egypt (see Figure 10.25). A series of pharaohs during the first (3100–2890 B.C.) and second (2890–2686 B.C.) dynasties ruled under the double crown, but consolidation of the two disparate regions was not a steady or easy process. The Egyptian kings adopted the strategy of establishing outposts, temples, and shrines throughout their domains, maintaining integration and preventing the monopoly of functions or power in any single place or capital. Intermarriage of the elite from north and south may have been used to solidify the unification.

The Egyptian population was less urban than Southwest Asian societies, which generally had larger centers. Apart from a few large sites, most of the Egyptian population continued to live in unwalled, largely self-sufficient villages. This may account for the preoccupation of the Egyptian elite with rural lifeways. Despite this preoccupation, a massive, hereditary bureaucracy developed, devoting official energy to tax collection, harvest yields, and the administration of irrigation. Each nome, administered by a local governor, was under overall central control. During the first dynasty, the Egyptian kings also supported an increasing number of craft specialists. Trade links were extended to what is now Sudan (Nubia) and Libya. With the elaboration of the court during the early dynasties, the demand for sub-Saharan products such as ivory and ebony intensified, thereby heightening interest in areas to the south.

Between the third dynasty in 2686 B.C. and the Persian conquest in 525 B.C., Egypt was ruled by no fewer than 23 dynasties. The third through sixth dynasties constitute what is known as the Old Kingdom (2686–2181 B.C.), a time of despotic pharaohs and grandiose pyramid construction. The largest Egyptian pyramids were constructed by these early dynasties. The first pyramid was a stepped stone structure constructed by the pharaoh Zoser as the centerpiece of his funeral complex (Figure 10.29). The step pyramids were soon

**Figure 10.29** Zoser's stepped pyramid at Saqqarah was an important first step in the construction of monumental pyramids in Egypt.

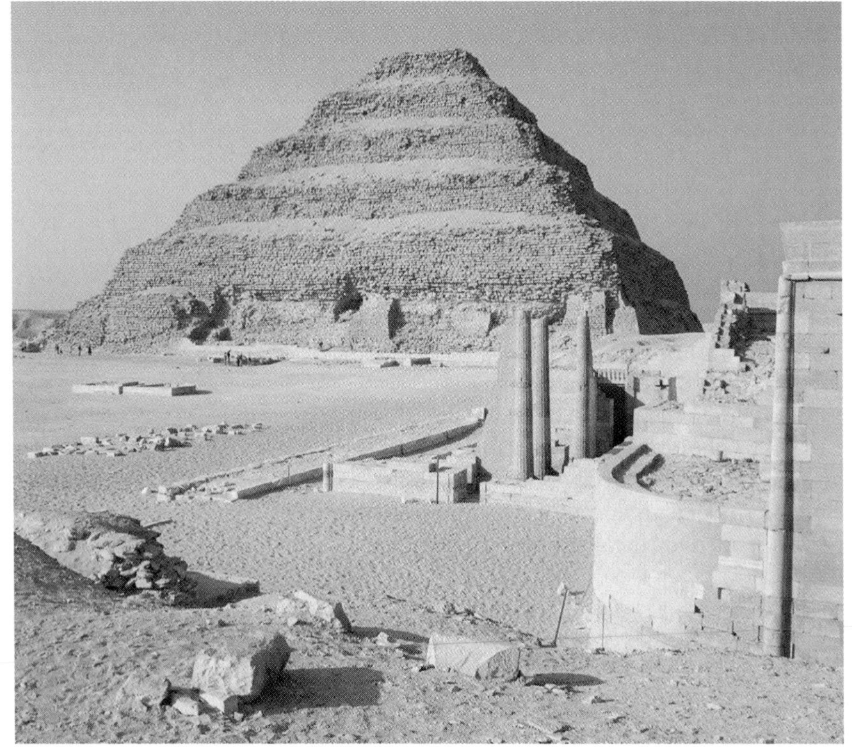

followed by the more familiar pyramids with smooth faces. Like all royal tombs until 1000 B.C., the pyramids were constructed in the desert on the west side of the Nile River and were surrounded by the tombs of contemporary officials.

Although few written records have survived from the Old Kingdom, sketchy accounts provide a perspective largely unavailable for earlier periods. Scribes were an important part of the government. Special schools trained writers for careers in the palace and the treasury. Contemporary documents on papyrus show that Egyptians were skilled in architecture, surgery, accounting, geometry, and astronomy. But most of the population, as in other early civilizations, consisted of illiterate peasant farmers who maintained the Egyptian agricultural base.

One major site of the Old Kingdom is Giza, located near modern Cairo (Figure 10.30). Just a short distance from the ancient capital city of Memphis, the Giza Plateau is where King Khufu (known as Cheops in Greek), of the fourth dynasty, built his massive pyramid. Called the Pyramid of Khufu, or the Great Pyramid, this monumental edifice required precise planning and complex engineering and serves as a clear reflection of state power and labor control. The pyramid is 150 m high (500 ft, almost as tall as the Washington Monument), covers 5.3 ha (13.1 acres), and contains a series of internal passages and chambers. Khufu's pyramid was constructed of 2.3 million stone blocks with an average weight of 2275 kg (2.5 tons). Its construction involved roughly 13.4 million man-days of labor and incorporated materials from areas as far away as Lebanon, Sinai, Aswan, and Nubia.

Surrounding the Pyramid of Khufu were the much smaller pyramids of three queens and the rectangular tombs of Khufu's closest royal relatives and high officials (Figure 10.31). Nearby was the king's palace complex and villages for the administrators and workmen. Two other large pyramids were constructed by his successors Khafre (known as Chephren in Greek) and Menkaure (Mycerinus in Greek) (Figure 10.32). Khafre's pyramid is almost as large as Khufu's, but its internal structure is much simpler, with a single tomb chamber at the base of the structure. One of the most famous ancient Egyptian structures, the king-headed lion, or Great Sphinx, bears Khafre's features. It was constructed to guard the sacred realm of the dead kings, whose power was believed to have continued to influence the universe in which their successors ruled. Although of the same design as the large pyramids, Menkaure's pyramid is much smaller, and its construction marks the end of the era of massive pyramid construction. Those built during the following dynasty were relatively small and poorly constructed.

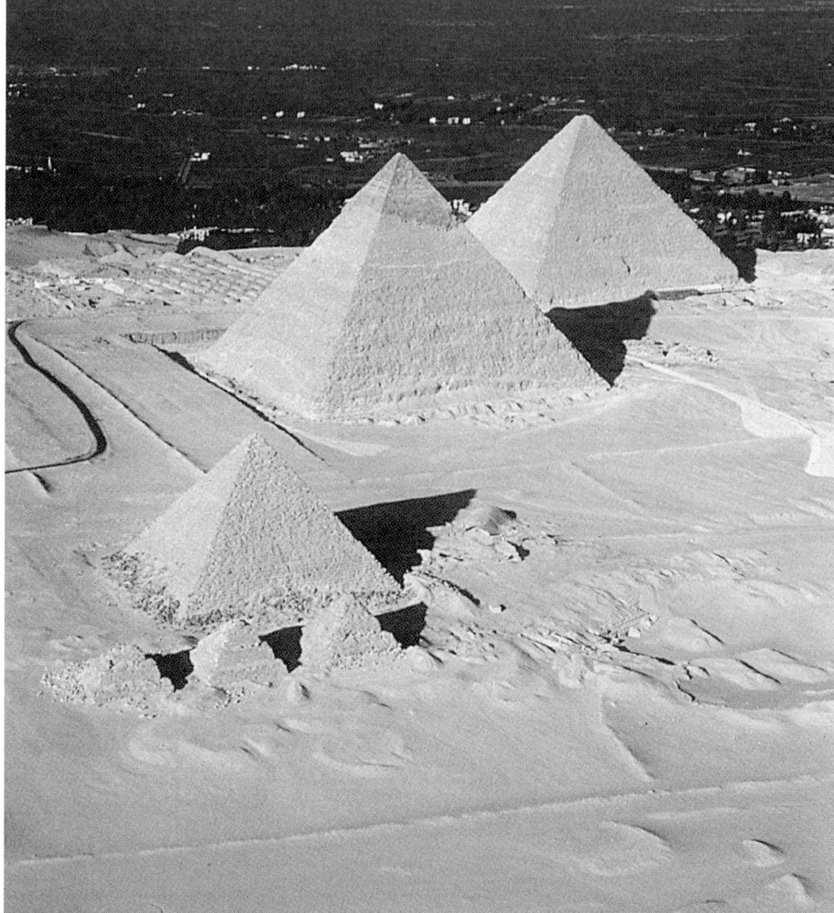

**Figure 10.30** The enormous pyramid complex at Giza, near modern Cairo, built during Old Kingdom Egypt (2686–2181 B.C.). The pyramids were constructed over a long period of time by a succession of pharaohs, each of whom had his own funerary monument.

During the early dynasties, pharaohs were central to the Egyptian state. They were considered divine, sometimes referred to as "the good god." These paramount rulers controlled economic exchange, served at the top of a great bureaucracy, and acted as the heads of state

Figure 10.31 The plan of Giza, showing the three large pyramids of the pharaohs, the smaller pyramids of the queens, and other smaller tombs.

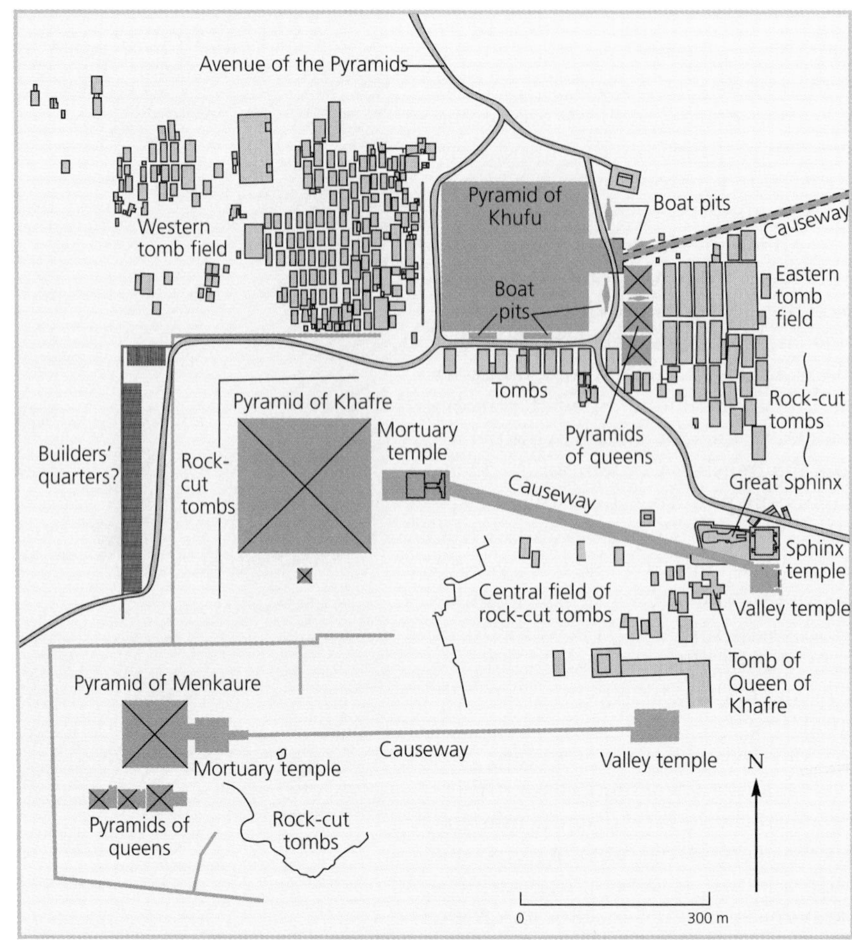


*Later Egyptian records mention at least seventeen kinds of beer, some of them referred to in poetic terms that sound, to modern ears, almost like advertising slogans: Different beers were known as "the beautiful and good," "the heavenly," "the joy-bringer," "the addition to the meal," "the plentiful," "the fermented." Beers used in religious ceremonies also had special names.*

—Tom Standage (2005)

Figure 10.32 The double statue of Menkaure and his sister, Khamerernebti II.

religion. Toward the end of the Old Kingdom, the construction of smaller pyramids paralleled a decline in royal power. Following the pattern that often occurred in ancient states and empires, the Old Kingdom collapsed after five centuries of strong central rule and was followed by a period of decentralization. The provinces became competitive petty kingdoms that fought with one another, either alone or in small alliances. With the fragmentation of the Egyptian state into these smaller territorial political groups, provincial governors and bureaucrats gained more power. Comparatively large mud-brick tombs were erected in these provinces, displaying the growing power of local authorities.

The beginning of the Middle Kingdom, around 2000 B.C., was marked by the reunification of Upper and Lower Egypt under a dynastic line centered at the city of Thebes in Upper Egypt. The rulers pacified southern Egypt and then overthrew the dynasty in power to the north. The capital was brought back to Memphis, and the fortified towns of the earlier decentralized period disappeared. With increased administrative centralization, a second era of ostentatious pyramid building began. Yet the Middle Kingdom pharaohs were less despotic. Trading contacts were extended, and parts of Nubia, just to the south of Egypt, were conquered. Huge fortresses were erected to solidify control of this frontier along the Nile.

During the first half of the second millennium B.C., central administrative authority again weakened, and a period of short-lived dynasties and regionalization followed. In the sixteenth century B.C., a later Theban dynasty began

**Figure 10.33** Using a shaduf to raise water from the Nile to a walled irrigation ditch.

a third era of unification and centralization, called the New Kingdom. The dynasties of this period are richly documented in historical texts. The kings of the New Kingdom reasserted control from the Nile Delta to Nubia and conquered parts of Lebanon, Palestine, and southern Syria. No earlier Egyptian polity had established such far-ranging external contacts. The highly centralized government of the New Kingdom depended on large external tribute levees for its maintenance and support.

During the New Kingdom, kings were considered quasi-divine, the mediators between humans and the gods. These rulers often married their own sisters to concentrate status and divinity in a dynastic line. The kings lived in elaborate complexes that contained throne rooms and extensive private chambers for the royal family, harems, court officials, and servants. The pharaohs adopted new burial customs; their mummies were buried in rock-cut tombs in the Valley of Kings near Thebes. Among the New Kingdom pharaohs were a number of historically renowned figures: Tuthmosis III, Ahkenaten, Tutankhamen (better known as King Tut), and Ramses II.

During the New Kingdom, an important innovation in irrigation permitted the agricultural development of the broad Nile Delta. The labor-saving **shaduf** enabled one to raise water from wells or ditches onto gardens and fields (Figure 10.33). This innovation, still in use today, may have contributed to the demographic buildup in the delta during the New Kingdom. The kings of the nineteenth dynasty divided their residence between the traditional centers of power, Thebes and Memphis, and a new royal residence that was established in the eastern delta.

The administrative centralization and stability that characterized the New Kingdom came to an end around 1000 B.C. Hostilities erupted when strong provincial leaders and local army commanders increased their regional power. A period of foreign intervention followed, and for millennia Egypt did not regain its autonomy for anything but a brief interlude. The Nile Valley was ruled in succession by

**shaduf** An Egyptian bucket-and-lever lifting device that enables one to raise water a few feet from a well or ditch onto fields and gardens.

Assyrians, Persians, and then Alexander the Great, king of the Macedonians (northern Greece). The almost-3000-year succession of pharaohs ended when Alexander appointed one of his generals ruler of Egypt.

Several hypotheses have been proposed to explain the highly centralized nature of the early Egyptian state. The constricted distribution and relatively small proportion of usable land (along the Nile) may have fostered the concentration and monopolization of wealth. Commoners and peasants would have had relatively few options when they were heavily taxed or asked to contribute to labor gangs. In an environment such as the fertile Nile Valley, surrounded by desert, it would be very difficult for people to move away and still maintain access to cultivable land.

The critical nature of water control (often requiring centralized maintenance and adjudication) also may have been a factor; however, according to Karl Butzer, of the University of Texas at Austin, early Egyptian irrigation systems were not highly centralized and were largely under local control. Nevertheless, the disastrous potential of Nile flooding may have encouraged the establishment of a central agency to help alleviate periodic local disasters.

Finally, Egypt had a number of military-political threats on its borders throughout much of its history, and that, too, may have encouraged the centralization of power in the hands of a few to coordinate a strong defense. Although none of these interpretations is convincing on its own, they do suggest questions and directions for future research.

# *Concept*

## Pyramids

### *Ancient monuments across the globe*

Pyramid-shaped structures were built by ancient civilizations in both the Eastern Hemisphere and the Americas, representing the wealth and power of those who erected them. Yet the building techniques and the specific uses of these constructions varied greatly from one ancient civilization to another.

The best-known pyramids in the world were erected by the ancient Egyptians during the third millennium B.C. The Egyptian pyramids were constructed of cut-stone blocks, with internal passageways and tombs. The first royal pyramid, built around 2680 B.C. at Saqqarah by Zoser, was a six-step pyramid (see Figure 10.29). Over the next century, the pyramid shape was perfected, culminating in the magnificent pyramids at Giza. The construction of these Old Kingdom pyramids required an enormous expenditure of energy and manpower, involving both unskilled labor to quarry and transport the stones and skilled masons who would cut, fit, and smooth the stones. Given the construction techniques known at the time, such large structures had to be in the shape of a pyramid to support their weight.

Constructed as monuments for kings, the Egyptian pyramids have as their origin the tomb architecture of predynastic Egypt. They were built in one long, contiguous episode of construction, without outside stairways, and were not meant to be climbed once they were completed. The large stone blocks likely were positioned through the use of temporary ramps that were subsequently dismantled. These pyramids served not only as tombs for the pharaohs but also as their houses for eternity. As such, the pyramids reflect the importance Egyptians placed on life in the afterworld.

Kurt Mendelssohn argues that the construction of monumental tombs for the pharaohs, who could have been interred at much less cost, was not the only goal. It was the erection of the pyramid itself that was important. He suggests that pyramid construction was a political strategy used by the pharaohs to institutionalize and materialize

AT LAST HAVE MADE WONDERFUL DISCOVERY IN VALLEY; A MAGNIFICENT TOMB WITH SEALS INTACT; RECOVERED SAME FOR YOUR ARRIVAL; CONGRATULATIONS.

—Telegram sent by Howard Carter, the investigator who discovered King Tut's tomb, to his sponsor, Lord Carnarvon, on November 6, 1922

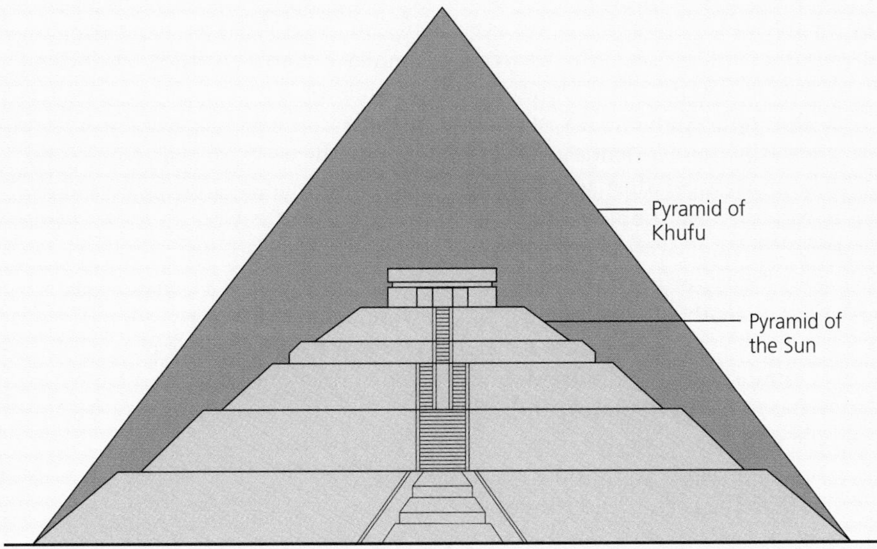


**Figure 10.34** A comparison of the Pyramid of the Sun at Teotihuacan and the Pyramid of Khufu at Giza, which is approximately 146 m high.

**Figure 10.35** The building episodes of a Late Postclassic pyramid in the Basin of Mexico. The earliest pyramid is represented by 0 and the latest by 5.

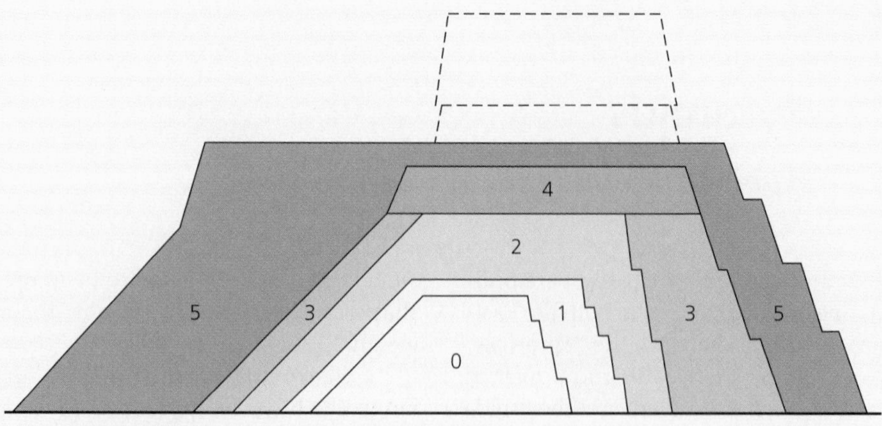

How did the nature of pyramids and their uses differ between Egypt and Mesoamerica?

the power of the state. The thousands of peasants who worked on the pyramids depended in part on the central government for food during a portion of the year. They were fed from food surpluses obtained from villages through taxation. One consequence was that the population became reliant on the state bureaucracy to redistribute food and organize labor. Recent excavations by Mark Lehner, of Harvard University, and Zahi Hawass have uncovered two communities near the Giza pyramids where builders of these great structures seem to have lived. On the basis of their excavations, Lehner and Hawass conclude that ordinary Egyptians (and not slaves) built the pyramids, some working as conscripts on a rotating basis and others as year-round workers.

Monumental structures in the Western Hemisphere were very different in form from their Egyptian counterparts. For example, in western Mexico, such buildings could be circular as well as square and rectangular. Throughout the Americas, most large structures were actually truncated pyramids, with flat tops. Most Mesoamerican pyramids were rubble-filled, with a cut-stone facing. However, some central Mexican pyramids have a core of adobe bricks with a stone facing held together by mortar. Other North American pyramids, such as Monks Mound at Cahokia, were built almost entirely of earthen fill.

Mesoamerican pyramids were smaller than the earlier Old Kingdom pyramids at Giza. Two of the most massive Mesoamerican pyramids, the Pyramid of the Sun and the Pyramid of the Moon, were constructed at Teotihuacan in central Mexico around 100 B.C. At its base, the Pyramid of the Sun is about the size of the Pyramid of Khufu at Giza, but it is only about half as high (Figure 10.34). In contrast to the Egyptian pyramids, Mesoamerican structures were often built in a series of construction episodes, in which they were enlarged and often changed drastically in appearance (Figure 10.35). The largest Mesoamerican pyramid, the Great Pyramid at Cholula (in the state of Puebla), was enlarged many times over hundreds of years.

Pyramids in the Americas generally served as foundations for other public buildings, such as temples, shrines, palaces, or elite residences. Stairways provided access to the structures above. The truncated pyramids emulated natural features, such as hills and mountains, raising structures above the ground level. The platforms increased the visibility of the public buildings while making direct access to them more difficult. Although many pyramids in the Americas include burial features, few were designed or used (as were the Egyptian pyramids) exclusively as the final resting place for a particular ruler or elite figure.

# An-yang

## *A late Shang city in China*

Decades ago, the emergence of Shang civilization in North China appeared to scholars to have no direct antecedents; it was formerly thought that early Chinese cities and states arose as a result of Mesopotamian contact. But as with Egypt and the Indus Valley, more recent archaeological fieldwork has demonstrated that the trajectory from the diversity of the Chinese Neolithic to the rise of early civilizations was more continuous, with outside influences playing a small role. The development of civilization in China was largely indigenous, with its own character and its own writing system. Wheat, barley, and the horse-drawn chariot were significant Western introductions into early China; however, those innovations were not the principal stimuli for the rise of Chinese civilization.

Between 5000 and 3000 B.C., the Huang (Yellow) River region of North China was settled by millet and pig farmers who resided in large villages of up to 100 houses. One such village was Ban-po-ts'un (see Chapter 6). The community included large central structures that may have served as clan meeting houses or the residences of certain influential villagers. Marks found on some Yangshao ceramic vessels resemble written Shang characters dating to more than several thousand years later. During the subsequent Longshan period (3000–2205 B.C.), significant changes took place in North Chinese social organization, including marked increases in social ranking. Compared with earlier burials, Longshan mortuary assemblages exhibit more variation; some include jade ornaments and ceremonial weapons. For the first time, many of the Longshan period settlements were walled, and the largest communities were much bigger than ever before.

While the Longshan period was a time of increasing political complexity, population growth, and economic specialization in the Yellow River Basin, similar developments were occurring in other parts of China as well. Thus Chinese civilization appears to have had multiple hearths during the late Neolithic period, with the largest and most complex polities eventually arising in the basin of the Yellow River during the third millennium B.C.

During Longshan times, scapulimancy, the interpretation of cracking patterns on heated bone, was practiced (see "Early Writing Systems," p. 451). Although no written inscriptions are found on Longshan bones, Chinese written characters have been found on numerous bones at later sites (Figure 10.36). In later times, such divination rituals involving **oracle bones** were addressed to royal ancestors and were carried out by religious specialists. In addition to scapulimancy, the manifestations of ritual were prevalent in many other ways during the Longshan period. Fantastic or mythical animals were crafted on objects of pottery, wood, and jade. Many of these objects were probably associated with shamanistic rituals that were important during the later Three Dynasties and Shang periods.

The era following Longshan in North China is known as the San dai, or Three Dynasties: Xia, Shang, and Zhou (pronounced "jo"). The Xia (Sha) dynasty (2205–1766 B.C.) is the first hereditary dynasty in recorded Chinese history. Although later historical texts suggest that there were 17 rulers in 471 years, the period is still somewhat of a mystery archaeologically. K. C. Chang has suggested that the Erlitou culture, with a spatial and temporal distribution that fits the historical accounts of

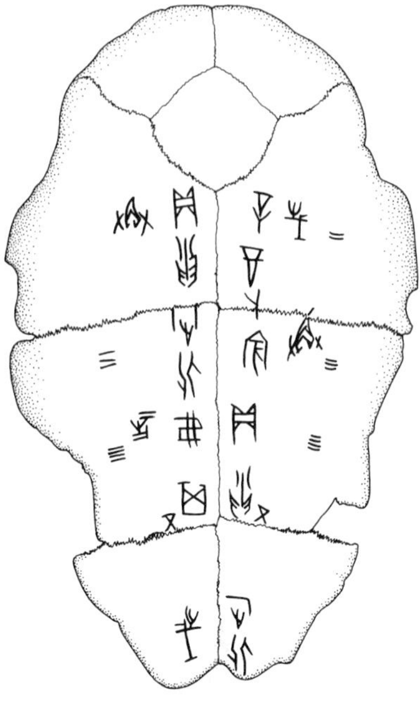

**Figure 10.36** An inscribed oracle bone from the Shang period.

**oracle bone** An animal bone with cracks (from heating) or other markings, used to foretell the future.

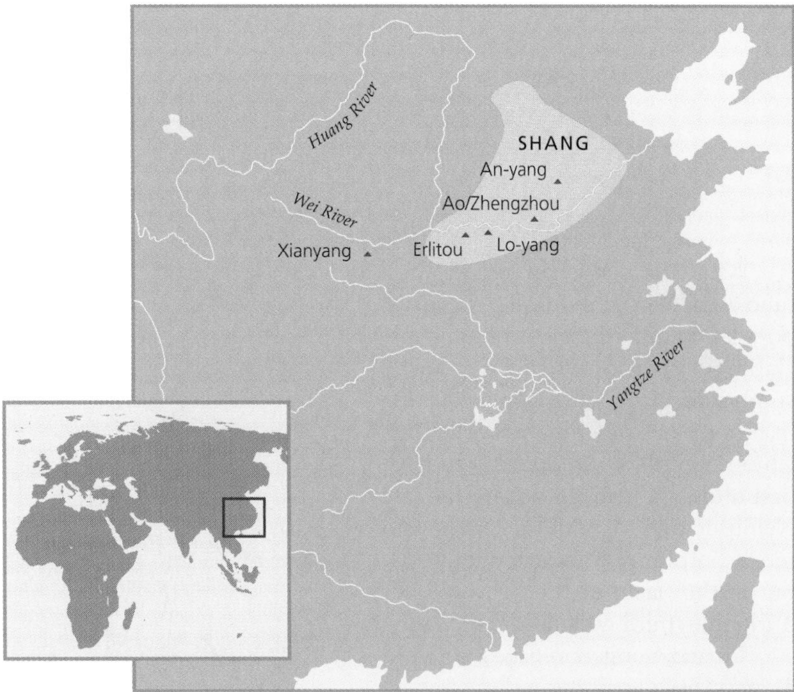


**Figure 10.37** The approximate extent of the Shang dynasty in North China, with important sites mentioned in the text.

*There is no need to emphasize the significance of Chinese civilization, which produced one of the few pristine states in the world nearly four thousand years ago. But it is rather surprising to note that, compared to other civilizations, little has been done in Chinese archaeology to systematically study the processes of state development.*

—Li Liu (2004)

the Xia dynasty, is the archaeological manifestation of that dynasty.

The Xia dynasty was transitional between the late Neolithic and the Shang dynasty. Scapulimancy continued to be practiced. Although there are no known inscriptions on oracle bones, signs and symbols have been found on pottery vessels. Bronzeworking, which was in evidence by the end of Longshan, became an increasingly important craft. According to a first-millennium B.C. text, the two principal affairs of the Chinese state were ritual and warfare. Most of the bronze was used to make ritual food and drink vessels, musical instruments, and weapons. Other valuable objects were fashioned from jade, turquoise, and lacquer. A few basic bronze implements were made, but most utilitarian tools, including knives, sickles, and hoes, were made in stone, shell, wood, antler, or bone. Wheel-thrown ceramic ware, first manufactured during the late Neolithic, increased in abundance, although handmade pottery also continued to be used.

Two palatial house foundations of stamped earth, found in later strata at the site of Erlitou, also indicate a possible important break with Longshan. Both palace foundations are much larger than the other houses at the site. The largest foundation, 108 × 100 m (350 × 330 ft), was associated with ritual burials (including one individual with bound hands).

The decline of the Xia dynasty coincided roughly with the rise of the Shang dynasty (1766–1122 B.C.). The Shang period is known from archaeological excavations at its last capital, An-yang; information from other ancient sites; and written records. The Chinese state had developed by Shang times. The major Shang centers were Ao (an early capital located underneath the modern industrial city of Zhengzhou), Lo-yang, and An-yang (Figure 10.37). Each had a clearly defined ceremonial core, inhabited by a royal household, and a series of nonresidential buildings (meeting halls and ancestral temples). The ceremonial core was surrounded by a service area and the pithouse residences of the commoners.

Today Ao is partially hidden by modern buildings, but at its height, it may have covered 3.4 sq km (1.3 sq mi). The central precinct was enclosed by a huge earthen wall 9 m (30 ft) high and 36 m (118 ft) wide at the base (Figure 10.38). The quantity and quality of artifacts indicate the presence of hundreds of skilled craftworkers. One area contained more than a dozen high-temperature pottery kilns, each associated with dense concentrations of oven-fired and broken pottery. In another area, human and animal bones were worked into fishhooks, awls, axes, and hairpins. Bronzeworking was one of the most highly developed crafts. Bronze was fashioned into ornaments as well as tools. In one workshop, molds were used to mass-produce bronze arrow points. As yet, the Shang materials contemporaneous with Ao have yielded no definitive indications of writing, chariots, or royal mausoleums, all features solidly linked with An-yang and its late Shang materials. However, the construction technology and the basic layout of the palace structure at Zhengzhou were nearly identical to those at subsequent An-yang (Figure 10.39).

Toward the end of the Shang dynasty, the capital was moved north to An-yang (ahn-yong). Like the earlier capital, An-yang was a large ceremonial and administrative center with monumental architecture surrounded by craft areas, including bronze foundries, stone and bone workshops, and pottery kilns. Circling the center were residential hamlets (small concentrations of wooden houses with thatched roofs), a royal cemetery area at Hsi-pei-kang, and more workshops.

An-yang consisted of three groups of buildings with a total of 53 rectangular structures built on top of stamped-earth platforms. The largest structure was 60 m (195 ft) long and is presumed to have been a royal palace. Between two of the building groups is a square, earthen foundation thought to have been a ceremonial altar. As a whole, this building complex appears to have been well planned, although it almost certainly was implemented in several construction stages.

Late Shang society was highly stratified into upper and lower classes. The extent of social distinctions, present as early as the Longshan period, was exaggerated by the establishment of An-yang. The king, his family, and officials were at the top. Kings were considered divine, with power flowing from the king to the nobility to the court, and finally to the commoners. Only those of high status possessed the spectacular Shang bronzes, used the Chinese script, and controlled the archives. The king and his court received grain and other forms of tribute, which they used to support a lavish style in death as well as in life. In the 11 large royal tombs at Hsi-pei-kang, Shang kings were buried with sacrificed retainers, horse-drawn chariots, and large quantities of luxury items, including bronze vessels, shell and bone ornaments, jade, and pottery (Figure 10.40). For each of these graves, moving the earth alone would have required thousands of working days. The royal tombs were surrounded by 1200 smaller and simpler graves, most of which lack any grave goods.

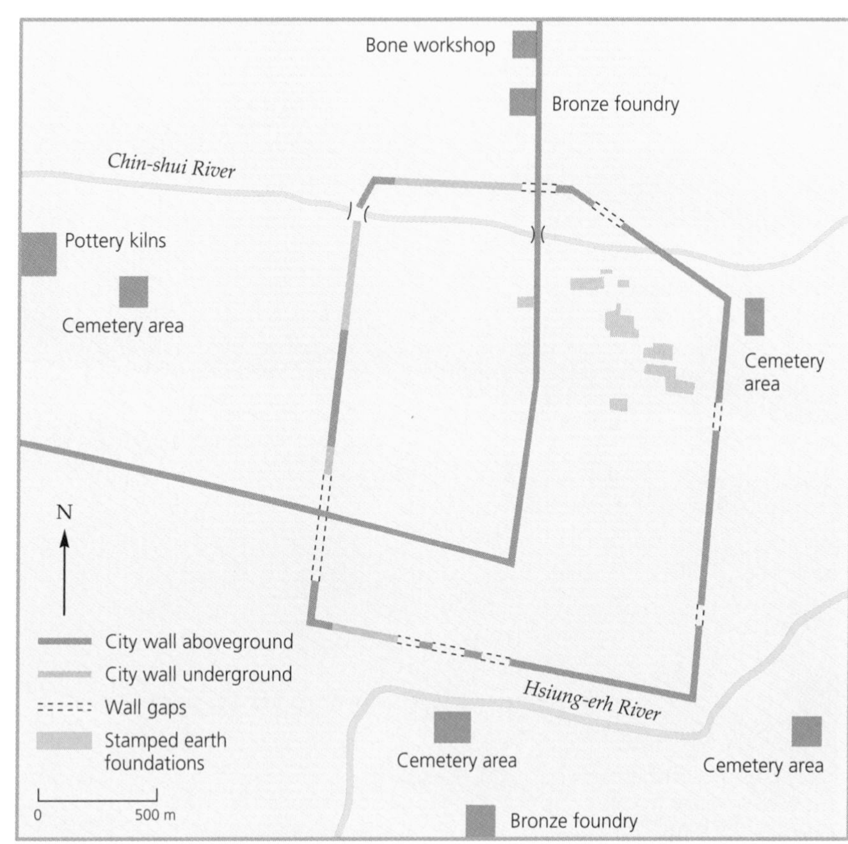


**Figure 10.38** The central precinct of Ao, enclosed by a huge earthen wall. Cemeteries and craft workshops have been found in many areas outside the city wall.

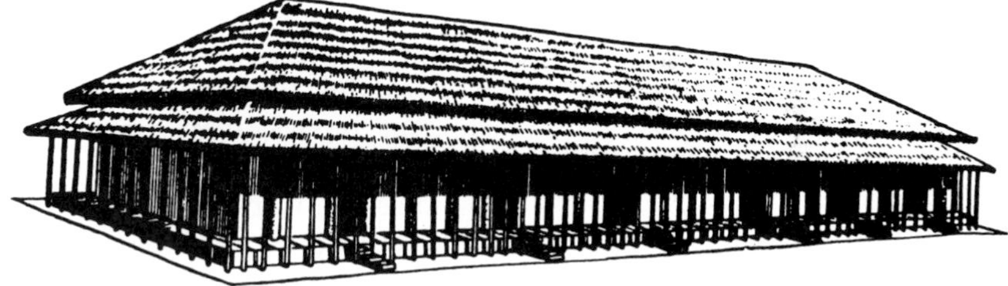

**Figure 10.39** An artist's reconstruction of a Shang palace at Ao.

The lower class consisted of farmers and craftworkers. Some of the more skillful and highly specialized ones (bronzesmiths, lacquerwarers, and wood carvers) may have had some of the privileges of the upper class; yet overall, the farmers and craftspeople used stone and bone implements and coarse gray pottery and lived in semi-subterranean pithouses. The commoners labored for public works and

**Figure 10.40** Sacrificial burials at An-yang.

military campaigns. At the bottom of the lower class were the war captives, who were kept as slaves or served as sacrificial victims for rituals and temple dedications.

Shang civilization is famous for its bronzework (Figure 10.41). Food and drinking vessels are the most common bronze items, but some weapons, chariot and cavalry fittings, and musical instruments also were made of bronze. Small objects, such as spearpoints, were made by pouring a molten mix of copper and tin into molds. Large ceremonial vessels were made by a more complex process involving clay prototypes. During the first half of the twentieth century, Western scholars familiar with the An-yang bronzes presumed that the metalworking technology was introduced from Europe or Southwest Asia. Yet the absence of such Western techniques as annealing, hammering, and lost wax casting and the presence of complex mold-casting technologies indicate an indigenous origin for Shang bronzeworking. The roots of late Shang metallurgy may lie in the sophisticated pottery kilns that were used as early as the late Neolithic.

At An-yang, scapulimancy became more complex and sophisticated. In addition to the shoulder blades of cattle and water buffalo, diviners used the carapaces of turtles. Once an answer was obtained, by consulting ancestral spirits and interpreting the cracks on the oracle bones, both the question and the answer were sometimes recorded on the surface of the bone. A symbol similar to the later written character for "book" is found on one bone, indicating the presence of scribes. The earliest Chinese writing may have been expressed on silk, bamboo, or wooden tablets. These surfaces commonly were used for written inscriptions in the last half of the first millennium B.C.; however, no texts on these highly perishable materials have been found for Shang. By late Shang times, Chinese written language had developed to the point where over 3000 phonetic, ideographic, and pictographic symbols were in use. Based on more than 150,000 inscribed turtle shells, in addition to inscriptions made in bronze, pottery, and stone, it is clear that early Chinese writing was related closely to the political, military, and ritual activities of the upper class and had little to do with mercantile matters.

The borders of the Shang state are unknown; however, late Shang rulers had at least some control over a fairly large area in northern China. The extent of their influence varied according to distance from the capital. Shang rulers traveled widely across their domain, and the extent of their influence was related in part to their actual physical presence. The rulers were assisted by a complex hierarchy of local nobles, who had considerable autonomy in their own territories. These local lords were responsible for collecting taxes and supplying men for public projects and military campaigns. On occasion, armies numbering 30,000 soldiers were assembled to wage war against "barbarians" at the edge of the Shang domain. Military success depended on the horse-drawn chariot. War was waged more for people than for land. In these campaigns, thousands of prisoners were taken, most of whom were sacrificed or used as slaves.

Despite major changes in political organization, written communication, and social stratification, the basic subsistence technology of the late Shang period changed little from earlier times. Millet remained the principal food crop in North China, supplemented by rice and wheat. Stone hoes, harvesting knives, and wooden digging sticks remained the primary cultivation implements. In some areas, two crops a year were grown, suggesting irrigation, yet large-scale water control was not implemented until the last centuries B.C.

Changes in labor practices may have constituted the most dramatic shift in the Shang economy. Larger numbers of people were employed in farming, thereby increasing production per unit of land as well as the amount of cultivated terrain. The reliance on human energy may help account for the kind of military campaigns that were waged, as well as the rapid demographic increases that occurred in China during this period. The importance of agricultural labor may have encouraged rural families to grow, since children could work in the fields at an early age. One consequence would have been large-scale population growth.

The Shang dynasty was overthrown by people living on its western periphery in the vicinity of Xianyang on the Wei River. It is unclear whether the defeat resulted from the internal rebellion of a distant Shang province or by the rebellion of an outside group of people forced by nomadic pressures to settle in or near the Shang state (as suggested by one 3000-year-old text). Whatever the case, the new dynasty did not create an entirely new civilization; it incorporated the existing network of towns and officials. It was on the foundation of the Shang dynasty that the subsequent Zhou dynasty established China's first empire.

**Figure 10.41** A bronze vessel from the Shang or early Zhou period.

*Western scholars tend to see civilization as a level of human attainment that lifts humans to a higher plane than that of "mere" animals and plants, and as an artificial environment that insulates us from unadulterated and hostile nature. But in ancient Chinese civilizations humans and nature were regarded as one; the Chinese were civilized precisely because they were able, or at least desirous, to be close to and harmonize with nature as a matter of conscious and deliberate choice.*

—Kuang-Chih Chang (1994)

*Concept*

## The Roots of Chinese Cuisine

### *Ancient culinary ritual and traditions*

**Figure 10.42** Late Neolithic noodles from China, revealed after the inverted earthenware bowl that had contained them was removed. These spectacular remains were found in northwestern China at the upper reaches of the Yellow River.

Archaeologists often study containers of fired clay, stone, and metal to infer information about chronology or past technologies. However, the main function of these vessels was the preparation and serving of food and drink. The pottery and bronze vessels of the Shang and Zhou dynasties provide one perspective on ancient Chinese culinary traditions.

This vantage recently has been supplemented by the recovery of actual food remains, such as the incredible discovery of millet noodles that were found in a sealed earthenware bowl and date back roughly 4000 years (Figure 10.42).

Historical texts and inscriptions also yield key insights on ancient Chinese cuisine. For example, *The Three Lis,* or *Three Books of Rites,* solemn texts from the Han period (206 B.C.–A.D. 220) that record ritual and courtly behavior from ancient China, provide detailed descriptions of food preparation and feasts, including the types and amounts of food and wine served on certain occasions. Oracle bone and bronze vessel inscriptions from the Shang period include written characters that refer to certain foods, rituals, and cooking techniques and whose shapes suggest ancient practices.

It is not surprising that many groups of people are strongly concerned with food. However, according to K. C. Chang, the Chinese are more concerned with food and eating than any other people. He pointed out that in contemporary China, a familiar greeting is "Have you eaten?" Chang believed that this preoccupation has a long history, as do many Chinese culinary traditions. According to one account, when a duke asked Confucius (551–479 B.C.) about military strategy, the sage replied, "I have indeed heard about matters pertaining to meat stands and meat platters, but I have not learned military matters" (quoted in Chang, 1973, p. 496). In ancient China, knowledge and skill in the preparation of food and drink were important personal characteristics; King T'ang, the founder of the Shang dynasty, chose a cook as his prime minister. According to several Zhou texts, a cooking vessel, called the *ting* cauldron, was the primary symbol of the state. Along with differences in dress and adornment, part of the definition of a "barbarian," or a non-Chinese, was a person who did not prepare and consume food in the customary manner. Included in the *Three Books of Rites* is a personnel roster of the king's palace; almost 60% of the 4000 people responsible for the king's private residential quarters were involved with food and wine, with specialists assigned to menu preparation, service, meat, fish, game, shellfish, wine, fruits and vegetables, pickling, and salt.

The dualism between *yin* and *yang,* central to much of contemporary Chinese culture, is also present in the categorization of food. A basic dichotomy exists between food and drink. Food is further divided into grain food and "dishes" that are combinations of meat and vegetables. These distinctions, and their associated rules, are integral to the Chinese way of eating today and seem not to have changed much since Zhou times. In the past as well as today, the basic or essential meal consists of grain and water. The basic word *shih,* for food (as opposed to drink), also, in a narrower sense, refers to grain. Meat and vegetable dishes are considered secondary in importance and are to be eaten in moderation.

The historical texts indicate that eating together was a major source of enjoyment in ancient China. Yet it also was a serious social affair, with strict rules to be observed, including correct table manners and an etiquette regarding the appropriate foods to be served at specific occasions. In Shang and Zhou times, people from the upper ranks ate individually, kneeling on mats. The number of dishes served to an individual was primarily determined by one's rank and age. Utensils and serving platters were placed beside the individual in specific arrangements, with certain foods on the right and others on the left. In addition, rules specified the arrangement of certain foods on the serving vessels and the way they were presented at the table. Children were trained early to eat with their right hand. In late Zhou times, crunching bones with one's teeth, eating too quickly, slurping down soup, and picking one's teeth were all specified as inappropriate etiquette.

In one contemporary Chinese cookbook, 20 methods for heating food are mentioned. Many of these procedures, including boiling, steaming, and roasting, also were important in Zhou texts. Yet the ancient accounts do not mention stir-frying, which is prevalent today. Nevertheless, in the past as well as the present, it is the preparation before cooking that is essential to Chinese cuisine. The word for cooking in the Zhou texts literally means "to cut and cook." Great significance is placed on the art of mixing flavors and ingredients into distinctive soups and stews before they are heated.

Social class was a major factor in dietary variation. Peasants relied on a basic grain diet, using the platters and vessels associated with such foods. According to the textual record, the meat dishes were intended for rituals or upper-class feasts. Meat was usually dried, cooked, or pickled. A few recipes for elaborate dishes of the Shang and Zhou times are known; these are for the so-called Eight Delicacies, which were prepared specifically for the elderly. They included the Rich Fry (pickled meat over rice), the Similar Fry (pickled meat over millet), the Bake (baked stuffed pig or ram), the Pounded (pounded meat fillets softened by pickle and vinegar), the Steeped (newly killed beef steeped in wine), the Grill (dried meat seasoned with cinnamon, ginger, and salt), the Soup Balls (fried cakes of meat and rice), and the Liver and Fat (roasted dog liver cooked in fat).

In ancient Chinese cooking, each variety of food and drink was associated with different ceramic and bronze vessels (Figure 10.43). There were vessels for boiling, for simmering, and for steaming. For serving and eating, ladles and chopsticks were used, although hands were used as often as chopsticks. There were special cups for water and wine. In the era of the Shang dynasty, bronze vessels were used to serve grains and drinks made from grain, but never to serve meat. The most important vessels for meat dishes were made from wood, basketry, and pottery.

Most excavated Zhou period burial assemblages contain ceramic vessels. The majority of the graves include not just one or two containers but a whole range of vessel forms. Chang reasoned that most of these individuals were interred with a set of containers for cooking and serving grain, serving meat, and drinking. Chang's deduction would have been difficult, if not impossible, to derive without the careful juxtaposition of texts with archaeology. Together, these complementary records are serving to uncover the deep traditions of Chinese cuisine.

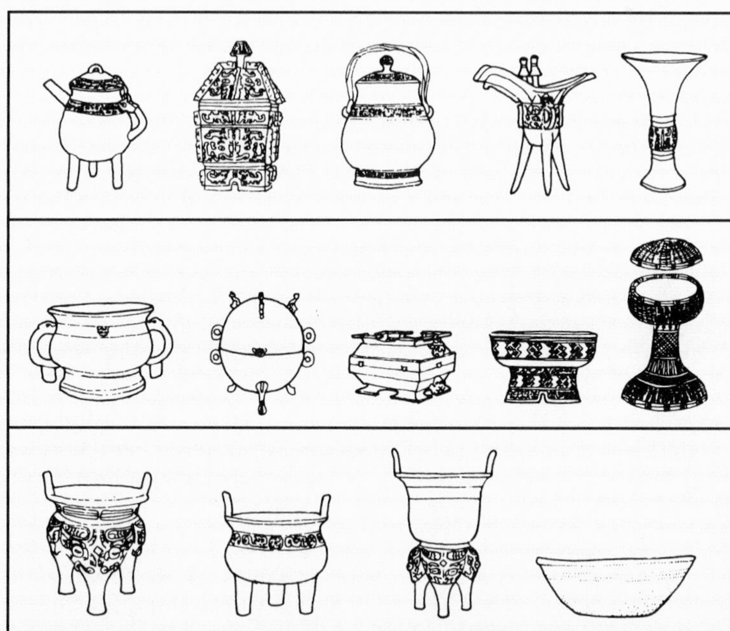

**Figure 10.43** Examples of Shang and Zhou food and drinking vessels: drinking vessels (top), serving vessels (center), cooking vessels (bottom).

Chinese food is one of the great cuisines of the world. Discuss its roots and its impact on material culture.

## Xianyang

*Terracotta soldiers and the Qin dynasty*

Figure 10.44 A reconstructed segment of the Great Wall of China in the mountains north of Beijing.

The Zhou dynasty (1122 to third century B.C.) marks the beginning of imperial China and its traditions, which persisted for the next 2000 years and into the present. Zhou society was highly stratified at its center, with the king and a royal court at the top. Away from this core, the adjacent areas were divided into partially independent provinces, and administration was enacted by semifeudal lords who had great control over their local domains. Periodic civil wars erupted between these lords and the king.

The Chinese state during the Three Dynasties (including the early Zhou) was built on a hierarchical network of large lineages in which the distance away from the main male line of descent determined relative political status and access to power. Each walled town was inhabited primarily by members of a particular lineage.

The latter half of the Zhou period was characterized by great political change and upheaval, with warring states and shifting capitals. It also was a time when Chinese urbanism spread over a much wider area than ever before. Great cities were built, many of which were larger and more nucleated than the earlier Shang cities. The largest

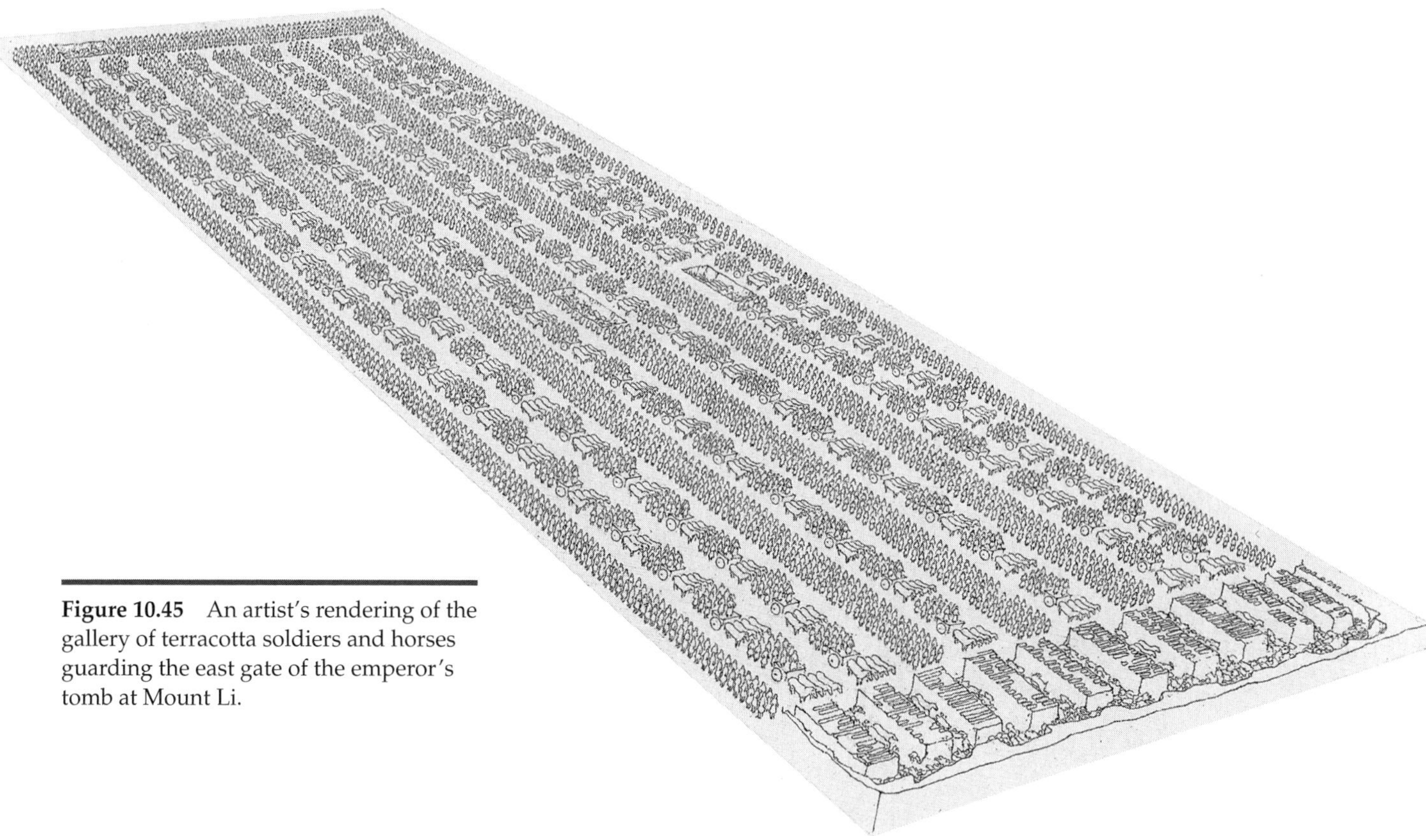

**Figure 10.45** An artist's rendering of the gallery of terracotta soldiers and horses guarding the east gate of the emperor's tomb at Mount Li.

Zhou settlement, G'a-to, had 270,000 people. All the large cities were walled. By 600 B.C., iron casting was practiced and iron agricultural tools were in use. Large irrigation works were constructed, and wet-rice irrigation became increasingly important. Changes in agricultural technology enabled rapid increases in population density. Late Zhou socioeconomic structure placed great emphasis on the taxation of peasants in lieu of labor drafts. Kinship bonds began to diminish, and territorial units and bureaucracies gained importance. Late Zhou was the time of Confucius (or Kongzi in Chinese), who preached order, deference, and family ties, perhaps in response to rapid social transition and transformation. Although large-scale political integration remained relatively weak and fragmentary, a single system of measurement was adopted across most of China. There was increased interregional trade and commercial activity, as well as greater cultural unity.

By the third century B.C., the descendants of the western Zhou kings ruled an increasingly small area outside their original homeland. As the Zhou polity weakened, other states rose in influence. The Qin polity expanded, and its short-lived dynasty (221–206 B.C.) eclipsed the Zhou, along with five other contemporary states.

Ying Zheng inherited the throne of the Qin (pronounced "chin") kingdom at age 13 in 246 B.C. During the first 25 years of his reign, he frequently engaged in battle, eventually conquering six other major kingdoms. For that reason, six was considered the lucky number of the Qin. Through military prowess, he unified China into a single imperial kingdom in 221 B.C. and declared himself China's first emperor, taking on the name Shihuangdi (literally, "first august emperor"). The empire was ruled from the capital city of Xianyang (she-ON-yong), to which he forced over 100,000 royal and wealthy families from throughout the empire, to

**Figure 10.46** Rows of terracotta soldiers in the large rectangular gallery guarding the emperor's tomb.

*The First Emperor of China controlled a vast territory and wielded enormous power. He ordered 120,000 families to move to the new capital, Xianyang; he summoned 700,000 men to build his tomb and other structures; and he was self-consciously aware of his authority and of the new era that this marked. Long inscriptions carved at his command on mountains in eastern China described his achievements and proclaimed his universal, indeed cosmic, rulership.*

—Jessica Rawson (2007)

move. Shihuangdi had luxurious palaces built in Xianyang that were replicas of royal residences in the conquered states. By moving local lords to Xianyang, he forcibly detached the feudal aristocracy from the land and its people, weakening their power. This move also served to centralize the Qin empire by concentrating economic and political power in a single capital.

According to historical records, Shihuangdi was an ambitious and ruthless emperor. He built the Great Wall along China's northern periphery by joining walls that had been constructed by earlier feudal states (Figure 10.44). Although the traditional view is that the wall was intended to protect the newly formed empire from the nomadic herders of Asia to the north, other scholars have suggested that its main function was to prevent heavily taxed peasants from escaping taxes and conscription. The 2400-km (1500-mi) wall, built by 700,000 conscripts and wide enough for six horses abreast, remains the longest fortification anywhere. Many men perished while working on the wall, inspiring some to call it "the longest cemetery in the world." Shihuangdi also established China's first standing army, a body that may have contained more than a million people.

To weaken regional autonomy, Shihuangdi destroyed the feudal structure that had existed for centuries. Because he saw Confucian philosophy as a threat to his authority, all the books of this school were burned, and Confucian scholars who refused to accept his reforms were buried alive.

The centralizing tendencies of Shihuangdi included increasing codification of a Chinese legal system and the standardization of Chinese character

Figure 10.47 Workers measuring a terracotta soldier guarding the tomb of Shihuangdi.

writing so that the written language could be understood throughout the empire. Weights and measures, coins, and the gauges of chariot wheels were increasingly regulated and made more homogeneous. Paper was invented during the Qin dynasty. In the grave of one Qin official, more than 1200 bamboo slips were found, bound into a series of books and containing an explicit legal code specifying particular crimes and their punishments. Under Shihuangdi, road building was intensified and a canal system was constructed to enhance communication and transportation. The canal system was one of the greatest inland water communication systems in the ancient world, and several canals are still functioning today.

As soon as Shihuangdi became emperor, he began building his tomb. According to history, 700,000 laborers from all parts of the country worked for 36 years on the project, a virtual subterranean palace for the emperor to live in for eternity. Recent DNA analysis has documented diverse origins for the workers. According to early Chinese records, the architects of the tomb conceived of it as a universe in miniature. All the country's major waterways were reproduced in mercury within the tomb, and they fed into a tiny ocean. Heavenly constellations were painted on the ceiling. The emperor's outer coffin was made of molten copper, and fine vessels, precious stones, and other rarities were buried with him.

The burial tomb, called Mount Li, was at one time 46 m (150 ft) tall. Built in the center of a spirit city, an area enclosed by an inner wall, it contained sacred stone tablets and prayer temples. Beyond this area was an outer

**Figure 10.48** A life-size terracotta figure from the gallery.

city enclosed by a high rectangular stone wall 7 m (23 ft) thick at the base. The total complex covered 200 ha (500 acres). Today, most of the walls and temples have been removed.

About 1370 m (4500 ft) east of Mount Li, excavations have revealed one of the most astonishing ancient spectacles. Guarding the east side of the emperor's tomb is a brick-floored, 1.2-ha (3-acre) gallery of terracotta soldiers and horses (Figure 10.45). Collapsed pillars indicate that a roof once covered the underground battlefield. In the royal tombs of the previous Shang dynasty, kings and high-ranking officials were interred with living warriors, women, servants, and horses. This practice, which had ceased centuries before the Qin dynasty, evidently was revived in symbolic fashion by Shihuangdi.

Although only parts of this large rectangular gallery, and two nearby smaller ones, have been excavated, some 8000 terracotta figures have been exposed, along with wooden chariots (Figure 10.46). The terracotta warriors are slightly larger than life-size (Figure 10.47); they are arranged in battle formations, dressed in uniforms of various rank, and carry real weapons—swords, spears, and crossbows. Traces of pigment indicate that the uniforms were brightly colored. Of the excavated figures, no two look exactly alike; their facial expressions vary, suggesting that they were realistic portraits of each individual in the emperor's honor guard (Figure 10.48). Even the horses were very finely crafted, appearing alert and tense as they would be in battle. The names of more than 80 master craftsmen, drawn from imperial workshops as well as other parts of China, have been identified on the backs of figures in the large gallery.

The army and horses are supplemented by a rich artifact assemblage, including gold, jade, and bronze objects, linen, silk, bamboo and bone artifacts, pottery utensils, and iron agricultural tools. Elemental analysis of the swords has revealed that they were made from an alloy of copper, tin, and 13 other elements. The designers of the tomb's security system, a series of mechanized crossbows, were sealed inside the tomb to die so that none of the tomb's secrets could be divulged.

Shihuangdi always lived and worked in guarded secrecy, because several assassination attempts were made on his life. Only a few trusted ministers ever knew where he was. He died on a journey to the eastern provinces, and his death was kept a secret from all except his youngest son. His prime minister and his chief eunuch (a castrated male) apparently plotted to keep the death secret for their own ambitious reasons. They wanted the emperor's youngest son to succeed to the throne, instead of an elder son, as Shihuangdi had decreed. The councillors thought they could more easily influence and manipulate the younger son. The elder son, exiled to the northwestern frontier to help build the Great Wall, was sent a fake order to commit suicide, which he did, paving the way for the younger son to become the new emperor. Nevertheless, Shihuangdi's efforts to expand his domain to both the north and the south sapped his treasury, so Qin preeminence was short-lived.

Although the Qin dynasty was brief, China's first episode of unification was not. Qin rule was followed by the Han dynasty, which lasted for 400 years (206 B.C.–A.D. 220). The Han unification was made possible in part by technological innovations developed in Zhou times: iron tools, wet-rice irrigation, the ox-drawn plow, improved roads, and the crossbow. Under Han rule, China continued as a unified empire, but with greater political stability. The economy was prosperous, and a standardized coinage circulated throughout China.

During the Han dynasty, China became even more densely settled. The world's first census, in the years A.D. 1 and 2, lists the population of the empire as 57.7 million, with cities of up to 250,000 people. One late Han city may have contained as many as 500,000 people. The decisions made by the Han monarchs were implemented through 1500 administrative provinces, each of which was centered at a walled town. No other political system of its era—not even the Roman Empire—was as vast in size or bureaucratic complexity.

# Angkor

## *Maritime kingdoms in Southeast Asia*

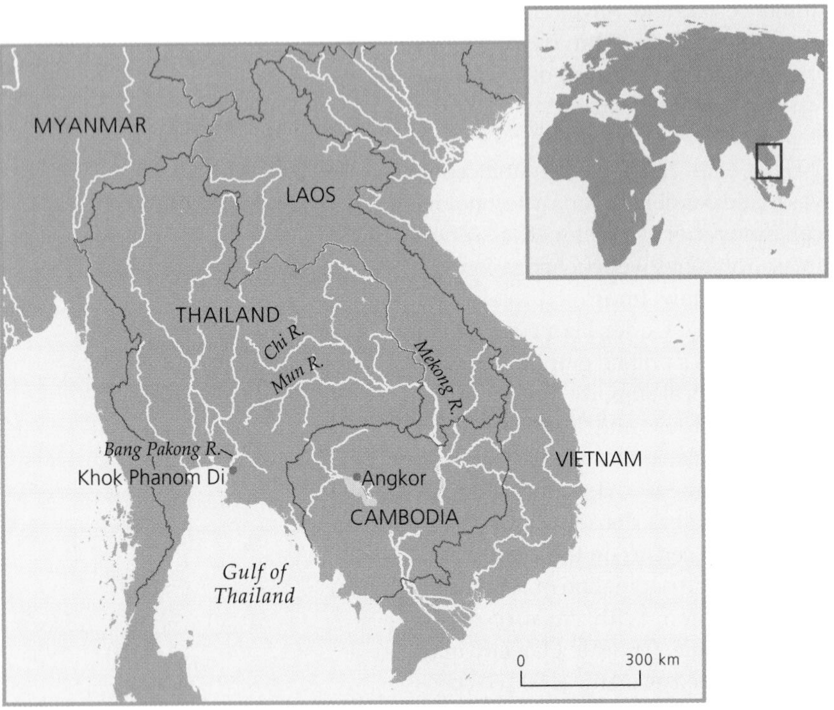


**Figure 10.49** Southeast Asia, with the location of Angkor, the Khmer ceremonial center situated in the jungles of Cambodia along a tributary of the Mekong River.

Until the introduction of cultivated rice in the third millennium B.C., Southeast Asia was populated by hunter-gatherers who lived in small communities along the coast and in forested uplands. At coastal sites such as Khok Phanom Di (see Chapter 6), villagers took advantage of rich coastal resources and rivers that facilitated exchange with distant regions to establish year-round settlements. With the introduction of cultivated rice from South China, small agricultural villages were settled throughout the area. Communities such as Khok Phanom Di engaged in exchange with the inland farming communities and soon cultivated rice themselves. Rice rapidly became the staple food crop across Southeast Asia.

Between 1500 and 1000 B.C., bronze casting was adopted in Southeast Asia, and after 500 B.C., iron was smelted to make ornaments, weaponry, and agricultural tools. Settlements began to grow in size, and more hierarchical forms of leadership and socioeconomic stratification were evidenced. Before the end of the first millennium B.C., Southeast Asians began to engage in maritime trade that linked them to offshore islands and China, as well as to the Indian subcontinent. With the introduction of new technologies and belief systems, some Southeast Asian societies became highly ranked kingdoms, focused on large centers that were presided over by an aristocratic class with close relationships to the ancestors. Ruling power was based in part on control of agricultural land, rice surpluses, and advantages in access to high-status imported goods. Public displays of feasting and ritual were important aspects of maintaining power and legitimacy to rule.

For hundreds of years, the landscape of Southeast Asia was peopled by small, competing polities that were often in a state of political flux and whose boundaries frequently shifted over time. Warfare is a recurrent theme in inscriptions, which describe military expeditions and the conquest of rivals. Social relations revolved around rulers, whose personal and spiritual qualities determined their success in forming alliances and defeating rivals.

Although belief systems were borrowed from South Asia, the distinctive form of kingship in Southeast Asia was markedly different from that of the much earlier Indus civilization, which did not emphasize specific individuals through elaborate graves or personalized inscriptions. Rather, one can draw parallels between Southeast Asian kings and the Classic Maya noble lords of Mesoamerica. As with the Classic Maya, Southeast Asian kingship emphasized their divine monar-

**Figure 10.50** The large ceremonial complex at Angkor. Rectangular reservoirs and ancient canals are visible in this aerial view. The large square to the right of the large reservoir is the city of Angkor Thom, with the smaller complex of Angkor Wat just below it.

chy and fostered the concentration of wealth and luxury in their hands.

After A.D. 550 in the Mekong Valley region of Cambodia, a series of kings tried to establish hegemony over as large an area as possible, but for several hundred years none was able to hold the kingdom together for long. The Angkor (AHN-cor) state that arose on a tributary of the Mekong River just after A.D. 800 was one of the largest and most centralized of these Southeast Asian polities (Figure 10.49).

The formation of this large, centralized state in A.D. 802 is attributed to Jayavarman II, a dynamic Khmer ruler who joined a series of smaller competing polities into a large state by first defeating rival rulers and then placing his followers in positions of authority. He established a succession of Khmer dynasties whose reign at Angkor endured for more than 600 years, in spite of periodic disruptions caused by civil wars and conflicts over succession.

Angkor, derived from the Sanskrit word for "holy city," is the modern name for a large complex of monuments, temples, reservoirs, and walls that was the political and ceremonial center of the Khmer civilization (Figure 10.50). The more than 100 temples at the site were constructed by a series of Khmer dynasties between the ninth and fifteenth centuries A.D. At its height, in the twelfth century, the site of Angkor stretched more than 1000 sq km (600 sq mi) and may have had between 500,000 and 1 million residents.

Majestic temples were an important symbol of rulership, and each new king built a massive religious structure

**Figure 10.51** Angkor Wat, the largest religious monument in the world. It was constructed as a representation of the Hindu universe by King Suryavarman II, who ruled from A.D. 1113 to 1150. Almost every surface of the temple and walls is covered with elaborately carved scenes.

to commemorate his reign. At his death, the temple became the deified ruler's mausoleum. The largest and most elaborate temple at Angkor, Angkor Wat, was constructed by Suryavarman II soon after he became king in A.D. 1113 (Figure 10.51). The construction of the temple may have taken the greater part of his 37-year reign. The walled complex measures 1500 m (5000 ft) by 1200 m (4000 ft) and incorporates a large moat, 200 m (660 ft) wide, that surrounds a second walled enclosure. The central precinct inside the smaller enclosure measures 215 × 187 m (710 × 620 ft) and includes three raised, covered terraces that culminate in a monument with five towers, the tallest of which stands 65 m (215 ft) above the surrounding terrain. These sandstone towers were carved in the form of giant lotus buds.

The walls of the complex are covered with elaborate scenes in bas-relief that depict the king and his court, processions, and battle scenes. Scenes on later temples portray activities of everyday life, including cooks preparing food for a feast, a wealthy Chinese merchant entertaining guests, men fishing, women selling fish in market stalls, and men playing chess. Many Angkorian inscriptions detail the punishments meted out to nonbelievers and the heavenly rewards awaiting the faithful. Small inscriptions on walls describe the punishment for particular crimes, including greed or gluttony; the theft of land, animals, and other goods; and inciting opposition. Temple inscriptions also reveal an intense concern with the quality of agricultural land and details of ownership and boundaries.

Construction of the temples and other public works, including the large reservoirs at Angkor, required enormous labor forces. Local labor was tied to the temples and provided them with goods and labor for rituals and for maintaining the ruling elite. The Khmer civilization had no currency; through taxation, the royal court received and distributed huge amounts of subsistence goods including rice, fish, salt, honey, oil, and cloth.

The Khmer rulers headed a bureaucracy of high-status families that included royal councillors, generals, and administrators. The bureaucracy controlled most aspects of Khmer life. There were numerous grades of officials, who oversaw royal warehouses and the payment of taxes, monitored land boundaries, commanded the army, and organized labor for construction projects.

The economy of the Angkor and other Southeast Asian states was based on surplus rice agriculture, and some scholars have argued that the huge reservoirs at Angkor were constructed for irrigating rice fields. The reservoirs are very large, holding millions of cubic meters of water, and are connected to canals and moats. But others disagree, arguing that there is plentiful groundwater in the region, so that irrigation was not necessary to produce rice surpluses. Inscriptions that mention the reservoirs do not link them with irrigation, and the reservoirs instead may have been constructed to provide drainage and help control floods. They also may have had symbolic importance, representing lakes surrounding sacred sites in the cosmos. Their very size may have been a measure of the power of the kings who constructed them.

During the twelfth century, Angkor was sacked by a rival. The Khmer rebuilt the center under the last of their major rulers, Jayavarman VII, who constructed the largest ceremonial precinct at the site, Angkor Thom, during his reign. This large precinct was surrounded by a massive wall 12.8 km (8 mi) long, entered through large, ornately carved gates 23 m (75 ft) tall (Figure 10.52). Eventually, warfare became endemic, and Angkor was abandoned in A.D. 1431 after it was sacked by the Thai following a long siege. After its abandonment, Angkor was visited by many explorers. By the end of the nineteenth century, clearing the jungle from the temples had begun, and restoration and maintenance continues to the present. Although the vegetation, war, and looting have taken their toll, even today the grandeur of Angkor inspires visitors, both Khmer and foreign, and archaeologists from around the globe.

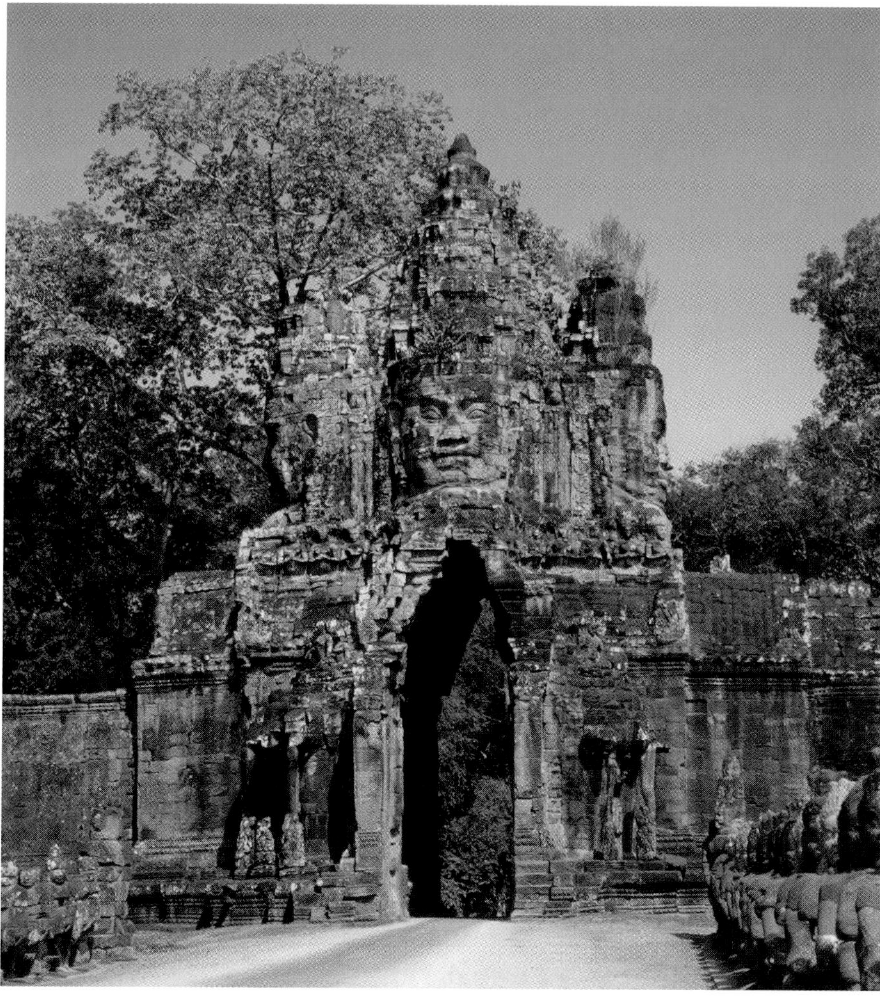

**Figure 10.52** The ornately carved southern entrance gate to the city of Angkor Thom, topped with five stone heads.

# Jenné-jeno

## *An ancient urban center in West Africa*

www.mhhe.com/priceip6e

For a Web-based activity on Jenné-jeno, see the Internet exercises on your online learning center.

The ancient Egyptian state, with its close ties to the Mediterranean world, had few direct contacts with regions far to the south and west. Only the area down to the Nile's first rapids (near the present Aswan Dam) was ruled consistently by the pharaohs, although slaves, ebony, and ivory were brought from farther south through trade. Early in the last millennium B.C., following New Kingdom penetrations into Upper Nubia, the Nubian kingdom of Kush (in what is now the Sudan) arose (Figure 10.53). The Kushites were ethnically and linguistically different from the Egyptians, and they had their own tomb style. Egypt later came briefly under Kushite control, and the intermingling of these two East African cultures intensified.

During the fourth century B.C., following an episode of Egyptian control, a major center on this portion of the southern Nile was established at Meroë. For almost a millennium (until the fourth century A.D.), the Meroitic kingdom maintained trade connections with both the Mediterranean world and the southern Sahara. Yet, after its collapse, the fertile grasslands around Meroë became the homeland for more rural lifeways. To the west, state-level societies did not develop on the southern fringes of the Sahara until the first millennium A.D.

The Sahara Desert has undergone several cycles of hyperaridity (extreme drought) that have affected human settlement in the region. Before 10,000 B.C., the desert was very dry and uninhabited. Several millennia later, after conditions improved, the Sahara consisted of a mosaic of shallow lakes and marshes linked by permanent streams where communities of hunter-fisher-collectors settled. The technology of these early groups included microliths, bone harpoons, comb-impressed pottery, and grinding stones used to process wild grains. Livestock were added to the subsistence base in the fifth millennium B.C. Sheep and goats were introduced first, most likely from Southwest Asia via Egypt or from North Africa. It is unclear, however, whether domestic cattle also were introduced from Southwest Asia or were domesticated indigenously from a wild local species.

**Figure 10.53** Africa, with places and names mentioned in the text.

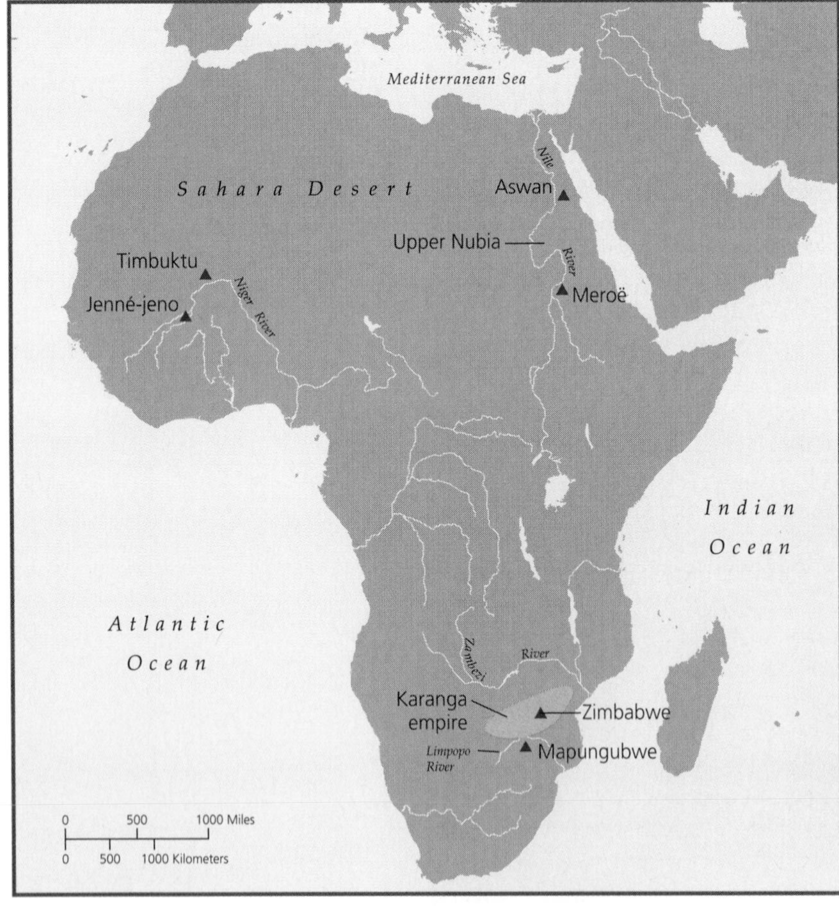

The central and southern Sahara continued to be occupied by **pastoralists** until about 2500 B.C., when a second pronounced dry period began, which continues to the present. Desiccation of the environment led to the southward movement of the Saharan peoples into sub-Saharan Africa. These herder-collectors brought their cattle with them, while the people remaining in the Sahara became more nomadic. The presence of the tsetse fly in the Sahel (the region at the southern edge of the Sahara) and the Sudanic savanna before 2500 B.C. had limited the expansion of pastoralists into the region. With the onset of drier conditions, the tsetse fly migrated farther south.

By 1000 B.C., pastoralists of the western Sahel had adopted or domesticated cereals. Early West African staples included sorghum and several genera of millet. Yet the subsistence economy remained variable as wild foods continued to be important, and lifeways based on hunting, gathering, and fishing remained dominant in some areas.

Iron metallurgy was introduced into West Africa during the first millennium B.C. In much of Africa (except Egypt), iron was the first metal to be used. This pattern contrasts with the development of metalworking in most of Eurasia, where ironworking followed copper and bronze. One explanation is that ironworking was introduced from the north, most likely by iron-using Phoenicians who established trading colonies in North Africa. Yet there is limited evidence for copper smelting in the West African Sahara almost a millennium earlier that may have led to the independent discovery of iron metallurgy in West Africa. Whatever its source, the great efficiency of iron tools spurred the rapid spread of this technology throughout Africa on its introduction.

The earliest identifiable iron-using society in West Africa is the Nok culture of central Nigeria, known for its distinctive sculpted terracotta heads. Iron-smelting furnaces from the region date to the last half of the first millennium B.C. One of the few other areas in West Africa that had iron at that time was southwestern Mali, where iron slag and artifacts have been recovered from the earliest occupation levels at the classic tell site of Jenné-jeno. Situated 3 km (1.8 mi) southeast of the present city of Jenné, the site consists of a mound of successive settlements 800 m (2600 ft) long and 6–8 m (20–26 ft) high (Figure 10.54).

**Figure 10.54** Jenné-jeno, located in the floodplain of the Niger River.

Jenné-jeno is located in the Inland Niger Delta in southwestern Mali along the middle course of the Niger River, an area lined with hundreds of ancient tells. This vast inland area of swamps and standing water is remarkably fertile, and the rivers have a great abundance of fish. The alluvial plain, however, is devoid of stone, copper, and iron ore.

The initial settlement at Jenné, dating to around 200 B.C., was confined to a few hectares in the central part of the site. The early inhabitants were mixed agriculturalists who constructed circular houses of straw coated with mud. The earliest direct evidence for domesticated African rice (*Oryza glaberrima*) in West Africa, dating to the first century A.D., was recovered at Jenné-jeno by the site's excavators, Susan and

**pastoralist** An animal herder; pastoralism is a subsistence strategy generally associated with a mobile lifeway.

**Figure 10.55** A funerary urn uncovered in the cemetery at Jenné-jeno.

Roderick McIntosh, of Rice University. Fish, reedbuck (African antelope), and domestic cattle (*Bos taurus*) also figured heavily in the inhabitants' diet. Craft skills are evident in the earliest materials recovered at the site, which include iron and slag and significant quantities of well-manufactured ceramics decorated with twine impressions.

Jenné-jeno's strategic location along a navigable river in a floodplain lacking raw materials encouraged exchange. The villagers traded their agricultural, fish, and animal products for iron ore and grindstones from at least 50 km (30 mi) away. The development of these regional trade networks within the Inland Niger Delta and immediately adjacent areas was an important factor in Jenné's early expansion.

The practice of camel domestication, which first occurred in Arabia, spread to the Sahara by early in the first millennium A.D. Camel transport had an important effect on the economy by providing a means of regular long-distance trading across the desert. With the development of long-distance trade, villages such as Jenné-jeno became important market centers. Jenné-jeno expanded its trading network to include copper and salt from the Sahara to the north and gold from the savanna and forest country to the south.

Jenné-jeno became increasingly urban after the mid-fourth century. The most frequent mode of interment in the crowded cemeteries of the site was urn burial (Figure 10.55). The deceased were placed in the bottom of jars measuring 60–90 cm (24–35 in) high and 45–50 cm (18–20 in) in diameter and were buried with few accompanying grave goods. This burial custom was practiced in the Inland Niger Delta into the late nineteenth century.

The city reached its height after A.D. 800, when it expanded to 33 ha (80 acres) and a city wall 3.6 m (11.8 ft) wide was constructed around the mound's 2-km (1.2-mi) circumference. Brick architecture replaced the coursed solid-mud technology that was in use earlier. Closely spaced house foundations of mud bricks are still visible on the surface; mud bricks used in constructing the city wall also are visible today along parts of the mound's periphery. Furnace parts, forge debris, and crucibles suggest that blacksmiths and coppersmiths worked the iron ore and copper that Jenné-jeno obtained through trade.

When Arabs penetrated western Africa at the end of the first millennium A.D., Jenné-jeno and other early West African towns were functioning as fully developed urban centers that were at the apex of regional settlement hierarchies. The rulers of Jenné-jeno presided over a large area of the floodplain extending 60 km (100 mi) downstream.

Jenné-jeno began to decline after A.D. 1150 and was abandoned by 1400, as were most of the rural settlements in its hinterland. The reasons for the abandonment are unknown; however, defensive concerns and the spread of

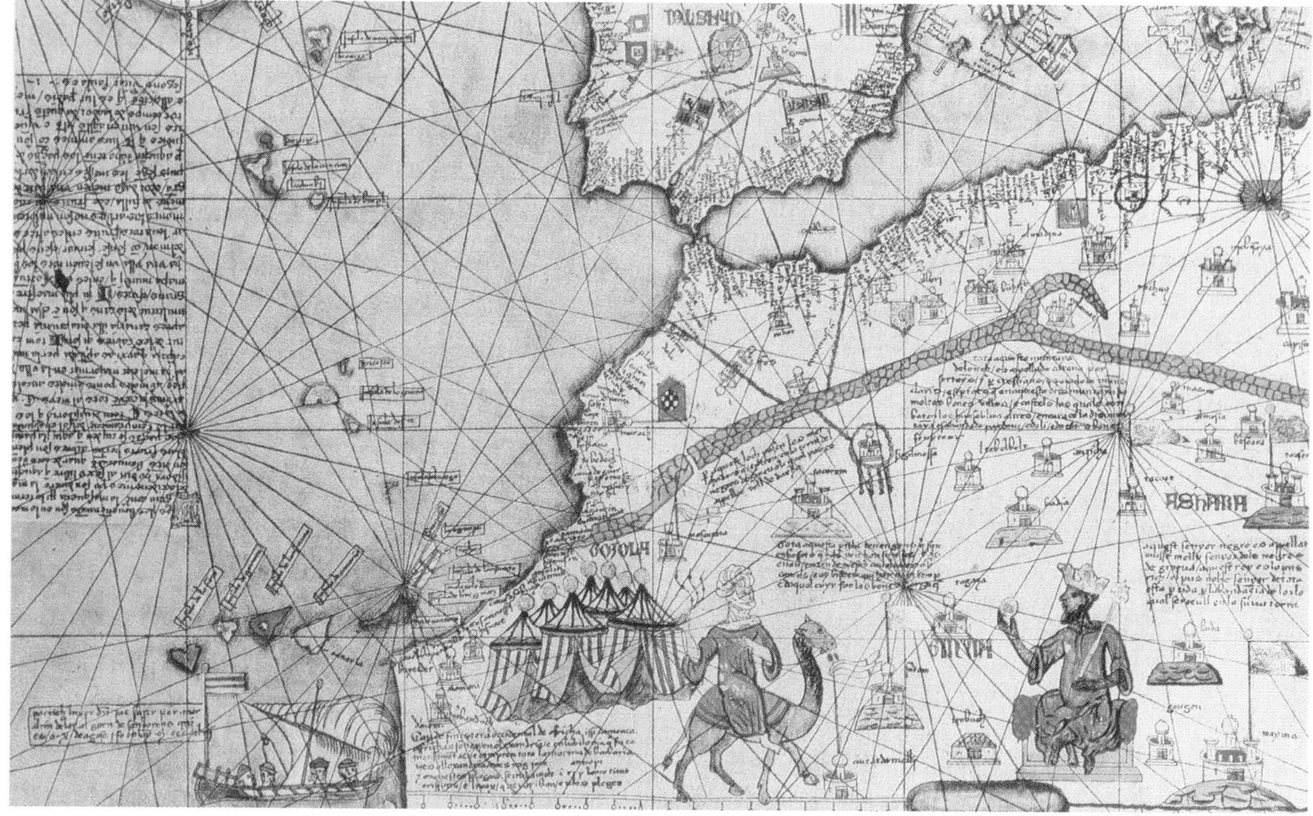

**Figure 10.56** Map of West Africa drawn in A.D. 1375 showing traders on camelback.
(The Granger Collection, New York.)

Islam after the arrival of the Arab traders are likely factors. The modern city of Jenné (Jenné-jeno means "ancient Jenné") was established nearby during the twelfth or thirteenth century when Jenné-jeno already was in decline. The new location in an area surrounded by water was easily defended, since it was accessible only by water most of the year. Given the long history of community displacement (both voluntary and coerced) associated with the spread of Islam throughout West Africa, the population base of the new center may have come largely from Jenné-jeno. The new Jenné not only continued to be an important commercial center but also became a center of Islamic learning.

The Inland Niger Delta remained an important thoroughfare for exchange throughout much of the second millennium A.D. Another important commercial center on the Niger River was Timbuktu, 500 km (300 mi) north of Jenné, at the edge of the Sahara. From at least the fourteenth century, the two towns served as major ports of trade in western Africa. North African pottery and blocks of Saharan salt arrived by camel caravan at Timbuktu, where they were shifted to canoes for transport up the Niger River to Jenné (Figure 10.56). At Jenné, they were traded for the rich agricultural produce of Jenné's hinterland and for gold mined from areas farther south. Historical texts refer to both cities and this "golden trade of the Moors." Today, modern Jenné is famous for its stunning mud architecture and distinctive mosque that reflects both indigenous and North African influences.

# Great Zimbabwe

*An important trading center in south-central Africa*

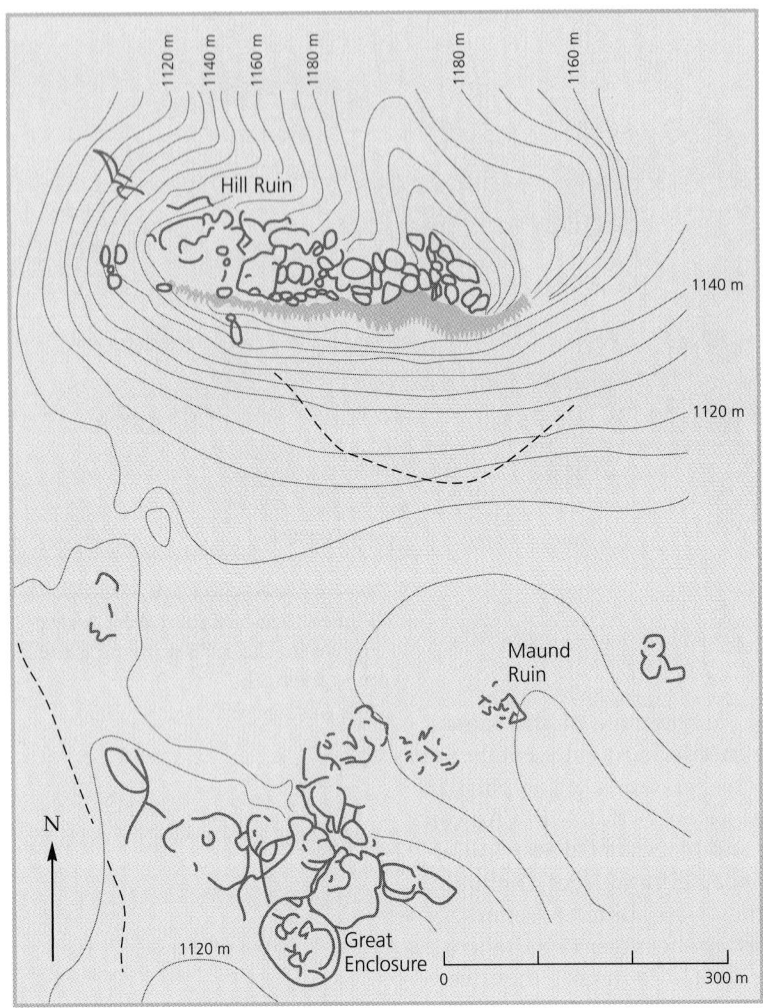


**Figure 10.57** The major ruins at Great Zimbabwe.

Peasant farmers first settled in south-central Africa, in what is now Zimbabwe (zim-BOB-way), during the fourth century A.D. Northeast of the Kalahari Desert, Zimbabwe is high plateau country (elevation 1200–1500 m, 4000–5000 ft) bounded by rivers. The gently rolling plains are cool and well watered, covered with savanna woodlands that are free of the disease-carrying tsetse fly, the scourge of equatorial Africa. Mineral deposits are abundant. Iron ores, widespread throughout much of southern and eastern Africa, are present, as are copper and gold.

The querns and grindstones found in these early farming villages indicate that grain was grown. Sheep and goats were kept, but hunting continued to provide an important source of meat. People lived in permanent villages, some as large as several hectares, located on open ground with little apparent concern for defense. Their huts were constructed of a wooden framework covered with mud. The presence of slag fragments suggests that ironworking was a common skill. Such small iron artifacts as arrowheads, razors, beads, and rings are found in every village. Copper items were rarer; usually no more than a few beads or small strips have been recovered in any one excavation. Handmade ceramics were produced, of which there were several distinct regional variants. Contact with the east coast of Africa is indicated by the presence of glass trade beads and occasional marine shells.

Relatively egalitarian political formations were more resilient in southern Africa than they were in West Africa. Farming and domesticated animals did not spread into southern Africa until the third century A.D., coincident with the appearance of ironworking and the spread of Bantu-speaking peoples. These herder-cultivators worked metal and made pottery. Before their arrival during the Early Iron Age, southern Africa was occupied by hunter-gatherers whose only tools were of stone.

Soon after their introduction, cattle became important both culturally and economically. As in many African societies today, the size of one's cattle herd was probably a sign of status and a basic means of converting grain surpluses into more permanent kinds of wealth. The advent of cattle herding did not eliminate hunting. Grain crops—particularly sorghum, finger millet, cowpeas, and ground beans—also were cultivated. Bananas were introduced from Indonesia by trans-Indian traders around the ninth century A.D.

During the later prehistory of Africa (in the past thousand years), complex states emerged in the central and southern regions. Groups such as the Karanga were led by powerful chiefs, priests, and traders. They had contacts with societies outside the continent, and at the advent of written history, several of them were still actively involved with foreign merchants.

Two of the largest early states in southern Africa were centered on Mapungubwe and Great Zimbabwe (see Figure 10.53). Mapungubwe, the earlier of the two, is located on top of a large sandstone outcrop that rises abruptly from the arid valley of the Limpopo River about 320 km (200 mi) south of Great Zimbabwe. The earliest farmers in the region built a number of villages close to the river after A.D. 800. Their economy was based on cattle, sheep, and goats, and they obtained such goods as cowrie shells and glass beads through Indian Ocean trade. Excavations at one of these early village sites (Bambandyanalo), only a few kilometers from Mapungubwe, revealed a large cattle enclosure, crude beakers and bag-shaped pots, grindstones, and a few iron tools. The first buildings were constructed on Mapungubwe Hill early in the twelfth century A.D. Excavations at the site have revealed a succession of houses and richly adorned burials accompanied by gold beads and bangles. Mapungubwe quickly became one of the largest towns in the region, controlling a hinterland of lesser settlements up to 60 km (37 mi) away. Its inhabitants specialized in various crafts, including working ivory into bracelets, making bone points, and weaving. However, the real base of Mapungubwe's power came from its intermediary role in coastal trade and the wealth of gold and animal products from its hinterland.

When Mapungubwe was at its peak, in the mid-thirteenth century A.D., Great Zimbabwe was a smaller district center. Mapungubwe later went into decline just as Great Zimbabwe was reaching its greatest size and influence. The eventual abandonment of Mapungubwe may in part have been due to Great Zimbabwe's seizure of the gold trade and exchange routes to the coast.

Great Zimbabwe, the largest and most famous site of the Karanga, is located in the central region of Zimbabwe, on a tributary that eventually drains into the Indian Ocean (Figure 10.57). The area is composed of granite hills, some of which are enormous, bare, rounded domes. Because of their size, these granite features affect rainfall patterns so that the prevailing southeasterly winds drop more rain here than in neighboring areas. To the north, the site is bounded by a narrow ridge of granite that forms a 91-m (300-ft) cliff, strewn with massive boulders. Just south of the Great Zimbabwe ruins, the land descends into drier, more open grasslands suitable for cattle. Slabs that break off the granite domes provide abundant building material.

The Karanga began to build stone structures, including field walls, terraces, and stone enclosures, sometime after A.D. 1000. The first stone structures at Great Zimbabwe, built after A.D. 1250, were placed on top of the

**Figure 10.58** The Hill Ruin at Great Zimbabwe consists of a series of stone enclosures built on top of a steep, rocky cliff, possibly for defense.

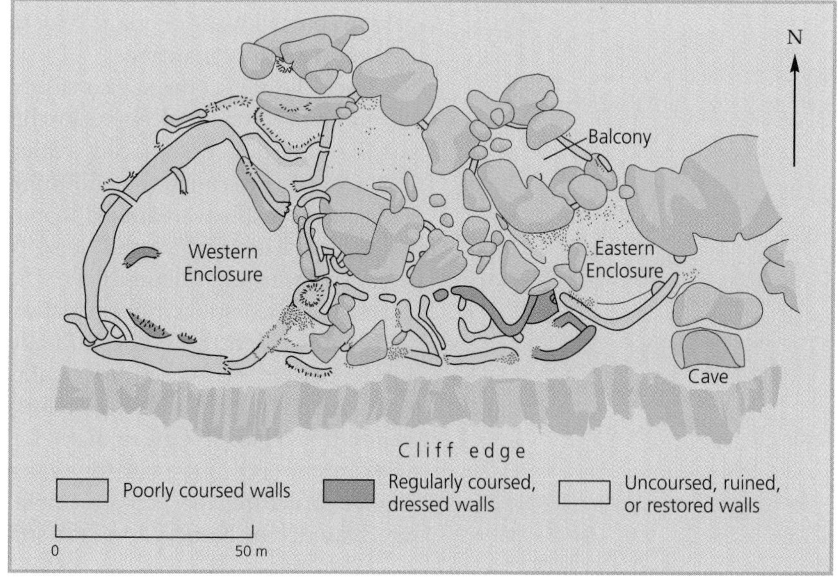

**Figure 10.59** The Great Enclosure and other stone ruins at Great Zimbabwe. The Great Enclosure is the largest known prehistoric structure in sub-Saharan Africa. Inside the Great Enclosure were smaller stone structures, which are thought to have housed the site's ruling families.

high cliff, possibly for defense. Simple stone walls enclosed platforms that held pole-and-mud houses. The walls do not follow an obvious plan. The only openings are narrow doorways, topped with simple stone lintels. The quality of the walls varies, from uncoursed sections of irregularly shaped rocks to coursed walls of granite blocks that were carefully matched.

The buildings at the site consist of two groups, one on the steep, rocky cliff and the other on the adjacent valley floor. On the cliff, called the Hill Ruin, well-coursed walls were linked to natural boulders, forming a series of easily defended enclosures (Figure 10.58). The largest and most substantial structure on the hill, called the Western Enclosure, consisted of two curved walls, over 9 m (30 ft) high, circling an area greater than 45 m (150 ft) in diameter. At the other end of the clifftop was a smaller structure, the Eastern Enclosure, bounded by boulders on the north and a stone wall on the south. Inside this structure were groups of circular stone platforms that held many monoliths. The presence of figurines, including seven carved soapstone birds, suggests that this enclosure was the ceremonial center of the site. The carved birds, about 36 cm (14 in) high, were placed on top of 1-m (3-ft) stone columns. Nothing like these stone carvings has been found elsewhere.

In the valley below, larger, freestanding walled enclosures were built surrounding circular pole-and-mud houses. This pattern is especially clear at the Maund Ruin at the edge of the site, where 29 separate stone walls were built. The walls abut ten circular dwelling huts, forming nine separate courtyards, each entered through doorways in the stone walls. These enclosures form single, functional units. Both in the valley and on the hill, large middens of domestic debris accumulated outside most of the enclosures.

Figure 10.60 The massive outer wall of the Great Enclosure, capped by the chevron pattern.

One enclosure at the opposite end of the valley from the Hill Ruin, the Great Enclosure, was especially large and complex, with a perimeter wall over 10 m (33 ft) high and 5 m (16 ft) thick (Figure 10.59). The outer wall was over 240 m (800 ft) long, forming an irregular ellipse with a diameter of 89 m (292 ft). The top of the wall is decorated with a band of two lines in a chevron pattern (Figure 10.60). There are several entrances into the enclosure on the north and west sides of the wall. Containing more stonework than all the rest of the ruins at Great Zimbabwe combined, this wall is the largest prehistoric structure in sub-Saharan Africa. Several smaller walled enclosures are situated within this outer wall, containing dwellings that housed the ruler and his family (Figure 10.61). The most striking construction inside the Great Enclosure is a solid circular stone tower rising 10 m (33 ft) from its base, which is 6 m (20 ft) in diameter. Called the Conical Tower, this structure was surrounded by platforms and large monoliths. The function of these monoliths, also associated with the Hill Ruin, remains somewhat of a mystery. Their distribution was not random; they were placed in areas having a sacred character.

The stone enclosures at the core of Great Zimbabwe—covering 40 ha (100 acres)—are the largest and most elaborate of the more than 150 similar stone structures constructed across the high granite region of the Zimbabwe plateau. Many of these sites were small, having between one and five small enclosures surrounded by freestanding walls. The pottery at all these sites was similar to that at Great Zimbabwe.

The architectural florescence at Great Zimbabwe was linked to the development of a powerful political authority. The construction of the extensive stone walls clearly required an organized labor effort. Centralized control of expanded trade links with Indian Ocean polities may have been a significant factor, and Great Zimbabwe became an important commercial center, both locally and regionally. Specialized craftworkers made simple forged iron tools, such as hoes, axes, and arrowheads. They alloyed copper with tin and made coiled wire bracelets and pins, needles, and razors, and used imported gold to make bracelets, anklets, and beads. These metals were worked

*African cities were in many ways similar to other cities worldwide and were easily recognized as such by Arab and European visitors.*

—Chapurukha Kusimba (2008)

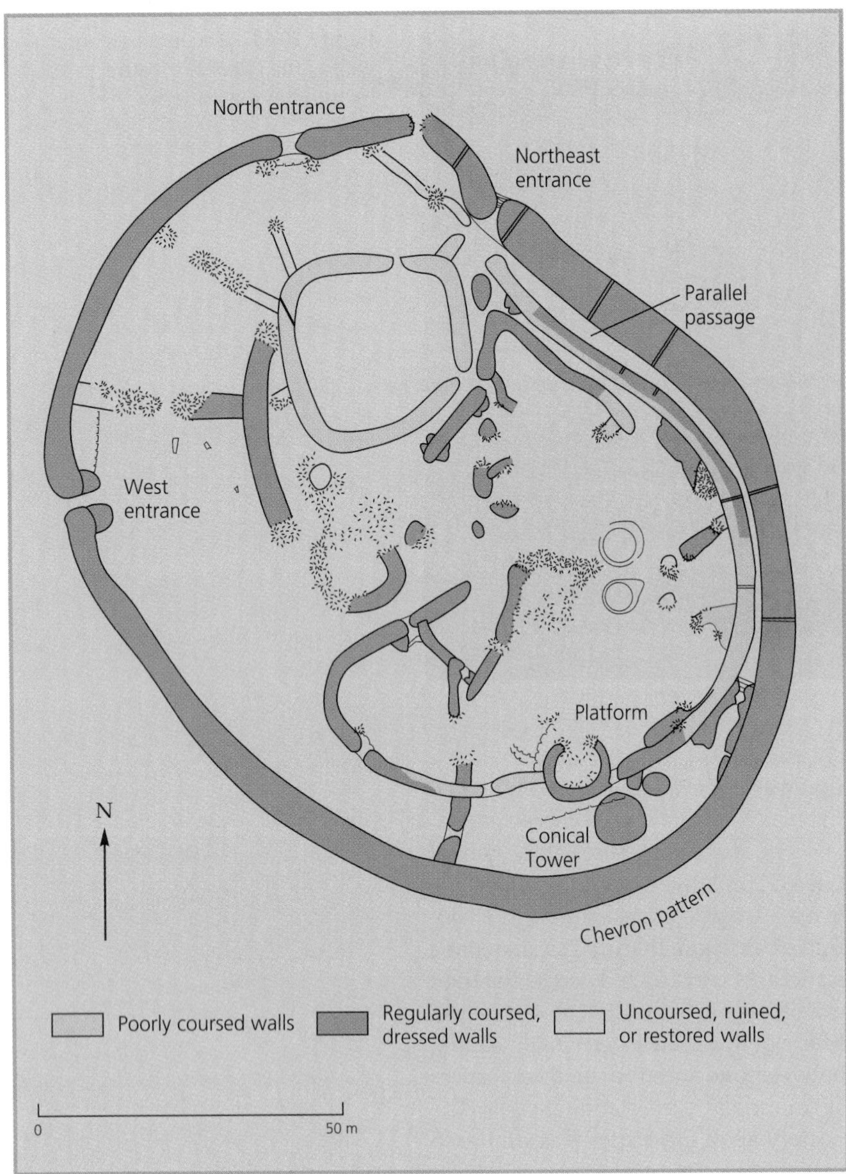


**Figure 10.61** The Great Enclosure, which contains more stonework than all the other ruins at Great Zimbabwe combined.

on a small scale in certain enclosures set aside for specific tasks. The presence of large numbers of spindle whorls, made from both potsherds and soapstone, indicates that cotton textiles were woven at Great Zimbabwe.

The prosperity of Great Zimbabwe was based largely on its monopolization of coastal and long-distance trade, which it had earlier wrested from Mapungubwe. Exchange with Africa's east coast, which was visited by Arab and Indian merchants, provided a large number of exotic objects, including Persian and Chinese pottery, Near Eastern glass, and cowrie shells from the beaches of the Indian Ocean. These items were prestige goods, essential to demonstrating rank. Porcelain, glass, and trinkets were found in one hoard at Great Zimbabwe in association with iron gongs, hoes, and seashells. The latter items are still recognized in the region today as symbols of chiefly authority. The traders at Great Zimbabwe also received products from the surrounding area, through either patronage or tribute. Copper was imported from the northern edge of the plateau in the form of standardized ingots. With the initiation of goldworking, the gold trade on the plateau became important by the late twelfth or early thirteenth century A.D.

Zimbabwe reached its period of greatest influence between A.D. 1350 and 1450, when the settlement, with a population estimated between 12,000 and 20,000, extended over 700 ha (1700 acres) and controlled an area of approximately 100,000 sq km (38,600 sq mi) between the Zambezi and Limpopo rivers. The balance of power then shifted to a more northerly center on the Zambezi River. The increasing importance of copper from the north may have been a factor in redirecting trade. Later, trade and communication routes, focused on the Zambezi, may have bypassed Great Zimbabwe. The Portuguese penetrated the area in the sixteenth century and established a fort on the east coast. Their attempt to control the gold exchange of south-central Africa further disrupted trade, and the Karanga empire disintegrated by the end of the century. Today, Karanga ruins stand tall in the plateau country of Zimbabwe. The word *zimbabwe* means "stone houses" or "venerated houses," and the Karanga used it to identify the houses of chiefs. It is these ruins that now give their name to a contemporary nation.

# *Images and Ideas*

## Theories of State Development

*Changing views on the rise of complex polities and urban societies*

The early civilizations that arose millennia ago in regions of Asia and Africa all were followed by episodes of political centralization and fragmentation. Over the past century, we have come to document and describe those waves of change more completely. In fact, in all regions of the globe, the emergence of urban societies was followed by episodes of change during which time-specific centers gained and lost in importance and power. Nevertheless, the timing and particular patterns of transition were not always the same.

It is important to note that the causal factors that account for those episodes of rise and fall, growth and collapse, remain a matter of debate. In the discussion that follows, we examine some of the ideas and models that have been advanced to account for the emergence of early civilizations. In many respects, the scholarly advances that have taken place over the past decades owe much to the comparative and systematic approaches that were outlined by the prehistorian Vere Gordon Childe.

*The regularities set forth by Steward, and the models constructed by Wittfogel, Carneiro, and others, have guided a great deal of fruitful research leading to knowledge about the material forces important in the rise of complex chiefdoms and states. What constructs, however, will guide us in the future?*

—Henry T. Wright (1986)

Over a half century ago, V. Gordon Childe described the essence of what we mean by civilization in a list of ten characteristics (even if he did not succeed in providing a scientifically precise or universally acceptable definition). Charles Redman, of Arizona State University, subsequently organized Childe's indices into a list of primary and secondary characteristics. The primary characteristics are economic, organizational, and demographic in nature and suggest fundamental changes in societal structure. They include (1) cities—dense, nucleated demographic concentrations; (2) full-time labor specialization; (3) state organization, based on territorial residence rather than kin connections; (4) class stratification—the presence of a privileged ruling stratum; and (5) the concentration of surplus. According to Redman, Childe's secondary characteristics serve to document the existence of the primary criteria. They are (1) monumental public works; (2) long-distance exchange; (3) writing; (4) arithmetic, geometry, and astronomy; and (5) highly developed, standardized artwork.

Childe's criteria, particularly the secondary ones, are certainly not without problems. For example, the Inca, who established the largest pre-Columbian empire in the Americas, did not have a formal system of writing in the traditional sense. Conversely, many societies that are not consensually recognized as civilizations built monumental edifices, engaged in long-distance exchange, crafted wonderful (and reasonably standardized) artwork, and were very aware of astronomical cycles. Even the primary criteria are subject to discussion, since kinship is known to have played a very strong organizational role in both Native American and early Chinese civilizations. Although it is next to impossible using archaeological data to distinguish full-time from part-time craft specialization, occupational specialization (of an unknown degree of intensity) is often found at archaeologically known sites that are not traditionally conceptualized as civilizations. Nevertheless, not only do Childe's criteria provide a valuable starting point for discussion, but most of them also can be examined archaeologically. To the researcher, they provide a more useful starting point than, for example, the frequently cited definition of the state as an institution that monopolizes force, a characteristic that cannot be subjected to straightforward archaeological investigation.

Given the difficulties in defining the state and civilization, as well as the evident variety in human societies and sequences of societal change, it is not surprising that no single, satisfactory explanation has been developed to account for these transformations. In anthropology, current interpretive perspectives can be subdivided into integrative and coercive models. Integrative approaches emphasize coordination and regulation as roles of emergent institutions. The alternative coercive theories stress the role of the developing state in the resolution of intra-societal conflicts that emerge from disparities in wealth. These alternative frameworks have their philosophical roots at least as early as the fifth century B.C., when the Greek writer Thucydides described the Peloponnesian War and its combatants. Thucydides compared different organizational frameworks, contrasting the democratic and the oligarchic. The former, typified by Athens under the ruler Pericles, was characterized by government through cooperation, with the populace described as benefitting from state policies and services. Sparta, which typified the latter, more coercive, governing structure, was ruled by a propertied class that controlled decision making to maintain their disproportionate wealth.

Most states integrate as well as coerce, although their degree of reliance on different governing strategies certainly can vary. For archaeologists, as well as other social and historical scientists, the decipherment of different organizational strategies is a promising domain for research. Yet in modeling the evolution of early states, researchers should recognize that government strategies can undergo change. For example, institutions may initially develop to serve integrative or regulative roles. Once established, they may become more coercive in the face of new challenges or to maintain whatever benefits their decision makers may have accrued. Therefore, the functions of a governing institution may not provide a complete picture of why that institution arose in the first place.

The preceding discussion contrasts the explanatory merits of integrative and coercive frameworks. A second analytical pathway compares the relative utility of different "prime-movers," key factors that are proposed to account for many, if not all, cases of state development. Karl Wittfogel proposed water control (irrigation) as the key variable in the rise of the "hydraulic state." Wittfogel saw water as having unique properties, essential for agriculture in the dry lands where many of the world's early states developed, yet manipulable by people in ways that other environmental resources are not. Nevertheless, although large-scale canal irrigation systems were eventually used in the domains of many early states (such as in Mesopotamia), the temporal sequence of state formation and the construction of these grand irrigation networks is not clear. In other areas, such as Mexico's Valley of Oaxaca, it appears that most pre-Colombian water-control devices could have been managed by a few households at most. Recent ethnographic research also indicates that large-scale irrigation networks do not necessarily require centralized administration.

*If population pressure was a problem in the Nile Valley, a circumscribed situation* par excellence, *the Pharaoh should have been delighted to see the last of Moses and his cogeners [followers]. That he was not, and indeed expended considerable effort to retain the Jews within his territories, suggests that population pressure was not perceived as a threat to social stability.*

—A. Terry Rambo (1991)

A second prime-mover, demographic pressure, places the primary cause of political change on imbalances between a human population and its available food supply. Influenced by the work of the agricultural economist Esther Boserup, proponents of this view have turned the work of Thomas Malthus on its head. In the late eighteenth century, Malthus argued that the advent of agriculture led to the production of food surpluses, thereby making human population growth possible and increasing the availability of leisure time. Yet anthropological work, spearheaded by Robert Carneiro, of the American Museum of Natural History in New York; Marshall Sahlins, of the University of Chicago; and Richard Lee, of the University of Toronto, has questioned the long-held dogma surrounding surplus and leisure time. As Kent Flannery synthesized,

> *The cold ethnographic fact is that the people with the most leisure time are the hunters and gatherers, who also have the lowest productivity; even primitive farmers don't produce a surplus unless they are forced to, and thus the challenge is getting people to work more, or more people to work. With better technology, people simply work less; what produces surplus is the coercive power of real authority, or the demands of elaborate ritual. (1972a, pp. 405–406)*

Recently, anthropologists have questioned the arguments of Carneiro, Lee, and Sahlins concerning leisure time. They note that most hunter-gatherer populations suffered seasonal or periodic food shortages or frequently lacked certain key resources, such as fat or protein. Yet the fact remains that, except when encouraged, few hunter-gatherers or village people produced a great deal more than their families required.

Primarily concerned with the contemporary Third World (where runaway demographic growth is not unusual), Boserup argues that technological changes and increased productivity also could be spurred by excessive population. Archaeological adherents of Boserup's position view ancient population growth as an independent variable and the principal cause of social and economic transformations. As we saw in many of the site discussions in this chapter and in Chapters 8 and 9, demographic growth often coincided with episodes of great social change, and in many regions, it was an important variable. Yet correlation does not equal causality. What is not clear in most cases is the nature of the interconnections—whether population growth was the cause or the consequence of political and economic transitions.

In rural, preindustrial contexts where child labor can be economically valuable, increases in tribute and the labor demands on households (often associated with political development) can spur cycles of demographic growth, as families opt to have more children. In other words, political and economic strategies can greatly influence demographic change. In many of the cases we have examined, the nucleation of population around an emerging center also may have been spurred by in-migration, as people were attracted by or coerced to settle near an increasingly powerful institution.

Furthermore, population growth does not necessarily imply population pressure, the latter being a notoriously difficult concept to measure. Archaeological and historical findings from many areas indicate that long-term population change is not regular, uniform, or ever-increasing, making it theoretically problematic to assume continuous and autonomous growth. Finally, in several cases, archaeological findings have shown that regional populations were markedly below any reasonable estimate of available agrarian production at the time of early state development.

Exchange also has been advanced as a prime-mover, although, like warfare, it is practically a human universal and therefore too broadly defined to account for the development of the state. Thus the occurrence of exchange is not as evolutionarily significant as are the nature and mode of the transactions, whether they are monopolized or controlled and by whom, the volume of the transactions involved, and the kinds of items moved (and their local importance). Until these considerations are empirically considered and refined theoretically, exchange cannot be convincingly employed as a prime-mover in state development.

Another general model for state development was proposed by Carneiro. Stimulated by his ethnographic work among tribal groups in the Amazon Basin of South America, Carneiro has suggested that warfare and bounded conditions may account for the origin of states. Carneiro recognized that warfare, almost universal in human society, cannot alone account for the rise of the state. Warfare was present (even endemic) in many places, yet the state never formed in those areas. In Carneiro's scenario, a population first must have increased in size beyond the limits of its local resources. **Circumscription** by either environmental (mountains, oceans, rivers) or social (neighboring groups) boundaries would then require warfare and conquest to obtain more food. Although warfare does appear to have been an important factor in some cases, such as the rise of Monte Albán in the Valley of Oaxaca, Mexico (see Chapter 8, p. 342), Carneiro's formulation, which tends to make warfare and population pressure into dual prime-movers, has not met with unanimous support. For example, it is hard to envision how circumscription played a major role on the extensive, flat North China Plain,

*The notion that the study of five or six precocious civilizations would inform us about the factors crucial in the rise of civilization in general is seductive. Throughout the second half of the twentieth century, research focused not only on these earlier developments but also on the supposed "core" areas of these developments, envisioned as the regions in which "breakthroughs" in cultural organization took place and from whence they "diffused" to peripheral regions. As research in the supposed peripheral regions has progressed, we have had some surprises, and empirical knowledge demands that we change our general conceptions. . . . I argue that the idea that civilizations have a single heartland is a product, in part, of the success of elites in particular regions in dominating the historical record and, in part, of the state of archaeology in the twentieth century.*

—Henry T. Wright (2005)

**circumscription** The process or act of being enclosed by either environmental boundaries, such as mountains, oceans, and rivers, or social boundaries, such as neighboring groups of people.

*I have sometimes compared models to ships. What interests me, once the ship is built, is to launch it, to see if it floats, then to make it sail wherever I please, up and down the currents of time. The moment of shipwreck is always the most meaningful.*
—Fernand Braudel (1970)

where the early Chinese state appears to have arisen. Even in Oaxaca, the connection between the concentration of political power and militarism began during a period when the regional population was small.

Today, most archaeologists have adopted multivariate approaches, recognizing that the process of state development was probably triggered by a suite of factors (including some of the prime-movers), rather than a single causal stimulus in each instance, and that even the same set of factors may not have been involved in each case. Our examination of state formation in Asia and Africa illustrates that factors such as population growth, new technologies, changing exchange and interaction (including warfare) patterns, and shifts in the organization of labor and specialization were often intertwined with episodes of managerial restructuring, yet we have sorted out neither the specific interlinkages between those factors nor their relative importance in each case. We also need to work hand-in-hand with natural scientists to document the web of interconnections between humans and their natural environments. Studies in many areas of the globe have now revealed the impacts that humans can have on their immediate settings: flora, fauna, patterns of erosion, desert creation, and more. Such **anthropogenic** processes and events also require careful analysis before we can understand long-term regional histories.

*Men make their own history, but they do not make it just as they please; they do not make it under circumstances chosen by themselves, but under circumstances directly encountered, given and transmitted from the past.*
—Karl Marx (1963 [1852])

The contingent or historical nature of social change provides a further challenge. In each region, earlier changes always constrain and underpin subsequent shifts. Consequently, the nature of the states in each of these regions varied somewhat because of the nature and organization of the specific polities that preceded them. If we concede that the rise of new forms of government are often accompanied by other significant (and interdependent) shifts at both higher and lower scales (e.g., households, boundary relations), then the analytical tasks in front of us seem all the more challenging. For each region, archaeologists will need to collect information at multiple scales from the activity area to the house, the community, and the region, and even learn to conceptualize at larger scales. All these vantages will have to be examined over time.

**www.mhhe.com/priceip6e**

For more review material and study questions, see the self-quizzes on your online learning center.

Nevertheless, we can take heart in the realization that there has been tremendous progress in the study of the state during the past several decades. Recent archaeological surveys, large-scale excavations, the study of ancient households, and ethnohistoric breakthroughs, which have helped us unravel some of the ideological changes that made new managerial formations possible, have enriched the empirical foundation necessary for examining this key societal transformation. In Southwest Asia, South Asia, Egypt, North China, and sub-Saharan Africa, recent findings enable us to refine and improve our models as we expand our knowledge of the history of each of those regions. If these contributions continue apace (especially in the face of our dwindling, threatened archaeological record), and if a series of crucial definitional and theoretical challenges are met, the opportunity for taking giant steps forward in our understanding lies immediately ahead.

## DISCUSSION QUESTIONS

1. How did the development and the role of writing vary in the early civilizations of Mesopotamia, the Indus Valley, Egypt, China, and Mesoamerica?
2. Was the development of irrigation systems a factor in the rise of most early complex societies? Why do you think so? If not, what other factors were important?
3. The early Egyptian state appears to have been more centralized than the Indus civilization. Can you offer some thoughts as to why?
4. Contrast the nature of rulership in two of the early civilizations discussed in this chapter. Can you account for or explain these differences?

**anthropogenic** The term used to describe an effect or process resulting from human activity. The creation of pasture from forest through intentional burning is an example. At times, human abandonment of a site or area (as well as initial occupation) also can set off environmental changes.

5. In sub-Saharan Africa and Southeast Asia, external contacts and exchange are thought to have had a role in the rise of early civilizations. How did such exogenous relations interplay with local traditions and developments in each region?

## SUGGESTED READINGS

For Internet links related to this chapter, please visit our Web site at www.mhhe.com/priceip6e.


Alcock, S. E., T. N. D'Altroy, K. D. Morrison, and C. M. Sinopoli, eds. 2001. *Empires: Perspectives from archaeology and history.* Cambridge: Cambridge University Press. *An edited collection that brings a comparative and global perspective to historically known empires.*

Carneiro, R. L. 2003. *Evolutionism in cultural anthropology: A critical history.* Boulder, CO: Westview. *Traces the interaction of evolutionary thought and anthropological theory from the nineteenth to the twenty-first century.*

Feinman, G. M., and J. Marcus, eds. 1998. *Archaic states.* Santa Fe, NM: School of American Research Press. *A recent collection of essays that highlights the diversity of ancient states.*

Kenoyer, J. M. 1998. *Ancient cities of the Indus Valley civilization.* Oxford: Oxford University Press. *A timely overview by an area specialist.*

Murowchick, R. E., ed. 1994. *Cradles of civilization: China.* Norman: University of Oklahoma Press. *A well-illustrated collection of articles examining the early civilizations of China.*

Rothman, M. S., ed. 2001. *Uruk Mesopotamia and its neighbors: Cross-cultural interactions in the era of state formation.* Santa Fe, NM: School of American Research. *A set of scholarly essays that presents up-to-date information on this early civilization.*

Smith, M. L., ed. 2003. *The social construction of ancient cities.* Washington, DC: Smithsonian Institution Press. *A collection of papers that provides a bottom-up perspective on ancient cities in several world areas.*

Trigger, B. G. 2003. *Understanding early civilizations: A comparative study.* Cambridge: Cambridge University Press. *A detailed comparative study of the seven best-documented early civilizations in the world.*

Wright, H. T. 1986. The evolution of civilizations. In *American archaeology, past and future,* ed. D. J. Meltzer, D. D. Fowler, and J. A. Sabloff. Washington, DC: Smithsonian Institution Press. *An analytical synthesis of long-term change in several world regions.*

Yoffee, N., and G. L. Cowgill, eds. 1988. *The collapse of ancient states and civilizations.* Tucson: University of Arizona Press. *A comparative collection of scholarly papers on collapse by experts from several disciplines.*

# CHAPTER 11

**Figure 11.1** Gold death mask from a shaft grave at Mycenae, Greece, ca. 1550 B.C.

# Prehistoric Europe

## Introduction
### From the First Farmers to the Roman Empire
*A story of change*

The funeral mask of "Agamemnon" from the shaft graves at Mycenae, Greece (Figure 11.1), captures several aspects of the later prehistory of Europe. It depicts a warrior-king (although almost certainly not Agamemnon) who ruled an agricultural society. It is made of an exotic raw material, gold, traded long-distance, probably from Bulgaria. From the appearance of the first farmers to the historic events of the Roman conquest, the archaeology of the past 9000 years in Europe is a story of the introduction of agriculture, of technological innovation and the use of metals, of the growth of regionalism and warfare, and of the development of economically and politically powerful groups.

This period is of interest today because many of the basic tenets of Western civilization come from prehistoric Europe. Languages, customs, traditions, forms of government, and many of our fundamental solutions to the uncertainties of the world emerged in Europe during this period. The period also interests us because, in the span of a few thousand years, we can trace the development of human societies from small, simple bands of hunter-gatherers to large, complex states with thousands of citizens. European archaeology is also fascinating because a long history of research has produced a number of remarkable finds.

It is useful to consider the prehistory of Europe in **millennia,** beginning with the arrival of agriculture before 7000 B.C. and ending with the decline of the Vikings around A.D. 1000. The millennia B.C. run backward; the first millennium B.C. is 1000–0 B.C., and the eighth millennium is 8000–7000 B.C. Dates designated A.D. run forward. We are now in the first years of the third millennium A.D.

**Eighth Millennium (8000–7000 B.C.)** Excavations at the site of Franchthi Cave in Greece document the introduction of agriculture to southeastern Europe shortly before 7000 B.C. Many major innovations—domesticated plants and animals, pottery, iron, writing, and others—came to Europe from Southwest Asia, appearing initially in the southeast and moving gradually to the north and west (Figure 11.2). Incipient farming communities appeared in the Aegean area and Greece shortly before 7000 B.C. and arrived in northwestern Europe around 4000 B.C.

**Seventh Millennium (7000–6000 B.C.)** During this millennium, farming and pottery followed two main pathways from Greece into Europe: by land into the center of the continent, and by sea along the north coast of the Mediterranean. This package of pottery, mud-brick houses, and domestic plants and animals had spread by 6500 B.C., via the Danube and other rivers, to the Balkan Peninsula of southeastern Europe (Bulgaria, Romania, Hungary, and the former Yugoslavia). Along the second path, distinctive Cardial pottery, decorated with the scalloped edge of a seashell, wheat, and the bones of domesticated sheep appeared in caves and rockshelters along the Mediterranean shore after 6000 B.C. The coastal location

CHAPTER OUTLINE

Figure 11.2 The spread of agriculture from Southwest Asia into Europe in time and space. The map shows the approximate dates for the major stages in the expansion of farming across Europe.

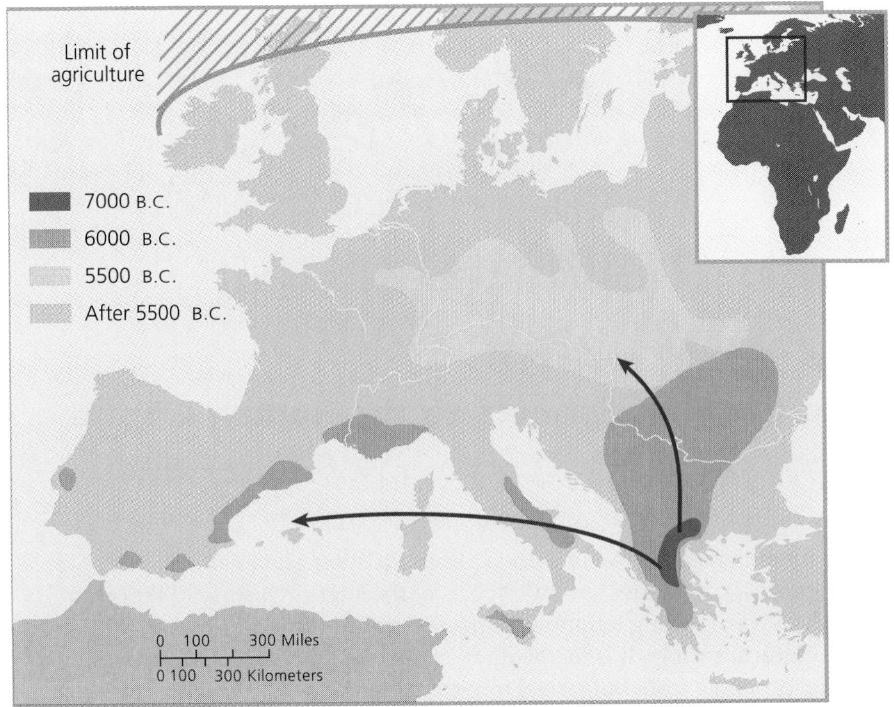


www.mhhe.com/priceip6e

For preview material for this chapter, see the comprehensive chapter outline and chapter objectives on your online learning center.

Was the spread of agriculture into Europe slow or fast? Gradual or jumpy?

**millennium** A period of 1000 years.

**lake dwelling** The former name for Early Neolithic lakeshore settlements originally thought to have been built over the water.

**Bandkeramik** An archaeological culture of the early Neolithic in central Europe, referring to the style of pottery: linear bands of incised designs on hemispherical bowls.

and sporadic distribution of these sites suggest a spread of agriculture arriving by sea.

**Sixth Millennium (6000–5000 B.C.)** This time witnessed the flowering of Neolithic cultures in southeastern Europe—the appearance of large settlements, elaborate religious systems, copper mining, and extensive trade networks. A number of the many large tells in the region, such as Starcevo outside Belgrade in Serbia and Karanovo in Bulgaria, have been excavated and provide a sequence of these events. These sites contain houses, elaborate pottery, and copper artifacts. Copper ore was mined from rich deposits in Serbia and elsewhere, providing raw material for the oldest metal production in the world. Finished axes and copper jewelry were traded throughout Europe. The cemetery at Varna documents the extraordinary wealth in copper and especially gold that accumulated in southeastern Europe during this period.

During this time, agriculture continued to spread across Europe. The coastal branch moved inland from the Mediterranean shore into Spain, France, and Italy. By 4000 B.C., farming communities were distributed across most of southern Europe. The Iceman came from one of these communities in northern Italy before he died at the top of the Alps. A number of very well preserved settlements, often described as **lake dwellings,** are known from Switzerland, France, and other countries around the Alps. As one example, the village of Charavines in southeastern France provides an extraordinary glimpse into the Neolithic because of the remarkable preservation of wood and other organic materials at the site.

The interior arm of agricultural expansion reached into central Europe during this same period. The early Neolithic communities in this area belong to the **Bandkeramik,** or Linear Pottery, culture. The Bandkeramik had its origin around 5700 B.C. in villages along the middle Danube and its tributaries in eastern Hungary. From this core area, farmers migrated east, north, and west, across the loess-covered valleys of central Europe to Belgium, southern Poland (Figure 11.3), and Ukraine. Within a period of a few hundred years, small farming villages appeared throughout this area. Both the rapid expansion of the Bandkeramik and the uniformity of its architecture, artifacts, burials, and settlement plan are remarkable.

Figure 11.3 A modern reconstruction of the interior of and the entrance to the Iron Age settlement at Biskupin, Poland. This lakeside site has a long history of occupation from the Bronze Age and the Iron Age.

**Fifth Millennium (5000–4000 B.C.)** This was a time of expansion and consolidation as Neolithic groups filled in much of southern and central Europe and regional differences emerged in ceramic styles. Neolithic groups began to develop local traditions as independent societies.

**Fourth Millennium (4000–3000 B.C.)** The beginning of this period witnessed the last stage in the spread of agriculture to northwestern Europe—the Netherlands, northern Germany, northern Poland, southern Scandinavia, and the British Isles. Neolithic farming societies in western Europe quickly began to erect megalithic structures—large stone tombs and monuments such as Stonehenge. Across Europe, in spite of such widespread traditions and growing trade, conflict and warfare are documented in the increasingly defensive nature of settlement location.

**Third Millennium (3000–2000 B.C.)** Major innovations appear, including the introduction of bronze, new weapons, the wheel, draft animals and the plow and oxcart, the horse and chariot, and extensive maritime contacts. Bronze first appeared in the form of weapons and jewelry and was largely in the possession of the elite. Bronze swords and spears must have provided a distinct military advantage. Trade and conflict appear to have escalated during this period as well.

**Second Millennium (2000–1000 B.C.)** The second millennium B.C. was important in the Aegean area. First on Crete, and later in Greece, Bronze Age lords directed powerful polities. The palaces of Knossos and Mycenae provide evidence of the vitality of these early states. The palace economy involved writing systems, craft specialization, taxation, and extensive trade networks. This commerce attracted goods and materials from most of temperate Europe to the Aegean. The second millennium B.C. was also the time of the Bronze Age north of the Alps. Large polities arose in those areas where raw materials and trade routes coincided. The elaborate tombs of elite individuals under large earthen mounds in southern England, the Czech Republic, Spain, and southern Scandinavia are evidence of local wealth and high status in these areas. The Danish site of Borum Eshøj provides examples of such tombs and the monuments of these societies.

**First Millennium (1000–0 B.C.)** This time is known as the Early Iron Age because of the introduction of this new metal. The classical civilizations of Greece and Rome arose in the Mediterranean region during this time. These literate polities with written histories are the subject of classical archaeology. North of the Alps, prehistory continued. In temperate western Europe, Celtic and Germanic tribes with distinctive traditions and art styles were present during the Iron Age. The fortresses of these warrior societies—known by their Roman name, **oppida,** centers of trade and warfare—dotted the landscape of western Europe. The princess burial at Vix in France documents the wealth and interaction of those Celtic elite; her tomb is located at the foot of Mont Lassois, one of the largest fortified towns of Celtic Europe. Iron Age sacrifices and executions preserved in the bogs of the north provide a startling glimpse of some of the inhabitants of that area.

The discipline and strength of the Roman legions finally overwhelmed the Celts, or Gauls, as Julius Caesar and his successors carried the legacy of Rome to western Europe. The Iron Age fortress of Maiden Castle in southern England was razed in A.D. 43 (Figure 11.4). By A.D. 125, the Romans had extended Hadrian's Wall across the northern border of England. Only those areas north and east of the Rhine River remained free of Roman rule and continued a tribal way of life for a short while longer. Eventually, in the first millennium A.D., the spread of Christianity brought a new religion, and the literate priesthood recorded history, closing the prehistoric part of Europe's past. The Vikings succumbed to history and Christianity around A.D. 1000.

**oppidum** A massive fortification in western Europe, often on a hilltop or a bluff, built for defensive purposes during the Iron Age.

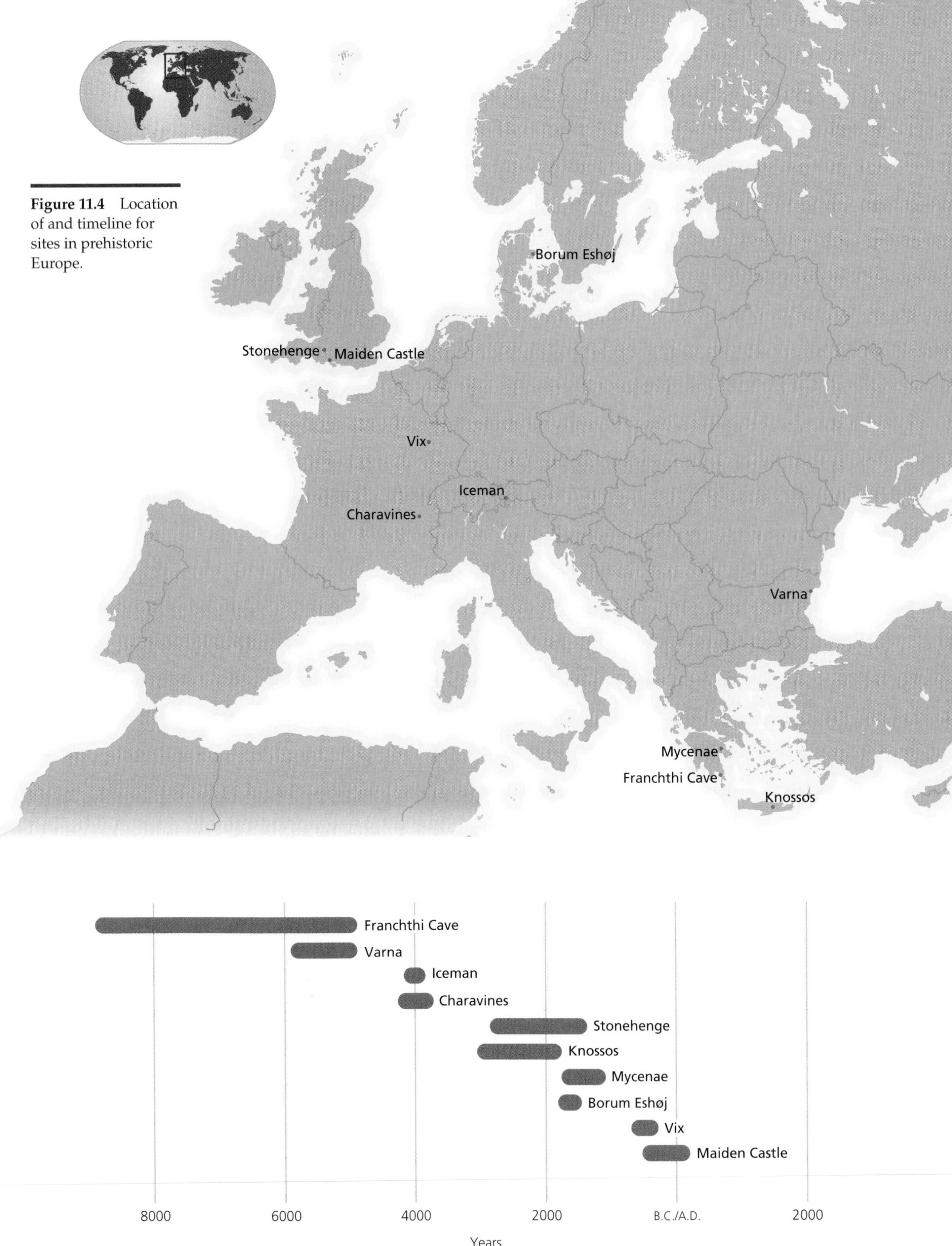


**Figure 11.4** Location of and timeline for sites in prehistoric Europe.

# Franchthi Cave

*The arrival of the Neolithic*

Franchthi (FRAUNK-tee) Cave in southern Greece provides early evidence for the introduction of agriculture to the European continent (Figure 11.5). Today, the cave is situated at the Aegean coast; in the early Holocene, however, the sea was some distance from the cave, and a fairly level plain stood where its waters are now. Investigations at the cave led by Thomas Jacobsen, of Indiana University, revealed layers of trash and other debris that contained a detailed picture of human residence there over the past 20,000 years (Figure 11.6). The early Mesolithic inhabitants of Franchthi exploited a wide range of terrestrial and marine resources at the end of the Pleistocene. Evidence for the hunting of red deer and other large game animals, the collecting of marine mollusks and land snails, and the use of several types of wild plants, including leafy greens, pistachio nuts, almonds, and various grasses, is found in the Upper Paleolithic deposits. The variety and seasonal availability of the foods at the site suggest that the cave may have been occupied year-round by 10,000 years ago.

The Mesolithic levels at the site indicate an increasing reliance on the sea. The remains of tuna and the presence of obsidian document the seafaring abilities of the residents around 10,000 years ago. Bones from large tuna constitute about 50% of the animal remains in these cave layers. Measuring up to 2.5 m (8 ft) long and weighing up to 200 kg (450 lb), tuna live only in the deeper waters of the Aegean. The obsidian in some of the artifacts at Franchthi comes from the island of Melos, some 150 km (100 mi) away.

After 7000 B.C., domesticated plants and animals were present at Franchthi. Sheep and goats were abundant in the cave levels from this period, as well as domesticated wheats and barley. Red deer and tuna were less common among the animal remains. Plant species consumed earlier declined, including wild oats, pistachios, and barley. Some stone blades have **sickle polish** along their edges, a substance that remains when blades are used to cut the stems of plants such as grasses and reeds. The presence of sickle polish indicates that the inhabitants of the cave were harvesting plants in substantial quantities. Coriander seeds were also found among the plant remains. Coriander grows as a weed in cultivated or disturbed areas; its presence suggests that crops may have been cultivated. Finally, the lentils preserved from this level at Franchthi are large, the same size as the later domesticated variety.

The occupation area increased in size at this time. A terrace in front of the cave was used for the houses of a

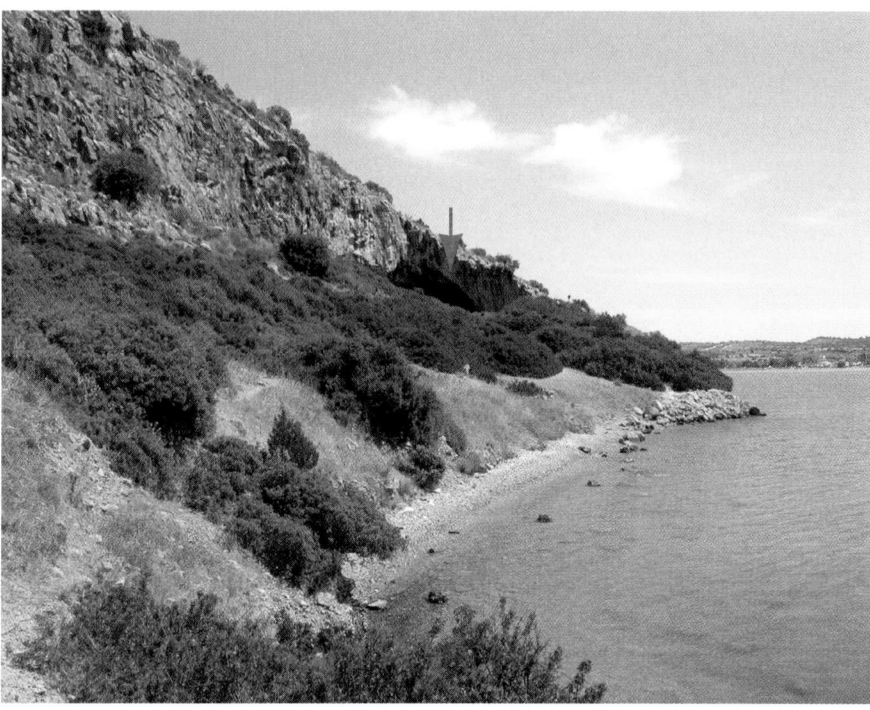

**Figure 11.5** Franchthi Cave, on the coast of the Aegean in southern Greece. During the first part of the occupation here, the Mediterranean was some distance from the cave, but rising sea levels gradually brought it closer.

**sickle polish** A clear polish that forms along the edges of flakes and blades that are used to cut reeds, grass, wheat, and other long-stemmed plants.

**TABLE 11.1 The Major Layers at Franchthi Cave**

| *Period* | *Sea Level* | *Proportion of Wild Animal Bones* | *Fish* | *Plants* | *Years B.P.* |
|---|---|---|---|---|---|
| Late Mesolithic | –25 m | Deer, pig | Large and common | Wild barley, vetch, lentils | 8500 |
| Middle Mesolithic | | Deer, pig | Small and rare | Wild barley, vetch, lentils | 10,500 |
| Early Mesolithic | | Deer, horse, goat, pig | Small and rare | Wild barley, vetch, lentils | 10,500 |
| | | Hiatus | | | |
| Late Paleolithic | –50 m | Deer, horse, cattle, goat | — | Wild barley, vetch, lentils | 12,500 |
| Upper Paleolithic | –90 m | Deer, horse | — | — | 22,000 |

small farming community with a population of perhaps 75 people. Contacts with other areas increased. New exotic materials such as marble appeared in the cave deposits for the first time. However, the introduction of domestic plants and animals, as well as pottery, did not disrupt all aspects of Franchthi Cave; there was some continuity with the previous way of life.

The domesticated plants and animals appeared rather suddenly at Franchthi and must have come from Southwest Asia. There are several possible scenarios for this introduction of agriculture. One involves the influx of people bringing domesticates to Greece and the Aegean islands. Another possibility is the adoption of exotic domesticates and pottery by the indigenous peoples of southeastern Europe. It seems unlikely that the inhabitants of the cave would have changed completely with the arrival of the Neolithic. Perhaps the domesticated plants and animals were introduced by seafarers from Turkey or Southwest Asia looking for exotic materials to trade or exchange. Whatever the initial mechanism of introduction, these innovations initiated a series of changes that would eventually be felt throughout Europe. Within 3000 years of their first appearance in Greece, farming societies had replaced hunter-gatherers across most of the European continent.

**Figure 11.6** A view down the "chimney" of Franchthi Cave to the excavations beneath. This large cave contains deposits from the Paleolithic, Mesolithic, and Neolithic of Greece.

# Varna

## *Golden burials on the Black Sea coast of Bulgaria*

In 1972, workers digging near the city of Varna on the Black Sea coast of Bulgaria uncovered several graves containing unusual metal objects. Thinking the metal was copper, they called in local archaeologists, who excavated the cemetery from 1973 to 1982. The discoveries at Varna have dramatically altered our impressions of early farmers in southeastern Europe because of the rare and valuable materials that accompanied the burials (Figure 11.7).

The discovery and use of metals in the Old World was a relatively slow process. A few small pieces of copper, in the form of jewelry, appeared in Southwest Asia by 7000 B.C. at early Neolithic sites. This was native copper, simply hammered from its original shape into a new form. The melting and casting of copper began in southeastern Europe and Southwest Asia shortly after 5000 B.C. Copper mines were opened in Yugoslavia, and various copper artifacts, primarily axes and jewelry, found their way throughout much of Europe. Gold objects also began to appear during the fifth millennium B.C.

The cemetery contained at least 190 graves in an area of 6500 sq m (1.6 acres). The graves are simple rectangular pits with rounded corners, dug into the earth to varying depths, up to 3 m (almost 10 ft). Red ochre was spread over most of the burials. The "copper" the workers discovered was, in fact, gold, and more than 6 kilos (about 14 lb) were found during the excavation of the cemetery. A wide range of other materials were uncovered in the graves as well, including flint, obsidian, bone, clay, ochre, shell, graphite, marble, and copper. Impressions of decayed textiles could be seen on the walls of the graves and were preserved with

**Figure 11.7** One of the richest graves at Varna. Note the gold discs around the head and on the chest, the arm rings, the axes, and especially the gold-handled stone axe in the man's hand.

**Figure 11.8** One example of the earliest use of gold for decorating pottery at Varna. The high temperatures involved in applying the gold to the ceramics imply sophisticated pyrotechnology.

some of the copper artifacts. Radiocarbon methods date the site to approximately 4500 B.C., contemporary with the Vinča culture in Yugoslavia.

The dead were buried with their heads toward the Black Sea. Most of the burials were males, lying extended on their backs. A few women were buried in a flexed position on their right sides. There were no graves with children; the youngest individual in the cemetery was about 14 years old. The graves contained relatively few furnishings. Most male burials included a copper axe or pottery and flint tools; female graves held only a few ceramic pots. Almost 20% of the graves did not contain a body—a pattern seen elsewhere in the Neolithic of southeastern Europe. Most of these empty graves, or **cenotaphs,** contained only a few offerings, usually gold rings and copper axes.

Several of the graves were quite distinctive. Three empty graves contained life-size clay masks of human faces. Certain facial features, such as the teeth and decorations on the ear, chin, or forehead, were made from gold plaques. In addition, thousands of gold pins and beads of *Spondylus* and *Dentalium* shell, copper needles, marble drinking cups, figurines, and graphite-and-gold-painted pottery were found in these three "mask" graves. The graphite and gold ceramics are exceptional examples of the technological sophistication of the potters of this period (Figure 11.8). Graphite is applied as a powder to the burnished clay surface of the pottery and must be fired at a temperature of at least 1000°C (1800°F) to fix the graphite. Gold powder may have been applied to pottery in a similar fashion, but the exact technique is unknown.

Three other empty graves, numbered 1, 4, and 36 during the excavations, contained even more wealth. The offerings and grave goods were arranged in these tombs as though a body were present. Grave 1 contained 1225 gold objects weighing 2093 g (4.5 lb), in 15 groups. (At the price of gold, the value would be roughly $1 million today.) These items included two gold tubes and parts of the shafts of axes. Golden masks were found in several of the graves. Grave 36 included a solid gold axe and shaft, two gold bull effigies, 30 miniature golden horns, and

**cenotaph** A grave that does not contain a skeleton.

**Figure 11.9** The contents of one grave at Varna include enormous flint blades, shell beads, gold plaques and rings, gold handles on a shaft, gold armbands, bracelets, and beads, and several copper axes and other tools.

various gold adornments and jewelry, a marble dish, four pottery vessels, and miscellaneous bone and flint tools.

Grave 4 contained 320 gold pieces, weighing 1500 g (3.3 lb). The list of items in the grave is remarkable:

*A stone axe of beautiful workmanship with a tubular gold shaft was placed as if at the right shoulder of the missing skeleton. Other grave goods included: a copper pickaxe of the same shape as found in the . . . copper [mines]; a shafthole axe; a flat axe; a chisel and awls [one with a preserved bone handle]; a dark green stone axe; an enormous flint blade [over 40 cm long]; oblong and rectangular breastplates of gold, having two small perforations in each corner; a circular convex gold disc 7 cm across, lying at the shoulder next to the golden shaft of the axe; one very large globular gold bead placed at the head; round gold earrings; a necklace of annular gold beads; three massive armrings of gold in the center of the grave; 41 circular convex discs of gold with perforations on the side, probably garment ornaments; and a mass of beads of* Spondylus *and* Dentalium *shell and of semiprecious orange, red, and black stone. At the head were a large gold-painted dish and vase and three other pots with lids. (Gimbutas, 1977, p. 48)*

The graves at Varna provide spectacular evidence for **status differentiation** in the Neolithic of southeastern Europe. Different categories of people in this society were distinguished by the wealth that accompanied the burials. The rich graves may have been those of religious or political leaders or merchants. Certainly, the location of this important cemetery points to the role of trade and exchange. Varna is located at the shore of a former inlet from the Black Sea, perhaps a natural harbor, and near the mouth of the Danube River. Trade routes for gold, copper, obsidian, marble, shell, pottery, and many other items must have run through or very near this area. Such a strategic location may well have led to the rise of an elite at Varna and the accumulation of extraordinary amounts of wealth. The fact that the wealth of the living was buried with the dead is both a remarkable testimony to the complexity of Neolithic society in the Balkan Peninsula and a boon to archaeology (Figure 11.9).

**status differentiation** Inequality in human society in which certain individuals or groups have access to more resources, power, and roles than others.

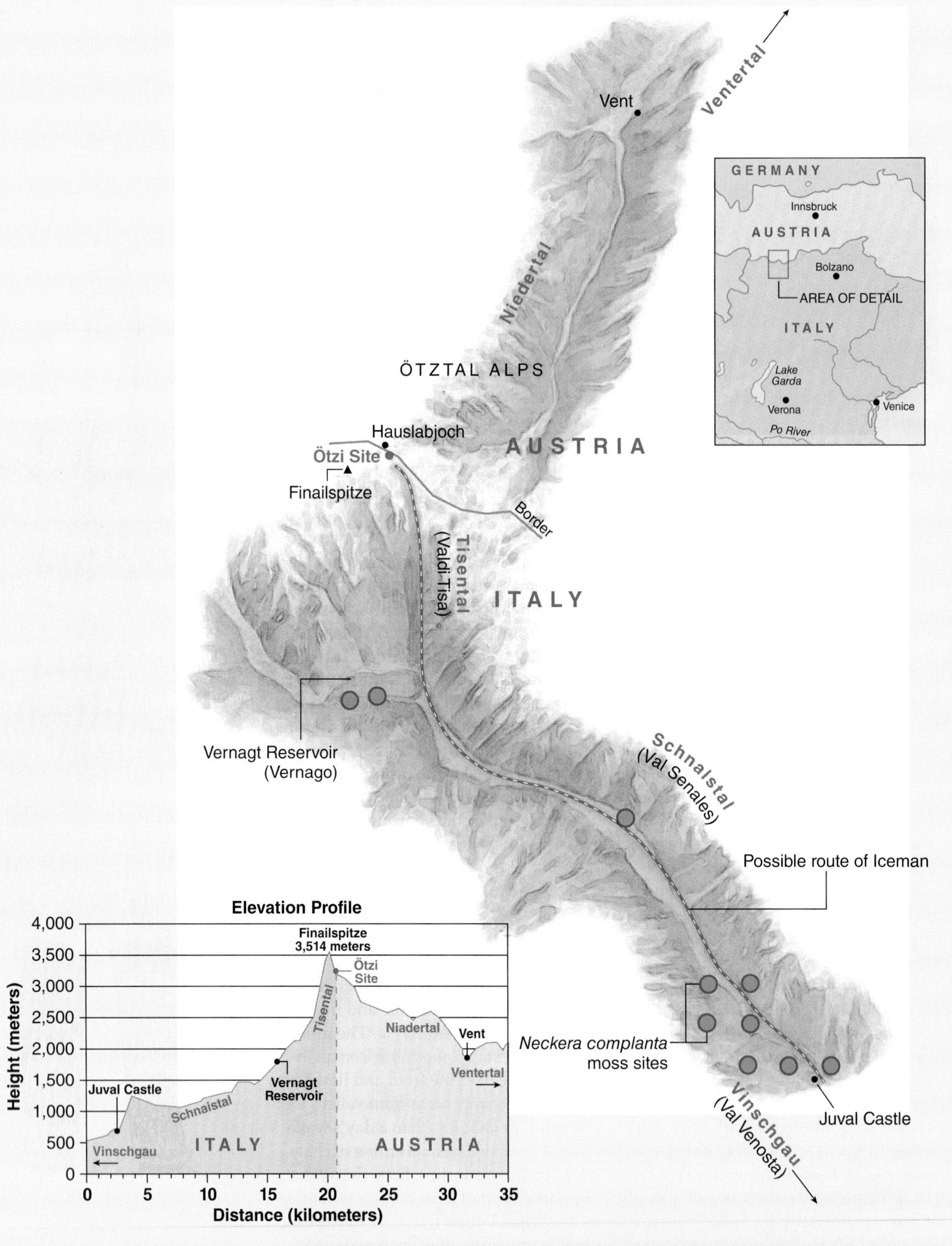


**Figure 11.13** The location of the find of the Iceman and relevant geographic areas. Several lines of evidence suggest that he came from the south into the high Alps.
From James H. Dickson, Klaus Oeggl, and Linda L. Handley. 2003. The Iceman Reconsidered. *Scientific American.*

as *Neckera complanata* were found in his intestines, perhaps used to cover and protect the food that he carried and ate. This species of moss grows only on the southern slopes of the Alps and also indicates that region of Italy as the place from where he came (Figure 11.13).

Another line of evidence comes from the isotopes in his teeth, which provide a record of the place of his birth. These isotopes originate in rocks and soil and differ from place to place. The isotopes get into our teeth through the foods we eat. Tooth enamel forms during childhood and does not change during our adult lives. Isotopes of strontium in the food that the Iceman ate as a young child, found in his tooth enamel, also point to a location to the south in Italy as his place of origin.

Until recently, there were several theories about how the Iceman died in the high Alps, involving either an accident or some kind of escape. Some suggested he may have been a shepherd in the mountains, caught by an early fall blizzard. However, more recent study of the body has revealed several wounds. Deep cuts to his hand and wrist suggest he was in an armed struggle, and an arrowhead lodged in his back may well have been the cause of death. It now seems that the Iceman died as a result of violent conflict.

The Iceman is one of those rare finds in archaeology that attract enormous public attention because of the unusual conditions of preservation. The mysteries of the Iceman—how the body was preserved for so long, and how and why he died—add to the aura of intrigue surrounding the discovery. Equally important, however, is how much we are learning from the Iceman about the artifacts, clothing, and equipment of the Neolithic—and, perhaps, especially how those people were not very different from us.

The Iceman has now been returned to the cold. His body today is displayed through a small window in a large freezer in a $1.9 million exhibit in a museum in northern Italy.

# Charavines

## *A Neolithic lakeside village*

The past is also found underwater. Underwater archaeology has been going on for some time. Although survey and excavation conditions are more difficult, the exceptional preservation of organic materials often makes the effort worthwhile. Perhaps the most famous finds have been of Greek and Roman ships in the Mediterranean, but earlier Bronze Age shipwrecks are also well known. In fact, there have been underwater finds from every period of European prehistory. The Upper Paleolithic cave of Cosquer off the southern coast of France is one example. Numerous Mesolithic sites have been found off the coasts of Denmark and Sweden in the Baltic Sea. Several submerged Neolithic settlements have been discovered and excavated in Switzerland and France. Originally described as lake dwellings, these settlements were thought to have stood over the water on raised pilings. It is clear today, however, that the lake levels are higher now than in the Neolithic, and these villages, once along the shoreline, were submerged after their abandonment.

One of the best examples of such a Neolithic lakeshore settlement is the site of Charavines (SHAR-ah-vans), located between Lyon and Grenoble in southeastern France. The site was originally noticed in 1906 when the tops of hundreds of large wooden posts were seen under the water, approximately 100 m (330 ft) off the shore of Lake Paladru (Figure 11.14).

Charavines was excavated by a team from the Institute for Alpine Prehistory at the University of Grenoble, headed by Amié Bocquet. These excavations, under 2–4 m (7–13 ft) of water, lasted from 1972 through 1986 and produced a remarkable array of food remains and items of wood, bone, fiber, and other materials, preserved in the oxygen-deficient mud of the lake bottom (Figure 11.15). The finds from

**Figure 11.14** Preserved wooden posts on the lake floor at Charavines. The posts were exposed during low lake levels in 1906, revealing the site for the first time. The location of the posts in the modern lake gave rise to the idea that prehistoric peoples lived over the water.

**Figure 11.15** Artist's interpretation of a diver at work. Underwater archaeology takes place all over the world, exploring a variety of time periods.

**TABLE 11.2 The Distribution of Animals during the Later Occupation at Charavines, Based on 504 Individuals**

| | *Percentage of Individuals* | *Percentage of Meat Used** | *Wild or Domestic* |
|---|---|---|---|
| Red deer | 60.5 | 61.0 | W |
| Wild boar | 22.7 | 29.3 | W |
| Goat | 6.0 | 1.7 | D |
| Sheep | 5.0 | 1.7 | D |
| Roe deer | 4.5 | 1.3 | W |
| Cattle | 1.3 | 5.0 | D |

**Estimated meat obtained, assuming all animals were eaten.*

*Centre de documentation de la Préhistoire Alpine*
*53 rue du Drac, 38000 Grenoble (France)*
*Tél/Fax: (33) 04 76 96 34 24*
*Préhistoire.CDPA@wanadoo.fr*
*http://perso.wanadoo.fr/..ctredocumprehistalpine/cha8an.htm*

this site prompted Bocquet to humorously suggest changing the other name for the Neolithic from the Stone Age to the "wood age." Hundreds of specialists have worked for years analyzing the various materials recovered in the excavations.

The excavations at Charavines revealed that there had been two major phases of occupation along this lakeshore more than 5000 years ago. Each one lasted 20–25 years, separated by about 3 years of abandonment. This detailed information is based on dendrochronological analysis of the wooden beams used in house construction. Most of the beams have traces of bark remaining, so the date when the trees were felled can be determined from the state of growth of the tree rings. Fir trees were felled during winter for timber to build the first two houses at Charavines; 9 years later, new posts were cut and used to rebuild the houses, and 8 years later they were rebuilt again.

The number of structures per settlement phase ranged from three to eight. The excavators were able to map

**Figure 11.16** Artist's interpretation of the Neolithic village at Charavines around 2600 B.C. The age has been determined by the dendrochronology of the wooden construction posts. The dendrochronology permits very detailed determination of the year of the construction of the houses.

the precise locations of the houses. The house contents were preserved on the mud floors. Houses were large, 10–12 m (40–50 ft) long and 3–4 m (10–14 ft) wide. Low platforms of clay were built on the floors for the hearths. Different activity areas and trash dumps were apparent from the distribution of artifacts and other materials at the site (Figure 11.16).

The food remains are remarkable; millions of fruit pits, nutshells, and seeds have been collected. The excellent preservation provides an unusual opportunity to reconstruct the complete diet of a prehistoric people. The diet of the inhabitants of Charavines was varied and nutritious. The occupants practiced farming, collecting, hunting, and fishing to obtain the foods they needed. A sizable portion of the diet came from wild sources.

The animal bones at Charavines provide evidence of meat in the diet. The bones from the later phase of settlement represent at least 504 animals from numerous species (Table 11.2). Although there are several domesticated animals, they represent fewer than 10% of the animals in the diet by weight. Wild animals provided the bulk of the meat.

The plant foods included a variety of dried or charred grains, seeds, nuts, berries, and fruits. More than 80 species of plants were found in the deposits at Charavines, including 17 species of weeds. Cultivated plants included three kinds of wheat, as well as barley, flax, and poppy. Several herbs, including oregano and thyme, were present. Fruits, nuts, and berries included wild apples, strawberries, plums, sloe berries, acorns, walnuts, hazelnuts, pine nuts, and beech seeds. Other wild plants included carrots, grapes, a material used as tinder for starting fires, and wild roses.

Food-preparation techniques can be determined from the preserved remains. Whole dried apples are preserved in the deposits at the site, along with baked breads and other materials (Figure 11.17). Cooking utensils such as wooden spoons and whisks, and baking stones for making bread, were also found. Both gardens and fields were used for growing plants. Small gardens next to the houses were used for herbs, spices, medicinal plants, and some vegetables. Agricultural fields were used for cereal crops of wheat and barley. Cultivating tools such as antler hoes were found in large numbers at the site.

A great deal of information on the technology of the inhabitants is preserved in the submerged layers at Charavines. The abundant wooden objects include bows and arrows; handles for axes, knives (Figure 11.18), and other tools; canoes and paddles; and planks for construction. Textiles and tools for cloth making are preserved as well, including spindle whorls for spinning yarn from wool and flax fiber, wooden combs used as weaving tools, and bone needles for sewing. Numerous pieces of rope and string were also found, as were beads and pendants of shell and various stones.

Other items at Charavines document long-distance trade during the Neolithic. Some of the flint used for daggers came from a source known as Grand Pressigny in northern France. An amber bead must have originally come from the shores of the Baltic, hundreds of kilometers to the north. Stone for a polished axe was brought from Switzerland or southwestern Germany. Clearly, there were connections for trade and exchange across large areas of Europe, even during the Neolithic.

Prehistoric sites with preservation such as that at Charavines are rare and for that reason are all the more important. Certainly, the information gained in the recovery of this underwater treasure was well worth the time, effort, and money expended.

**Figure 11.17** Apples dried for storage. They were preserved among the many organic materials from Charavines in the wet lake sediments.

**Figure 11.18** Two hafted flint knives. These extraordinarily rare examples show the craftsmanship involved in the technology of the Neolithic. The haft is wood, lashed to the flint blade with strands of bark fiber.

*Concept*

# The Megaliths of Western Europe

## *Trademark tombs of the first farmers*

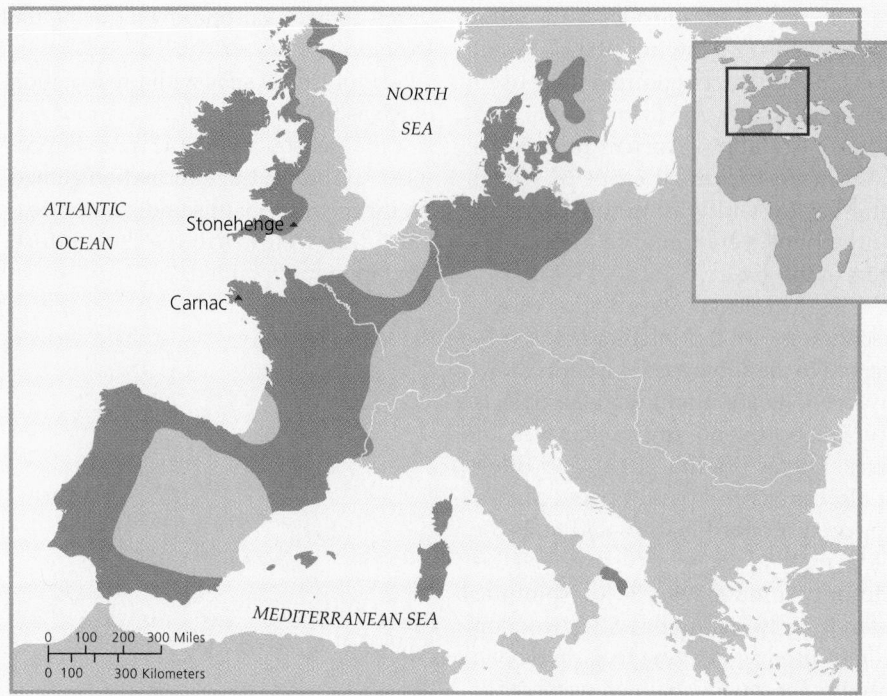


**Figure 11.19** The distribution of megalithic tombs (shaded areas) in western Europe and the location of Stonehenge, England, and Carnac, France. Notice that there are concentrations of tombs in some areas and a relative absence in other regions. Generally, the distribution of the tombs follows the Atlantic and North Sea coasts of Europe.

Agriculture spread to western and northern Europe at the beginning of the fourth millennium B.C. Almost immediately, farming societies began to erect structures made of massive stone slabs and boulders. These **megaliths,** as they are called, usually involved a burial area in or on the ground, surrounded by a chamber made of huge stones laid on top of one another without mortar. The entire stone tomb was then buried beneath a mound of earth to create an artificial cave. Often, a covered passage at the edge of the mound provided an entrance for later use of the tomb.

Tens of thousands of these structures are found along the western fringe of Europe, still highly visible today, in Portugal, Spain, France, Belgium, Ireland, Britain, the Netherlands, Germany, Denmark, and Sweden (Figure 11.19). The megaliths are distributed geographically in a curious, patchy pattern that defies current explanation. Different traditions of pottery and house construction were associated with these monuments; apparently, different groups of people built the same kinds of tombs.

The absence of metal objects in these structures makes it clear that they predate the Bronze Age in western Europe. Radiocarbon dates indicate an age between 4000 and 2000 B.C., during the Neolithic. Most of the megalithic structures were built early in this period. Varying greatly in size and in the number of stones used for construction, they were all built to withstand the test of time—to last for many, many generations (Figure 11.20).

The megaliths fall into three major categories: menhirs, henges, and tombs. **Menhirs** are large standing stones, erected either singly or collectively in linear arrangements. Standing stones, either selected as long narrow blocks or

**megalith** A large stone monument.

**menhir** A large standing stone, found either alone or collectively in lines.

shaped intentionally to be set upright in the ground, occur in various heights, usually in the range of 1–5 m (3–15 ft). The largest known menhir comes from the town of Locmariaquer on the peninsula of Brittany in northwestern France. It now lies on the ground, broken into five huge pieces. Originally, this menhir was 23 m (75 ft) tall, the height of a six-story building, and weighed at least 350 tons.

Figure 11.20 A megalithic tomb, or dolmen, in Denmark. The grave itself lies under the capstone. Many of these dolmens and other megalithic tombs would have been buried under a mound of earth.

Perhaps the most impressive of the linear arrangements of these stones is found at Carnac, also in Brittany, where approximately 3000 large stones have been arranged in 13 parallel lines, stretching almost 6 km (4 mi) across the landscape (Figure 11.21). The stones are smaller at the eastern end, around 1 m (3 ft) high, and reach up to 4 m (13 ft) at the western end. The purpose of these linear arrangements is unclear, but they may have been intended to measure the cycles of the moon and predict eclipses. What is intriguing is that a smaller arrangement of wooden poles could easily have been used in place of such massive stone sentinels.

**Henge** monuments, or circles, are defined by an enclosure, usually a circular ditch and bank system, up to 500 m (1600 ft) in diameter. Not all henges contain stones; some appear to have been large timber structures. Stone circles, found primarily in the British Isles, are a special form of alignment with a definite astronomical significance. The best known of these is at Stonehenge (see p. 528), but hundreds of other stone circles dot the landscape of northern England and Scotland.

Figure 11.21 The largest series of aligned menhirs in Europe at Carnac. There are approximately 3000 standing stones at the site in a series of rows. The standing stones are usually larger at one end of the row than at the other.

**henge** A monument defined by the presence of an enclosure, usually made by a circular ditch and bank system, up to 500 m in diameter.

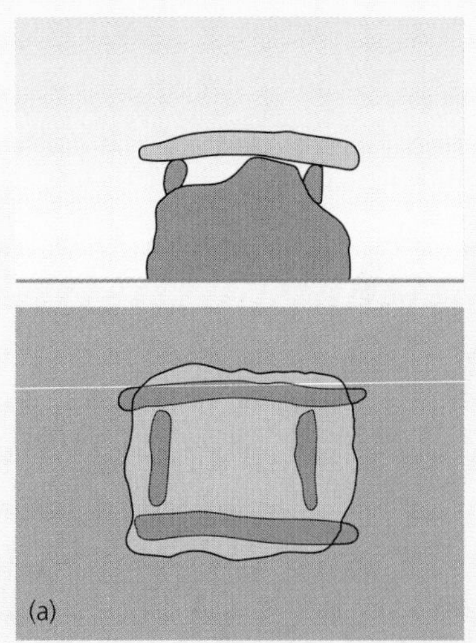


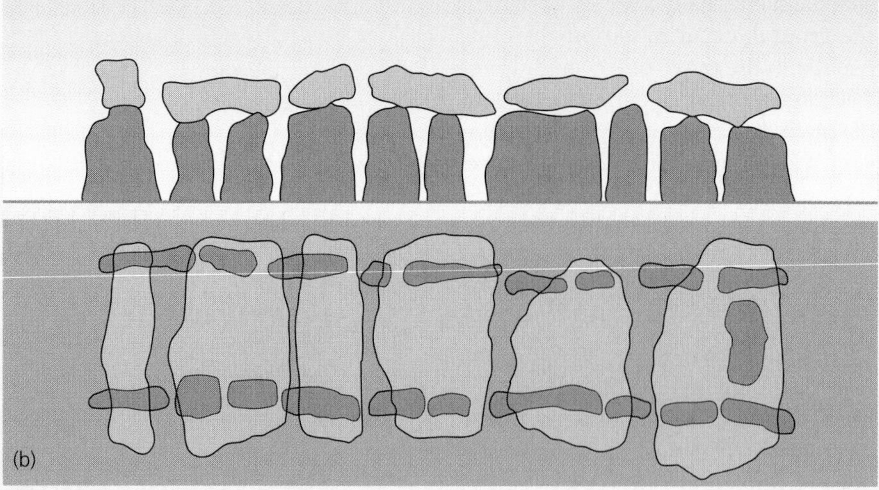


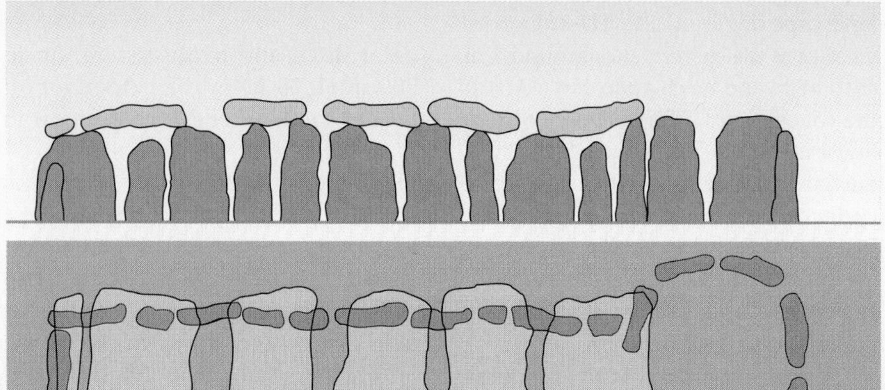


**Figure 11.22** The three major types of megalithic tombs in western Europe: (a) dolmen, (b) gallery grave, and (c) passage grave. The chronological and geographic relationships among these tomb types are not clear.

**dolmen** A generic term for a megalithic tomb or chamber with a roof.

**passage grave** A megalithic tomb entered via a long, low, narrow passage that opens into a wider room, generally near the center of the structure.

**gallery grave** A megalithic tomb lacking an entrance passage; the burial room or rooms form the entire internal structure.

A **dolmen** is a small megalithic tomb or chamber with a roof. Large stones and piles of earth were used to create these chambers. In spite of the enormous amount of labor required to obtain the stones and move them to the site of the tomb, the entire structure was often buried under a mound of earth. Megalithic tombs range from small, single-chamber structures to enormous hills of rock and soil that may hide a number of rooms and crawlways. Passage and gallery graves are two types of these larger tombs. A **passage grave** is entered via a long, low, narrow passage that opens into a wider room, generally near the center of the structure. A **gallery grave,** or long tomb, lacks an entrance passage, and the burial room or rooms form the entire internal structure (Figure 11.22). Some of the tombs had a movable stone door that could be opened to permit the interment of new bodies. Remains of the previous occupants were pushed to the sides to make room. These tombs may have been intended for all the members of a related group of farmsteads or hamlets; the tomb symbolized the collective and cooperative nature of the group.

The earliest examples of megalithic tombs come from Brittany, dating to around 4000 B.C., the time of the transition to agriculture in this area. The first large tombs in Scandinavia at

"WELL, SO MUCH FOR
WOODHENGE."

about the same time were earthen long **barrows,** or mounds, with a single log tomb inside, apparently imitating the plan of a Neolithic house. These earthen structures, intended for the burial of a single individual, could be transformed into larger stone chambers for the collective burial of several individuals.

These tombs served an important purpose for the living as well. Such "cults of the dead" likely involved both ancestor worship and property rights. Elaborate burial rituals and monument construction integrated the cult. Ancestor veneration may have supported claims to agricultural fields for local communities of farmers. The construction of a permanent burial monument provides dramatic evidence of one's tenure in place and the inheritance of rights to the land.

Part of the ritual associated with a cult of the dead apparently dictated that burials be placed in large stone tombs after lengthy ceremonies and activities elsewhere. Only the bones of the deceased were placed in the tombs; the flesh had decomposed or had been removed before entombment. The tombs do not appear to have been major repositories for wealth or elaborate furnishings for the dead. Grave goods are rare; usually, only a few pots, stone tools, and animal bones are found. There is, however, evidence that pottery vessels with food and drink were regularly placed at the entrance of the tombs in ceremonial offerings for the deceased.

Megalithic structures provide dramatic and enduring evidence of the impact of agriculture on the inhabitants of western Europe. Construction of monumental architecture is one clue to the increasing complexity of societies in this area. Shortly after farming was adopted, a pronounced trend toward regionalization began. In spite of the evidence of a widespread cult such as megalithic burials, various regional styles in material culture arose in conjunction with the fortification of settlements and increasing evidence for warfare. It appears that more distinct and delineated societies were identifying themselves across the continent, and this pattern continued into the succeeding Bronze Age and Iron Age.

Megalithic tombs represent a statement placed on the landscape by Neolithic peoples. What is that statement?

**barrow** An earthen mound covering a burial.

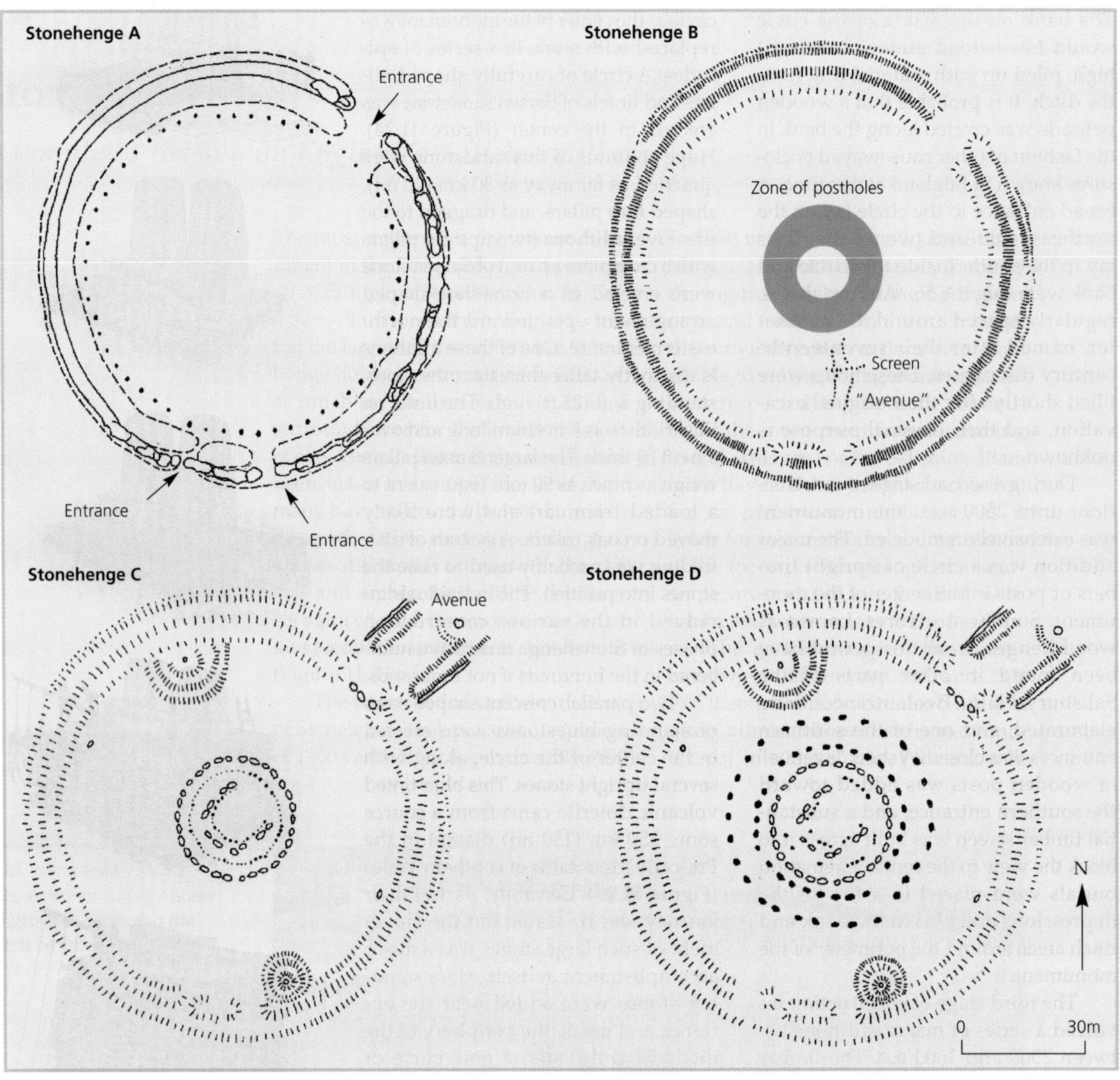


**Figure 11.26** Four major stages in the construction of Stonehenge: (a) a causewayed enclosure with an internal palisade, c. 3000–2900 B.C.; (b) a timber construction with avenue and screen and central zone of postholes, 2900–2500 B.C.; (c) the major stone structure, 2500–1600 B.C.; and (d) the final phase with two rings of pits surrounding the central stones, 1600–1500 B.C.

standing bluestones was placed inside the horseshoe of trilithons. In the final stage of construction, a ring of bluestone pillars was raised inside the Sarsen circle, but outside the horseshoe. In addition, two rings of large holes were dug around the outer circle. These may have held standing stones that are now missing (Figure 11.26).

An "avenue" some 500 m (1600 ft) long and 15 m (50 ft) wide, flanked on either side by an earthen ditch and bank, was constructed running to the northeast from the circle of Stonehenge, leading to the River Avon. This avenue runs through one of the densest concentrations of prehistoric burial monuments in England. The Heel Stone was brought to the site at this time and erected in the avenue about 10 m (33 ft) from the northeastern edge of the circle. This irregular boulder rises almost 5 m (16 ft) above ground level and weighs at least 35 tons (equivalent to an 18-wheel truck).

Stonehenge functioned in part as an observatory to record the summer solstice. On the 21st or 22nd of June each year, the dawn sun rises directly over the Heel Stone. When the weather is clear, the first sunlight passes across the Heel Stone and through the double standing stones at the entrance, bisects the two horseshoes of standing stones, and reaches the altar stone in the very center of the circle. Today, the sun just misses the exact top of the Heel Stone as a result of small changes in the earth's axis since the monument's construction. This shift was used in 1905 by the Royal Astronomer, Sir Norman Lockyer, to estimate the date of the monument as 1900 B.C., an accurate prediction made many years before other methods of absolute dating were available.

Some have argued that Stonehenge was an astronomical computer, used to record various lunar and stellar alignments. One of the more popular theories is that the circle of stone and holes could have been used to predict lunar eclipses. There is no strong evidence, however, for any alignment other than that of the summer solstice.

The last stage of Stonehenge reflects its declining use in the period between 1600 and 1500 B.C. Two concentric rings of pits were added around the stone circles in the middle of the monument. Their function is unknown. In addition, several carvings were added to the trilithons, including a depiction of a bronze dagger.

New fieldwork has begun at Stonehenge in recent years, and the discoveries increase rapidly. Stonehenge was first built about the same time as the timber rings at Durrington Walls and Woodhenge. These wood henges are connected to Stonehenge by an avenue of parallel banks and ditches over a distance of 8 km (5 mi). In addition, the remains of a potentially very large Neolithic village may underlie the construction of the henges at Durrington Walls. Stonehenge served as an important burial ground from its earliest beginnings and for several hundred years. The scientists in charge of the new excavations, Mike Parker Pearson and his colleagues, believe that this avenue connected the living (wood) with the dead (stone) domains in this sacred landscape.

Preserving Stonehenge has been a problem for British archaeology in recent years. Although it is a mecca for tourists to England, just behind the Tower of London in popularity, the wear and tear wrought by visitors has led to more careful regulation of the monument grounds. Years of postwar tourism had dire consequences—inquisitive fingers wore down the engravings on the stones, and the weight borne by millions of feet eroded the ground down to the chalk bedrock. At the summer solstice in late June, huge festivals celebrated the summer as present-day Druids welcomed the sunrise. Today, most of the monument is not directly accessible; walkways direct the visitor past the mute sentinels of the past. While such means of protection distance the visitor from the stones, they do serve to help ensure that Stonehenge and its heritage will remain for the future as a monument to and from the ancient Britons.

*What is Stonehenge: it is the roofless past;*
*Man's ruinous myth; his uninterred adoring*
*Of the unknown in sunrise cold and red;*
*His quest of stars that arch his doomed exploring.*
*And what is Time but shadows that were cast*
*By these storm-sculptured stones while centuries fled?*
*The stones remain; their stillness can outlast*
*The skies of history hurrying overhead.*

—Siegfried Sassoon (1961)

Concept

# The Aegean Bronze Age

*Home of the heroes of Homer's legends*

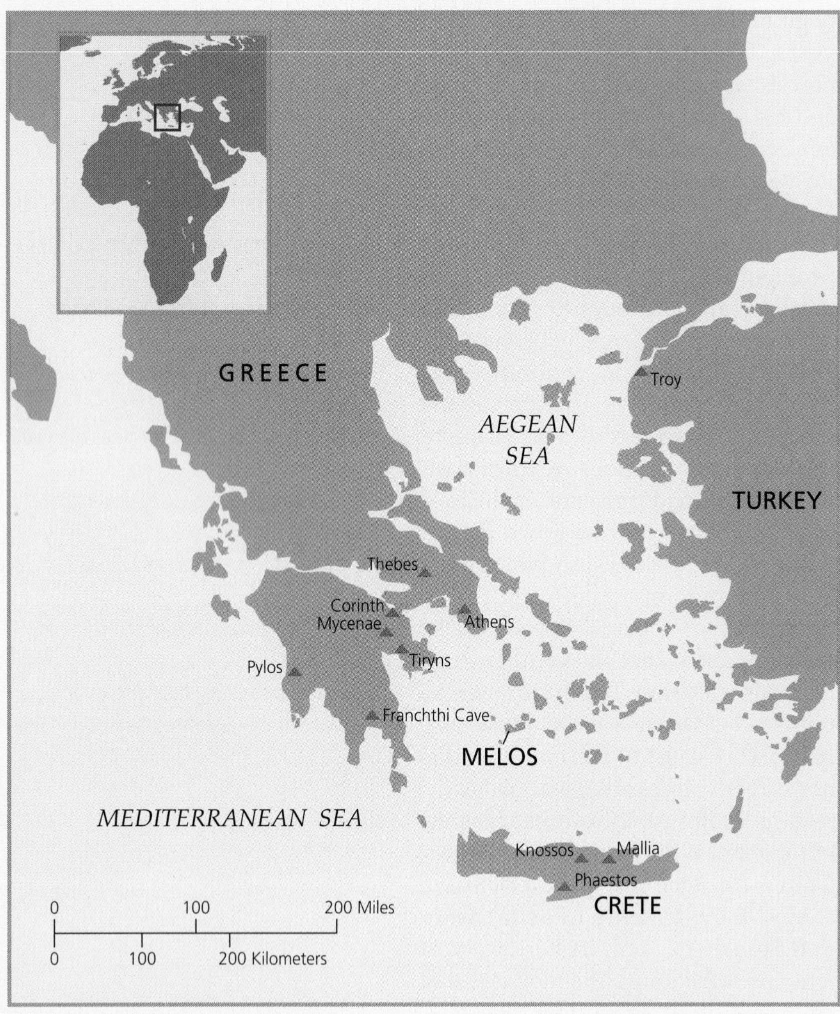


**Figure 11.27** Locations of important Minoan and Mycenaean sites in the Aegean region. Only a small number of the Aegean islands are shown, including Melos, the source of obsidian during the Mesolithic.

The wine-dark waters of the Aegean Sea bathe the shores of Turkey to the east and Greece to the north and west. The long, mountainous island of Crete marks the southern limits of this sea. The Aegean is splattered with small, rocky, volcanic islands, actually the summits of a submerged mountain range, with thin, poor soils and a dry climate (Figure 11.27).

These rugged, barren conditions may have been a hidden benefit for the early inhabitants. The absence of large areas of fertile farmland meant that crops other than cereals had to be cultivated. Wheat could be grown in more sheltered areas with deeper soils, but grapes, olive trees, and sheep flourished on the rocky slopes of the islands. Olives are remarkably nutritious and provide oil that can be burned, eaten, cooked, or rubbed on the skin and hair. Not only are grapes a delicious fruit, but their fermented juice is wine. Oil, wine, and wool became important exports for the economies of these small islands. The inhabitants must have also relied on the sea for fish and other foods; sailing and a knowledge of the sea would have been an essential part of life.

Seafaring and trade permitted the movement of goods and foods between islands, and between the islands and the mainland. The strategic location of Crete and the Aegean islands along the main avenues of sea trade enabled the inhabitants to become the middlemen in moving goods between the civilizations of Egypt and Southwest Asia and the settlements of Europe.

The demand for wine, olive oil, pottery, textiles, and other goods enhanced the economic well-being of the people of the Aegean islands. A pattern was apparently established rather early in which raw materials were taken to the islands and made into finished products. Craftworkers used the potter's wheel to make fine ceramic vessels. Others carved stone, bone, and ivory seals for marking economic transactions; produced wooden tools; sculpted figurines and bowls of marble, obsidian, and other colorful stones; or created jewelry and other luxury items. After 3000 B.C., the craftworkers of the Aegean also began to make objects of metal: bronze, silver, and gold. Smiths produced bronze tools and weapons by the thousands for both

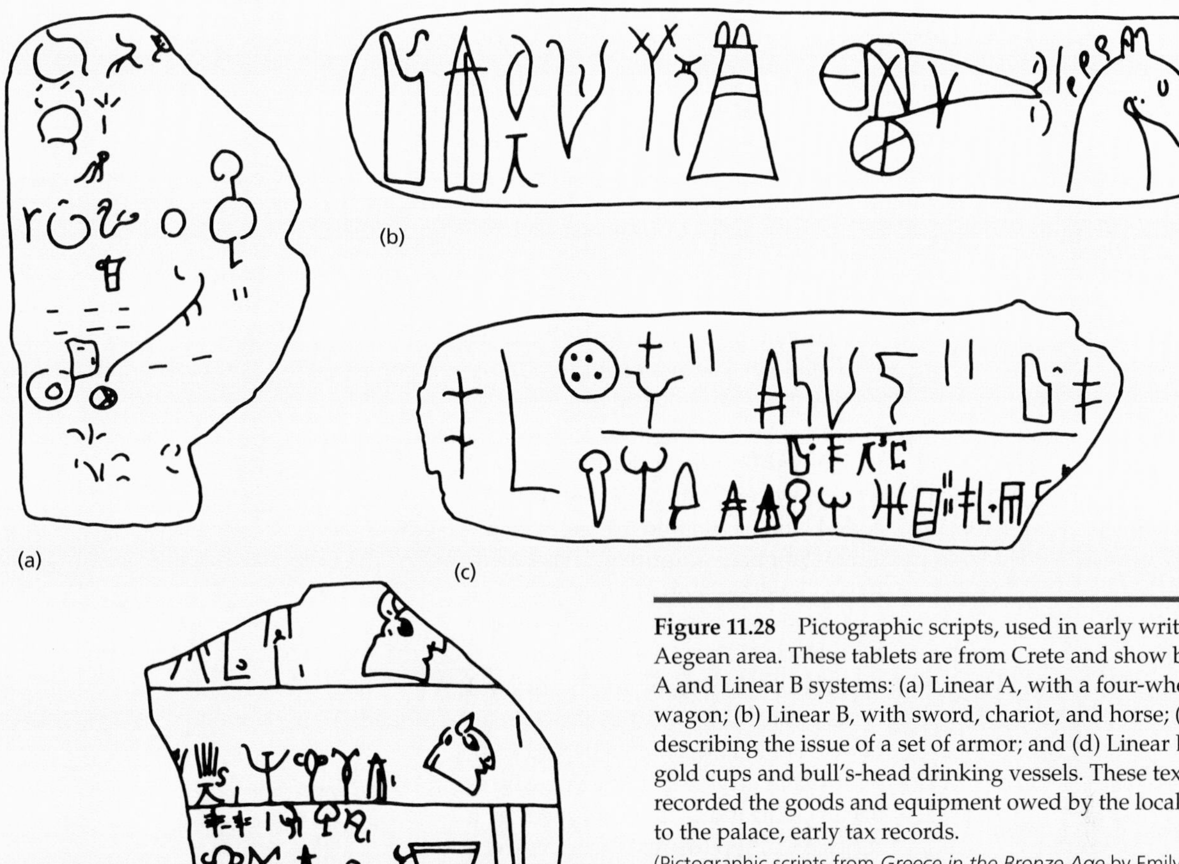


**Figure 11.28** Pictographic scripts, used in early writing in the Aegean area. These tablets are from Crete and show both Linear A and Linear B systems: (a) Linear A, with a four-wheeled wagon; (b) Linear B, with sword, chariot, and horse; (c) Linear B, describing the issue of a set of armor; and (d) Linear B, counting gold cups and bull's-head drinking vessels. These texts often recorded the goods and equipment owed by the local populace to the palace, early tax records.



local use and export. This metal was the signature material of the Bronze Age, and its production was one of the primary reasons for the explosion of economic and political power in the Aegean region.

**Bronze** was discovered, probably by accident, shortly before 3000 B.C. Bronze is a mixture of copper and tin or arsenic. Copper ores often contain some arsenic naturally. In all likelihood, early smiths discovered that those ores that included arsenic produced a slightly harder material that was easier to cast. Further experimentation must have led to the discovery of tin as another alloy, and bronze metallurgy had begun. Bronze has several advantages over copper. It can be recycled repeatedly, whereas copper loses its tensile strength in recasting. Bronze also holds an edge much better than copper, and most of the early bronze objects were weapons: swords, daggers, spearheads, and arrowheads.

The advent of metallurgy, first of copper and then of bronze, silver, and gold, greatly increased trade and the movement of goods throughout the Aegean region and the rest of Europe. Much of Europe was involved in the movement of materials and goods into the economic magnet of the eastern Mediterranean.

The Aegean Bronze Age dates to about 3000–1000 B.C., ending with the beginning of the Iron Age and the rise of the classical Greek civilization of Plato and Homer. There were two major centers of development and power in the Aegean: one on Crete and one on mainland Greece. The civilization that emerged on the island of Crete was known as the Minoan and reached

**bronze** A hard, durable metal made from a mixture of copper and tin or arsenic.

its peak between 2000 and 1450 B.C. During this period, the Minoans dominated the Aegean through sea power and the control of trade in the eastern Mediterranean. The seats of power on Crete were palaces and villas, residences of the local rulers who directed this early state. Defensive fortifications were not needed by the islanders; they were protected by their ships.

Three writing systems were used on Crete, including an early hieroglyphic system, replaced around 1700 B.C. by a system known as Linear A, which is still undeciphered. A second writing system, Linear B, has been decoded and is related to the archaic Greek language (Figure 11.28). Linear B was developed on mainland Greece and later introduced to Crete by the Mycenaeans.

The Mycenaeans on mainland Greece controlled most of the Aegean between 1600 and 1100 B.C. and took over Crete after 1450 B.C. The Mycenaean civilization was dominated by a series of hilltop fortresses, or **citadels,** interconnected by roads. These citadels were ruled by powerful warrior-kings, whose graves are among the richest ever uncovered in Europe. Episodic alliances among the citadels led to greater political, economic, and military power, and the Mycenaeans became the major force in the Aegean around 1500 B.C. The collapse of Mycenaean power and the abandonment of the heavily fortified citadels after 1100 B.C. is one of the more intriguing mysteries of Aegean archaeology.

The Bronze Age in the Aegean marks a watershed in the prehistory of Europe. In the Mediterranean Basin, early civilizations rose in the Aegean, on mainland Greece, and later on the peninsula of Italy. These societies were literate and ruled by kings; they inhabited large towns, maintained armies and navies, collected taxes, and established laws. These states controlled trade over large areas and extracted a variety of raw materials and other products from the rest of Europe.

North of the Alps, there was less political integration; societies operated at a tribal or a chiefdom level, on a smaller scale. This pattern continued essentially until the Roman conquest of France and much of Britain, shortly before the birth of Christ. The Romans introduced writing systems and true statecraft into northwestern Europe for the first time. Prehistory ended much earlier south of the Alps, where the literate civilizations of Greece, in the first half of the first millennium B.C., and of Rome, in the second half, dominated the Mediterranean Basin.

**citadel** A hilltop fortress, the characteristic settlement of the ruling elite of Mycenaean civilization, 1700–1100 B.C.

# Knossos

*The mythical halls of the Minotaur on the island of Crete*

Sir Arthur Evans, then keeper of the Ashmolean Museum in Oxford, England, traveled to Crete in 1894 and "discovered" an extensive group of ruins, buried under a low mound of soil and collapsed walls, at a place known as Knossos (kuh-NOS-sus). Of course, the local people had known about these ruins for millennia, but his was the first report back to the English-speaking world. Beginning in 1900, Evans spent the remaining 35 years of his life excavating at Knossos. He restored many of the areas he had excavated, rebuilding the walls and repainting the plaster in the vivid colors that had been preserved in the ruins. Today, the palace that he uncovered is a monument to his labor and his vision of the restoration (Figure 11.29).

The first Bronze Age palace at Knossos was erected around 3000 B.C. on top of 7 m (22 ft) of Neolithic deposits that had accumulated for several thousand years. A series of palaces were built one on top of another, each larger and more elaborate, as the settlement and its administrative structure grew.

www.mhhe.com/priceip6e

For a Web-based activity on the Minoan ruins at Knossos, see the Internet exercises on your online learning center.

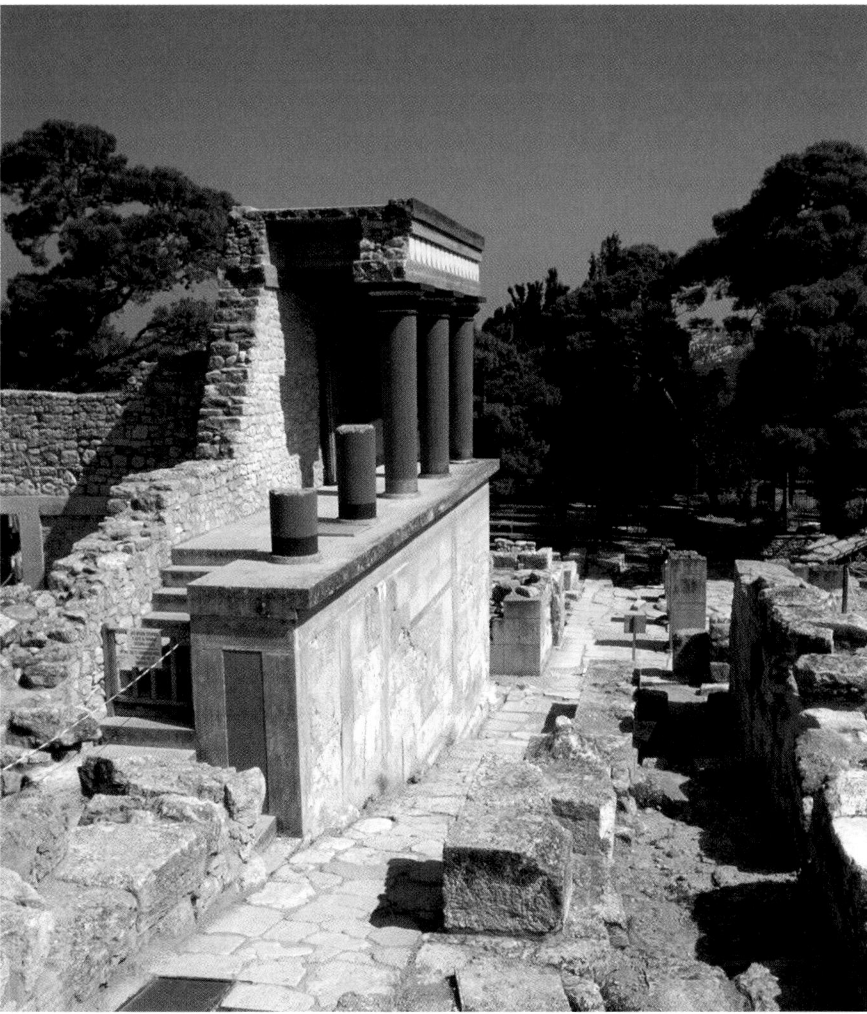

**Figure 11.29** A portion of the reconstructed palace at Knossos, Crete, showing a street and the facade of a building. Large parts of the central area of the site were extensively reconstructed by the excavator Arthur Evans.

Figure 11.30 The plan of Knossos around 1900 B.C., including the palace, several adjacent mansions, smaller houses, and other buildings, along with a system of paved roads. The original settlement at this location was a Neolithic village at the junction of the two streams.

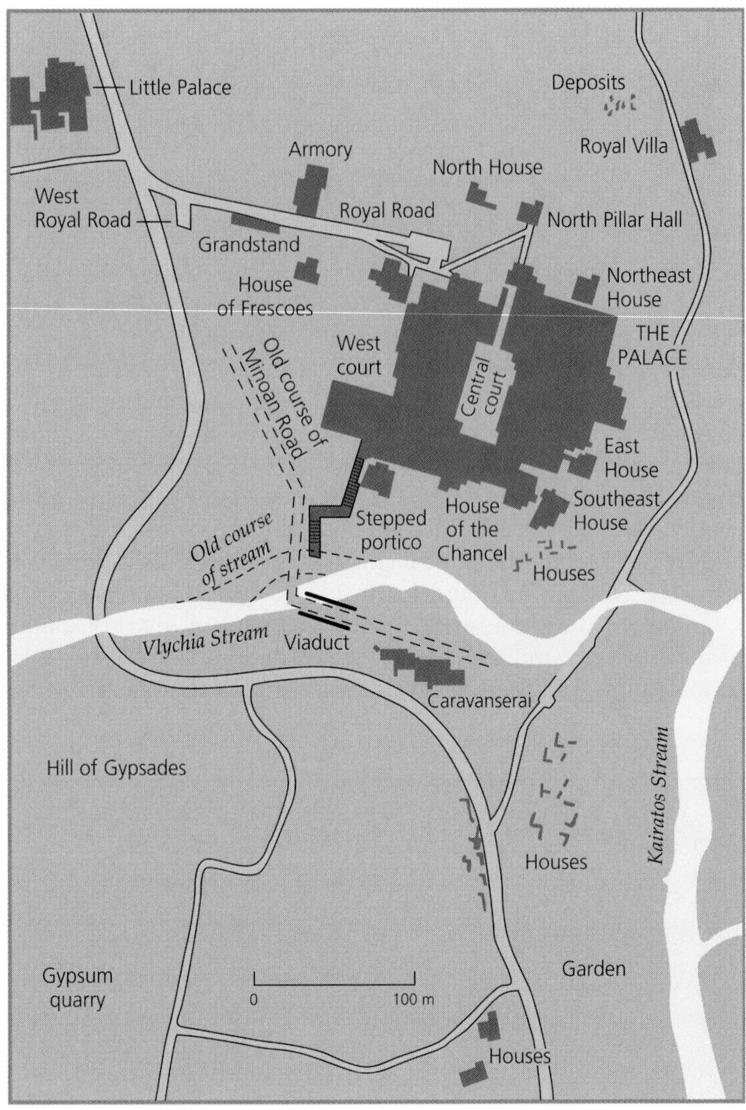


Knossos covers almost 25,000 sq m (6 acres, an area the size of a large basketball arena), in a complex of buildings and construction that included the palace itself, several surrounding large mansions, and many smaller houses, connected by roads (Figure 11.30).

The palaces were the centers of the Minoan state, laid out and built according to plan, with a large, rectangular central court surrounded by myriad rooms, numerous corridors, a maze of courtyards, grand staircases, private apartments, administrative chambers, enormous storerooms, baths, and even a sophisticated plumbing system (Figure 11.31). The complex of rooms and buildings housed many of the administrative, economic, and religious functions of the government. Many important craft workshops were also located in the palace or housed in adjacent buildings. Functional space was carefully designed and separated according to residential, administrative, storage, religious, and manufacturing uses. The palace was a multistory building with extensive storerooms. Long, narrow rooms held enormous storage jars, or ***pithoi,*** along the walls for oils, wine, and other liquids, and stone-lined pits in the floor were filled with wheat and other cereals (Figure 11.32). It is clear from this arrangement that the palace complex controlled the economic activities of the state.

***pithos*** A large clay storage jar.

Frescoes and murals decorated the walls of the palace, depicting various

**Figure 11.31** An artist's reconstruction of the palace at Knossos, showing the multistory building, the large central plaza, and the open nature of the construction.

aspects of Minoan life. Shrines are scattered throughout the palace as well, documenting the integration of church and state in the early Aegean civilizations. Much attention has been focused on the open-bodice costumes of the goddesses and the acrobatic bullfighters who are often depicted. Religious ceremonies appear to have combined several elements, including the bull, a sacred axe, and snakes.

The extensive network of trade that was directed from Knossos and other Minoan centers is evidenced by the variety of raw materials found in the palace: copper from Cyprus and Turkey; ivory, amethyst, carnelian, and gold from Egypt; lapis lazuli from Afghanistan; and amber from Scandinavia. These commodities, and the Cretan ships that carried them, were the foundation of the wealth and power of the Minoan state. The Egyptians feared the "great green sea," but the sturdy Minoan ships, with their deep keels and high prows, weathered the storms of the Mediterranean and controlled the sea lanes.

The palace of Knossos was destroyed at least twice during its history. The first destruction, in 1700 B.C., was marked by extensive wall collapse and evidence of a major fire. Many of the other palaces and villas on Crete show evidence of similar destruction at the same time; it seems clear that a major earthquake must have occurred. Most of the palaces were rebuilt following this episode of destruction. The second period of destruction at Knossos dates to approximately 1450 B.C. and marks the end of the Minoan civilization. The palace was reoccupied following this episode, but the pottery and other artifacts indicate that Mycenaeans from the mainland were in control. Other palaces on Crete also were destroyed at this time, but not simultaneously, as in 1750 B.C. The reason for this last episode of destruction and the collapse of the Minoans is less clear but probably involves the growing power of the Mycenaeans.

**Figure 11.32** Basement storerooms at Knossos. These palace basements were warehouses with storage pits in the floor for grains and huge storage jars, or *pithoi,* for liquids along the walls. Such storage areas reflect the economic primacy of the palace.

# Mycenae

*Fortress of the warrior-kings of Bronze Age Greece*

The Bronze Age in Europe, and its accompanying weaponry, ushered in a period of conflict and warfare in which the skills, attitude, and power of the military seemed to take precedence over other aspects of society. A new warrior class emerged during this period; weapons and armor were the primary burial goods, and martial and hunting scenes dominated decorative art. A military presence is strongly visible in the Bronze Age citadels of southern Greece, the "halls of the heroes." These are the people, so vividly described in *The Iliad* of Homer, who sailed to Troy, on the west coast of Turkey, and eventually sacked the city around 1250 B.C. This is the civilization of Agamemnon and Ulysses. These early Greeks gradually wrested power away from Crete and the Minoans and came to dominate the Aegean between 1600 and 1100 B.C., a time known as the Mycenaean period in prehistoric archaeology.

The citadels, of which the site of Mycenae (my-SEEN-ee) is best known, were fortified palace towns, located on high, defensible points on the landscape (Figure 11.33). The early rulers of the citadel of Mycenae were buried in **shaft graves,** straight-sided pits 6–8 m (20–25 ft) deep, cut into the soft rock of their hilltop settlement. Groups of shaft graves were enclosed in a circle of standing limestone slabs (Figure 11.34). Two such grave circles have been excavated at Mycenae, and several tombs were found in each shaft. The walls of the tombs were lined with brick or stone, and the entire structure was covered with a timber roof. At a

**Figure 11.33** An aerial photograph of the citadel of Mycenae in Greece. The fortresses of the Mycenaeans usually were situated in highly defensible locations.

**shaft grave** A vertical tunnel cut into rock and holding the tombs of Mycenaean elite.

later date, the shaft was reopened and another tomb added. Nineteen individuals were buried in the six shafts of grave circle A at Mycenae, two to five people in each shaft. There were nine men, eight women, and two children.

The grave goods from Mycenae are among the most spectacular finds from the Bronze Age. The graves included precious metals and stone in the form of weapons, vessels, masks, and other objects (Figure 11.35). One early grave in these tombs contained more than 5 kg (11 lb) of gold. There are gold and bronze masks and drinking cups, necklaces, earrings, a crystal bowl carved in the shape of a goose, and swords and daggers with gold and lapis inlays. Ninety swords were found in the graves of three individuals. Amber from northern Europe, ivory from Africa, silver from Crete, glass from Egypt, and great amounts of gold were entombed along with these early rulers. In addition, the corpses were apparently covered with hundreds of leaves, flowers, butterflies, and stars cut from thin sheets of gold.

Heinrich Schliemann, excavator of the graves, described opening one of the shafts in a letter to a friend in 1876:

*There are in all five tombs, in the smallest of which I found yesterday the bones of a man and a woman covered by at least five kilograms of jewels of pure gold, with the most wonderful archaic, impressed ornaments; even the smallest leaf is covered with them. To make only a superficial description of the treasure would require more than a week. Today I emptied the tomb and still gathered more than 6/10 kilogram of beautifully ornamented gold leafs; also many earrings and ornaments representing an altar with two birds. . . . There were also found two scepters with wonderfully chiselled crystal handles and many large bronze vessels and many gold vessels. (Quoted in Vermeule, 1972, p. 86)*

Schliemann was convinced that he had found the gold death mask and body of Agamemnon, who was murdered by his wife's lover when he returned from the conquest of Troy. Although that individual was probably not

*A kind of radiance, like that of the sun or moon, lit up the high roofed halls of the great king . . . the interior of the well-built mansion was guarded by golden doors hung on posts of silver which sprang from the bronze threshold. . . . On the other side stood gold and silver dogs . . . to keep watch over the palace.*

—Homer, describing the home of a legendary Greek king

**Figure 11.34** The massive outer walls of the citadel, enclosing one of the shaft-grave circles and several of the elite burials at the site. The grave shafts were originally filled and covered in the construction of the burial ground.

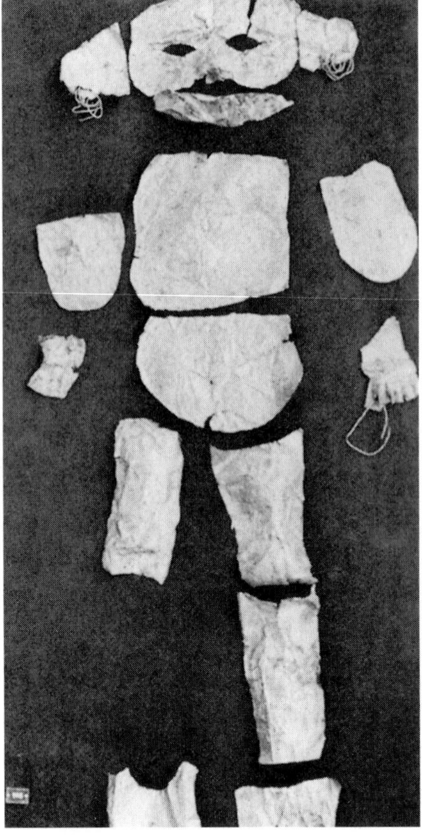

**Figure 11.35** A gold suit placed over a buried child at Mycenae. Gold masks were placed on the faces of several of the individuals buried here and at other Mycenaean sites.

*Not even those who lived long ago before us and were sons of our lords, the gods, themselves half-divine, came to an old age and the end of their days without hardship and danger, nor did they live forever.*

—Simonides, in Vermeule (1972)

***tholos*** A large, beehive-shaped tomb, constructed using the corbel arch technique, characteristic of the Mycenaean civilization of Greece.

**Cyclopean** A term describing the huge stone walls of Mycenaean tombs and fortresses; from Cyclops, the mythical giant.

Agamemnon, and the mask may well have been a forgery brought in by Schliemann, the contents of the graves of Mycenae clearly document the wealth of this civilization and its rulers.

By 1400 B.C., a new kind of grave, the huge, vaulted, beehive-shaped ***tholos*** tomb, was constructed for the major rulers. Several of these architectural wonders still stand today. The Treasury of Atreus at Mycenae is the finest example of a *tholos* tomb. The roof of the vault stands more than 13 m (40 ft) above the floor, which is 15 m (50 ft) in diameter. The dramatic doorway to the tomb is 5 m (16 ft) high, and the lintel across the door weighs more than 100 tons (Figure 11.36). Unfortunately, the contents of the tomb were stolen long ago.

Many large and small settlements from this time period were scattered across southern Greece. A sophisticated system of graveled roads for chariots and carts, with stone bridges and culverts, connected the towns and villages. Mycenaean towns were heavily fortified with stone walls known as **Cyclopean** walls because of their massive size. Major citadels from this period are known from Mycenae itself: Tiryns, Pylos, and Thebes. At the citadel of Tiryns, the great walls are 15 m (50 ft) thick and contain internal passages.

At Mycenae, the hilltop was leveled and terraced to accommodate the walls of the fortress as well as the inhabitants of the palace and town. A long, narrow road, flanked by high stone walls, leads up to the Lion Gate, the entrance to the citadel, so named because of the enormous stone sculpture of two lions that crowns the gate. The monumental stone walls of Mycenae encircle an area 1100 m (3500 ft) in diameter (the equivalent of two city blocks), enclosing the palace of the king as well as a number of residences and other structures.

The Mycenaean palaces combined many of the administrative, military, and manufacturing functions of the kingdom within the residence of the ruler. Workshops for crafts, guardrooms, storerooms, and kitchens were attached to the rear of the palace. There was a small postern gate at the back of the citadel. During a siege, fresh water was available from a cistern, located at the bottom of a rock-cut tunnel and staircase deep inside the hill of Mycenae.

The surrounding villages supplied plant foods and meat, men, and materials to the lord of the citadel. This information comes from preserved clay tablets with Linear B script. In some instances, these soft clay tablets were accidentally burned in fires that swept the citadels and hardened the clay, thereby preserving the script. The subjects of the texts are primarily economic, dealing with inventories, shipments, and quotas of items to be paid to the palace in tribute.

At the palace of Pylos, where a major hoard of tablets was preserved, a list of different occupations in the kingdom was recorded: bakers, bronzesmiths, carpenters, heralds, masons,

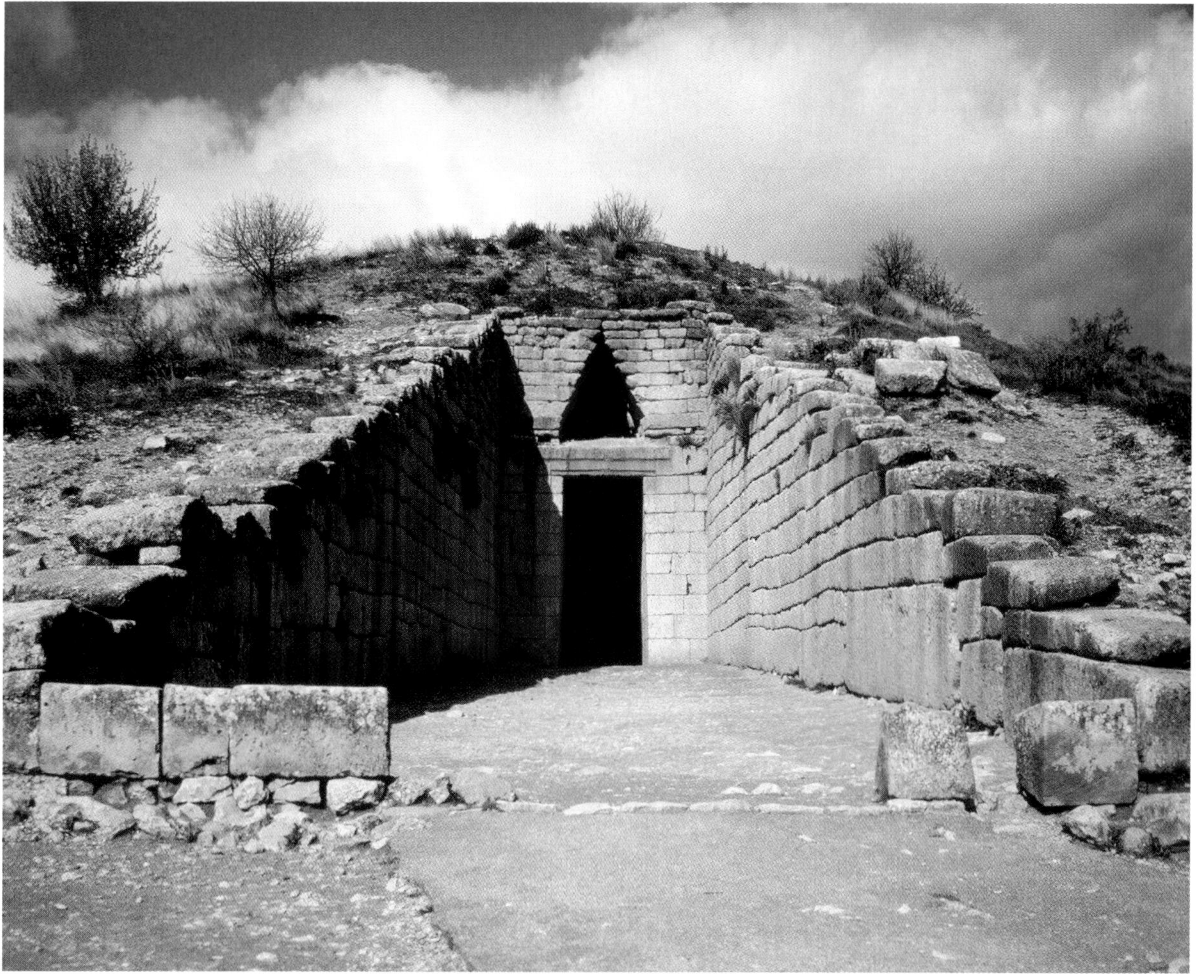

**Figure 11.36** The entrance to a *tholos* tomb, in which the later kings of Mycenae were buried. This example at Mycenae is called the Treasury of Atreus and dates to 1400 B.C. These monumental constructions were architectural wonders both then and now.

messengers, potters, shepherds, and "unguent boilers." Many other skills are also evidenced in the artifacts and architecture of the citadel, such as delicate ivory carving, fresco painting, metal inlaying, and arms manufacturing.

The reason for the collapse of Mycenaean civilization remains a mystery. Unrelated to drought or outside conquest, perhaps it was simply the result of a culmination of centuries of conflict and competition. After 1100 B.C., Athens began to assert its importance in Greece as the center of the new industry of ironworking, and the citadels of the Mycenaeans fell into disuse. Power shifted for a brief period to the north, to Macedonia, the realm of Philip and his son Alexander the Great. The Iron Age civilization of classical Greece blossomed from 600 to 300 B.C. and gave rise to the golden age of Athens, the exploits of Pericles, the wisdom of Socrates and Plato, the inventions of Archimedes, the writings of Homer, and the foundations of much of Western civilization.

Concept

# The Bronze Age North of the Alps

## *Innovation and growing populations*

One of the more pronounced trends in the European Neolithic was regionalization, the development of distinctly local traditions. Initial farming cultures expanded over broad regions (Figure 11.37). Settlements were generally located in open and unprotected spaces, and pottery styles were similar across very large areas. Very quickly, however, population growth and the development of permanent field systems resulted in competition and conflict between groups. By 3000 B.C., the continent was occupied by well-entrenched farming populations making stone tools and pottery—cultivating, trading, and fighting.

Later Neolithic settlements were often located in defensible positions and heavily fortified. Pottery styles became more limited in their distribution. At the same time, trade and exchange expanded in scope. A variety of materials and finished goods were moved long distances across Europe. Obtaining raw materials, manufacturing trade items, and transporting finished goods became an important part of Neolithic economic systems. Flint, for example, was mined in Denmark, Belgium, England, and elsewhere and polished into fine axes for trade.

Metals appeared later in the northern part of Europe than in the Aegean area. Copper first appeared north of the Alps around 4000 B.C., coming primarily from southeastern Europe. Bronze objects began to appear in graves and cemeteries of farming settlements in this region after 2000 B.C. By this time, Bronze Age cultures in the eastern Mediterranean had developed into powerful political entities through a combination of alliances, sea power, craft production, and the control of trade.

The eastern Mediterranean acted like a magnet for the valued raw materials from the rest of Europe (Figure 11.38). Copper, tin, and gold from sources in Ireland and England moved across the English Channel, down the Seine and Rhone rivers in France, to the Mediterranean for shipment to the Aegean. Copper ores and ingots from the Carpathian Mountains in eastern Europe were brought overland through the Brenner Pass in the Alps to Greece. Amber from the Baltic and North Sea coasts of Denmark and Poland was imported to the Aegean. Other exports, such as furs and slaves, may have also been sent in exchange for finished bronze weapons, pottery vessels, and bronze and gold jewelry.

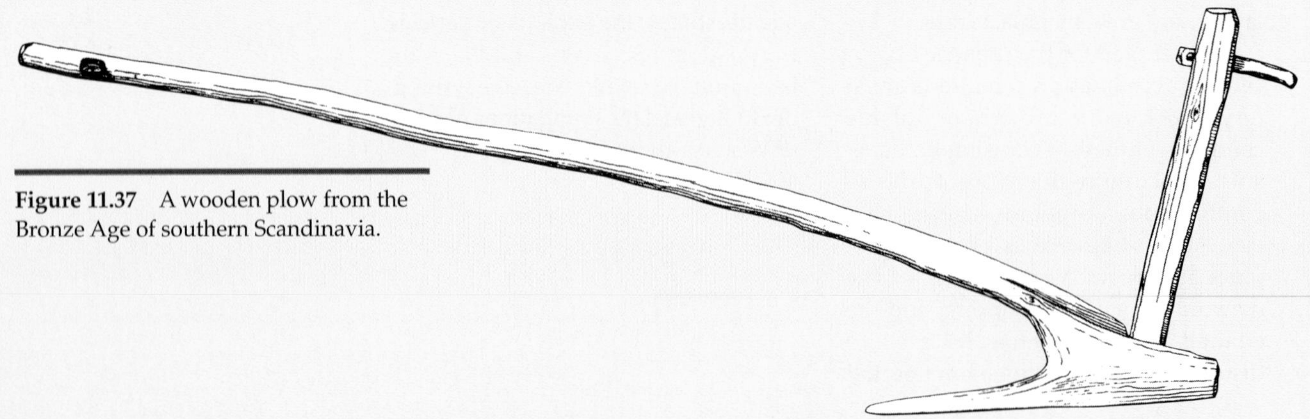

**Figure 11.37** A wooden plow from the Bronze Age of southern Scandinavia.

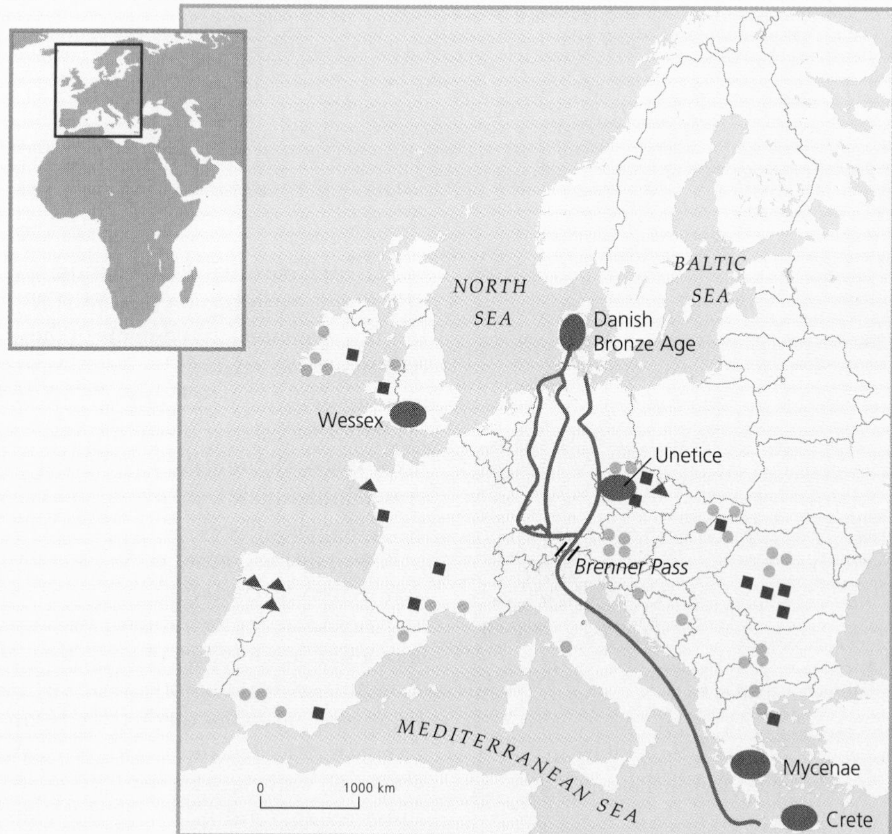


**Figure 11.38** The major sources of gold, copper, tin, and amber in Europe and some of the trade routes to the Mediterranean. Three of the major centers of the Bronze Age north of the Alps were in southern England, Denmark, and the Czech Republic. The exchange of rare and valued materials between the Aegean and the rest of Europe gave rise to a number of powerful societies.

New things and ideas filtered back into Europe along these corridors of trade. The third millennium B.C. in northern and western Europe witnessed a number of major innovations, including bronze and gold, the oxcart and oxen as draft animals, the wheel, the horse and chariot, and new weapons. Secondary animal products such as milk and wool became more important and fostered new industries.

Wealthy and powerful hierarchical societies arose at the centers of these important trade routes in the early Bronze Age after 2500 B.C. The Wessex culture in England elaborated the construction of Stonehenge and erected hundreds of burial mounds, or barrows, across southern England. The Unetice culture in the Czech Republic, known from several "princely" burials, dominated central Europe. The Bronze Age in Denmark and southern Sweden was spectacular in terms of the quantity of fine metal objects that were buried in many funerary mounds and caches. In fact, much of what is known about the Bronze Age comes from large barrows or caches of metal objects hidden in the ground; relatively few houses or settlements have been discovered or excavated. Such information provides a limited but spectacular view of only a small, wealthy segment of Bronze Age society north of the Alps.

*Site*

# Borum Eshøj

## *A Bronze Age tomb in Denmark*

**Figure 11.39** Two Bronze Age barrows (burial mounds) along the coast of Denmark. These burial mounds dot the landscape of northern Europe and were constructed along roads and other routes of transport.

Bronze Age barrows dot the landscape of southern Scandinavia (Figure 11.39). In a few instances, the contents of these barrows have survived, providing a glimpse of the elite of Bronze Age society in northwestern Europe. Dressed in their finest clothing and jewelry, deceased individuals were placed in a coffin, a huge log of oak, split in half and hollowed inside (Figure 11.40). This coffin was then covered with a pile of stones and buried under a mound of cut sods and soil. The coverings of these tombs sometimes sealed the contents from the air, and the log coffins quickly filled with groundwater. Recent studies suggest that water may have been intentionally added during construction. These conditions preserved both the coffins and the contents to a remarkable extent.

Borum Eshøj (BORE-um ES-hoy) was one of the largest Bronze Age barrows in Denmark, located slightly north

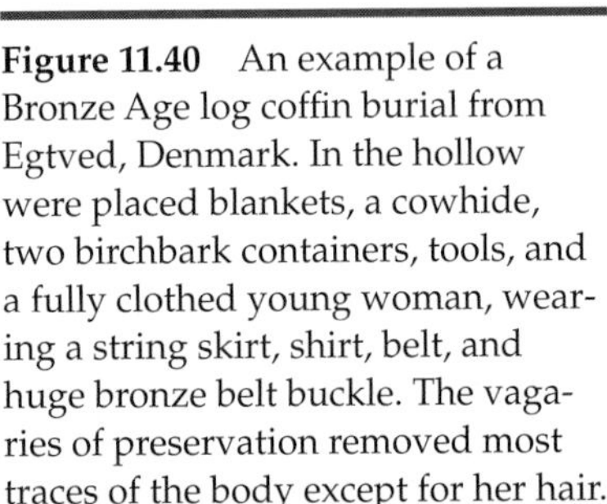

**Figure 11.40** An example of a Bronze Age log coffin burial from Egtved, Denmark. In the hollow were placed blankets, a cowhide, two birchbark containers, tools, and a fully clothed young woman, wearing a string skirt, shirt, belt, and huge bronze belt buckle. The vagaries of preservation removed most traces of the body except for her hair.

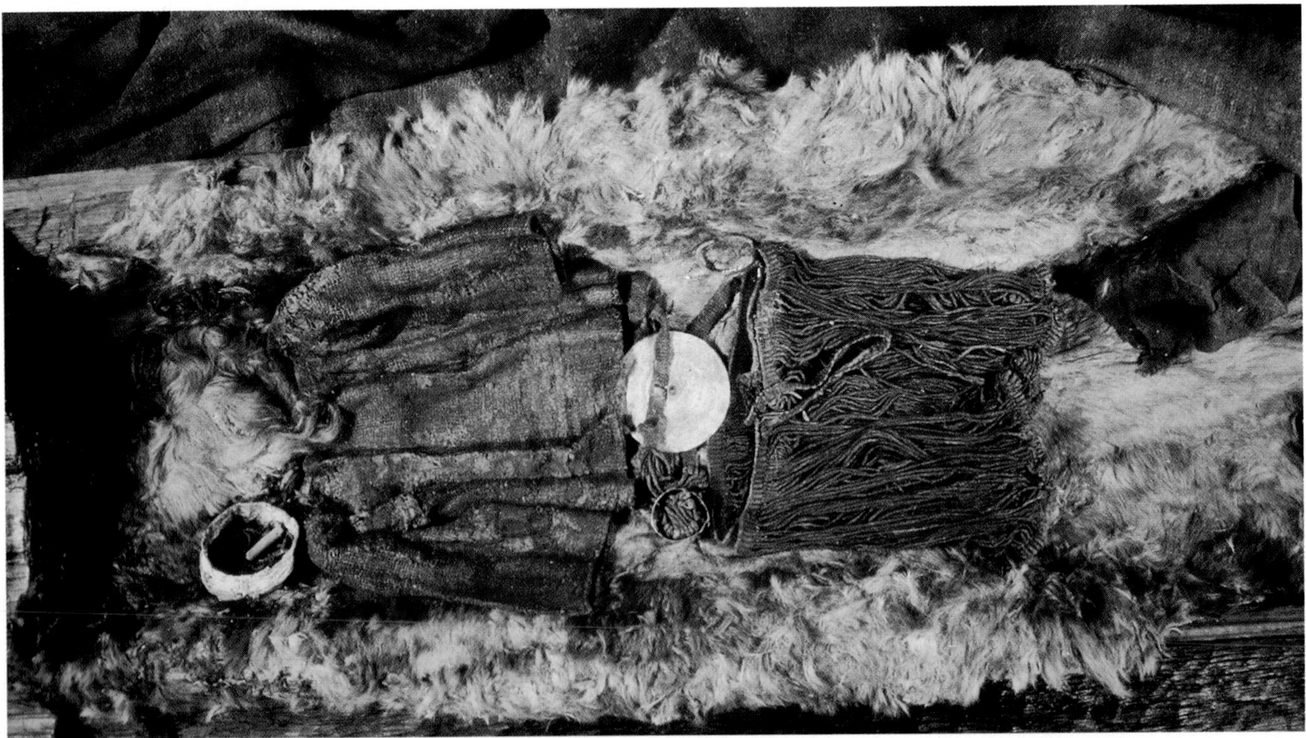

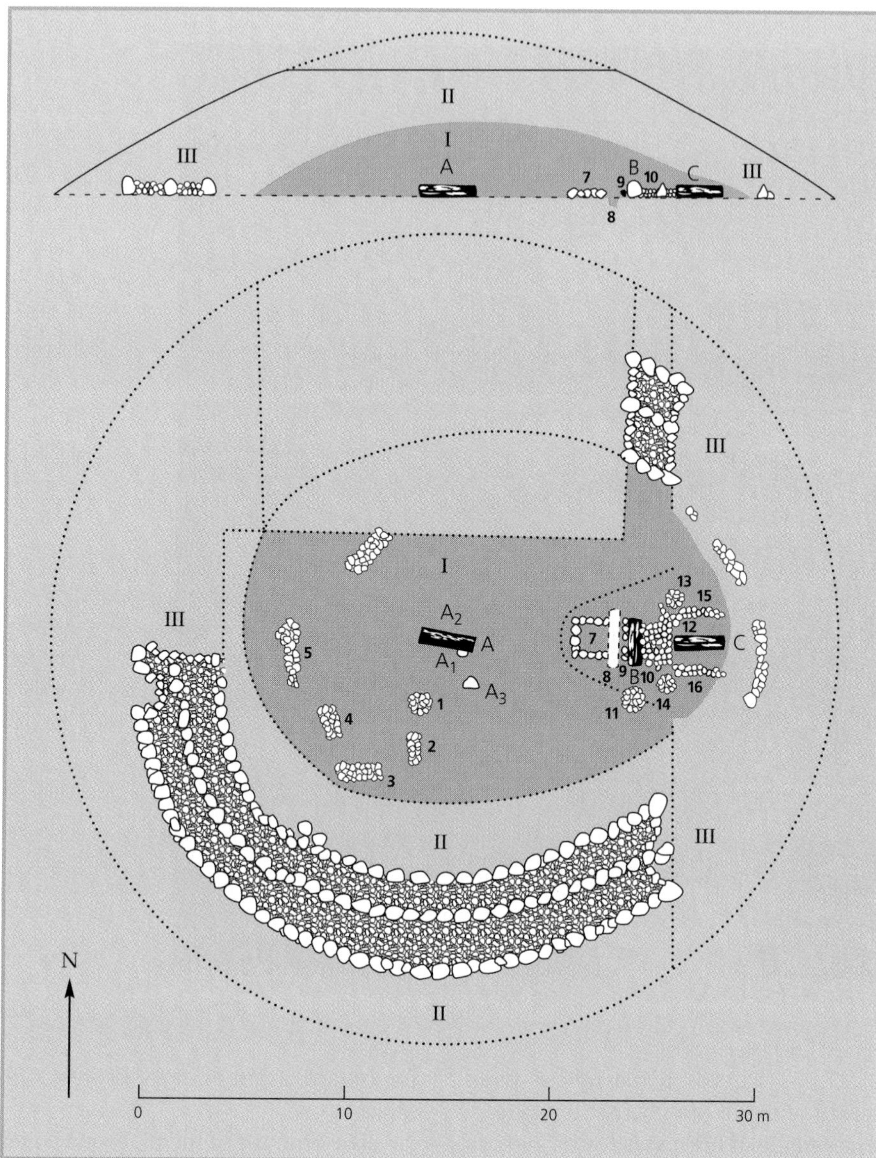


**Figure 11.41** The ground plan of an excavated Bronze Age burial mound at Borum Eshøj in Denmark. The cross section at the top shows the stages of mound building and the location of the log coffins. The plan view shows the stone rings in the mound, the coffins, and other burial features.

**Figure 11.42** A woman's woolen tunic and belted skirt from one of the Bronze Age log coffins, one of the earliest examples of preserved clothing anywhere in the world.

of the modern city of Aarhus (Figure 11.41). The original mound was almost 9 m (30 ft) high (equivalent to a three-story building) and 40 m (130 ft) in diameter. The barrow was first opened in 1875 by the landowner, who was removing the rich soil of the mound to add to his fields. Three oak coffins were found in the mound, containing an elderly man, an elderly woman, and a younger man. The central log coffin was 3 m (10 ft) long and contained the body of a 50- to 60-year-old man, lying on a cowhide. He wore a wool cap over hair that was once blond, now stained black by tannic acid. His chin, also stained dark, was clean-shaven, and his teeth were in good condition. He was dressed in a wool skirt with a rope belt. The body of the younger man, age 20, was found in another coffin. Wearing a wool shirt held together by a leather belt and a wooden button, he was buried with a bronze dagger in a wooden sword scabbard, a bone comb, a round bark container, and a wooden pin to fasten his cloak.

The elderly woman was extremely well preserved. She was 50–60 years old and 1.57 m (5 ft, 2 in) tall. The first item found when the coffin was opened was a cowhide with the hairs still intact. Beneath the hide was a wool rug on top of the woman's body. She was buried wearing a skirt and tunic of brown wool, and a tasseled belt (Figure

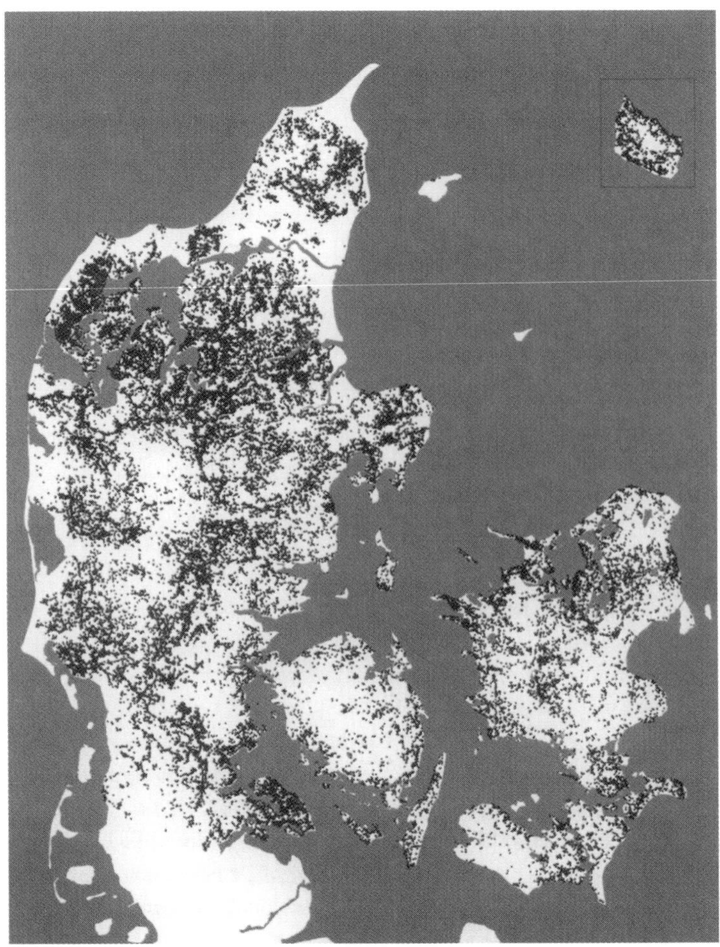

**Figure 11.43** The geographic distribution of Bronze Age barrows in Denmark. Note the distinct concentrations in certain areas and especially the linear patterns that appear in the southern half of Jutland, probably following old road systems.

11.42), as well as a hairnet of wool thread with her long hair still inside. A comb made of horn was found next to her hair. Various bronze objects in the coffin included a pin, a dagger with a horn handle, a belt disk, and rings for the fingers, arms, and neck.

Bronze Age barrows were built for the wealthier members of society and placed near where they had died. Most barrows in Denmark are located in areas of productive farmland, evidence of the strong relationship between wealth and the control of agricultural resources (Figure 11.43). These high, circular mounds were often placed dramatically on the horizon to emphasize the importance of the buried individuals. Lines of barrows follow the high points on the landscape, along old roads and routes of movement. The distribution of thousands of such barrows in Denmark provides some information on the use of the landscape and the organization of early Bronze Age society.

The amount of metal, bronze, and gold in these burials provides some indication of the wealth of the deceased individuals as well. All bronze and gold in southern Scandinavia had to be imported because the ores are not indigenous. Gold was more valuable; only 1 g (0.04 oz) of gold is found for every 1000 g (2.2 lb) of bronze. There are pronounced differences in buried wealth between the sexes and between individuals. Male graves are more frequent than female graves, and they contain more wealth. Some individuals were buried with a great deal of bronze and gold, and some without any, suggesting that social differentiation was pronounced in this region. An elite segment of the population must have controlled most of the resources as well as the trade.

# Vix

## *A princess burial from the Iron Age*

Iron has a melting temperature of over 3000°C (5400°F), and sophisticated furnaces and smelting techniques are required for reducing the ore. Iron making was discovered in Turkey shortly before 2000 B.C. The technology was probably a well-guarded secret for some time, to gain military advantage—iron can cut bronze. The new metal was used initially to make stronger, more durable weapons and later for making more practical tools and equipment. Iron came to Europe around the beginning of the first millennium B.C., slightly earlier in the eastern Mediterranean and slightly later in the northwestern part of the continent.

The Iron Age in western Europe, the time of the Celtic tribes, can be divided into two phases: Hallstatt and La Tène. Hallstatt, the earlier period, approximately 800–500 B.C., was centered in Austria, southern Germany, and the Czech Republic. During the early Iron Age, salt and iron mines in these regions led to economic boom times. The La Tène period followed Hallstatt. The major concentrations of sites from this period are found in eastern France, Switzerland, southern Germany, and the Czech Republic. The Celtic Iron Age came to an end in most of western Europe around 50 B.C. with the Roman conquest, led by Julius Caesar. The emperor Claudius conquered most of England shortly thereafter. Remnants of the Celtic traditions continued in Ireland for centuries, however, largely untouched by the Roman Empire. Germanic tribes in central and northern Europe also remained in the Iron Age on the fringes of the Roman Empire for another 1000 years, essentially until the arrival of Christianity.

**Figure 11.44** Part of the decoration of the Gundestrup cauldron from Denmark, a classic example of Celtic art. This large silver bowl was found in pieces buried in a bog, perhaps as a sacrifice.

Figure 11.45 The ground plan of the princess burial at Vix. The wagon bed in the center was used as a burial platform, and the wheels of the wagon were placed along the wall to the right. An enormous bronze krater (storage vessel) was placed in the upper-left corner of the tomb, along with a number of other vessels.

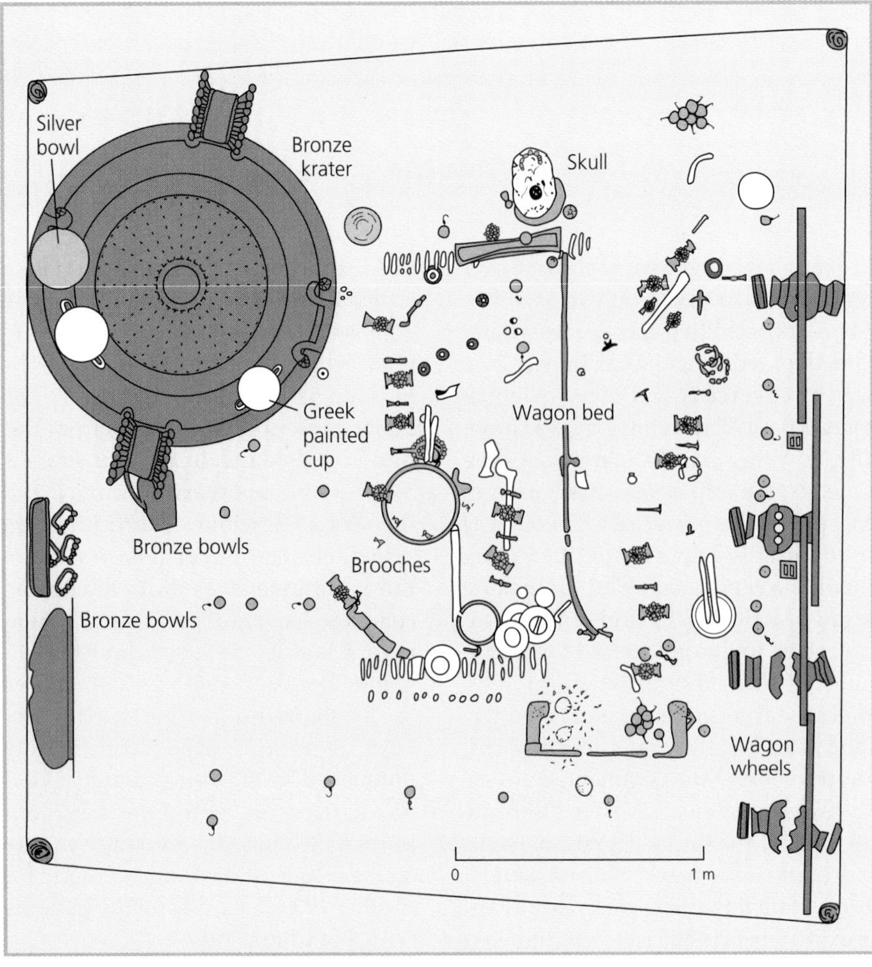

Why did the introduction of bronze cause such dramatic changes in European societies?

A distinctive Celtic art style was practiced throughout western Europe during the pre-Roman Iron Age (Figure 11.44). Both Hallstatt and La Tène are defined primarily by styles of artistic depiction and decoration and by types of pottery. Designs from the La Tène period are both flamboyant and hypnotic. Complex patterns of concentric circles, spirals and meanders, and a variety of bird and animal figures appear on metal and ceramic objects. Disembodied heads with almond-shaped eyes and fierce mustaches; long, fanciful horse heads; and willowy statues of women characterize the tradition. Weapons, tools, jewelry, and everyday equipment were ornamented with this distinctive art.

This art style, along with certain religious practices and beliefs, was shared by several distinct societies in western Europe. These groups were headed by strong leaders and organized along similar lines. Some areas had elected magistrates. Julius Caesar, who encountered these groups in battle and in negotiations, wrote of their social structure, describing three major groups below the king: an aristocratic class of warriors and priests, the common people, and slaves—a stratified society.

The tombs of the elite of Celtic society are among the best-known finds from this period. The grave at Vix (pronounced "vicks") was excavated in 1953 by René Joffroy at the foot of an Iron Age hillfort (oppidum) known as Mont Lassois in northern France. A princess had been buried there beneath an earthen mound, along the headwaters of the Seine River, around 500 B.C. A large square chamber was dug into

# The Past as Present and Future

## *Introduction* The Past as Present and Future

Archaeology is beautiful. The Square Tower House ruin in Mesa Verde National Park in Colorado contains some of the largest and most beautiful of the cliff dwellings in the southwestern United States (Figure 12.1). Archaeology is also fragile; the past doesn't live forever. Archaeology is worth protecting.

To conclude *Images of the Past,* it seems appropriate to turn toward the present and the future, to examine what we have learned in the context of our lives today. The following pages bring together several diverse aspects of archaeology that don't really fit in the review of major sites, finds, and concepts that has filled the preceding chapters. Under separate headings, we consider issues of the relevance of archaeology, archaeological heritage, and ethics. Although these topics are discussed separately, they are in fact closely related aspects of the past in the present. In case you are interested, there is also a section on careers in archaeology.

CHAPTER OUTLINE



*There is no present or future—only the past, happening over and over again—now.*

—Eugene O'Neill


www.mhhe.com/priceip6e

For preview material for this chapter, see the comprehensive chapter outline and chapter objectives on your online learning center.


### THE VALUE OF THE PAST

A very reasonable question concerns the relevance of archaeology. Why should we study archaeology? Why is it important to know about what happened in prehistory?

One simple reason to learn about archaeology is to be able to participate in the contemporary fascination with the subject. Public opinion in the United States is very positive with regard to archaeology. A recent poll revealed that 76% of those questioned expressed a real interest in archaeology and 90% thought archaeology should be taught in school. Reasons for that interest were varied; learning about how people lived in the past, connecting the past to the present, and the thrill of discovery were mentioned. Archaeology is clearly of inherent interest to the general public. Stories appear almost daily in our newspapers and on television. The Internet is crowded with sites about archaeology and our human past.

But the public's fascination with archaeology stems from the inherent significance of the subject. There is, of course, an exciting mystery involved in unearthing treasures from the earth, but, more than that, archaeology tells us about ourselves and how we got to be the way we are. Ultimately, it is the lessons archaeology teaches about our past that convey its significance. The human condition is one that has changed and will change over time. To know our place and to have confidence about where we are going are essential ingredients in the success of our species.

**Figure 12.2** The Rock of Cashel, Ireland, a fortress and religious center dating back to the fourth century A.D.

*Study the past if you would define the future.*

—Confucius, 561–479 B.C.

Gathering and/or hunting constituted most of our human career. The roots of human behavior are to be found in our past as hunter-gatherers. The changes that took place in that period were both biological and cultural: primarily biological at the beginning, almost exclusively cultural toward the end. Our earliest hominid ancestors appeared 5–4 m.y.a. in Africa. The first groups of farmers have been found in western Asia around 11,000 years ago. During the intervening period of roughly 4 million years, our activities shifted from a peripatetic quest for food by small groups of a generic apelike ancestor to an elaborate pattern of intensive food collecting and storing by large groups of fully modern humans living in permanent communities. In fact, hunter-gatherers have continued to exist at the margins of modern society until very recently. Understanding the archaeology of the beginnings of humanness, the origins of fully modern behavior, and our background as foragers is essential to understanding ourselves and our place in nature. In a sense, our life in megapolistic societies with highly structured hierarchical organizations, highly advanced technologies, and extraordinary communication and exchange is too new to be understood without knowledge of the baseline behaviors from which it derived.

Archaeology tells how humans, over thousands and millions of years, have survived and succeeded in the face of the difficult challenges of changing environments and competitive neighbors. We learn how past societies dealt with issues such as environmental change, overpopulation, and political competition. Maybe one of the most important lessons of archaeology is that we are only building on what has been done before.

The role of archaeology ultimately is to describe the course of human development, to tell us about our origins. That knowledge can provide both pride and confidence in our species, along with a much greater awareness of our oneness. Of course, that may not seem so important in an age when recent polls indicate that the majority of Americans do not know that the earth travels around the sun every 365 days and continue to believe that humans and dinosaurs did battle in the past. But then again, maybe that is why it is so important. Archaeology has the opportunity to greatly extend the fundamental contributions that are made to human knowledge and society.

Figure 12.3 Standing stone giant of Easter Island, South Pacific, dating to approximately A.D. 1500.

## THE HERITAGE OF THE PAST

But we also learn larger lessons from the past. The Spanish American philosopher Santayana wrote that those who cannot remember the past are condemned to repeat it. Certainly, there are lessons about the long span of our prehistory on earth and about the evolution of our species and our behavior. In the vastness of geological or archaeological time, the role of humans on the planet is minuscule indeed. Yet the impact of our species is immeasurable.

Although relative newcomers to earth's history, we have an obligation and a responsibility toward all that is around us. Humans have tremendous destructive power as well as creative abilities. Through looting, careless development, and the wanton destruction of archaeological resources, we even have the potential to eliminate our capacity to reconstruct and understand our own past.

*That's the thing about history, it's over before you know it.*

—Garrison Keillor

There is a note, rather a crescendo, of urgency in our quest for scientific understanding of our ancestral history. The archaeological record, under attack from growing populations and global economies, is rapidly disappearing in many areas. The growth of modern cities and transportation networks is covering the earth's surface with concrete, asphalt, and mountains of trash from our consumer society. The industrialization of agriculture results in the deep plowing of sites, the mixing of layers of soil, and the lowering of the groundwater table, destroying the archaeological record. If we are to have any archaeology at all in the future, it is essential that the fundamental information on our past that remains buried in the ground be recorded and protected, before there remains nothing for us to study. This challenge should be a major focus of concern and action in the twenty-first century.

There are a number of ways to help protect the past. One of them is simply to learn more and to tell others of the importance of our archaeological heritage. Public interest and awareness is needed to safeguard the past. A number of organizations of archaeologists and others are working to increase public awareness and support. In the United States, the Society for American Archaeology is notably active in this effort.

Another step is to recognize that no one owns the past—it belongs to all of us; important archaeological sites and artifacts should not be the property of individuals (Figures 12.2 and 12.3). Dealers in antiquities and the market they supply are responsible for the looting of hundreds of archaeological sites each year. Enforcing existing legislation against the import and sale of antiquities is a large part of the battle to save the past.

**TABLE 12.1 The Mission of UNESCO's World Heritage Program**

- Encourage countries to sign the 1972 Convention and to ensure the protection of their natural and cultural heritage.
- Encourage countries to nominate sites within their national territory for inclusion on the World Heritage List.
- Encourage countries to set up reporting systems on the state of conservation of World Heritage sites and establish management plans.
- Help countries safeguard World Heritage sites by providing technical assistance and professional training.
- Provide emergency assistance for World Heritage sites in immediate danger.
- Support activities that increase public awareness of World Heritage conservation.
- Encourage participation of the local population in the preservation of their cultural and natural heritage.
- Encourage international cooperation in conservation of cultural and natural heritage.

A number of organizations are actively working to protect archaeological sites. Two of the larger ones are the Archaeological Conservancy and the UNESCO World Heritage Site program. Both are worthy programs deserving support.

The Archaeological Conservancy, established in 1980, is the only national non-profit organization dedicated to acquiring and preserving remaining archaeological sites in the United States. Since its founding in 1980, the conservancy, based in Albuquerque, New Mexico, has acquired more than 245 sites in 37 states across America. These range in size from a few acres to more than 1000 acres and include the earliest habitation sites in North America, a nineteenth-century frontier army post, and remains from nearly every major cultural period in between.

The United Nations Educational, Scientific, and Cultural Organization (UNESCO) was chartered in 1972 to encourage the identification, protection, and preservation of cultural and natural heritage around the world considered to be of outstanding value. "Cultural heritage" refers to monuments, buildings, and sites with historical, aesthetic, archaeological, scientific, ethnological, or anthropological value. "Natural heritage" refers to outstanding physical, biological, and geological formations; habitats of threatened species of animals and plants; and areas with scientific, conservation, or aesthetic value. The mission of this program is described in Table 12.1. To date, 830 sites have been enscribed in the program, some of which are listed in Table 12.2.

## WHO OWNS THE PAST?

One issue facing archaeology today is growing concern about who owns the past. This issue involves both national and individual ownership. When archaeology was just beginning and European empires controlled much of the known world, soldiers and merchants from the conquering nations returned home with many treasures, both ancient and modern, from the countries they had visited. For example, Napoleon returned from his invasion of Egypt with a number of marvelous ancient Egyptian artifacts and monuments.

A well-known example involving ownership of the past concerns the Elgin marbles. These statues have a long and storied history. After the Greeks defeated the Persians in 479 B.C., the Greeks returned to Athens to resurrect their city, ruined during the war. Their leader, Pericles, rebuilt the city as an artistic and cultural center with many wonderful structures—including the Parthenon—during the 30 years of his rule. The Parthenon took 15 years to construct and was finally dedicated in 432 B.C. as the temple of the goddess Athena, sitting on the Acropolis above Athens as the pinnacle of Greek power and creativity.

**TABLE 12.2 A Partial List of World Heritage Archaeological Sites***

| *Site* | *Location* |
|---|---|
| Prehispanic city of Chichén Itzá | Mexico |
| Stonehenge, Avebury, and associated sites | United Kingdom |
| Angkor | Cambodia |
| Prehispanic city and national park of Palenque | Mexico |
| Heart of Neolithic Orkney | United Kingdom |
| Imperial tombs of the Ming and Qing dynasties | China |
| The Great Wall | China |
| Acropolis, Athens | Greece |
| Archaeological sites of Mycenae and Tiryns | Greece |
| Prehispanic city of Teotihuacan | Mexico |
| Archaeological park and ruins of Quirigua | Guatemala |
| Decorated grottoes of the Vézère Valley | France |
| Archaeological site of Vergina | Greece |
| Chan Chan archaeological zone | Peru |
| Prehistoric rock-art sites in the Côa Valley | Portugal |
| Altamira Cave | Spain |
| Neolithic flint mines at Spiennes (Mons) | Belgium |
| Thracian tomb of Kazanlak | Bulgaria |
| Pont du Gard (Roman aqueduct) | France |
| Archaeological ensemble of the Bend of the Boyne | Ireland |
| Petra | Jordan |
| Lines and geoglyphs of Nasca and Pampas de Jumana | Peru |
| Rock carvings in Tanum | Sweden |
| Rapa Nui National Park | Chile |
| Memphis and its necropolis—the pyramid fields from Giza to Dahshur | Egypt |
| Persepolis | Iran |
| Great Zimbabwe National Monument | Zimbabwe |
| Archaeological ruins at Mohenjo-daro | Pakistan |
| Lower valley of the Awash | Ethiopia |
| Fatehpur Sikri | India |
| Hadrian's Wall | United Kingdom |
| Archaeological site of Troy | Turkey |
| San Agustín Archeological Park | Colombia |
| Jelling mounds, runic stones, and church | Denmark |
| Rock drawings of Alta | Norway |
| Chavín archaeological site | Peru |
| Koch'ang, Hwasun, and Kanghwa dolmen sites | Republic of Korea |
| Rock-art of the Mediterranean Basin on the Iberian Peninsula | Spain |
| Ban Chiang archaeological site | Thailand |
| Mesa Verde | United States |
| Chaco Culture National Historical Park | United States |
| Tiwanaku: spiritual and political center of the Tiwanaku | Bolivia |
| Joya de Ceren archaeological site | El Salvador |
| Lower valley of the Omo | Ethiopia |
| Archaeological sites of Bat, Al-Khutm, and Al-Ayn | Oman |
| City of Cuzco | Peru |
| Birka and Hovgården | Sweden |
| Cahokia Mounds State Historic Site | United States |
| Archaeological areas of Pompei, Herculaneum, and Torre Annunziata | Italy |
| Archaeological site of Atapuerca | Spain |
| Peking Man site at Zhoukoudian | China |
| Roman theater and its surroundings and the "Triumphal Arch" of Orange | France |
| Sangiran early man site | Indonesia |
| Fossil hominid sites of Sterkfontein, Swartkrans, Kromdraai, and environs | South Africa |
| Megalithic temples of Malta | Malta |
| Maya site of Copan | Honduras |
| L'Anse aux Meadows National Historic Site | Canada |
| Head-Smashed-In Buffalo Jump | Canada |

**The sites listed here constitute only a part of the 830 places of great historical, archaeological, cultural, or natural importance protected by United Nations Convention. The list is growing, but not quickly enough.*

Figure 12.4 The Elgin marbles at the British Museum.

Atop the Parthenon, just under the roofline, was a frieze of more than 400 human and 200 animal marble statues. The frieze has a maximum height of more than 2 m (about 7 ft) and a total length of 160 m (about 500 ft) around the four sides of the temple. One of the marvels of antiquity, the frieze depicts the most important annual festival of ancient Athens. During the six-day celebrations, various musical, literary, and athletic competitions were held, including beauty contests, track-and-field events, horse and chariot races, and regattas.

In 1801, Thomas Bruce, Lord Elgin and the British ambassador to Constantinople (Turkey), obtained permission to remove large portions of the Parthenon frieze. From Athens, the marble statues of the Parthenon were shipped to the British Museum in London, where they remain today, known as the Elgin marbles (Figure 12.4).

The Greek government has been petitioning the British government for many years for the return of these treasures, but to no avail. The United Nations, the British populace, and world opinion support the Greek claim, but British authorities counter with statements about setting a precedent for the return of other museum treasures around the world. The British also argue that the marbles were purchased legitimately from the Turks who controlled Athens at that time, that the marbles were removed in order to save them from destruction, and that the Greeks did not care then about the marbles. More recently, the buildup of corrosive air pollution in Athens has been added to the arguments against returning the marbles. One moral of such cases is that there are rarely easy answers to questions about the ownership and/or return of cultural heritage.

To reiterate: No one owns the past; it belongs to all of us. Important archaeological sites and artifacts should not be the property of individuals. Archaeological materials are valuable cultural resources and part of our inheritance. It is essential that everyone understands their significance and works toward their care and curation. Trading in antiquities or disturbing archaeological sites without permission is illegal in most states and punishable by fines and/or imprisonment. Dealers in antiquities and the market they supply are ultimately responsible for the looting of hundreds of archaeological sites each year. Enforcing existing legislation against the import and sale of antiquities is a large part of the battle to save the past.

**TABLE 12.3 Major Stipulations of the Native American Graves Protection and Repatriation Act (NAGPRA) of 1990**

- Federal agencies and museums must identify cultural items in their collections that are subject to NAGPRA and prepare inventories and summaries of the items.
- Federal agencies and museums must consult with lineal descendants, Indian tribes, and Native Hawaiian organizations regarding the identification and cultural affiliation of the cultural items listed in their NAGPRA inventories and summaries.
- Federal agencies and museums must send notices to lineal descendants, Indian tribes, and Native Hawaiian organizations describing cultural items and lineal descendancy or cultural affiliation and stating that the cultural items may be repatriated. The law requires the secretary of the interior to publish these notices in the Federal Register.

## U.S. LEGISLATION AND ARCHAEOLOGY

The first U.S. government legislation to protect the past was signed by President Theodore Roosevelt in 1906. The Antiquities Act described the study of archaeology as a scientific undertaking and protected 167 million acres of cultural and natural significance. The act gave the president unilateral power to create national monuments on government property; the act also enumerated punishment for individuals caught looting or damaging national monuments and listed qualifications for individuals permitted to conduct research. This act was the precursor to a series of subsequent legislative decisions.

The U.S. Congress reiterated the importance of the historic and prehistoric past of the country in 1966 with the passage of the Natural Historic Preservation Act. This act recognized the importance of cultural resources and established the National Register of Historic Places and the legal framework for the protection of cultural resources. Because of growing public interest in the past and a substantial increase in looting and the illicit trade in antiquities, Congress passed the Archaeological Resources Protection Act in 1979 to further help preserve archaeological materials on public and Indian lands. This law defined archaeological resources to be any remains of past human life or activities that are of archaeological interest and are at least 100 years old; encouraged cooperation between groups and individuals in possession of archaeological resources from public or Indian lands with special permit and disposition rules for the protection of archaeological resources on Indian lands; provided that information regarding the nature and location of archaeological resources remain confidential (to prevent looting and disturbance); and established civil and criminal penalties, including forfeiture of vehicles, fines of up to $100,000, and imprisonment of up to 5 years for second violations for the unauthorized appropriation, alteration, exchange, or other handling of archaeological resources, with rewards for furnishing information about such unauthorized activities.

An even more sensitive and contentious issue involves the disposition of ancient human skeletal remains. North American archaeologists have been excavating burials, along with other cultural materials, for many years. By some estimates, more than 100,000 Native American graves have been excavated in the United States and the skeletons placed in museums. The Smithsonian Institution in Washington, DC, for example, houses the remains of more than 16,000 Native Americans collected over the years. Because of growing concern about the excavation of native remains and the desire of native peoples to rebury these remains, Congress passed the Native American Graves Protection and Repatriation Act (NAGPRA) in 1990.

NAGPRA provides a mechanism for museums and federal agencies to return certain Native American cultural materials—human remains, funerary and sacred artifacts, and objects of cultural patrimony—to lineal descendants, culturally affiliated Indian tribes, and Native Hawaiian organizations. The major features of NAGPRA are listed in Table 12.3. Items requested for return must be repatriated to a lineal descendant or related group. Several different lines of evidence are required to determine cultural affiliation, including geographic, biological, archaeological, linguistic, and anthropological evidence. The law also forbids trafficking in Native American cultural or human material and establishes procedures for notification of and consultation with tribes for planned excavation or accidental discovery of cultural materials on tribal property. Because of NAGPRA and similar legislation, the Smithsonian has repatriated more than 4000 sets of human remains to native tribes for reburial, out of a total collection of some 16,000, since 1984.

The repatriation of human skeletal remains is not always a clear-cut issue, however, and this legislation has created several controversial situations, such as the case of Kennewick Man.

### Kennewick Man

The story of Kennewick Man, introduced in Chapter 4, involves one of the earliest known human skeletons in the Americas. Discovered accidentally along the Columbia River in Kennewick, Washington, in 1996, the bones have been dated to 7500 B.C. Shortly after the discovery, a local newspaper story about the find initiated a series of ethical dilemmas, legal actions, court decisions, and publications concerning the questions that arise from the discovery of prehistoric human remains in the United States.

Five Native American tribes in the area claimed these remains for reburial under the NAGPRA legislation. The Army Corps of Engineers took possession of the skeleton, which had been found on Corps lands, and agreed to return it to the tribes. Shortly thereafter, eight archaeologists and biological anthropologists filed an injunction to prevent the immediate return of the skeleton and to allow scientific investigation of this important find. The scientists argued that the remains were important and that they were not demonstrably Native American, questioning the legality of the tribes' claim.

This issue was in the courts and the media for almost a decade (Figure 12.5). In 2002, a judge ruled that the "remains were so old, and information as to his era so limited, that it is impossible to say whether the Kennewick Man is related to the present-day Tribal Claimants." The judge also ordered that the remains be given over for scientific investigation. The tribes appealed this ruling, but an appeals court in 2004 upheld the judge's decision. The issue now seems to have been settled.

**Figure 12.5** The cover of *Time* in March 2006, continuing the saga of Kennewick Man and the first Americans.

The ongoing conflict between science and belief is highlighted in such issues. The public battle over burial rights and the right to pursue knowledge about the past has both underscored and brushed aside the importance of the Kennewick find. This skeleton is important because of its antiquity and also because of the unusual nature of the remains. Questions raised by certain features of the skull demand further investigation to better understand the original inhabitants of the Americas. At the same time, the importance of learning more about the past of all of us is lost in the debate about who should control these remains and how they should be handled.

Kennewick is a special case, a very old skeleton with distinct and unusual characteristics. Thousands of human remains have been excavated in the United States that are not as old and not as unusual. These remains are by law to be given to identifiable descendants who request their return. The issue of responsibility for human remains is one of the thorniest in archaeology. On the one hand, these materials are the remains of ancestors and significant, even sacred, in many cultures. On the other hand, the bones and tissues of these ancestors hold an enormous amount of information about the individual represented and about our common human past. As the Kennewick case shows, the issue is not easily resolved when diverse interests fight for control of such remains.

## ETHICS IN ARCHAEOLOGY

Ethics represent a common understanding among people about what is right and dutiful behavior in human society. Ethics are an important and growing concern in modern life. Ethical behavior in archaeology is increasingly complex, related to issues of heritage, native peoples, treatment of the dead, and the preservation of the past. Several books on the subject have appeared in recent years, and panels on ethical issues are frequently found at scientific conferences. In addition, national organizations have added ethical statements to their bylaws.

The major professional organization for archaeologists in the United States is the Society for American Archaeology (SAA). Founded in 1934, the society has more than 6500 professional archaeologists and students as members today. The SAA seeks to stimulate interest and research in American archaeology, advocate and aid in the conservation of archaeological resources, encourage public access to and appreciation of archaeology, oppose all looting of sites and the purchase and sale of looted archaeological materials, and serve as a bond among those interested in the archaeology of the Americas.

The promotion of ethical behavior is an important aspect of the society's activities. The major principles of ethical practice have been set down by the SAA and are summarized in Table 12.4. These principles encompass the major concerns of archaeology. Stewardship concerns the protection of our common archaeological and cultural heritage; unless this heritage is protected, it will disappear. This principle of protection and preservation also extends to the collections and records that archaeologists accumulate. Accountability concerns archaeology's interaction with the individuals or groups involved with particular archaeological sites or materials. These individuals and groups include the landowners of sites where archaeological projects may take place and Native American groups whose beliefs incorporate ancient artifacts and human remains.

**Figure 12.6** Diver bringing a bucket from the surface to collect glass remains found on the *Glass Wreck,* an eleventh-century ship that sank off the coast of Turkey with over 200 pieces of glasswork.

## THE RESPONSIBLE ARCHAEOLOGIST

It is important to remember that archaeology is not a do-it-yourself activity. Amateur archaeologists in most cases work hand in hand with professionals. Most professional archaeologists have advanced degrees and have spent a great deal of time in the field and the classroom learning the many facets and skills of the discipline (Figure 12.6).

Historical archives may be studied over and over again, but archaeological sites are nonrenewable resources. Excavations involve moving earth and all its contents from a site. Every excavation means the destruction of all or part of an

**TABLE 12.4 Eight Ethical Principles of the Society for American Archaeology**

1. **Stewardship.** The archaeological record is irreplaceable, and it is the responsibility of all archaeologists to practice and promote stewardship of the archaeological record.
2. **Accountability.** Responsible archaeological research requires a commitment to consult with affected group(s) to establish a working relationship that can be beneficial to all parties involved.
3. **Commercialization.** The buying and selling of objects contributes to destruction of the archaeological record on the American continents and around the world. Archaeologists should discourage and avoid activities that enhance the commercial value of archaeological objects.
4. **Public education and outreach.** Archaeologists should work with the public to improve the preservation, protection, and interpretation of the record.
5. **Intellectual property.** A researcher may have primary access to original materials and documents for a limited and reasonable time, after which those materials and documents must be made available to others.
6. **Public reporting and publication.** The knowledge that archaeologists obtain in their investigations should be presented to the public.
7. **Records and preservation.** Archaeologists should work actively for the preservation of archaeological collections, records, and reports.
8. **Training and resources.** Archaeologists must ensure that they have the training, experience, facilities, and other support necessary to conduct a program of research.

archaeological site. It is for this reason, and in recognition that new methods and techniques in the future will be available to reveal more about the past, that archaeologists usually leave a substantial portion of a site undisturbed.

All that is left when an excavation is over are the finds themselves, the unexcavated parts of the site, and the samples, photographs, drawings, measurements and other notes that the archaeologists made. Accurate notes and records of the layers, structures, and finds at a site are essential, not only for the investigator but also as a permanent archive of information that is available to others.

In addition to keeping accurate records for a permanent archive, it is essential that archaeologists make their work public—known to other archaeologists and to the general public. Publication—making things public—in print or other media is part of the responsibility that archaeologists have to make their work and conclusions known so that the information can be checked and added to the general body of knowledge about the past. Books, articles in scientific journals, and reports are part of the permanent record that archaeology creates to document what is learned.

In addition to scientific publication, archaeologists try to make their discoveries known to the general public through magazines, newspapers, television, and the Web. Hardly a day goes by without mention of a new discovery or revelation about the past in the popular media. Keeping the public informed is part of the responsibility of being an archaeologist. One of the popular means of keeping the public informed has been the creation of an Archaeology Week in many states (Figure 12.7). This is an annual event at which lectures, exhibitions, and other public activities provide more information to the public and raise awareness of the importance of archaeology.

A third responsibility regards the commercialization of the past, and particularly the illegal trade in antiquities that remains a major force in the destruction of the past by looters and thieves. The archaeologist must discourage and avoid such activities. For example, an archaeologist should not provide estimates of the value of antiquities to collectors and retailers.

Public education is an important role for archaeologists, intended to increase both interest and support. The more people who understand and appreshaped marks to convey a message or text.

**cutmark** A trace left on bone by a stone or metal tool used in butchering a carcass; one of the primary forms of evidence for meat-eating by early hominins.

**Cyclopean** A term describing the huge stone walls of Mycenaean tombs and fortresses; from Cyclops, the mythical giant.

***danzante*** (Spanish) Dancer; a life-size carving of a captive or a prisoner of war depicted in bas-relief on stone slabs at San José Mogote and Monte Albán, Oaxaca.

***débitage*** A term referring to all the pieces of shatter and flakes produced and not used when stone tools are made.

**dendrochronology** The study of the annual growth rings of trees as a dating technique to build chronologies.

**division of labor** The differentiation of economic roles in a specific sociopolitical context.

**dolmen** A generic term for a megalithic tomb or chamber with a roof.

**domestication** The taming of wild plants and animals by humans. Plants are farmed and become dependent on humans for propagation; animals are herded and often become dependent on their human caretakers for food and protection.

**dryopithecine** The generic term for the Miocene fossil ancestor of both the living apes and modern humans, found in Africa, Asia, and Europe.

**ecofact** Any of the remains of plants, animals, sediments, or other unmodified materials that result from human activity.

**economy** The management and organization of the affairs of a group, a community, or an establishment to ensure their survival and productivity.

**edge hypothesis** The theory that the need for more food was initially felt at the margins of the natural habitat of the ancestors of domesticated plants and animals; a revised version of the population pressure hypothesis about the origins of agriculture.

**effigy** A representation or image of a person or an animal.

**egalitarian** A term that refers to societies lacking clearly defined status differences between individuals, except for those due to sex, age, or skill. *See also* hierarchical.

**E group** An arrangement of buildings designed to mark the position of the rising sun during important solar events, such as equinoxes and solstices, in Mesoamerica.

**El Niño** (Spanish) A warm-water countercurrent that periodically appears off the Peruvian coast, usually soon after Christmas, and alters the normal patterns of water temperature, flow, and salinity. These changes diminish the availability of nutrients to marine life, causing large schools of fish and flocks of seabirds to either migrate or die.

**emblem glyph** A set of Maya hieroglyphs; generally, each emblem glyph is specific to a given Classic Maya city. Although most Maya epigraphers agree that emblem glyphs have a geographic referent, they do not agree on whether such glyphs stand for a place or for the royal family that ruled the place.

**empire** A union of dispersed territories, colonies, states, and unrelated peoples under one sovereign rule.

**endocast** A copy or cast of the inside of a skull, reflecting the general shape and arrangement of the brain and its various parts.

**epigraphy** The study of inscriptions.

**epiphysis** The end of a long bone in humans and other mammals that hardens and attaches to the shaft of the bone with age.

**epoch** A subdivision of geological time, millions of years long, representing units of eras.

**equinox** A time when the sun crosses the plane of the equator, making the night and the day the same length all over the earth, occurring about March 21 and September 22.

**era** A major division of geological time, tens or hundreds of millions of years long, usually distinguished by significant changes in the plant and animal kingdoms; also used to denote later archaeological periods, such as the prehistoric era.

**estrus** The cycle of female sexual receptivity in many species of animals.

**estuary** A low area along a coast where the wide mouth of a river meets the sea and the waters of the two mix.

**ethnocentrism** Evaluating other groups or societies by standards that are relevant to the observer's culture.

**ethnography** The study of human cultures through firsthand observation.

**ethnohistory** The study of ancient (often non-Western) cultures using evidence from documentary sources and oral traditions, and often supplemented with archaeological data. Traditionally, ethnohistorians have been concerned with the early history of the Americas, the time of European contact, and later settlement and colonization by Europeans.

**evolution** The process of change over time resulting from shifting conditions of the physical and cultural environments, involving mechanisms of mutation and natural selection. Human biology and culture evolved during the Late Miocene, Pliocene, Pleistocene, and Holocene.

**excavation** The exposure and recording of buried materials from the past.

**extrasomatic** Literally, "outside the body"; nonbiological, nongenetic.

**facade** The face, or front, of a building.

**feature** An immovable structure or layer, pit, or post in the ground having archaeological significance.

**Fertile Crescent** An upland zone in Southwest Asia that runs from the Levant to the Zagros Mountains, with adequate rainfall and many wild species that were domesticated.

**fieldwork** The search for archaeological sites in the landscape through surveys and excavations.

**flake** A type of stone artifact produced by removing a piece from a core through chipping.

**flint** A fine-grained, crystalline stone that fractures in a regular pattern, producing sharp-edged flakes; highly prized and extensively used for making flaked stone tools.

**flintknapping** The process of making chipped stone artifacts; the striking of stone with a hard or soft hammer.

**floodwater farming** A method of farming that recovers floodwater and diverts it to selected fields to supplement the water supply.

**flotation** A technique for the recovery of plant remains from archaeological sites. Sediments or pit contents are poured into water or heavy liquid; the lighter, carbonized plant remains float to the top for recovery, while the heavier sediments and other materials fall to the bottom.

**fluted point** The characteristic artifact of the Paleoindian period in North America. Several varieties of fluted points were used for hunting large game. The flute refers to a large channel flake removed from both sides of the base of the point to facilitate hafting.

**Folsom** An archaeological culture during the Paleoindian period in North America, defined by a distinctive type of fluted point and found primarily in the Great Plains.

**fossil** The mineralized bone of an extinct animal. Most bones associated with humans in the Pliocene, Pleistocene, and Holocene are too young to have been mineralized, but the term *fossil skull* or *fossil bone* is often used generically in those cases as well.

**frieze** A decorative band or feature, commonly ornamented with sculpture, usually near the top of a wall.

**galena** A common heavy mineral that is the principal ore of lead.

**gallery grave** A megalithic tomb lacking an entrance passage; the burial room or rooms form the entire internal structure. Gallery graves are found in Neolithic western Europe.

**gazelle** One of several species of small-to-medium, swift, and graceful antelopes native to Asia and Africa.

**geoglyph** Ground markings, such as the lines and life-form representations found in the Nazca desert.

**geomorphic** Having the form or attributes of surface features of the earth or other celestial bodies.

**glacial** A cold episode of the Pleistocene, in contrast to a warmer interglacial period; also called an ice age. The classic European sequence of the Günz, Mindel, Riss, and Würm glacials has recently been revised, with the recognition of a large number of cold/warm oscillations in the Pleistocene.

**glaciation** The expansion of continental glacial ice during a period of cold climate.

**glume** The tough seed cover of many cereal kernels. In the process of the domestication of wheat, the tough glume became more brittle, making threshing easier.

**glyph** (Greek) A carving; a drawn symbol in a writing system that may stand for a syllable, a sound, an idea, a word, or a combination of these. *See also* emblem glyph.

**gorget** A circular ornament, flat or convex on one side and concave on the other, usually worn over the chest.

**grave goods** The items that are placed in graves to accompany the deceased.

**ground-penetrating radar (GPR** or **georadar)** An instrument for remote sensing or prospecting for buried structures using radar maps of subsoil features.

**guano** Bird excrement.

**half-life** A measure of the rate of decay in radioactive materials; half the radioactive material will disappear within the period of one half-life.

**hammerstone** A stone used to knock flakes from cores.

**handaxe** A large, teardrop-shaped stone tool bifacially flaked to a point at one end and a broader base at the other. The characteristic artifact of the Lower Paleolithic; for general-purpose use that continued into the Middle Paleolithic.

**handedness** Preferential use of the right or the left hand; related to the organization of the brain in two hemispheres.

**hard-hammer technique** A flintknapping technique for making stone tools by striking one stone, or core, with another stone, or hammer. *See also* soft-hammer technique.

**hematite** A common heavy mineral that is the principal ore of iron.

**hemp** A tall annual plant whose tough fibers are used to make coarse fabrics and ropes.

**henge** A monument defined by the presence of an enclosure, usually made by a circular ditch and bank system, up to 500 m in diameter. Henges were erected during the Neolithic and early Bronze Age in western Europe.

**hierarchical** A term referring to societies that have a graded order of inequality in ranks, statuses, or decision makers. *See also* egalitarian.

**hieroglyph** Originally, the pictographic script of ancient Egypt; any depictive, art-related system of writing, such as that of Mesoamerica; also may refer to an individual symbol.

**historical archaeology** Archaeology in combination with the written record.

**Hohokam** One of three major cultural traditions of the American Southwest during late prehistoric times. The Hohokam were centered in the deserts of southern Arizona.

**hominid** An obsolete term that refers to the human members of the primates, both fossil and modern forms.

**hominin** A term that refers to the human, chimp, and gorilla members of the primates, both fossil and modern forms.

**hominoid** A descriptive term for any human or ape, past or present, characterized by teeth shape, the absence of a tail, and swinging arms.

**Hominoidea** The taxonomic group (family) that includes the human and ape members of the primates, both fossil and modern forms.

**Hopewell Interaction Sphere** A complex network involving the exchange of goods and information that connected distinct local populations in the midwestern United States from approximately 100 B.C. to A.D. 400.

**horizon** A widely distributed set of cultural traits and artifact assemblages whose distribution and chronology suggest they spread rapidly. A horizon is often composed of artifacts associated with a shared symbolic or ritual system.

**household archaeology** The archaeological analysis of past houses and associated residential remains to learn about domestic life and activities.

***huaca*** (Quechua) An Andean word for pyramid.

**hunter-gatherer** A hunter of large wild animals and gatherer of wild plants, seafood, and small animals, as opposed to farmers and food producers. Hunting and gathering characterized the human subsistence pattern before the domestication of plants and animals and the spread of agriculture. Hunter-gatherers are also known as foragers.

**hyoid bone** A delicate bone in the neck that anchors the tongue muscles in the throat.

**iconography** The study of artistic representations or icons that usually have religious or ceremonial significance.

**ideograph** A written symbol that represents an abstract idea rather than the sound of a word. *See also* pictograph.

**ideology** A conceptual framework by which people structure their ideas about the order of the universe, their place in that universe, and their relationships among themselves and with objects and other forms of life around them.

***incensario*** (Spanish) An incense burner made of pottery and sometimes stone, used in Mesoamerican religious and political ceremonies.

**inflorescence** The flowering part of a plant.

**intaglio** An engraving in stone or other hard material that is depressed below the surface; an impression of the design produces an image in relief.

**interglacial** A warm period of the Pleistocene, in contrast to a colder period called a glacial.

**isotope** One of several atomic states of an element; for example, carbon occurs as $^{12}C$, $^{13}C$, and $^{14}C$, also known as carbon-14 or radiocarbon.

**isotopic technique** A method for absolute dating that relies on known rates of decay in radioactive isotopes, especially carbon, potassium, and uranium.

**jasper** A high-quality flint, often highly colored; often used as a raw material for the manufacture of stone tools, beads, and other ornaments.

**jet** A compact, black coal that can be highly polished; used to make beads, jewelry, and other decorative objects.

**Jomon** The archaeological culture of late Pleistocene and early Holocene Japan; primarily associated with groups of hunter-gatherers, but recent evidence suggests that these groups were practicing some rice cultivation.

**jujube** A small, edible fruit from an Asian tree of the buckthorn family. The fruit has one seed in the center, somewhat like a cherry.

**kiln** A furnace or oven for baking or drying objects, especially for firing pottery.

**kiva** A semisubterranean ceremonial room found at sites throughout the American Southwest.

**krater** A large metal vessel for mixing and storing wine, traded over a large part of Europe during the Iron Age.

**lactational amenorrhea** The suppression of ovulation and menstruation during breast-feeding.

***laguna*** (Spanish) Lagoon; a man-made depression in Mesoamerica that may have begun as a borrow pit for the construction of an earthen mound. *Lagunas* were often lined with waterproof bentonite blocks and may have been used for ritual bathing.

**lake dwelling** Former name for Early Neolithic lakeshore settlements originally thought to have been built over the water.

**lapidary** Of or related to the practice of working or cutting precious or semiprecious stone.

**lapis lazuli** A semiprecious stone of deep blue; used and traded widely in antiquity in the form of beads, pendants, and inlay.

**lateralization** The division of the human brain into two halves. One side controls language; the other regulates perception and motor skills.

**leguminous plants** Vegetables used as food.

**Levallois** A technique for manufacturing large, thin flakes or points from a carefully prepared core; first used during the Lower Paleolithic and remaining common during the Middle Paleolithic. The method wasted flint and was generally not used in areas of scarce raw materials.

**Levant** A mountainous region paralleling the eastern shore of the Mediterranean, including parts of the countries of Turkey, Syria, Lebanon, and Israel.

**lintel** A horizontal beam of wood or stone that supports the wall above a doorway or window.

**lithic** Pertaining to stone or rock.

**llama** A woolly South American camelid; used as a beast of burden.

**locomotion** A method of animal movement, such as bipedalism.

**loess** Wind-blown silt deposited in deep layers in certain parts of the Northern Hemisphere.

***lomas*** (Spanish) Vegetation that is supported by fog in otherwise arid environments.

**Long Count** The Classic Maya system of dating that records the total number of days elapsed from an initial date in the distant past (3114 B.C.). The system is based on multiples of 20 beginning with the *kin* (1 day), *uinal* (20 *kins* or 20 days), *tun* (18 *uinals* or 360 days), *katun* (20 *tuns* or 7200 days), and *baktun* (20 *katuns* or 144,000 days).

**longhouse** A wooden structure that is considerably longer than it is wide that served as a communal dwelling, especially among native North Americans in the Northeast and on the Northwest Coast.

**lost wax casting** A technique for casting metal in which a sand or clay casing is formed around a wax sculpture; molten metal is poured into the casing, melting the wax. The cooling metal takes on the shape of the "lost" wax sculpture preserved on the casing.

**macaw** Any of several varieties of parrots from Mexico and Central and South America that were prized for their colorful feathers.

**magnetite** A black iron oxide that can be polished to a lustrous surface.

**maguey** Any of several species of arid-environment plants with fleshy leaves that conserve moisture. The fiber and needles of magueys were used to make rope and clothing in Mesoamerica and the southwestern United States.

**mano** The hand-held part of a stone-milling assembly for grinding maize or other foods.

**marketing** An exchange system that frequently involves currencies and generally extends beyond close kinsmen and a small group of trading partners. Market participants try to minimize their costs and maximize their returns to make a profit.

**Maya Blue** A steadfast blue pigment made by fusing an extract from the plant indigo with a fine white clay, palygorskite. The Maya and other Mesoamerican peoples applied this pigment on a range of materials, including ceramics, sculptures, and murals.

**megalith** A large stone monument.

**menhir** A large, standing stone, found either alone or collectively in lines.

**Mesoamerica** The region consisting of central and southern Mexico, Guatemala, Belize, El Salvador, and the western parts of Honduras and Nicaragua that was the focus of complex, hierarchical states at the time of Spanish contact. The people of this area shared a basic set of cultural conventions. Also called Middle America.

**Mesolithic** The period of time of hunter-gatherers in Europe, North Africa, and parts of Asia between the end of the Pleistocene and the introduction of farming; the Middle Stone Age.

**Mesopotamia** The flat plain between the Tigris and Euphrates rivers in southern Iraq where the world's first civilization developed.

**mesquite** A tree or shrub of the southwestern United States and Mexico whose beanlike pods are rich in sugar.

**metallurgy** The art of separating metals from their ores.

**metate** The stone basin, often trough-shaped, or lower part of a stone-milling assembly for grinding maize or other foods.

**mica** A colored or transparent mineral silicate that readily separates into very thin sheets. Mica was carved to make ornaments and crushed as an inclusion to clay in the fabrication of pottery.

**microband** A small family group of hunter-gatherers.

**midden** An accumulated pile of trash and waste materials near a dwelling or in other areas of an archaeological site.

**Milankovitch forcing** A term describing the phenomenon considered to be the prime reason for glacial fluctuations and climatic change. Changing factors are the distance between the earth and the sun and the tilt of the earth's axis, which play major roles in the amount of sunlight reaching the earth, atmospheric temperature, and the expansion and retreat of continental glaciation. The cyclical nature of variation in these factors was recognized by Yugoslav mathematician Milutin Milankovitch.

**millennium** A period of 1000 years.

**Mississippian** The collective name applied to the agricultural societies that inhabited portions of the eastern United States from approximately A.D. 800–1700. Mississippian peoples constructed earthen platform mounds and shared certain basic cultural conventions.

***mit'a* system** A means of tribute in prehispanic Andean South America that involved the use of conscripted laborers to complete discrete organizational tasks.

***mitmaq*** A system of colonization used by the Inca to minimize provincial rebellion by moving people around to break up dissident groups.

**mitochondrial DNA** Genetic material in the mitochondria of human cells that mutates at a relatively constant rate. Because mitochondrial DNA is inherited only from the mother, it provides an unaltered link to past generations.

**Mogollon** One of three major cultural traditions of the American Southwest during late prehistoric times. The Mogollon were centered in the mountainous areas of southeastern Arizona and southwestern New Mexico.

**monochrome** One color; describing pottery decorated with only one color that contrasts with the underlying color of the paste of the vessel.

***montaña*** (Spanish) Mountain, specifically referring to the wet, tropical slopes of the Amazonian Andes.

**mortar** A bowl-shaped grinding tool, used with a wood or stone pestle for grinding various materials.

**motif** A recurring thematic design element in an art style.

**Mousterian** A term describing the stone tool assemblages of the Neanderthals during the Middle Paleolithic, named after the site of Le Moustier in France. *See also* Acheulean.

**multivallate** A term describing complex defenses of multiple ditches and ramparts at large Iron Age hillforts.

**mural art** One of the two major categories of Paleolithic art, along with portable art. Mural art consists of painting, engraving, and sculpting on the walls of the caves, shelters, and cliffs of southwestern Europe; one of the hallmarks of the Upper Paleolithic.

**m.y.a.** Abbreviation for *millions of years ago.*

**natural habitat hypothesis** The theory about the origins of agriculture associated with Robert Braidwood, suggesting that the earliest domesticates appeared in the area that their wild ancestors inhabited.

**necropolis** (Greek) Cemetery.

**Neolithic** The period of time of early farmers with domesticated plants and animals, polished stone tools, permanent villages, and often pottery; the New Stone Age.

**net-sinker** A small weight attached to fishing nets.

**nome** A geographic province incorporated within the ancient Egyptian state.

**oasis hypothesis** The theory about the origins of agriculture associated with V. Gordon Childe and others, suggesting that domestication began as a symbiotic relationship between humans, plants, and animals at oases during the desiccation of Southwest Asia at the end of the Pleistocene.

**obsidian** Translucent, gray to black or green, glasslike rock from molten sand; produces extremely sharp edges when fractured and was highly valued for making stone tools.

**oca** A South American wood sorrel (*Oxalis crenata*) that is cultivated for its edible tuber.

**occipital bun** A distinctive shelf or protrusion at the base of the skull; a feature usually associated with Neanderthals.

**Oldowan** The name given to the assemblages of early pebble tools and flakes belonging to the Basal Paleolithic, derived from *Olduvai.*

**Olmec** The Aztec name for the late prehispanic inhabitants of the Gulf Coast region of Mexico. This term has been extended by archaeologists to describe the sites, monuments, and art found in the same region during the Formative period. Aspects of this art style and related motifs had a wider distribution across Mesoamerica during the Early and Middle Formative periods (1150–700 B.C.). This broader distribution is called the Olmec Horizon.

**oppidum** A massive fortification in western Europe, often on a hilltop or a bluff, built for defensive purposes during the Iron Age; described in some detail and often conquered by the Romans.

**oracle bone** An animal bone with cracks (due to heating) or other markings, used to foretell the future.

**organization** The arrangements between individuals and groups in human society that structure relationships and activities.

**oxygen isotope ratio** The ratio of different isotopes of oxygen in ocean water, varying with the temperature of the water; measured in seashells and used as an indicator of temperature change over time.

**paleoanthropology** The branch of anthropology that combines archaeology and physical anthropology to study the biological and behavioral remains of the early hominins.

**Paleoindian** The period of large-game hunters in North America at the end of the Pleistocene. Paleoindian remains are characterized by the presence of fluted points and frequently the bones of extinct animals.

**Paleolithic** The first period of human prehistory, extending from the time of the first tools, more than 2.5 m.y.a., until the end of the Pleistocene, 10,000 years ago. Characterized by the use of flaked stone tools, it is also known as the Old Stone Age.

**palisade** A fence of posts or stakes erected around a settlement for defensive purposes.

**panpipe** A wind instrument consisting of bound sets of short pipes in graduated lengths.

**pantheon** The officially recognized gods of a people.

**papyrus** A tall marsh plant, or reed, of the Nile Valley that the ancient Egyptians cut into strips and pressed into a kind of paper to write on.

**Paranthropus** Genus of early hominins, contemporary with *Australopithecus*, that includes *boisei* and *robustus* as species.

**passage grave** A megalithic tomb entered via a long, low, narrow passage that opens into a wider room, generally near the center of the structure.

**pastoralist** An animal herder. Pastoralism is a subsistence strategy generally associated with a mobile lifeway.

**patrilocal** Describing a residence pattern in which married couples live with or near the husband's family.

**pectoral** A large ornament worn across the chest, especially for defensive purposes.

**percussion flaking** A technique for producing stone artifacts by striking or knapping crystalline stone with a hard or soft hammer. *See also* pressure flaking.

**petroglyph** A drawing that has been carved into rock.

**petty state** A small, socially stratified political unit prevalent in Mesoamerica at the time of the Spanish conquest. Similar political formations have been found in other regions as well.

**phonetic** Pertaining to the sounds of speech.

**pictograph** A written or painted symbol that more or less portrays the represented object. *See also* ideograph.

**pipal tree** A species of fig tree on the South Asian subcontinent that has had sacred significance for many cultures and religions throughout the region for thousands of years.

***pithos*** A large clay storage jar.

**pithouse** A prehistoric semisubterranean dwelling in which the lower parts of the walls were the earthen sides of a shallow pit; the top parts of the walls often consisted of a framework of poles intertwined with small twigs, covered with mud.

**Plio-Pleistocene** A term used to describe the time between the appearance of the earliest hominins during the Pliocene and the beginning of the Pleistocene.

***pochteca*** A privileged, hereditary guild of long-distance Aztec traders.

**polychrome** Multicolored; describing pottery that has been decorated with three or more colors.

**polygynous** Having more than one mate.

**population pressure hypothesis** Lewis Binford's theory that population increase in Southwest Asia upset the balance between people and food, forcing people to turn to agriculture as a way to produce more food.

**porphyry** An igneous rock with visible quartz or feldspar crystals embedded in a finer-grained base.

**portable art** One of the two major categories of Paleolithic art, along with mural art. Portable art includes all decorated materials that can be moved or carried; found throughout Europe and much of Eurasia.

**post mold** The circular remains, often just a dark stain in the soil, of a wooden post that formed part of the frame of a prehistoric structure; also called a posthole.

**potassium-argon dating** *See* radiopotassium dating.

**potlatch** A large feast among Northwest Coast Native Americans that included the display and dispersal of accumulated wealth to the assembled guests.

**potsherd** A fragment of a clay vessel or object.

**prehistory** In general, the human past; specifically, the time before the appearance of written records.

**pressure flaking** A technique for producing stone artifacts by removing flakes from a stone core by pressing with a pointed implement. *See also* percussion flaking.

**primary context (*in situ*)** An object found where it was originally located in antiquity, not redeposited.

**primate** The order of animals that includes lemurs, tarsiers, monkeys, apes, and humans; characterized by grasping hands, flexible limbs, and a highly developed sense of vision.

**provenience** The place of origin for archaeological materials, including location, association, and context.

**pueblo** A stone-masonry complex of adjoining rooms found in the American Southwest.

***puna*** (Spanish) High grassland plateaus in the Peruvian Andes.

**quern** A stone grinding surface for preparing grains and other plant foods and for grinding other materials.

**quinoa** A pigweed (*Chenopodium quinoa*) of the high Andes. Seeds of the plant were ground and used as food in the past and still are today.

***quipu*** The Inca word for an elaborate knotted-string device used by the Inca and other peoples in Peru for record keeping. A *quipu* consists of a horizontal cord from which a series of smaller knotted strings hang. The placement, color, and nature of the knots on the cords convey numbers and other information.

**rachis** The stem that holds seeds to the stalk in wheat and other plants; changes from brittle to tough when wheat is domesticated.

**radiocarbon dating** An absolute dating technique based on the principle of decay of the radioactive isotope of carbon, $^{14}C$; used to date archaeological materials within the past 40,000 years.

**radiopotassium dating** An absolute dating technique based on the principle of decay of the radioactive isotope of potassium, $^{40}K$; used to date materials ranging in age from 500,000 years old to the age of the oldest rocks in the universe. Also called potassium-argon dating.

**ramón** A tree that grows abundantly in the tropical forests of the Maya Lowlands and bears an edible fruit; also called breadnut.

**rank** A relationship of inequality between members of society in which status is determined by kinship relations of birth order and lineage.

**reciprocity** The exchange of goods between known participants, involving simple barter and face-to-face exchanges.

**redistribution** The accumulation and dispersal of goods through a centralized agency, individual, or institution.

**red ochre** An iron mineral that occurs in nature; used by prehistoric peoples in powdered form as a pigment for tanning animal skins; often found in burials from the late Paleolithic and Mesolithic.

**reduction technique** In archaeology, a manufacturing process involving the removal (as opposed to the addition) of materials from a core that becomes the finished product; includes techniques such as flintknapping and wood carving.

**relative dating** A technique used to *estimate* the antiquity of archaeological materials, generally based on association with materials of known age or simply to say that one item is younger or older than another.

**repoussé** (French) The process of forming a raised design on a thin sheet of metal by placing it over a mold and hammering it in place.

**retouch** The shaping or sharpening of stone artifacts through percussion or pressure flaking.

**rhizome** An edible, rootlike subterranean plant stem.

**robust** "Big-boned," heavy, thick-walled skeletal tissue. Robust early hominins also had very large teeth.

**roof comb** An architectural feature, frequently carved with glyphs and figures, that is placed on the top of Mesoamerican temples.

***sacbe*** The Maya word for a raised causeway constructed of stone blocks and paved with gravel and plaster.

**sarcophagus** A stone coffin, usually decorated with sculpture and/or inscriptions.

**scapulimancy** The ancient practice of seeking knowledge by reading cracks on bones. Symbols were written on an animal's scapula (shoulder blade); the bone was heated until a series of cracks formed; then diviners interpreted the pattern of cracking to foretell the future.

**scepter** A staff or baton borne by a ruler as an emblem of his or her position and authority.

**scheduling** The process of arranging the extraction of resources according to their availability and the demands of competing subsistence activities.

**seal stamp** A piece of inscribed stone used by administrators to impress a symbol on wet pieces of clay or bitumen in order to keep track of goods.

**seasonality** The changing availability of resources according to the different seasons of the year.

**sedentism** Living in permanent, year-round contexts, such as villages.

**serpentine** A stone of dull green color that often has a mottled appearance.

***setaria*** A wild grass with edible seeds.

**sexual dimorphism** A difference in size between the male and female members of a species; for example, male gorillas are significantly larger than females.

**sexual division of labor** The cooperative relationship between the sexes in hunter-gatherer groups involving different male and female task activity.

**shaduf** An Egyptian bucket-and-lever lifting device that enables one to raise water a few feet from a well or ditch onto fields and gardens.

**shaft grave** A vertical tunnel cut into rock and holding the tombs of Mycenaean elite.

**shaman** An anthropological term for a spiritualist, curer, or seer.

**shattering** A natural mechanism of seed dispersal.

**shell midden** A mound of shells accumulated from human collection, consumption, and disposal; a dump of shells from oysters, clams, mussels, or other species found along coasts and rivers, usually dating to the Holocene.

***shicra*** The Inca word for meshed bags containing rocks, used as fill in the construction of ancient Andean structures.

**sickle** A tool for cutting the stalks of cereals, especially wheat. Prehistoric sickles were usually stone blades set in a wood or antler handle.

**sickle polish** A clear polish that forms along the edges of flakes and blades that are used to cut reeds, grass, wheat, and other long-stemmed plants.

**site** The accumulation of artifacts and/or ecofacts, representing a place where people lived or carried out certain activities.

**slash and burn** A type of farming in which the ground is cleared by cutting and burning the vegetation on the spot. The burned vegetation serves as a natural fertilizer. The field is farmed until yields decrease; then it is allowed to lie fallow. Also called swidden farming.

**slate** A fine-grained rock, with a dull, dark bluish-gray color, that tends to split along parallel cleavage planes, often producing thin plates or sheets.

**soapstone** A soft stone with a soapy feel that is easy to carve; often referred to as steatite.

**social hypothesis** The theory that domestication allowed certain individuals to accumulate food surplus and to transform those foods into more valued items, such as rare stones or metals, and even social alliances.

**sodality** An alliance or association among some members of a society, often based on age and sex, with a specific function. Sodalities can be ceremonial, political, or economic; examples include dance societies, warrior groups, sororities, clubs, and fraternal organizations.

**soft-hammer technique** A flintknapping technique that involves the use of a hammer of bone, antler, or wood, rather than stone. *See also* hard-hammer technique.

**solifluction** A phenomenon in which freezing and thawing of the ground results in slippage of the surface.

**solstice** The time of year when the sun is at its greatest distance from the equator, occurring about June 21 and December 22.

***sondage*** (French) A test excavation or test pit made at an archaeological site to determine the content and/or the distribution of prehistoric materials.

**Southeastern Ceremonial Complex** A network of interaction, exchange, and shared information present over much of the southeastern (and parts of the midwestern) United States from around A.D. 1200 until the early 1500s; also previously referred to as the Southern Cult.

**spindle whorl** A cam or balance wheel on a shaft or spindle for spinning yarn or thread from wool, cotton, or other material; usually made of clay.

**split inheritance** An Andean practice by which the successor to the throne inherited only the office of the dead ruler; his junior kinsmen received the lands, palace, and personal wealth of the dead ruler.

**state** A form of government with an internally specialized and hierarchically organized decision-making apparatus. A state generally has three or more administrative levels.

**status differentiation** Inequality in human society in which certain individuals or groups have access to more resources, power, and roles than others. Differentiation occurs through ranking of descent groups or the creation of classes of people.

**steatite** Soapstone, a variety of talc with a soapy or greasy feel; often used to make containers or carved ornaments.

**stela** (Latin, pl. **stelae**) An erect stone monument that is often carved.

**stingray spine** Bony tail spines of stingrays that were used in the past to draw blood in human autosacrificial rites.

**stirrup spout** A distinctive curving spout on pottery vessels that is shaped like the stirrup of a saddle; characteristic of Moche pottery.

**stone boiling** The process of heating stones in a fire and then adding them to containers to boil water or cook other foods.

**stratigraphic section** The excavation of trenches and squares across man-made layers to expose a cross section of the deposits and reveal the sequence and methods of construction.

**stucco** A type of plaster, often made out of lime, used for decoration.

**survey** A systematic search of the landscape for artifacts and sites on the ground through aerial photography, field walking, soil analysis, and geophysical prospecting.

**sweat bath** A hut or other space heated by steam that is created by pouring water over hot stones. Used by many peoples for ritual cleansing and therapeutic sweating.

***talud-tablero*** (Spanish) An architectural style characteristic of Teotihuacan during the Classic period, in which recessed rectangular panels (the *tablero*) are separated by sloping aprons (the *talud*).

***tampu*** A roadside lodging and storage place (principally for food, fodder, firewood, and other commodities) along the Inca road system, placed roughly one day's walk apart.

**technology** The combination of knowledge and manufacturing techniques that enables people to convert raw materials into finished products.

**tell** A mound composed of mud bricks and refuse, accumulated as a result of human activity. The mound of Jericho built up at a rate of roughly 26 cm (10 in) per 100 years, almost a foot per century.

**temper** A nonplastic material (such as sand, shell, or fiber) that is added to clay to improve its workability and to reduce breakage during drying and firing.

**temporal marker** A morphological type, such as a design motif on pottery or a particular type of stone tool, that has been shown to have a discrete and definable temporal range.

**teosinte** (Aztec *teōcentli*) A tall annual grass, native to Mexico and Central America, that is the closest relative of maize.

**terracotta** A hard, brown-orange earthenware clay of fine quality, often used for architectural decorations, figurines, etc.

***tholoi*** Ancient Mesopotamian round structures that often were attached to a rectangular antechamber or annex, resulting in a keyhole shape. They may have been used as storage facilities or as religious features for the interment of important individuals.

***tholos*** A large, beehive-shaped tomb, constructed using the corbel arch technique, characteristic of the Mycenaean civilization of Greece.

***tlachtli*** The Aztec word for their ritual ballgame.

**tool** Any equipment, weapon, or object made by humans to change their environment.

**total station** A computerized surveying and mapping instrument that uses a laser beam or radio waves to measure the distance and angle between the instrument and the target, and then calculates the exact position of the target.

**totem pole** A pole or post that has been carved and painted with totems or figures, such as animals, that serve as the emblems of clans or families. Native Americans of the Pacific Northwest often erected these poles in front of their houses.

**transhumance** A pattern of seasonal movement usually associated with pastoralists who take their herds to the mountains in summer and to the valleys in winter; more generally, a regular pattern of seasonal movement by human groups.

**trilithon** A massive stone lintel occurring in prehistoric structures, such as Stonehenge and the *tholos* tombs in Greece.

**trophic level** An organism's place in the food chain.

**tuber** A fleshy, usually oblong or rounded outgrowth (such as the potato) of a subterranean stem or root of a plant.

**tumpline** A strap that is passed over the forehead or the chest to facilitate the transportation of a heavy load carried on the back.

***tzompantli*** The Aztec word for skull rack. The Aztec and other Mesoamerican peoples often placed the skulls of sacrificial victims on a wooden pole or frame; in some cases, large blocks of stone were sculpted to look like skull racks.

**UNESCO World Heritage Site** A property around the world considered by the World Heritage Committee to have outstanding universal value. UNESCO (United Nations Educational, Scientific and Cultural Organization) encourages the protection and preservation of cultural and natural heritage that is considered to be of outstanding value to humanity.

**unifacial** A term describing a flaked stone tool in which only one face or side is retouched to make a sharp edge.

**vallum** A Roman wall-and-ditch fortification.

**vault** An arched structure of masonry that forms a ceiling or roof. The construction of vaults with corbelled, or stepped, ceilings was a common building technique of the Maya.

**wadi** (Arabic) A dry streambed.

***waranqa*** A subdivision of the Inca empire that was used for administrative purposes, consisting of 1000 taxpayers.

**wattle and daub** A building technique that uses a framework of poles, interspersed with smaller poles and twigs; the wooden frame is plastered with mud or a mud mixture. This building technique also was employed in the Southeast and other parts of the world.

**weaning** The process of transferring the young from dependence on its mother's milk to other forms of nourishment.

**were-jaguar** A representation of a supernatural figure that is half jaguar and half human, a common symbol in Preclassic Mesoamerica.

**wet-site excavation** The technique of excavating waterlogged sites by pumping water through garden hoses to spray the dirt away and expose archaeological features and artifacts.

**wheel-thrown pottery** Pottery that is made using the potter's wheel.

**woodhenge** A circular feature demarcated by large upright timbers; probably used by prehistoric groups as astronomical observatories.

**Zapotec** A Mesoamerican cultural tradition generally associated with the Valley of Oaxaca and several smaller adjacent valleys in central Oaxaca (state of Oaxaca, Mexico). The Zapotec language is part of the Otomanguean language family, a language family that is distinct from the Maya or Utoaztecan, which includes Nahuatl, the language of the Aztecs.

**ziggurat** A large pyramid in Mesopotamia consisting of many stepped levels.

**zoomorphic** Having animal form or attributes.

# References


Aaris-Sørensen, K., and E. Brinch Petersen. 1986. The Prejlerup aurochs—an archaeozoological discovery from Boreal, Denmark. *Striae* 24:111–117.

Abbott, D. R., S. L. Stinson, and S. van Keuren. 2001. The economic implications of Hohokam buff ware exchange during the early Sedentary period. *Kiva* 67:7–29.

Acker, R. 1998. New geographical tests of the hydraulic thesis at Angkor. *South East Asia Research* 6(1):5–47.

Adams, D. 1980. *The hitchhiker's guide to the galaxy.* New York: Harmony.

Adams, J. L. 2002. *Ground stone analysis: A technological approach.* Salt Lake City: University of Utah Press.

Adams, R. E. W. 1991. *Prehistoric Mesoamerica,* rev. ed. Norman: University of Oklahoma Press.

Adams, R. E. W., W. E. Brown, and T. P. Culbert. 1981. Radar mapping, archeology and ancient Maya land use. *Science* 213:1457–1463.

Adams, R. E. W., and M. J. MacLeod, eds. 2000. *The Cambridge history of the native peoples of the Americas.* Vol. 2, *Mesoamerica, part 1.* Cambridge: Cambridge University Press.

Adams, R. McC. 1966. *The evolution of urban society.* Chicago: Aldine.

Adams, R. McC. 1981. *Heartland of cities.* Chicago: University of Chicago Press.

Adler, D. S., G. Bar-Oz, A. Belfer-Cohen, and O. Bar-Yosef. 2006. Ahead of the game: Middle and Upper Paleolithic hunting behaviors in the southern Caucasus. *Current Anthropology* 47:89–118.

Aiello, L. C. 1993. The fossil evidence for modern human origins in Africa: A revised view. *American Anthropologist* 95:73–96.

Aikens, C. M., and T. Higuchi. 1982. *The prehistory of Japan.* New York: Academic Press.

Aikens, R. J. C. 1956. *Stonehenge.* Baltimore: Pelican.

Aitken, M. J. 1985. *Thermoluminescence dating.* New York: Academic Press.

Aitken, M. J. 1990. *Science-based dating in archaeology.* New York: Longman.

Akazawa, T. 1980. Fishing adaptation of prehistoric hunter-gatherers at the Nittano site, Japan. *Journal of Archaeological Science* 7:325–344.

Alcock, S. E., T. N. D'Altroy, K. D. Morrison, and C. M. Sinopoli, eds. 2001. *Empires: Perspectives from archaeology and history.* Cambridge: Cambridge University Press.

Alcock, S. E., and R. G. Osborne. 2005. *Classical archaeology.* Oxford: Blackwell.

Algaze, G. 2001. Initial social complexity in southwestern Asia: The Mesopotamian advantage. *Current Anthropology* 42:199–233.

Allchin, B., and R. Allchin. 1982. *The rise of civilization in India and Pakistan.* Cambridge: Cambridge University Press.

Alperson-Afil, N., D. Richter, and N. Goren-Inbar. 2007. Phantom hearths and the use of fire at Gesher Benot Ya`Aqov, Israel. *PaleoAnthropology* 2007:1–15.

Alva, W. 1990. New tomb of royal splendor: The Moche of ancient Peru. *National Geographic* 177(6):2–15.

Alva, W. 2001. The royal tombs of Sipán: Art and power in Moche society. In *Moche: Art and archaeology in ancient Peru,* ed. J. Pillsbury. Studies in History of Art 63. Washington, DC: National Gallery of Art.

Alva, W., and C. B. Donnan. 1993. *Royal tombs of Sipán.* Los Angeles: Fowler Museum of Cultural History, University of California.

Alvarado Tezozomoc, F. 1975. *Crónica Mexicáyotl,* trans. E. O'Gorman. Universidad Nacional Autónoma de México, Mexico City: Originally written 1609.

Ames, K. M. 1981. The evolution of social ranking on the Northwest Coast of North America. *American Antiquity* 46:789–805.

Ammerman, A. J., and L. L. Cavalli-Sforza. 1984. *The Neolithic transition and the genetics of populations in Europe.* Princeton, NJ: Princeton University Press.

Anawalt, P. R. 1982. Understanding Aztec human sacrifice. *Archaeology* 35(3):38–45.

Anderson, A. 1987. Recent developments in Japanese prehistory: A review. *American Antiquity* 61:270–281.

Anderson, D. G. and M. K. Faught. 1998. The distribution of fluted Paleoindian projectile points: Update 1998. *Archaeology of Eastern North America* 26:163–187.

Anderson, D. G., and M. K. Faugh. 2000. Palaeoindian artefact distributions: Evidence and implications. *Antiquity* 74:507–513.

Appenzeller, T. 1994. Clashing Maya superpowers emerge from a new analysis. *Science* 226:733–734.

Arens, W. 1979. *The man-eating myth: Anthropology and anthropophagy.* New York: Oxford University Press.

Arnold, B., and D. B. Gibson, eds. 1998. *Celtic chiefdom, Celtic state.* Cambridge: Cambridge University Press.

Arnold, D. E., J. R. Branden, P. R. Williams, G. M. Feinman, and J. P. Brown. 2008. The first direct evidence for the production of Maya Blue: Rediscovery of a technology. *Antiquity* 82:151–164.

Arsuaga, J. L., J. M. Carretero, A. Gracia, and I. Martínez. 1990. Taphonomical analysis of the human sample from the Sima de los Huesos Middle Pleistocene site (Atapuerca/Ibeas, Spain). *Human Evolution* 5:505–513.

Arsuaga, J. L., I. Martínez, A. Gracia, J. M. Carretero, and E. Carbonell. 1993. Three new human skulls from the Sima de los Huesos Middle Paleolithic site in Sierra de Atapuerca, Spain. *Nature* 362:534–537.

Arsuaga, J. L., I. Martínez, C. Lorenzo, A. Gracia, A. Muñoz, O. Alonso, and J. Gallego. 1999. The human cranial remains from Gran Dolina Lower Pleistocene site (Sierra de Atapuerca, Spain). *Journal of Human Evolution* 37:431–457.

Atwood, Roger. 2004. *Stealing history: Tomb raiders, smugglers, and the looting of the ancient world.* New York: St. Martin's Press.

Aveni, A. F. 1986. The Nazca lines: Patterns in the desert. *Archaeology* 39(4):32–39.

Bahn, P. G., ed. 1995. *The story of archaeology: The 100 great discoveries.* New York: Barnes & Noble.

Bahn, P. G., ed. 1996. *The Cambridge illustrated history of archaeology.* Cambridge: Cambridge University Press.

Bahn, P. G. 1999. *Bluff your way in archaeology.* London: Oval Books.

Bahn, P. G., ed. 2003. *Written in bones: How human remains unlock the secrets of the dead.* Toronto: Firefly Books.

Bahn, P. G,. and J. Vertut. 1997. *Journey through the Ice Age: Art and architecture.* Berkeley: University of California Press.

Bailey, G., and P. Spikins, eds. 2008. *Mesolithic Europe.* Cambridge: Cambridge University Press.

Baines, J., and J. Málek. 1980. *Atlas of ancient Egypt.* New York: Facts on File.

Balme, J., and A. Paterson. 2005. *Archaeology in practice. A student guide to archaeological analyses.* Oxford: Blackwell.

Balter, V., J. Blichert-Toft, J. Braga, P. Telouk, F. Thackeray, and F. Albarède. 2008. U-Pb dating of fossil enamel from the Swartkrans Pleistocene hominid site, South Africa. *Earth and Planetary Science Letters* 267:236–246.

Banning, E. B., and B. F. Byrd. 1987. Houses and changing residential units: Domestic architecture at PPNB 'Ain Ghazal, Jordan. *Proceedings of the Prehistoric Society* 53:8–65.

Barber, R. L. N. 1988. *The Cyclades in the Bronze Age.* Iowa City: University of Iowa Press.

Bareis, C. J., and J. W. Porter, eds. 1984. *American Bottom archaeology.* Urbana: University of Illinois Press.

Barker, G. 1985. *Prehistoric farming in Europe.* Cambridge: Cambridge University Press.

Bar-Yosef, O. 1986. The walls of Jericho: An alternative explanation. *Current Anthropology* 27:157–162.

Bar-Yosef, O. 1998. The Natufian culture in the Levant: Threshold to the origins of agriculture. *Evolutionary Anthropology* 6:159–177.

Bar-Yosef, O., and A. Belfer Cohen. 1992. Foraging to farming in the Mediterranean Levant. In *Transitions to agriculture in prehistory,* ed. A. B. Gebauer and T. D. Price. Madison, WI: Prehistory Press.

Basu, S., J. Dickhaut, G. Hecht, K. Towry, and G. Waymire. 2009. Recordkeeping alters economic history by promoting reciprocity. *Proceedings of the National Academy of Sciences* 106:1009–1014.

Bauer, B. S., and R. A. Covey. 2002. Processes of state formation in the Inca heartland (Cuzco, Peru). *American Anthropologist* 104:846–864.

Bawden, G. 1996. *The Moche.* Malden, MA: Blackwell.

Bayard, D. 1971. *Non Nok Tha: The 1968 excavation procedure, stratigraphy, and a summary of evidence.* Studies in Prehistoric Anthropology, Vol. 4. Dunedin, NZ: University of Otago.

Bayard, D. 1980. East Asia in the Bronze Age. In *The Cambridge encyclopedia of archaeology,* ed. A. Sherratt. New York: Crown.

Beadle, G. 1980. The ancestry of corn. *Scientific American* 242:112–119.

Becker, M. J. 1979. Priests, peasants, and ceremonial centers: The intellectual history of a model. In *Maya archaeology and ethnohistory,* ed. N. Hammond and G. R. Willey. Austin: University of Texas Press.

Bellwood, P. 1978. *Man's conquest of the Pacific.* Oxford: Oxford University Press.

Bellwood, P. 1990. Foraging towards farming: A decisive transition or a millennial blur? *Review of Archaeology* 11:14–24.

Bellwood, P. 2005. *First farmers: The origins of agricultural societies.* Malden, MA: Blackwell.

Bender, B. 1978. Gatherer-hunter to farmer: A social perspective. *World Archaeology* 10:204–222.

Bennett, W. C. 1934. Excavations at Tiahuanaco. *Anthropological Papers of the American Museum of Natural History* 34(3):359–494.

Bennett, W. C. 1947. The archaeology of the central Andes. In *Handbook of South American Indians.* Vol. 2, *The Andean civilizations,* ed. J. Steward. Bureau of American Ethnology, Bulletin 143. Washington, DC: Smithsonian Institution.

Benson, E. P., ed. 1968. *Dumbarton Oaks conference on the Olmec.* Washington, DC: Dumbarton Oaks.

Benson, E. P., ed. 1971. *Dumbarton Oaks conference on Chavín.* Washington, DC: Dumbarton Oaks.

Benson, E. P., ed. 1981. *The Olmec and their neighbors: Essays in memory of Matthew W. Stirling.* Washington, DC: Dumbarton Oaks.

Berdan, F. 1982. *The Aztecs of central Mexico: An imperial society.* New York: Holt, Rinehart & Winston.

Berger, R., R. Chohfi, A. V. Zegarra, W. Yepez, and O. F. Carrasco. 1988. Radiocarbon dating Machu Picchu, Peru. *Antiquity* 62:707–710.

Berlo, J. C., ed. 1992. *Art, ideology, and the city of Teotihuacan.* Washington, DC: Dumbarton Oaks.

Bermudéz de Castro, J. M. A. 1998. Hominids at Atapuerca: The first human occupation in Europe. In *The first Europeans: Recent discoveries and current debate,* ed. E. Carbonell, J. Bermudéz de Castro, J. L. Arsuaga, and X. P. Rodriguez. Burgos, Spain: Aldecoa.

Bernal, I. 1965. Archaeological synthesis of Oaxaca. In *Handbook of Middle American Indians.* Vol. 3, *Archaeology of southern Mesoamerica,* ed. G. R. Willey. Austin: University of Texas Press.

Bernal, I. 1980. *A history of Mexican archaeology: The vanished civilizations of Middle America.* London: Thames & Hudson.

Bicchieri, M. G. 1972. *Hunters and gatherers today.* New York: Holt, Rinehart & Winston.

Bickerton, D. 1991. *Language and species.* Chicago: University of Chicago Press.

Bidwell, P. T. 1985. *The Roman fort of Vindolanda.* HBMCE. Arch, Rep 1. London.

Binford, L. R. 1968. Post-Pleistocene adaptations. In *New perspectives in archeology,* ed. S. R. Binford and L. R. Binford. Chicago: Aldine.

Binford, L. R. 1983. *In pursuit of the past.* New York: Thames & Hudson.

Binford, L. R. 2001. *Constructing frames of reference: An analytical method for archaeological theory building using hunter-gatherer and environmental data sets.* Berkeley: University of California Press.

Binford, L. R., and S. R. Binford. 1966. A preliminary analysis of functional variability in the Mousterian of Levallois facies. In *Recent studies in paleoanthropology,* ed. J. D. Clark and F. C. Howell. *American Anthropologist,* special issue 68(2):238–295.

Binford, L. R., and C. K. Ho. 1985. Taphonomy at a distance: Zhoukoudien, the cave home of Beijing man. *Current Anthropology* 26:413–442.

Bingham, H. 1915. The story of Machu Picchu: The Peruvian expeditions of the National Geographic Society and Yale University. *National Geographic* 27(2):172–216.

Bingham, H. 1948. *Lost city of the Incas.* New York: Duell, Sloan & Pearce.

Black, D. 1931. On an adolescent skull of *Sinanthropus pekinensis* in comparison with an adult skull of the same species and with other hominid skulls, recent and fossil. *Palaeontologica Sinica,* Series D, Vol. 7, Fasicule 2.

Blanton, R. E. 1978. *Monte Albán: Settlement patterns at the ancient Zapotec capital.* New York: Academic Press.

Blanton, R. E. 1983. The ecological perspective in highland Mesoamerican archaeology. In *Archaeological hammers and theories,* ed. J. A. Moore and A. S. Keene. New York: Academic Press.

Blanton, R. E., G. M. Feinman, S. A. Kowalewski, and L. M. Nicholas. 1999. *Ancient Oaxaca.* Cambridge: Cambridge University Press.

Blanton, R. E., S. A. Kowalewski, G. M. Feinman, and L. M. Finsten. 1993. *Ancient Mesoamerica: A comparison of change in three regions.* 2d ed. Cambridge: Cambridge University Press.

Blumenschine, R. J. 1987. Characteristics of the early hominid scavenging niche. *Current Anthropology* 28:383–407.

Bocherens, H. 2001. New isotopic evidence for dietary habits of Neanderthals from Belgium. *Journal of Human Evolution* 40:497–505.

Bocquet, A., J. L. Brochier, A. Emery-Barbier, K. Lundstrom-Baudais, C. Orcel, and F. Vin. 1987. A submerged Neolithic village: Charavines "Les Baigneurs" in Lake Paladru, France. In *European wetlands in prehistory,* ed. J. M. Coles and A. J. Lawson. Oxford: Clarendon Press.

Bogucki, P. 1988. *Forest farmers and stockherders.* Cambridge: Cambridge University Press.

Bolger, D. Gender and human evolution. In *Handbook of gender in archaeology,* ed. S. M. Nelson. London: AltaMira.

Bonnichsen, R., ed. 2004. *Who were the first Americans?* Corvallis, OR: Center for the Study of the First Americans.

Bordaz, J. 1971. *Tools of the Old and New Stone Age.* New York: American Museum of Natural History.

Bordes, F. 1968. *The Old Stone Age.* New York: McGraw-Hill.

Bordes, F. 1972. *A tale of two caves.* New York: Harper & Row.

Bordes, F., and D. de Sonneville-Bordes. 1970. The significance of variability in Paleolithic assemblages. *World Archaeology* 2:61–73.

Boserup, E. 1965. *The conditions of agricultural growth: The economics of agrarian change under population pressure.* Chicago: Aldine.

Boule, M. 1911–1913. L'homme fossile de La Chapelle-aux-Saintes. *Annales de Paléontologie,* VI–VIII.

Bourget, S. 2001. Rituals of sacrifice: Its practice at Huaca de la Luna and its representation in Moche iconography. In *Moche art and archaeology in ancient Peru,* ed. J. Pillsbury. New Haven, CT: National Gallery of Art.

Bowen, D. Q. 1978. *Quaternary geology.* Oxford: Pergamon Press.

Bradley, R. 1984. *The social foundations of prehistoric Britain.* Harlow, England: Longman.

Bradley, R. 1998. *The significance of monuments.* London: Routledge.

Braidwood, R. J. 1960. The agricultural revolution. *Scientific American* 203(3):130–148.

Brain, C. K. 1981. *The hunters or the hunted? An introduction to African cave taphonomy.* Chicago: University of Chicago Press.

Braudel, F. 1970. History and the social sciences: The long term. *Social Science Information* 9:145–174.

Breeze, D., and B. Dobson. 2000. *Hadrian's Wall,* 3d ed. London: Allen Lane.

Brewer, D. J., and E. Teeter. 1999. *Egypt and the Egyptians.* Cambridge: Cambridge University Press.

Brier, B. 2007. How to build a pyramid. *Archaeology* 60(3):22–27.

Brodie, N., and K. W. Tubb, eds. 2002. *Illicit antiquities: The theft of culture and the extinction of archaeology.* London: Routledge.

Brose, D., J. Brown, and D. Penney. 1985. *Ancient art of the American Woodland Indians.* New York: Harry N. Abrams.

Brothwell, D. 1987. *The bog man and the archaeology of people.* Cambridge, MA: Harvard University Press.

Brothwell, D., and A. M. Pollard, eds. 2001. *Handbook of archaeological sciences.* New York: Wiley.

Browman, D. L. 1981. New light on Andean Tiwanaku. *American Scientist* 69:408–419.

Bruhns, K. O. 1994. *Ancient South America.* Cambridge: Cambridge University Press.

Brumfiel, E. M., and G. M. Feinman, eds. 2008. *The Aztec world.* New York: Abrams.

Brunhouse, R. L. 1973. *In search of the Maya.* New York: Ballantine Books.

Bryan, A. L. 1978. *Early man in America from a circum-Pacific perspective.* Edmonton: Archaeological Researches International.

Bryan, A. L. 1986. *New evidence for the Pleistocene peopling of the Americas.* Orono, ME: Center for the Study of Early Man.

Bryant, V. 2007. Microscopic evidence for the domestication and spread of maize. *Proceedings of the National Academy of Science* 104:19,659–19,660.

Buchanan, B., M. Collard, and K. Edinborough. 2008. Paleoindian demography and the extraterrestrial impact hypothesis. *Proceedings of the National Academy of Science* 105:11,651–11,654.

Buikstra, J., and L. Beck. 2006. *Bioarchaeology. The contextual analysis of human remains.* San Diego: Elsevier.

Burenhult, G. 1993. *People of the Stone Age: Hunter-gatherers and early farmers.* San Francisco: HarperCollins.

Burenhult, G., ed. 1994. *Old World civilizations: The rise of cities and states.* New York: HarperCollins.

Burenhult, G., ed. 1999. *Arkeologi i Norden* 1–2. Stockholm: Bokförlaget Natur och Kultur.

Burger, R. L. 1984. *The prehistoric occupation of Chavín de Huantar, Peru.* Berkeley: University of California Press.

Burger, R. L. 1985. Concluding remarks: Early Peruvian civilization and its relation to the Chavín horizon. In *Early ceremonial architecture in the Andes,* ed. C. B. Donnan. Washington, DC: Dumbarton Oaks.

Burger, R. L. 1989. An overview of Peruvian archaeology (1976–1986). *Annual Review of Anthropology* 18:37–69.

Burger, R. L. 1992. *Chavín and the origins of Andean civilization.* London: Thames & Hudson.

Burger, R. L., and L. C. Salazar. 2004. *Machu Picchu: Unveiling the mystery of the Incas.* New Haven, CT: Yale University Press.

Burl, A. 1976. *Stone circles of the British Isles.* New Haven, CT: Yale University Press.

Butzer, K. W. 1980. Civilizations: Organisms or systems? *American Scientist* 68:148–160.

Butzer, K. W. 1982. *Archaeology as human ecology.* Cambridge: Cambridge University Press.

Cabrera Castro, R., S. Sugiyama, and G. L. Cowgill. 1991. The Templo de Quetzalcoatl project at Teotihuacan. *Ancient Mesoamerica* 2:77–92.

Calnek, E. E. 1976. The internal structure of Tenochtitlan. In *The Valley of Mexico: Studies in pre-Hispanic ecology and society,* ed. E. R. Wolf. Albuquerque: University of New Mexico Press.

Campbell, B. G., and J. D. Loy. 2000. *Humankind emerging,* 8th ed. Boston: Longman.

Cann, R. L., M. Stoneking, and A. C. Wilson. 1987. Mitochondrial DNA and human evolution. *Nature* 325:31–36.

Carbonell, E., J. Castro, J. Pares, A. Perez-Gonzalez, G. Cuenca-Bescos, A. Olle, et al. 2008. The first hominin of Europe. *Nature* 452:465–469.

Carman, J. 2002. *Archaeology and heritage: An introduction.* London: Continuum.

Carneiro, R. L. 1970. A theory of the origin of the state. *Science* 169:733–738.

Carneiro, R. L. 2003. *Evolutionism in cultural anthropology: A critical history.* Boulder, CO: Westview.

Carr, C., and T. Case, eds. 2005. *Gathering Hopewell: Society, ritual, and ritual interaction.* New York: Kluwer.

Carrasco, D., ed. 2001. *The Oxford encyclopedia of Mesoamerican cultures: The civilizations of Mexico and Central America.* Oxford: Oxford University Press.

Carter, H., and A. C. Mace. 1923–1933. *The tomb of Tut-ankh-Amen.* London: Macmillan.

Caso, A., and I. Bernal. 1965. Ceramics of Oaxaca. In *Handbook of Middle American Indians.* Vol. 3, *Archaeology of southern Mesoamerica,* ed. G. R. Willey. Austin: University of Texas Press.

Cauvin, J. 2000. *The birth of the gods and the origins of agriculture,* trans. T. Watkins. Cambridge: Cambridge University Press.

Cela-Conde, C. J., and F. J. Ayala. 2003. Genera of the human lineage. *Proceedings of the National Academy of Sciences* 100:7684–7689.

Chadwick, J. 1976. *The Mycenaean world.* Cambridge: Cambridge University Press.

Chakrabarti, D. 1980. Early agriculture and the development of towns in India. In *The Cambridge encyclopedia of archaeology,* ed. A. Sherratt. New York: Crown.

Chang, K. C. 1973. Food and food vessels in ancient China. *Transactions of the New York Academy of Sciences* 35:495–520.

Chang, K. C. 1977a. Chinese archaeology since 1949. *Journal of Asian Studies* 36:623–646.

Chang, K. C. 1977b. The continuing quest for China's origins, I: Early farmers in China. *Antiquity* 30:116–123.

Chang, K. C. 1977c. The continuing quest for China's origins, II: The Shang civilization. *Antiquity* 30:187–193.

Chang, K. C. 1981. In search of China's beginnings: New light on an old civilization. *American Scientist* 69:148–160.

Chang, K. C. 1986. *The archaeology of ancient China.* New Haven, CT: Yale University Press.

Chang, K. C. 1989. Ancient China and its anthropological significance. In *Archaeological thought in America,* ed. C. C. Lamberg-Karlovsky. Cambridge: Cambridge University Press.

Chang, K. C. 1994. Ritual and power. In *Cradles of civilization: China,* ed. R. E. Murowchick. Norman: University of Oklahoma Press.

Changeux, J.-P., and J. Chavillon, eds. 1995. *Origins of the human brain.* Oxford: Oxford University Press.

Chapman, R., I. Kinnes, and K. Randsborg, eds. 2009. *The archaeology of death.* Cambridge University Press.

Chesterton, G. K. 1933. *All I survey: A book of essays.* London: Methuen.

Childe, V. G. 1950. The urban revolution. *Town Planning Review* 21:3–17.

Childe, V. G. 1951. *Man makes himself.* New York: New American Library.

Childe, V. G. 1956. *A short introduction to archaeology: Man and society.* London: F. Muller.

Chippendale, C. 1983. *Stonehenge complete.* Ithaca, NY: Cornell University Press.

Churchill, S. E. 1998. Cold adaptation, heterochrony, and Neandertals. *Evolutionary Anthropology* 7:46–61.

Cieza de León, P. 1959. *The Incas,* ed. V. von Hagen, trans. H. de Onis. Norman: University of Oklahoma Press.

Clark, J. D. 1970a. *Kalambo Falls.* Cambridge: Cambridge University Press.

Clark, J. D. 1970b. *The prehistory of Africa.* London: Thames & Hudson.

Clark, J. D., and S. A. Brandt, eds. 1984. *From hunters to farmers.* Berkeley: University of California Press.

Clark, J. D., and J. W. K. Harris. 1985. Fire and its roles in early hominid lifeways. *African Archaeological Review* 3:3–28.

Clark, J. E. 1986. From mountains to molehills: A critical review of Teotihuacan's obsidian industry. In *Research in Economic Anthropology, Supplement 2,* ed. B. L. Isaac. Greenwich, CT: JAI Press.

Clottes, J. 2008. *Cave art.* London: Phaidon.

Clutton-Brock, J. 1999. *A natural history of domesticated animals.* Cambridge: Cambridge University Press.

Coe, M. D. 1977. *Mexico,* 2d ed. New York: Praeger.

Coe, M. D. 2005. *The Maya,* 7th ed. London: Thames & Hudson.

Coe, M. D., and R. A. Diehl. 1980. *In the land of the Olmec: The archaeology of San Lorenzo Tenochtitlan.* Austin: University of Texas Press.

Coe, M., D. Snow, and E. Benson. 1986. *Atlas of ancient America.* New York: Facts on File.

Coe, W. R. 1965. Tikal: Ten years of study of a Maya ruin in the lowlands of Guatemala. *Expedition* 8(1):5–56.

Coe, W. R. 1988. *Tikal: A handbook of the ancient Maya ruins,* 2d ed. Philadelphia: University Museum.

Coe, W. R., and W. A. Haviland. 1982. Introduction to the archaeology of Tikal, Guatemala. *University Museum Monograph 46.* Philadelphia: University of Pennsylvania.

Coggins, C. 1979. A new order and the role of the calendar: Some characteristics of the Middle Classic period at Tikal. In *Maya archaeology and ethnohistory,* ed. N. Hammond. Austin: University of Texas Press.

Cohen, M. N. 1977. Population pressure and the origins of agriculture: An archaeological example from the coast of Peru. In *The origins of agriculture,* ed. C. Reed. The Hague: Mouton.

Cole, S. 1975. *Leakey's luck: The life of Louis Seymour Bazett Leakey, 1903–1972.* New York: Harcourt Brace Jovanovich.

Coles, J. M. 1982. The Bronze Age in northwestern Europe. *Advances in World Archaeology* 1:265–321.

Coles, J. M., and E. S. Higgs. 1969. *The archaeology of early man.* London: Faber & Faber.

Collis, J. 2001. *Digging up the past: An introduction to archaeological excavation.* Stroud, UK: Sutton.

Conkey, M. W. 1980. The identification of prehistoric hunter-gatherer aggregation sites: The case of Altamira. *Current Anthropology* 21:609–630.

Conkey, M. W. 1981. A century of Paleolithic cave art. *Archaeology* 34(4):20–28.

Conrad, G. W. 1981. Cultural materialism, split inheritance, and the expansion of ancient Peruvian empires. *American Antiquity* 46:3–26.

Conyers, L. B. 2004. *Ground-penetrating radar for archaeology.* Walnut Creek, CA: AltaMira.

Coope, G. R. 1975. Climatic fluctuations in northwest Europe since the last interglacial, indicated by fossil assemblages of Coleoptera. In *Ice ages: Ancient and modern,* ed. A. E. Wright and F. Moseley. Liverpool: Seel House Press.

Cordell, L. S. 1979. Prehistory: Eastern Anasazi. In *Handbook of North American Indians.* Vol. 9, *Southwest,* ed. A. Ortiz. Washington, DC: Smithsonian Institution Press.

Cordell, L. S. 1997. *Archaeology of the Southwest,* 2d ed. San Diego: Academic Press.

Cordell, L. S., and B. D. Smith. 1996. Indigenous farmers. In *The Cambridge history of the native peoples of the Americas.* Vol. 1, *North America, part 1,* ed. B. G. Trigger and W. E. Washburn. Cambridge: Cambridge University Press.

Costantini, L. 1984. The beginning of agriculture in the Kachi Plain: The evidence of Mehrgarh. In *South Asian archaeology 1981,* ed. B. Allchin. New York: Cambridge University Press.

Costin, C. L. 2004. Craft economies of ancient Andean states. In *Archaeological perspectives on political economies,* ed. G. M. Feinman and L. M. Nicholas. Salt Lake City: University of Utah Press.

Cowan, C. W., and P. J. Watson. 1992. *Origins of agriculture in world perspective.* Washington, DC: Smithsonian Institution Press.

Cowgill, G. L. 1975. Population pressure as a non-explanation. In *Population studies in archaeology and biological anthropology,* ed. A. C. Swedlund. *American Antiquity, Memoir* 30:127–131.

Cowgill, G. L. 1997. State and society at Teotihuacan, Mexico. *Annual Review of Anthropology* 26:129–161.

Crawford, G. W., and C. Shen. 1998. The origins of rice agriculture: Recent progress in East Asia. *Antiquity* 72:858–866.

Crawford, G. W., and H. Takamiya. 1990. The origins and implications of late prehistoric plant husbandry in northern Japan. *Antiquity* 64:889–911.

Croes, D. R. 2003. Northwest Coast wet-site artifacts: A key to understanding resource procurement, storage, management, and exchange. In *Emerging from the mist: Studies in Northwest Coast culture history,* ed. R. G. Matson, G. Coupland, and Q. Mackie. Vancouver, BC: UBC Press.

Crook, J. H. 1972. Sexual selection, dimorphism, and social organization in the primates. In *Sexual selection and the descent of man, 1871–1971,* ed. B. Campbell. Chicago: Aldine.

Crown, P. L., and W. J. Judge, eds. 1991. *Chaco and Hohokam: Prehistoric regional systems in the American Southwest.* Santa Fe, NM: School of American Research Press.

Crumley, C. L. 1995. Heterarchy and the anaysis of complex societies. In *Hetararchy and the analysis of complex societies,* ed. R. M. Ehrenreich, C. L. Crumley, and J. E. Levy. Archeological Papers No. 6. Arlington, VA: American Anthropological Association.

Culbert, T. P. 1988. Political history and the Maya glyphs. *Antiquity* 62:135–152.

Culbert, T. P., and D. S. Rice, eds. 1990. *Precolumbian population history in the Maya Lowlands.* Albuquerque: University of New Mexico Press.

Cunliffe, B. 1994. *The Oxford illustrated prehistory of Europe.* Oxford: Oxford University Press.

Cunliffe, B. 2001. *Facing the ocean: The Atlantic and its people, 8000 B.C. to A.D. 1500.* Oxford: Oxford University Press.

Cunliffe, B. 2008. *Europe between the oceans: 9000 B.C.–A.D. 1000.* New Haven, CT: Yale University Press.

Cunliffe, B., C. Gosden, and R. A. Joyce, eds. 2009. *The Oxford handbook of archaeology.* Oxford: Oxford University Press.

Curry, A. 2007. Digging into a desert mystery. *Science* 317:446–447.

Dahlin, B. H. 1984. The colossus in Guatemala: The Preclassic Maya city of El Mirador. *Archaeology* 37(5):18–25.

Dales, G. F. 1986. Some fresh approaches to old problems in Harappan archaeology. In *Studies in the archaeology of India and Pakistan,* ed. J. Jacobson. New Delhi: Oxford and IBH Publishing.

D'Altroy, T. N. 1992. *Provincial power in the Inka empire.* Washington, DC: Smithsonian Institution Press.

D'Altroy, T. N. 2001. Empires in a wider world. In *Empires: Perspectives from archaeology and history,* ed. S. E. Alcock, T. N. D'Altroy, K. D. Morrison, and C. M. Sinopoli. Cambridge: University of Cambridge Press.

D'Altroy, T. N., and T. K. Earle. 1985. Staple finance, wealth finance, and storage in the Inka political economy. *Current Anthropology* 26:187–206.

Dart, R. A. 1953. The predatory transition from ape to man. *International Anthropological Linguistics Review* 1:201–219.

Darwin, C. 1981. *The descent of man, and selection in relation to sex.* With an introduction by J. Bonner and R. M. May. Princeton, NJ: Princeton University Press. Originally published 1871.

Davidson, B. 1970. *The lost cities of Africa,* rev. ed. Boston: Little, Brown.

Day, M. 1977. *Guide to fossil man.* London: Cassell.

Deacon, H. 1989. Late Pleistocene paleoecology and archaeology in the southern Cape, South Africa. In *The human revolution,* ed. P. A. Mellars and C. B. Stringer. Princeton, NJ: Princeton University Press.

Deacon, H. J., and J. Deacon. 1999. *Human beginnings in South Africa: Uncovering the secrets of the Stone Age.* Cape Town: David Philip.

Dearborn, D. S. P., and K. J. Schreiber. 1986. Here comes the sun: The Cuzco–Machu Picchu connection. *Archaeoastronomy* 9:15–37.

Dearborn, D. S. P., K. Schreiber, and R. E. White. 1987. Intimachay: A December solstice observatory at Machu Picchu, Peru. *American Antiquity* 52:346–352.

de Borhegyi, S. F. 1980. The pre-Columbian ballgames: A pan-Mesoamerican tradition. *Contributions in Anthropology and*

*History: 1.* Milwaukee: Milwaukee Public Museum.

Decker-Walters, D., T. Walters, C. W. Cowan, and B. D. Smith. 1993. Isozymic characterization of wild populations of *Cucurbita pepo. Journal of Ethnobiology* 13:55–72.

de Lumley, H. 1969. A Paleolithic camp at Nice. *Scientific American* 220(5):42–50.

Demarest, A. 2004. *Ancient Maya: The rise and fall of a rainforest civilization.* Cambridge: Cambridge University Press.

de Mortillet, G. 1872. Classification des ages de la pierre. *Comptes rendues congress International d'Anthropologie et d'Archéologie prehistorique, VI session.* Brussels.

Denevan, W. M. 1992. The pristine myth: The landscape of the Americas in 1492. *Annals of the Association of American Geographers* 82:369–385.

Denham, T., S. Haberle, and C. Lentfer. 2004. New evidence and revised interpretations of early agriculture in Highland New Guinea. *Antiquity* 78:839–857.

Denham, T. P., S. G. Haberle, C. Lentfer, R. Fullagar, J. Field, M. Therin, N. Porch, and B. Winsborough. 2003. Origins of agriculture at Kuk Swamp in the highlands of New Guinea. *Science* 301:189–193.

Dennell, R. C. 1983. *European economic prehistory: A new approach.* New York: Academic Press.

d'Errico, F., C. Henshilwood, and P. Nilssen. 2001. An engraved bone fragment from ca. 70,000-year-old Middle Stone Age levels at Blombos Cave, South Africa: Implications for the origin of symbolism and language. *Antiquity* 75:309–318.

Deuel, L. 1977. *Memoirs of Heinrich Schliemann.* New York: Harper & Row.

Diamond, J. 1997. *Guns, germs, and steel: The fates of human societies.* New York: Norton.

Diamond, J. 2002. Evolution, consequences and future of plant and animal domestication. *Nature* 418:700–707.

Diáz del Castillo, B. 1956. *The discovery and conquest of Mexico.* New York: Farrar, Straus & Giroux.

Diehl, R. A. 1976. Pre-Hispanic relationships between the Basin of Mexico and north and west Mexico. In *The Valley of Mexico,* ed. E. R. Wolf. Albuquerque: University of New Mexico Press.

Diehl, R. A. 1981. Tula. In *Supplement to the handbook of Middle American Indians,* ed. J. A. Sabloff. Austin: University of Texas Press.

Diehl, R. A. 1983. *Tula: The Toltec capital of ancient Mexico.* London: Thames & Hudson.

Diehl, R. A., and J. C. Berlo, eds. 1989. *Mesoamerica after the decline of Teotihuacan,* A.D. *700–900.* Washington, DC: Dumbarton Oaks.

Dikov, N. N. 1994. The Paleolithic of Kamchatka and Chukotka and the problem of the peopling of America. In *Anthropology of the North Pacific Rim,* ed. W. W. Fitzhugh and V. Chausronnet. Washington, DC: Smithsonian Institution Press.

Dillehay, T. 1984. A late Ice-Age settlement in southern Chile. *Scientific American* 254(4):100–109.

Dillehay, T. 1987. By the banks of the Chinchihuapi. *Natural History* 98(4):8–12.

Dillehay, T. 1997. *Monte Verde, a late Pleistocene settlement in Chile.* Washington, DC: Smithsonian Institution Press.

Dillehay, T. D. 2009. Probing deeper into first American studies. *Proceedings of the National Academy of Science* 106:971–978.

Dillehay, T. D., J. Rossen, T. C. Andres, and D. E. Williams. 2008. Preceramic adoption of peanut, squash, and cotton in northern Peru. *Science* 316:1890–1893.

Dinacauze, D. F. 2002. *Environmental archaeology, principles and practice.* Cambridge: Cambridge University Press.

Dixon, J. E., J. R. Cann, and C. Renfrew. 1968. Obsidian and the origins of trade. *Scientific American* 211(3):44–53.

Doebley, J. 1990. Molecular evidence and the evolution of maize. *Economic Botany* 44(3 Supplement):6–27.

Domínguez-Rodrigo, M., and T. R. Pickering. 2003. Early hominid hunting and scavenging: A zooarchaeological review. *Evolutionary Anthropology* 12:275–282.

Donnan, C. B. 1976. *Moche art and iconography.* Los Angeles: UCLA Latin American Center Publications.

Donnan, C. B. 1990. Masterworks of art reveal a remarkable pre-Inca world. *National Geographic* 177(6):16–33.

Donnan, C. B., ed. 1985. *Early ceremonial architecture in the Andes.* Washington, DC: Dumbarton Oaks.

Dorweiler, J., A. Stec, J. Kermicle, and J. Doebley. 1993. Teosinte glume architecture 1: A genetic locus controlling a key step in maize evolution. *Science* 262:233–235.

Doyel, D. E., S. K. Fish, and P. R. Fish, eds. 2000. *The Hohokam village revisited.* Fort Collins, CO: Southwestern and Rocky Mountain Division of the American Association for the Advancement of Science.

Drewett, P. 1999. *Field archaeology: An introduction.* London: Routledge.

Drucker, P. 1955. *Indians of the Northwest Coast.* New York: McGraw-Hill.

Drucker, P., R. Heizer, and R. Squier. 1959. *Excavations at La Venta, Tabasco.* Bureau of American Ethnology, Bulletin 170. Washington, DC: Smithsonian Institution.

Dubois, E. 1894. *Pithecanthropus erectus, eine Menschenahnliche Übergangsform aus Java.* Cologne: Batavia.

Duby, G. 1974. *The early growth of the European economy: Warriors and peasants from the seventh to the twelfth century.* Ithaca, NY: Cornell University Press.

Dye, D. 1989. Death march of Hernando de Soto. *Archaeology* 42(3):27–31.

Earle, T. 1997. *How chiefs come to power: The political economy in prehistory.* Stanford, CA: Stanford University Press.

Elvin, M. 1973. *The pattern of the Chinese past.* Stanford, CA: Stanford University Press.

Emerson, T. E., R. E. Hughes, M. R. Hynes, and S. U. Wisseman. 2003. The sourcing and interpretation of Cahokia-style figurines in the trans-Mississippi South and Southeast. *American Antiquity* 68:287–313.

Engel, F. A. 1976. *An ancient world preserved.* New York: Crown.

English, N. B., J. L. Betancourt, J. S. Dean, and J. Quade. 2001. Strontium isotopes reveal distant sources of architectural timber in Chaco Canyon, New Mexico. *Proceedings of the National Association of Science* 98:11891–11896.

Erickson, C. L. 1992. Prehistoric landscape management in the Andean highlands: Raised field agriculture and its environmental impact. *Population and Environment* 13:285–302.

Erickson, D. L., B. D. Smith, A. C. Clarke, D. H. Sandweiss, and N. Tuross. 2005. An Asian origin for a 10,000-year-old domesticated plant in the Americas. *Proceedings of the National Academy of Sciences* 102:18315–18320.

Evans, D., C. Pottier, R. Fletcher, S. Hensley, I. Tapley, A. Milne, and M. Barbetti. 2007. A comprehensive archaeological map of the world's largest preindustrial settlement complex at Angkor, Cambodia. *Proceedings of the National Academy of Sciences* 104(36):14,277–14,282.

Evans, J., and T. O'Connor. 2001. *Environmental archaeology, principles and method.* Stroud, UK: Sutton.

Evans, S. T. 2004. *Ancient Mexico and Central America: Archaeology and culture history.* London: Thames & Hudson.

Evans, S. T., and D. L. Webster, eds. 2001. *Archaeology of ancient Mexico and Central America: An encyclopedia.* New York: Garland.

Fagan, B. M. 1978. *Quest for the past: Great discoveries in archaeology.* Prospect Heights, IL: Waveland.

Fagan, B. M. 1987. *The great journey.* London: Thames & Hudson.

Fagan, B. M., ed. 1996. *The Oxford companion to archaeology.* Oxford: Oxford University Press.

Fagan, B. M. 1998. 50 years of discovery. *Archaeology* 51(5):33–34.

Fagan, B. M. 2000. *Ancient North America,* 3d ed. London: Thames & Hudson.

Fagan, B. M. 2003. *Archaeologists: Explorers of the human past.* Oxford: Oxford University Press.

Fagan, B. M. 2004. *People of the earth: An introduction to world prehistory,* 11th ed. Upper Saddle River, NJ: Prentice-Hall.

Fagan, G. G., ed. 2006. *Archaeological fantasies: How pseudoarchaeology misrepresents the past and misleads the public.* London: Routledge.

Fairservis, W. A. 1983. The script of the Indus Valley civilization. *Scientific American* 248(3):58–66.

Falk, D. 1984. The petrified brain. *Natural History* 93(9):36–39.

Farnsworth, P., J. E. Brady, M. J. deNiro, and R. S. MacNeish. 1985. A reevaluation of the isotopic and archaeological reconstructions of diet in the Tehuacán Valley. *American Antiquity* 50:102–116.

Fash, W. L. 1991. *Scribes, warriors, and kings: The city of Copán and the ancient Maya.* London: Thames & Hudson.

Feder, K. L. 2001. *Frauds, myths, and mysteries: Science and pseudoscience in archaeology,* 4th ed. New York: McGraw-Hill.

Feder, K. L., and M. A. Park. 2001. *Human antiquity,* 4th ed. New York: McGraw-Hill.

Fedigan, L. M. 1986. The changing role of women in models of human evolution. *Annual Review of Anthropology* 15:25–66.

Fedje, D. W., and H. Josenhans. 2000. Drowned forests and archaeology on the continental shelf of British Columbia, Canada. *Geology* 28:99–102.

Feinman, G. M. 2001. Mesoamerican political complexity: The corporate-network dimension. In *Leaders to rulers: The development of political centralization,* ed. J. Haas. New York: Kluwer/Plenum.

Feinman, G. M., S. A. Kowalewski, L. Finsten, R. E. Blanton, and L. M. Nicholas. 1985. Long-term demographic change: A perspective from the Valley of Oaxaca. *Journal of Field Archaeology* 12:333–362.

Feinman, G. M., and L. Manzanilla, eds. 2000. *Cultural evolution: Contemporary viewpoints.* New York: Kluwer/Plenum.

Feinman, G. M., and J. Marcus, eds. 1998. *Archaic states.* Santa Fe, NM: School for American Research Press.

Feinman, G. M., and L. M. Nicholas. 2004. Unraveling the prehispanic highland Mesoamerican economy: Production, exchange, and consumption in the Classic period Valley of Oaxaca. In *Archaeological perspectives on political eocnomies,* ed. G. M. Feinman and L. M. Nicholas. Salt Lake City: University of Utah Press.

Feinman, G. M., and T. D. Price, eds. 2001. *Archaeology at the millennium: A sourcebook.* New York: Kluwer/Plenum.

Feldman, R. A. 1983. From maritime chiefdom to agricultural state in Formative coastal Peru. In *Civilization in the ancient Americas: Essays in honor of Gordon R. Willey,* ed. R. M. Leventhal and A. L. Kolata. Albuquerque: University of New Mexico Press.

Fiedel, S. J. 1992. *Prehistory of the Americas.* Cambridge: Cambridge University Press.

Findlayson, C. 2004. *Neanderthals and modern humans: An ecological and evolutionary perspective.* Cambridge: Cambridge University Press.

Finlayson, W. D. 1985. The 1975 and 1978 rescue excavations at the Draper site: Introduction and settlement patterns. *National Museum of Man Mercury Series,* Paper #130. Ottawa: Archaeological Survey of Canada.

Finney, F. A., and J. B. Stoltman. 1991. The Fred Edwards site: A case of Stirling phase culture contact in southwestern Wisconsin. In *New perspectives on Cahokia,* ed. J. B. Stoltman. Madison, WI: Prehistory Press.

Firestone, R. B., A. West, J. P. Kennett, L. Becker, T. E. Bunch, Z. S. Revay, P. H. Schultz, T. Belgya, D. J. Kennett, J. M. Erlandson, O. J. Dickenson, A. C. Goodyear, R. S. Harris, G. A. Howard, J. B. Kloosterman, P. Lechler, P. A. Mayewski, J. Montgomery, R. Poreda, T. Darrah, S. S. Que Hee, A. R. Smith, A. Sticr, W. Topping, J. H. Wittke, and W. S. Wolbach. 2007. Evidence for an extraterrestrial impact 12,900 years ago that contributed to the megafaunal extinctions and the Younger Dryas cooling. *Proceedings of the National Academy of Science* 104:16,016–16,021.

Fish, P. R. 1998. Hohokam culture area. In *Archaeology of prehistoric Native America: An encyclopedia,* ed. G. Gibbon. New York: Garland.

Fish, S. K., and P. R. Fish, eds. 2007. *The Hohokam millennium.* Santa Fe, NM: School for American Research Press.

Fish, S. K., P. R. Fish, and J. H. Madsen, eds. 1992. *The Marana community in the Hohokam world.* Tucson: University of Arizona Press.

Fish, S. K., and S. A. Kowalewski, eds. 1990. *The archaeology of regions: A case for full-coverage survey.* Washington, DC: Smithsonian Institution Press.

Fisher, H. E. 1983. *The sex contract: The evolution of human behavior.* New York: Quill.

Fitting, J. E. 1978. Regional cultural development, 300 B.C. to A.D. 1000. In *Handbook of North American Indians.* Vol. 15, *Northeast,* ed. W. C. Sturtevant and B. G. Trigger. Washington, DC: Smithsonian Institution Press.

Flannery, K. V. 1968a. Archaeological systems theory and early Mesoamerica. In *Anthropological archeology in the Americas,* ed. B. J. Meggers. Washington, DC: Anthropological Society of Washington.

Flannery, K. V. 1968b. The Olmec and the Valley of Oaxaca: A model for interregional interaction in Formative times. In *Dumbarton Oaks conference on the Olmec,* ed. E. Benson. Washington, DC: Dumbarton Oaks.

Flannery, K. V. 1972a. The cultural evolution of civilizations. *Annual Review of Ecology and Systematics* 3:399–426.

Flannery, K. V. 1972b. The origins of the village as a settlement type in Mesoamerica and the Near East: A comparative study. In *Man, settlement, and urbanism,* ed. P. J. Ucko, R. Tringham, and G. W. Dimbleby. London: Duckworth.

Flannery, K. V. 1973. The origins of agriculture. *Annual Review of Anthropology* 2:271–310.

Flannery, K. V., ed. 1976. *The early Mesoamerican village.* New York: Academic Press.

Flannery, K. V., ed. 1986. *Guilá Naquitz: Archaic foraging and early agriculture in Oaxaca, Mexico.* New York: Academic Press.

Flannery, K. V., and J. Marcus. 1976. Evolution of the public building in Formative Oaxaca. In *Cultural change and continuity: Essays in honor of James Bennett Griffin,* ed. C. Cleland. New York: Academic Press.

Flannery, K. V., and J. Marcus. 1983. The growth of site hierarchies in the Valley of Oaxaca: Part 1. In *The cloud people: Divergent evolution of the Zapotec and Mixtec civilizations,* ed. K. V. Flannery and J. Marcus. New York: Academic Press.

Flannery, K. V., and J. Marcus. 1994. *Early Formative pottery of the Valley of Oaxaca, Mexico.* Memoirs of the Museum of Anthropolog, No. 27. Ann Arbor: University of Michigan.

Flannery, K. V., and J. Marcus, eds. 1983. *The cloud people: Divergent evolution of the Zapotec and Mixtec civilizations.* New York: Academic Press. Reprint, Clinton Corners, NY: Percheron Press, 2003.

Flinders Petrie, W. M. 1904. *Methods and aims of archaeology.* London: Macmillan.

Flint, R. F. 1971. *Glacial and quaternary geology.* New York: Wiley.

Foley, R. 1987. Hominid species and stone-tool assemblages: How are they related? *Antiquity* 61:380–392.

Foley, R. 1999. Evolutionary geography of Pliocene African hominids. In *African biogeography, climate change, and human evolution,* ed. T. G. Bromage and F. Schrenk. New York: Oxford University Press.

Folkens, P. A., and T. D. White. 2000. *Human osteology.* New York: Academic Press.

Ford, J. A., and C. H. Webb. 1956. *Poverty Point: A Late Archaic site in Louisiana.* Anthropological Papers, vol. 46, part 1. New York: American Museum of Natural History.

Ford, R. I., ed. 1984. *The origins of plant husbandry in North America.* Ann Arbor: University of Michigan Museum of Anthropology.

Foster, J. 2003. *Life and death in the Iron Age.* Oxford: Ashmolean Museum

Foster, M. S., and P. C. Weigand, eds. 1985. *The archaeology of west and northwest Mesoamerica.* Boulder, CO: Westview.

Fowler, M. L. 1974. *Cahokia: Ancient capital of the Midwest.* Reading, MA: Addison-Wesley.

Fowler, M. L. 1975. A pre-Columbian urban center on the Mississippi. *Scientific American* 233(2):92–101.

Fowler, M. L. 1991. Mound 72 and Early Mississippian at Cahokia. In *New perspectives on Cahokia,* ed. J. B. Stoltman. Madison, WI: Prehistory Press.

Fowler, M. L., and R. L. Hall. 1978. Late prehistory of the Illinois area. In *Handbook of North American Indians.* Vol. 15, *Northeast,* ed. W. C. Sturtevant and B. G. Trigger. Washington, DC: Smithsonian Institution Press.

Frankfurt, H. 1956. *The birth of civilization in the Near East.* Garden City, NY: Doubleday.

Frayer, D. W., M. H. Wolpoff, A. G. Thorne, F. H. Smith, and G. G. Pope. 1993. Theories of modern human origins: The paleontological test. *American Anthropologist* 95:14–50.

French, E. 2002. *Mycenae: Agamemnon's capital.* Stroud, UK: Tempus.

Friedman, R. 2003. City of the hawk. *Archaeology* 56(6):50–56.

Fullagar, R., J. Field, T. Denham, and C. Lentfer. 2006. Early and mid Holocene tool-use and processing of taro (*Colocasia esculenta*), yam (*Dioscorea* sp.) and other plants at Kuk Swamp in the highlands of Papua New Guinea. *Journal of Archaeological Science* 33:595–506.

Funk, R. E. 1978. Post-Pleistocene adaptations. In *Handbook of North American Indians.* Vol. 15, *Northeast,* ed. W. C. Sturtevant and B. G. Trigger. Washington, DC: Smithsonian Institution Press.

Fyfe, C. 1994. The development of African states: 3000 B.C.–A.D. 1500. In *Old World civilizations: The rise of cities and states,* ed. G. Burenhult. San Francisco: HarperCollins.

Galik, K., B. Senut, M. Pickford, D. Gommery, J. Treil, A. J. Kuperavage, and R. B. Eckhardt. 2004. External and internal morphology of the BAR 1002'00 Orrorin tugenensis femur. *Science* 305:1450–1452.

Galinat, W. C. 1971. The origin of maize. *Annual Review of Genetics* 5:447–478.

Gamble, C. 1986. *The Paleolithic settlement of Europe.* Cambridge: Cambridge University Press.

Gamble, C. 1999. *The Paleolithic societies of Europe.* Cambridge: Cambridge University Press.

Gamble, C. 2007. *Origins and revolutions: Human identity in earliest prehistory.* Cambridge: Cambridge University Press.

Garlake, P. S. 1973. *Great Zimbabwe.* London: Thames & Hudson.

Garlake, P. S. 1980. Early states in Africa. In *The Cambridge encyclopedia of archaeology,* ed. A. Sherratt. New York: Crown.

Garrod, D. A. E., and D. M. A. Bate. 1937. *The Stone Age of Mount Carmel.* Oxford: Clarendon Press.

Gates, C. 2003. *Ancient cities.* London: Routledge.

Geertz, C. 1963. The transition to humanity. *Anthropological Series* 3:1–9. Washington, DC: Voice of America, United States Information Service.

Gibbon, G., ed. 1998. *Archaeology of prehistoric North America: An encyclopedia.* New York: Garland.

Gibson, J. L. 1987. The Poverty Point earthworks reconsidered. *Mississippi Archaeology* 22:15–31.

Gibson, J. L. 1990. Earth sitting: Architectural masses at Poverty Point, northeastern Louisiana. In *Recent research at the Poverty Point site,* ed. K. M. Byrd. Lousiana Archaeology No. 13. Lafayette: Louisiana Archaeological Society.

Gibson, J. L. 1996. *Poverty Point: A terminal Archaic culture of the lower Mississippi Valley,* 2d ed. Baton Rouge: Department of Culture, Recreation and Tourism, Louisiana Archaeological Survey and Antiquities Commission.

Gibson, J. L. 2001. *Ancient mounds of Poverty Point: Place of rings.* Gainesville: University Press of Florida.

Gibson, J. L. 2006. Navels of the earth: Sedentism in the early mound-building cultures in the Lower Mississippi Valley. *World Archaeology* 38(2):311–329.

Gilbert, W. H., and B. Asfaw. 2009. *Homo erectus: Pleistocene evidence from the Middle Awash, Ethiopia.* Berkeley: University of California Press.

Gimbutas, M. 1977. Varna, a sensationally rich cemetery of the Karanova culture about 4500 B.C. *Expedition* 19, no. 4 (1977):39–47.

Gingerich, P. D. 1985. Nonlinear molecular clocks and ape–human divergence times. In *Hominid evolution: Past, present, and future,* ed. P. V. Tobias. New York: A. R. Liss.

Gleeson, P., and M. Fisken. 1977. *Ozette archaeological project, interim final report, phase X.* Pullman: Washington Archaeological Research Center, Washington State University.

Gleeson, P., and G. Grosso. 1976. Ozette site. In *The excavation of water-saturated archaeological sites (wet sites) on the Northwest Coast of North America,* ed. D. R. Croes. Ottawa: Archaeological Survey of Canada.

Glob, P. V. 1970a. *The bog people.* Ithaca, NY: Cornell University Press.

Glob, P. V. 1970b. *The mound people.* Ithaca, NY: Cornell University Press.

Glover, I. C. 1977. The Hoabinhian: Hunter-gatherers or early agriculturalists in Southeast Asia? In *Hunters, gatherers, and first farmers beyond Europe,* ed. J. V. S. Megaw. Leicester: Leicester University Press.

Glover, I. C. 1980. Agricultural origins in East Asia. In *The Cambridge encyclopedia of archaeology,* ed. A. Sherratt. New York: Crown.

Goebel, T., A. P. Derevianko, and V. T. Petrin. 1993. Dating the Middle-to-Upper Paleolithic transition at Kara-Bom. *Current Anthropology* 34:452–458.

Goebel, T., M. Waters, and D. O'Rourke. 2008. The Late Pleistocene dispersal of modern humans in the Americas. *Science* 319:1497–1502.

Good, I. 2001. Archaeological textiles: A review of current research. *Annual Review of Anthropology* 30:209–226.

Goodall, J. 1986. *The chimpanzees of Gombe Reserve.* Cambridge, MA: Harvard University Press.

Goren-Inbar, N., N. Alperson, M. E. Kislev, O. Simchoni, Y. Melamed, A. Ben-Nun, and E. Werker. 2004. Earliest signs of human-controlled fire uncovered in Israel. *Science* 5671:663–665.

Gorman, C. H. 1970. Excavations at Spirit Cave, North Thailand: Some interim interpretations. *Asian Perspectives* 13:79–107.

Gorman, C. H. 1971. The Hoabinhian and after: Subsistence patterns in Southeast Asia during the Late Pleistocene and Early Recent periods. *World Archaeology* 2:300–320.

Gorman, C. H. 1977. A priori models and Thai prehistory: A reconsideration of the beginnings of agriculture in southeastern Asia. In *The origins of agriculture,* ed. C. A. Reed. The Hague: Mouton.

Goudie, A. 1983. *Environmental change.* Oxford: Clarendon Press.

Gould, S. J. 1984. A short way to corn. *Natural History* 93(3):12–20.

Gowlett, J. A. J. 1984a. *Ascent to civilization: The archaeology of early man.* New York: Knopf.

Gowlett, J. A. J. 1984b. Mental abilities of early man. In *Community ecology and human adaptation in the Pleistocene,* ed. R. A. Foley. London: Academic Press.

Gowlett, J. A. J. 1987. The archaeology of accelerator radiocarbon dating. *Journal of World Prehistory* 1:127–170.

Graham, I. 1967. *Archaeological explorations in El Petén, Guatemala.* Middle American Research Institute, Publication 33. New Orleans: Tulane University.

Grayson, D. K. 1987. Death by natural causes. *Natural History* 96(5):8–12.

Grayson, D. K. 1991. Late Pleistocene mammalian extinctions in North America: Taxonomy, chronology, and explanations. *Journal of World Prehistory* 5:193–232.

Grayson, D. K. 1993. *The desert's past: A natural history of the Great Basin.* Washington, DC: Smithsonian Institution Press.

Grayson, D. K., and D. J. Meltzer. 2002. Clovis hunting and large mammal extinction: A critical review of the evidence. *Journal of World Prehistory* 16:313–359.

Greber, N. B. 1998. Ohio Hopewell. In *Archaeology of prehistoric Native America: An encyclopedia,* ed. G. Gibbon. New York: Garland.

Greber, N. B. 2003. Chronological relationships among Ohio Hopewell sites: Few dates and much complexity. In *Theory, method, and practice in modern archaeology,* ed. R. J. Jeske and D. K. Charles. Westport, CT: Praeger.

Green, M. W. 1981. The construction and implementation of the cuneiform writing system. *Visible Language* 15:345–372.

Greene, K. 2002. *Archaeology: An introduction,* 4th ed. Philadelphia: University of Pennsylvania Press.

Griffin, J. B. 1967. Eastern North American archaeology: A summary. *Science* 156:175–190.

Griffin, J. B. 1980. Agricultural groups in North America. In *The Cambridge encyclopedia of archaeology,* ed. A. Sherratt. New York: Crown.

Griffin, J. B. 1983. The Midlands. In *Ancient North Americans,* ed. J. Jennings. San Francisco: Freeman.

Grove, D. C. 1981. The Formative period and the evolution of complex culture. In *Supplement to the handbook of Middle American Indians,* Vol. 1, ed. J. A. Sabloff. Austin: University of Texas Press.

Grove, D. C. 1984. *Chalcatzingo: Excavations on the Olmec frontier.* London: Thames & Hudson.

Grube, N., ed. 2001. *Maya: Divine kings of the rain forest.* Cologne: Könemann Verlagsgesellschaft mbH.

Gumerman, G. J., ed. 1991. *Exploring the Hohokam: Prehistoric desert peoples of the American Southwest.* Dragoon, AZ: Amerind Foundation; Albuquerque: University of New Mexico Press.

Gumerman, G. J., and E. W. Haury. 1979. Prehistory: Hohokam. In *Handbook of North American Indians.* Vol. 9, *Southwest,* ed. A. Ortiz. Washington, DC: Smithsonian Institution Press.

Guthrie, R. D. 2005. *The nature of Paleolithic art.* Chicago: University of Chicago Press.

Haas, J. S. 1982. *The evolution of the prehistoric state.* New York: Columbia University Press.

Haas, J., ed. 2001. *Leaders to rulers: The development of political centralization.* New York: Kluwer/Plenum.

Haas, J., W. Creamer, and A. Ruiz. 2004. Dating the Late Archaic occupation of the Norte Chico region in Peru. *Nature* 432:1020–1023.

Haas, J., W. Creamer, and A. Ruiz. 2005. Power and the emergence of complex polities in the Peruvian preceramic. In *Foundations of power in the prehispanic Andes,* ed. K. J. Vaughn,

D. Ogburn, and C. A. Conlee. Archeological Papers No. 14. Arlington, VA: American Anthropological Association.

Haas, J., S. Pozorski, and T. Pozorski, eds. 1987. *The origins and development of the Andean state.* Cambridge: Cambridge University Press.

Habu, J. 2004. *Ancient Jomon of Japan.* Cambridge: Cambridge University Press.

Haddingham, E. 1979. *Secrets of the Ice Age.* London: Walker.

Hall, M. 1996. Mapungubwe and Toutswemogala. In *The Oxford companion to archaeology,* ed. B. M. Fagan. New York: Oxford University Press.

Hall, M., and S. Silliman. 2005. *Historical archaeology.* Malden, MA: Blackwell.

Hall, R. L. 1977. An anthropocentric perspective for eastern United States prehistory. *American Antiquity* 42:499–518.

Halloway, R. L. 1983. Cerebral brain endocast pattern of *Australopithecus afarensis. Nature* 303:420–422.

Hammond, N. 1982. *Ancient Maya civilization.* New Brunswick, NJ: Rutgers University Press.

Hammond, N. 1987. The discovery of Tikal. *Archaeology* 40(3):30–37.

Hantman, J. L. 1990. Between Powhatan and Quirank: Reconstructing Monacan culture and history in the context of Jamestown. *American Anthropologist* 92:676–690.

Hantman, J. L., and G. Dunham. 1993. The enlightened archaeologist. *Archaeology* 46(3):44–49.

Harding, A. F. 2000. *European societies in the Bronze Age.* Cambridge: Cambridge University Press.

Harlan, J. R. 1967. A wild wheat harvest in Turkey. *Archaeology* 20(3):197–201.

Harlan, J. R. 1992. *Crops and man,* 2d ed. Madison, WI: American Society of Agronomy and Crop Science Society of America.

Harlan, J. R. 1995. *The living fields: Our agricultural heritage.* Oxford: Oxford University Press.

Harlan, J. R., J. M. J. de Wet, and A. B. L. Stemler, eds. 1976. *Origins of African plant domestication.* The Hague: Mouton.

Harlan, J. R., and D. Zohary. 1966. Distribution of wild wheats and barley. *Science* 153:1074–1080.

Harner, M. 1977. The enigma of Aztec sacrifice. *Natural History* 86(4):47–52.

Harris, D. R., and G. C. Hillman, eds. 1989. *Foraging and farming: The evolution of plant exploitation.* London: Unwin Hyman.

Harrison, P. D. 1999. *The lords of Tikal: Rulers of an ancient Maya city.* London: Thames & Hudson.

Harrison, R. J. 1980. *The Beaker folk.* London: Thames & Hudson.

Hart, J. P., D. L. Asch, C. M. Scarry, and G. W. Crawford. 2002. The age of the common bean (*Phaseolus vulgaris* L.) in the northern Eastern Woodlands of North America. *Antiquity* 76:377–385.

Harvati, K., and T. Harrison, eds. 2007. *Neanderthals revisited: New approaches and perspectives.* New York: Springer.

Hassan, F. A. 1981. *Demographic archaeology.* New York: Academic Press.

Hassan, F. A. 1997. Global population and human evolution. *Human Evolution* 12:3.

Hassan, F. A. 2007. The lie of history: Nation-states and the contradictions of complex societies. In *Sustainability or collapse: An integrated history and future of the people on Earth,* ed. R. Costanza, L. J. Graumlich, and W. Steffen. Cambridge, MA: MIT Press.

Hastings, C. M., and M. E. Moseley. 1975. The adobes of Huaca del Sol and Huaca de la Luna. *American Antiquity* 40:196–203.

Hastorf, C. A., ed. 1999. *Early settlement at Chiripa, Bolivia: Research of the Taraco archaeological project.* Contributions of the Archaeological Research Facility No. 57. Berkeley: University of California.

Hastorf, C. A., and V. S. Popper. 1989. *Current paleoethnobotany.* Chicago: University of Chicago Press.

Haury, E. W. 1976. *The Hohokam: Desert farmers and craftsmen.* Tucson: University of Arizona Press.

Hayden, B. 1990. Nimrods, piscators, pluckers and planters: The emergence of food production. *Journal of Anthropological Archaeology* 9:31–69.

Haynes, G. 2009. *American megafaunal extinctions at the end of the pleistocene.* New York: Springer.

Heckenberger, M. J., A. Kuikuro, U. T. Kuikuro, J. C. Russell, M. Schmidt, C. Fausto, and B. Franchetto. 2003. Amazonia 1492: Pristine forest or cultural parkland? *Science* 301:1710–1714.

Heckenberger, M. J., J. B. Petersen, and E. Goés Neves. 1999. Village size and permanence in Amazonia: Two archaeological examples from Brazil. *Latin American Antiquity* 10:353–376.

Hedges, R. E. M. 1981. Radiocarbon dating with an accelerator. *Archaeometry* 23:3–18.

Helbaek, H. 1960. The paleoethnobotany of the Near East and Europe. In *Prehistoric investigations in Iraqi Kurdistan,* ed. R. J. Braidwood and B. Howe. Studies in Oriental Civilization 31. Chicago: Oriental Institute.

Henderson, J. S. 1981. *The world of the ancient Maya.* Ithaca, NY: Cornell University Press.

Henke, W., and I. Tattersall. 2006. *Handbook of paleoanthropology.* London: Springer.

Henry, D. 1989. *From foraging to agriculture: The Levant at the end of the Ice Age.* Philadelphia: University of Pennsylvania Press.

Henshilwood, C. S., F. d'Errico, R. Yates, Z. Jacobs, C. Tribolo, G. A. T. Duller, N. Mercier, J. C. Sealy, H. Valladas, I. Watts, and A. Wintle. 2002. Emergence of modern human behaviour: Middle Stone Age engravings from South Africa. *Science* 295:1278–1280.

Hesse, B. 1982. Slaughter patterns and domestication: The beginnings of pastoralism in western Iran. *Man* 17:403–417.

Higham, C. F. W. 1977. Economic change in prehistoric Thailand. In *The origins of agriculture,* ed. C. A. Reed. The Hague: Mouton.

Higham, C. F. W. 1984. Prehistoric rice cultivation in Southeast Asia. *Scientific American* 250(4):138–146.

Higham, C. F. W. 2001. *The civilization of Angkor.* Berkeley: University of California Press.

Higham, C. F. W. 2002. *Early cultures of mainland Southeast Asia.* Chicago: Art Media Resources.

Higham, C. F. W., R. Bannanurag, G. Mason, and N. Tayles. 1992. Human biology, environment, and ritual at Khok Phanom Di. *World Archaeology* 24:35–54.

Higham, C. F. W., and A. Kijngam. 1982. Prehistoric man and his environment: Evidence from the Ban Chiang faunal remains. *Expedition* 24(4):17–24.

Higham, C. F. W., and T. L.-D. Lu. 1998. The origins and dispersal of rice cultivation. *Antiquity* 72:867–877.

Higham, C. F. W., and R. Thosarat. 1994. *Khok Phanom Di: Prehistoric adaptation to the world's richest habitat.* Fort Worth: Harcourt Brace.

Hill, B., and R. Hill. 1974. *Indian petroglyphs of the Pacific Northwest.* Saanichton, Canada: Hancock House.

Hill, J. N. 1970. *Broken K Pueblo: Prehistoric social organization in the American Southwest.* Tucson: University of Arizona Press.

Hillman, G. C., and M. S. Davies. 1990. Measured domestication rates in wild wheats and barley under primitive cultivation, and their archaeological implications. *Journal of World Prehistory* 4:157–222.

Hodder, I. 2000. *Towards reflexive method in archaeology: The example at Çatalhöyük.* Cambridge: McDonald Institute for Archaeological Research.

Hodder, I., ed. 2001. *Archeological theory today.* Cambridge: Polity Press.

Hodder, I. 2006. *The leopard's tale: Revealing the mysteries of Çatalhöyük.* New York: Thames & Hudson.

Hoffecker, J. F., W. R. Powers, and T. Goebel. 1993. The colonization of Beringia and the peopling of the New World. *Science* 259:46–53.

Hoffman, M. A. 1976. The city of the hawk. *Expedition* 18(3):32–41.

Hoffman, M. A. 1983. Where nations began. *Science* 83:42–51.

Hole, F., K. V. Flannery, and J. A. Neely. 1969. *Prehistory and human ecology of the Deh Luran Plain.* Ann Arbor: University of Michigan Press.

Holliday, V. T. 2004. *Soils in archaeological research.* Oxford: Oxford University Press.

Holloway, R. L. 1975. *The role of human social behavior in the evolution of the brain.* New York: American Museum of Natural History.

Hood, S. 1973. *The Minoans.* London: Thames & Hudson.

Hsu, C. 1965. *Ancient China in transition.* Stanford, CA: Stanford University Press.

Huckell, B. B. 1996. The Archaic prehistory of the North American Southwest. *Journal of World Prehistory* 10:305–373.

Hyslop, J. 1984. *The Inka road system.* New York: Academic Press.

Ikawa-Smith, F. 1980. Current issues in Japanese archaeology. *American Scientist* 68:134–145.

Ikram, S. 2009. *Ancient Egypt: An introduction.* Cambridge: Cambridge University Press.

Iltis, H. H. 1983. From teosinte to maize: The catastrophic sexual transmutation. *Science* 222:886–894.

Isaac, G. 1977. *Olorgesailie: Archaeological studies of a Middle Pleistocene lake basin in Kenya.* Chicago: University of Chicago Press.

Isaac, G. 1984. The archaeology of human origins: Studies of the Lower Pleistocene in East Africa, 1971–1981. *Advances in World Archaeology* 3:1–87.

Isaac, G., and R. Leakey. 1979. *Human ancestors. Readings from Scientific American.* San Francisco: Freeman.

Isbell, W. H. 1978. The prehistoric ground drawings of Peru. *Scientific American* 238(4):140–153.

Isbell, W. H., and H. Silverman, eds. 2002a. *Andean archaeology I: Variations in sociopolitical organization.* New York: Kluwer/Plenum.

Isbell, W. H., and H. Silverman, eds. 2002b. *Andean archaeology II: Art, landscape, and society.* New York: Kluwer/Plenum.

Jackson, H. E. 1989. Poverty Point adaptive systems in the lower Mississippi Valley: Subsistence remains from the J. W. Copes site. *North American Archaeologist* 10:173–203.

Jackson, H. E. 1998. Poverty Point objects. In *Archaeology of prehistoric Native America: An encyclopedia,* ed. G. Gibbon. New York: Garland.

Jacobsen, T. 1976. Seventeen thousand years of Greek prehistory. *Scientific American* 234(6):76–87.

Jacobson, J. 1979. Recent developments in South Asian prehistory and protohistory. *Annual Review of Anthropology* 8:467–502.

Jacobson, J. 1986. The Harappan civilization: An early state. In *Studies in the archaeology of India and Pakistan,* ed. J. Jacobson. New Delhi: Oxford and IBH Publishing.

Jameson, J. H. 1997. *Presenting archaeology to the public: Digging for truths.* Walnut Creek, CA: AltaMira.

Janusek, J. W. 2004. Tiwanaku and its precursors: Recent research and emerging perspectives. *Journal of Archaeological Research* 12:121–183.

Jarrige, J.-F., and R. H. Meadow. 1980. The antecedents of civilization in the Indus Valley. *Scientific American* 243(2):122–133.

Jawad, A. J. 1974. The Eridu material and its implications. *Sumer* 30:11–46.

Jefferson, T. 1797. *Notes of the state of Virginia.* London: J. Stockdale.

Jeffries, R. W. 1987. *The archaeology of Carrier Mills.* Carbondale: Southern Illinois University Press.

Jefferies, R. W. 2009. *Holocene hunter-gatherers of the Lower Ohio River Valley.* Tuscaloosa: University of Alabama Press.

Jeffries, R. W., and M. Lynch. 1985. Dimensions of Middle Archaic cultural adaptation at the Black Earth site, Saline County, Illinois. In *Archaic hunters and gatherers in the American Midwest,* ed. J. L. Phillips and J. A. Brown. New York: Academic Press.

Jelinek, A. J. 1982. The Tabun Cave and Paleolithic man in the Levant. *Science* 216:1369–1375.

Jelinek, A. J. 1988. Technology, typology, and culture in the Middle Paleolithic. In *Upper Pleistocene prehistory,* ed. H. Dibble and A. Montet-White. Philadelphia: University of Pennsylvania Press.

Jennings, J. D., ed. 1983. *Ancient South Americans.* San Francisco: Freeman.

Jiang, L., and L. Liu. 2006. New evidence for the origins of sedentism and rice domestication in the Lower Yangzi River, China. *Antiquity* 80:355–361.

Jiménez Moreno, W. 1941. Tula y los toltecas según las fuentes históricas. *Revista Mexicana de Estudios Antropológicos* 5:79–83.

Joffroy, R. 1962. *Le Trésor de Vix. Histoire et portée d'une grande découverte.* Paris: Fayard.

Johansen, K. L., S. T. Laursen, and M. K. Holst. 2004. Spatial patterns of social organization in the Early Bronze Age of South Scandinavia. *Journal of Anthropological Archaeology* 23:33–55.

Johanson, D. C. 1976. Ethiopia yields first "family" of early man. *National Geographic* 150(6):790–811.

Johanson, D. C., and M. A. Eddy. 1981. *Lucy: The beginnings of humankind.* New York: Simon & Schuster.

Johnson, M. 1999. *Archaeological theory.* Oxford: Blackwell.

Jolly, C. 1970. The seed eaters: A new model of hominid differentiation based on a baboon analogy. *Man* 5:5–26.

Jones, A., ed. 2008. *Prehistoric Europe: Theory and practice.* Oxford: Blackwell.

Jones, C. 1977. Inauguration dates of three Late Classic rulers of Tikal, Guatemala. *American Antiquity* 42:28–60.

Jones, C., and L. Satterthwaite. 1982. *The monuments and inscriptions of Tikal: The carved monuments.* University Museum Monograph 44. Philadelphia: University of Pennsylvania.

Jones, M. 2003. *The molecule hunt: Archaeology and the search for ancient DNA.* New York: Arcade.

Jones, M. K., R. G. Allaby, T. A. Brown, F. Hole, M. Heun, B. Borghi, and F. Salamini. 1998. Wheat domestication. *Science* 279:202–204.

Jurmain, R., H. Nelson, and W. A. Turnbaugh. 1987. *Understanding physical anthropology and archaeology,* 3d ed. St. Paul, MN: West.

Kantner, J. 2004. *Ancient Puebloan Southwest.* Cambridge: Cambridge University Press.

Kay, R. F., and F. E. Grine. 1988. Tooth morphology, wear and diet in Australopithecus and Paranthropus from southern Africa. In *Evolutionary history of the "robust" Australopithecines,* ed. F. E. Grine. New York: Aldine de Gruyter.

Keatinge, R. W., ed. 1988. *Peruvian prehistory.* Cambridge: Cambridge University Press.

Keeley, L. H. 1981. *Experimental determination of stone tool uses: A microwear analysis.* Chicago: University of Chicago Press.

Keeley, L. H., and N. Toth. 1981. Microwear polishes on early stone tools from Koobi Fora, Kenya. *Nature* 293(8):464–465.

Keightley, D. N., ed. 1983. *The origins of Chinese civilization.* Berkeley: University of California Press.

Kelly, R. L. 1995. *The foraging spectrum: Diversity in hunter-gatherer lifeways.* Washington, DC: Smithsonian Institution Press.

Kelly, R. L., and M. Prasciunas. 2004. Did the ancestors of Native Americans cause animal extinctions in Late Pleistocene North America? In *Reconsidering the ecological Indian,* ed. M. E. Harkin and D. R. Lewis. Lincoln: University of Nebraska Press.

Kennedy, G. E. 2005. From the ape's dilemma to the weanling's dilemma: Early weaning and its evolutionary context. *Journal of Human Evolution* 48:123–145.

Kennett, D. J., J. P. Kennett, A. West, C. Mercer, S. S. Que Hee, L. Bement, T. E. Bunch, M. Sellers, and W. S. Wolbach. 2009. Nanodiamonds in the Younger Dryas Boundary Sediment Layer. *Science* 323:94.

Kenoyer, J. M. 1984. Shell working industries of the Indus civilization: A summary. *Paleorient* 10(1):49–63.

Kenoyer, J. M. 1985. Shell working at Mohenjo-daro, Pakistan. In *South Asian archaeology 1983,* ed. J. Schotsmans and M. Taddei. Naples: Instituto Universitario Orientale.

Kenoyer, J. M. 1991. The Indus Valley tradition of Pakistan and western India. *Journal of World Prehistory* 5:331–385.

Kenoyer, J. M. 1998a. *Ancient cities of the Indus Valley civilization.* Oxford: Oxford University Press.

Kenoyer, J. M. 1998b. Birth of a civilization. *Archaeology* 51(1):54–61.

Kense, F. J., and J. A. Okoro. 1993. Changing perspectives on traditional iron production in West Africa. In *The archaeology of Africa: Food, metals and towns,* ed. T. Shaw, P. Sinclair, B. Andah, and A. Okpoko. London: Routledge.

Kenyon, K. 1954. Ancient Jericho. *Scientific American* 190(4):76–82.

Kenyon, K. 1960. *Excavations at Jericho. I.* Jerusalem: British School of Archaeology.

Kidder, T. R. 2008. Poverty Point and the archaeology of singularity. *The SAA Archaeological Record* 8(5):9–12.

King, A. 2003. Over a century of explorations at Etowah. *Journal of Archaeological Research* 11(4):279–306.

Kirchhoff, P. 1952. Mesoamerica: Its geographic limits, ethnic composition, and cultural characteristics. In *Heritage of conquest,* ed. S. Tax. New York: Free Press.

Kirk, R., and R. D. Daugherty. 1978. *Exploring Washington archaeology.* Seattle: University of Washington Press.

Kislev, M. E., A. Hartmann, and O. Bar-Yosef. 2006. Early domesticated fig in the Jordan Valley. *Science* 312:1372–1374.

Kittler, R., M. Kayser, and M. Stoneking. 2003. Molecular evolution of *Pediculus humanus* and the origin of clothing. *Current Biology* 13:1414–1417.

Klein, R. G. 1995. Anatomy, behavior, and modern human origins. *Journal of World Prehistory* 9:167–198.

Klein, R. G. 1999. *The human career,* 2d ed. Chicago: University of Chicago Press.

Klein, R. G., and K. Cruz-Uribe. 1984. *The analysis of animal bones from archaeological sites.* Chicago: University of Chicago Press.

Klein, R. G., and K. Cruz-Uribe. 1987. Large mammal and tortoise bones from Eland's Bay Cave Province, South Africa. In *Papers in the prehistory of the Western Cape, South Africa,* ed. J. Parkington and M. Hall. Oxford: British Archaeological Reports.

Klein, R. G., and B. Edgar. 2002. *The dawn of human culture.* New York: Wiley.

Klima, B. 1962. The first ground plan of an Upper Paleolithic loess settlement in middle Europe and its meaning. In *Courses toward urban life,* ed. R. J. Braidwood and G. R. Willey. Chicago: Aldine.

Klima, B. 1963. *Dolni Vestonice.* Prague: Nakladatelstvi Ceskoslovenske Akademie Ved.

Knight, V. J., Jr. 1990. Social organization and the evolution of hierarchy in southeastern chiefdoms. *Journal of Anthropological Research* 46:1–23.

Knight, V. J., Jr., and V. P. Steponaitis, eds. 1998. *Archaeology of the Moundville chiefdom.* Washington, DC: Smithsonian Institution Press.

Kobayashi, T. 2004. *Jomon reflections: Forager life and culture in the prehistoric Japanese archipelago.* Oxford: Oxbow Books.

Kojan, D. 2008. Paths of power and politics: Historical narratives at the Bolivian site of Tiwanaku. In *Evaluating multiple narratives: Beyond nationalist, colonialist, imperialist archaeologies,* ed. J. Habu, C. Fawcett, and J. M. Matsunaga. New York: Springer.

Kolata, A. L. 1983. The South Andes. In *Ancient South Americans,* ed. J. D. Jennings. San Francisco: Freeman.

Kolata, A. L. 1986. The agricultural foundations of the Tiwanaku state. *American Antiquity* 51:748–762.

Kolata, A. L. 1987. Tiwanaku and its hinterland. *Archaeology* 40(1):36–41.

Kolata, A. L. 1993. *The Tiwanaku: Portrait of an Andean Civilization.* Cambridge, MA: Blackwell.

Kolata, A. L., ed. 2003. *Tiwanaku and its hinterland: Archaeology and paleoecology of an Andean civilization.* Washington, DC: Smithsonian Institution Press.

Kowalewski, S. A., G. M. Feinman, L. Finsten, R. E. Blanton, and L. M. Nicholas. 1989. *Monte Albán's hinterland, part II: Prehispanic settlement patterns in Tlacolula, Etla, and Ocotlán, the Valley of Oaxaca, Mexico.* Memoirs of the Museum of Anthropology, No. 23. Ann Arbor: University of Michigan.

Kowalski, J. K., and C. Kristan-Graham, eds. 2007. *Twin Tollans: Chichén Itzá, Tula, and the Epiclassic to Early Postclassic Mesoamerican world.* Washington, DC: Dumbarton Oaks.

Kramer, S. N. 1988. The temple in Sumerian literature. In *Temple in society,* ed. M. V. Fox. Winona Lake, IN: Eisenbrauns.

Krings, M., A. Stone, R. W. Schmitz, H. Krainitzki, M. Stoneking, and S. Pääbo. 1997. Neanderthal DNA sequences and the origin of modern humans. *Cell* 90:19–30.

Kristiansen, K. 2000. *Europe before history. The European world system in the 2nd millennium* B.C. Cambridge: Cambridge University Press.

Kuman, K., and R. J. Clarke. 2000. Stratigraphy, artefact industries and hominid associations for Sterkfontein, Member 5. *Journal of Human Evolution* 38:827–847.

Kurtén, B. 1968. *Pleistocene mammals of Europe.* Chicago: Aldine.

Kurtén, B., and E. Anderson. 1980. *Pleistocene mammals of North America.* New York: Columbia University Press.

Kusimba, C. M. 2008. Early African cities: Their role in the shaping of urban and rural interaction spheres. In *The ancient city: New perspectives on urbanism in the Old and New Worlds,* ed. J. Marcus and J. A. Sabloff. Santa Fe, NM: School for Advanced Research Press.

Laitman, J. T. 1984. The anatomy of human speech. *Natural History* 93(9):20–27.

Lamberg-Karlovsky, C. C., and J. A. Sabloff. 1995. *Ancient civilizations: The Near East and Mesoamerica,* 2d ed. Prospect Heights, IL: Waveland Press.

Lambert, J. 1997. *Traces of the past: Unraveling the secrets of archaeology through chemistry.* New York: Addison Wesley Longman.

Lanning, E. P. 1967. *Peru before the Incas.* Englewood Cliffs, NJ: Prentice-Hall.

Larsen, C. S. 1999. *Bioarchaeology: Interpreting behavior from the human skeleton.* New York: Cambridge University Press.

Larsen, C. S. 2000. *Skeletons in our closet: Revealing our past through bioarchaeology.* Princeton, NJ: Princeton University Press.

Larsen, C. S., R. M. Matter, and D. L. Cabo. 1998. *Human origins: The fossil record.* Prospect Heights, IL: Waveland Press.

Larsson, L. 1988. *The Skateholm Project. I, Man and environment.* Lund, Sweden: Almqvist & Wiksell International.

Lawton, G. 2004. Urban legends. *New Scientist* (18 September):32–35.

Leacock, E. B. 1971. *North American Indians in historical perspective.* New York: Random House.

Leakey, M. D. 1971. *Olduvai Gorge.* Cambridge: Cambridge University Press.

Leakey, M. D. 1978. Pliocene footprints at Laetoli, Tanzania. *Antiquity* 52:133.

Leakey, M. D., and J. M. Harris, eds. 1987. *Laetoli: A Pliocene site in northern Tanzania.* Oxford: Clarendon Press.

Leakey, M. D., and R. E. Leakey, eds. 1978. *Koobi Fora research project.* Oxford: Clarendon Press.

Leakey, M. G., F. Spoor, F. H. Brown, P. N. Gathogo, C. Klarle, L. N. Leakey, and I. McDougall. 2001. New hominin genus from eastern Africa shows diverse middle Pliocene lineages. *Nature* 410:433–440.

Leakey, R. 1981. *The making of mankind.* London: M. Joseph.

Leakey, R., and R. Lewin. 1977. *Origins reconsidered.* New York: Dutton.

Lechevallier, M., and G. Quivron. 1985. Results of the recent excavations at the Neolithic site of Mehrgarh, Pakistan. In *South Asian archaeology 1983,* ed. J. Schotsmans and M. Taddei. Naples: Instituto Universitario Orientale.

Lee, R. B., and R. Daly, eds. 1999. *Cambridge encyclopedia of hunters and gatherers.* Cambridge: Cambridge University Press.

Lee, R. B., and I. DeVore. 1968. *Man the hunter.* Chicago: Aldine.

Legge, A. J., and P. A. Rowley-Conwy. 1988. *Star Carr revisited.* London: University of London.

LeGros Clark, W. E., and B. G. Campbell. 1978. *The fossil evidence for human evolution.* Chicago: University of Chicago Press.

Lekson, S. H. 1999. *The Chaco meridian: Centers of political power in the ancient Southwest.* Walnut Creek, CA: AltaMira.

Lekson, S. H., T. C. Windes, J. R. Stein, and W. J. Judge. 1988. The Chaco Canyon community. *Scientific American* 259(1):72–81.

León-Portilla, M. 1987. Ethnohistorical record for the Huey Teocalli. In *The Aztec Templo Mayor,* ed. E. H. Boone. Washington, DC: Dumbarton Oaks.

Lepper, B. 2005. *Ohio archaeology: An illustrated chronicle of Ohio's ancient American Indian cultures.* Wilmington, OH: Orange Frazer Press.

Leroi-Gourhan, A. 1957. *Prehistoric man.* New York: Philosophical Library.

Leroi-Gourhan, A. 1968. The archaeology of Lascaux Cave. *Scientific American* 219(4):104–111.

Leroi-Gourhan, A. 1984. *The dawn of European art: An introduction to Paleolithic cave paintings.* Cambridge: Cambridge University Press.

Leroi-Gourhan, A., and M. Brezillon. 1972. Fouilles de Pincevent: Essai d'analyse ethnographique d'un habitat Magdalenien (sec. 36). VII supplément à *Gallia Prehistoria.* Paris: Éditions du Centre National de la Recherche Scientifique.

Levtzion, N. 1976. The early states of the western Sudan to 1500. In *History of West Africa,* vol. 1, 2d ed., ed. J. F. A. Ajayi and M. Crowder. New York: Columbia University Press.

Levy, T. E. 2009. *The new biblical archaeology: From text to turf.* London: Equinox.

Lewin, R. 1984. *Human evolution: An illustrated introduction.* San Francisco: Freeman.

Lewin, R. 1988. *In the age of mankind.* Washington, DC: Smithsonian Institution Press.

Lewin, R. 1998. *Principles of human evolution.* Malden, MA: Blackwell.

Lewis-Williams, D. 2002. *The mind in the cave: Consciousness and the origins of art.* London: Thames & Hudson.

Lieberman, D. E. 2001. Another face in our family tree. *Nature* 410:419–420.

Lieberman, P. 1991. *Uniquely human: The evolution of speech, thought, and selfless behavior.* Cambridge, MA: Harvard University Press.

Lipe, W. 1983. The Southwest. In *Ancient North Americans,* ed. J. Jennings. San Francisco: Freeman.

Lister, R. H., and F. C. Lister. 1981. *Chaco Canyon, archaeology and archaeologists.*

Albuquerque: University of New Mexico Press.

Little, B. J. 2002. *Public benefits of archaeology.* Gainesville: University Press of Florida.

Liu, L. 2004. *The Chinese Neolithic.* Cambridge: Cambridge University Press.

Lloyd, S., and F. Safar. 1943. Tell Uqair: Excavations by the Iraq government directorate of antiquities in 1940 and 1941. *Journal of Near Eastern Studies* 2:131–189.

Loewe, M., and E. L. Schaughnessy. 1999. *The Cambridge history of ancient China.* Cambridge: Cambridge University Press.

Londo, J. P., Y. C. Chiang, K. H. Hung, T. Y. Chiang, and B. A. Schaal. 2006. Phylogeography of Asian wild rice, *Oriyza rufipogon,* reveals multiple independent domestications of cultivated rice, *Oryza sativa. Proceedings of the National Academy of Sciences* 103(25):9578–9583.

Long, A., B. F. Benz, D. J. Donahue, A. J. T. Jull, and L. J. Toolin. 1989. First direct AMS dates on early maize from Tehuacán, Mexico. *Radiocarbon* 31:1035–1040.

Lovejoy, C. O. 1981. The origin of man. *Science* 211:341–350.

Lu, H., X. Yang, M. Ye, K. Liu, Z. Xia, X. Ren, L. Cai, N. Wu, and T. Liu. 2005. Millet noodles in late Neolithic China. *Nature* 437:967–968.

Lumbreras, L. 1974. *The peoples and cultures of ancient Peru,* trans. B. J. Meggers. Washington, DC: Smithsonian Institution Press.

Lynch, T. F. 1980. *Guitarrero Cave: Early man in the Andes.* London: Academic Press.

Lynch, T. F., R. Gillespie, J. A. J. Gowlett, and R. E. M. Hedges. 1985. Chronology of Guitarrero Cave, Peru. *Science* 229:864–867.

MacNeish, R. S. 1978. *The science of archaeology?* North Scituate, MA: Duxbury Press.

MacNeish, R. S. 1981. Tehuacán's accomplishments. In *Supplement to the handbook of Middle American Indians,* vol. 1, ed. J. A. Sabloff. Austin: University of Texas Press.

MacNeish, R. S., and J. G. Libby, eds. 1995. *Origins of rice agriculture: The preliminary report of the Sino-American Jiangxi (PRC) Project.* Publications in Anthropology No. 13. El Paso: Centennial Museum, University of Texas.

MacNeish, R. S., F. A. Peterson, and K. V. Flannery. 1970. *Prehistory of the Tehuacán Valley.* Vol. 3, *Ceramics,* ed. R. S. MacNeish. Austin: University of Texas Press.

Majewski T., and D. Gaimster, eds. 2009. *International handbook of historical archaeology.* New York: Springer.

Malek, J., ed. 1993. *Cradles of civilization: Egypt.* Norman: University of Oklahoma Press.

Maloney, B. K., C. F. W. Higham, and R. Bannanurag. 1989. Early rice cultivation in Southeast Asia: Archaeological and palynological evidence from the Bang Pakong Valley, Thailand. *Antiquity* 63:363–370.

Mann, C. C. 2003. Cracking the khipu code. *Science* 300:1650–1651.

Mann, C. C. 2005. *1491: New revelations of the Americas before Columbus.* New York: Knopf.

Mannion, A. M. 1999. Domestication and the origins of agriculture: An appraisal. *Progress in Physical Geography* 23:37–56.

Manzanilla, L. 1997. Corporate groups and domestic activities at Teotihuacan. *Latin American Antiquity* 7:228–246.

Manzanilla, L., L. Barba, R. Chávez, A. Tejero, G. Cifuentes, and N. Peralta. 1994. Caves and geophysics: An approximation of the underworld of Teotihuacan, Mexico. *Archaeometry* 36:141–157.

Marcus, J. 1976a. *Emblem and state in the Classic Maya Lowlands: An epigraphic approach to territorial organization.* Washington, DC: Dumbarton Oaks.

Marcus, J. 1976b. The origins of Mesoamerican writing. *Annual Review of Anthropology* 5:35–67.

Marcus, J. 1980. Zapotec writing. *Scientific American* 242(2):50–64.

Marcus, J. 1983a. The conquest slabs of Building J, Monte Albán. In *The cloud people: Divergent evolution of the Mixtec and Zapotec civilizations,* ed. K. V. Flannery and J. Marcus. New York: Academic Press.

Marcus, J. 1983b. Lowland Maya archaeology at the crossroads. *American Antiquity* 48:454–488.

Marcus, J. 1987. Prehistoric fishermen in the kingdom of Huarco. *American Scientist* 75:393–401.

Marcus, J. 1989. Zapotec chiefdoms and the nature of Formative religions. In *Regional perspectives on the Olmec,* ed. R. J. Sharer and D. C. Grove. Cambridge: Cambridge University Press.

Marcus, J. 1992a. *Mesoamerican writing systems: Propaganda, myth, and history in four ancient civilizations.* Princeton, NJ: Princeton University Press.

Marcus, J. 1992b. Political fluctuations in Mesoamerica. *National Geographic Research and Exploration* 8:392–411.

Marcus, J., ed. 1990. *Debating Oaxaca archaeology.* Anthropological Papers of the Museum of Anthropology, No. 84. Ann Arbor: University of Michigan.

Marcus, J. 2008. The archaeological evidence for social evolution. *Annual Review of Anthropology* 37:251–266.

Marcus, J., and K. V. Flannery. 1996. *Zapotec civilization: How urban society evolved in Mexico's Oaxaca Valley.* London: Thames & Hudson.

Marcus, J., and J. A. Sabloff, eds. 2008. *The ancient city: New perspectives on urbanism in the Old and New Worlds.* Santa Fe, NM: School for Advanced Research Press.

Marean, C. W., M. Bar-Matthews, J. Bernatchez, E. Fisher, P. Goldberg, A. I. R. Herries, Z. Jacobs, A. Jerardino, P. Karkanas, T. Minichillo, P. J. Nilssen, E. Thompson, I. Watts, and H. M. Williams. 2007. Early human use of marine resources and pigment in South Africa during the Middle Pleistocene. *Nature* 449:908–910.

Marshack, A. 1972a. *The roots of civilization.* New York: McGraw-Hill.

Marshack, A. 1972b. Upper Paleolithic symbol and notation. *Science* 178:817–828.

Martin, P. S., and F. Plog. 1973. *The archaeology of Arizona: A study of the Southwest region.* New York: Natural History Press.

Martin, P. W., and H. E. Wright Jr. 1967. *Pleistocene extinctions: The search for a cause.* New Haven, CT: Yale University Press.

Martin, S., and N. Grube. 1995. Maya superstates. *Archaeology* 48(6):41–46.

Marx, K. 1963. *The eighteenth Brumaire of Louis Bonaparte.* New York: International Publishers.

Mason, R. J. 1981. *Great Lakes archaeology.* New York: Academic Press.

Masuda, S., I. Shimada, and C. Morris. 1985. *Andean ecology and civilization: An interdisciplinary perspective on Andean ecological complementarity.* Tokyo: University of Tokyo Press.

Matheny, R. T., ed. 1980. *El Mirador, Petén, Guatemala: An interim report.*

Papers 45. Provo, UT: New World Archaeological Foundation.

Matheny, R. T. 1986. Investigations at El Mirador, Petén, Guatemala. *National Geographic Research* 2:332–353.

Mathien, F. J., and R. H. McGuire, eds. 1986. *Ripples in the Chichimec Sea: New considerations of Southwestern-Mesoamerican interactions.* Carbondale: Southern Illinois University Press.

Matos Moctezuma, E. 1984. The great temple of Tenochtitlán. *Scientific American* 251(2):80–89.

Matsuoka, Y., Y. Vigouroux, M. Goodman, J. Sanchez, G. E. Buckler, and J. Doebley. 2002. A single domestication for maize shown by multilocus microsatellite genotyping. *Proceedings of the National Academy of Sciences* 99(9):6080–6084.

Mayr, E. 1970. *Population, species, and evolution.* Cambridge, MA: Harvard University Press.

McDonald, K. 1996. Early Iron-Age settlement of sub-Saharan Africa. In *The Oxford companion to archaeology,* ed. B. M. Fagan. New York: Oxford University Press.

McHenry, H. M. 1982. The pattern of human evolution: Studies on bipedalism, mastication, and encephalization. *Annual Review of Anthropology* 11:151–173.

McIntosh, S. K., ed. 1995. *Excavations at Jenné-jeno, Hambarketolo, and Kaniana (Inland Niger Delta, Mali), the 1981 seasons.* Berkeley: University of California Press.

McIntosh, S. K., ed. 1999. *Beyond chiefdoms: Pathways to complexity in Africa.* Cambridge: Cambridge University Press.

McIntosh, S. K., and R. J. McIntosh. 1980. Jenné-jeno: An ancient African city. *Archaeology* 33(1):8–14.

McIntosh, S. K., and R. J. McIntosh. 1981. West African prehistory. *American Scientist* 69:602–612.

McIntosh, S. K., and R. J. McIntosh. 1983. Current directions in West African prehistory. *Annual Review of Anthropology* 12:215–258.

McIntosh, S. K., and R. J. McIntosh. 1984. The early city in West Africa: Towards an understanding. *African Archaeological Review* 2:73–98.

McIntosh, S. K., and R. J. McIntosh. 1993. Cities without citadels: Understanding urban origins along the middle Niger. In *The archaeology of Africa: Food, metals and towns,* ed. T. Shaw, P. Sinclair, B. Andah, and A. Okpoko. London: Routledge.

Mckillop, H. 2004. *The ancient Maya.* Santa Barbara, CA: ABC-Clio.

McManamon, F. P., L. S. Cordell, K. G. Lightfoot, and G. R. Milner, eds. 2008. *Archaeology in America: An encyclopedia.* Westport, CT: Greenwood.

Mead, J. I., and D. J. Meltzer. 1985. *Environments and extinctions: Man in late glacial North America.* Orono, ME: Center for the Study of Early Man.

Meadow, R. H. 1984. Animal domestication in the Middle East: A view from the eastern margin. In *Animals and archaeology 3,* ed. J. Clutton-Brock and C. Grigson. Oxford: British Archaeological Reports.

Meggers, B. J., and C. Evans. 1957. *Archaeological investigations at the mouth of the Amazon.* Bureau of American Ethnology, Bulletin 167. Washington, DC: Smithsonian Institution.

Mellaart, J. 1964. Excavations at Çatal Hüyük, 1963: Third preliminary report. *Anatolian Studies* 14:39–119.

Mellaart, J. 1967. *Çatal Hüyük: A Neolithic town in Anatolia.* London: Thames & Hudson.

Mellaart, J. 1975. *The Neolithic of the Near East.* New York: Scribner.

Mellars, P. 2006. A new radiocarbon revolution and the dispersal of modern humans in Eurasia. *Nature* 439:931–935.

Mellars, P., and C. Stringer. 1989. *The human revolution: Behavioural and biological perspectives on the origins of modern humans.* Edinburgh: Edinburgh University Press.

Meltzer, D. J. 2006. *Folsom.* Berkeley: University of California Press.

Meltzer, D. J. 2009. *First peoples in a New World: Colonizing Ice Age America.* Berkeley: University of California Press.

Mendelssohn, K. 1974. *The riddle of the pyramids.* New York: Praeger.

Menotti, F. 2004. *Living on the lake in prehistoric Europe.* London: Routledge.

Mercader, J., H. Barton, J. Gillespie, J. Harris, S. Kuhn, R. Tyler, and C. Boesch. 2007. 4,300-year-old chimpanzee sites and the origins of percussive stone technology. *Proceedings of the National Academy of Science* 104:3043–3048.

Merriman, N., and T. Schadla-Hall. 2002. *Public archaeology.* London: Routledge.

Milisauskas, S. 1978. *European prehistory.* New York: Academic Press.

Milisauskas, S., ed. 2002. *European prehistory, a survey.* New York: Springer.

Millon, R. 1967. Teotihuacan. *Scientific American* 216(6):38–48.

Millon, R. 1973. *Urbanization at Teotihuacan, Mexico.* Vol. 1, *The Teotihuacan map.* Austin: University of Texas Press.

Millon, R. 1976. Social relations in ancient Teotihuacan. In *The Valley of Mexico,* ed. E. R. Wolf. Albuquerque: University of New Mexico Press.

Millon, R. 1981. Teotihuacan: City, state, and civilization. In *Supplement to the handbook of Middle American Indians.* Vol. 1, *Archaeology,* ed. J. A. Sabloff. Austin: University of Texas Press.

Mills, B. J. 2002. Recent research on Chaco: Changing views on economy, ritual, and society. *Journal of Archaeological Research* 10:65–117.

Milner, G. R. 1998. *The Cahokia chiefdom: The archaeology of a Mississippian society.* Washington, DC: Smithsonian Institution Press.

Milner, G. R. 2003. Archaeological indicators of rank in the Cahokia chiefdom. In *Theory, method, and practice in modern archaeology,* ed. R. J. Jeske and D. K. Charles. Westport, CT: Praeger.

Milner, G. R. 2004. *The moundbuilders: Ancient peoples of eastern North America.* London: Thames & Hudson.

Montague, A. 1964. *The concept of race.* New York: Free Press.

Moore, A. M. T. 1985. The development of Neolithic societies in the Near East. *Advances in World Archaeology* 4:1–70.

Moore, A. M. T., G. C. Hillman, and A. J. Legge. 2000. *Village on the Euphrates: The excavation of Abu Hureyra.* Oxford: Oxford University Press.

Moore, C. B. 1905. Certain aboriginal remains of the Black Warrior River. *Journal of the Academy of Natural Sciences of Philadelphia* 13:125–244.

Moore, J. D. 1996. *Architecture and power in the ancient Andes: The archaeology of public buildings.* Cambridge: Cambridge University Press.

Moorehead, W. K. 1922. *The Hopewell mound group of Ohio.* Anthropological Series 6(5). Publication 211. Chicago: Field Museum of Natural History. Reprinted in 1968.

Morley, S. G. (ed. R. J. Sharer). 1994. *The ancient Maya,* 5th ed. Stanford, CA: Stanford University Press.

Morley, S. G., and G. W. Brainerd. 1956. *The ancient Maya,* 3d ed. Stanford, CA: Stanford University Press.

Morrell, V. 2001. The pyramid builders. *National Geographic* 200(5):78–99.

Morris, C. 1998. Inka strategies of incorporation and governance. In *Archaic states,* ed. G. M. Feinman and J. Marcus. Santa Fe, NM: School of American Research Press.

Morris, C., and D. E. Thompson. 1985. *Huánuco Pampa: An Inca city and its hinterland.* London: Thames & Hudson.

Morris, C., and A. von Hagen. 1993. *The Inka empire and its Andean origins.* New York: Abbeville Press.

Moseley, M. E. 1975a. Chan Chan: Andean alternative of the preindustrial city? *Science* 187:219–225.

Moseley, M. E. 1975b. *The maritime foundations of Andean civilization.* Menlo Park, CA: Benjamin/Cummings.

Moseley, M. E. 1975c. Prehistoric principles of labor organization in the Moche Valley, Peru. *American Antiquity* 40:191–196.

Moseley, M. E. 1983. Central Andean civilization. In *Ancient South Americans,* ed. J. D. Jennings. San Francisco: Freeman.

Moseley, M. E. 2001. *The Incas and their ancestors: The archaeology of Peru,* rev. ed. London: Thames & Hudson.

Moseley, M. E., and K. C. Day, eds. 1982. *Chan Chan: Andean desert city.* Albuquerque: University of New Mexico Press.

Movius, H. L. 1948. The Lower Paleolithic culture of southern and eastern Asia. *Transactions of the American Philosophical Society* 38:329–351.

Muller, J. 1983. The Southeast. In *Ancient North Americans,* ed. J. Jennings. San Francisco: Freeman.

Mulvaney, D. J. 1975. *The prehistory of Australia,* 2d ed. Baltimore: Pelican.

Mulvaney, J., and J. Kamminga. 1999. *The prehistory of Australia.* Washington, DC: Smithsonian Institution Press.

Muro, M. 1998. New finds explode old views of the American Southwest. *Science* 279:653–654.

Murowchick, R. E., ed. 1994. *Cradles of civilization: China.* Norman: University of Oklahoma Press.

Murra, J. V. 1962. Cloth and its function in the Inca state. *American Anthropologist* 64:710–728.

Murra, J. V. 1972. El "control vertical" de un máximo de pisos ecológicos en la economía de las sociedades andinas. In *Visita de la provincia de Leon de Huanuco (1562),* vol. 2, ed. J. V. Murra. Huánuco, Peru: Universidad Nacional Hermilio Valdizan.

Ndoro, W. 1996. Great Zimbabwe. In *The Oxford companion to archaeology,* ed. B. M. Fagan. New York: Oxford University Press.

Neitzel, J. 1989. The Chacoan regional system: Interpreting the evidence for social complexity. In *The sociopolitical structure of prehistoric southwestern societies,* ed. S. Upham, K. G. Lightfoot, and R. A. Jewett. Boulder, CO: Westview.

Neitzel, J. E., ed. 1999. *Great towns and regional polities in the prehistoric American Southwest and Southeast.* Albuquerque: University of New Mexico Press.

Neuman, R. W. 1990. *An introduction to Louisiana archaeology.* Baton Rouge: Louisiana State University Press.

Neumann, T. N., and R. M. Sanford. 2001. *Cultural resources archaeology.* Walnut Creek, CA: AltaMira Press.

Nicholas, L. M., and G. M. Feinman. 1989. A regional perspective on Hohokam irrigation in the lower Salt River Valley, Arizona. In *The sociopolitical structure of prehistoric southwestern societies,* ed. S. Upham, K. G. Lightfoot, and R. A. Jewett. Boulder, CO: Westview.

Nissen, H. J. 1986. The archaic texts from Uruk. *World Archaeology* 17:317–334.

Nissen, H. J. 1988. *The early history of the ancient Near East, 9000–2000 B.C.* Chicago: University of Chicago Press.

Noble, D. G., ed. 2004. *In search of Chaco: New approaches to an archaeological enigma.* Santa Fe, NM: School for American Research Press.

Normile, D. 1997. Yangtze seen as earliest rice site. *Science* 275:309.

Oakley, K. P. 1955. Fire as a Paleolithic tool and weapon. *Proceedings of the Prehistoric Society* 21:36–48.

Oates, J. 1980. The emergence of cities in the Near East. In *The Cambridge encyclopedia of archaeology,* ed. A. Sherratt. New York: Crown.

Oates, J., A. McMahon, P. Karsgaard, S. Al Quntar, and J. Ur. 2007. Early Mesopotamian urbanism: A new view from the north. *Antiquity* 81:585–600.

O'Connor, D. 1980. Egypt and the Levant in the Bronze Age. In *The Cambridge encyclopedia of archaeology,* ed. A. Sherratt. New York: Crown.

Oliver, R., and B. M. Fagan. 1975. *Africa in the Iron Age: c. 500 B.C. to A.D. 1400.* Cambridge: Cambridge University Press.

Ortiz de Montellano, B. 1978. Aztec cannibalism: An ecological necessity? *Science* 200:611–617.

Osborne, R. 2009. *Greece in the making 1200–479 B.C.* London: Routledge.

Otto, M. P. 1979. Hopewell antecedents in the Adena heartland. In *Hopewell archaeology: The Chillicothe conference,* ed. D. S. Brose and N. Greber. Kent, OH: Kent State University Press.

Parkington, J. E. 1972. Seasonal mobility in the Late Stone Age. *African Studies* 31:223–243.

Parkington, J. E. 1981. Stone tools and resources: A case study from South Africa. *World Archaeology* 13:16–30.

Parkington, J. E. 1984. Changing views of the Later Stone Age of South Africa. *Advances in World Archaeology* 3:89–142.

Parpola, A. 1986. The Indus script: A challenging puzzle. *World Archaeology* 17:399–419.

Parsons, J. R. 1972. Archaeological settlement patterns. *Annual Review of Anthropology* 1:127–150.

Pauketat, T. R. 1998. Refiguring the archaeology of greater Cahokia. *Journal of Archaeological Research* 6:45–89.

Pauketat, T. R. 2003. Resettled farmers and the making of a Mississippian polity. *American Antiquity* 68:39–66.

Pauketat, T. R. 2004a. *Ancient Cahokia and the Mississippians.* Cambridge: Cambridge University Press.

Pauketat, T. R. 2004b. The economy of the moment: Cultural practices and Mississippian chiefdoms. In *Archaeological perspectives on political economies,* ed. G. M. Feinman and L. M. Nicholas. Salt Lake City: University of Utah Press.

Pauketat, T. R. 2009. *Cahokia: Ancient America's great city on the Mississippi.* New York: Viking Adult.

Pauketat, T. R., and T. E. Emerson, eds. 1997. *Cahokia: Domination and ideology in the Mississippian world.* Lincoln: University of Nebraska Press.

Pauketat, T. R., and N. H. Lopinot. 1997. Cahokian population dynamics. In *Cahokia: Domination and ideol-*

*ogy in the Mississippian world,* ed. T. R. Pauketat and T. E. Emerson. Lincoln: University of Nebraska Press.

Paul, A., and S. A. Turpin. 1986. The ecstatic shaman theme of Paracas textiles. *Archaeology* 39(5):20–27.

Pearsall, D. 1989. *Paleoethnobotany.* Orlando, FL: Academic Press.

Pearsall, D. 1992. The origins of plant cultivation in South America. In *Origins of agriculture in world perspective,* ed. C. W. Cowan and P. J. Watson. Washington, DC: Smithsonian Institution Press.

Pearson, M. P. 1996. Mortuary analysis. In *The Oxford companion to archaeology,* ed. B. M. Fagan. New York: Oxford University Press.

Pearson, M. P., R. Cleal, P. Marshall, S. Needham, J. Pollard, C. Richards, C. Ruggles, A. Sheridan, J. Thomas, C. Tilley, K. Welham, A. Chamberlain, C. Chenery, J. Evans, and C. Knüsel. 2007. The age of Stonehenge. *Antiquity* 811(313):617–639.

Pearson, R., and A. Underhill. 1987. The Chinese Neolithic: Recent trends in research. *American Anthropologist* 89:807–822.

Peebles, C. S., and C. A. Black. 1987. Moundville from 1000–1500 A.D. as seen from 1840 to 1985 A.D. In *Chiefdoms in the Americas,* ed. R. D. Drennan and C. A. Uribe. Lanham, MD: University Press of America.

Peebles, C. S., and S. Kus. 1977. Some archaeological correlates of ranked society. *American Antiquity* 42:421–448.

Peltenberg, E., S. Colledge, P. Croft, A. Jackson, C. McCartney, and M. A. Murra. 2000. Agro-pastoralist colonization of Cyprus in the 10th millennium B.P.: Initial assessments. *Antiquity* 74:844–853.

Peregrine, P. N., and M. Ember, eds. 2003. *Encyclopedia of prehistory.* New York: Springer Verlag.

Perlès, C. 2001. *The Early Neolithic in Greece.* Cambridge: Cambridge University Press.

Perony, D. 1930. Le Moustier. *Revue Anthropologique* 14.

Perrot, J. 1966. Le gisement natoufien de Mallaha (Eynan), Israel. *L'Anthropologie* 47:437–484.

Perry, L., R. Dickau, S. Zarrillo, I. Holst, D. M. Pearsall, D. R. Piperno, M. J. Berman, R. G. Cooke, K. Rademaker, A. J. Ranere, J. S. Raymond, D. H. Sandweiss, F. Scaramelli, K. Tarble, and J. A. Zeidler. 2007. Starch fossils and the domestication and dispersal of chili peppers (*Capsicum* sp. L) in the Americas. *Science* 315:986–988.

Perry, L., D. H. Sandweiss, D. R. Piperno, K. Rademaker, M. A. Malpass, A. Umire, and P. de la Vera. 2006. Early maize agriculture and interzonal interaction in southern Peru. *Nature* 440:76–79.

Peterson, I. 1988. Tokens of plenty. *Science News* 134:408–410.

Pfeiffer, J. E. 1982. *The creative explosion: An enquiry into the origins of art and religion.* New York: Harper & Row.

Pfeiffer, J. E. 1985. *The emergence of humankind.* New York: Harper & Row.

Phillipson, D. 1977. *The later prehistory of eastern and southern Africa.* London: Heinemann.

Phillipson, D. 1980. Iron Age Africa and the expansion of the Bantu. In *The Cambridge encyclopedia of archaeology,* ed. A. Sherratt. New York: Crown.

Phillipson, D. 1985. *African archaeology.* Cambridge: Cambridge University Press.

Phillipson, D. W. 1996. Prehistory of Africa. In *The Oxford companion to archaeology,* ed. B. M. Fagan. New York: Oxford University Press.

Pickering, T. R., T. D. White, and N. Toth. 2000. Cutmarks on a Plio-Pleistocene hominid from Sterkfontein, South Africa. *American Journal of Physical Anthropology* 111:579–584.

Pickford, M., and B. Senut. 2001. The geological and faunal context of Late Miocene hominid remains from Lukeino, Kenya. *Comptes Rendus de l'Académie de Sciences* 332:145–152.

Pikirayi, I. 2006. The demise of Great Zimbabwe, A.D. 1420–1550: An environmental re-appraisal. In *Cities in the world, 1500–2000,* ed. A. Green and R. Leech. Leeds, UK: Maney.

Pilbeam, D. 1985. Distinguished lecture: Hominoid evolution and hominoid origins. *American Anthropologist* 88:295–312.

Piperno, D. R., and K. V. Flannery. 2001. The earliest archaeological maize (*Zea mays* L.) from highland Mexico: New accelerator mass spectrometry dates and their implications. *Proceedings of the National Academy of Sciences* 98:2101–2103.

Pitts, M. 2008. Stonehenge: One of our largest excavations draws to a close. *British Archaeology.* York, England: Council for British Archaeology.

Pleger, T. C. 2000. Old copper and red ocher social complexity. *Midcontinental Journal of Archaeology* 25:169–190.

Plog, S. 2008. *Ancient peoples of the American Southwest,* 2d ed. London: Thames & Hudson.

Pollock, S. 1999. *Ancient Mesopotamia: The Eden that never was.* Cambridge: Cambridge University Press.

Pope, K. O., M. E. D. Pohl, J. G. Jones, D. L. Lentz, C. von Nagy, F. J. Vega, and I. R. Quitmyer. 2001. Origin and environmental setting of ancient agriculture in the lowlands of Mesoamerica. *Science* 292:1370–1373.

Popson, C. P. 2002. Grim rites of the Moche. *Archaeology* 55(2):30–35.

Portal, J., ed. 2007. *The first emperor: China's terracotta army.* London: British Museum Press.

Possehl, G. L. 1990. Revolution in the urban revolution: The emergence of Indus urbanization. *Annual Review of Anthropology* 19:261–282.

Possehl, G. L. 1997. The transformation of the Indus civilization. *Journal of Archaeological Research* 11:425–472.

Possehl, G. L. 2002. *The Indus civilization: A contemporary perspective.* Walnut Creek, CA: AltaMira.

Postgate, J. N. 1994. *Early Mesopotamia: Society and economy at the dawn of history.* New York: Routledge.

Powell, T. G. E. 1980. *The Celts.* London: Thames & Hudson.

Praetzellis, A. 2000. *Death by theory: A tale of mystery and archaeological theory.* Walnut Creek, CA: AltaMira Press.

Prag, J., and R. Neeve. 1999. *Making faces.* London: British Museum Press.

Price, T. D. 1987. The Mesolithic of western Europe. *Journal of World Prehistory* 1:225–305.

Price, T. D., ed. 1989. *The chemistry of prehistoric bone.* Cambridge: Cambridge University Press.

Price, T. D., ed. 2000. *Europe's first farmers.* Cambridge: Cambridge University Press.

Price, T. D., and E. Brinch Petersen. 1987. A Mesolithic community in Denmark. *Scientific American* 255(3): 111–121.

Price, T. D., and J. A. Brown, eds. 1985. *Prehistoric hunter-gatherers.* Orlando, FL: Academic Press.

Price, T. D., and A. B. Gebauer. 2005. *Smakkerup Huse: A coastal Late Mesolithic site in Denmark.* Aarhus: Aarhus University Press.

Price, T. D., and A. B. Gebauer, eds. 1995. *Last hunters—first farmers: New perspectives on the prehistoric transition to agriculture.* Santa Fe, NM: School for American Research Press.

Pringle, H. 1997. Oldest mound complex found at Louisiana site. *Science* 277:1761–1762.

Prufer, K. M., and J. E. Brady. 2005. *Stone houses and earth lords: Maya religion in the cave context.* Boulder: University Press of Colorado.

Prufer, O. 1964. The Hopewell cult. *Scientific American* 211(6):90–102.

Puleston, D. E. 1973. Ancient Maya settlement patterns and environment at Tikal, Guatemala: Implications for subsistence models. Ph.D. diss., University of Pennsylvania, Philadelphia.

Puleston, D. E. 1977. The art and technology of hydraulic agriculture in the Maya Lowlands. In *Social processes and Maya prehistory,* ed. N. Hammond. New York: Academic Press.

Puleston, D. E. 1978. Terracing, raised fields, and tree cropping in the Maya Lowlands: A new perspective on the geography of power. In *Prehispanic Maya agriculture,* ed. P. D. Harrison and B. L. Turner II. Albuquerque: University of New Mexico Press.

Quilter, J. 1985. Architecture and chronology at El Paraíso, Peru. *Journal of Field Archaeology* 12:279–297.

Quilter, J. 1991. Late preceramic Peru. *Journal of World Prehistory* 5:387–438.

Quilter, J., B. Ojeda, D. M. Pearsall, D. H. Sandweiss, J. G. Jones, and E. S. Wing. 1991. Subsistence economy of El Paraíso, an early Peruvian site. *Science* 251:277–283.

Quilter, J., and T. Stocker. 1983. Subsistence economies and the origins of agriculture. *American Anthropologist* 85:545–562.

Rambo, A. T. 1991. The study of cultural evolution. In *Profiles in cultural evolution: Papers from a conference in honor of Elman R. Service,* ed. A. T. Rambo and K. Gillogly. Anthropological Papers of the Museum of Anthropology, No. 85. Ann Arbor: University of Michigan.

Randsborg, K. 1975. Social dimensions of early Neolithic Denmark. *Proceedings of the Prehistoric Society* 41:105–118.

Rawson, J. 2008. The first emperor's tomb: The afterlife universe. In *The first emperor: China's terracotta army,* ed. J. Portal. London: British Museum Press.

Raymond, J. S. 1981. The maritime foundations of Andean civilization: A reconsideration of the evidence. *American Antiquity* 46:806–821.

Redman, C. 1978. *The rise of civilization: From early farmers to urban society in the ancient Near East.* San Francisco: Freeman.

Redmond, E. M. 1983. *A fuego y sangre: Early Zapotec imperialism in the Cuicatlán Cañada, Oaxaca.* Memoirs of the Museum of Anthropology, No. 16. Ann Arbor: University of Michigan.

Reed, C. A., ed. 1977. *The origins of agriculture.* The Hague: Mouton.

Renfrew, C. 1974. *Before civilization.* New York: Knopf.

Renfrew, C., and P. Bahn. 1998. *Archaeology: Theories, methods, and practice.* London: Thames & Hudson.

Renfrew, J. 1973. *Palaeoethnobotany.* New York: Columbia University Press.

Renfrew, C. 2009. *Prehistory: The making of the human mind.* Modern Library Chronicles.

Rice, G. 1987. La Ciudad: A perspective on Hohokam community systems. In *The Hohokam village: Site structure and organization,* ed. D. E. Doyel. Glenwood Springs, CO: Southwestern and Rocky Mountain Division of the American Association for the Advancement of Science.

Richards, J. C. 2007. *Stonehenge: The story so far.* Swindon, England: English Heritage.

Richards, M. P., P. B. Pettitt, M. C. Stiner, and E. Trinkaus. 2001. Stable isotope evidence for increasing dietary breadth in the European mid–Upper Paleolithic. *Proceedings of the National Academy of Science* 98:6528–6532.

Richerson, P. J., and R. Boyd. 2001. Institutional evolution in the Holocene: The rise of complex societies. In *The origin of human social institutions,* ed. W. G. Runciman. Oxford: Oxford University Press.

Rindos, D. 1984. *The origins of agriculture: An evolutionary perspective.* New York: Academic Press.

Robson, J. R. K., R. I. Ford, K. V. Flannery, and J. E. Konlande. 1976. The nutritional significance of maize and teosinte. *Ecology of Food and Nutrition* 4:243–249.

Roe, D. 1981. *The Lower and Middle Paleolithic periods in Britain.* London: Routledge.

Rogers, A. R., D. Iltis, and S. Wooding. 2004. Genetic variation at the MC1R locus and the time since loss of human body hair. *Current Anthropology* 45:105–108.

Rolland, N., and H. L. Dibble. 1990. A new synthesis of Middle Paleolithic variability. *American Antiquity* 55:480–499.

Rollefson, G. O. 1985. The 1983 season at the Early Neolithic site of 'Ain Ghazal. *National Geographic Research* 1(1):44–62.

Rollo, F., M. Ubaldi, L. Ermini, and I. Marota. 2002. Ötzi's last meals: DNA analysis of the intestinal content of the Neolithic glacier mummy from the Alps. *Proceedings of the National Academy of Sciences* 99:12594–12599.

Ronen, A., ed. 1982. *The transition from Lower to Middle Paleolithic and the origin of modern man.* Oxford: British Archaeological Reports.

Roosevelt, A. 1989. Lost civilizations of the lower Amazon. *Natural History* 98(2):74–82.

Roosevelt, A. C., R. A. Housley, M. Imazio da Silveira, S. Maranca, and R. Johnson. 1991. Eighth millennium pottery from a prehistoric shell midden in the Brazilian Amazon. *Science* 254:1621–1624.

Rosenberg, M., R. Nesbitt, R. W. Redding, and B. L. Peasnall. 1998. Hallan Çemi, pig husbandry and post-Pleistocene adaptations along the Taurus-Zagros archaeology (Turkey). *Paléorient* 24:25–41.

Rosman, A., and P. G. Rubel. 1971. *Feasting with mine enemy: Rank and exchange among Northwest Coast societies.* New York: Columbia University Press.

Rothman, M. S., ed. 2001. *Uruk Mesopotamia and its neighbors: Cross-cultural interactions in the era of state formation.* Santa Fe, NM: School of American Research Press.

Rouse, I. 1992. *The Tainos: Rise and decline of the people who greeted Columbus.* New Haven, CT: Yale University Press.

Rowe, J. H. 1947. Inca culture at the time of Spanish conquest. In *Handbook of South American Indians.* Vol. 2, *The Andean civilizations,* ed.

J. H. Steward. Bureau of American Ethnology, Bulletin 143. Washington, DC: Smithsonian Institution.

Rowe, J. H. 1967. What kind of settlement was Inca Cuzco? *Nawpa Pacha* 5:59–76.

Rowe, J. H. 1987. Machu Pijchu: A la luz de los documentos del siglo XVI. *Kuntur* 4:12–20.

Ruddiman, W. F., and J. E. Kutzbach. 1991. Plateau uplift and climatic change. *Scientific American* 264(3):66–75.

Ruz Lhuillier, A. 1973. *El Templo de las Inscripciones: Palenque.* Mexico City: Instituto Nacional de Antropología e Historia.

Sabloff, J. A. 1990. *The new archaeology and the ancient Maya.* New York: Freeman.

Sabloff, J. A., ed. 2003. *Tikal: Dynasties, foreigners, and affairs of state.* Santa Fe, NM: School of American Research Press.

Sagan, C. 1987. Billions and billions. *Parade,* May 31, 9.

Sage, R. F. 1995. Was low atmospheric $CO_2$ during the Pleistocene a limiting factor for the origin of agriculture? *Global Change Biology* 1:93–106.

Sahagún, F. B. 1950–1982. *Florentine codex: General history of the things of New Spain,* trans. A. J. O. Anderson and C. E. Dibble. 11 vols. Santa Fe, NM: School for American Research; Provo: University of Utah Press.

Sahlins, M. D. 1968. Notes on the original affluent society. In *Man the hunter,* ed. R. B. Lee and I. DeVore. Chicago: Aldine.

Sahlins, M. D. 1972. *Stone Age economics.* Chicago: Aldine.

Sanders, W. T., J. R. Parsons, and R. S. Santley. 1979. *The Basin of Mexico: Ecological processes in the evolution of a civilization.* New York: Academic Press.

Sanders, W. T., and B. Price. 1968. *Mesoamerica: The evolution of a civilization.* New York: Random House.

Sarich, V. 1983. Retrospective on hominid macromolecular systematics. In *New interpretations of ape and human ancestry,* ed. R. L. Ciochon and R. S. Corrucini. New York: Plenum.

Sassaman, K. 2004. Complex hunter-gatherers in evolution and history: A North American perspective. *Journal of Archaeological Research* 12:227–280.

Sassaman, K. 2005. Poverty Point as structure, event, process. *Journal of Archaeological Method and Theory* 12:335–364.

Saturno, W. A., K. A. Taube, D. Stuart, and H. Hurst. 2005. *The murals of San Bartolo, El Petén, Guatemala. Part 1, The north wall.* Ancient America, No. 7. Barnardsville, NC: Center for Ancient American Studies.

Sauer, C. O. 1952. *Agricultural origins and dispersals.* New York: American Geographical Society.

Saunders, J. W., and T. Allen. 1994. Hedgepeth mounds, an Archaic mound complex in north-central Louisiana. *American Antiquity* 59:471–489.

Saunders, J. W., R. D. Mandel, R. T. Saucier, E. T. Allen, C. T. Hallmark, J. K. Johnson, E. H. Jackson, C. M. Allen, G. L. Stringer, D. S. Frink, J. K. Feathers, S. Williams, K. J. Gremillion, M. F. Vidrine, and R. Jones. 1997. A mound complex in Louisiana at 5400–5000 years before the present. *Science* 277:1796–1799.

Scarborough, V. L., and D. R. Wilcox, eds. 1991. *The Mesoamerican ballgame.* Tucson: University of Arizona Press.

Scarre, C., and G. Scarre. 2006. *The ethics of archaeology.* Cambridge: Cambridge University Press.

Schele, L., and M. E. Miller. 1986. *The blood of kings: Dynasty and ritual in Maya art.* Fort Worth, TX: Kimball Art Museum.

Schmandt-Besserat, D. 1978. The earliest precursor of writing. *Scientific American* 238(6):50–59.

Schmandt-Besserat, D. 1980. The envelopes that bear the first writing. *Technology and Culture* 21:357–385.

Schmandt-Besserat, D. 1990. Accounting in the prehistoric Middle East. *Archeomaterials* 4:15–23.

Schrenk, F. 2008. *The Neanderthals.* London: Routledge.

Schwartz, J. H. 1995. *Skeleton keys.* Oxford: Oxford University Press.

Schwartz, J. H., and T. D. White. 2003. Another perspective on hominid diversity. *Science* 301:763–764.

Senut, B., et al. 2001. First hominid from the Miocene (Lukeino Formation, Kenya). C. R. Acad. Sci. Paris, *Earth and Planetary Sciences* 332:137–144.

Serjeantson, D. 2009. *Birds.* Cambridge Manuals in Archaeology. Cambridge: Cambridge University Press.

Service, E. R. 1975. *Origins of the state and civilization: The process of cultural evolution.* New York: Norton.

Shackleton, N. J., and N. D. Opdyke. 1973. Oxygen isotope and paleomagnetic stratigraphy of equatorial Pacific core V28-238: Oxygen isotope temperatures and ice volume on a $10^5$ and $10^6$ year scale. *Quarternary Research* 3:39–55.

Shady Solis, R., J. Haas, and W. Creamer. 2001. Dating Caral, a preceramic site in the Supe Valley on the central coast of Peru. *Science* 292:723–726.

Sharer, R. J., and D. C. Grove, eds. 1989. *Regional perspectives on the Olmec.* Cambridge: Cambridge University Press.

Sharer, R. J., and L. P. Traxler. 2006. *The ancient Maya,* 6th ed. Stanford, CA: Stanford University Press.

Shea, J. J. 2003. Neandertals, competition, and the origin of modern human behavior in the Levant. *Evolutionary Anthropology* 12:173–187.

Sherratt, A., ed. 1980. *The Cambridge encyclopedia of archaeology.* New York: Crown.

Shipman, P. 1983. Early hominid lifestyle: Hunting and gathering or foraging and scavenging? In *Animals and archaeology: Hunters and their prey,* ed. J. Clutton-Brock and C. Grigson. Oxford: British Archaeological Reports.

Shipman, P. 2002. Hunting the first hominid. *American Scientist* 90:25–27.

Shopland, N. 2006. *A finds manual: Excavating, processing and storing.* Stroud, UK: Tempus.

Shutler, R., Jr. 1983. *Early man in the New World.* Beverly Hills, CA: Sage Publications.

Siemens, A. H., and D. E. Puleston. 1972. Ridged fields and associated features in southern Campeche: New perspectives on the lowland Maya. *American Antiquity* 37:228–239.

Simon, M. 2003. In line of the founder: A view of dynastic politics at Tikal. In *Tikal: Dynasties, foreigners, and affairs of state,* ed. J. A. Sabloff. Santa Fe, NM: School of American Research Press.

Simons, E. 1972. *Primate evolution.* New York: Macmillan.

Simpson, G. G. 1967. *The meaning of evolution,* rev. ed. New Haven, CT: Yale University Press.

Singer, R., and J. Wymer. 1982. *The Middle Stone Age at Klasies River Mouth in South Africa.* Chicago: University of Chicago Press.

Skelton, R. R., H. M. McHenry, and G. M. Drawhorn. 1986. Phylogenetic analysis of early hominids. *Current Anthropology* 27:21–43.

Smith, B. D. 1986. The archaeology of the southeastern United States: From Dalton to de Soto, 10,500–500 B.P. *Advances in World Archaeology* 5:1–92.

Smith, B. D. 1989. Origins of agriculture in eastern North America. *Science* 246:1566–1571.

Smith, B. D. 1992. *Rivers of change: Essays on early agriculture in eastern North America.* Washington, DC: Smithsonian Institution Press.

Smith, B. D. 1996. Agricultural chiefdoms of the Eastern Woodlands. In *The Cambridge history of the native peoples of the Americas.* Vol. 1, *North America, part 1,* ed. B. G. Trigger and W. E. Washburn. Cambridge: Cambridge University Press.

Smith, B. D. 1997. Reconsidering the Ocampo caves and the era of incipient cultivation in Mesoamerica. *Latin American Antiquity* 8:342–383.

Smith, B. D. 1998. *The emergence of agriculture.* New York: Scientific American Library.

Smith, B. D. 2001. Documenting plant domestication: The consilience of biological and archaeological approaches. *Proceedings of the National Academy of Sciences* 98:1324–1326.

Smith, B. D. 2005. Reassessing Coxcatlan Cave and the early history of domesticated plants in Mesoamerica. *Proceedings of the National Academy of Sciences* 02(27):9438–9445.

Smith, B. D. 2006. Eastern North America as an independent center of plant domestication. *Proceedings of the National Academy of Sciences* 103(33):12,223–12,228.

Smith, C. E. 1980. Plant remains from Guitarrero Cave. In *Guitarrero Cave,* ed. T. F. Lynch. New York: Academic Press.

Smith, F. H., and F. Spencer, eds. 1984. *The origins of modern humans.* New York: A. R. Liss.

Smith, M. E. 1996. *The Aztecs.* Malden, MA: Blackwell.

Smith, M. E., and M. A. Masson, eds. 2000. *The ancient civilizations of Mesoamerica: A reader.* Malden, MA: Blackwell.

Smith, M. L., ed. 2003. *The social construction of ancient cities.* Washington, DC: Smithsonian Institution Press.

Snow, D. R. 2009. *Archaeology of Native North America.* Englewood Cliffs, NJ: Prentice-Hall.

Soffer, O. 1985. *The Upper Paleolithic of the central Russian plains.* New York: Academic Press.

Solecki, R. 1971. *Shanidar: The first flower people.* New York: Knopf.

Solheim, W. G., II. 1972a. An earlier agricultural revolution. *Scientific American* 226(4):34–41.

Solheim, W. G., II. 1972b. Early man in Southeast Asia. *Expedition* 14(3):25–31.

Spence, M. W. 1974. Residential practices and the distribution of skeletal traits in Teotihuacan, Mexico. *Man* 9:262–273.

Spence, M. W. 1981. Obsidian production and the state in Teotihuacan. *American Antiquity* 46:769–787.

Spencer, C. S. 1982. *The Cuicatlán Cañada and Monte Albán: A study of primary state formation.* New York: Academic Press.

Spindler, K. 1994. *The man in the ice.* London: Weidenfeld & Nicholson.

Spooner, B., ed. 1972. *Population growth: Anthropological implications.* Cambridge, MA: MIT Press.

Standage, T. 2005. *A history of the world in 6 glasses.* New York: Walker.

Stanford, C. 1998. The social behavior of chimpanzees and bonobos. *Current Anthropology* 39:399–420.

Stanish, C. 2002. Tiwanaku political economy. In *Andean archaeology I: Variations in sociopolitical organization,* ed. W. H. Isbell and H. Silverman. New York: Kluwer/Plenum.

Stanish, C. 2003. *Ancient Tiwanaku: The evolution of complex society in southern Peru and northern Bolivia.* Berkeley: University of California Press.

Stein, G. J. 1998. Heterogeneity, power, and political economy: Some current research issues in the archaeology of Old World complex societies. *Journal of Archaeological Research* 6:1–44.

Stein, G. J. 2001. Understanding ancient state societies in the Old World. In *Archaeology at the millennium: A sourcebook,* ed. G. M. Feinman and T. D. Price. New York: Kluwer/Plenum.

Stein, G. J., and M. S. Rothman. 1994. *Chiefdoms and early states in the Near East.* Madison, WI: Prehistory Press.

Stephens, J. L. 1841. *Incidents of travel in Central America, Chiapas, and Yucatán.* 2 vols. New York: Harper & Row. Reprint, New York: Dover, 1962.

Stephens, J. L. 1843. *Incidents of travel in Yucatán.* 2 vols. New York: Harper & Row. Reprint, New York: Dover, 1963.

Steponaitis, V. 1983. *Ceramics, chronology, and community patterns: An archaeological study at Moundville.* New York: Academic Press.

Steponaitis, V. 1986. Prehistoric archaeology in the southeastern United States, 1970–1985. *Annual Review of Anthropology* 15:363–404.

Steponaitis, V. 1991. Contrasting patterns of Mississippian development. In *Chiefdoms: Power, economy, and ideology,* ed. T. Earle. Cambridge: Cambridge University Press.

Stille, A. 2003. *The future of the past.* New York: Picador Books.

Stirling, M. W. 1943. *Stone monuments of southern Mexico.* Bureau of American Ethnology, Bulletin 138. Washington, DC: Smithsonian Institution.

Stoltman, J. B., ed. 1991. *New perspectives on Cahokia: Views from the periphery.* Madison, WI: Prehistory Press.

Storey, A. A., D. Quiroz, J. M. Ramírez, N. Beavan-Athfield, D. J. Addison, R. Walter, T. Hunt, J. Athens, L. Huynen, and E. A. Matisoo-Smith. 2008. Pre-Columbian chickens, dates, isotopes, and mtDNA. *Proceedings of the National Academy of Science* 105:E99.

Storey, G. R., ed. 2006. *Urbanism in the preindustrial world: Cross-cultural approaches.* Tuscaloosa: University of Alabama Press.

Stringer, C. B. 1985. Middle Pleistocene hominid variability and the origin of Late Pleistocene humans. In *Ancestors: The hard evidence,* ed. E. Delson. New York: A. R. Liss.

Stringer, C. B. 1988. *The Neanderthals.* London: Thames & Hudson.

Stringer, C. B. 1990. The emergence of modern humans. *Scientific American* 259(12):98–103.

Stringer, C., and P. Andrews. 2005. *The complete world of human evolution.* London: Thames & Hudson.

Sudgen, D. E., and B. S. John. 1976. *Glaciers and landscape.* London: E. Arnold.

Susman, R. L., and J. T. Stern. 1982. Functional morphology of *Homo habilis. Science* 217:931–934.

Sutliffe, A. J. 1985. *On the track of Ice Age mammals.* Cambridge, MA: Harvard University Press.

Sutton, M. Q., and B. S. Arkush. 1998. *Archaeological laboratory methods.* Dubuque, IA: Kendall/Hunt.

Swaminathan, M. S. 1984. Rice. *Scientific American* 250(1):80–93.

Tanner, N. 1981. *On becoming human.* London: Cambridge University Press.

Tattersall, I. 1995. *The fossil trail: How we know what we think we know about human evolution.* Oxford: Oxford University Press.

Tattersall, I. 1999. *The last Neanderthal: The rise, success, and mysterious extinction of our closest human relatives.* Boulder, CO: Westview.

Tattersall, I., C. Delson, and J. V. Couvering, eds. 1988. *Encyclopedia of human evolution and prehistory.* New York: Garland.

Tattersall, I. 2001. *The human odyssey: Four million years.* Lincoln, NE: Universe Press.

Tattersall, I., and J. H. Schwartz. 2001. *Extinct humans.* Boulder, CO: Westview.

Tauber, H. 1981. $^{13}$C evidence for dietary habits of prehistoric man in Denmark. *Nature* 292:332–333.

Taylor, R. E. 1988. *Radiocarbon dating.* New York: Academic Press.

Taylour, W. 1989. *The Mycenaeans.* London: Thames & Hudson.

Te-k'un, C. 1959. *Archaeology in China.* Vol. 1, *Prehistoric China.* Cambridge: W. Heffer & Sons.

Te-k'un, C. 1960. *Archaeology in China.* Vol. 2, *Shang burials.* Cambridge: W. Heffer & Sons.

Te-k'un, C. 1966. *Archaeology in China: New light on prehistoric China.* Cambridge: W. Heffer & Sons.

Tello, J. C. 1943. Discovery of the Chavín culture in Peru. *American Antiquity* 9:135–160.

Teltser, P. 1996. Mississippian culture. In *The Oxford companion to archaeology,* ed. B. M. Fagan. Oxford: Oxford University Press.

Templeton, A. R. 1993. The "Eve" hypothesis: A genetic critique and reanalysis. *American Anthropologist* 95:51–72.

Thiel, J. H., and J. B. Mabry, eds. 2006. Rio Hondo archaeology, 2000–2003: *Investigations at the San Agustín Mission and Mission Gardens, Tucson Presidio, Tucson Pressed Brick Company, and Clearwater site.* Technical report No. 2004-11. Tucson, AZ: Desert Archaeology.

Thieme, H. 1997. Lower Paleolithic hunting spears from Germany. *Nature* 385:807.

Thomas, D. H. 1983. *The archaeology of Monitor Valley 2: Gatecliff Shelter.* New York: American Museum of Natural History.

Thomas, D. H. 1989. *Archaeology.* New York: Holt, Rinehart & Winston.

Thomas, D. H. 2000. *Skull wars: Kennewick man, archaeology, and the battle for Native American identity.* New York: Basic Books.

Thompson, D. E., and J. V. Murra. 1966. The Inca bridges in the Huánuco region. *American Antiquity* 31:632–639.

Thorne, A. G., and M. H. Wolpoff. 1992. The multiregional evolution of humans. *Scientific American* 266(4):76–83.

Tobias, P. 1971. *The brain in hominid evolution.* New York: Columbia University Press.

Todd, I. A. 1976. *Çatal Hüyük in perspective.* Menlo Park, CA: Cummings.

Toffler, A. 1970. *Future shock.* London: Pan Books.

Topic, T. L. 1982. The Early Intermediate period and its legacy. In *Chan Chan,* ed. M. E. Moseley and K. C. Day. Albuquerque: University of New Mexico Press.

Topping, A. 1978. The first emperor's army, China's incredible find. *National Geographic* 153(4):440–459.

Toth, N. 1987. The first technology. *Scientific American* 256(2):112–121.

Townsend, R. F., ed. 1992. *The ancient Americas: Art from sacred landscapes.* Chicago: Art Institute of Chicago.

Townsend, R. F., ed. 2004. *Hero, hawk, and open hand: American Indian art of the ancient Midwest and South.* Chicago: Art Institute of Chicago.

Trask, L. 1998. The origins of speech. *Cambridge Archaeological Journal* 8:69–94.

Trigger, B. G. 1978. Early Iroquoian contacts with Europeans. In *Handbook of North American Indians.* Vol. 15, *Northeast,* ed. W. C. Sturtevant and B. G. Trigger. Washington, DC: Smithsonian Institution Press.

Trigger, B. G. 1980a. Archaeology and the image of the American Indian. *American Antiquity* 45:662–675.

Trigger, B. G. 1980b. *Gordon Childe: Revolutions in archaeology.* New York: Columbia University Press.

Trigger, B. G. 1998. *Sociocultural evolution: Calculation and contingency.* Malden, MA: Blackwell.

Trigger, B. G. 2003. *Understanding early civilizations: A comparative study.* Cambridge: Cambridge University Press.

Trigger, B. G. 2006. *A history of archaeological thought.* Cambridge: Cambridge University Press.

Trigger, B. G., B. J. Kemp, D. O. O'Connor, and A. B. Lloyd. 1985. *Ancient Egypt: A social history.* Cambridge: Cambridge University Press.

Tringham, R. 1971. *Hunters, fishers, and farmers of Eastern Europe 6000–3000 B.C.* London: Hutchinson University Library.

Trinkaus, E., ed. 1990. *The emergence of modern humans.* Cambridge: Cambridge University Press.

Trinkaus, E. 2005. Early modern humans. *Annual Review of Anthropology* 34:207–230.

Trinkhaus, E. 2007. European early modern humans and the fate of the Neandertals. *PNAS* 104:7367–7372.

Trinkaus, E., and W. W. Howells. 1979. The Neanderthals. *Scientific American* 241(6):94–105.

Trubitt, M. B. 2003. Mississippian period warfare and palisade construction at Cahokia. In *Theory, method, and practice in modern archaeology,* ed. R. J. Jeske and D. K. Charles. Westport, CT: Praeger.

Tuck, J. A. 1978a. Northern Iroquoian prehistory. In *Handbook of North American Indians.* Vol. 15, *Northeast,* ed. W. C. Sturtevant and B. G. Trigger. Washington, DC: Smithsonian Institution Press.

Tuck, J. A. 1978b. Regional cultural development, 3000 to 300 B.C. In *Handbook of North American Indians.* Vol. 15, *Northeast,* ed. W. C. Sturtevant and B. G. Trigger. Washington, DC: Smithsonian Institution Press.

Turner, B. L., II, and P. D. Harrison, eds. 1983. *Pulltrouser Swamp: Ancient Maya habitat, agriculture, and settlement in northern Belize.* Austin: University of Texas Press.

Tyler, N. 1999. *Historic preservation: An introduction to its history, principles, and practice.* New York: Norton.

Tylor, E. B. 1960. *Anthropology.* Ann Arbor: University of Michigan Press. Originally published 1881.

Ubelaker, D. H. 1978. *Human skeletal remains.* Washington, DC: Taraxacum Press.

Ucko, P. J., and A. Rosenfeld. 1967. *Paleolithic cave art.* London: Weidenfeld & Nicholson.

Underhill, A. 1997. Current issues in Chinese Neolithic archaeology. *Journal of World Prehistory* 11:103–160.

Underhill, A. P. 2002. *Craft production and social change in northern China.* New York: Kluwer/Plenum.

Underhill, A. P., G. M. Feinman, L. M. Nicholas, G. Bennett, H. Fang, F. Luan, H. Yu, and F. Cai. 2002. Regional survey and the development of complex societies in southeastern Shandong, China. *Antiquity* 76:745–755.

Underhill, A., G. Feinman, L. Nicholas, H. Fang, F. Luan, H. Yu, and F. Cai. 2008. Changes in regional settlement patterns and the development of complex societies in southeastern Shandong, China. *Journal of Anthropological Archaeology* 27:1–29.

Ungar, P. S., ed. 2006. *Evolution of the human diet: The known, the unknown, and the unknowable.* Oxford: Oxford University Press.

Urton, G. 2003. *Signs of the Inka Khipu: Binary coding in the Andean knotted-string records.* Austin: University of Texas Press.

U.S. Congress, Office of Technology Assessment. 1986. *Technologies for prehistoric and historic preservation.* OTA-E-319. Washington, DC: U.S. Government Printing Office.

Vaillant, G. C. 1966. *Aztecs of Mexico.* Harmondsworth, England: Pelican.

Vermeule, E. 1972. *Greece in the Bronze Age.* Chicago: University of Chicago Press.

Vigne, J. D., J. Guilaine, K. Debue, L. Haye, and P. Gérard. 2004. Early taming of the cat in Cyprus. *Science* 304:259–260.

Villa, P. 1982. Conjoinable pieces and site formation processes. *American Antiquity* 47:276–290.

Vitelli, K. D. 1996. *Archaeological ethics.* Walnut Creek, CA: AltaMira.

Vitelli, K. D., and C. Colwell-Chanthphonh. 2006. *Archaeological ethics,* 2d ed. Blue Ridge Summit, PA: AltaMira.

Wainwright, G. 1989. *The henge monuments.* London: Thames & Hudson.

Walker, A. 1981. Diet and teeth: Dietary hypotheses and human evolution. *Philosophical Transactions of the Royal Society of London* B292:57–64.

Wallace, A. R. 1869. *Malay archipelago.* New York: Harper & Brothers.

Warren, P. 1975. *The Aegean civilizations.* Oxford: Elsevier Phaidon.

Warrick, G. A. 1983. *Reconstructing Iroquoian village organization.* National Museum of Man Mercury Series, Paper No. 124. Ottawa: Archaeological Survey of Canada.

Warrick, G. A. 1988. Estimating Ontario Iroquoian village duration. *Man in the Northeast* 36:21–60.

Watson, W. 1960. *Archaeology in China.* London: Max Parrish.

Waters, M. R., and T. W. Stafford Jr. 2007. Redefining the age of Clovis: Implications for the peopling of the Americas. *Science* 315:1122–1126.

Weaver, M. P. 1981. *The Aztecs, Maya, and their predecessors: Archaeology of Mesoamerica.* New York: Academic Press.

Webb, C. H. 1982. *The Poverty Point culture,* 2d ed. Baton Rouge: Louisiana State University School of Geoscience.

Webster, D. 2002. *The fall of the ancient Maya.* London: Thames & Hudson.

Weiss, E., M. E. Kislev, and A. Hartmann. 2006. Autonomous cultivation before domestication. *Science* 312:1608–1610.

Weiss, H. 2005. *Collapse: How sudden climate change destroyed civilization and shaped history.* London: Routlege.

Wenke, R. J. 1999. *Patterns in prehistory: Humankind's first three million years,* 4th ed. New York: Oxford University Press.

Wenke, R. J. 2009. *The ancient Egyptian state: The origins of Egyptian culture (c. 20,000–1900 B.C.).* Cambridge: Cambridge University Press.

Wheeler, R. E. M. 1943. *Maiden Castle, Dorset.* London: Society of Antiquaries 12.

Wheeler, R. E. M. 1968. *The Indus civilization.* Cambridge: Cambridge University Press.

Wheeler, T. S., and R. Maddin. 1976. The techniques of the early Thai metalsmith. *Expedition* 18(4):38–47.

White, J. C. 1982. *Discovery of a lost Bronze Age: Ban Chiang.* Philadelphia: University of Pennsylvania Press.

White, L. A. 1959. *The evolution of culture.* New York: McGraw-Hill.

White, R. 1986. *Dark caves, bright visions: Life in ice age Europe.* New York: American Museum of Natural History.

White, T., G. Suwa, and B. Asfaw. 1994. *Australopithecus ramidus,* a new species of early hominid from Aramis, Ethiopia. *Nature* 371:306–312.

Whittle, A. 2003. *The archaeology of people: Dimensions of Neolithic life.* London: Routledge.

Wilcox, D. R., T. R. McGuire, and C. Sternberg. 1981. *Snaketown revisited.* Arizona State Museum Archaeological Series 155. Tucson: University of Arizona.

Willey, G. R. 1953. *Prehistoric settlement in the Virú Valley, Peru.* Washington, DC: Smithsonian Institution Press.

Willey, G. R. 1966. *An introduction to American archaeology.* Vol. 1, *North and Middle America.* Englewood Cliffs, NJ: Prentice-Hall.

Willey, G. R. 1971. *An introduction to American archaeology.* Vol. 2, *South America.* Englewood Cliffs, NJ: Prentice-Hall.

Willey, G. R. 1974. The Classic Maya hiatus: A rehearsal for the collapse? In *Mesoamerican archaeology: New approaches,* ed. N. Hammond. London: Duckworth.

Wills, W. H. 1988. Early agriculture and sedentism in the American Southwest: Evidence and interpretations. *Journal of World Prehistory* 2:445–488.

Wilmsen, E. N. 1974. *Lindenmeier: A Pleistocene hunting society.* New York: Harper & Row.

Wilmsen, E. N. 1978. *Lindenmeier, 1934–74.* Washington, DC: Smithsonian Institution Press.

Wilson, A. C., and R. L. Cann. 1992. The recent African genesis of humans. *Scientific American* 266(4):68–73.

Wilson, D. J. 1981. Of maize and men: A critique of the maritime hypothesis of state origins on the coast of Peru. *American Anthropologist* 83:93–120.

Wilson, S. M., ed. 1997. *The indigenous people of the Caribbean.* Gainesville: University Press of Florida.

Wing, E. S. 1980. Faunal remains. In *Guitarrero Cave: Early man in the Andes,* ed. T. S. Lynch. New York: Academic Press.

Wiseman, J. R., and F. El-Baz, eds. 2007. *Remote sensing in archaeology.* New York City: Springer.

Wittfogel, K. 1957. *Oriental despotism.* New Haven, CT: Yale University Press.

Wolf, E. R. 1982. *Europe and the people without history.* Berkeley: University of California Press.

Wolpoff, M. 1999. *Paleoanthropology,* 2d ed. Boston: McGraw-Hill.

Wood, B. Palaeoanthropology: Hominid revelations from Chad. *Nature* 418:133–135.

Wood, B., and B. G. Richmond. 2000. Human evolution: Taxonomy and paleobiology. *Journal of Anatomy* 196:19–60.

Wood, J. W., D. Lai, P. L. Johnson, K. L. Campbell, and I. M. Masler. 1985. Lactation and birth spacing in highland New Guinea. *Journal of Biosocial Science,* Supplement 9:159–173.

Woodman, P. C. 1981. A Mesolithic camp in Ireland. *Scientific American* 245(2):120–132.

Woolley, C. L. 1954. *Excavations at Ur.* London: Benn.

Wright, G. A. 1969. *Obsidian analyses and prehistoric Near Eastern trade: 7500–3500 B.C.* Ann Arbor: University of Michigan. Anthropological Papers of the Museum of Anthropology, No. 37.

Wright, H. E. 1971. Late Quaternary vegetational history of North America. In *The Late Cenozoic ice ages,* ed. K. K. Turekian. New Haven, CT: Yale University Press.

Wright, H. T. 1986. The evolution of civilizations. In *American archaeology, past and future,* ed. D. J. Meltzer, D. D. Fowler, and J. A. Sabloff. Washington, DC: Smithsonian Institution Press.

Wright, H. T. 2005. The polycentricity of the archaic civilizations. In *A catalyst for ideas: Anthropological archaeology and the legacy of Douglas W. Schwartz,* ed. V. L. Scarborough. Santa Fe, NM: School of American Research Press.

Wright, H. T., and G. A. Johnson. 1975. Population, exchange and early state formation in southwestern Iran. *American Anthropologist* 77:267–289.

Wright, H. T., and E. S. A. Rupley. 2001. Calibrated radiocarbon age determinations of Uruk-related assemblages. In *Uruk Mesopotamia and its neighbors: Cross-cultural interactions in the era of state formation,* ed. M. S. Rothman. Santa Fe, NM: School of American Research Press.

Wright, R. P. 2009. *The ancient Indus: Urbanism, economy, and society.* Cambridge: Cambridge University Press.

Wymer, J. 1968. *Lower Paleolithic archaeology in Britain.* London: John Baker.

Xi, Z., F. Zhang, B. Xu, J. Tan, S. Li, C. Li, H. Zhou, H. Zhu, J. Zhang, Q. Duan, and L. Jin. 2008. Mitochondrial DNA evidence for a diversified origin of workers building mausoleum for first emperor of China. *PLoS One* 10(3):1–7.

Yates, R. D. S. 1994. The birth of imperial China. In *Cradles of civilization: China,* ed. R. E. Murowchick. Norman: University of Oklahoma Press.

Yen, D. E. 1977. Hoabinhian horticulture: The evidence and the questions from northwest Thailand. In *Sunda and Sahul: Prehistoric studies in Southeast Asia, Melanesia, and Australia,* ed. J. Allen, J. Golson, and R. Jones. London: Academic Press.

Yen, D. E. 1982. Ban Chiang pottery and rice. *Expedition* 24(4):51–64.

Yerkes, R. W. 1988. The Woodland and Mississippian traditions in the prehistory of midwestern North America. *Journal of World Prehistory* 2:307–358.

Yoffee, N., and G. L. Cowgill, eds. 1988. *The collapse of ancient states and civilizations.* Tucson: University of Arizona Press.

Zarrillo, S., D. M. Pearsall, J. S. Raymond, M. A. Tisdale, and D. J. Quon. 2008. Directly dated starch residues document Early Formative maize (Zea mays L.) in tropical Ecuador. *Proceedings of the National Academy of Sciences* 103(33):5006–5011.

Zeder, M. A. 2006. Central questions in the domestication of plants and animals. *Evolutionary Anthropology* 15:105–117.

Zeder, M. A., D. Bradley, E. Emshwiller, and B. D. Smith, eds. 2006. *Documenting domestication: New genetic and archaeological paradigms.* Berkeley: University of California Press.

Zimmer, C. 2001. *Evolution: The triumph of an idea.* New York: HarperCollins.

Zimmerman, L. J., K. D. Vitelli, and J. Hollowell-Zimmer, eds. 2003. *Ethical issues in archaeology.* Walnut Creek, CA: AltaMira.

Zohary, D., and M. Hopf. 2000. *Domestication of plants in the Old World: The origin and spread of cultivated plants in West Asia, Europe, and the Nile Valley,* 3d ed. Oxford: Oxford University Press.

zur Nedden, D., K. Wicke, R. Knapp, H. Seidler, H. Wilfing, G. Weber, K. Spindler, W. A. Murphy, G. Hauser, and W. Platzer. 1994. New findings on the Tyrolean "Ice Man": Archaeological and CT-body analyses suggest personal disaster before death. *Journal of Archaeological Science* 21:809–818.

Zvelebil, M., and P. M. Dolukhanov. 1991. The transition to farming in eastern and northern Europe. *Journal of World Prehistory* 5:233–278.

# Photo Credits

**Chapter 1** 1.1, © Boxgrove Project; 1.2, Courtesy NASA, ESA and J. Hester (ASU); 1.6, Courtesy James B. Stoltman; 1.7, T.D. Price; 1.8, Courtesy Michael Kienitz; 1.9, Courtesy Lawrence Conyers; 1.10, T.D. Price; 1.13, © John W. Rick; 1.14, T.D. Price; 1.15, © Michael A. Hampshire/NGS Image Collection; 1.16, Courtesy Michael Kienitz; 1.17, T.D. Price; 1.18, Courtesy of James B. Stoltman; 1.19, Courtesy Sönke Hartz; 1.20, 1.21, Courtesy Michael Kienitz; 1.22, T.D. Price; 1.23, © Statens Historiska Museum. Photo: Soren Hallgren; 1.25, 1.29, 1.33, T.D. Price; 1.34, © Warren & Genny Garst/ Tom Stack and Associates **Chapter 2** 2.1, © John Reader/Photo Researchers, Inc.; 2.2, © Kevin O'Farrell Concepts; 2.3, Courtesy of Hominidae.com; 2.9, Micrographs courtesy of Dr. Frederick E. Grine, SUNY, Stony Brook; 2.10, © John Reader/Photo Researchers, Inc.; 2.12, © Institute of Human Origins; 2.13, 2.14, 2.15, 2.16, © John Reader/Photo Researchers, Inc.; 2.17, Courtesy Department of Library Services, AMNH. Photo D. Finnin/C. Chesek. Neg. #4936-300; 2.19, © John Reader/Photo Researchers, Inc.; 2.21, Courtesy Richard Potts; 2.22, © E.E. Kingsley/Photo Researchers, Inc.; 2.27, Robert F. Sisson, © National Geographic Image Collection; 2.28, © John Reader/Photo Researchers, Inc.; 2.30, © AP/Wide World Photos **Chapter 3** 3.1, © Royal British Columbia Museum, Canada; 3.3, © National Museums of Kenya; 3.4, © Tom McHugh/Photo Researchers, Inc.; 3.6, Photo courtesy F. Clark Howell; 3.12, From Professor Huang Weiwen. Institute of Paleontology & Paleoanthropology, Beijing; 3.13, Courtesy Department of Library Services. American Museum of Natural History. Neg #335651; 3.14, © Dean Conger/Corbis; 3.18 (left), Staatliches Museum fur Naturkunde, Stuttgart; 3.18 (right), © Laboratoire de Préhistoire du Musée de l'Homme; 3.19, Courtesy of F. Clark Howell; 3.21, © Javier Trueba/Madrid Scientific Films; 3.22, © Maurício Antón/Madrid Scientific Films; 3.23, © Javier Trueba/Madrid Scientific Films; 3.24, *The Age of Mammals,* a mural by Rudolph F. Zallinger. Copyright © 1966, 1975, 1989, 1991, 2000 Peabody Museum of Natural History, Yale University, New Haven, Connecticut, USA.; 3.25, Aaris-Sorensen and Brinch Petersen, STRIAE, 24: 111–117, photo by Geert Brovad; 3.27, Courtesy J. Desmond Clark; 3.30, © Dr. Harmut Thieme, Niedersächsisches Landesamt für Denkmalpflege, Hannover, Germany. Photo: Peter Pfarr **Chapter 4** 4.1, © Erich Lessing/Art Resource, NY; 4.3, © Kenneth Garett/NGS Image Collection; 4.7, © John Reader/Photo Researchers, Inc.; 4.8, T.D. Price; 4.15, © John Reader/Photo Researchers, Inc.; 4.16, Reconstruction of Homo sapiens neanderthalensis by Jay H. Matternes, © Copyright 1981.; 4.23, T.D. Price; 4.27, © The National Museum of Denmark; 4.29, Courtesy Peter Vemming Hansen; 4.31, © Musée de l'Homme. Photo by D. Destable; 4.32, Courtesy of Archeologicky Ustav, Brno, Czech Republic; 4.35, Collection of the Institute fur Ur-and Fruhgeschichte, University of Tubingen, Germany; 4.38, Photo by Jean Vertut, Issey-les-Molineaux, France; 4.44, © Charles & Josette Lenars/Corbis; 4.45, Courtesy J.-M. Chauvet, French Ministry of Culture and Communication, Regional Direction for Cultural Affairs - Rhône-Alpes region - Regional Department of Archaeology; 4.47, Courtesy Department of Library Services. American Museum of Natural History. Neg # 39686. Photo by Kirschner; 4.48, © Professor Leroi-Gourhan. From The Old Stone Age, p. 236. Weidenfeld & Nicholson Ltd.; 4.53, © Réunion des Musées Nationaux/Art Resource, NY; 4.54, © Medford Taylor/NGS Image Collection; 4.55, © Anthropology Photographic Archive, University of Auckland; 4.62, © Dr. Mike Waters, Texas A&M University; 4.63, Courtesy of the Royal Ontario Museum, Toronto, Canada; 4.66, From The National Anthropological Archives, Smithsonian Institution; 4.68, © Keren Su/Corbis; 4.69, 4.71, © Tom Dillehay; 4.72, Courtesy Vance Holliday; 4.73, From The National Anthropological Archives, Smithsonian Institution; 4.76, © National Geographic Society Image Collection **Chapter 5** 5.1, © Lennart Larsen/The National Museum of Denmark; 5.3, Courtesy Tom Pleger; 5.9, T.D. Price; 5.12, © The National Museum of Denmark; 5.13, © Lennart Larsen/The National Museum of Denmark; 5.17, T.D. Price; 5.19, Courtesy John Parkington, Department of Archaeology, University of Capetown; 5.22, 5.23, 5.24, Courtesy Sannai-Maruyama Site Preservation Office, Cultural Properties Protection Division, Aomori Prefectural Board of Education; 5.25, © Board of Trustees, Southern Illinois University; 5.27, Courtesy Richard Jeffries; 5.28, © Southern Illinois University; 5.30, © Board of Trustees, Southern Illinois University; 5.32, © Michael A. Hampshire/NGS Image Collection; 5.34, © Lee/Anthro-Photo **Chapter 6** 6.1, © Biblioteca Medicea-Laurenziana, Florence, Italy/The Bridgeman Art Library; 6.2, © Erich Lessing/Art Resource, NY; 6.4, T.D. Price; 6.6, Reprinted by permission from the Florentine Codex: General History of the Things of New Spain by Fray Bernardino de Sahagun, Book IV, Which Telleth of the Book of Days Which the Mexicans Handed Down, translated by Arthur J.O. Anderson and Charles E. Dibble. © 1981 by the School of American Research, Santa Fe.; 6.8, Photo by Peter Dorell and Stuart Laidlaw, Courtesy University of London, Institute of Archaeology; 6.9, Courtesy of James L. Phillips, The Field Museum; 6.16, Courtesy Charles M. Niquette, Cultural Resource Analysts, Inc.; 6.17, © Gil Stein; 6.18, Courtesy Institute of Archaeology, University College, London; 6.20, © Albatross Aerial Photography; 6.21, © Ann Hatfield; 6.23, © Barry Kass/Images of Archaeology; 6.29, Courtesy Ian Hodder, Catalhöyük Project, Stanford University; 6.31, Courtesy James Mellaart; 6.34, © C. Jarrige/CNRS-Guimet; 6.37, Courtesy Susan Kepecs; 6.39, Courtesy Linda Nicholas; 6.46, 6.47, 6.48, © Charles Higham; 6.51, Courtesy Kent V. Flannery; 6.52, Courtesy Linda Nicholas; 6.53, Courtesy Kent V. Flannery; 6.54, © David Cavagnaro/Peter Arnold, Inc.; 6.57, 6.58, © Robert S. Peabody Museum of Archaeology. Phillips Academy, Andover, MA. All rights reserved.; 6.62, 6.63, 6.64, 6.65, © Thomas F. Lynch; 6.66, © Chip Clark; 6.68, T.D. Price **Chapter 7** 7.1, Courtesy Cahokia Mounds State Historic Site, Collinsville, Illinois; 7.4, © Richard A. Cooke/Corbis; 7.6, Courtesy Poverty Point State Historic Site, Louisiana Office of State Parks. Photo by Steven Carricut; 7.7, © The Field Museum, Neg. #94855; 7.12, © The Field Musuem, A113968. Photo by John Weinstein; 7.13, © The Field Museum, A110016C. Photo by Ron Testa; 7.14, Panther Effigy Pipe, USA, Indiana, Posey County, Mann Site. Allison-Copena, Middle Woodlands period, AD 1-400. Black steatite. 2 3/8 x 1 9/16 x 6 5/16, L49.5. Anonymous loan. © The Brooklyn Museum of Art; 7.15, © The Field Museum, A113969. Photo by John Weinstein; 7.16, © The Field Museum, Neg. #A110028c; 7.17, Photo © Sam Noble Oklahoma Museum of Natural History, University of Oklahoma. Used with permission of the Caddo Nation and the Witchita & Affilitated Tribes; 7.19, Courtesy Cahokia Mounds State Historic Site, Collinsville, Illinois. Painting by William R. Iseminger; 7.20, Courtesy Dr. Melvin Fowler, University of Wisconsin, Milwaukee; 7.21, Courtesy Cahokia Mounds State Historic Site, Collinsville, Illinois; 7.22, Courtesy Missouri Historical Society, St. Louis; 7.24, Library, Academy of Natural Sciences, Philadelphia; 7.31, Photo by William D. Finlayson/This Land Archaeology, Inc.; 7.32, © The Field Museum, Neg. #CSA78062; 7.34, Arizona State Museum, The University of Arizona. Photo by Helga Teiwes; 7.35, Arizona State Museum, The University of Arizona. Photo by Emil Haury; 7.36, © The Field Museum, cat. #83350. Photograph by Linda Nicholas; 7.37, Arizona State Museum, The University of Arizona. Photo by Helga Teiwes; 7.38, Courtesy the Arizona State Museum, the University of Arizona, photographer, Jannelle Weakly. #7301; 7.42, Courtesy Linda Nicholas; 7.43, © The Field Museum, Neg. #CSA77994; 7.44, © The Field Museum, Neg. #A88593; 7.45, Courtesy Paul Logsdon; 7.47, © Ruth &

Louis Kirk; 7.48, © Ruth Kirk; 7.52, Courtesy Allan May; 7.53, © Birmingham Public Library, Cat. #245; 7.54, © The Field Museum, Neg. #A97603 **Chapter 8** 8.1, Photo: © David Hiser/NGS Image Collection, Overlay: Ned M. Seidler, © National Geographic Society; 8.3, 8.7, Courtesy Linda Nicholas; 8.9, Richard H. Stewart, © National Geographic Society Image Collection; 8.11, © Museo Nacional de Antropologia, Mexico City, Mexico/Bridgeman Art Library/Giraudon; 8.14, Courtesy Department of Library Services, American Museum of Natural History. Neg #1298; 8.16, 8.19, Courtesy Dr. Ray T. Matheny/Project El Mirador; 8.25, 8.27, Courtesy Linda Nicholas; 8.28, Courtesy of Stephen Kowalewski/University of Georgia; 8.32, 8.33, Courtesy Linda Nicholas; 8.36, Courtesy Jennifer Blitz; 8.39, © Arvind Garg/Corbis; 8.40, © Charles & Josette Lenars/Corbis; 8.41, © University of Pennsylvania Museum, Tikal Project, Neg. #65-4-1094; 8.44, From *Science,* " Pre-Historic Raised Field Agriculture in the Maya Lowlands," by B.L Turner, Volume 213, pp. 399–405, July 1981. © 1981 by the AAAS; 8.48, © Werner Foreman/Art Resource, NY; 8.49, 8.55, Courtesy Linda Nicholas; 8.57, Courtesy Susan Kepecs; 8.58, © Bates Littlehales/NGS Image Collection; 8.60, 8.61, Courtesy Linda Nicholas; 8.62, © The Field Museum, Neg. #CSA45113; 8.64, © Kenneth Garrett; 8.68, © The Bodleian Library, Oxford University. MS. Arch Seld. A.1, fol. 47r; 8.71, Codex Florentino: Illustrations for Sahagun's Historia General de las Cosas de Nueva España, edited by Francisco del Paso Troncoso, Vol. 5, Madrid, 1905.; 8.73, © Boltin Picture Library/Bridgeman Art Library **Chapter 9** 9.1, © Nathan Benn; 9.3, © Jonathan Haas/Getty Images; 9.4, R.A. Feldman, Ph.D dissertation, Harvard University; 9.5, 9.8, Courtesy Jeffrey Quilter; 9.10, © Johan Reinhard; 9.12, © Wilfredo Loayza; 9.14, © John W. Rick; 9.16, Courtesy Dumbarton Oaks Research Library and Collections, Washington, DC; 9.17, Courtesy Department of Library Services. American Museum of Natural History. Neg. #334913; 9.21, Courtesy Department of Library Services. American Museum of Natural History. Neg #122461; 9.23, © William Albert Allard/NGS Image Collection; 9.24, © Bill Ballenberg/NGS Image Collection; 9.25, Photo by Guillermo Cock; 9.27, © Nathan Benn; 9.28, © Martha Cooper/NGS Image Collection; 9.31, © 2006 Peabody Museum, Harvard University. 50-1-20/22982 T268; 9.32, Courtesy Richard F. Townsend; 9.37, Courtesy Michael E. Moseley; 9.38, Courtesy Department of Library Services. American Museum Natural History. Neg #334878; 9.41, Courtesy Jennifer Blitz; 9.42, © Robert Frerck/Woodfin Camp and Associates; 9.44, Courtesy John Hyslop, American Museum of Natural History; 9.48, Courtesy Donald E. Thompson **Chapter 10** 10.4, © John Sanders of the The Oriental Institute, Chicago; 10.9, © Hirmer Verlag; 10.10, © Gil Stein/Oriental Institute, University of Chicago; 10.11, Courtesy Denise Schmandt-Besserat. With permission of Deutsches Archaologisches Institut; 10.12a, © University of Pennsylvania Museum (Image #141589); 10.12b, © University of Pennsylvania Museum (Image #142672); 10.12c, © University of Pennsylvania Museum (Image #141589); 10.13, 10.14, Courtesy Denise Schmandt-Besserat. With permission of Deutsches Archaologisches Institut; 10.16, © Dilip Mehta/Woodfin Camp and Associates; 10.19, Courtesy George Dales and the Harappa Project, University of California at Berkeley; 10.20, Photo by J.M. Kenoyer, courtesy of the Department of Archaeology and Museums, Government of Pakistan; 10.21, Courtesy George Dales and the Harappa Project, University of California at Berkeley; 10.24, © Ashmolean Museum, Oxford; 10.25, © Erich Lessing/Art Resource, NY; 10.29, © Sandro Vannini/Corbis; 10.30, © Photri, Inc.; 10.32, Acct. no. 11.1738, King Menkaure (Mycerinus) and Queen. Harvard University/Museum of Fine Arts Expedition. Photograph © Museum of Fine Arts, Boston; 10.40, Courtesy of the Institute History and Philology, Academy Sinica, Taiwan; 10.41, Courtesy the Metropolitan Museum of Art, Gift of Mrs. John Marriott, Mrs. John Barry Ryan, Gilbert W. Kahn, Roger Wolfe Kahn, 1949. #49. 136.5; 10.42, Photo courtesy Mr. Ye Maolin. Reprinted by permission from Macmillan Publishers Ltd: *Nature*, Vol. 437, Issue 7061. Copyright 2005; 10.44, © Audrey R. Topping; 10.45, 10.47, Courtesy Linda Nicholas; 10.48, © Asian Art & Archaeology, Inc./Corbis; 10.50, Courtesy NASA/JPL/Caltech; 10.51, Glen Allison/Getty Images/PhotoDisc; 10.52, © Luca I. Tettoni/Corbis; 10.54, 10.55, © Dr. Roderick James McIntosh; 10.56, © The Granger Collection, New York; 10.60, © Robert Holmes; 10.61, © Walter Edwards/NGS Image Collection **Chapter 11** 11.1, © Scala/Art Resource, NY; 11.3, © 1991 by Peter Bogucki. Used by permission; 11.5, © Natalie Munro; 11.6, Courtesy Thomas Jacobsen; 11.7, 11.8, Courtesy of the Museum of Archaeology in Varna, Bulgaria; 11.9, © V. Vitanov/Ancient Art & Architecture Collection; 11.10, Forschungsinstitut für Alpine Vorzeit; 11.11, © Gerha Hinterleitner/Gamma/Eyedea; 11.14, Courtesy Musee Dauphinois. Grenoble, France; 11.17, 11.18, A. Bocquet/Centre de Documentation de la Prehistoire Alpine; 11.20, T.D. Price; 11.21, From *Ancient Europe from the Beginnings of Agriculture to Classical Antiquity*, by Stuart Piggott. Reprinted with permission from Edinburgh University Press; 11.23, © British Crown Copyright/ M.O.D. Reproduced with the permission of the Controller of Her Britannic Majesty's Stationary Office; 11.29, © Vincenzo Lombardo/Taxi/Getty Images; 11.31, Courtesy John Bennet, Oxford University, Department of Classics; 11.33, © Kevin Fleming/Corbis; 11.34, Courtesy Walter M. Shandruk; 11.35, Photo by J. McCredie, National Archaeological Museum, Athens; 11.36, © Gianni Dagli Orti/Corbis; 11.39, Four bronze age barrows along the coast of Denmark. *From Danish Prehistoric Monuments*, by P.V. Glob, 1971, page 27, figure 4. Reprinted with permission of Glydendal, Copenhagen; 11.40, © Lennart Larsen/The National Museum of Denmark; 11.43, From J. Jensen, Danmarks oldtid bd. 2, Bronzealderen 2000-500 f.Kr. 2002 Gyldendal. København. Used by permission of the author; 11.44, © The National Museum of Denmark; 11.47, Musee Archeologique, Chatillon Sur Seine, France/Giraudon/Bridgeman Art Library; 11.46, Cliche Musee Archeologique de Chatillon sur Seine; 11.48, © Forhistorisk Museum, Moesgard; 11.49, © Ira Block; 11.50, © Dae Sasitorn/www.lastrefuge.co.uk; 11.52, Courtesy the Society of Antiquaries of London; 11.54, © UK Alan King/Alamy **Chapter 12** 12.1, K.L Feder; 12.2, Digital Vision/Getty Images; 12.3, Jeremy Woodhouse/PhotoDisc/Getty Images; 12.4, © Reuters/Corbis; 12.5, Photo by Time Inc./Time Life Pictures; 12.6, © Jonathan Blair/Corbis; 12.7, Poster courtesy of the State Historic Preservation Office, Arizona State Parks, Phoenix, Arizona; 12.9, © Diego Meozzi/Stone Pages

# Text Credits

**Chapter 1** 1.12, Courtesy of Goran Burenhult; 1.26, Courtesy of Sonke Hartz; 1.28, Adapted from A. Sherratt (ed.), *Cambridge Encyclopedia of Archaeology.* Copyright © 1980 Cambridge University Press; 1.31, Courtesy of Ullrich Rossing; 1.32, With permission from Annual Review of Ecology and Systematics, Vol. 3. © 1972 by Annual Reviews: www.annualreviews.org **Chapter 2** 2.4, Kottak, C., *Anthropology: The Exploration of Human Diversity,* 9/e, fig. 6.3, p. 146. Copyright © The McGraw-Hill Companies, Inc. Used with permission from The McGraw-Hill Companies; 2.6, From P. Gagneux et al., "Mitochondrial Sequences Show Diverse Evolutionary Histories of African Hominids," *Proceedings of the National Academy of Sciences,* Vol. 96, April 27, 1999, pp. 5077–5082. Copyright © 1999 National Academy of Sciences, U.S.A. Used with permission; 2.7, From Pat Shipman, "Hunting the First Hominid," *American Scientist,* Vol. 90, No. 1, Jan–Feb 2002, p. 27. Illustration credit: Barbara Aulicino/American Scientist. Copyright © 2002 American Scientist. Reprinted by permission of American Scientist, magazine of Sigma Xi, The Scientific Research Society; 2.11, From Johansen & Edey, *Lucy: The Beginnings of Humankind,* Simon & Schuster; 2.18, From footprints on PBS website; 2.25, Mary Leakey, *Olduvai Gorge,* Vol. 3. Copyright © Cambridge University Press; 2.30, Nicholas Toth, "The First Technology," *Scientific American,* April 1987, art by Edward L. Hanson. Art copyright © Edward L. Hanson. Used by permission of the artist **Chapter 3** 3.7, From Andre Leroi-Gourhan, 1957, *Prehistoric Man.* New York: Philosophical Library. Reprinted with permission; 3.24, *The Age of Mammals,* a mural by Rudolph F. Zallinger. Copyright © 1966, 1975, 1989, 1991, 2000 Peabody Museum of Natural History, Yale University, New Haven, CT; 3.26, Courtesy of Richard Klein; 3.28, Adapted from J. Desmond Clark, *Kalambo Falls Prehistoric Site,* Vol. 1, Cambridge University Press, 1969; 3.29, From Francois Bordes, *The Old Stone Age.* Copyright © 1968 The McGraw-Hill Companies, Inc. Used with permission from The McGraw-Hill Companies **Chapter 4** 4.6, From Roger Lewin, *In the Age of Mankind,* (Washington, DC: Smithsonian Institution Press), page 181. Used by permission. Copyright © 1989; 4.10, Courtesy of Richard Klein; 4.12, From *Mosaic,* Vol. 10, No. 2, March/April 1979; 4.13, Feder, K. and M. Park, *Human Antiquity: An Introduction to Physical Anthropology and Archaeology,* 4/e, f4.1, p. 71. Copyright © The McGraw-Hill Companies, Inc. Used with permission from The McGraw-Hill Companies; 4.18, From Francois Bordes, *The Old Stone Age.* Copyright © 1968 The McGraw-Hill Companies, Inc. Used with permission from The McGraw-Hill Companies; 4.19, Kottak, C., *Anthropology: The Exploration of Human Diversity,* 9/e, fig. 7.4, p. 176. Copyright © The McGraw-Hill Companies, Inc. Used with permission from The McGraw-Hill Companies; 4.20, From Turnbaugh et al., *Understanding Physical Anthropology & Archaeology,* 7/e, p. 439. Copyright © 1999. Reprinted with permission of Wadsworth, a division of Cengage; www.cengage.com.; 4.21, © John Sibbick/NHMPL. Used with permission; 4.24, "Out on a Limb" from P. Kahn & A. Gibbons, "Anthropology: DNA From an Extinct Human," *Science,* Vol. 277, July 10, 1997 pp. 176–178. Copyright © 1997 AAAS. Reprinted with permission of Svante Pääbo, MPI-EVA; 4.25, From *Oxford Illustrated Prehistory of Europe* by Barry Cunliffe. Copyright © 1994. Reprinted by permission of Paul Mellars; 4.33, From B. Kilma, 1963, *Dolni Vestonice,* Prague: Academy of Science of the Czech Republic. Reproduced with permission; 4.34, Feder, K. and M. Park, *Human Antiquity: An Introduction to Physical Anthropology and Archaeology,* 4/e, f13.5, p. 395. Copyright © The McGraw-Hill Companies, Inc. Used with permission from The McGraw-Hill Companies; 4.36, H. Muller-Karpe, *Handbuch Vor Vorgeschichte,* 1966. C.H. Beck; 4.37, From B. Kilma, 1963, *Dolni Vestonice,* Prague: Academy of Science of the Czech Republic. Reproduced with permission; 4.40, From A. Leroi-Gourhan, 1982. *The Dawn of European Art: An Introduction to Paleolithic Cave Painting.* New York: Cambridge University Press. Reprinted with permission of Cambridge University Press; 4.41, Copyright © Zdenek Burian. Used by permission of Jiri Hochman; 4.42, *Secrets of the Ice Age* by Evan Hadingham, 1979, Walker & Co. Reprinted by permission of Walker & Co.; 4.47 Drawing by Ann Hatfield, from *Plato Prehistorian* by Mary Settegast. Illustrations copyright Lindisfarne Books. Reprinted with permission; 4.49, From A. Leroi-Gourhan, *The Old Stone Age,* Cambridge University Press; 4.50, After Leroi-Gourhan and Brezillion, 1966. Reprinted with permission of the publisher, Editions du Centre National de la Recherche Scientifique, Paris; 4.51, © 2006 President and Fellows of Harvard College, Peabody Museum, Alexander Marshack; 4.52, © 2006 President and Fellows of Harvard College, Peabody Museum, Alexander Marshack; 4.58, Bruce D. Smith, the Emergence of Agriculture, WH Freeman, 1995, p. 39. Used with permission; 4.61, © Estate of Bunji Tagawa. Used with permission; 4.64, Anderson & Faugt, *Archaeology of Eastern North America,* Vol. 26, pp. 163–187. Copyright © 1998. Used by permission of Eastern States Archaeological Federation; 4.67, Reprinted from *Environments & Extinctions,* Mead, Jim I. and Meltzer, David J., 1985, with permission from the Center for the Study of the First Americans; 4.74, C. Kottak, *Anthropology: The Exploration of Human Diversity,* 9/e, fig 9.6, Copyright © The McGraw-Hill Companies, Inc. Used with permission from The McGraw-Hill Companies 4.75, D.H. Thomas, *Archaeology,* f2.1, p. 64. Copyright © 1979. Reprinted with permission of Wadsworth, a division of Cengage: www.cengage.com; **Chapter 5** 5.7, Legge & Rowley-Conway, Star Carr Revisited, 1990. Copyright © Anthony Legge. Used with permission; 5.8, Courtesy of Lars Larsson, Institute of Archaeology, Lund University, Sweden; 5.12, Illustration by Eric Claudell. Courtesy of Erik Brinch Petersen, Institute of Archaeology, University of Copenhagen; 5.18, Courtesy of Richard Klein; 5.19, Reprinted with permission from John Parkington, University of Capetown, South Africa; 5.20, Drawing adapted from the original of Tatsuo Kobayashi in *Image and Life: 50,000 Years of Japanese Prehistory* by Gordon Miller, Museum Note No. 5, Illustration by Gordon Miller. Copyright © Gordon Miller. Used with permission; 5.21, Reprinted from *The Prehistory of Japan,* by C. Aikens & T. Higuchi, Copyright © 1982. With permission from Elsevier; 5.26, Figure 1-2, p. 9, from The Archaeology of Carrier Mills: 10,000 Years in the Saline Valley of Illinois, by Richard W. Jefferies, 1987. Illustrated by Thomas W. Gatlin. © Board of Trustees, Southern Illinois University. Reprinted with permission; 5.28, Figure 3-6, p. 84, from *The Archaeology of Carrier Mills: 10,000 Years in the Saline Valley of Illinois,* by Richard W. Jefferies, 1987. Illustrated by Thomas W. Gatlin. © Board of Trustees, Southern Illinois University. Reprinted with permission; 5.29, Figure from E. J. Bassett, "Osteological Analysis of Carrier Mills Burials." In *The Carrier Mills Archaeology Project: Human Adaptation in the Saline River Valley, Illinois,* ed. R. W. Jeffries and B. M. Butler, 2, pp. 1027–1114. Cent. Archaeolo. Invest. Res. Pap. 33. Carbondale, IL: Center for Archaeological Investigations, 1982. Used with permission of the Center for Archaeological Investigations. Copyright 1982 by the Board of Trustees, Southern Illinois University **Chapter 6** 6.3, Feder, K. & M. Park, *Human Antiquity* 4/e, f14.1, p. 437. Copyright © 2001 by The McGraw-Hill Companies, Inc. Used with permission from The McGraw-Hill Companies; 6.7, R.F. Sage, "Was Low Atmospheric $CO_2$ During the Pleistocene a Limiting Factor for Origin of Agriculture?," *Global Change Biology,* fig. 2, pp. 93–106, 1995. Copyright © 1995 Blackwell Publishing. Used with permission; 6.10, After Jean Perrot, Centre de Recherche Francais de Jerusalem; 6.11, *The Rise of Civilization* by Charles Redman. Copyright © 1978 by W.H. Freeman and Company. Used with permission; 6.13, *Village on the Euphrates: The Excavation of Abu Hureyra* edited by Andrew M.T. Moore and A. Legge. Copyright © 1999 by Oxford University Press, Inc. Used by permission of Oxford University Press; 6.14, Fig 13.14 from

*Principles of Archaeology*, Price. McGraw-Hill. Adapted from Figures 14.1 and 14.4 from A.M.T. Moore, G.C. Hillman, and A.J. Legge, *Village on the Euphrates: From Foraging to Farming at Abu Hureyra.* Oxford University Press, 2000, pp. 484, 498. Used with permission; 6.15, Reprinted with permission from the artist, Jonathan Mabry; 6.19, Courtesy Institute of Archaeology, University College London. And from Feder, K. & M. Park, *Human Antiquity* 4/e, f14.23, p. 475. Copyright © 2001 by The McGraw-Hill Companies, Inc. Used with permission from The McGraw-Hill Companies; 6.21, Drawing by Ann Hatfield, from *Plato Prehistorian* by Mary Settegast. Illustrations copyright Lindisfarne Books. Reprinted with permission; 6.22, Courtesy Institute of Archaeology, University College, London; 6.26, Clifford Jolly & White, *Physical Anthropology and Archaeology* 5/e. Copyright © 1995 The McGraw-Hill Companies, Inc. Used with permission from The McGraw-Hill Companies; 6.27, Legge & Rowley-Conway, *Star Carr Revisited*, 1990. Copyright © Anthony Legge. Used with permission; 6.28, Figure 1 from *Antiquity*, December 2001, p. 718. Reprinted with permission from Antiquity Publications Ltd; 6.30, Drawing by Ann Hatfield, from *Plato Prehistorian* by Mary Settegast. Illustrations copyright Lindisfarne Books. Reprinted with permission; 6.32, Drawing by Ann Hatfield, from *Plato Prehistorian* by Mary Settegast. Illustrations copyright Lindisfarne Books. Reprinted with permission; 6.33, James Mellaart, *Catal-Huyuk: A Neolithic Town in Anatolia*, 1966; 6.35, M. Lechevallier and G. Quivron, 1985, "Results of the Recent Excavations at the Neolithic Site Mehrgarh, Pakistan," *South Asian Archaeology*, 1983. J. Schotmans and M. Taddei, eds., Instituto Universitario Orientale, Seminario di Studi Asiatici, Series Minor 23, Naples; 6.55, Feder, K. & M. Park, *Human Antiquity* 4/e, f14.23, p. 475. Copyright © 2001 by The McGraw-Hill Companies, Inc. Used with permission from The McGraw-Hill Companies; 6.57, Figure redrawn from G. Beadle, "The Ancestry of Corn," *Scientific American*, 242:113. Art by Nelson Prentiss. © 1980. Reprinted with permission; 6.59, From "The Origins of New World Civilizations" by Richard MacNeish, *Scientific American*, 1964. Illustration by Eric O. Mose. Used by permission of the Estate of Eric Mose; 6.67, Reprinted by permission from *Economic Botany*, Vol. 35, Issue 3, p. 235, Hugh D. Wilson. Copyright © 1981 The New York Botanical Garden Bronx, New York **Chapter 7** 7.3, From *Prehistory of North America* 2/e by Jesse Jennings. Copyright © Jesse Jennings. Used by permission of the Estate of Jesse Jennings; 7.4, Adapted from *Journal of Archaeological Method and Theory*, Vol. 12, No. 4, December 2005, "Poverty Point as Structure, Event, Process" by Kenneth E. Sassaman (© 2005), with kind permission from Springer Science and Business Media and the author; 7.8, From Clarence Webb, *The Poverty of Culture*, 2/e, p. 51. Reprinted with permission from LSU Geoscience Publications; 7.18, Fig. 1.5 from *Cahokia: Domination and Ideology in the Mississippian World.* Copyright © 1997. Used courtesy of the Illinois Transportation Archaeological Research Program, University of Illinois at Urbana-Champaign; 7.25, Adapted from Archaeology of the Moundville Chiefdom, ed. by Vernon James Knight and Vincas P. Steponaitis, Fig. 1.1, p. 3. Smithsonian Institution Press. Used with permission. Also adapted from George R. Holley: Moundville, fig 2.6, p. 26 from *Great Towns and Regional Politics*, Jill Neitzel, ed. Copyright © 1999 University of New Mexico Press. Used with permission; 7.26, Redrawn from C.B. Moore, "Certain Aboriginal Remains of the Black Warrior River," *Journal of the Academy of Natural Science of Philadelphia*, Vo. 13, pp. 125–244, 1905; 7.27, Steven Patricia's rendering of Moundville. Used with permission; 7.29, Artist's reconstruction of the main palisaded village and enclosed longhouses at the Draper site, courtesy Canadian Museum of Civilization, artist Ivan Kocsis, Mercury Series, no. 130. Used with permission; 7.31, Excavated longhouses at the Draper site, courtesy Canadian Museum of Civilization, artist Ivan Kocsis, Mercury Series, no. 130. Used with permission; 7.45, D.H. Thomas, *Archaeology*, 2/e, f.9.2. Copyright © 1989. Reprinted with permission of Wadsworth, a division of Cengage: www.cengage.com; 7.48, Illustration by Chris Walsh Heady from *Archaeology in Washington* by Ruth Kirk with Richard D. Daugherty. Copyright © 2007. Used with permission; 7.50, Illustration by Chris Walsh Heady from *Archaeology in Washington* by Ruth Kirk with Richard D. Daugherty. Copyright © 2007. Used with permission; 7.51, Illustration by Chris Walsh Heady from *Archaeology in Washington* by Ruth Kirk with Richard D. Daugherty. Copyright © 2007. Used with permission **Chapter 8** 8.4, K.V. Flannery & J. Marcus, eds. *The Cloud People: Divergent Evolution of the Zapotec and Mixtex Civilizations.* Copyright © 1983. Courtesy of Joyce Marcus & Kent V. Flannery. Reprinted with permission; 8.5, K.V. Flannery & J. Marcus, eds. *The Cloud People: Divergent Evolution of the Zapotec and Mixtex Civilizations.* Copyright © 1983. Courtesy of Joyce Marcus & Kent V. Flannery. Reprinted with permission; 8.6, K.V. Flannery & J. Marcus, eds. *The Cloud People: Divergent Evolution of the Zapotec and Mixtext Civilizations.* Copyright © 1983. Courtesy of Joyce Marcus & Kent V. Flannery. Reprinted with permission; 8.8, K.V. Flannery & J. Marcus, eds. *The Cloud People: Divergent Evolution of the Zapotec and Mixtext Civilizations.* Copyright © 1983. Courtesy of Joyce Marcus & Kent V. Flannery. Reprinted with permission; 8.10, From Rebecca Gonzalez Lauck, "La Venta: An Olmec Capital" in *Olmec Art of Ancient Mexico*, Elizabeth Benson and Beatriz de la Fuente, eds., National Gallery of Art, Washington D.C. Copyright © Rebecca Gonzalez Lauck. Reprinted with permission; 8.14, K.V. Flannery & J. Marcus, eds. *The Cloud People: Divergent Evolution of the Zapotec and Mixtext Civilizations.* Copyright © 1983. Courtesy of Joyce Marcus & Kent V. Flannery. Reprinted with permission; 8.15, Drawing from *In the Land of the Olmec: The Archaeology of San Lorenzo Tenochtitlan*, Volume I, by Michael Coe and Richard Diehl, Copyright © 1980. By permission of the University of Texas Press; 8.17, © T.W. Rutledge; 8.20, K.V. Flannery & J. Marcus, eds. *The Cloud People: Divergent Evolution of the Zapotec and Mixtext Civilizations.* Copyright © 1983. Courtesy of Joyce Marcus & Kent V. Flannery. Reprinted with permission; 8.21, K.V. Flannery & J. Marcus, eds. *The Cloud People: Divergent Evolution of the Zapotec and Mixtext Civilizations.* Copyright © 1983. Courtesy of Joyce Marcus & Kent V. Flannery. Reprinted with permission; 8.23, K.V. Flannery & J. Marcus, eds. *The Cloud People: Divergent Evolution of the Zapotec and Mixtext Civilizations.* Copyright © 1983. Courtesy of Joyce Marcus & Kent V. Flannery. Reprinted with permission; 8.24, K.V. Flannery & J. Marcus, eds. *The Cloud People: Divergent Evolution of the Zapotec and Mixtext Civilizations.* Copyright © 1983. Courtesy of Joyce Marcus & Kent V. Flannery. Reprinted with permission; 8.25, K.V. Flannery & J. Marcus, eds. *The Cloud People: Divergent Evolution of the Zapotec and Mixtext Civilizations.* Copyright © 1983. Courtesy of Joyce Marcus & Kent V. Flannery. Reprinted with permission; 8.26, "A Fuego y Sangre: Early Zapotec Imperialism in Cuicatlan," by Elizabeth Redmond, Memoirs, no. 16. Museum of Anthropology, University of Michigan, 1983. Used with permission; 8.35, Arthur G. Miller, fig. 173, p. 100 from *The Mural Painting of Teotihuacan*, with drawings by Felipe Davalos G. Copyright © Dumbarton Oaks. Used with permission; 8.37, Figure 23 from *The Sculpture of Elajin, Veracruz, Mexico* by Michael Kampen. Reprinted with permission of the University Press of Florida; 8.42, Description: Stella 29, Credit: Reprinted from John S. Henderson: *The World of the Ancient Maya–Second Edition.* Copyright © 1981 by Cornell University. Used by permission of the publishers, Cornell University Press and John Murray, Ltd.; 8.43, Reprinted from John S. Henderson: *The World of the Ancient Maya–Second Edition.* Copyright © 1981 by Cornell University. Used by permission of the publishers, Cornell University Press and John Murray Ltd.; 8.47, © Merle Greene Robertson. Used by permission; 8.50, Courtesy Andromeda Oxford Ltd., now part of the Brown Reference Group plc.; 8.51, Courtesy Andromeda Oxford Ltd., now part of the Brown Reference Group plc.; 8.52, From *Everyday Life of the Aztecs* by Warwick Bray, 1968. B.T. Batsford, Ltd., London; 8.55, From *Tula: The Toltec Capital of Ancient Mexico* by Dr. Richard A. Diehl, published by Thames and Hudson. Reprinted with permission; 8.56, Reprinted with permission from *Tula of the Toltecs* by Dan Healan, published by the University of Iowa Press; 8.60, Morley, Brainerd, and Sharer, *The Ancient Maya*, 3rd Edition. Copyright © 1946, 1947, 1956, 1983, 1994 by the Board of Trustees of the Leland Stanford Junior University. All rights reserved. Used with the permission of Stanford University Press: www.sup.org; 8.65, From *Everyday Life of the Aztecs* by Warwick Bray, 1968. B.T. Batsford, Ltd., London; 8.67, Frances Berdan et al., *Aztec Imperial Strategies*, fig. 11.1, p. 112. Copyright © 1996 Dumbarton Oaks. Used with permission; 8.68, From *Everyday Life of the Aztecs* by Warwick Bray, 1968. B.T. Batsford, Ltd., London; 8.70, *Codex Florentino: Illustrations For Sahagen's Historia*

*General De Las Cosas De Nueva Espana,* Francisco Del Pas Troncose, Vol. 5, Madrid, 1905; 8.71, F. Berdan, *The Aztecs of Central Mexico: An Imperial Society,* f. 5.3. Copyright © 1982. Reprinted with the permission of Wadsworth, a division of Cengage: www.cengage.com; 8.72, F9.6b, p. 222 from Michael Smith, *The Aztecs.* Copyright © 1996 Michael E. Smith. Published by Blackwell Publishing, Ltd. Used with permission **Chapter 9** 9.6, Chavin de Huantar, R.A. Feldman doctoral dissertation; 9.7, Copyright © Bernardino Ojeda. Used with permission; 9.9, Michael K. Mosely, *Ocean Currents, The Maritime Foundations of Andean Civilization.* Copyright © 1975 Michael Moseley. Reprinted with permission; 9.11, Michael K. Moseley, *Ocean Currents, The Maritime Foundations of Andean Civilization.* Copyright © 1975 Michael Moseley. Reprinted with permission; 9.13, Images from p. 131, *Chavin and the Origins of Andean Civilization* by Richard L. Burger. © 1992 Thames and Hudson, Ltd., London. Reprinted with permission; 9.15, G. R. Willey *Introduction to American Archaeology: South America.* © 1971 Gordon R. Willey; G. R. Willey, *Introduction to American Archaeology: South America.* © 1971 Gordon R. Willey; 9.18, From *American Antiquity,* Vol. 40, 1975. Reprinted by permission of the Society for American Archaeology; 9.19, From "Prehistoric Principles of Labor Organization in the Moche Valley, Peru," by Michael E. Moseley and Charles Hastings, *American Antiquity,* 40(2): 191–196, 1975. Reprinted with permission; 9.22, Christopher Donnan, *Moche Art and Iconography,* Los Angeles: UCLA Latin American Center Publications, 1976. Reproduced with permission of The Regents of the University of California; 9.26, Courtesy of Christopher Donnan, drawing by Alberto Gutierrez. Reprinted with permission from Walter Leonel Alva Alva; 9.29 Courtesy Andromeda Oxford Ltd., now part of the Brown Reference Group plc.; 9.33, W. Bennett, 1947. *Handbook of South American Indians,* Vol. 2, J. Stewart, ed. US Government Printing Office; 9.35, Courtesy Andromeda Oxford Ltd., now part of the Brown Reference Group plc.; 9.36, Courtesy Andromeda Oxford Ltd., now part of the Brown Reference Group plc.; 9.40 From *Prehistory of North America,* 2/e by Jesse Jennings. Copyright © Jesse Jennings. Used by permission of the Estate of Jesse Jennings; 9.46, From Guaman Poma de Ayala, Noevo Coronica, c. 1610; 9.47, Adapted from R.W. Keating, ed., *Peruvian Prehistory: An Overview of Pre-Inca and Inca Society.* Copyright © 1988 Cambridge University Press; 9.49, From Craig Morris and Donald E. Thompson, *Huanuco Pampa: An Inca City and its Hinterland,* 1985. London: Thames and Hudson. Reproduced with permission of the authors **Chapter 10** 10.6, From *Art of the Ancient Near East* by Seton Lloyd. Copyright © 1961 Thames & Hudson, Ltd., London. Reprinted with permission; 10.7, © State Antiquities and Heritage Organization, Baghdad; 10.17, M. Wheeler, *The Indus Civilization.* Copyright © 1968 Cambridge University Press. Reprinted with permission; 10.18, From Michael Jansen, *Civilizations Anciennes Du Pakistan,* 1989. Bruxelles: Musees Royaux d'Art et d'Histoire. Copyright © 1989 Michael Jansen. Reprinted with permission; 10.22, Redrawn with permission from original illustration by J.M Kenoyer; 10.26, From *The Riddle of the Pyramids* by Kurt Mendelssohn © 1974 by Kurt Mendelssohn. Thames & Hudson, Ltd., London. Reprinted with permission; 10.28, From Michael Hoffman, "Where Nations Began," *Science,* October 1983, pp. 42–51. 1983; 10.34, From *The Riddle of the Pyramids* by Kurt Mendelssohn © 1974 by Kurt Mendelssohn. Thames & Hudson, Ltd., London. Reprinted with permission; 10.35, After *The Riddle of the Pyramids* by Kurt Mendelssohn. Thames & Hudson, Ltd., London; 10.38, From Wenwu, 1984; 10.39, K.C. Chang, *Studies of Shang Archaeology.* Copyright © 1986 Yale University Press. Reprinted by permission of the publisher, Yale University Press; 10.43, From K.C. Chang, "Food & Vessels In Ancient China," *Translations of the NY Academy of Sciences,* Vol. 35, No. 6, 1973. Copyright © 1973 NY Academy of Sciences. Used with permission; 10.46, © Hsien-Min Yang National Geographic Image Collection; 10.57, From *Great Zimbabwe* by Peter S. Garlake. Copyright © 1973 Thames & Hudson. Ltd., London. Reprinted with permission; 10.58, From *Great Zimbabwe* by Peter S. Garlake. Copyright © 1973 Thames & Hudson. Ltd., London. Reprinted with permission; 10.59, From *Great Zimbabwe* by Peter S. Garlake. Copyright © 1973 Thames & Hudson. Ltd., London. Reprinted with permission **Chapter 11** 11.12, Courtesy the Forschungsinstitut fur Alpine Vorzeit; 11.13, Courtesy the Forschungsinstitut fur Alpine Vorzeit; 11.15, Courtesy Dr. Ullrich Ruoff; Table 11.2 The Distribution of Animals During the Later Occupation at Charavines, Based on 504 Individuals. Centre de Documentation de la Prehistoire Alpine. Reprinted with permission from Aimé Bocquet; 11.16, Courtesy of A. Houot/Centre de Documentation de la Prehistoire Alpine. Reprinted with permission from Aimé Bocquet; 11.25, Christopher Chippendale, *Stonehenge Complete,* Illustration 240, p. 269. Copyright © Crown. NMR. Used with permission; 11.27, After *Stonehenge Complete* by Christopher Chippendale, Thames & Hudson, Ltd. Reprinted with permission; p. 571, Siegfried Sassoon, from "The Heart's Journey: 1928." With permission from Heinemann Publishers, Ltd.; 11.31, *Past Worlds: The Times Atlas of Archaeology,* edited by Chris Scarre. Reprinted by permission of HarperCollins Publishers Ltd. and Chris Scarre. © Chris Scarre 1988; 11.39, J. Jensen, 1979, Bronzealderen, Vol 1, Copenhagen: Sesam Publishers. Published by permission of the National Museum of Denmark; 11.42, Peter Vilhelm Glob, *The Mound People;* 11.44, J. Jensen, 1979, Bronzealderen, Vol 1, Copenhagen: Sesam Publishers. Published by permission of the National Museum of Denmark; 11.46, Reprinted from *Prehistoric Europe* by T. Champion et al., Copyright © 1984. With permission from Elsevier; 11.52, Wheeler's interpretation of the construction phases at Maiden Castle. Copyright © Society of Antiquaries of London. Used with permission **Chapter 12** Table 12.1, The Mission of UNESCO's World Heritage Program. Credit: Mission Statement of UNESCO's World Heritage Centre. Used with permission; Table 12.2, A Partial List of World Heritage Archaeological Sites. Credit: Partial list of UNESCO's World Heritage List. Used with permission; Table 12.4, 8 ethical principles from website saa.org/aboutSAA/ethics.html. Courtesy of the Society of American Archaeology: www.saa.org.

# Index

Page numbers for illustrations and tables are italicized.